University of Cambridge Oriental Publications
published for the
Faculty of Oriental Studies
See pages 418–19 for the complete list

Published by the Press Syndicate of the University of Cambridge
The Pitt Building, Trumpington Street, Cambridge CB2 1RP
32 East 57th Street, New York, NY 10022, USA
10 Stamford Road, Oakleigh, Melbourne 3166, Australia

First published 1986

Printed in Great Britain at the University Press, Cambridge

British Library cataloguing in publication data

Wink, André
Land and sovereignty in India: agrarian society and
politics under the eighteenth-century Maratha Svarājya.
– (University of Cambridge oriental publications; no. 36)

Library of Congress cataloguing in publication data

Wink, André
Land and sovereignty in India.
Bibliography.
Includes index.
1. Marathas – Politics and government.
2. India – History – 18th century.
3. Land tenure – India – History. I. Title
DS485.M349W56 1986 954.03 85-22333

ISBN 0 521 32064 X

CE

Land and Sovereignty in India

Agrarian Society and Politics under the Eighteenth-century Maratha Svarājya

ANDRÉ WINK
University of Leiden

The right of the University of Cambridge to print and sell all manner of books was granted by Henry VIII in 1534. The University has printed and published continuously since 1584.

CAMBRIDGE UNIVERSITY PRESS
CAMBRIDGE
LONDON NEW YORK NEW ROCHELLE
MELBOURNE SYDNEY

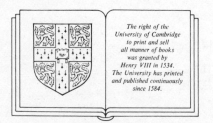

University of Cambridge Oriental Publications No. 36

Land and Sovereignty in India

CONTENTS

MAPS AND DIAGRAMS

PREFACE

The research for this book was done mainly in London, Bombay, Poona, and New Delhi from 1980 to 1983. For financial support during more than three years I am indebted to the Netherlands Foundation for the Advancement of Tropical Research (WOTRO). I would also like to acknowledge a six-month research fellowship which I was awarded by the Department of Rural Sociology of the Tropics and Subtropics of the Agricultural University, Wageningen, and an additional grant which I received from the Leiden University Foundation.

Invaluable to me were the services provided by the staff of the India Office Library and Records, and the British Museum in London; the Archives of Poona and Bombay; the Bharat Itihas Samshodak Mandal in Poona; the Kern Institute in Leiden; also a very large number of other specialized libraries which I visited from time to time. In Poona there were Shri B. D. Apte and Shri M. M. Omkar and other veterans of Modi and Persian always ready to answer questions and prepared to part with information not asked for.

Among friends and colleagues, I would like to thank especially Dr Annie Montaut for her hospitality in New Delhi; Dr Chris Bayly, Dr Frank Perlin, and Dr Muzaffar Alam, Mandira Mitra, Geert Horringa, and Dr Dirk Kolff for suggestions, references and criticism; Bert Keizer for the efforts he made to amend my English and for checking virtually the entire manuscript with great dedication; Professor A. R. Kulkarni for sponsoring my stay in India and facilitating research in a variety of ways.

Of former tutors I would like to acknowledge the support and encouragement I received in an initial, uncertain stage from Professor R. A. J. Van Lier, to whom I am also indebted for a very stimulating introduction to sociology, and Dr J. H. B. Den Ouden, who first made me familiar with Indian studies.

Above all my gratitude goes to Professor Jan Heesterman who made incisive comments on almost every chapter of this work during long hours of discussion from which I always derived much benefit and great pleasure. Needless to say that the responsibility for the final result is entirely mine.

A.W.

ABBREVIATIONS

B.A.: R.D.	*Bombay Archives: Revenue Department*
BG	*Gazetteer of the Bombay Presidency*, vols I–XXIII (Bombay, 1879–96)
BGS	*Selections from the Records of the Bombay Government* (Bombay, 1852–84)
BISM	*Bhārat Itihās Saṃśodak Maṇḍaḷ*
BISMQ	*Bhārat Itihās Saṃśodak Maṇḍaḷ Quarterly*
CIS	*Contributions to Indian Sociology*
CSSH	*Comparative Studies in Society and History*
EIP	*Selections of Papers from the Records at the East-India House Relating to the Revenue, Police, and Civil and Criminal Justice under the Company's Governments in India*, 4 vols (London, 1820–6)
IESHR	*The Indian Economic and Social History Review*
IS	*Itihās Saṃgraha* (Poona, 1908–16), ed. by D. B. Parasnis
JAS	*The Journal of Asian Studies*
JBBRAS	*Journal of the Bombay Branch of the Royal Asiatic Society*
JESHO	*Journal of the Economic and Social History of the Orient*
MAS	*Modern Asian Studies*
MIS	*Marāṭhyāṇcyā Itihāsācīṇ Sādhaneṇ*, 22 vols (Poona, Bombay, etc., 1898–1919), ed. by V. K. Rajvade
MITSA	*Mahārāṣṭre Itihāsācī Sādhaneṇ*, 3 vols (Bombay, 1967), ed. by V. S. Bendre
P.A.	*Poona Archives*
PRC	*Poona Residency Correspondence*, 13 vols (Bombay, 1936–58), ed. by J. Sarkar, G. S. Sardesai *et al.*
SCS	*Śivcaritra Sāhitya*, 13 vols (Poona, 1926–65), ed. by *BISM*
SKPSS	*Śivkālīn Patrasārsaṃgraha*, 3 vols (Poona, 1930–7), ed. by *BISM*
SPD	*Selections from the Peshwa Daftar*, 45 vols (Bombay, 1930–4), ed. by G. S. Sardesai
SSRPD	*Selections from the Satara Rajas' and the Peishwas' Diaries*, 9 vols (Poona and Bombay, 1905–11), ed. by R. B. G. C. Vad, D. B. Parasnis *et al.*

TKKP	Tārābāīkālīn Kāgadpatre, 3 vols (Kolhapur, 1969–72), ed. by A. Pawar
WZKSOA	*Wiener Zeitschrift für die Kunde Süd- und Ostasiens*

GLOSSARY

(Marathi orthography is maintained unless otherwise indicated)

adhikārī: right
agrahāra: religious foundation of brahmans
ain: nett-
ajmās: estimate
amal: fraction, right
amānat: sequestrated
aṇtastha: secret payment
artha (*śāstra*) (Skt): (science of) politics
'*aṣabīya* (Ar.): tribal or political cohesion
aṣṭapradhān: council of eight ministers

bāb: cess
bābtī: one-fourth of the cauth or other Maratha levies
bāgāīt: garden land
balutedār: village-artisan
bakhar: chronicle
baṭāī: crop-sharing
bhaṭ: a brahman
bhāūbaṇd: brotherhood
bheda: drawing away from allegiance, rebellion, sedition
bhūpati: lord of the land
bighā: a measure of surface or capacity

caḍh: cess
cakravartī: universal emperor
caudharī: hereditary local official
caukī: guarding post
cauth: one-fourth (of land-revenue, etc.)
chatrapati: lord of the umbrella, title of Maratha kings
ciṭṇis: an auditing official or clerk

daftar: record-office
darakdār: hereditary auditor

dār al-ḥarb (Ar.): the House of War, territory not under Muslim sovereignty
dār al-islām (Ar.): the House of Islam, territory under Muslim sovereignty
darbār: court
dastūrammal: assessment regulation
daulat: hereditary or pseudo-hereditary dominion or assignment
dāya: sharing
dāyadā: co-sharer
dehajhāḍā: register of villages
desāī: district-zamindar
deśkuḷkarṇī: hereditary district-accountant
deśmukh: district-zamindar
deśpāṇḍe: hereditary district-accountant
devasthān: religious establishment or temple
dhārā: settlement, assessment
dharma (*śāstra*) (Skt): (science of) religion
dharmādāya: religious gift or foundation
dīwān: revenue and civil administrator

faḍṇīs: secretary (one of the darakdārs)
fāṇd (fitur): rebellion, sedition
farmān: official document or decree issued by a Muslim sovereign
fasād (Ar., P.): rebellion, sedition
faujdār(ī): Mughal military governor(ship)
fauj-saraṇjām: assignment of land or land-revenue for the upkeep of troops
fitna (Ar., P.), *fitvā* (Mar.): drawing away from allegiance, rebellion, sedition

gallā: crop-sharing
gāṇv: village
gardī kā vakt: period of trouble
gatkūḷ: land of which the cultivating family is extinct or absent
ghairsanadī: without sanad
ghāsdāṇā: grass and grain, fodder for the horses
ghugrī: grain
girāśī: chieftain
gosāīn: ascetic
gosāvī: religious mendicant or ascetic
gota: judicial assembly
gotra: family
grassia: chief
gutkā, *guttā*, *gutā*: contract, farm

hak: right
hakīkat: account, chronicle
hakīm: commander, authority

haklājimā: rights and privileges
havālā: bill of exchange
hiśeb: account
hissā: share
hon: a gold coin
hujat: draft document
huṇḍī: bill of exchange
huzrāt: household troops
huzūr: court

ijāra(*dār*): (holder of a) farm of revenue
inām(*dār*): (holder of a) hereditary tax-exempt or privileged tenure
*iqṭā*ʻ (Ar., P.): assignment of land or land-revenue
istāvā: lease with annually increasing rate
izāfat: additional inām village given to zamīndārs

jāgīr(*dār*): (holder of an) assignment of land or land-revenue
jamā: collection, assessment, valuation
jamābaṇḍī: rent-roll
janapada: land-cum-people
japt: sequestrated
jarīb: measurement survey
jarīpaṭkā: standard
jathā: family, lineage
jīrāīt: agricultural land
jiziya: Islamic poll-tax

kaccā: detailed, supervised, regulated
kacerī: office, court
kamāl: perfection, completion, total; also the name of a revenue survey
kamāvīsdār: official, collector
kārkūn: clerk or auditor
kaul (nāmā): assurance-deed or document of agreement
k͟halīfa (Ar., P.): leader of the Muslims
khālsā: crown domain
khaṇḍaṇī: tribute
k͟harāj (Ar., P.): land-revenue
khāsgī, *khāzgī*: private domain
khidmat: post of service
khilāt: robe of honour
khotī: farm of revenue
khurdkhat: draft document
k͟huṭba (Ar., P.): friday-prayer
killedār: fort-commander
kuḷkarṇī: accountant
kulmukhtyārī: delegate with full powers

kuṇbī: cultivator, peasant

mahāl: a territorial unit
mahār (or *dher*): a low caste
majumdār: an auditing official or clerk
mahzar: a written statement used in a suit
maktā: contract, farm
māmlatdār: official, collector
mānkarīs: persons entitled to special honours
mansab (*dār*): (holder of) a noble rank
masnad: throne
maṭh: a religious establishment or monastery
mauza: village
mauzevār: village-wise
mavās: bandit, leader, chief
mestak: table
mirāsdār: hereditary cultivator
mokadam: village headman
mokāsā(*dār*): (holder of an) assignment of land or land-revenue; also the designation of the 3/4 fraction of the Maratha levies
moṇglāī: Mughal sovereignty or fiscal claim
mukām: temporary residence
mukhya pradhān: prime minister; equivalent of Peshwa
mulk (Ar.): sovereignty
mulk ṭabīʿī (Ar.): natural power
mulūkhgirī: expedition of conquest
muśāhirā: salary
mutālīk: agent, representative
mutālīk śikka: deputy seal

nāīb: deputy
nawāb: Mughal regional governor
nāyak: chief, leader
nazar: honorary present
nāẓim: Mughal provincial governor
nimtānā: sample-estimate
nokar: servant

pādśāh: emperor
pakkā: unsupervised, unregulated
pāḷegār: chief
pāṇḍharpeśas: village artisans and brahmans in the Northern Konkan
paradaulatdār: the enemy's retainers
parāgaṇdā: fugitive, absconding
parakīya: opposing
paramulūkh: the enemy's territory,

parbhāre: 'in, through or by another'
pararājya: the enemy's sovereignty
pargaṇā: a territorial division
parvānā: order, licence
pāṭīl: village-headman
patra: deed, document
paṭṭī: cess
peśkaś: tributary or honorary payment
peshwa, *peśvā*: prime minister
peśvāī: rule of the Peshwas
pradhān: minister
prajbhāg: the cultivators' share
prāṇt: province
pujārī: temple officiant
puṇḍa: rebellion, plundering

rājā: king, sovereign
rājbhāg: the king's share
rājmaṇḍal: royal council
rājyābhiṣeka: royal consecration
rayat: cultivator, peasant
rayatvār: cultivator-wise
rāye: rates (of assessment)
rivāj: custom
rusūm: emolument of zamindars

sādilvārī: fund for 'contingent' expenses
sāhotrā: 6%
sāheb: lord, sovereign
sākukār (also *sāvkār*): banker, merchant
saṃsthānik: tributary chieftain
sanad: official document or decree
sanyasi: renouncer
saraṇjām: assignment of land or land-revenue
sardār: captain, commander, high official
sardārī: dominion
sardesai: hereditary district official
sardeśmukh(*ī*): head-deśmukh(ship) or emolument ad 10–12% of idem
sardeśpāṇḍgirī: hereditary head-accountantship of a district or province
sarkār: government, superior
sarsubhedār: government official
sārvabhaum: lord of all land
savār: cavalry
śerī: government land
śerṇī: fee
śetsanadīs: armed retainers, police-force

sharia, *shar'īya* (Ar.): Islamic law
śibandi: soldier
śikkekaṭyār: seal-and-dagger; emblem of delegated sovereignty
śiledār: armed horseman
śivāy jamā: extra collections or assessments
ṣubahdār (P.): Mughal provincial governor
subhā: province
subhedār: provincial governor
sulṭān (A., P.): sovereign
svakīya: 'one's own'
svarājya: self-rule
swaddle: cess

tahnāmā: treaty document
taināt jābtā: deed of assignment
ṭakā, a coin
tākīdpatra: deed of injunction
ṭālebaṇd: account of receipt and expenditure
tālukā: territorial division
tappa: a territorial division
tarf: territorial division
ṭhāṇa: garrison, military post

'ulamā' (Ar.): Muslim jurists or theologians
umma (Ar.): the brotherhood of Islam
uparī: temporary cultivator or tenant

vakīl: ambassador
vāṇṭekarī: share-cropper
varāt: bill of exchange issued by the government
varṣāsan: cash allowance paid annually
vasūl: collections
vatan(*dār*): (holder of) hereditary vested right
vazīr: high official
veṭh begār: forced labour
vilāyat: domain of a zamindar
vṛtti: hereditary estate

waqf (Ar.): Islamic religious foundation

yādī: document, attestation

zabardastī: illegitimate force
zakāt: customs
zamīndār(*ī*): hereditary landed gentry
zāt saraṇjām: personal assignment of land or land-revenue
zilhā: province
zortalabī: refractoriness
zulūm: oppression

INTRODUCTION

It is one of the axioms of classical Indian thought that a society without a king (*a-rājaka*) is not viable. A kingless society would be prone to the 'logic of the fish' (*matsya-nyāya*). The king's sovereignty was instituted as a guarantee of safety and protection.[1]

Such a conception of sovereignty as the precondition of order in society is also characteristic of the political theory of modern Europe. For Bodin sovereignty was the supreme legal power of the state and the essential constituent of a political community. In Hobbes' view the covenant by which individuals resigned self-help and subjected themselves to a sovereign generated 'that great Leviathan, or rather . . . that Mortal God, to which we owe under the Immortal God, our peace and defence'.[2] Rousseau conceived of sovereignty as a power 'wholly absolute, wholly sacred, wholly inviolable', but it was not founded on a covenant between a superior and an inferior but on a social contract through which individuals 'profitably exchanged an uncertain and precarious life for a better and more secure one'.[3] In Europe sovereignty, the guarantee of order, was seen as absolute, but not as unlimited. Under Rousseau's social contract, most explicitly, sovereignty did not pass 'the bounds of public advantage'. Less philosophically-minded European observers typically took the hereditary aristocracy with its inalienable landed interests as the crucial mitigator of sovereign power, while they attributed unmitigated sovereignty, the brutal imposition of *force majeure*, to the East. Thus Bacon: 'A monarchy where there is no nobility at all, is ever pure and absolute tyranny; as that of the Turks. For nobility attempers sovereignty,

[1] Cf. R. Lingat, *Les Sources du Droit dans le Système Traditionnel de l'Inde* (Paris and The Hague, 1967), pp. 231–2.
[2] T. Hobbes, *Leviathan* (Oxford, 1946), ch. 17.
[3] J. J. Rousseau, *Du Contrat Social* (Paris, 1973), II, 4.

and draws the eyes of the people somewhat aside from the line royal.'[4] The alleged absence of a landed nobility in the Oriental states of the seventeenth and eighteenth centuries gave rise to the lapidary notion of Oriental Despotism which, throughout modern history, served to conjure up a vaguely defined complex of persistent apprehensions about the non-European civilized world which seemed less innocent than 'Barbary'. The conception of the despotic Oriental state still dominates even the contemporary scholarly debate but there is an increasing awareness of its inadequacy. Perry Anderson, in his comparative study of Absolutism, retains the term, but 'in a strictly provisional and merely descriptive sense' and he concedes that 'scientific concepts for the analysis of Oriental states in this epoch are still largely lacking.'[5]

The theory of Oriental Despotism has of course never been anything other than provisional. Yet, it could be argued that even when taken as provisional, the theory, including as minimal ingredients the postulates of the absence of vested intermediary rights of an agrarian and commercial gentry ('civil society') and state-monopoly of land (sometimes of people as well), contains a curious self-contradiction. While its adherents are commonly at pains to point out the development of proto-democratic features in feudal and post-feudal Europe, in the East they observe but 'decadence', 'anarchy' and 'rebellions' setting in with a supposed 'decline' of the power of the despot. Nothing good could come out of despotism. Indeed, reading the descriptive accounts of European travellers and historians, one is tempted to believe that an East without despotism was almost naturally bound to veer towards the other extreme of the 'logic of the fish'. The delicate question which remains unanswered however concerns the transition between the two conditions: how can an allegedly all-powerful despotism 'decline' or 'disintegrate' at all? *Prima facie* it seems fairly obvious that the two great despotisms of the Turkish Ottoman and Mughal dynasties – the ones of which Europeans were most manifestly aware – were caught in a parallel development. Consolidated systems of 'total power' in their heyday, they are thought to have lapsed into anarchic disorder almost at the same time, at about the turn of the seventeenth century, or somewhat earlier, when their 'natural' expansionism overreached itself. At that fateful point the

[4] *The Essays or Counsels Civil and Moral* (1632), quoted from P. Anderson, *Lineages of the Absolutist State* (London, 1980), p. 398.

[5] P. Anderson, *Lineages of the Absolutist State*, p. 365, note 7.

autonomist aspirations of provincial governors, in combination with local 'revolts' led by *a'yān* or *zamīndārs* disrupted the respective imperial dominions.[6] In the case of India the transition from 'despotism' to 'anarchy' appeared particularly abrupt and was felt to have coincided with the death of the last great Mughal Emperor Aurangzeb in 1707. To the present day the eighteenth century in India is first of all the period 'between the Mughal and the British empires', although it is equally avowed that this period 'defies categories'.[7] Understandably, the interest of most historians was until very recently practically confined to those periods in which they thought some kind of unitary order could be relatively easily detected while the eighteenth century was patched over with a plethora of decline theories. The most influential of these theories is perhaps the one advanced by the leading Mughal historian Irfan Habib, which holds that the Mughal Empire, from the late seventeenth century onwards, destroyed itself by 'excessive exploitation' of the peasantry and *zamīndārs* leading to 'agrarian revolts' of Jats, Sikhs, Marathas and other autochthonous groups in the eighteenth century.[8] The Mughal order, although unmitigatedly despotic, was thus 'destroyed' and 'no new order was, or could be, created by the forces ranged against it . . . the gates were opened to reckless

[6] The parallel has often been drawn but awaits a systematic study. For the Ottoman case, see K. K. Barbir, *Ottoman Rule in Damascus, 1708–1758* (Princeton, 1981); C. V. Findley, *Bureaucratic Reform in the Ottoman Empire: The Sublime Porte, 1789–1922* (Princeton, 1980); H. Islamoğlu & Çağlar Keyder, 'Agenda for Ottoman History', *Review*, 1, 1 (Summer 1977), pp. 31–55; K. H. Karpat, 'The Stages of Ottoman History', in: *idem* (ed.), *The Ottoman State and its Place in World History* (Leiden, 1974), pp. 79–98; B. McGowan, *Economic Life in Ottoman Europe* (Cambridge, 1981); V. P. Mutafcieva, 'L'Institution de l'Ayanlik pendant les dernières décennies du XVIIIe siècle', *Études Balkaniques*, 2–3 (1965), pp. 233–47; Y. Özkaya, *Osmanli Imparatorluğunda Âyânlik* (Ankara, 1977); K. Röhrborn, *Untersuchungen zur osmanischen Verwaltungsgeschichte* (Berlin and New York, 1973); D. R. Sadat, 'Urban Notables in the Ottoman Empire: The Âyân' (unpublished PhD thesis, Rutgers University, 1969); D. R. Sadat, 'Rumeli Ayanlari: The Eighteenth Century', *Journal of Modern History*, 44,3 (1972), pp. 346–63; S. J. Shaw, *History of the Ottoman Empire and Modern Turkey*, vol. 1 (Cambridge, 1976); A. Sućeska, 'Bedeutung und Entwicklung des Begriffes A'yān im Osmanischen Reich', *Südostforschungen*, 25 (1966), pp. 3–26.

[7] R. B. Barnett, *North India between Empires: Awadh, the Mughals, and the British, 1720–1801* (Berkeley, 1980), p. 1.

[8] I. Habib, *The Agrarian System of Mughal India* (Bombay, 1963), pp. 317–51; *idem*, 'The Social Distribution of Landed Property in Pre-British India (a Historical Survey)', in: R. S. Sharma & V. Jha (eds), *Indian Society: Historical Probings in memory of D. D. Kosambi* (New Delhi, 1964), p. 315. J. F. Richards did much to discredit another widely held view, that a shortage of jagirs in the Deccan was a major factor in the 'decline' (cf. *Mughal Administration in Golconda* (Oxford, 1975), esp. pp. 200–1, 214).

rapine, anarchy and foreign conquest'.[9] The view that the eighteenth century as a whole was a period of decline and dissolution has been expressed countless times by the British in the nineteenth century and in one way or another – but hardly ever toned down – pervades the literature on the last phase of Mughal history. There have been in the past decades a few isolated attempts to see the eighteenth century 'in its own terms' by a closer reading of especially the earliest British documentation.[10] A reconstruction and rehabilitation of the eighteenth century was held up as a possibility, but appeared difficult to achieve and in effect the picture remained one of fragmentation.

In the meantime it did become evident that the proliferation of decline theories was matched by a virtually complete absence of quantitative economic data exhibiting such decline as an overall process. The late Mughal chronicles cry out about 'rebellion' and 'oppression', but so do the earlier ones and these appear to have been the stereotype repudiations (religiously sanctioned at that) of virtually everything that was beyond the pale of Mughal regulation – everything non-Mughal or sub-Mughal, which was a lot. Far from being the detached observations of Mughal economic historians these were the counterpart of the condemnations of the feud system by the churchmen of medieval Europe. Writing from early British sources mainly, C. A. Bayly has recently rejected the general charge of 'decline' and 'native misgovernment' in a forceful argument attesting that 'the Black Legend of the eighteenth century' was an issue in British imperial ideology which served to counter Indian nationalism.[11] Bayly's detailed reconstruction of a section of the intermediate economy associated with a service gentry and a homogeneous merchant class which solidified between state and peasantry and which were to become an important 'indigenous component in European expansion' is at the same time an argument for continuity and development. It convincingly demonstrates the adaptability of the eighteenth-century economy and points to a balanced redistribution of resources rather than any significant overall corrosion.

9 Habib, *Agrarian System*, p. 351.

10 Amongst these B. S. Cohn's essay 'Political Systems in Eighteenth Century India: The Banaras Region', *Journal of the American Oriental Society*, 82 (1962), pp. 312–20 was in many respects seminal.

11 *Rulers, Townsmen and Bazaars: North Indian society in the age of British expansion, 1770–1870* (Cambridge, 1983), esp. pp. 11–12, 35–7, 72, 162–3, 267.

The present book, the evidence and inspiration for which were found in the eighteenth-century Maratha sources, does not attempt to provide new quantitative economic data. Not only in India but perhaps everywhere in the world the *ancien régime* documentation preserved by conquerors and revolutionaries is shallow and often contradictory on economic aspects while these are not really differentiated or isolated from other (social, religious, juridical) aspects of institutions. A few British statements which we will bring up as bearing on the question point unambiguously to agricultural expansion and prosperity in the districts under Maratha rule in the second part of the eighteenth century and wholly fit the profile sketched by Bayly. These statements, to be sure, coming from the first generation of British administrators, can be put next to a much larger number of others made by the same men in which the Maratha rule is depicted with more venom than even the Mughals were accustomed to employ. Then again sanctimonious moralizing rather than dispassionate and objective assessments of economic or political processes seem to determine the content of these statements. The British historian of the Marathas and Political Agent at the Satara court, James Grant Duff, saw them as 'very corrupt'; in his view

> perfidy and want of principle are the strongest features in their character, and their successes have perhaps been less owing to their activity and courage than to their artifice and treachery. Their presence of mind, patience, and intrepidity are truly surprising since they appear to have no point of honour to fight for, few feelings of generosity or gratitude, and little *esprit de corps*.[12]

Thomas Broughton, a camp-follower of Scindhia, wrote the following summary description of Maratha character for his brother in England:

> They are deceitful, treacherous, narrow-minded, rapacious, and notorious liars; the only quality they are endowed with which could, according to our system of ethics, be placed ... to the credit side of the account, being candour: for there is not one of the propensities I have enumerated to which a Maratha would not immediately plead guilty; in his idea of things, they are requisite to form a perfect character: and to all accusations of

Cf. also T. Raychaudhuri & I. Habib (eds), *The Cambridge Economic History of India*, vol. I (Cambridge, 1982), pp. 177–8.

12 *EIP*, 4, p. 215; and cf. *History of the Mahrattas* (orig. publ. 1826), 2 vols (New Delhi, 1971).

falsehood, treachery, extortion, &c., he has one common answer: *Marāṭhā darbār āhe* ('tis a Maratha court).[13]

Others, like William Chaplin, selected the Maharashtrian brahmans for particular criticism; these were 'an intriguing, lying, corrupt, licentious and unprincipled race of people, who are in no respect to be trusted, unless numerous checks are established to guard against their knavery and dishonesty'.[14] In Henry Pottinger's opinion the brahmans were 'the most unprincipled, dishonest, shameless, and lying race in India'.[15] What should be noted is that such evaluations are all expressed in the same mentalistic jargon. There is at best an acknowledgement of a different system of 'ethics' but never of a different political system. Broughton however noted the incongruity of the observed propensities being 'requisite to make a perfect character'. Chaplin, interestingly, wrote earlier that in India 'treason or rebellion does not seem to have been regarded so serious a crime as in Europe'.[16] In sharp conflict with the conventional image of the Marathas as a predatory, rapacious horde is further, apart from the British observations of the flourishing condition of the country under their rule, the fact that they left a most detailed and complete administrative record, the largest single body of indigenous material which has been preserved of the eighteenth century. The Maratha documentation, if taken in its entirety, reaches behind the Mughal semantic idiom to show the socio-political forces at work. It thus allows for a reappraisal of the most important aspects of the late Mughal development which the Mughal sources themselves merely hide behind a façade of moralistic or religious condemnation, the categoric charge of 'revolt' (which was the parallel of the British perception of 'anarchy'), or which they reduce to uniformity by the superposition of a universalist and centralist bureaucratic grid. Most present-day Mughal historians would probably, due to the centralist bias of so much of their source material, be prepared to subscribe to the assumption, made explicit by J. F. Richards, that the Mughal state (in the despotic stage of the seventeenth century at least) represented 'a realm of public order' analogous to our own conception of the modern state, although the latter would be more effective and 'limited'.[17] Starting from this premise the rise to

[13] T. D. Broughton, *Letters from a Mahratta Camp* (Calcutta, 1977), pp. 71–2.
[14] *EIP*, 4, p. 278. [15] *Ibid.*, p. 301. [16] *Ibid.*, p. 271.
[17] *Golconda*, p. 311; and see *ibid.*, pp. 314–15.

power of the Marathas in the late seventeenth and early eighteenth century could only be seen as a disturbance of order.

In this book an attempt is made to look at the other side of this process. It is not directly concerned with the refutation of the moral or political accusations which were so profusely brought against Indian rulers, and in particular against the Marathas. Its purpose is rather to avoid anachronistic conceptions which derive from the 'formal rationality' (as Max Weber called it) of the modern state, and thus to introduce, analyse, illustrate and assess a new set of key 'scientific' concepts and substitute these for the standard prejudicial or provisional vocabulary of 'despotism', 'treason', 'rapaciousness', 'corruption', 'rebellion', etc. Instead of seeing the rise of Maratha power in the eighteenth century as a disturbance of a despotic, quasi-modern but unlimited Mughal order, elements of continuity can be brought out next to significant dynamic and conflictive change. This continuity is first of all evident in the political and administrative terminology and practices of the eighteenth century which clearly refer back to the preceding centuries of Muslim domination. But also the rise of gentry groups such as the Marathas can be placed firmly within the context of the expansion of Muslim power in India, from perhaps the fourteenth century onwards, rather than seeing this exclusively as a force rallying against it. The Marathas especially could almost without effort intensify and exploit the factional politics of the Mughals in the Deccan. The gentry of the north, Jats, Rajputs, Bundelas, Sikhs, Bhumihars, and others seem to have benefited from an enduring Mughal overlordship in a variety of ways, rising to prosperity with it and gathering strength from it so as to be able eventually to create rival foci of autonomous power with close links to agrarian society, and with close links to the Marathas. A case can be made, then, that Muslim domination in India, after a chequered process of expansion which went on for centuries, in the end fell prey to its own success. The political dissolution of the Empire, in this view, went hand in hand with the expansion of the agrarian and mercantile economy and the rise of the intermediate sections of society (which then became a stepping-stone for the establishment of British power, as Bayly argues). In all this, the Islamic idiom of legitimation shows a remarkable resilience up to the Mutiny of 1857 and beyond, creating a third element of continuity in the eighteenth century.

In summary, the primary aim of this book is to show how the

establishment and consolidation of Maratha sovereignty or *svarājya* over the larger part of the Mughal domains, i.e., over most of the Indian subcontinent, took place within the political and socio-economic context of Mughal expansion itself. Secondly, how it related to the structures of dominance established by the Mughals and how the *svarājya*, as a political structure in its own right, represented precisely that intermediary gentry or *zamīndārī* stratum which the universalist Islamic ideology of empire dismissed as illegitimate and which the theory of despotism excluded as non-existent.[18] The eighteenth century is thus evinced to be the century of the 'gentrification' of the Muslim empire. On the other hand, as already indicated, it is not suggested that this process is without antecedents and cannot be traced further back to preceding centuries. The Indo-Persian chronicles disclose a growing awareness of the Marathas and of *zamīndārs* generally from the fourteenth century onwards. In numerous ways, in agrarian management and in politico-military statebuilding, Hindu gentry and Muslim conquerors mutually supported each other in a system of 'symbiotic dissent' from the point of first contact. The Marathas of the Western Deccan rose to the fore in the Delhi Sultanate, later in the Sultanates of Bidar, Ahmadnagar and Bijapur which had branched off from the former. In the final stage they could, through a process which was referred to as *fitna*, 'sedition' or 'rebellion' aligning with internecine Muslim conflict, penetrate into the expanding Mughal Empire of the late seventeenth century. It is with the inwardness of this process of *fitna*, of the expansion of Maratha *zamīndārī* power and the way that it was subsequently institutionalized within a realigning and dissolving Mughal Empire in the eighteenth century and led to a new agrarian *mise en valeur*, that the following pages are concerned.

[18] Attempts to describe the rise of *zamīndārī* power in Northern India in the eighteenth century on the basis of local indigenous sources in terms of a shift of sovereignty are rare, and unsystematic and restricted in scope; to support our argument we may yet adduce the following case-studies: Ph.B. Calkins, 'The Formation of a Regionally Oriented Ruling Group in Bengal, 1700–1740', *JAS*, 29, 4 (1970), pp. 799–806; R. P. Rana, 'Agrarian Revolts in Northern India during the Late 17th and Early 18th Century', *IESHR*, 18, 3–4 (1981), pp. 287–326; M. Alam, 'Aspects of Agrarian Disturbances in North India in the Early Eighteenth Century' (Mimeograph, Jawaharlal Nehru University, 1983); M. Alam, 'Mughal Centre and the Subas of Awadh and the Punjab, 1707–1748' (Thesis, Jawaharlal Nehru University, New Delhi, 1976), esp. pp. vii, xv, 22, 33, 37–8, 64, 88, 91–2, 99, 100, 121, 144, 210, 213, 215, 218–19, 232, 235, 238, 262, 354.

1

Brahman, king and emperor

1 Sovereignty and universal dominion*

Under the impact of external physical threats to the survival of the state in the unstable international environment of continental Europe, Machiavelli and later political 'realists' redefined the relationship between religion and politics in its modern form. Fundamental to this redefinition was the insight that politics is inseparable from armed violence and characterized by a special morality and rationale of its own. Political expediency was radically put beyond all religious or ethical considerations. As Machiavelli wrote: 'A prince .. should have no other object or thought, nor acquire skill in anything, except war, its organization, and its discipline'.[1]

Reason of state, the power-interest of the state as foundation of an aggressive foreign policy, and the correlated concept of sovereignty had been unknown in the Middle Ages. The Christian West constituted a spiritual and temporal unity under the condominium of Pope and Emperor – a unity which manifested itself as such to the outside world. The decomposition of this medieval fabric into a multiplicity of states during the Renaissance led, via the Reformation, Hobbes and Locke, the French Encyclopaedists and the French Revolution, to the modern concept of the 'national state', in which religion and politics are separated, and in which natural law and human reason regulate the lives of 'free' citizens. Machiavelli accused the Christian faith of having weakened the military *virtù*, but on the other hand attempted to make use of religion as a

* This subchapter appeared earlier in an adapted form under the title 'Sovereignty and Universal Dominion in South Asia', in *IESHR*, 21, 3 (1984), pp. 265–92.

[1] '*Deve . . . un principe non avere altro oggetto nè altro pensiero, nè prendere cosa alcuna per sua arte, fuora della guerra ed ordini e disciplina di essa*', *Il Principe* (Florence, 1857), Cap. XIV.

weapon against anarchy, a means of mass domestication, and to enhance patriotism. This was the contradiction which characterized nationalism in Europe, where it had to be detached from a Christian universalist order which transcended national boundaries and national identifications. The only solution which offered itself was to restore the faith to its origin and disentangle it from temporal affairs.

Concomitant with the development of a system of territorially demarcated national states the notion of 'sovereignty' was introduced to give expression to the internal unity of these states, their centrally co-ordinated and autonomous character *vis-à-vis* the subject population which came to be defined as 'society'. Thus the modern state acquired the 'sovereign' capacity to create new laws and the exclusive power to impose obedience to them on subjects who were addressed in their abstract non-particularist capacity of 'citizenship' which lent them equality and which was obtained merely by virtue of an individual's birth within the state's territory. At the same time, the concept of sovereignty expressed the political autonomy of modern states with regard to each other. Any alliance between states or 'linkage politics' is at best a supplementary asset to what is in essence a closed and independent entity complete within itself, a matter of transitory agreement dictated by self-interest, but never constitutive of sovereign power or enforceable by a paramount supra-national arbiter. The modern state, in other words, is transcendent and cannot be transcended.[2] The 'balance of power' of the international state system could be upset at any time by the application of the logic of reason of state, which proclaims the acquisition of territory through war as the first national ambition. Modern territorial sovereignty emerged out of feudalism, but it came to be conceived of as a form of absolute ownership in the sense of Roman property law. From this derived the assumption of international law that the sovereign states are, relative to each other, in a state of nature.[3] The pre-feudal institution of tribal kingship had no territorial basis, and it could only transcend itself by resuscitating the Roman tradition of universal imperial dominion.[4] This universalist conception of

[2] The transcendence of the state is also postulated in those theories which deduce sovereignty from a 'social contract'; see for instance Rousseau, *Contrat Social*, II, 4: '*le pouvoir souverain, tout absolu, tout sacré, tout inviolable qu'il est, ne passe ni peut passer les bornes des conventions générales*'.

[3] H. J. S. Maine, *Ancient Law* (London, 1924), p. 65.

[4] *Ibid.*, pp. 61–2.

Empire could integrate the medieval feudal order, but it was incompatible with the idea of the national state.

a. Indian nationalism

It was one of the great claims of Indian nationalism that the South Asian subcontinent had historically not merely been a geographical and cultural unity but also a political one.[5] This claim was set against the tendency of British authors to stress the heterogeneity of the subcontinent and to attribute to the British conquerors the exclusive merit of its political unification. Under the British Raj, in effect, the boundaries of the subcontinent coincided with the territory under the control of the British army. The Partition of 1947 however caused the formation of *two* territorially demarcated states: Pakistan, founded on an Islamic inspiration, and India, a secular state in which religion was not to meddle with politics. The frontiers of these states were to a large extent artifacts. The politicians of the Congress saw the Partition as a tragedy, and it can hardly be denied that it had a deep traumatic effect on the newly created nations.[6] For the nationalists the evidence of pan-Indian historical unity was to be found in the periodic recurrence of imperial structures on a subcontinental or nearly subcontinental scale.[7] Their claim was not founded on an allegedly religious heritage, but it did have the convenience that it could refer back to pre-Muslim as well as Muslim and even post-Muslim periods of domination. It was in fact a claim of political territory which should have allowed Indian nationalism to keep religion out of politics or work out a Hindu–Muslim coalition. There were certain clues in the Indian tradition which seemed to justify this stand. The ancient Brahmanical, Buddhist and Jain literature commonly took the whole of the subcontinent as an almost self-evident frame of reference. Later, Indian Islam, and the Marathas in its wake, tended to do the same. The paradox is that the imperial unification of pre-British India always took place explicitly under the aegis of religion, while modern Indian nationalism singled out the pan-Indian territorial dimension of this imperial tradition to justify the creation of a *secular* national Indian state. As Louis Dumont has

[5] Cf. Markovits, 'L'Inde Coloniale: Nationalisme et Histoire', *Annales ESC*, 37, 4 (1982), p. 657.
[6] Cf. A. Jussawalla (ed.), *New Writing in India* (Penguin Book, 1977).
[7] Markovits, 'Nationalisme et Histoire', *loc. cit.*

stressed, territory is, apart from the will of a people to form a nation, the only element which is absolutely indispensable for the realization of a nation, while other elements such as a common history and culture are perhaps useful but can be left out.[8] This explains the nationalist emphasis on the 'national unity' of the South Asian subcontinent, but it is nonetheless evident that the role played by religion in Indian nationalism is at least as contradictory and ambiguous as in the nationalisms of Europe. Much of the distorted character of these nationalist views is now taken for granted. The historical and social sciences again underscore the complexity and variety of the Indian tradition, replacing the simplistic views of national unity with a picture of an irreducible heterogeneity.

b. The 'science of politics' (*arthaśāstra*)

A source of confusion common to both the historiographical and the nationalist views of Indian political history lies in an anachronistic interpretation of the relationship between religion and politics in the traditional setting. This came out clearly in 1905 with the discovery of the single extant political treatise of ancient India, Kautilya's *Arthaśāstra* – a text often attributed to a brahman minister of Candragupta Maurya (324–300 BC), although this remains disputable – which provided new arguments to nationalist intellectuals to support the claim to a specifically Indian political tradition, while to others it seemed rather a confirmation of the picture of a 'hopeless' political fragmentation. In any case the political 'realism' of this treatise appeared to warrant an emancipation from the cloudy obscurantism and otherworldliness that had thus far stigmatized Indian thought in general, particularly in the British estimate. Kautilya was at once hailed as an Indian Machiavelli *avant la lettre*.

This comparison was easily drawn on account of the primacy that both authors give to politics over religion and ethics. A detailed analysis however reveals the anachronistic element in it and provides a completely different model of Indian sovereignty. To begin with, it may be asked what conception we find here of ancient Indian 'politics' and how this relates to our own conceptions. Secondly, how does this conception relate to 'religion'?

[8] 'Nationalism and Communalism', in: *Religion, Politics and History in India* (Paris and The Hague, 1970), p. 107.

At the very outset the Science of Politics (*artha-śāstra*) states to have as its object 'the acquisition and protection of the earth'.[9] The author addresses himself primarily to the king as the political agent. This king is not specified by name, but is referred to as the *vijigīṣu* or 'conqueror-to-be'.[10] Political action however is not undertaken by the king on his own, but by a complement of seven *prakṛtis* or 'constituents': next to the king (*rāja*), these are the minister (*amātya*), the country (*janapada*), the fortified city (*durga*), the treasury (*kośa*), the army (*daṇḍa*), and the ally (*mitra*).[11] Thus is constituted a polity which is essentially open-ended, since it includes what we would call an 'extraneous' constituent, the ally. The ally is a king who 'has no separate interest from the *vijigīṣu*'.[12] He is likewise complemented by six constituents. It is an axiom of the science that the *janapada* or 'country' of the conqueror-to-be is surrounded on all sides by another constituent which does not belong to him and which is called 'enemy' (*ari, amitra*).[13] In Kautilya's schematic representation the enemy's country, in its turn, is encircled by the conqueror-to-be's ally; the ally, again, is encircled by the enemy's ally; the latter by the conqueror-to-be's ally's ally.[14] Kautilya calls this the 'circle of kings'. Both the conqueror-to-be and his enemy have a circle of six times as many constituents as they have allies, eighteen in Kautilya's scheme. Beyond the circle there is however not a void, but a 'middle king' who is either a potential ally or a potential enemy of the conqueror-to-be, depending on the latter's strength.[15] Beyond the middle king there is a 'neutral king' who may ally himself with the middle king, the enemy, or with the conqueror-to-be, depending on the strength of each.[16] The postulate of the presence of these middle and neutral kings implies in fact that the circle of kings does not stop with the *vijigīṣu*'s ally's ally, but goes on *ad infinitum*. Basically the scheme of the circle of kings can be reduced to that of a political realm defined by the distinction ally/enemy. Kautilya thus speaks of two 'dominions' (*viṣaya*): there is the *sva-viṣaya* or the dominion of the conqueror-to-be himself, and the *para-viṣaya* or the dominion of the enemy.[17] But these dominions should not be seen as consolidated territorial states which are to be defended and extended by

[9] R. P. Kangle (ed.), *The Kauṭilīya Arthaśāstra*, 3 vols (Bombay, 1965–72), 1.1.1. (compare 15.1.2.)

[10] *Ibid.*, 6.2.13. [11] *Ibid.*, 6.1.1. [12] *Ibid.*, 6.1.12. [13] *Ibid.*, 6.2.14.

[14] *Ibid.*, 6.2.15 ff. see H. Scharfe, *Untersuchungen zur Staatsrechtslehre des Kauṭalya* (Wiesbaden, 1968), pp. 120–7 for a useful explication of this topic.

[15] *Arthaśāstra*, 6.2.21. [16] *Ibid.*, 6.2.22. [17] *Ibid.*, 1.13–14.

warfare against neighbouring states. In Kautilya's conception a 'dominion' extends over a *janapada*; this is a 'country', but it differs from our own abstract conception of territory in that it compounds territory and the indwelling people into a single undifferentiated entity of 'people-cum-territory'.[18]

A second difference, which results partly from the first and partly from the proximity of the enemy, is that 'the *janapada* is shared with the enemy'.[19] In the scheme of alliances and rivalries that is envisaged in Kautilya's circle of kings this means that the constituents of the conqueror-to-be and those of his enemy are intermingled. The reason for this is that each king's dominion is made up of two categories of people: 'those who are likely to be won over (by the enemy)' and 'those who are not likely to be won over (by the enemy)'.[20] The difference is a matter of degree, but it is especially the first category which constitutes the point of impact of the enemy within the country of the conqueror-to-be. *Vice versa*, it is through the same category of people in the enemy's country that the conqueror-to-be can extend his own dominion or sovereignty over that of his enemy. The category of 'those likely to be won over' is divided by Kautilya into four classes or *vargas*. He refers to these as the classes of 'the enraged' (*kruddhavarga*), 'the frightened' (*bhītavarga*), 'the greedy' (*lubdhavarga*), and 'the proud' (*mānivarga*).[21] They are all people who have grievances and feel that in one way or another their interests are damaged under the existing dispensation of the king or have other egoistic motives for supporting the king's enemy. Now the policy-recommendations of the *Arthaśāstra* amount to no more than stratagems which the king should employ to keep both categories of his subjects and servants on his side, at the same time to prevent the enemy from winning them over, and furthermore extend his dominion by winning over the subjects and servants of the enemy. In principle the stratagems to be employed by the king are the same in his own dominion and in that of his enemy. There is therefore no distinction of kind between 'external' and 'internal' politics. Kautilya draws up a list of four general political 'means' (*upāya*), with the following order of precedence: conciliation (*sāntva, sāma*), gift-giving (*dāna*), sedition and winning over (*bheda*), and force (*daṇḍa*).[22] The application of

[18] *Janapada* is a *tatpuruṣa* or dependent noun-compound of *jana*, 'people', and *pada*, 'abode', thus meaning literally 'abode of people'.

[19] '*jānapadāstvamitrasādhāraṇāḥ iti*' (*Arthaśāstra*, 8.1.27).

[20] *Ibid.*, 1.13–14. [21] *Ibid.*, 1.13.22; 1.14.2–5. [22] *Ibid.*, 9.6.51–61.

force comes in the last place and is also explicitly discredited in favour of sedition (*bheda*) in all those situations which involve multitudes of people.[23] Such depreciation of force as a means of conquest or politics is not a peculiarity of Kautilya. It recurs in Indian political writings until as late as the eighteenth century as the scheme of the four *upāya*.[24] It is likewise found in Manu: 'A king should try to conquer his enemies by conciliation (*sāma*), by gifts (*dāna*), and by sedition (*bheda*), used either separately or conjointly, never by fighting'.[25]

The conquest which is desired by the conqueror-to-be is not primarily a matter of military action, but of expansion of his sovereignty or *svaviṣaya* by effecting alliances with 'those who are likely to be won over' under the enemy's sovereignty or *paraviṣaya*. This is done by sending spies or double agents (often disguised as holy men) and envoys practising a policy of instigation (*upajāpa*; lit. 'whispering') and the four political *upāya*, so that the conqueror-to-be can 'make terms' with them and employ them for his own purpose.[26] The king's agents should also infiltrate among 'those who are not likely to be won over' and cause there sedition (*bheda*) and create dissensions by 'pointing out (to them) the defects of the enemy'.[27] At the same time, spies are set everywhere in the king's own dominion to check and ensure by the same means the loyalties of his subjects and servants and guard them against the instigations of the enemy (*paropajāpa*).[28] In this way there is throughout the *Arthaśāstra* a constant obsession with secret tests, secret servants, spies and counter-spies, the guarding of secrets, methods of interrogation, the ascertainment of loyalties and disloyalties, secret intentions and conspiracies of officials and subjects. As long as there is an enemy, this enemy appears to be everywhere. Obviously the elimination of the enemy would render 'politics' entirely redundant. However, in order to eliminate his enemy the king has to eliminate not only the enemy with proximate country but also his enemy's ally, and his enemy's ally's ally, and so on. It is logical then that Kautilya makes the conquest of the entire earth the ultimate aim of the *vijigīṣu*: 'one possessed of high personal qualities, though ruling over a small country, being united with the excellences of the constituents [of his kingdom] and conversant with [the science of]

[23] *Ibid.*, 9.5.2; 9.6.30; 11.1.2. [24] See p. 33.
[25] G. S. Nene (ed.), *Mānava Dharmaśāstra* (Benares, 1970), 7.198.
[26] *Arthaśāstra*, 1.14.1–12. [27] *Ibid.*, 1.16.26–34; 1.14.12.
[28] *Ibid.*, 1.13.11–26.

politics, does conquer the entire earth (*pṛthivīṃ kṛtsnam*) and never loses'.[29] This conquest of the earth is to be effected in stages: 'After conquering the enemy's country the *vijigīṣu* should seek to seize the middle king, after succeeding in this, the neutral king'.[30] Kautilya also concretely equates 'the world' with 'the region extending northwards between the Himalayas (*himavat*), i.e., 'snow-mountains') and the sea, one thousand *yojanas* in extent across'; this is 'the realm of the universal Emperor' or *cakravarti-kṣetra*, which is coterminous with the whole South Asian subcontinent within its natural frontiers.[31]

It is an argument which seems to give us a clue to what has been called the 'imperative' of Indian history: the political unification of the subcontinent. But it is quite significant that Kautilya, once arrived at this point, does not describe any further how such a pan-Indian Empire should be administered. Kautilya merely adds that 'after conquering the world, the king should enjoy it divided into *varṇas* (castes) with *āśramas* (life-stages) in accordance with his *dharma*'.[32] Clearly, the elimination or final conquest of the enemy paves the way for the establishment of the religious order of the *varṇas*. The king's universal dominion is not a dominion or sovereignty in the political sense, as with the circle of kings, which was inherently unstable as it was based on shifting alliances and antagonisms. When the political process has run its full course it transcends its own temporality and makes place for the universal *dharma*. It can be concluded then that in Kautilya's case, in contrast with that of Machiavelli, there is no question of a 'divorce' of religion and politics; for although in the *Arthaśāstra* politics has its own autonomous logic (in which however armed violence has a subordinate role or has no place) and is not directly linked to an ethical or religious doctrine, the ultimate aim of political power is

[29] *Ibid.*, 6.1.18. [30] *Ibid.*, 13.4.54. (For alternatives see 13.4.56–61.)

[31] *Ibid.*, 9.1.18. The term *cakravarti* denotes a king 'who makes turn the wheel (of the *dharma*)' as well as one 'who has driven (his war chariot) around the entire earth (conceived as a circle)' (G. Fussman, 'Le concept d'empire dans l'Inde ancienne', in: M. Duverger (ed.), *Le Concept d'Empire* (Paris, 1981), pp. 380–2). *Cakravarti* and *sārvabhauma*, 'possessing the entire earth', are also used as adjectives qualifying the title of *rāja*. Kingship is thus always ideologically associated with universal dominion, but, as Fussman points out, there does not appear to have been any real difference in ancient India between a king and an emperor (called *saṃrāja*, or otherwise) nor does the Sanskrit political literature know a term for an empire as a territorial, administrative or political entity (*ibid.*, pp. 383–8). For a further analysis of the term *cakravarti* see J. Gonda, *Ancient Indian Kingship from the Religious Point of View* (Leiden, 1966), pp. 123–8.

[32] *Arthaśāstra*, 13.5.62.

the establishment of the king's universal dominion and the universal *dharma*. It may also be noted that in contrast with the Christian doctrine the *Arthaśāstra* makes no attempt to lift politics as such to a spiritual plane. In the next section it will be seen that the *dharma* legitimates politics by being its antithesis. The aim of 'world conquest' derives from a political logic, but the *dharma* transcends politics and an exposition of its contents properly belongs in the *dharmaśāstra* or 'science of religion', not in the *arthaśāstra*.

c. The 'science of religion' (*dharmaśāstra*)

In post-Vedic Hinduism it was the king (*rāja, svāmi, pati*, etc.) who represented *artha*, while the *brahman* represented the universal *dharma*. This separation of functions itself was a triumph of the *dharma*, a rationalization of thought which we associate with the 'axial age'.[33] The Vedic Aryans already knew a disjunction of priesthood and kingship but their priesthood did not yet form an exclusive caste of religious specialists.[34] The Vedic age of heroic sacrifice was characterized by cyclical patterns of reciprocity, co-operation and agonistic rivalry. The caste system or *varṇa* order is first introduced in the mythical projection of the *Puruṣasūkta*, the sacrifice of Primeval Man, where it signals the dissolution of the body politic, *vi-rāj*: 'his mouth became the brāhmaṇa, his arms the rājanya, his thighs the vaiśya and from his feet the śūdra was born.' By breaking up the complementarity and interdependence of social relations between the *varṇas* the *dharma* made kingship problematic. The Hindu king derived a qualification of sacrality and even divinity from his integrative function, from his pivotal role of arbiter in a process of redistribution of power through a network of alliances and rivalries. The *dharma* however could only transcend politics and conflict by dissolving this network of interdependencies on which the king's power was based. It introduced a renunciatory principle and a kind of ultramundane cosmopolitanism aiming at the desacralization of society and hinged on the apolitical individual. As 'universal religion' it opposed itself to all 'sacral religion' or cults of royalty.

By being renunciatory and universal the *dharma* should legiti-

33 J. C. Heesterman, 'Ritual, Revelation and Axial Age', in: *The Inner Conflict of Tradition: Essays in Indian Ritual, Kingship and Society* (Chicago and London, 1985), pp. 95–107.

34 *Idem*, 'Brahmin, Ritual and Renouncer', *WZKSOA*, 8 (1964), pp. 1–31.

mate temporal politics, but it could never be directly linked to it. *Artha* or politics was reduced to an attribute of the king in the scheme of duties of the *varṇa* order – it became the duty of the king to protect this order. The ultimate aim of the king's political function, his own *dharma* and legitimation, was the elimination of conflict and the establishment of the *varṇa* order under his universal dominion. In the meantime the *dharma* not only divided society into exclusive *varṇas*, but went on to dissolve the internal unity of the *varṇas* themselves. This is evident for example in the connubial regulations forbidding marriages within the circle of known relatives (*sapiṇḍa*) within one *varṇa*, which, if applied, would isolate the patrilineage.[35] Again the *dharmaśāstra* (e.g. Manu 9.111), though allowing joint arrangements, recommends partition of family estates and the separation of the patrilineal relatives while denying them birthright in property. Ownership, including ownership of land, was conceived of as purely a relationship with the object (*sva-svāmī-saṃbandha*).[36] The legal foundation of joint family property does not lie in the religious law of dharma but rather in custom. It was codified in Vijñāneśvara's *Mitākṣara on Yājñavalkya* in the eleventh century AD with the concept of *dāya* or 'sharing', which expressed the vested interest on an inheritance or joint family property deriving from birthright. This code was irreconcilably opposed to the Brahmanic, individualistic conception, but it was, as Vijñāneśvara says, 'property as known to the world' (*laukikameva svatvam*).[37] Conspicuously absent in the *dharmaśāstra* is not only collective property but also a landed gentry with free-standing rights of its own such as we know from historical sources to have existed in later times and which beyond doubt also existed earlier. Apart from the sovereign *rāja*, Manu recognizes nothing but the desacralized principle of labour in the 'right of the first clearer', and further only mentions a hierarchy of

35 *Idem*, 'Caste and Karma: Max Weber's analysis of Caste', in: *The Inner Conflict of Tradition*, p. 200; *idem*, 'Power and Authority in Indian Tradition', in: R. J. Moore (ed.), *Tradition and Politics in South Asia* (New Delhi, etc., 1979), pp. 82–3.

36 J. D. M. Derrett, *The Concept of Property in Ancient Indian Theory and Practice* (Groningen, 1968); *idem*, 'The Development of the Concept of Property in India c. AD 800–1800', *Zeitschrift für vergleichende Rechtswissenschaft*, 64 (1962), pp. 53–62, 102.

37 This conception of *laukika* property, it is added by the same writer, may be found even among tribals (*pratyantavāsināḥ*) 'who never heard of the *śāstra*' (N. P. Parvatiya (ed.), *Mit. on Yājñ.* (Benares, 1914), Dāyavibhāgapr. 4).

temporarily appointed royal servants, 'lords' of 1, 10, 20, 100 and 1,000 villages.[38]

The *dharma* texts in general offer an extremely artificial schematism, discounting all social realities, to underpin the king's universal dominion. It is not the king's sacral character which lends him legitimacy, but the transcendent *dharma* as represented by the brahman. Legitimate Hindu sovereignty was a condominium of king and brahman, but their relationship was fraught with the contradiction of religious universalism and political finality. The brahman, in order to preserve his transcendent position had to stand aloof from politics. But the king needed him for the legitimation of his power, while the brahman needed the king's gifts for his subsistence. Gifts, as we saw, were an *upāya* of politics. This is why the classical *dānadharma* or 'gift code' had to introduce a fiction to deny the brahman's dependence on the royal donor.[39] 'For a brahman', writes Medātithi, 'the accepting of a gift' is not constituted by 'merely taking a thing', but only by the acceptance of something which was given with the idea that the donor would derive some 'unseen' (*aḍṛṣṭa*) benefit from it.[40] In this way the *dharma* could allow the brahman to participate in the king's sovereignty, but the need for this fiction could only arise from the existence of a fundamental rift between politics and transcendent religion.

d. The Maurya Empire

The question which now arises is how we should understand the 'imperial unifications' of the Indian subcontinent which are alleged to have occurred in pre-British times (cf. section b). Did these prefigure modern territorial sovereignty or should they be interpreted as realizations of 'universal dominion' as understood by and in accordance with the *dharma*? Discounting Islam, the present-day Indian republic set up the former Maurya Empire as the symbol of Indian unity. Founded by Candragupta Maurya in the year 313

38 *Mānava Dharmaśāstra*, 7.114–19; 9.44.

39 Cf. M. Mauss, 'Essai sur le Don', in: *Sociologie et Anthropologie* (Paris, 1973), p. 249: 'Toute cette théorie est même assez comique. Cette caste entière, qui vit de dons, prétend les refuser'. What is at stake here is however not, as Mauss thought, the 'superiority' of the brahman, but his independence (Heesterman, 'Brahmin, Ritual and Renouncer').

40 Medātithi on Manu 4.5, quoted in: P. V. Kane, *History of Dharmaśāstra*, 5 vols (Poona, 1968–77), 2, p. 842.

BC, this Empire was enlarged by his successors Bindusāra and Aśoka (261–226?) until, as it is maintained, it comprised virtually the entire peninsula.[41] It was eminently suited to become a symbol of unity since each of the three successive Maurya Emperors appears to have been the patron of one of the three great non-Islamic religions: the first was presumably a Jain, the second a Hindu, and the third a Buddhist. Aśoka's *dharma*, as many have noted, in actual fact suited the Hindu or Jain conceptions as much as it suited those of the Buddhists.[42] There is a certain concord of its principles with the natural morality taught by the Buddha for the usage of laymen (which does not touch the religious doctrines intended for his religious followers), but more fundamentally it taught concord between all sects and seems to rest on a foundation common to all doctrines. Aśoka's *dharma* superimposed itself on a great diversity of confessions without intending to absorb them.[43] In all this, Aśoka himself was a paternalistic Buddhist variant of the Indian *cakravarti* or 'universal Emperor', propagating 'abstinence from sin' and 'virtuous action'.

In his capacity of world-ruler Aśoka tried to establish harmony between sects but did not interfere in sectarian doctrine, Buddhist or otherwise.[44] There is also nothing which indicates that under Aśoka the political reality or *artha* had merged into this transcendent *dharma*; in other words it cannot be shown that there was anything like an imperial–political unification of the Indian peninsula in his time. From contemporary evidence, all that can be claimed is that Aśoka's 'world conquest' or *digvijaya* consisted of the propagation of the *dharma* in edicts on rocks and pillars throughout the subcontinent.[45] The latter, the so-called 'pillars of Aśoka' became the emblem of the Indian Republic. None of these edicts, however, has any political reference. They do not give any information about the methods used by Aśoka's administration; they are completely silent on questions of revenue or tribute collection, the army, or the tasks of officials beyond the propa-

41 G. Fussman, 'Pouvoir central et régions dans l'Inde ancienne', *Annales ESC*, 37, 4 (1982), p. 621.

42 *Ibid.*, p. 630; E. Lamotte, *Histoire du Bouddhisme Indien* (Leuven, 1958), pp. 233–5.

43 Lamotte, *Bouddhisme Indien*, pp. 249, 255, 258.

44 H. Bechert, 'Aśokas "Schismenedikt" und der Begriff Samghabheda', *WZKSOA*, 5 (1960), pp. 18–52; *idem*, 'Einige Fragen zur Religionssoziologie und Struktur des Südasiatischen Buddhismus', in: *Internationales Jahrbuch für Religionssoziologie*, Bd. IV (Cologne and Opladen, 1968), pp. 251–95.

45 Lamotte, *Bouddhisme Indien*, p. 235.

gation of the *dharma*.[46] The edicts of Aśoka are addressed to the whole Indian peninsula, but not a single name of a province or a city is mentioned in them. The ancient kingdoms of Avanti, Kosala, Anga and others which the Buddhist chronicles describe are not referred to as political or administrative entities, nor is any mention made of special adjustments to other local situations. Aśoka merely says 'everywhere in my Empire', or sometimes 'everywhere in the world'. Another phrase has it that Aśoka's activity extended over the *Jambudvīpa*, the Isle of the Jambu-tree, i.e. the Indian peninsula considered as the totality of the world inhabited by human beings. Everything, in short, points to the conclusion that Aśoka, conforming to the Buddhist conception of *cakravarti*, superimposed his *dharma* on existing structures of sovereignty, like it was superimposed on the various existing religions, but did not absorb them.[47] A (relatively) centralized imperial administration may have existed in a limited region around the Maurya capital, but the political situation of the Indian subcontinent at large did not transcend the normal situation of the 'circle of kings'. Later texts, amongst which those of Megasthenes, confirm beyond doubt the existence of large autonomous kingdoms and systems of clan- or tribal sovereignty within Aśoka's 'Empire of *dharma*'.

e. Sovereignty and *fitna* in the House of Islam

The South Asian constellation of the circle of kings at irregular intervals attracted invaders from outside the subcontinent. It was the Greeks who brought down the Mauryas. After the Mauryas and the Greeks there were many other conquerors-to-be, either originating from within the Hindu-Buddhist realm or coming from the north-west. The imperial ambition had its most notable revival under the Gupta dynasty in the fourth to sixth centuries AD, but was checked by Hun invasions. Subsequent attempts at imperial unification all took place under the banner of Islam.

Northern India was at the periphery of the Arabian conquests as early as the eighth century AD, about 800 years before Babar founded the Mughal Empire. Early Persian chronicles referred to the region as *Hindūstān*, the 'land of the Hindus', a term without an exact territorial reference, used vaguely to denote the country to

46 Fussman, 'Pouvoir Central', pp. 623, 625, 626–8, 630–1, 634, 640.
47 Cf. U. N. Ghoshal, *A History of Indian Political Ideas* (Oxford, 1966), pp. 77–8.

the south-east of the core lands of Muslim power.[48] Islam had the potential to draw the subcontinent into the orbit of an even wider universal dominion with a centre and origin outside its geographical limits. However, it had already become clear in the first century of Islamic history that the unity of Muslims was not to be seen as a political reality. In fact, like in the case of the Hindu *dharma*, the universalist pretension of Islam precluded even the conception of a political theory of sovereignty. In the classical Muslim version there was a *khalīfa* chosen through 'consultation' (*shūrā*) to represent the prophet Muhammad as the 'leader of the faithful' (*amīr al-mu'minīn*) on earth. Under the leadership of the *khalīfa* the Muslims (those who had 'submitted' to Allah) were united in the great brotherhood of the *umma* through a supra-tribal contract which made them 'equal'.[49] The classical Muslim state coincided with the number of Muslims and had no territorial references except the holy cities of Mecca and Madina. Only secondarily did it have a territorial aspect in the sense that it extended over those territories which were under Muslim control. The *khalīfa* was merely the 'leader of the faithful' and his territory was left out of consideration until the jurists introduced the term *dār al-islām* or 'House of Islam', a concept which derives its meaning from the complementary concept of *dār al-ḥarb* or 'House of War', i.e., those territories belonging to infidels which the Muslims are enjoined to conquer by *jihād* or 'holy war'. The *dār al-islām* was a 'house', but it was not a replica of the agnatic patriarchal house or *oikos* as was the ancient Greek democracy.[50] Islam was a city civilization but it did not give a place to the city in its law. The city was called *ma-dīna*, 'place of law', but it was the antithesis of a community based on the cohesion of the agnatic clan. The Muslim law or *shar'īya* was trans-temporal and trans-spatial; it referred only to Muslims as persons, postulating a strictly individual freehold title to property and partition of estates at death. Opposing itself to all manifestations of political particularism deriving from tribal cohesion and alliance known as *'aṣabīya*, it was, again like the Hindu *dharma*, completely desacralized.

48 Cf. W. H. Moreland, *The Agrarian System of Moslem India* (New Delhi, 1968), p. 21.

49 On the concept of *umma* see L. Massignon, 'L'Umma et ses synonymes: notion de "communauté sociale" en Islam', *Revue des Études Islamiques* (Cahier unique 1941–46), pp. 150–7.

50 Cf. O. Brunner, 'Das "Ganze Haus" und die alteuropäische Ökonomik', in: *Neue Wege der Sozialgeschichte* (Göttingen, 1956), pp. 33–62.

Given this desacralized or depoliticized basis it may cause little surprise that the universal brotherhood of Islam fell apart almost immediately after it was conceived. The beginning of what is known as the great *fitna* or 'schism' is commonly dated from the 35th year Hijrī or AD 657, the end of the rule of the first four 'well-guided' Caliphs who were still chosen through 'consultation'. As the Arab historian Ibn Khaldun (1332–1406) explained, this was caused by the wide-scale intrusion of the very same political and tribal divisive loyalties and alliances which Islam had sought to overcome, but with which it was bound to live in a tragic, complementary relationship.[51] *'Aṣabīya*, derived from clan-cohesion and the support of clientele and followers (*mawālī*) as well as political alliances (*ḥilf*), was the constituent factor of sovereignty or *mulk*. Ibn Khaldun says that the four 'well-guided' Caliphs lived in a time when sovereignty (*mulk*) as such did not yet exist and the sole restraining influence (*wāzi'*) was Islam.[52] The transformation of the Caliphate into dispersed foci of political sovereignty took place *pari passu* with the *fitna*. Islam by itself could not constitute sovereign power. In Ibn Khaldun's 'realist' conception *'aṣabīya* is seen as an indispensable constituent of the Muslim monarchy, but at the same time as a threat to Islamic universalism. From the beginning of the *fitna* onwards the universal dominion of Islam was no longer a political reality (if it had ever been so) and the Caliphate became hereditary in the Ummayad dynasty (661–750) and subsequently in the Abbasid dynasty (750–1258), resting on non-Arab groupings of *mawālī*, especially Persians, who attempted to build up an administration on a Sassanid–Zoroastrian model.

The *fitna* was essentially the political disruption of the unitary *umma*, a cataclysm which followed the accumulation of land and fortunes (*al-ḍiyā' wa-l-māl*) in the wake of Arabian expansion and led to a permanent *morcellement* of the House of Islam into three main political and doctrinal divisions (each with numerous subdivisions): the *khawārij* or 'seceders', representing the puritan forces of nomadism; the *shī'a* or partisans of Ali who introduced the hereditary principle in the Caliphate; and the *sunnī* or 'orthodox' Muslims. Tradition maintains that the prophet presaged this: 'after

[51] A. Wafi (ed.), *Muqaddimat Ibn Khaldūn*, 4 vols (Cairo, 1960–2). The best translation is by V. Monteil: *Ibn Khaldūn, Discours sur L'Histoire Universelle*, 3 vols (Beirut, 1968). For a good secondary treatment which gives special attention to Khaldun's theory of the great *fitna* see M. M. Rabi, *The Political Theory of Ibn Khaldun* (Leiden, 1967).

[52] Wafi, *Muqaddima*, 2, pp. 708–18, 723, 728, 730.

me there will be *fitna*'.[53] But Ibn Khaldun's interpretation of the event – which remains one of the most controversial issues of Muslim history – still stands out as the single sociological rationalization.[54] For Khaldun the *fitna* marked the transition of the properly universal Islamic dominion of the Caliphate to political sovereignty. After the Abbasid power began to decline in the ninth century the Caliphate was continued for five centuries in Baghdad and for three more in Cairo, but it became an institution serving merely the legitimation of regional Muslim monarchs or Sultans. A prisoner in the hands of Turkish mercenaries, the real power of the Caliph crumbled to nothing, and his role with regard to the rising power of the regional Sultans was but the acceptance of the rights they acquired by 'natural power' (*mulk ṭabī'ī*) in return for their recognition of the symbolic function of the Caliph and the formal supremacy of the Sharia. Henceforth it became the task of Islamic jurisprudence to maintain a nominal unity of the *umma*. To all practical purposes the later Islamic régimes can be defined as a condominium of the Sultan and the '*ulamā*', the jurists interpreting the Sharia.

Under the post-classical sultanates the term *fitna* continued to be used to denote any social–religious deviation, 'rebellion', or 'disorder'.[55] As instigators of *fitna* Muslims were stigmatized as 'inno-

[53] '*yakūnu ba'adī fitna*..': H. Laoust, *La Profession de Foi d'Ibn Baṭṭa* (Damas, 1958), fol. 3b.

[54] Rabi, *Ibn Khaldun*, pp. 14–15, 18, 83–5, 100–10; *Encyclopaedia of Islam* (Leiden and London, 1965), s.v.; A. J. Wensinck, *The Muslim Creed* (Cambridge, 1932), p. 109; H. Laoust, *Essai sur les doctrines sociales et politiques de Taḳī-d-Dīn Aḥmad B. Taimīya* (Cairo, 1939), pp. 213, 291; H. Laoust, *Les Schismes dans l'Islam* (Paris, 1977); J. Wellhausen, *The Religio-Political Factions in Early Islam* (Amsterdam and Oxford, 1975).

[55] R. P. Mottahedeh, *Loyalty and Leadership in an Early Islamic Society* (Princeton, 1980), pp. 161, 183; M. A. Shaban, *The 'Abbāsid Revolution* (Cambridge, 1970), p. 47; Laoust, *Ibn Baṭṭa*, fols 4a, 9a, 16b, 21a; *idem, Aḥmad B. Taimīya*, pp. 217, 315, 501, 619; W. L. Wright (tr.), *Ottoman Statecraft: The Book of Counsel for Vezirs and Governors (Naṣā'iḥ ül-vüzera ve'l-ümera) of Suri Meḥmed Pasha, the Defterdār* (Princeton, 1935), p. 87; T. P. Hughes, *Dictionary of Islam* (Lahore, n.d., orig. publ. 1885), p. 129. For India see for instance *Tārīkh-i-Fīroz Shāhī of Zia ad-Din Barani* (ed. Sayyid Ahmad Khan, Calcutta, 1862), pp. 236, 444, 447–8, 478–80; *Akbarnāma of Abul Fazl*, 3 vols (ed. Maulawi Abd ur-Rahim, Calcutta, 1878–9), I, fols 255, 260, 308, 311–2; *Ma'āṣir-i-Jahāngirī of Khwaja Kamgar Husaini* (ed. Azra Alavi, Bombay, 1978), pp. 129–31; *Asrār-i-Ṣamadī* (eds M. Shuja ud-Din and Bashir Husain, Lahore, 1965), p. 6; In'amullah bin Khurram Shah, *Auṣāf al-Āṣaf* (*ms* 480/ 1F, Abd us-Salam Collection, Maulana Azad Library, Aligarh). The primary religious meaning of *fitna* was 'putting to the proof' or 'discriminatory test'. This was not a matter of inner temptation but always of external circumstances. 'Your goods and children are *fitna*' (*Qur'ān*, VIII, 28; LXIV, 15). Beautiful women are also seen as a cause of *fitna*

vators' (*muḥdith*),[56] while the Good Muslim was enjoined 'to abstain from participation in *fitna* and keep himself apart'.[57] The concept of *fitna* is very frequently found in numerous texts throughout Muslim history – in law-books and religious manuals as well as in political historiography – and if these texts are taken at face-value the meaning always appears to be in agreement with the translations found in the dictionaries of Arabic, Persian, Turkish and the Indian languages which adopted it: 'sedition', 'insurrection caused by factionalism', 'revolt', 'chaos', 'dissension', or 'civil war'. The corresponding Arabic verb is *fatana*, which stands for 'leading into rebellion', 'to entice', etc. In India the term *fitna* is found from at least the thirteenth century onwards, and most likely was introduced much earlier.[58] In the Indo-Persian chronicles it recurs *passim* in combination with, or as an equivalant of, the term *fasād* and derivations thereof. For the Muslims, *fasād*, like *fitna*, was a religiously or theologically charged concept which they employed historically to denote the decline of unitary Islamic dominion by referring to it as *fasād az-zamān*, 'the corruption brought by time' which was always reducible to individual immorality. Instigators of *fitna* may then be described as *mufsidān*, 'rebels', or, more rhetorically, the chronicles speak of 'the fire of *fitna* and *fasād*' (*ātish-i-fitna-o-fasād, nā'ira' fitna-o-fasād*). Or they refer to *fitna* as a form of terror: *fitna-o-ḥawādiṣ*, *fitna-o-āshob*, etc. The raising of the 'head of sedition' (*sar-i-fitna*) is also commonly described as a conspiracy originating under a 'veil' (*parda*) which has to be 'lifted' (*gushā*), while the quelling of *fitna* – by diplomacy, conciliation or possibly by military action – can be called an 'act of worship' (*'ibādat*). In a more prosaic frame of reference the term *fitna* occurs very often in the eighteenth-century Maratha documentation in a slightly corrupted form as *fitvā*, for which term the dictionary gives a similar array of meanings: 'rebellion', 'defection', 'drawing off from allegiance',

(F. Mernissi, *Beyond the Veil*, New York, etc., 1975), pp. 4, 10–13. The dominant connotation of *fitna* became that of 'rebellion'.

56 Laoust, *Ibn Baṭṭa*, p. 21.

57 '*al-kaff wa-l-qu'ūd fī-l-fitna*' (Laoust, *Ibn Baṭṭa*, fol. 21a). The duty of abstinence is common to all Islamic doctrines ('*aqīda*) and may be expressed by a variety of terms: *kaff, imsāk, qu'ūd, luzūm al-bait* (*ibid.*, p. 126, note 1).

58 For references cf. note 55; P. Hardy, 'Force and Violence in Indo-Persian writing on History and government in Medieval South Asia', in: M. Israel and N. K. Wagle (eds), *Islamic Society and Culture: Essays in Honour of Professor Aziz Ahmad* (New Delhi, 1983), pp. 165–208.

etc.[59] These standard translations of the dictionaries however lead us into a methodological problem. The pejorative connotations which are invariably attached to *fitna* seem to indicate that the word refers to a disruption of the social order, i.e., of sovereignty and its transcendent, religious consecration which makes it 'just' government. But we saw that according to Ibn Khaldun's interpretation of the great *fitna* of 657 – the *fitna par excellence* – sovereignty or *mulk* could not be constituted without it and that a sociological conception of *fitna* can dispense with the pejorative or negative connotations. In fact *fitna*, although it could be a very temporary 'flame', was as indispensable a foundation of Muslim or pseudo-Muslim sovereignty as was 'national war' for the territorial sovereignty of the modern unitary state of the West. But terms like 'revolt', 'sedition', and 'civil war' in their normal present-day application always presuppose the existence of a unitary sovereign state and are therefore singularly inadequate translations of the term *fitna*.[60] In the Islamic world *fitna* was the normal political mechanism of state-formation or annexation and, as it were, the negative basis of universal dominion. Objectively *fitna* implies no more than the forging of alliances; it is thus – unlike state expansion in modern Europe – not primarily determined by the use of military power. The latter might have a (limited) role in it, but this was not necessarily so. A common lever in the *fitna* mechanism was what students of war refer to as the 'political use of military power'. Actual physical battles involving entire armies, apart from skirmishes or strategic outmanoeuvring, were rare and seem to have occurred largely accidentally, while even then they were of themselves of little political consequence. In eighteenth-century India only one real massacre occurred in the so-called Third Battle of Panipat of 1761 between the assembled armies of the Marathas and the Afghans; both sides were entrenched in the field for months and were greatly embarrassed with the situation until starvation and

[59] The corruption of *fitna* into *fitvā* can perhaps be explained as due to the insertion of the Marathi causative suffix *-av*. The infinitive of the Marathi verb is *fitṇeṇ*, 'to revolt from'; the causative 'to draw away from allegiance' is *fitaviṇeṇ* or *fitāviṇeṇ*. Thus from the Arabic maṣdar *fatn* we may arrive at the Marathi verb *fitṇeṇ*, hence at *fitaviṇeṇ* and the substantive *fitvā*.

[60] The methodological problem involved here can be compared with that of the medieval *feud* (German Fehde, Dutch *vete*), which equally implied a form of 'self-help' which is incompatible with the modern conception of unitary territorial sovereignty (cf. O. Brunner, *Land und Herrschaft: Grundfragen der territorialen Verfassungsgeschichte Österreichs im Mittelalter* (Darmstadt, 1973), esp. pp. 4, 38, 106–7.

general hysteria made a final clash of arms inevitable. This battle however effected little change in the overall political situation of northern India. Persian chroniclers, although apt to exaggerate the heroism displayed in military campaigning, are equally emphatic that 'the fame of the sword' of an approaching general was sufficient to bring to a stop 'the ravaging of the country' and that in most cases no real battle had to take place.[61]

As opposed to a purely military operation *fitna* was at least a mixture of coercion and conciliation and characteristically implied intervention in and making use of existing local conflicts. *Fitna* can be equated with the political expedient of *upajāpa* of the Indian *arthaśāstra*, comprising conciliation, gift-giving, sowing dissension among and 'winning over' of an enemy's local supporters, and involving the use of force only secondarily. Such a mechanism of conquest or political expansion was not unknown to post-medieval Europe, but here, with the centralist consolidation of the Absolutist state and the establishment of territorial sovereignty on the principles of Roman law, it was progressively replaced by a new type of 'international' warfare in which military force predominated.[62] In India, as in all Islamic states, sovereignty was primarily a matter of allegiances; the state organized itself around conflict and remained essentially *open-ended* instead of becoming terri-

61 Thus the Mughal historian Khafi Khan described Nizam al-Mulk's campaign against the Marathas at Aurangabad in 1712 (H. M. Elliot and J. Dowson, *The History of India as told by its own Historians*, 8 vols (London, 1867–7), 7, p. 450).

62 P. Anderson characterizes the Absolutist states as 'machines built overwhelmingly for the battlefield' (*Lineages of the Absolutist State*, p. 32). He points at 'the virtual permanence of international armed conflict' as 'one of the hallmarks of the whole climate of Absolutism' (*ibid.*, p. 33). Yet, for the sixteenth and early seventeenth centuries he gives examples of Absolutist rulers extending their sovereignty through sedition. He thus writes that 'Charles V and Philip II had both profited from the internal weakness of the French state, by utilizing provincial dissaffections to invade France itself', and that later 'a maturing French Absolutism was able to exploit aristocratic sedition and regional separatism in the Iberian peninsula to invade Spain' (*ibid.*, p. 79). Particularly instructive in this respect is Anderson's description of the long-drawn-out conflict of the Habsburgs and the Ottomans in Hungary; his conclusion is that 'the tenacity of Magyar particularism was (thus) also a function of its potent backstops across the Ottoman frontier' (*ibid.*, p. 315; and see pp. 316, 324). The Ottoman conquest of the Balkans, according to Anderson, swept away the local nobility, but at the same time, led to 'an actual regression to clannic institutions and particularist traditions among the Balkan rural population' (*ibid.*, pp. 372–3). The clannic and tribal institutions in question, Anderson explains further, were being severely undermined before the Ottoman conquest. They thus appear to have owed their revival to Ottoman support against the local nobles. The latter conclusion is not drawn by Anderson, who opts for a model of Ottoman Despotism, untrammelled by local particularisms.

torially circumscribed.[63] Modern European states again conformed to this pattern while expanding into indigenous polities in Asia, Africa and America during the open frontier period.[64] But such forms of sovereignty, characterized by dispersal through shifting combinations with local powerholders, have become alien to Europe and the modern state in general, where sovereignty is always expressed in terms of political territory and not of allegiances.[65]

What the Muslims called *fitna* is a process which can only be interpreted as 'rebellion' or 'sedition' from the perspective of the unitary state, a state which in the Muslim world did not exist but which was postulated in the universalist religion precisely to transcend *fitna* and make it legitimate sovereignty. This process

[63] In what way, and to what extent, the Absolutist states in Europe were *internally* determined as products of conflicting interests is still a controversial question. Engels was the first to pronounce the Absolutist state the product of an equilibrium between the landowning nobility and the bourgeoisie (cf. Anderson, *ibid.*, pp. 15–16). Anderson denies that this was the case and sees in it the political instrument of class rule by the nobility in the period following the decline of serfdom, 'the redeployed political apparatus of a feudal class' which in Western Europe served as 'a compensation for the disappearance of serfdom', while in Eastern Europe it would have been 'a device for the consolidation of serfdom' (*ibid.*, pp. 195, 212; and see pp. 169, 260, 269, 430). Anderson does not deny however that the Absolute sovereign could not with impunity violate 'social laws' and he speaks of 'the impotence of the personal will of the ruler, once it transgressed the collective interests of the class which Absolutism historically functioned to defend' (*ibid.*, p. 321). Engels' equilibrium model is perhaps best worked out in N. Elias, *Über den Prozess der Zivilisation*, 2 vols (Suhrkamp ed., 1976). Elias highlights 'die Angewiesenheit der Gruppen und Schichten dieser Gesellschaft auf einen obersten Koordinator, der den Austausch und die Zusammenarbeit der verschiedenen, gesellschaftlichen Funktionen und Bezirke in Gang hält' (2, p. 293). The Absolutist state was thus, according to the same author, a 'multipolares Balancesystem' in which the rivalry between nobility and bourgeoisie became ever more important: 'In der Tat erlangt die gesellschaftliche Institution des Königtums ihre grösste, gesellschaftliche Stärke in jener Phase der Gesellschaftsgeschichte, in der ein schwächer werdender Adel mit aufsteigenden, bürgerlichen Gruppen bereits in mannigfachen Hinsicht rivalisieren muss, ohne dass einer den anderen entscheiden aus dem umstrittenen Felde zu schlagen vermag' (*ibid.*, p. 243; and see pp. 242, 248–50).

[64] This is exemplified by British expansion in India, to which attention will be paid in Chapter I-III. For the American and African frontiers see especially H. Lamar and L. Thompson (eds), *The Frontier in History: North America and Southern Africa Compared* (New Haven and London, 1981), pp. 123–48: C. A. Milner, 'Indulgent Friends and Important Allies: Political Process on the Cis-Mississipi Frontier and Its Aftermath'; pp. 149–71: Ch. Saunders, 'Political Processes in the Southern African Frontier zones'.

[65] Otherwise it is always an anomaly: for instance, the attempt of the present Russian–Afghan government to buy the support of the Shinwari tribe in the Eastern province of Nangahar to block the road from Pakistan for the guerrillas. The tribesmen used to offer free passage to the latter in return for a smaller payment than that received from the Russians (*NRC-Handelsblad*, 15 December 1982).

which is of pivotal importance in the Muslim state is marginalized in modern Europe. But the conception of the national state, in which religion and politics are separated and which is transcendent and autonomous within an abstract, geographically delimited territory in which it claims the monopoly of legitimate violence, has the corollary of a permanent crisis *between the states*, the 'state of nature' which is the logical starting point but by no means the sure foundation of the Grotian system of international law. The modern sovereign state could only develop historically by disengaging itself, through the reception of Roman law, from the idea of a Christian universal community. In the modern constellation 'sedition' then came to mean a disturbance of the internal sovereignty of the state, or, as Webster's dictionary defines it, 'any act aimed at disturbing peace of realm or producing insurrection'. From this perspective we cannot but see the entire Muslim history as well as that of India as an uninterrupted story of betrayals and rebellions. This is, hard to reconcile with the picture of despotism and self-contradictory as it may be, not far removed from its current interpretations. Nehru, for example, in his prison diary poses this question, put to him by Kripalani: 'Why should the Indian people breed so many traitors – now and throughout history?'[66] His answer is that 'they have had and have splendid opportunities'. Obviously the question is considered in a wholly anachronistic framework and cannot even be asked in this way. *Fitna* was anathematized in Islam by being set off against the transcendent conception of universal dominion, not against the absolute, unitary sovereignty of the nation state which derives from Roman law. In India it was immaterial whether the transcendent idea of universality and just kingship was brought in from Brahmanism or Buddhism or from Islam. Essential was only that nothing but a truly *universal* dominion could transcend *fitna*, since in actual political life *fitna* had no end. In India therefore we find *fitna* set off against Islam, but also against the Hindu *dharma*. Speaking generally, in the Indian context the *dharma* is understood as any 'universal religion'. While sovereignty is the precondition of immanent order in society, the *dharma* is the universal law of transcendent order and can comprise any religious doctrine which relates justice to a universal norm. It thus comprised Islam as the *islāmdharma*. The *dharma* invariably postulates a completely desacralized or, in other words, atomized

66 S. Gopal (ed.), *Selected Works of Jawaharlal Nehru*, 13 vols (New Delhi, 1972–80), 13, p. 106 (diary of 13 April, 1943).

society on a transcendent and apolitical basis. In its transcendent, universal aspect Islam was no real innovation in India. The concept of *fitna* could of course only have come in vogue after the Muslim invasions, but for this too there were equivalent concepts in the pre-Islamic history of India. The Sanskrit texts equated 'universal dominion' or 'world-dominion' with 'dominion over the South Asian subcontinent'. Indian Islam soon adjusted itself to the same idea, but the intention still remained that of universality. The imperial ambition which was concomitant with this universality was a logical imperative of Indian history, but could never be achieved since expansion could not cancel the limitations inherent in *fitna* and the form of sovereignty which was based on it.

In principle the paradigm of Muslim sovereignty found under the first Sultanates in India was not different from that of the coeval Middle East. The Sultans of Delhi (1206–1526) buttressed their position by an explicit reference to the Caliphate of Baghdad and later Cairo.[67] Some even went so far as to style themselves *nā'ib-i-khalīfa* or 'deputy of the *khalīfa*'. In the later period however there was a tendency to drop this practice, or the Sultan assumed the Caliphate in his own name. From a very early date the Muslim rulers of India assumed two typically Persian symbols of sovereignty: the use of a throne (also an Indian practice) and the title of *pādshāh*, which in Persia reflected the Shiite orientation but in India (as in the Ottoman Empire) was detached from it and continued to be used until the end of independent Muslim rule alternately with the title of *sulṭān* by rulers who considered themselves either Shiite or Sunnite.[68] When the Mughals (a Central-Asian Timurid dynasty) took the throne of Delhi in 1526, they initially did not even acknowledge the Caliphate. To the alarm of the orthodox *'ulamā'*, Akbar (1556–1605) restored the idea of the divinity or sacrality of the Hindu king. But the coinage of Akbar also bore the inscription of 'the great Sulṭān, the exalted Khalīfa'.[69] The Mughal capitals of Delhi and Agra, as well as the temporary residences of the Mughal Emperors, were considered in India, from Akbar's reign until as late as that of Shah Alam II (1760), as

[67] R. P. Tripathi, *Some Aspects of Muslim Administration* (Allahabad, 1966), pp. 26ff.

[68] The Persian word *pādshāh* has the same root as the Sanskrit *pati*, Greek *despotes*, Latin *potens*, 'ruler'. *Sulṭān* is an Arabic title of the sovereign which came in use in the eleventh century AD (*Enzyclopaedia der Islam*, Bd. III (Leiden and Leipzig, 1936), s.v. *pādishāh and sulṭān*).

[69] *Encyclopaedia of Islam*, s.v. *khalīfa*.

the *dār al-khilāfa*.[70] A strong reaction against religious syncretism with the Hindus asserted itself under Aurangzeb, who of all Mughal Emperors was the one who gave the most weight to Islamic, specifically Sunnite, legitimation and who was most intransigent in his ambition to bring the entire subcontinent under the *dār al-islām*.

Through *fitna* the Mughals had entered the circle of kings and continually expanded their 'sphere of influence' in Hindustan until by the late sixteenth century they began to get seriously involved in the politics of the states to the south of the Narmada river, the part of India which was known as the Deccan (Skt. *dakṣiṇa*, 'southern'). When Hindustan was brought under Mughal sovereignty there remained in the Deccan three independent Shiite Sultanates which had originally evolved out of a break-away governorship of the Delhi Sultanate and now, after the dissolution of the Vijayanagar kingdom, extended as far south as Rameshvara. To bring the Deccan under their sovereignty even the Mughals were dependent on the formation of local alliances and intervention in local conflicts, on *fitna* in short, or, as it was called in the Deccan, *fitvā*.[71] Mughal intervention in the continual conflicts in and among the Deccan Sultanates greatly benefited the autochthonous Hindu *zamīndārs* or gentry, the prop of Muslim domination everywhere in the subcontinent, which could increase their power as different Muslim sovereigns sought for a rapprochement with them to fend off competitors. It was in this way that the Marathas in the Western Deccan began their rise to sovereign power as part of a process of 'gentrification' of the Deccan Muslim polities which took place under the pressure of the Mughals. But Maratha *fitna* continued unabated under the Mughals after they had eliminated the Deccan Sultanates and established the 'universal dominion' of Islam throughout India. Rather than a 'revolt' against the Empire, the *fitna* of the Marathas in the eighteenth century represents – along with that of other groups like the Jats, Bundelas, Sikhs, etc., in the north – the ultimate result of Muslim expansion in India. This was, in the last analysis, but the continuation of a process which had begun in the period of the fourteenth to seventeenth centuries in Hindustan with the ascent of the Rajputs ('king's sons'), which provided the Marathas with a model and might be seen as the first stage of the gentrification of Indo-Muslim sovereignty. From the

70 *Ibid.*; S. P. Blake, 'The Patrimonial–Bureaucratic Empire of the Mughals', *JAS*, 39, 1 (1979), p. 93.

71 Cf. Chapter I-II and I-III.

fourteenth century onwards the 'native inhabitants' or *mutawaṭṭi-nān* of Hindustan and the Deccan begin to loom large in the Indo-Muslim chronicles as *fitna*-mongers, and they can be identified, if not as Rajputs or predecessors of Rajputs, as Jats (*jatwān*), Marathas (*marhatta*) or 'other gentry groups' ('tribes'; *ṭawā'īf-i-dīgar*) who henceforward are also designated by the generic term *zamīndārs*.[72] Even close to Delhi, Muslim rule had brought power and wealth to the *zamīndārs* and had provided avenues for upward mobility to formerly often obscure clans and rural Hindu gentry, in a symbiotic development of mutual reinforcement which reached its breaking point in the seventeenth century. At that stage, a part of this gentry, foremost the Marathas, made good their claims to sovereignty.

Thus a process of *fitna* followed in the wake of Muslim expansion in India as it had done in the early Caliphal Empire. Through *fitna* the Marathas in the course of the eighteenth century established their own sovereignty or *svarājya* over the larger part of India but they did so without denying the legitimacy of Muslim universal

[72] Cf. p. 184, note 4; *Asrār-i-Ṣamadī*, p. 6; Barani, *Tārīkh-i-Fīroz Shāhī*, (ed. Khan) esp. pp. 61, 84, 208–10, 390, 515; Khwaja Kamgar Husaini, *Ma'āṣir-i-Jahāngirī*, pp. 129–31. That expansion and the generation of surplus causes *fitna* is a recurrent theme in Barani's *Tārīkh* (ed. Khan) (cf. esp. pp. 224, 343) of the fourteenth century, as in most later chronicles. For the Rajputs see also D. H. A. Kolff, 'An Armed Peasantry and its Allies: Rajput Tradition and State Formation in Hindustan, 1450–1850' (PhD thesis, Leiden, 1983), esp. chapter III; N. P. Ziegler, 'Some Notes on Rajput Loyalties during the Mughal Period', in: J. F. Richards (ed.), *Kingship and Authority in South Asia* (Madison, Wisc., 1978), pp. 215–51. For the Jats see M. C. Pradhan, *The Political System of the Jats of Northern India* (Bombay, 1966). For the Sikhs, Jats and Rajputs in Northern India at the turn of the seventeenth century see especially Rana, 'Agrarian Revolts'; M. Alam, 'Sikh Uprisings under Banda Bahadur, 1708–1715', *Studies in History*, vol. 1, no. 2 (1979), pp. 197–213. In the first of these articles, focusing on the subas of Agra, Delhi and Ajmer it is concluded that 'the rebellions did not necessarily arise from the zamindars' economic depression; on the contrary, most of the disturbances were created by their attempts to expand their zamindaris' (p. 289; compare similar remarks on pp. 305, 322). The same article also provides glimpses of how the resurgence of zamindari power was bound up with the factional politics of the Mughal court (p. 309). In the second article, M. Alam suggests that 'the rise of the Jats may possibly be explained in the light of the extension of irrigated agriculture which had made the region among the most prosperous in the Mughal empire in the 17th century' (p. 202). See also Alam, 'Agrarian Disturbances', which (on the evidence of local Persian sources) relates the rise of Rajput zamindars in Awadh, Benares and the Moradabad-Bareilly region to their 'growing strength and prosperity' (p. 1), to a 'considerable increase in cultivation since the time of Jahangir' (p. 11), a 'substantial increase in commercialized agriculture' (p. 13), etc; cf. further Alam 'Mughal Centre', esp. pp. vii, xv, 22, 99, 144, 215, for similar statements supported by abundant Persian source material.

dominion and they never really shed the status of *zamīndārs*. In a way which is reminiscent of Kautilya's distinction of *svaviṣaya* and *paraviṣaya* the Marathas opposed their *svarājya* to the *pararājya* or 'enemy's sovereignty', identifying the latter usually as the *moṇglāī* or Mughal dominion, but of this they nominally remained the servants. At the same time the Maratha sovereigns decked themselves out as 'upholder of the *dharma* and protector of gods and brahmans'. The Maratha political treatise *Ājñāpatra* recalls the classical political means of the Hindu monarchy, 'conciliation, gifts, sedition, force, alliance, separation (etc.)'.[73] Posing as the servants of the Mughal Emperor, the Marathas however most commonly described the political actions of their rivals – including the Mughal mansabdars themselves – as *fitvā*. This was also, from the point of view of universal dominion, the mechanism of conquest on which their own sovereignty had been based from the outset.[74] *Fitvā* meant the 'drawing away from allegiance' of *zamīndārs* or *rayats*, 'sedition' in forts, the 'rebellion' or 'conspiracy' of commanders and officials, or any 'disloyalty'.[75] In eighteenth-century India *fitvā* was primarily a matter of 'political arithmetic',[76] assignments or grants of land-revenue, gifts of cash or the bestowal of other 'monetized honours', and not so much of kinship or clan- or tribal alliances as it had been in earlier times in other parts of the Islamic world. Behind the negative moral undertone stands the political contest for sovereignty with an enemy who uses always *zabardastī* or 'illegitimate power' since he stands in the way of universal dominion. The most comprehensive Marathi term for all acts of *fitna*, all 'seditious risings and revolts', is *fitvāfāṇḍā*, in which *fāṇḍā* denotes the 'fork of a tree' or 'bifurcated stick', a 'digression'. Sovereignty in the Islamic state was thus not unitary in practice but 'bifurcated'. The unitary order against which *fitna* was set was

[73] '*sāma, dāna, bheda, daṇḍ saṃdhivigrah mitrabheda mitrasaṃdhānādi*' (N. Banhatti (ed.), *Ājñāpatra* (Poona, 1974), ch.4).

[74] Thus, for instance, the Kolhapur branch of the Bhonsle dynasty accused Shahu (the Satara king) of *fitvā*, each party putting itself up as the Mughal representative in the Deccan (cf. Chapter I-3-c).

[75] E.g. *SSRPD*, 4, nos 3, 76, 130, 141, 150, 379; 5, no.102; 8, no.866; 9, no.303; *MIS*, 8, no.12; 20, no.254; V. G. Khobrekar (ed.), *Records of the Shivaji Period* (Bombay, 1974), nos 28, 106, 108; V. V. Khare (ed.), *Aitihāsik Lekh Saṃgraha*, 5 (1918), pp. 2466, 2638, 2664, 2671; R. B. G. C. Vad, P. V. Mawji and D. B. Parasnis (eds), *Kaifiyats, Yadis, & c.* (Bombay, 1908), p. 187; Banhatti, *Ājñāpatra*, ch.8.

[76] The term is Petty's (cf. G. Ardant, *Histoire de l'Impôt*, 2 vols (Paris, 1971–2), 1, pp. 115–18, 383).

merely the postulate of universal dominion, of just rule. What the rise of Maratha *svarājya* exemplifies most of all is not the loss or depletion of centralist and unified Mughal power but that 'illegitimate' power and *fitna* in India (as in the Islamic world generally) were the constituent factors of sovereignty; that *fitna*, in other words, was the beginning and the end of sovereign dominion.

f. Maratha *svarājya* and Mughal Empire

The Mughal Empire represented a form of sovereignty, a balancing system of continually shifting rivalries and alliances which differed in its dimension but not in its basic constitution from preceding sultanates of Hindu kingdoms in Hindustan or the Deccan. At no stage did it transcend *fitna*. The politic incorporation of ever more aspiring gentry groups and nobility of indigenous or foreign extraction which rose to fortune and power was the essential task posed to its continued existence. It is only to the external observer that Mughal expansion until the early eighteenth century shows itself primarily as the extension of centralist Muslim power. Concomitant with expansion, however, competition for local alliances among the conquering Mughal nobility striving for independent power-bases in the provinces occasioned a further participation in the system of sovereignty of the Hindu gentry, of the *zamīndārs*. This was the powerful dynamic of *fitna* moving in the opposite direction of universalism and centralism, a dynamic which is misleadingly referred to as the 'decline' of the Empire. Expansion and *fitna* were both bound up with increasing wealth among nobles and gentry. *Fitna* was therefore the inevitable result of Mughal expansion, and the eighteenth century brought only a further localization or gentrification of Islamic sovereignty, not the destruction of a once unitary, despotic state. Economic and agricultural decline really is in evidence only in the period immediately preceding the establishment of British supremacy over the Marathas. This was the so-called *gardī kā vakt* or 'period of trouble' which is dated roughly from 1800 to 1818 and for which British interference is partly if not mainly responsible. As Max Weber has clearly seen, the Marathas were the only native rulers who, in co-operation with the brahmans, reintroduced an independent fiscal economy on a vast scale and whose administrative technique was actually better adjusted to local diversities and complexities than that of the Mughals.[77] The British Resident at the court of Nagpur, T. Jenkins, wrote in a report of 1827 that 'from the first establishment of the Maratha power until the year AD 1792, the country was prosperous ... but from this period the inhabitants begin to date the period of misrule and oppressive assessment, though it was not carried, at first, to the ruinous excess of exaction which marks the conduct of Raghuji after the Maratha war of 1802'.[78] There are more very positive evaluations of the Maratha economy by the first generation of British officials. As exemplary (not as exceptional) beneficent revenue administrators are often singled out Ahalyabai Holkar in Malwa and Peshwa Madhav Rao I and Nana Fadnis in the Deccan.[79] They are sometimes recalled in lyrical terms or at least with a tinge of admiration, if not self-denial, as in the case of H. Pottinger: 'As far as my experience goes, I am led to think that no European administration of the revenue of this country can, or will ever be so effective as that of the Marathas during the time of Nana Fadnis'.[80] The Maratha rulers, wrote Jenkins in the aforementioned report, 'have never left the plain manners of their nation; they are connected by the ties of blood and by constant familiar intercourse with every one of their principal officers, and born in the class of cultivators, consequently having a hereditary respect for that order'.[81] Something of this must have been intended when the Mughals remarked that 'the Maratha leaders did not behave as rulers but as *zamīndārs*'.[82]

The Maratha gentry of the Western Deccan originally owed its rise to Mughal pressure on the Deccan Sultans. This allowed them to grow stronger through *fitna* and alternating alliances with the different Muslim sovereigns of the Deccan against the Mughals and each other until they felt urged to bring forward a claim to independent Hindu sovereignty. Thus was consecrated in the person of Shivaji Bhonsle, in 1674, the first Hindu king since the dismemberment of Vijayanagar, unique in the seventeenth century, when all the Hindu kings of the north (including the Solar

77 M. Weber, *Gesammelte Aufsätze zur Religionssoziologie*, II (Hinduismus und Buddhismus) (Tübingen, 1972), pp. 71–2.

78 T. Jenkins, *Report on the Territories of the Raja of Nagpur* (Nagpur, 1827, reprinted 1923), p. 96.

79 Cf. *ibid.*, p. 76; Grant Duff, *History*, I, p. 452; *B.A.: R.D.*, vol. II/698 of 1836, pp. 37–9; J. Malcolm, *A Memoir of Central India*, 2 vols (New Delhi, 1970), I, pp. 179–80.

80 *EIP*, 4, p. 745.

81 *Nagpur*, p. 76.

82 Thus Azad Bilgrami in 1761, as quoted by M. Athar Ali, 'The Passing of Empire: The Mughal Case', *MAS*, 9, 3 (1975), p. 392.

dynasty of Udaipur) had become tributaries of the Mughal emperor. Shivaji's *rājyābhiṣeka* or 'royal consecration' was much resented by his Deccan peers of often older standing. A chronicle called *Śivdigvijaya* ('Shivaji's World Conquest') explains that 'Shivaji was unwilling to share the leadership of the Marathas with others, and although he had formerly been on one level with many other Maratha sardars as (mere) servants of Bijapur, he could justify his new claims to pre-eminence amongst them by pointing out that this dependence, through his efforts, no longer existed'.[83] One of his attendants suggested to him, according to the same *bakhar*, that in order to be recognized as an independent maharaja he should consecrate himself and acquire the *chatra* or umbrella of kingship and a throne.[84] A brahman Gangabhat is then mobilized from Benares for the role of chief officiant or *mukhya adhvaryu* of the *rājyābhiṣeka*. The latter's initial objection that only kshatriyas were entitled to undergo the ceremony – while Shivaji was a shudra – was overcome by proclaiming the Bhonsle a Shisodia Rajput, a descendant of the royal house of Udaipur and of Chitor and consequently of kshatriya lineage.[85] It was a claim which, despite repeated attempts to prove genealogically its correctness, was destined to remain disputed forever.[86] That Shivaji himself at first did not have such kshatriya pretensions is proven by the fact that in 1657 he married three women of three different Maratha families. Titles like *mahārāja* and even *chatrapati* or 'lord of the umbrella' he had already used on occasion from 1647 onwards.[87] Shivaji thought of himself as a king 'by virtue of his power to protect the *dharma* and his subjects'.[88] On the day of the consecration a new era was instituted, called the *rājyābhiṣeka śaka*, but an old mestak states that Shivaji ruled for thirty years before he became a *śakakartā* ('maker of an era') and for six years, from 1674 up to his death, afterwards.[89] Satara became the seat of sovereignty of the Chatra-

[83] P. R. Nandurbarkar and L. K. Dandekar (eds), *Śivdigvijaya* (Poona, 1895), pp. 406–7.

[84] *Ibid.*, p. 409. [85] *Ibid.*, p. 411. [86] Cf. *SPD*, 42, nos 18, 43.

[87] Cf. *SCS*, 2, no. 344; 3, no. 534; *MIS*, 15, no. 440; *SKPSS*, no. 1209; R. B. G. C. Vad, P. V. Mawji and D. B. Parasnis (eds), *Sanadāpatreṇ* (Bombay, 1913), p. 120.

[88] Nandurbarkar and Dandekar, *Śivdigvijaya*, p. 412. It is perhaps noteworthy in this context that the Vedic royal consecration is not understood by most *dharma* commentators to be the decisive sacrament or *saṃskāra* that legitimates the king. An indispensable *saṃskāra* is only the *upanayana* or sacred thread ceremony that any member of the twice-born *varṇas* must undergo (cf. Lingat, *Sources du Droit*, p. 234, note 1).

[89] *BISM-Vārṣik Itivṛtt* (1914), p. 174.

pati who, although repudiating the title of Badshah, dealt on terms of equality with the Deccan Muslim sovereigns.[90]

Shivaji's kingdom further retained a strong patrimonial imprint. A rudimentary body of officials with Persian titles which had already been constituted in 1669 when the Bhonsles were formally still *jāgirdārs* of Bijapur was given a Sanskrit nomenclature and converted into a regular *rājmaṇḍal* or *aṣṭapradhān* council of 'eight ministers' modelled upon the ancient examples.[91] The pradhans were non-hereditary, salaried royal delegates – six of them brahmans in Shivaji's time – still to a large degree household officials as they had been in origin. As household officials we find their duties only vaguely defined in an abstract blueprint. First among the eight ministers was the *Peśvā*, an originally Persian denomination, who became *Mukhya Pradhān* or 'head minister'. There had been a *Muzumdār* (Mar.) who became *Amātya* with the general supervision of the finances of the kingdom.[92] The *Senāpati* was the commander-in-chief of the army. The *Paṇḍit Rāo* or *Dānādhyakṣa* had the 'supervision of *dharma* and *adharma*'. The *Saciv* (formerly the Persian *Sūr-Nawīs*) and the *Maṇtrī* were both assigned unspecified governmental and military functions. The *Nyāyādīś* was especially charged with the administration of justice, while the *Sumaṇt* had to receive the vakils of the *pararājya*, i.e., the emissaries of other kingdoms.

The small kingdom which was thus constituted by the shudras-turned-kshatriyas in the seventeenth-century Western Deccan remained only the nucleus of a second much wider Maratha *svarājya* spreading to the north, east and south in the eighteenth century. Maratha sovereignty, after the Mughal retreat from the Deccan, kept expanding and never became territorially fixed. Constitutionally it evolved further as a loose association or 'confederacy' of military leaders denoted as *sardārs* (Persian for 'captain') who had the Bhonsle dynasty as their pivot and who did not claim for themselves a contiguous and circumscribed territory, but had a standard (*jarīpaṭka*) 'to be planted on the Himalayas'.[93]

[90] Cf. G. S. Sardesai (ed.), *Shivaji Souvenir* (Poona, 1927), pp.240–3.

[91] 'Kānūjābtā rājyābhiṣeka śaka 1 . . . etc', in: G. S. Sardesai, Y. M. Kale and V. S. Vakaskar (eds), *Aitihāsik Patreṇ Yādī Vagaire* (Poona, 1930), no.2; R. V. Hervadkar (ed.), *Saptaprakaraṇātmak Caritra* (Poona, 1967), pp. 228–9.

[92] In the term *amātya*, lit. 'inmate of the house', the patrimonial origin of the officialdom is clearly in evidence.

[93] A statement attributed to the Maratha king Shahu (cf. Grant Duff, *History*, 1, p. 270). The designation 'confederacy' was often used by the British in the

Formally all Maratha *sardārs* merely held temporary assignments of the land-revenue, but in practice these tended to become hereditary when they were large. The *sardārs* were often titled (the titles becoming meaningful only by being associated with a particular *sardār*) and commanded stipulated quota of troops in the service of the Maratha sovereign. Among these confederate sardars who, through *fitna*, conquered most of India in the eighteenth century, the monarchic ideal continued to prevail. After Shivaji's death the *rājmaṇḍal* was revived in Jinji during the Mughal occupation of the capital; a new member was added with the denomination of *Pratinidhi*, who, as the king's 'representative' for some time overshadowed the other *pradhāns*, until the *Peśvā* became supreme. With the exception of the latter the eight ministers gradually lost all political consequence except as holders of extensive *jāgīrs*. As such the Pratinidhi remained the most considerable until the early nineteenth century. The estates of a number of other sardars who established Maratha sovereign power in Northern and Central India were much larger however than those of the obsolete pradhans; they too were referred to as *jāgīrs*, but more commonly as *sardārīs, saraṇjāms* or *daulats*. The sardars who held these vast estates, although subject to periodic checks and auditing by the central court, were themselves formally equipped with sovereign power. It became inevitable of course that with the extension of the *svarājya* the essential tasks of government were delegated. Emblematic of such delegation was the *śikkekaṭyār* or 'seal and dagger'. But the *śikkekaṭyār* was not merely an emblem of sovereignty, for the seal was at the same time a 'deputy' seal (*mutālīk-* or *taināt-śikka*) and its possession implied the right to make grants and assignments of land or confirm hereditary rights and hence was a precondition of the extension of Maratha *svarājya* through *fitna* in the Mughal domains.[94]

Now a most remarkable feature is that in the eighteenth century, during the expansion of Maratha sovereignty, the political–ideological leverage of the universal Empire of the Mughals was entirely preserved, even when the Marathas were, as Morlat put it in 1787,

eighteenth and nineteenth centuries and was taken over by many modern Indian historians, first by M. G. Ranade.

94 Vad, Mawji and Parasnis, *Kaifiyats, Yadis*, p. 206; *EIP*, 4, p. 271; *SSRPD*, 1, no. 103; 6, no. 610; *MITSA*, 1, nos 12, 17; *MIS*, 4, pp. 35, 54, 60; C. Malet to Sir J. Shore, 17 March 1794, *PRC*, 2, p. 337. The 'deputy' seal is distinguished from the seal of the central court, the *huzūr śikka* (cf. Malet to G. T. Cherry, Persian Translator, Fort William, 8 June 1790, *PRC*, 2, p. 160).

'la seule puissance réelle dans l'Inde'.[95] Maratha *fitna* thus left intact the fiction of Mughal plenitude of power. We will meet with numerous concrete examples (cf. Chapter I–III) of this phenomenon, which the British saw as a curious paradox. Malcolm for instance noted with surprise that of the eighteenth-century rulers the Marathas most of all 'affected a scrupulous sense of inferiority in all their intercourse and correspondence with the Emperors, and with their principal chiefs, particularly with the Rajput princes ... [and] in hardly any instance considered the right of conquest as a sufficient title to the smallest possession'.[96] The Marathas, observed also Grant Duff, 'notwithstanding their predatory character, are at all times exceedingly eager to have any right formally recognized'.[97] Contemporary documents make clear that from the outset Shivaji in his relationship with the Mughal Emperor spoke of his kingdom as a mere gentry right, a *vatan* or *zamīndārī*.[98] These are terms which point to subservience to the Mughal and imply a denial of any independent sovereign or vested right.

In Mughal parlance *zamīndār* was a generic concept for the indigenous Indian gentry – a gentry which was either subservient or rebellious – and if necessary it could be stretched considerably to perpetuate the fiction of universal Mughal dominion. It could then be applied not only to the kings of the Marathas but also to those of the Rajputs and Bundelas. Sometimes, as in the case of the Mughal historian Bhimsen, this appellation is extended to all sovereigns of the Deccan. Bhimsen writes about Ahmad Nizam-al-Mulk, the founder of the Ahmadnagar Sultanate, as 'the *zamīndār* of the Deccan who called himself a king'.[99] Writing in the early eighteenth century, Bhimsen explains further that Shah Jahan and Aurangzeb conquered most of the Deccan, but that 'there are still as many as one thousand forts in the possession of *zamīndārs*'.[100] The same author entirely denies the legitimacy of the claims to royal status

[95] Quoted in E. Thompson, *The Making of the Indian Princes* (London and Dublin, 1978), p. 2.

[96] *Central India*, I, p. 81. [97] *History*, I, p. 225.

[98] '*mulūk vatanī sahebācā āhe*', '*āplā vatan mulūk*' (*MIS*, 8, nos 10, 21; 15, no.340; and see S. N. Joshi, *Arvācīn Mahārāṣṭre-itihāsakāḷāṇtīl Rājyakārbhārācā Abhyās*, vol. I (Poona, 1959), pp. 151, 191). Habib, *Agrarian System*, p. 349, note 57 quotes a British report mentioning that Shivaji in 1675 had agreed 'to be the Kings Desy [i.e., *desāī*, a synonym of *deśmukh*, a district *zamīndār*] of all his countrys of Deccan'.

[99] V. G. Khobrekar (ed.), *Tarikh-i-Dilkasha of Bhimsen* (English translation by J. Sarkar) (Bombay, 1972), p. 7.

[100] *Ibid.*, pp. 10–11.

among the Marathas: after the death of Shahaji (Bhonsle) his eldest son Shivaji 'developed the *zamīndārī* to such an extent that he turned his head of obedience away from the subordination of the ruler of Bijapur and extended his hand of possession and oppression on his country'; and after Shivaji's death 'the *zamīndārī* passed on to Sambha'.[101] In the eighteenth century, Maratha expansion continued to evolve along the same double-track of subservience and sovereign power acquired through *fitna* or 'rebellion'. In the numerous treaties concluded with the Mughals the Maratha king remains a *zamīndār* and it is repeated again and again that he has to 'populate the land, organize cultivation and expel robbers'. It is never openly said that the Maratha king actually conquered a district and that it was therefore ceded to him in perpetuity. The structure of sovereignty and conquest through *fitna* submerged under a universalist idiom as soon as the conquests had been successfully consolidated.

The Marathas themselves also gave the impression at all times that they were to be servants of the Empire. The *Ājñāpatra* speaks of the Emperor of Delhi (*dillīśvaro*) as the 'lord of the universe' (*jagadīśvaro*).[102] Of Shahu it is said that he objected to the building of a Delhi Gate (*darvāzā*) in Poona facing the north (a project undertaken by the Peshwa minister) as this implied open defiance of the Badshah.[103] The Maratha letters of his reign – and till as late as the Battle of Panipat – often refer to the Mughal Emperor as the *sārvabhaum*, the 'lord of all land' or 'Universal Emperor'.[104] Peshwa Baji Rao I calls the Emperor the *pṛthvipatī* or 'lord of the earth' in a letter of 1736 to his mother in which he informs her of his probable success in a campaign against him.[105] Nana Fadnis still uses the same title in his late eighteenth-century autobiographical memoir when he describes the visit to the Delhi court which he

101 *Ibid.*, pp. 16, 231. 102 Banhatti, *Ājñāpatra*, ch. 1.

103 S. N. Sen, *Administrative System of the Marathas* (Calcutta, 1976), p. 112.

104 G. S. Sardesai, *Marāṭhī Riyāsat*, madhya-vibhāg 1 (Bombay, 1925), p. 99; D. B. Parasnis (ed.), *Brahmendrasvāmī Dhavaḍśīkar* (Bombay, 1945), no. 35; K. N. Sane (ed.), *Aitihāsik Patreṇ Yādī Vagaire* (Poona, 1889), no.32. Other kings, for example the Bidar Badshah, may also be called *sārvabhaum* (cf. *BISM-Aitihāsik Saṃkīrṇa Sāhitya*, vol.1 (Poona, 1931), p. 56). The Maratha king may refer to himself as *sārvabhaum*, as in the *Śivdigvijaya* (Nandurbarkar and Dandekar eds, p. 247); in a letter of 1739 from the Peshwa's brother Chimnaji Ballal to the Chatrapati the latter is again addressed as *sārvabhaum* (cf. *MITSA*, 2, no.418). *Sārvabhaum* has the general connotation of universal dominion, and the Mughal Emperor is merely the *sārvabhaum par excellence*.

105 *SPD*, 14, no.51.

made in 1759 or 1760.[106] With the Badshah the 'lord of the earth', his darbar was the 'centre of the earth'.[107] The Marathas remained 'steadfast in his service'[108]; to destroy him was seen as 'unprofitable',[109] and at Panipat the Maratha army fought the Afghans 'to protect the Sultan of Taimur'.[110] After 1761 we find such explicit avowals of subservience only in official treaties or agreements, but still then the Rajas of Satara and the Peshwas acknowledged the universal authority of the Emperors of Delhi by addressing them in the form of petitions or *arjīs* and by coining their money with the Mughal impression.[111] The Nizams of the Deccan were also addressed by *arjīs*, but the Peshwas, with the increase of their power began to address them by *mihrbān mukhlisāna*, in the latter of which honorifics an acknowledgement of superiority is preserved to a minimal degree.[112]

An umbrella of imperial universalism was thus set over the *svarājya* despite the fact that at the same time the Maratha *svarājya* and the Mughal *pararājya* were intertwined rival networks of political allegiances. *Fitna* and Mughal universalism determined the substance and form of the Maratha *svarājya* but equally of the other sub-polities which in the same period were formed within the Mughal sphere and which were all linked up with the rise of Maratha power. Whether it was in the Deccan, in Gujarat, Malwa, Bengal or Hindustan, the Maratha conquests were always at one stage or another supported or invited by Mughal governors who, through a Maratha alliance, attempted to boost their own independence from the imperial centre and to secure more solid local roots. In all cases the Marathas also found support from Hindu clan-leaders, local chiefs or *zamīndārs* such as Rajputs, Jats and Bundelas against the Empire which was further weakened, in the period of 1739–67, by the repeated invasions from the north-west by the Persian Emperor Nadir Shah and the Afghan leader Ahmad Shah Abdali.

Still in the time of Aurangzeb, the Mughal mode of provincial administration had been a *dualist* one: to each district there were appointed on a temporary basis a *faujdār* or military governor, and

106 A. Macdonald, *Memoir of the Life of the late Nana Farnavis* (Oxford, 1927), App.2: 'The Autobiography of Nana Farnavis', p. 167.

107 '*bādśāhī darbār pṛthvicā madhya āhe*' (*MIS*, 2, p. 95).

108 *Ibid.* 109 Parasnis, *Brahmendrasvāmī* (patravyavahār section), no. 27.

110 *IS*, 2, 8, (1910), 'Aitihāsik Ṭipaṇeṇ', no.33.

111 Malet to Cherry, 8 January 1790, *PRC*, 2, pp. 165–7.

112 As the Peshwa's regent, Nana Fadnis continued to address the Nizam by *arjī*.

a *dīwān*, a revenue and civil administrator. The military commanders of large provinces were called *ṣubahdārs* (Mar. *subhedārs*) or *nāẓims*, and these also had appointed to them a *dīwān* as counterpart and supervisor. In the early decades of the eighteenth century three of the most powerful of such Mughal *ṣubahdārs*, Murshid Quli Khan in Bengal, Asaf Jah in the Deccan, and Barhan-al-Mulk in Awadh, took the preliminary step to dynasty-building (common in the Islamic world) of permanently merging the two offices into one and bringing the regulatory process of office rotation to a standstill.[113] Mirza Najaf Khan took the same course in the Delhi province when the three first-mentioned *ṣubahdārs* were already practically independent of the Delhi court and had for several decades denied it its share of the revenues of their provinces where they ruled as hereditary *nawābs* in their provincial capitals, appointing their revenue officials without reference to the Emperor.[114] The Emperor could not prevent the fusion of the offices of *ṣubahdār* and *dīwān* but none of the *nawābs* gave up the practice of having the *k͟huṭba*, the Friday prayer in the central mosque, read in the Emperor's name and of coining their money with the Mughal impression, while they never openly denied the legitimacy of Mughal imperial suzerainty and always took the opportunity to obtain farmans or authorizations from the Emperor; for as much as they needed Maratha support to enhance their position they could invoke the Emperor's name to prop themselves up against the Marathas if these encroached farther than was intended. In the establishment of the *nawābīs* it seems plausible to assign a crucial importance to the invasion of Nadir Shah in 1739 – who, incidentally, had the *k͟huṭba* read at Delhi in his own name for two months. The Persian Emperor himself however gave as his motive for invading the Mughal domains the 'rebellion' of the Hindustani and Deccani *zamīndārs*. Nadir Shah did not withdraw without enjoining the Marathas to obey the Mughal Emperor.[115] Primarily we thus witness an endogenous rising of the power of Hindu *zamīndārs* aspiring to sovereignty in combination with

[113] Cf. pp. 316ff.

[114] The title of *nawāb* is the honorific Arabic plural of *nā'ib*, 'representative'. As Barnett (*North India*, p. 21) points out it was not a specific Mughal title but it came into popular use to designate the eighteenth-century regional governors. Originally it denoted any high-ranking imperial deputy.

[115] In effect, the Persian Emperor seems to have claimed certain rights of protection and suzerainty over the Mughals (cf. F. W. Buckler, 'The Political Theory of the Indian Mutiny', *Transactions of the Royal Historical Society*, 4th series, vol. 5 (London, 1922), pp. 82ff).

Mughal governors attempting to set themselves up permanently in their own more compact domains with closer ties to agrarian society and who, retaining the revenue surpluses which were formerly siphoned off by the imperial centre, presided over a redistribution of surplus which favoured landed gentry. While the rise of the nawabis was linked up in particular with the rise of the Marathas, in other provinces such as Malwa and Gujarat it is found that the Mughal governors, after first inviting Maratha assistance, were eventually ousted by them, and such districts were then brought under complete Maratha control instead of remaining under shared sovereignty.

The concept of *svarājya* in the eighteenth century came in general use to denote Maratha sovereignty anywhere in India. As will be seen, the eighteenth-century usage of the term refers to Maratha rights or claims, in both their political and fiscal aspects, irrespective of their regional location. It was then not merely a term for the Maratha 'homeland' in the Western Deccan, as is often still erroneously supposed. In its eighteenth-century context the term bears the mark of the contradiction of conquest and subservience, of kingship and *zamīndārī*. *Sva-rājya* is an original Sanskrit compound which means 'self-rule' and which was not current in the Indo-Persian diplomatic vocabulary.[116] Maratha *svarājya* was a form of 'zamindari sovereignty' not merely in the eyes of the Mughals but actually established by people who were often just one or two generations away from village or district zamindari status and the practice of 'organizing cultivation and expelling robbers'. We do not know if the term *svarājya* by itself was already used under Shivaji.[117] Perhaps it was not until the early eighteenth century that it was first applied to those districts which were then alleged to have been included in Shivaji's kingdom before it was overrun by the Mughal armies. These districts were formally restored by the Emperor to the Maratha king Shahu in 1719, after the Mughal retreat from the Western Deccan. In the *jābtā svarājya* or 'statement of *svarājya*' of 1719 they were aggregated into one territorial entity on the two sides of the Western Ghats extending from the river Tapti in the north to the Krishna in the south, with a

[116] In the Brahmanas it has perhaps more specific meanings but even then these included 'independent sovereignty' (cf. P. K. Chaudhuri, *Political Concepts in Ancient India: A Glossary of Political Terms* (New Delhi, 1977), s.v.).

[117] The late seventeenth-century bakhar of Sabhasad makes an analogous distinction between the Maratha 'homeland' (*āple mulakh*) and the 'foreign land' (*paramulakh*) (V. S. Vakaskar (ed.), *Sabhāsadācī Bakhar* (Poona, 1973), p. 27).

few gaps around Aurangabad and Burhanpur; some of Shivaji's conquests in the Karnataka are also included: Kopbal, Gadag, Bellari, Jinji, Vellore, and Thanjavur. This territorial definition of *svarājya* however was requisite only for incorporating Maratha sovereignty into the universalist, pan-Indian Mughal scheme of district demarcations, and the Marathas never abided by the boundaries determined in 1719. The treaty of 1719 was, like all Maratha–Mughal treaties of the eighteenth century, based on the fiction that the Marathas could only be the *zamīndārī* servants of the Empire. All these treaties, therefore, had to deny *fitna a posteriori* and the territorial designations in them are of little significance. A Maratha document announced as early as 1718 that 'the King has established *svarājya* from the Badshah and has obtained control of all *ṭhāṇas*'.[118] *Svarājya* was established in the Western Deccan when the *ṭhāṇas*, the garrisons or military posts where the revenue officials were stationed, were under Maratha control, for, as Grant Duff says, 'the cultivators consider him their master who is in possession of the *ṭhāṇa*'.[119] However, while *svarājya* was not a form of territorial sovereignty it also did not necessarily imply direct administration. Whereas often the Marathas penetrated into regions which were inaccessible to the Mughals (e.g., in Deogarh and Orissa) and which had been left by them with a great measure of autonomy, the Maratha *svarājya* comprised at all times innumerable tributary relationships with chiefs and local rajas under a form of suzerainty which left them free in their internal administration.

Finally, *svarājya* is not necessarily the 'exclusive' Maratha sovereignty over an area. There never were clear-cut boundaries to the *mahāls* which were under Maratha control and in many of them sovereignty was shared. Besides the revenue of the districts which were later defined as his *svarājya* by the Mughals, Shivaji levied what was called the *cauth* or 'one-quarter' of the revenue of some surrounding Mughal districts (Junnar, Ahmadnagar, Parenda) during his *mulūkhgirī*[120] campaigns and he had secured this right, with that of the *sardeśmukhī* or 'dues of the head-*deśmukh*', nominally 10 or 12½% of the assessed land-revenue, from Bijapur and Golconda, which kingdoms on account of these paid him 3 and

118 '*svāmīs svarājya pātśahāni bahal karūn avāghi ṭhāṇi dilhī*' (*SCS*, 5, no.863).

119 *History*, 1, p. 506. Likewise, 89 of the 145 forts which were formally restored in the grant of *svarājya* of 1719 were already in the actual possession of the Marathas.

120 Lit. 'seizing of country'.

5 lacs of rupees respectively.[121] Both levies are derived from *zamīndārī* claims. The *sardeśmukhī* was a right associated with the hereditary *vatan* of the house of Bhonsle.[122] It was a particular *zamīndārī* right which had already been in vogue in the Konkan before the Bhonsles claimed it in areas in the Deccan.[123] Imperial recognition for this claim on the part of the Bhonsles was not obtained before Shahu's time.[124] The *cauth* was another claim deriving from the traditional right of *zamīndārs* under the Mughal government to a fourth of the land or the land-revenue under their charge.[125] In the Deccan the *cauth* as payment for *zamīndārs* is found as early as the Bahmani period.[126] The *cauth* of the land-revenue did not remain the usual remuneration of any type of *zamīndārs* in the eighteenth century but there were then still traces of it[127] and the term continued to be used to denote the fictive *zamīndārī* right to one-quarter of the Maratha kings.

Cauth and *sardeśmukhī* were originally *zamīndārī* claims, but in the former (and in the latter in some areas in conjunction with the former) was amalgamated in a peculiar way the idea of aid. To back and justify its imposition there was the potential of military support, the 'political' use of military power, and the threat of plunder and burning which might have been used to make an entry. In the eighteenth century the *cauth* became the fulcrum of Maratha expansion to the north, and the aid which the Marathas provided in return for its payment was primarily military–political intervention in local internecine rivalries, commonly also the restraining of rival parties of Marathas and the co-ordination of troops: it was a recognition of their sovereignty therefore, even if partial or shared, and the villages indeed begged for it.[128] The *cauth*

121 J. Sarkar, *House of Shivaji* (New Delhi, 1978), p. 127; Grant Duff, *History*, 1, p. 112.
122 Sardesai, *Marāṭhī Riyāsat*, madhya-vibhag 1, p. 100.
123 Cf. A. R. Kulkarni, *Maharashtra in the Age of Shivaji* (Poona, 1967), p. 133; Sen, *Administrative System*, pp. 66, 111–12.
124 Grant Duff, *History*, 1, p. 112; Sarkar, *House of Shivaji*, p. 129; Sen, *Administrative System*, p. 66.
125 Habib, *Agrarian System*, pp. 148ff.
126 In a document of 1426 the Bidar Badshah declares that a *mavāsī rājā* who refused to pay his revenue has to be brought to terms; a promise is made that 'whoever subdues this rebel and recovers the revenue will be entitled to the *cauthāī* along with the *deśmukhī* of the region' (*SPD*, 31, no.1).
127 Cf. pp. 203–4.
128 Cf. A. Pawar (ed.), *Tarabai Papers: A Collection of Persian Letters* (Kolhapur, 1971), pp. xvi–b–c; Malcolm, *Central India*, 1, pp. 70–2; Q. Ahmad, 'Mughal–Maratha Relations, 1719–1739', in: A. Pawar (ed.), *Maratha History Seminar* (Kolhapur, 1971), p. 157; Elliot and Dowson, *History of India*, 7, pp. 464–5.

was a kind of protection-rent or *rakhvālī*, akin to the *Huldigung* of feudal Europe, an agreement concluded by peasant communities with the 'enemy of their land',[129] or akin to the *khafāra* which was levied by 'brigands' (*shuṭṭār*) as the price of protection in parts of the Arab world,[130] or, again, the *rakhī* levied by the Sikhs on their neighbours,[131] and it was basically not different from the insurance system which worked for merchants in most parts of the pre-modern world.[132] The only typical feature of the Maratha *cauth* and *sardeśmukhī* was that these levies were nominally claimed and given out as the rightful remuneration of *zamīndārī* service to the Mughal Emperor. In order to encompass the *svarājya* within the Mughal universal dominion it had to be conceptualized in treaty documents as a simulacrum of the original local *zamīndārī* system. It is for this reason that, in the last year of the reign of Aurangzeb, the two claimants of the Maratha throne attempted to obtain from the Emperor a farman for what in the Maratha letters of that time is called the *zamīndārī* or the *zamīndārī-rājya*.[133] The imperial grant of 1719 then equated the Maratha *svarājya* with this zamindari dominion of the Bhonsle dynasty in the Western Deccan, adding to it the concessions of the *cauth* and *sardeśmukhī* of the six subhas of the Mughal Deccan. After that it soon became the normal practice of the Marathas to subsume the *cauth* and *sardeśmukhī* of the Mughal subhas under the appellation of *svarājya* as well.[134] Later, in Gujarat, Malwa, or Berar, the *cauth* – always under sanction or pretended sanction of the Emperor – was nothing but a prelude to the establishment of complete Maratha sovereignty. These provinces were simply 'brought under *svarājya*' in their entirety.

In sum, Maratha sovereignty or *svarājya* is not to be defined as an

129 Brunner, *Land und Herrschaft*, pp. 86–8.

130 Wafi, *Muqaddima*, 2, p. 640.

131 G. Forster to Earl Cornwallis, Gov. Gen., 27 December 1786, *PRC*, 1, p. 161.

132 Cf. Ardant, *Histoire de l'Impôt*, 1, pp. 358–9. Some Hindu writers are apt to point at Muslim antecedents of the *cauth*; thus C. V. Vaidya made a futile attempt to show that the *turuṣkdaṇḍ* or 'Turkish punishment' paid by Raja Pratihar of Kanoj on behalf of his people to the Sultans of Ghazni was probably the prototype of the Maratha *cauth* ('Cauth āṇi Sardeśmukī', *BISMQ*, 12, 1 (1953), pp. 1–13).

133 *MIS*, 8, no. 56.

134 Cf. R. B. G. C. Vad, P. V. Mawji and D. B. Parasnis (eds), *Treaties, Agreements and Sanads* (Bombay, 1924), p. 26: yadi of 1798 which mentions '*425000 [rupees] bedar subhyāce svarājya-paikīṇ*'; R. V. Hervadkar (ed.), *Thorle Śāhū Mahārāja yāṇce Caritra* (Poona, 1973), p. 80: '*bhāgānagar lagat dāhā vīs mahāl yethīl cauth sardeśmukhī vagaire svarājyāce aṃmal āhet* (etc.)'; *ibid.*, p. 53: '*sarlaṣkar (yāṇs) gaṇgātīr moṇglāīṇtīl svarājya yāce amal yāṇcā subhā dilhā*'. Countless other examples can be found in the Peshwa Daftar.

abstract, territorially circumscribed, dominion complete in itself. Unlike modern territorial sovereignty the conception of *svarājya* is only determined by its complementary opposite, the *pararājya*, the 'enemy's sovereignty'.[135] As such the Maratha *svarājya* was most commonly identified as the non-*moṇglāī*. On the other hand, Maratha *svarājya*, while based on conquest, on *fitna* or 'rebellion', was conceptualized in the Mughal universalist idiom as a service-tenure, a *zamīndārī*. Hence, in many areas of the eighteenth-century subcontinent where we find the sovereignty, and *ipso facto* the land-revenue, shared by the Marathas and the Mughals (either temporarily or permanently), the shares of the Marathas, no matter how large in practice, were invariably indicated as *cauth* and *sardeśmukhī*, the remunerations of the fictive *zamīndārī* rights of the Maratha king. The term *svarājya* could thus, in the areas where sovereignty was shared, denote merely these shares of sovereign power or their fiscal equivalents. A complication is further that the *sardeśmukhī* is sometimes added to the *svarājya* in a purely fiscal sense as a special *vatan* of the Maratha king distinct from his other rights; it is in other words not always comprised in the *svarājya* as the *cauth* always is. This detail should not distract us and we shall assume that in the *svarājya* all Maratha rights are comprised unless explicitly stated otherwise.

Svarājya then denoted partial or complete Maratha sovereignty anywhere in India and it is intermingled with the *moṇglāī* or *pararājya* to such an extent (down to the village level) that the concept of territory becomes fallacious. When *svarājya* is territorially defined, as in the treaty with the Mughals of 1719, it is to reduce the question of power and loyalty to a question of exclusive and asymmetrical subservience. A territorial reference to a Maratha homeland is present furthermore in such (far less common) alternative expressions as *mahārāṣṭra rājya* but there it is also secondary.[136] This secondary reference to territory stands out most sharply in a definition of the term *svarājya* given by Govind Rao Chitnis in 1765 in reply to a query then made about its meaning: 'the *svarājya* is the country West of the Bhima, and all else which you call *svarājya*; beyond that is *zabardastī*'.[137] There was always the territorial link with the Maharashtrian homeland,

135 E.g. *MIS*, 12, p. 222; 14, p. 54.

136 *BISM-Vārṣik Itivṛtt* (1913), p. 234 (doc. of 1707); *BISMQ*, 1, 1–3 (1920–1), no.6 of 1707; *BISMQ*, 40, 1–4 (1964–5), no.75 (undated); D. V. Apte and N. C. Kelkar (eds), *Śivcaritra Pradīpa* (Poona, 1925), p. 43.

137 Quoted by Grant Duff, *History*, 1, p. 548.

and this accounts for that 'genuine patriotism' and 'national attachment' of the Marathas so often remarked upon by the British, but it was an emotional bond of union nevertheless which became weaker the further they expanded beyond Maharashtra and the less it was a strategic desideratum.[138] The justifying mystique of *mahārāṣṭra dharma* paradoxically dates from the period when the Marathas were most under threat, at the turn of the seventeenth century, when a rallying cry was needed against the Mughals.[139] It was an appeal which became fashionable under the impact of nationalism in the twentieth century, particularly through the writings of M. G. Ranade and R. S. Bhagvat.[140] These two authors regard it as a parallel of Protestantism in Western Europe. But, notably, Grant Duff does not give any attention to it. The anonymous author of the *Śivdigvijaya* also does not attempt a systematic elucidation of *mahārāṣṭra dharma*, but merely mentions the wretched condition of *hiṇdū dharma* in the first and second quarter of the seventeenth century, and he further expounds that

> the *dharma* of establishing sovereignty (*svāmitva*) enjoins us to bring everywhere holders of rights (*adhikārīs*), *ināmdārs, zamīndārs*, and rayats under its sway, to commit everyone's estate (*vṛtti*) to its charge, and so sovereignty is established.[141]

This conception of *dharma* concerns merely the extension of political dominion and has no connection with a geographical territory. The compound *mahārāṣṭra dharma* occurs (as far as is known) for the first time in a fifteenth-century Marathi work, the *Guru Caritra*, where the author, rather than vaunting a conscious national or proto-national self-awareness and legitimation (of a mental territory), reaches out towards the pan-Indian, universalist ideals of Sanskritic Hinduism, the acceptance of the Veda, the *varṇāśrama* scheme, and so on. Again in the seventeenth century Ramdas, the guru of Shivaji, vigorously advocates its spread, and Shivaji in effect appears as the 'protector of gods, brahmans, holy places and the cow'. Still, this *mahārāṣṭra dharma* never became anything else than a parochial blend of elements of Hindu dharma that prevailed everywhere in India. Present-day Indian authors more often call the claim that the Marathas attempted to establish a

138 Cf. Thompson, *Indian Princes*, pp. 1, 19, 46; R. O'Hanlon, 'Maratha History as Polemic: Low Caste Ideology and Political Debate in late Nineteenth-century Western India', *MAS*, 17, 1 (1983), pp. 2–3.

139 Cf. *SCS*, 5, p. 767.

140 *MIS*, 4, p. 106.

141 Quoted by Rajvade, *ibid.*, p. 113.

hiṇdūpādśāhī or Hindu Empire 'chauvinistic'. That the Maratha rajas, and later the brahman Peshwas, became 'the upholders of Hindu dharma' did not exclude a nominal subservience to the Mughals nor a sustained effort to participate in Indo-Islamic political culture. In the eighteenth century there were several attempts to bring the sacred cities of Hindu pilgrimage under Maratha control. These took the characteristic form, for the first time in 1736, when Peshwa Baji Rao I demanded Prayag, Benares, Gaya, and Mathura in *jāgīr* from the Emperor.[142] There were more such demands, and attempts to have the pilgrim-tax abolished, to obtain farmans prohibiting cow-slaughter, etc.

Against this backdrop of an interlocked structure of Maratha and Mughal sovereignties there developed a form of diplomacy or mediation which was to adjust the relationship between 'rebels' and a universal Empire which could not but treat all political foci within its orbit as subordinate to itself. The possession of a 'minister of foreign affairs' and the sending of 'ambassadors' to different courts constituted in the eighteenth century one of the formal attributes of sovereign power. Yet it is easy to see that here too there are crucial differences with the type of diplomatic intercourse that goes with the modern system of closed, juxtaposed sovereign states. In Shivaji's Council of Eight there had been a Sumant who was to be 'in charge of the affairs of the *pararājya*'. But the Maratha–Mughal treaty of 1719 was not negotiated through him. This was done by a former Saciv of Rajaram (a *kārkūn* under Shivaji) who during the Mughal siege of Jinji had retired as sanyasi to Benares.[143] His service was engaged by Husain Ali Khan, the Mughal subhedar of the Deccan, after he had become gravely distracted by factionalism and Maratha intrusions at his court. On the request of the Deccan subhedar the sanyasi–diplomat opened a correspondence with the Maratha court at Satara and was subsequently dispatched hence to effect an arrangement between the Mughals and his own countrymen. At Satara he quickly won the confidence of Shahu and it was his mediation which led to the final treaty of 1719. As it turns out, such a procedure was fairly typical of eighteenth-century diplomacy in general. The Marathas always remained dependent on outsiders of one kind or another in their contacts with the Mughal courts.[144] The so-called *vakīls* or 'ambassadors' sent from one court to

[142] *SPD*, 15, no.86 (p. 96). [143] Hervadkar, *Thorle Śāhū*, p. 56.
[144] Cf. T. S. Shejwalkar (ed.), *Nagpur Affairs* (Selection of Marathi Letters from the Menavli Daftar), 2 vols (Poona, 1954–9), I.

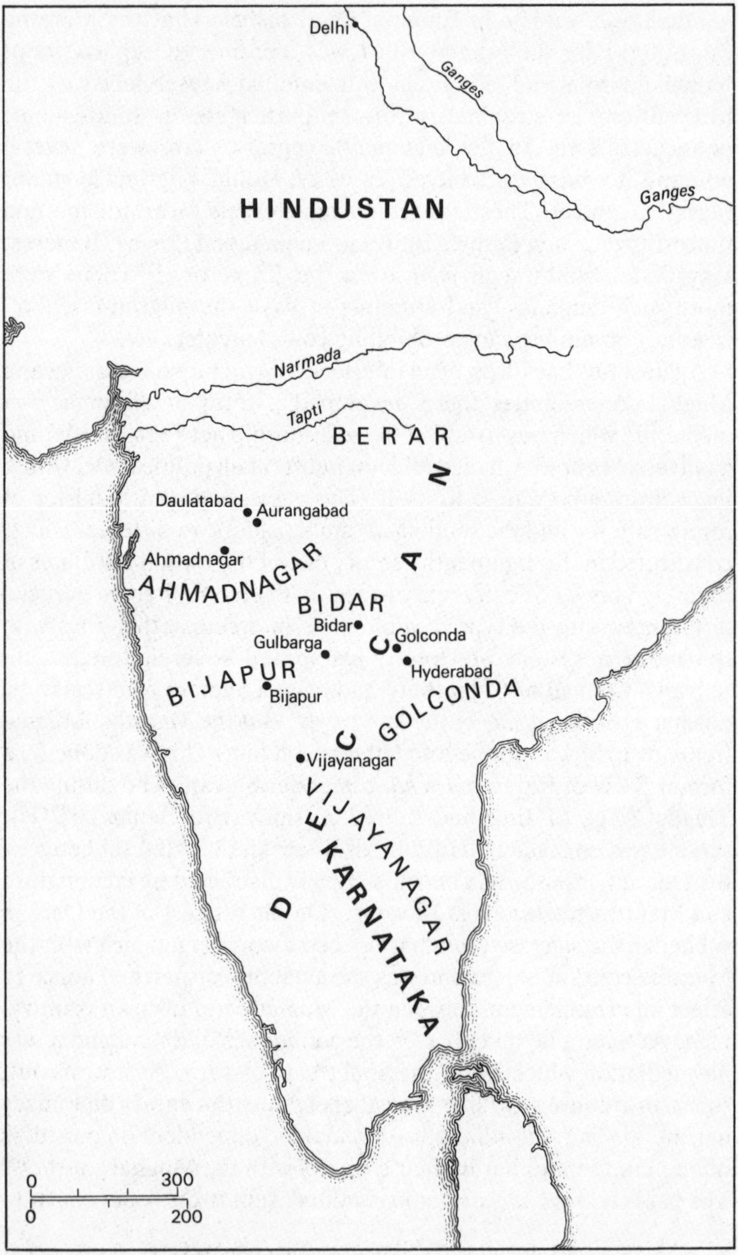

India in the sixteenth century

another are always found working for both parties simultaneously, and they were – irregularly – paid by both parties.[145] After 1719 a Maratha envoy lived at Delhi almost uninterruptedly. This permanent vakil belonged to the Hingane family, a member of which had been stationed at Delhi after a personal visit of the Peshwa and which had originally been the head priests at Nasik and the Peshwa's domestic priests at that place.[146] Next to them there was a body of professional news-writers, *waqī'a-nawīs* or *akhbār-nawīs*, independent of Hingane, who wrote in Persian and were mostly North-Indian Kayasthas or Khatris but were salaried by the Peshwas. The first Hingane owed his appointment, which became hereditary in the family, to his talents and qualifications as a Marathi and Persian scholar. Characteristically the remuneration of the Hinganes consisted of hereditary grants of revenue made by both the Emperor and the Peshwa from the *moṇglāī* as well as from the *svarājya*.[147]

II Mughal expansion in the Deccan

In the preceding subchapter the argument was put forward that in India and in the Muslim world as a whole the immediate constituents of sovereignty were not an army and a territory but political allegiances. The argument has so far remained rather abstract and was intended to offer an alternative to the modern theories of power politics which assume that the historical military empires of Asia tended to pursue expansionist goals almost 'naturally' and that there is a certain 'natural' limit to imperial expansionism, the transgression of which led to the 'decline' of the empires. In this subchapter and the following we shall describe in as much detail as is needed the actual historical process of Mughal expansion in the seventeenth century and then attempt to demonstrate how the subsequent involution of imperial dominion in the eighteenth century – the development of Maratha *svarājya* – can be seen as the ultimate consequence of the expansion of Mughal power.

Under the Delhi Sultans the political constellation in Hindustan had still been in a constant flux; in Indian terms the Muslim sultan

145 *Ibid*.

146 Cf. D. B. Parasnis (ed.), *Dillī yethīl Marāṭhyāṇcīṇ Rājkāraṇeṇ*, 2 vols (Bombay, 1913–14); G. H. Khare (ed.), *Hiṇgaṇe Daftar*, 2 vols (Poona, 1945–7); D. Verma (ed.), *Newsletters of the Mughal Court* (Reign of Ahmad Shah, 1751–2 AD) (Bombay, 1949); *P.A.*: *List 13, Ru.74, File 1044*, pp. 26–7.

147 P.A.: *List 13, Ru.55, File 751*, Report C 16.

was merely one king in the 'circle of kings'. In an Indo-Persian chronicle it is observed with sarcasm that in the late thirteenth century 'the Empire of the King of the World extended from Delhi to Palam'.[1] The sway of the Sultanate reached its maximum extent under Muhammad bin Tughluq (1325–51), who first established it ephemerally over a part of the Deccan. From 1340 to the accession of Akbar in 1556 Islamic dominion lost ground again, while in the south its spread was checked by the establishment of the powerful Hindu kingdom of Vijayanagar. In 1347 an Afghan or Turki official of the Delhi Sultan, called Zafar Khan, broke away to establish the independent Bahmani dynasty at Gulbarga, later at Bidar. Provincial governors of that dynasty made themselves strong, in the typical fashion of the circle of kings, by allying themselves with the Vijayanagar power and playing it off against the Bahmani, then setting themselves up as independent Badshahs or Sultans.[2] In this way five new sultanates took the Bahmani's place in the period 1482–1518. Two of the smaller sultanates, the Imad Shahi of Berar and the Barid Shahi of Bidar were in the period 1574–1619 incorporated in the three bigger ones which survived into the seventeenth century: the Nizam Shahi of Ahmadnagar, the Adil Shahi of Bijapur, and the Qutub Shahi of Golconda.[3] The Deccan Sultans, while owing their rise to shifting alliances with the Bahmani and Vijayanagar kings, later periodically re-allied themselves with Vijayanagar against each other and against their internal rivals, but subsequently formed a transitory confederation to bring down the Hindu kingdom. As a result of this Vijayanagar fell in 1565, after which the supremacy of Islam was established over the entire Deccan, although not under a single sovereignty but under three independent sultanates reaching from the Narmada down to Rameshvara on the Southern tip of the peninsula.[4]

From the outset, mutual competition and rivalry among the Deccan Sultans and the Vijayanagar King made them seek close

[1] '*pādshāhī shāh 'ālam az dehlī tā pālam*' (Elliot and Dowson, *History of India*, 5, p. 74). Palam is only a few miles away from the city of Delhi.

[2] Cf. 'Jāvlikar More yāṇcī choṭī Bakhar', in: *IS*, 1, 10 (1909), 'Aitihāsik Sfuṭ Lekh', pp. 21–3; 'they turned away from Ramraja (*rāmrājāsīṇ bebadal jāhlā*), ... then they rose the *chatra* upon themselves ... [and] thus their *pādśāhā* began'.

[3] In the telescoped chronology of the *More Bakhar* only the last three are mentioned.

[4] Cf. 'More Bakhar', *op. cit.*, p. 23; 'The three united, and they dropped their Vidyānagar obligations (*vidyānagarāvar nimakharām hoūn*), ... they killed the Raja and divided his country. Then in this country there were 3 *pādśāhās* from the Narmada up to Rāmeśvar.'

connections with the local Hindu chiefs, the *zamīndārs* and *nāyaks*. The *More Bakhar* mentions a host of Maratha families who first served Krishnadeva Raja and Ramraja of Vijayanagar, and then, after the extinction of their rule, became *nokar* ('servant') of one of the Sultans: Moite, Surave, Yadhava Rao, Kadam, Scindhia, Ravi Rao, Bhadvalkar, More, Ghatge, Junjar Rao, Nalcade, Salonkhi, Patankar, Mane Mhasvadkar, Dahiganvkar, Yelahurkar.[5] 'All Marathas leaving Ramraja began to eat the *saraṇjām* of whoever was the strongest. Some became *mansabdār* in Bijapur, some in Bhaganagar (Golconda), some in Devgiri Daulatabad.'[6] In a part of the eastern Deccan the *zamīndārs* and *nāyaks* continued to receive support from the Vijayanagar ruling élite to whom they were linked by tributary and kinship ties, and their assimilation remained a crucial problem for the Golconda Sultans.[7] Elsewhere in the Deccan the Sultans were successful in absorbing them through a multifarious conciliation-policy comprising 'honourable employment' and concessions of revenue or immunizations but also the playing down of Islam as a compliant form of Shiism and the introduction of an official bilingualism (Persian/Marathi or Persian/Telugu). These conciliatory policies were the parallel of what happened in the coeval Mughal Empire under Akbar, who made the Rajputs the cornerstone of the polity. Also in parallel to the Deccan Sultanates, the Mughal Sultanate had originated from within the Delhi Sultanate. This occurred when in 1526 the nobles under Ibrahim Lodi made an appeal to Babar to assist them in the restoration of their equality and independence within the Sultanate. Babar's intervention however quickly led to a transfer of sovereignty to the Mughal–Timurids, a dynasty which headed a retinue or 'nobility' of a very mixed provenance, including Iranis, Turanis, Uzbeks, and Afghans next to Mughals proper. In Hindustan the alliance made by Babar's grandson Akbar with the Rajputs and the famous *Dīn-i-Ilāhī*, a syncretist religious concoction of Hindu, Muslim and other elements that aroused a violent animosity of the Sunni orthodoxy, were only the culmination of assimilative trends which had been constitutive of Mughal power from the start, but more specifically they were prompted by the need to counterbalance older sections of Turani and Mughal nobles threatening the Emperor's sovereign position.[8] The alliance with the Rajputs – the

[5] *Ibid.*, p. 21. [6] *Ibid.*, p. 23. [7] Cf. Richards, *Golconda*, pp. 10, 12, 18.

[8] S. Chandra, *Parties and Politics at the Mughal Court, 1707–1740* (Aligarh, 1959), p. xxviii; and see p. xxvi.

indigenous Hindu rulers and *zamīndārs* ramifying all over the north – was extended under Jahangir and Shah Jahan but the Shiite elements of the Mughal variant of Islam were gradually eliminated and became more and more exclusively identified with the Iranis when the Mughals – through them and through the Rajputs – became embroiled with the Deccan Sultanates and began to harbour designs of further expansion beyond the Narmada. From 1590 onwards the Mughal Emperors were almost uninterruptedly involved in the political struggles of the Deccan Sultanates – until, in effect, the latter were successively extinguished as independent centres of Muslim power in the final quarter of the seventeenth century.

To the Mughal Empire the incorporation of the Deccan Muslim polities did not pose a new political problem, but it did pose a problem of legitimation. Not surprisingly, we witness at this stage of Mughal expansion a polarization within Indian Islam of which the northern, Mughal component – that of expansion – was an exact reversal of the syncretist tendencies followed earlier which served the incorporation of the Rajputs. Orthodox Sunni Islam related to the Shiism prevailing in the Deccan as the transcendent Brahmanical conception of *dharma* to popular Hinduism, to the 'sacral cults' of royalty, the little kingdom, 'idolatry' and tribalism. This polarization of Sunni universalism versus Shia Islam, versus Hinduized Islam, reached its apex under Aurangzeb (*alias* Alamgir) and assumed a most tangible form in the re-introduction of the Muslim poll-tax or *jiziya* on 'unbelievers' throughout the subcontinent in 1679. In the Deccan Aurangzeb always maintained to be motivated by the desire to propagate the pure Muslim faith in a 'region of idolatry' and never by a desire to possess its resources or its territory.[9] In the same vein the Mughal chronicler of the *Ma'āṣir-i-'Ālamgirī* or 'The Glories of Alamgir' merely gives as the Emperor's motivation that in the Deccan 'no respect was left for Islam and its adherents; mosques were without splendour while idol-temples flourished'.[10]

Politically, what we see first of all is that the imperial expansion in the Deccan was not primarily a military venture but a form of intervention which always followed the lines of local conflicts: the Mughals, despite their apparent might, remained dependent on

9 Cf. Grant Duff, *History*, I, p. 83.

10 J. Sarkar (ed. and transl.), *Ma'āṣir-i-'Ālamgirī of Saqui Musta'id Khan* (Calcutta, 1947), p. 174.

'dissension', 'conciliation', the 'enticing away' of their enemy's supporters, in short, on the exploitation and integration of conflict. It may again seem fairly obvious that a power looming as large as the Mughal Empire in the late sixteenth century would soon be drawn into the factional politics and disputes which were endemic in the apparently much less mighty Deccan Sultanates; but while it is certainly true that the Mughals were 'drawn' into the Deccan, it should not be thought that the Mughals themselves had any choice whether or not to resist the Deccan 'pull'. In the Mughal political system itself a very precariously balanced equilibrium had to be preserved and the alliances or 'intrigues' made among individual members of the Mughal nobility, especially also those made with 'outside powers', never failed to have direct repercussions on the equilibrium of the polity at large and would demand counter-alliances: *graves amicitiae principum.* The process of alliance, counter-alliance and 'sowing dissension' first 'unbalanced' and then 'paralyzed' the Deccan monarchies and it could not deeply affect the Mughal equilibrium until the frontier of expansion became closed. *Fitna* then had no outlet any more. Turning exclusively inward, it intensified factional strife and shifting alliances, interlacing ever more the Mughal nobility with Hindu chiefs and gentry. In the process the imperial dominion was not so much eroded as pushed upward.

In the Deccan the process of expansionist subversion started with 'the king with proximate country' and it is no coincidence that when Akbar began the Deccan conquests the kingdom of Ahmadnagar was in particular, as Grant Duff observed, 'a prey to disorder'.[11] The other Deccan kingdoms were also plagued by 'internal dissensions' but in Ahmadnagar factionalism had proceeded farthest and had brought into sharp opposition two groups of Hindu and Abyssinian nobles. The Hindu faction first invited Mughal intervention and allowed Akbar, after his conquest of Khandesh, to wrest from the Nizam Shah the greater part of Berar and the fort of Ahmadnagar with adjacent districts.[12] In 1607 the Mughals effected an alliance with Ahmadnagar against Bijapur. When this proved fruitless they attempted again to intervene in political factionalism at Ahmadnagar and temporarily allied themselves with Bijapur. Abul Fazl made out that 'religious strife', 'oppression of the peasantry' and 'misgovernment' were the cause of Mughal

[11] Grant Duff, *History*, I, p. 46. [12] *Ibid.*

intervention.[13] After 1622 both the Bijapur Sultan and Malik Ambar, the Abyssinian regent of Ahmadnagar, sought a Mughal alliance; the Mughals considered it more expedient to isolate Malik Ambar and, jointly with Bijapur, Shah Jahan eventually succeeded in bringing down the Nizam Shahi in 1636, after which its holdings were partitioned between the Mughals and Bijapur.[14] Shortly later in the same year Bijapur and Golconda – now the two kingdoms proximate to the Empire – were forced to enter into a tributary relationship with Shah Jahan and had to accept a Mughal Resident or *ḥājib* at their court.[15] The terms of submission acceded to by Abdullah Qutub Shah further stipulated that his coins should bear the Mughal impression and that in the Friday prayers the names of the four 'well-guided' Caliphs should be read instead of those of the Twelve Shia Imams and that they should mention the Mughal Emperor as the legitimate suzerain instead of the Safavid monarch of Persia.[16] At the Mughal court however the relationship with the two remaining Deccan kingdoms very soon became an issue of dissension among the Emperor's sons Aurangzeb and Dara Shikoh. The latter tried to maintain the relationship as defined by Shah Jahan up to 1658, but Aurangzeb, who was appointed governor of the Deccan for the second time in 1650, was a proponent of further expansion. As governor of the Deccan Aurangzeb established his seat at Khirki, the former residence of Malik Ambar, which he renamed Aurangabad.[17] At the Golconda court he soon found an ally in the powerful minister Mir Jumla, the conqueror of the Southern Karnataka, who had an open dispute with Abdullah Qutub Shah.[18] Mir Jumla first tacitly concurred with Aurangzeb in the latter's plan to annex the entire Deccan, then willingly became his tool to stir up faction until the minister was enrolled as a Mughal *mansabdār* and Aurangzeb invaded Golconda on the pretext of Mir Jumla's son being imprisoned. Shah Jahan and Dara Shikoh however made Aurangzeb withdraw and the tributary relationship remained in force. In 1656 the death of Muhammad Adil Shah induced Aurangzeb to invade Bijapur, but he was called away by tidings of the mortal illness of his father Shah

13 S. Chandra, 'The Deccan Policy of the Mughals – A Reappraisal (I)', *The Indian Historical Review*, 4, 2 (1978), p. 328.
14 *Ibid.*, p. 331.
15 Richards, *Golconda*, pp. 35–7; Grant Duff, *History*, 1, p. 80.
16 Richards, *Golconda*, pp. 35–6. 17 Grant Duff, *History*, 1, p. 78.
18 *Ibid.*, pp. 78–83; Richards, *Golconda*, pp. 37–8.

Jahan. This appeared premature but Aurangzeb dislodged Shah Jahan from power and mounted the throne in 1658.

So far, Mughal policies in the Deccan had been ostensibly directed against the Muslim powers. But already Jahangir had recognized the Marathas as the real political bed-rock of the Deccan and had begun to make attempts to win them over to his side.[19] In the period between the subversion of the Vijayanagar kingdom in 1565 and Shivaji's consecration in 1674 the future royal dynasty of Bhonsle was one of numerous Maratha families which rose to the fore by means of quickly alternating alliances with the Mughals on the one hand and the threatened Deccan Sultans on the other. The *More Bakhar* does not yet mention the Bhonsles as servants of Vijayanagar. The earliest history of the dynasty is more obscure than that of many other contemporary Maratha families. Some scanty evidence shows that in the final decade of the sixteenth century the Bhonsles were *mokāsadārs* or *jāgirdārs* under the Nizam Shah and that, until Shivaji became a formally independent Chatrapati, they shifted their allegiance at least five times: from the Nizam Shah to the Adil Shah, for a while enjoying a *mansab* under Shah Jahan, then returning to the Nizam Shah, and finally continuing in the service of the Adil Shah.[20] The bakhar of Sabhasad refers back to the late sixteenth century when it mentions Shivaji's grandfather Maloji and the latter's brother Vithoji Bhonsle as 'high officers, enjoying a large assignment (*daulat*) and much influence under the Nizam Shah'.[21] The family gradually accumulated more and more holdings in temporary service or hereditary tenure. While Maloji can be shown to have been in the possession of his father's jagir of Padepedganv (on the bank of the Bhima) and some dispersed *mokāsā* and *inām* villages in Daulatabad newly given to him by the Nizam Shahi regent Malik Ambar, there is no indication that he had already acquired the district of Poona.[22] Probably his son Shahaji received it first, in *mokāsā* or 'assignment', after Maloji's death, in 1623 or 1627, as a reward for expelling the Adil Shahis.[23] The Poona assignment Shahaji held from the Nizam Shah

19 Chandra, 'Deccan Policy', p. 330.

20 G. S. Sardesai, *New History of the Marathas*, 3 vols (Bombay, 1971), 1, chapters, 2–4; *MIS*, 15, nos 367, 372, 385, 400; *SKPSS*, 1, no. 10.

21 Vakaskar, *Sabhāsadācī Bakhar*, p. 2.

22 *MIS*, 15, nos 369, 371; *SKPSS*, 1, no. 30; C. V. Vaidya, 'Mālojīcī Jahāgīr Puṇeṇ Navhtī', *BISMQ*, 11, 3 (1931), pp. 23–4.

23 *SCS*, 1, nos 21 (p. 35), 47; *BISMQ*, 1, 3 (1920), no. 3 (p. 35); Vad, Mawji and Parasnis, *Sanadāpatreṇ*, p. 101; *EIP*, 4, p. 412; *MIS*, 15, nos 404, 406, 415; 20, nos 230–1.

until 1636, when the rule of that dynasty came to an end. Soon after that, it is stated in one of the chronologies, 'Shahaji Raje Bhonsle obtained from the Adil Shah a command of 12,000 horse with a provision of land for his expenses, [and] this land included the country of Poona.'[24] Apart from Poona it comprised Chacun, Junnar, Supe, Baramati, Indapur, the Twelve Mavals, and perhaps Vai and Sirval.[25] When Shahaji entered the service of the Adil Shah in 1636, his son Shivaji obtained the sub-*mokāsā* of Karyat Maval from him.[26] Of the rest of his father's assignment Shivaji took control without authorization during Shahaji's absence in the Karnataka; he never received a formal sanad for it from the Adil Shah. After capturing the fort Sinhagarh in 1644, he alarmed the Sultan in 1645 by organizing the Mavale troops and taking over the fort Rohida. At that time Shivaji is first described as being 'disloyal (*bemāngī*) to Shahaji'.[27] His own letters now begin to abound with new self-justifications and epithets of ancient derivation which make him 'the protector of cows and brahmans' (*gobrahmāṇce pratipālak*) and 'the upholder of the *dharma*' (*dharmaparāyeṇa*). When Shivaji had established himself throughout the country between the Bhima and the Nira, the Adil Shah tried to bring him to terms by arresting his father. This perplexed him for a while, but as soon as Shahaji was released he re-asserted his power in 1653.[28] Upon this followed the punitive expedition by the Bijapuri general Afzal Khan, which ended with his assassination by Shivaji. It took a Mughal invasion of the Western Deccan led by the Rajput Raja Jai Singh to effect Shivaji's submission.[29] This was formalized in the

24 'Sahā Kalamī Śakavalī', in: Apte and Kelkar, *Śivcaritra Pradīpa*, pp. 70–1. Sabhasad confirms that Shahaji, after the extinction of the Nizam Shahi, became a servant of the Adil Shah and a commander of 12,000, and adds that on that occasion the title of Maharaja was conferred on him (Vakaskar, *Sabhāsadācī Bakhar*, p. 3). The title of Maharaja is sometimes found in Shahaji's letters and sanads (cf. *SCS*, 2, nos 120, 122; Vad, Mawji and Parasnis, *Sanadāpatreṇ*, p. 111; *MIS*, 20, no. 13). P. M. Candarkar mentions as *farmān* of Muhammad Ibrahim Adil Shah in which Shahaji is addressed as *Mahārāja* by the Shah himself ('Śahājīrāje va Vataneṇ', *BISMQ*, 1–4 (1922), p. 108).

25 *EIP*, 4, p. 412; V. S. Vakaskar (ed.), *91 Kalamī Bakhar* (Poona, 1962), sect. 20; R. V. Hervadkar, (ed.), *Saptaprakaraṇātmak Caritra* (Poona, 1967), p. 30.

26 *MIS*, 18, no. 22 (p. 44). Other parts of the Poona jagir of Shahaji were given out in sub-assignment to others, e.g. Sandas Khurd to Mambaji Bhonsle (*ibid.*), Chacun to Dilavar Khan (*MIS*, 15, no. 436).

27 *MIS*, 15, no. 267.

28 Vad, Mawji and Parasnis, *Sanadāpatreṇ*, p. 113.

29 Jai Singh being a Rajput was instrumental in this; cf. Khobrekar, *Tarikh-i-Dilkasha*, p. 45; 'Shivaji said (to J. S.) that he saw his welfare in his obedience to the Emperor. He said: "Considering you as my father, I want to get my crimes pardoned by the Emperor through you"'.

Treaty of Purandar of 1665, whereby under 'the strongest oaths which a Hindu can possibly take' Shivaji agreed to give up 20 of his 32 forts and to content himself with a *jāgīr* yielding 5 lacs of rupees, which was given to him as a 'mark of imperial grace', while he was made to promise 'never to act disobediently or plunder the imperial dominions', and to perform service for the Mughal Emperor in the Deccan whenever he was called upon. His son Sambhaji was given a mansab of 5,000 to attend upon the Deccan subhedar.[30] In addition to this a future partition was agreed upon of the districts of Bijapur, the conquest of which was projected as a joint venture.

This treaty was nullified very soon afterwards. Shivaji and his son made a visit to Agra but were put in confinement and probably were only saved from execution by political pressure of Rajput nobles (especially Jai Singh) at the Mughal court. They reached the Deccan in 1666 as refugees but could easily compensate for the set-back received from the Mughal invasion by the exploitation of internal rifts which were opening up at the court of Bijapur, after the accession of Sikandar Adil Shah in 1672 caused a drawn-out conflict between Afghan and Deccani factions.[31] Furthermore, at Golconda brahmans had by 1674 gained sufficient political influence to be able to induce the Sultan to enter into an alliance with Shivaji and accede to the payment of *cauth* and *sardeśmukhī*. This alliance and similar tributary links which would soon afterwards be established with Bijapur were maintained after Shivaji's death in 1680 by his son Sambhaji.[32] The nexus of alliances which had thus developed in 1681 again induced the Mughal prince Akbar, like his father Aurangzeb before him when still the subhedar of the Deccan, to make an attempt to oust the Emperor through the formation of a Maratha–Rajput–Bijapur–Golconda coalition under his leadership. Unlike Aurangzeb he failed in taking effective control of the imperial throne and fled to Sambhaji's court, from where in 1683 he crossed to Persia. This attempt, though it failed, made the Emperor acutely aware of the potential threat of the Deccan powers allying with any of his sons or nobles. The Deccan threat forced Aurangzeb to move south in 1682, after the conclusion of campaigns in Rajastan, with a large army and with his entire court. It was allegedly the 'disobedience' of his nobles which forced the Emperor to remain in the Deccan and personally co-ordinate the Mughal conquests up to his death in 1707. In fact, the Mughal

[30] Sarkar, *House of Shivaji*, p. 126; Grant Duff, *History*, I, p. 112.

[31] Richards, *Golconda*, p. 44.

[32] *Ibid.*, pp. 44–5; and cf. *ibid.*, p. 28.

nobles attempted only to enhance their own power by colluding with and appeasing the enemy in very much the same way as earlier the princes Aurangzeb and Akbar had done themselves. Bhimsen writes that 'Raja [Jai Singh] caused defection among many nobles of Bijapur by giving them the promise of safety and protection and awarding them suitable ranks.'[33] In such numbers did the Bijapuris come over that their names would fill 'a volume of record', but yet this policy 'proved distasteful to the Emperor'.[34] Why such defections should be 'distasteful' is easy to surmise. The Deccanis did not so much defect to the Mughal Emperor as rather to his generals and governors, and they thus increased conflict in the imperial camp. Collusions and secret alliances criss-crossed the Mughal and Deccani courts from the first beginnings of Mughal involvement in the Deccan but with the progress of expansion this process of double or plural linkage accelerated.[35] Secret alliances were formed, despite the Emperor's countervailing presence, with factions at the Deccani courts or with the Sultans of Bijapur and Golconda themselves, or with the Marathas – always in opposition to Mughal factions which urged immediate annexation of the Deccan states to check such alliances. In the earlier part of Aurangzeb's reign his son Shah Alam was subhedar of the Deccan and colluded with the Rajput Raja Yaswant Singh and the Marathas in opposition especially to the 'imperialist' Dilir Khan. In 1682–3 secret alliances were again reported to have been made between the Bijapur Sultan and Shah Alam, Saiyid Abdullah Khan, Munim Khan and others of the most prominent Mughal nobles. Together with Bahadur Khan Kokaltash, one of the highest imperial mansabdars, Shah Alam once more sought a rapprochement with Abul Hasan, the Sultan of Golconda, and with the Maratha King Sambhaji but was arrested in 1685 and remained under arrest for seven years. But still the number of factions and groupings among the Mughal nobility which sympathized with different powers in the Deccan increased. Rajput mansabdars such as Yaswant Singh were always closely linked to the Marathas; Afghan mansabdars sympathized with a large number of their compatriots at the Bijapur court; Persian nobles and Iranis were easily appeased by the Shiite Qutub Shah. In the meantime the Marathas remained united with the Hindu section at Golconda.

33 Khobrekar, *Tarikh-i-Dilkasha*, p. 48. 34 *Ibid.*, pp. 42, 51.

35 Cf. M. Athar Ali, *The Mughal Nobility under Aurangzeb* (Bombay, etc., 1970), pp. 102–11.

It is thus evident that the Mughal campaign in the Deccan was not primarily a military operation. Certainly the mechanism of *fitna* put a premium on wiliness rather than dashing courage, and hence imperial warfare was of a sort that aroused the scorn of Europeans. It became notorious that the Mughals did not fight hard, accepted bribes from the enemy to put off a battle, or negotiated mock-captures; or they were thought to be guilty of the worst of military sins, 'cowardice' and 'loss of morale'.[36] Bernier observed that the generals sent against Bijapur 'conduct every operation with languor, and avail themselves of any pretext for the prolongation of war which is alike the source of their emolument and dignity. It became a proverbial saying that the Deccan is the bread and support of the soldiers of Hindustan.'[37] The subjugation of Bijapur and Golconda occupied Aurangzeb until 1686–7. Bijapur was besieged for eighteen months, after which the fort surrendered. The fort of Golconda was besieged for seven months and was finally taken by 'treason'.[38] The two kingdoms were then made the Mughal subhas of Bijapur and Hyderabad, both extending over the Karnataka down to the extreme south of the peninsula. Both these conquests were consolidated through the most lenient and far-reaching concern for the assimilation of the Deccan nobles, especially if they were Muslims. Lavish promotions, rewards for desertion, the confirmation of assignments of land-revenue and immunities were all part of a great 'exercise in public relations' which excluded only the two monarchs themselves and, at Golconda, two of the leading brahman ministers.[39] All 'infidel customs', however, were ordered to be abandoned and with the dispersal of the Persian nobility of Golconda the connections with Safavid Persia were greatly reduced.

Expedience dictated that along with the Deccan Muslim nobility a large number of Marathas were given mansabdari status in the imperial service, but Maratha mansabdars never reached positions quite as high nor did they become provincial governors.[40] There were several clear reasons why the Marathas could not be integra-

36 Cf. M. N. Pearson, 'Shivaji and the Decline of the Mughal Empire', *JAS*, 35, 2 (1976), p. 233. In medieval Europe this type of 'imperial warfare' was associated in particular with the Byzantines and already then was looked at with much disdain by the Western knights (S. Painter, *A History of the Middle Ages 284–1500* (London and Basingstoke, 1979), pp. 40–1).

37 F. Bernier, *Travels in the Mughal Empire* (London, 1891), pp. 196–7; for similar evidence see Athar Ali, *Mughal Nobility*, p. 102.

38 Cf. Richards, *Golconda*, pp. 46–51.

39 *Ibid.*, pp. 52–63, 66–7, 73.

40 Cf. Athar Ali, *Mughal Nobility*, p. 35, Table 2 (b).

ted into the imperial dominion in the same way as the Muslims of the Deccan. It was first of all evident that only the Emperor himself stood to benefit from a final and definitive conclusion of the Deccan campaigns but none of the Mughal nobles participating in them. Thus all attempts to subdue the Marathas were bound to fail and with the end of the Deccan expansion 'war' in sight, the Mughal nobility allowed it to reach a stalemate. Natives to the Deccan, diffused in small and mobile parties, in the east operating in close conjunction with the Telugu *nāyaks* and *zamīndārs*, the Marathas eluded frontal assault and remained the indispensable lever for the Mughal nobles' self-enhancement. Political rivalries and collusions had no end and an internecine contest for power engulfed the Deccan. For the invading Mughals war meant not only the possibility of an alliance with the Maratha *zamīndārī* chiefs, but also, as Bhimsen pointed out, 'expectation of promotion' and this also accounted for the 'delay in conquering the Deccan', for the Mughal officers would, after the conclusion of the Deccan war, have 'no other work than to conquer Qandahar'.[41] There are other testimonies that a number of Mughal mansabdars gave up all allegiance to the Emperor and joined the Marathas.[42] The Maratha capital fort Rajgarh was taken in 1689 and the Maratha king Sambhaji was executed by Aurangzeb. But Sambhaji's successor Rajaram set up a provisional government in Jinji on the Coromandel coast, from where he issued thousands of sanads restoring, sanctioning or giving lands to Maratha *zamīndārs* and *ināmdārs*, offering these as rewards for their loyalty – in areas of the Deccan which were then facing the physical, military presence of the Mughals.[43] Command over the Maratha army was delegated to a number of generals under the co-ordination of the Amatya and the Saciv as the King's lieutenants in the west. *Fitna*, competition with the Mughals, became virtually synonymous with the extension of hereditary gentry rights across the Deccan. Countless were the Maratha *zamīndārs* who crossed over several times back and forth; as writes Bhimsen, 'when they took service under the Emperor, they professed great loyalty, but as they have no constancy of faith, their

[41] Khobrekar, *Tarikh-i-Dilkasha*, p. 208. As Pearson remarks, 'the real significance of Qandahar was as a testing point, a limited arena, where each side (the Mughals and the Safavids) could probe the strength of the other' ('Shivaji', pp. 230–1). In a period of two centuries Qandahar was besieged fifteen times and transferred twelve times.

[42] Athar Ali, *Mughal Nobility*, pp. 106–10.

[43] See Chapter 2–1.

loyalty is not certain'.[44] 'Bribing', self-aggrandizement by Mughal nobles through alliances with Marathas, was enhanced by the drought, famine and epidemic which affected most of the Deccan in the period 1700–4, but to speak here of 'demoralization' seems out of place;[45] this was rather a period of unprecedented opportunities. By the end of the century even a former hard-core imperialist like Dilir Khan was making attempts to reach a private settlement with a rival disputant of the Maratha kingship, Sambhaji Bhonsle.[46] The prince Kam Bakhsh tried to do the same with Rajaram at Jinji but was arrested by the vazir Asad Khan.[47] It was now no longer a matter of 'imperialists' versus 'Deccan autonomists' but of the exploitation of internal Maratha schisms. Far from being induced by demoralization this represented an irreversible and purely political mechanism which forced Aurangzeb to relax the system of rotation of governorships. Of the greatest importance was also the anticipated succession struggle for the Mughal throne which would inevitably follow the impending death of the aged Emperor and which necessitated his three sons to search for as many allies for themselves as possible. Here it becomes ever more evident that the increase of Maratha power was a direct consequence of Mughal involvement. As earlier the Emperor Akbar had been forced to enter into an alliance with the Rajputs to counterpoise the older Turani and Mughal nobles, so Aurangzeb's three sons had only the choice to perish in the approaching succession struggle or to develop a local entrenchment in the Deccan. The reticence of one would be an opportunity for the other and Aurangzeb, as long as he was alive, could only attempt to keep a balance among them and keep the Marathas divided.

The first permanent governor of Hyderabad and Bijapur after the Mughal conquest was Jan Sipar Khan, who was appointed by Aurangzeb in 1689–90.[48] He stayed on in this function until his

[44] Khobrekar, *Tarikh-i-Dilkasha*, p. 240.

[45] Cf. J.F. Richards, 'The Imperial Crisis in the Deccan', *JAS*, 35, 2 (1976), pp. 244–9. Richards speaks of 'demoralization', 'loss of emotional security', 'sense of frustration and futility' (p. 249). He notes that there was 'frequent unwillingness of Mughal governors and *faujdārs* to meet raiders and bandits in open battle' and that the former 'often preferred to negotiate with and bribe the attackers to withdraw' (*ibid.*). As 'perhaps the most damaging sign of demoralization' Richards considers 'the tendency of powerful Mughal officers – not transferred by Aurangzeb as frequently as by his predecessors – to start building alliances with locally important chiefs' (*ibid.*).

[46] Sarkar, *House of Shivaji*, p. 178.

[47] Richards, *Golconda*, p. 216.

[48] *Ibid.*, pp. 215–19.

death in 1700 and was then replaced by prince Kam Bakhsh but the Emperor appointed the governor's son Rustam Dil Khan as deputy. After the death of the Maratha king Rajaram in 1700 his widow Tarabai continued to levy the *cauth* in the Deccan and Rustam Dil Khan's administration was unwilling to expel the 'marauders'. As the European traders on the coast could observe, Rustam, instead, paid large sums to the Marathas and at the same time, through concessions, also consolidated his ties with the Telugu *zamīndārs*. In 1704 Aurangzeb was thus induced to attempt to bring to an end a fifteen-year dominance of Rustam Dil Khan and his father by replacing the former as deputy governor by Saiyid Muzaffar Khan.[49] The latter in his turn was replaced within a year by Daud Khan Panni, the deputy governor of the Hyderabad Karnataka who was now supposed to drive the Marathas out. But in 1705 Mughal authority in the province had dwindled rapidly and the Emperor had to re-appoint Rustam Dil Khan and through him the absentee governor Muhammad Kam Bakhsh could continue to build up his power base in the Deccan, until, after the death of Aurangzeb, he took the administration of Hyderabad and Bijapur in his own hands and executed his deputy.[50]

With the succession struggle approaching its dénouement, *fitna* among the Mughal nobility re-aligned along the old divisions of Turanis and Iranis.[51] These became the two parties which in the subsequent decades exploited, or rather created, a dispute about the succession to the Maratha kingship between Rajaram's widow Tarabai and her son Shivaji, and Shahu, the son of the executed Maratha king Sambhaji, the grandson of the Chatrapati Shivaji who was made prisoner by the Mughals when Rajgarh was taken in 1689. Due to this all-pervading schism among the Mughal nobles the two Maratha disputants could still more extend their power by supporting one side against the other. At the time of the death of Aurangzeb both Irani and Turani nobles were equally involved in the Deccan and the succession struggle promised further opportunities for both.[52] The Iranis were led by the vazir Asad Khan and his son Zulfiqar Khan, the Mir Bakhshi; these two had a long record of service in the Deccan and in 1706 Aurangzeb had Shahu transferred to the camp of Zulfiqar Khan in an attempt to negotiate through him a settlement with the Marathas in opposition to Kam

[49] *Ibid.*, p. 224. [50] *Ibid.*, pp. 236–41.
[51] Chandra, *Parties and Politics*, pp. 1–9.
[52] *Ibid.*, pp. 12, 16–18.

Bakhsh who co-operated with Tarabai. After Aurangzeb's death in the following year Asad Khan and Zulfiqar Khan received further support from Rao Dalpat Bundela, the Rajput Rao Ram Singh Hara of Kota, and from Daud Khan Panni, a noble who was also very influential among the Deccani Hindus but who was a rival of Kam Bakhsh and his deputy Rustam Dil Khan. Among the most prominent Turanis we find Chin Qulich Khan (the later Nizam-al-Mulk), his brother Hamid Khan Bahadur, his father Ghazi-ad-Din Firuz Jang, and his cousin Muhammad Amin Khan. When he died, Aurangzeb left three sons: Azam Shah, the governor of Gujarat; Shah Alam or Sultan Mauzam, the governor of Kabul; and Kam Bakhsh, the governor of Hyderabad and Bijapur. Asad Khan and Zulfiqar Khan initially supported Azam Shah, but their subsequent sudden withdrawal led to the defeat of Azam Shah at Jajau, after which Shah Alam proclaimed himself Emperor and assumed the title of Bahadur Shah. Before he was defeated however Azam Shah, at the instance of Zulfiqar Khan, allowed Shahu to be released and was further induced to give high mansabs to the Rajput rajas Jai Singh and Ajit Singh. After becoming Emperor, Bahadur Shah began to make attempts to reconcile the rival Turanis in order to isolate Kam Bakhsh, the third son of Aurangzeb who still survived and had long consolidated his position in Hyderabad and Bijapur and in 1708 proclaimed himself King of Golconda, struck coins and read the *khuṭba* in his name.[53] Bahadur Shah, it may be recalled, had earlier been subhedar of the Deccan but on charge of collusions with Sambhaji and the Sultan of Golconda he was arrested and kept in confinement up to 1692. Already in 1681 he had been giving out promises to Rajputs to abolish the *jiziya* in return for their support in the contest with his brothers.[54] The Turanis around Chin Qulich Khan now came over to his side but still resented the concessions made to the Rajputs and the Marathas by Bahadur Shah at the instigation of the vazir Munim Khan and Zulfiqar Khan.[55] Kam Bakhsh failed to counter desertions to Bahadur Shah, particularly in the Karnataka due to the opposition of Daud Khan, the deputy of Zulfiqar Khan. He was killed in 1709 and Zulfiqar Khan, the Mir Bakhshi, became governor of the six Mughal subhas of the Deccan under Bahadur Shah, with Daud Khan as his deputy.[56] In the period which follows,

53 *Ibid.*, p. 40; Richards, *Golconda*, pp. 236–41.
54 Chandra, *Parties and Politics*, pp. 23–4.
55 *Ibid.*, pp. 24–39. 56 *Ibid.*, pp. 42–3.

the post of Deccan subhedar, in combination with that of the vazirate of the Empire, became the chief bone of contention among the Mughal factions of Iranis and Turanis. Through appeasement of the Hindus, relaxation of Islamic orthodoxy, and most of all through alliances with Rajputs and Marathas, the vazir could arrogate to himself the substance of imperial sovereignty, leaving the Emperor with a merely nominal universality. The rise of the Mughal vazir in the early decades of the eighteenth century was thus intimately bound up with the *fitna* of the Marathas. After Zulfiqar Khan's death the vazirate was handed over to the Saiyid brothers who increased its independent authority still further.[57] This eventually provided the occasion for far-reaching concessions to the Maratha king Shahu (1709–49) in the Deccan aiming in particular to outrival the opposition of the Turanis who in their turn were allied with the rival branch of the Bhonsle dynasty which centred at Kolhapur. From that time onwards we can also begin to date the rise of the brahman minister, the Peshwa, at Satara, a process which runs to a large extent parallel to the rise of the vazir at the Mughal court and led, in its turn, to a gradual loss of effective power of the Raja of Satara.

This intricate process of *fitna*, then, chanelled the imperial power and resources into the growth of local centres which in their turn intensified the agrarian *mise en valeur* of the areas under their sway, thereby further enhancing their capacity. Though this raised the stakes of conflict it did not directly threaten imperial dominion. It drew away imperial resources into local development and conflict but left the Empire's universalist claim intact. Even if increasingly drained of power the imperial court still was the ultimate arena of conflict and source of legitimation in the eighteenth century. We shall illustrate this further in the next subchapter by detailing the continuation of the process which resulted in the expansion of Maratha *svarājya* over most of the subcontinent.

III The Maratha svarājya in the eighteenth century

The sections of this subchapter each provide a part of a chronological analysis of the main political developments under the expanding Maratha *svarājya* in the eighteenth century. The rise of the Peshwas is treated first since it is of pivotal importance; in the subsequent sections the same events or parallel events in so far as affecting the various Maratha sardars and

[57] *Ibid.*, pp. 45, 55, 60 ff.

sovereigns on a more localized level but closely linked to the Peshwas' rise are recorded. For genealogical tables of the various dynasties the reader should refer to Chapter I–IV.

a. The brahman ascent

In classical India, but also in later kingdoms like those of the Vijayanagar and Maratha dynasties which rose within the context of expanding Muslim power, legitimate sovereignty resulted from the conjoint authority of king and brahman. The transcendent or universal basis of sovereignty which was postulated in religious theory and which was acquired by the brahmanical consecration of kingship allowed it to adjust itself to every conceivable situational compromise. The brahman was, ideally, not to partake in temporal power.

The Indian law-books on the other hand could hardly deny a mundane function to the brahman. At royal courts almost invariably brahman literati served as councillors or ministers of the king, or as his judges. Vasishtha says that 'a realm where a brahman minister is appointed *purohita* flourishes'.[1] This *purohita* or brahman minister was 'the real brain of the king'.[2] The *Ājñāpatra* allegorically asserts that 'the minister (*pradhān*) is like the goad of an elephant'.[3] In theory again the two functions of king and councillor were strictly juxtaposed and the king retained the plenitude of power. In practice the brahman *purohita* or *pradhān*, like his Muslim counterpart the *vazīr*, had to share in the king's power in order to be effective. Hence we find the ambiguous situation that for brahmans to be a royal minister was an acknowledged and sought-after occupation, but that association with the court still remained suspect and that brahmans who did so ranked low on the brahman purity-scale or were considered brahmans in name only.[4] Islam required a similar political aloofness from its doctors of law but among them this was equally exceptional. There is then a recurrent pattern in Indian history of an intelligent and politically adroit brahman minister or a vazir replacing the king all but nominally.[5] This also happened with the Maratha kings of Satara.

[1] Lingat, *Sources du Droit*, p. 242. [2] *Ibid.* [3] Banhatti, *Ājñāpatra*, ch. 4.
[4] Cf. pp. 228 ff.
[5] Cf. Tripathi, *Muslim Administration*, pp. 161 ff; J. D. M. Derrett, *The Hoysalas: A Medieval Indian Royal Family* (Madras, 1957), p. 179.

In the Maratha Deccan the administrative bureaucracy was from a very early date the virtually exclusive domain of the brahmans.[6] The latter formed the only status group of local provenance which did not flaunt an outspoken disdain for literacy. Agrarian society in the Deccan was fissured by a pervasive dualism in all matters of administration: on the village level of brahman *kuḷkarṇī* or 'accountant' was juxtaposed to an executive, non-brahman *pāṭīl*; in each small district a brahman *deśpāṇḍe* or *deśkuḷkarṇī* stood next to an executive, non-brahman *deśmukh*. These were the main (hereditary) groupings of what the Muslims referred to as the *zamīndārs*, with complementary functions but always operating through 'management by conflict'.[7] The *Ājñāpatra*, on the eve of the eighteenth-century Maratha expansion, advocates a dualist authority of 'warriors' and 'ministers' which almost reads like a replica of the original local *zamīndārī* system.

> The protection of the country and forts is not possible without those warriors who conquer new lands. If, however, the authority (*yakhtyār*) over these lands is entrusted to them alone they would be inclined to fighting only.... Therefore the entire administration of the kingdom (*saṃpūrṇa rājyabhār*) and the supervision over its lands should never be entrusted to a single person. The army-commanders (*senānāyak*) should be made dependent in each case on a minister (*sarkārkūn*) who gives them orders and inquires into their affairs. They must be made to agree with each other in administrative matters. If attention is paid to their co-operation, with increased confidence even the impossible can be achieved by making use of their rivalry (*irṣene*).[8]

Brahmans, of which the subcastes can no longer be identified, had risen to the higher administrative posts under the Adil Shahs from 1555 and under the Nizam Shahs from 1529 onwards. The Maratha bakhars establish that under Shivaji's reign Citpavan or Konkanastha brahmans, but no less members of the other two great subcastes of Deccan brahmans, the Saraswats or Shenavis and the Deshasthas occupied six of the eight posts in the *aṣṭapradhān* council and were generally employed as provincial administrators,

[6] Cf. Chapter 4–1.

[7] Thus R. N. Gooddine describes how in the Deccan villages severe conflicts could occur, the population of a village becoming divided into two parties, one headed by the *kuḷkarṇī* and the other by the *pāṭīl* ('Report on the Village Communities of the Deccan', *BGS*, o.s. no. 4 (Bombay, 1852), p. 16. For a parallel system in Vijayanagar, see B. Stein, *Peasant State and Society in Medieval South India* (Delhi, 1980), p. 413.

[8] Banhatti, *Ājñāpatra*, ch. 4.

while Prabhus often served as karkuns. Brahmans of all subcastes figure prominently in the very early period of expansion during Shahu's reign, but in the 1730s the Citpavans had already taken a decisive lead. At that stage the Emperor acknowledged the Citpavan Prime Minister or Peshwa as the *sardeśpāṇḍe* or 'head-district-accountant' of the Deccan.[9] In the mid eighteenth century the Citpavans became all-powerful throughout the Western Deccan. Here the Prabhus lost their prominence from the time of Peshwa Balaji Baji Rao, after whom there stands out from their ranks only one great name (that of Sakharam Hari, a commander under Raghunath Rao), but in Baroda and Nagpur they continued to play a role of some importance as ministers and military commanders. The Shenavis also regained influence only under the northern Maratha sardars, particularly under Mahadaji Scindhia, who by employing them reinforced his independence from the Citpavan minister to which his ancestors had owed their rise.

The migration of numberless Citpavan brahmans from the Konkan to the Maratha court at Satara started when for the first time a member of their subcaste was promoted to the Peshwaship by Shahu. Before the elevation of Balaji Vishvanath, the Konkanastha brahmans were not very often employed as clerks or karkuns but more generally as messengers and spies. In the brahman hierarchy they occupied a low position, but the story of their origination from fourteen drowned bodies of different castes which were brought ashore the Konkan by Vishnu (as narrated in the *Sahyādri Khaṇḍ*), was systematically suppressed by the Peshwas, who quickly began to derive a sense of caste superiority from their political prominence in the Maratha country.[10] Their low origin and relative impurity indeed greatly facilitated the Citpavan political ascent and their contest with the Maratha military chieftains. Crucial factors in the consolidation of Citpavan power were, in addition to the possession of literacy and a measure of prestige which they shared with other brahmans, an extremely circumspect and methodical mode of conduct, great industry and assiduousness, and a perfectioning of strategic generalship. The British Resident C. W. Malet, who observed the Poona court at the height of its power in the 1780s and 90s, mentions all these among

9 Cf. p. 98.

10 Grant Duff, *History*, I, p. 477; M. L. P. Patterson, 'Chitpavan Brahman Family Histories: Sources for a Study of Social Structure and Social Change in Maharashtra', in: M. Singer and B. S. Cohn (eds), *Structure and Change in Indian Society* (Chicago, 1968), pp. 397–411.

the 'circumstances of advantage' which the Peshwa enjoyed over the British and the Nizam of Hyderabad.[11] The Peshwa, as Malet explained, possessed 'the most accurate information of every state in India by means of his tribe, as intriguing, as artful, as industrious and much more numerous than the Jesuits ever were'.[12]

It will be remembered that in the Maratha government the Peshwa was originally only the *mukhya pradhān* or 'prime minister' of the Council of Eight and that his post was not hereditary.[13] Up to the accession of Balaji Vishvanath in 1714 only in one case (that of Moro Trimbak Pingle) was a father allowed to be succeeded as Peshwa by his son. Balaji Vishvanath was the fifth incumbent of the office, but the *Peshwa Bakhar* treats him as the first.[14] This is because only now the Peshwa begins to outstrip the other Pradhans and the Pratinidhi (who was added on a higher salary than the Peshwa) and becomes a hereditary prime minister. The system of government by a Council of Eight was upheld in the early years of Shahu's reign, then fell gradually into disuse and completely ceased to function when the Peshwa transferred his capital to Poona. When he became Shahu's chief adviser, Balaji Vishvanath still had only a very small military command. In fact the Peshwa's military importance had diminished during the Mughal invasions in Rajaram's reign when the command of the entire army was given over to generals like Ghorpade and Yadhava whose reputation reached much further than his. On the death of Dhanaji Yadhava his son Candrasen was appointed to the office of Senapati, but when the latter joined the Nizam the office was bestowed on Khande Rao Dabhade. When Balaji Vishvanath's successor attempted to increase his military power the Senapati was the first to offer resistance. Shahu's intervention could but temporarily postpone an open conflict with Dabhade, who was killed in 1731 at Dabhoi in Gujarat by Baji Rao, the 'second' Peshwa. Thereafter the Senapati hardly played any role in Maratha history.

When Shahu ascended the throne in 1708, the post of Peshwa went to a son of Moro Trimbak Pingle. Dhanaji Yadhava, whose family had become renowned already under Shivaji and who was instrumental in enabling Shahu to establish his sovereignty, was confirmed as Senapati. Balaji Vishvanath appears in this period to have been one of the dependants of his family and the Peshwas later

[11] C. W. Malet to Earl Cornwallis, Gov. Gen., 29 March 1788, *PRC*, 2, p. 132; *idem* to Captain W. Kirkpatrick, 6 June 1794, *PRC*, 4, p. 58.

[12] *PRC*, 4, *op. cit.*, p. 61. [13] Cf. p. 37. [14] *MIS*, 4, pp. 23–69.

always carried a sign on their umbrella (*abdāgīr*) in commemoration of this circumstance or rather as a memorial of gratitude to their benefactor Dhanaji whom they considered the original agent behind Balaji Vishvanath's rise.[15] Soon however he was taken into the direct service of the king and appointed *mutālīk* or 'deputy' to the Amatya, with the title of *Senākarte*.[16] In 1713, when the succession dispute with the rival house of the Bhonsles of Kolhapur was still undecided, he was sent on an important diplomatic mission to effect an accommodation with Angria of Kolaba, a sardar who until then had adhered to the opposing party. Without resorting to armed force Balaji Vishvanath won over the most powerful chieftain on the Kolhapur side. On condition of receiving ten forts and sixteen fortified places and being confirmed in the command of his fleet and his title of *Sarkhel*, Angria agreed to renounce Sambhaji Bhonsle.[17] The Kolhapur branch, thus deprived of their supporter, soon afterwards accepted a separate dominion around Panhala. Balaji was received home with the greatest honours, his agreement was ratified by the King of Satara, and he was allowed to replace Pingle and received the *śikkekaṭyār* and the robes of Peshwaship.[18] Ambaji Pant Purandare of Sasur was nominated his *dīvān* and received from the Raja the authority of *mutālīk*.[19]

The Peshwas, in reorganizing the administration and regulating Maratha expansion, exploited to the maximum the principle of rivalry, of 'management by conflict', through an elaborate scheme of quota repartition of the revenue which was promulgated by Balaji Vishvanath after his return from Delhi in 1719 with the farmans for *svarājya*, *cauth* and *sardeśmukhī*. The revenue aggregates of villages or districts were generally split up into *amals* or 'fractions', varying between 3 and 75%, which were separately assigned or alienated to different parties.[20] This procedure was followed in the *svarājya* in the Western Deccan, but also in the Mughal subhas where only the *cauth* and *sardeśmukhī* were levied. Of the *cauth* the Raja of Satara nominally retained only one-fourth, called the Raja's *bābtī*, and the balance or *mokāsā* was repar-

15 *P.A.: List 13, Ru.75, File 1044*, pp. 12–13; Vad, Mawji and Parasnis, *Kaifiyats, Yadis*, p. 53; Grant Duff, *History*, I, p. 238.

16 Vad, Mawji and Parasnis, *Kaifiyats, Yadis*, *loc. cit.* At this date he is also referred to as *sarsubhā* (*SPD*, 7, no. 1).

17 Hervadkar, *Śāhū Caritra*, pp. 42–5; Vad, Mawji and Parasnis, *Treaties*, pp. 197–9; Grant Duff, *History*, I, p. 243.

18 'Peśvyāṇcī Bakhar', *MIS*, 4, p. 34.

19 *P.A.: List 13, Ru. 75, File 1044*, pp. 10–11.

20 Cf. Chapter 4–II–a.

titioned in various ways, usually as assignments to military commanders. The Peshwa soon persuaded the Raja also to give out sanads for the collection of *cauth* in those subhas which were not specified in the Mughal farmans of 1719. Here, initially, the imposed repartition scheme was less elaborate and more *ad hoc* than in the coeval Deccan.

In 1719 the members of the *aṣṭapradhān* council and other important sardars received large but rather imprecisely circumscribed assignments of *amals* of revenue and tribute either in the Deccan or beyond, where Maratha claims still had to be established.[21] The Peshwa himself on this occasion obtained from the Raja the assignment of *cauth* in the strategically vital Mughal subhas of Malwa and Khandesh (perhaps also in Baglana). Malwa in particular was important as the political and commercial connecting link of the Deccan with Hindustan. At the same time it could serve the Peshwa as a wedge between the subhas of Gujarat in the west and Berar, Gondwana and Katak in the east, the *cauth* of which was assigned to the Senapati and to Kanhoji Bhonsle respectively. Only under Balaji Vishvanath's son Baji Rao, who succeeded him in the Peshwaship in 1720, did the projected Maratha expansion to the north really begin to gain momentum. The expansionist design itself was not entirely new – Rajaram appears to have contemplated it as early as 1691[22] – and as part of a reconnaissance regular campaigns had begun to be undertaken in Gujarat and Malwa during the last years of Aurangzeb's reign. But when the decision was finally taken to direct the expansion to the north this proved to be of momentous importance for the establishment of the power of the Peshwa in opposition both to the older *maṇḍala* or 'circle' of Maratha sardars – adherents of the Raja of Satara, but envious of the Peshwa's supremacy – and the Mughal subhedar of the Deccan, Nizam-al-Mulk. In an attempt to give legitimacy to their expansion and to back their claims, the Peshwas pretended to have received sanads from the Emperor for what was called the 'established tribute', the *cauth* and *sardeśmukhī*, of the two provinces of Gujarat and Malwa. The *Śāhū Caritra* describes how the Peshwa's proposals to extend Maratha sovereignty into Malwa, Gujarat and Hindustan were for some time successfully

21 Hervadkar, *Śāhū Caritra*, p. 53; Grant Duff, *History*, 1, p. 255.

22 Cf. *SCS*, 5, pp. 9–12, a letter from Rajaram to Ghorpade in which he offers rewards of *saraṇjām* for the capture of Rajgarh, Bijapur, Hyderabad, Aurangabad, and Delhi.

opposed by the Pratinidhi.[23] The latter perhaps genuinely feared a renewal of hostilities with the Mughals and Nizam-al-Mulk, but certainly also perceived the Peshwa's influence as dangerous for his own position. Instead he proposed an expansionist policy into the Konkan to expel the Sidi of Janjira, and into the Karnataka, to complete the conquests begun by Shivaji. This more cautious policy was rejected and the Peshwa obtained the Raja's sanction to pursue – as his delegate – the expansion scheme to the north. From then onwards the Peshwa's resources began to increase steadily. His meetings with the Raja became rarer and of shorter duration, while the latter preferred the luxury of his palace.[24] A British envoy to the Satara Court reported in 1739 that

> Baji Rao is so powerful that he takes small account of the Raja. . . . As his power is uncontrolled by whomsoever, the Raja is compelled to an exercise of an outward civility to him. The sentiments of most are that Baji Rao has in view to throw off his allegiance to the Raja . . . [and] although a civil correspondence with the Raja may not be amiss, care must be taken that he is not solicited for what interferes with Baji Rao whose authority at court is even such, that in the absence of the Raja, and contrary to the advice of the seven principal counsellors, he can enforce a complete obedience to his sole mandates.[25]

Under Shahu's authority Baji Rao granted sanads to his sardars Pawar, Holkar and Scindhia allowing them to levy the *cauth* and *sardeśmukhī* in Malwa and to retain the *mokāsā* portion for the payment of their troops. The Peshwa too was incessantly campaigning from the time of his accession in 1720 up to his death in 1740: in Malwa in 1723 and 1724, in the Deccan against the Nizam in 1728, and against his rival Dabhade in Gujarat in 1731. When the Senapati was reduced Baji Rao made a secret compact with the Nizam which for a time greatly reinforced his position. In 1733 a campaign was launched against the Sidi of Janjira. He was thrown back on his rock-island, and under a treaty in 1736 dual government was established in eleven mahals in the Konkan which were formerly administered by him solely.[26] The conquest of Bassein in 1739 marked the end of Portuguese rule in the Northern Konkan. In that same year the invasion of Nadir Shah profoundly shook the Empire. Baji Rao took the opportunity to profess anew his

23 Hervadkar, *Śāhū Caratra*, pp. 60–1.
24 Cf. V. G. Dighe, *Peshwa Baji Rao I & Maratha Expansion* (Bombay, 1944), p. 197.
25 Quoted by Dighe, *ibid.*
26 Vad, Mawji and Parasnis, *Treaties*, pp. 107–13.

submission to the Emperor, who in his turn, under acceptance of a *nazar*, confirmed the Peshwa in his rank and in his jagirs in the Deccan.[27]

Baji Rao left three sons, of which the eldest, Balaji Baji Rao *alias* Nana Saheb, succeeded him in 1740 as Peshwa. Under Balaji Baji Rao the conquests of Malwa and Gujarat were completed and it is only from this period that a good many of the brahman families who were prominent at the turn of the eighteenth century could date their rise. In three generations the ascent of the Peshwas created two distinctly rival groups of sardars. Firstly there were the relations and adherents of the Raja of Satara – ever more empathically loyal to him – the Bhonsle of Nagpur, the remaining members of the *aṣṭapradhān* council and the Pratinidhi, all of whom were unwilling to accept the Peshwa's pre-eminence. Secondly, the new men put forward by the Peshwa: Scindhia, Holkar and Rastia the most prominent among them. In the first part of Balaji's Peshwaship from 1740 up to the death of Shahu in 1749 he was still under the restraint of the Raja to the degree that the latter effectively managed to regulate the Maratha expansion to the north. This expansion had from an early date predominantly been the work of the Peshwas and their sardars, but there were royalists with a stake in it: in the eastern region the Bhonsles of Nagpur, in Gujarat the Dabhades, and in Malwa the Pawars and the Yadhavas. The south always remained primarily a field for the campaigns of old sardars like the Pratinidhi and Shahu's adopted son Fattesingh Bhonsle. From all these Balaji Baji Rao met with constant opposition but not enough to outbalance the increase of power which he derived from his new conquests in the north. In the first year of Balaji's reign, northern politics culminated in the recognition of his claim on Malwa by an imperial farman of the *nāīb-subhedārī* or 'deputy governorship' of that province. In effect, Malwa was then lost to the Empire. In the same period also the Marathas penetrated further to the north, beyond Delhi into the Panjab as far as Attock, and to the east, into the Doab, Awadh, Allahabad, Bihar, Bengal, and Orissa. All these conquests of the

[27] Grant Duff, *History*, I, p. 308. The Marathas, in actual fact, appear to have conspired with Nizam-al-Mulk to furnish a pretext for inviting Persian intervention; to counter their influence Barhan-al-Mulk also seems to have entered into negotiations with the Persian Emperor at this time (cf. Buckler, 'Indian Mutiny', p. 72; J. R. I. Cole, 'Imami Shi'ism from Iran to North India, 1722–1856: State, Society and Clerical Ideology in Awadh' (Thesis, University of California, Los Angeles, 1984), p. 16).

Marathas without exception started as 'conquests on invitation', as *fitna*: their assistance was sought by one party in a succession dispute among local chiefs or *zamīndārs*, or they were called in to back an appropriation of rights. Huge tributes, under the denomination of *cauth*, were demanded for this, and if these were not paid in time they were quick to assist the other party. Such demands then served as a lever for the further consolidation of sovereignty. Between 1740 and 1748 Balaji organized four expeditions to the north. The first, in 1740–1, was to Rajastan, then even more than usually prey to succession rivalries and disputes among the Rajputs. In a second expedition, from 1741 to 1743, he entered Bihar and Bengal via Bundelkhand on the invitation of the usurping Mughal subhedar Ali Vardi Khan. There he came into conflict with Raghuji Bhonsle, who claimed the whole region from Berar to Bengal as his own sphere of interest. The Peshwa aimed to check Raghuji's growing power and establish his own claims to the *cauth* in these provinces. In 1743 he drove Raghuji's army from the region but the latter sought redress with Shahu. After Dabhade in Gujarat this was the second time that the Raja's intervention had to settle a conflict with the overambitious Peshwa. A demarcation of rights was made and the Peshwa and Raghuji were ordered not to interfere in each other's spheres. On his return from Bengal the Peshwa persuaded the rajas of Bundelkhand to accept Maratha sovereignty in return for the *cauth* but a third campaign was necessary to settle his claims, in Bundelkhand and again in Rajastan in 1744–5. The fourth expedition was undertaken with the chief aim to aid the Emperor against the Afghan Ahmad Shah Abdali who invaded India in 1747. When Abdali turned back in 1748 Maratha sovereignty was not yet decisively established anywhere in Northern India. Constant expeditioning remained necessary to realize the *cauth*. Particularly the Rajputs, with their disputes decided, easily turned against the Maratha invaders.

In the second period of his reign, after the death of Shahu, Balaji succeeded in dislodging the Raja of Satara from sovereign power and assuming it for himself in all but name. The king was childless and was alleged to have intended the adoption of Sambhaji of Kolhapur. This plan Tarabai, the widow of Rajaram, sought to frustrate by revealing the existence of her grandson Ramraja. For a while the Peshwa supported her assertion. He had, according to Grant Duff, a private meeting with Ramraja in which he obtained a deed authorizing him to take over the government on condition of perpetuating the Raja's name and keeping up the dignity of the house of Bhonsle through the grandson of Tarabai and his descendants.[28] Two undated *yādīs* to the same effect have been brought to light, containing orders from Shahu to Balaji enjoining him to keep up the dynasty (*vaṃś*) of Bhonsle and not to adopt 'one of Kolhapur', and confirming to him the ministry and administration of the *rājya* in the name of the Raja to be.[29] And so, a few days after Shahu's death, Ramraja was ushered into Satara and installed on the throne.[30] He was left there in almost complete isolation, while the Peshwa, after securing for himself the support of Raghuji Bhonsle, gradually removed all the offices of government to Poona. Several unsuccessful attempts were made by the Raja to collect followers and regain control over the administration. Balaji safeguarded his new position by concluding arrangements which he held up to be in conformity with the will of the late Raja Shahu. In the latter's name Raghuji Bhonsle received new sanads for Berar, Gondwana and Bengal; half of Gujarat was confirmed to Yaswant Rao Dabhade, while Malwa was partitioned among Holkar, Scindhia and a small number of other jagirdars among whom Anand Rao Pawar was the most prominent.[31] The *aṣṭapradhān* council was maintained but only *pro forma* and without any intention to employ it. Fattesingh Bhonsle was confirmed in his jagirs and other holdings and was given the title of Raja of Akulkot. A relation of the Mantri whom Shahu had appointed *ajahat sardeśmukh* or 'vice-sardeśmukh', in practice the general collector of the *sardeśmukhī*, was deprived of his right to interfere in the collections of the 10% of the six Mughal subhas of the Deccan but he was assigned a jagir in compensation.[32] Shahu's death, finally, provided the Peshwa with an opportunity to reduce Angria, the most powerful sardar in the Konkan and a stubborn loyalist of the Raja refusing to submit to the brahman minister. In 1735 the Peshwa had divided the Angria jagir between the two brothers Sambhaji and Manaji. The latter was assigned a part of the Northern Konkan around Kolaba. Sambhaji continued to hold the title of *Sarkhel* with the fleet, and had his capital at Vijayadurg; his jagir shrank to a strip of unfertile land stretching from Bankot to Malvan. When Sambhaji died Manaji tried to obtain the Sarkhelship from the King, but it

[28] *Ibid.*, p. 338.
[29] Published with the original *moḍi* texts in G. S. Sardesai, *Marāṭhī Riyāsat*, madhya vibhāg 2 (Bombay, 1921), pp. 127–8.
[30] Cf. *SPD*, 6. [31] Grant Duff, *History*, 1, p. 345. [32] *Ibid.*, p. 341.

was conferred in 1743 on Tulaji Angria, Sambhaji's brother, who again managed to increase his naval power but only as long as Shahu was alive. In 1753 the Peshwa announced that he would not tolerate Angria's 'persecution of brahmans and vatandars' any longer,[33] and in 1755 Suvarnadurg and three other forts of Angria fell under the joint assault of the Peshwa and the British. After this the Peshwa's troops overran the entire estate and captured the forts of Anjanvel, Gavalkot and Ratnagiri. The whole of the Southern Konkan then finally came under the direct administration of the Peshwa. He also continued to encroach on the jagir of the other branch of the family, that of Manaji Angria, and took a number of his forts. Their relationship remained strained until the last decade of the eighteenth century, when Manaji's son Raghuji died and the estate fell in the hands of a usurping regent of his infant son.

In 1751 the Raja of Satara renounced all sovereign power and agreed to sanction the Peshwa's policies unconditionally. The only stipulation made was that he should receive some land around Satara under his direct management; this was acceded to but never given effect. Tarabai once again attempted to incite Ramraja to resume power but when she saw he had lapsed into utter apathy she conspired with Damaji Gaikwar to subvert the brahman government and remove the Raja from its control. To prevent this the Raja was at last put under strict confinement in the fort of Satara. The Gaikwar was won over by allowing him to replace Dabhade in the possession of the half share of Gujarat. Disputes with Tarabai continued till as late as 1758 but her basic submission seems to have been secured in 1753.[34]

The Raja of Satara henceforward remained a prisoner of state – powerless, but always a potential focus for all disaffection of the Maratha sardars. Appearances were therefore scrupulously maintained. The Chatrapati invested every new Peshwa with the *khilat* or robes and he always confirmed the Peshwas' orders to continue the other hereditary pradhans and sardars in their titles and jagirs.[35] Every year the Peshwa came to Satara to submit the revenue accounts. This he did to the last as the King's prime minister. No Peshwa could ever embark on a campaign without first formally taking leave of the Raja. The royal family and their domestic servants enjoyed an exemption from all taxes and duties and the country surrounding Satara, as Tone could still observe in 1799,

33 *SSRPD*, 1, no. 240. 34 *TKKP*, 3, nos 28, 81, 123, 126.
35 *SSRPD*, 4, nos 179, 205–6, 226, 231; 9, no. 122; etc.

was always exempted from military exactions of all sorts and whenever any chief entered it his great drum or *nagārā* ceased to beat.[36]

After the confinement of the Raja, Balaji Baji Rao's *Peśvāī* saw a number of indecisive *mulūkhgirī* campaigns to the south, while in the north tensions built up between the Marathas and the Afghans, contending with each other for the 'protection' of the Mughal throne. These reached a climax in the Battle of Panipat and the defeat of the Maratha army in 1761, a catastrophe which the Peshwa did not survive. Nana Saheb's son Madhav Rao came to Satara as a minor, attended by his uncle Raghunath Rao, and received the investiture from the Raja. The latter remained in confinement in the same manner until shortly afterwards Tarabai died and he was allowed to live in the town of Satara. Madhav Rao subsequently also permitted him to appoint agents for the collection of his *pāṭīl* dues in several villages and of his *deśmukhī vatan* of Indapur.[37] For some time Raghunath Rao acted as the young Peshwa's regent and attempted to keep him in a state of tutelage. But Madhav Rao was soon able to take the government in his own hands, imprisoned Raghunath, and reigned for eleven years. During this period he did much to recover prestige for the Poona court which had suffered from the disaster of Panipat that was attributed both by the Marathas and the other brahmans to the 'incompetence' of the Citpavans. Immediately after Panipat the Nizam attempted to boost his own power by supporting Janoji Bhonsle in an abortive attempt to overturn the Poona government. He suffered a defeat in 1762, and after this date only two new threats arose: from Raghunath Rao (again with the support of Janoji Bhonsle) in 1767, and once again at the time of Madhav Rao's death in 1772 (then with the support of the British). Both times Raghunath aimed to acquire the Peshwaship, causing widespread *fitvā*, but was in the end unsuccessful.

Citpavan power reached its summit under Balaji Janardan *alias* Nana Fadnis, a former personal karkun of Madhav Rao who became regent in the name of the child of Madhav Rao's murdered brother Narayan Rao. In the new arrangements that evolved in the years 1773–4 it was accepted, or rather taken for granted, that the Chatrapati of Satara should continue as the *de jure* sovereign and the Peshwa of Poona as the *de facto* sovereign. For want of an heir it

36 Sen, *Administrative System*, p. 117.

37 Grant Duff, *History*, 1, p. 412.

was first decided that the office of *Peśvāī* was to be represented by a council of ministers called the *Bārbhāī* or Twelve Brothers.[38] According to a British account of 1781 this council was in the beginning merely a body of five brahmans but these thought it necessary 'to establish their system on a basis more extended' on the presumption that 'when supported by the joint interest of the brahmans and warriors' it would become 'immovable'.[39] Scindhia and Holkar and five other Maratha chiefs were therefore associated with it and the whole was called the Twelve Barbhai. The infant Narayan was acknowledged Peshwa and the robes were procured for him from the Raja. The Barbhai council never functioned as a regular governmental body; the persons who composed it used it solely to assert their private interests against their own rivals. Nana Fadnis finally succeeded in extricating himself as the regent of Peshwa Narayan Rao's child. The sardars of the Barbhai considered themselves safe and the council dissolved. For about twenty years, from 1775 to 1795, Nana Fadnis' power was supreme, but he lived under the constant fear of being overthrown by the Maratha community rallying around the Chatrapati.[40] As a measure to conciliate the Marathas, there was much talk about 'taking the Raja out' (*rājā bahar kāḍhāvā*) – a project strongly supported by the British – but this plan was dropped when in 1773 Madhav Rao Narayan was born and made Peshwa.[41]

The Raja was not 'taken out'; if anything his situation became worse. In 1787 Malet wrote that he again lived 'under a very jealous, rigid inspection in the fort of Satara under the management of Babu Rao Apte, a brahman appointed from hence and instructed with the entire control and direction of the Raja's revenues, household, &c.'.[42] Malet considered at that time the Raja of Kolhapur the most dangerous of the rivals of the brahman government 'on the strength of his claim to the Rajaship of the Marathas'.[43] Indeed the Citpavan hegemony did not go unchallenged for long – not for more than the twenty years of Nana Fadnis' regency – but the new threats did not come from Kolhapur or the

38 S. Athavale, 'Restoration of the Chhatrapati', in: *Maratha History Seminar*, p. 230.

39 *An Historical Account of the Settlement and Possession of Bombay by the English East India Company, and the Rise and Progress of the War with the Mahratta Nation* (London, 1781), p. 61.

40 Athavale, 'Restoration of the Chhatrapati', p. 231.

41 *Ibid.* 42 Malet to Gov. Gen., 15 March 1787, *PRC*, 2, p. 94.

43 Malet to Earl Cornwallis, K. G., Gov. Gen., 29 March 1788, *ibid.*, p. 132.

Maratha royal clique but from the Peshwa's own sardars, first from Scindhia and later from Holkar.

Scindhia had grown more and more powerful in Hindustan and, after reinstating the Emperor Shah Alam, was appointed *Vakīl-i-muṭlaq* of the Empire. This aroused the Peshwa's protest and the same title was subsequently assumed by himself while Scindhia was invested as his 'deputy'. Still the *mānkarīs*, the one-time mansabdars of the Mughal, and the old officials of the Raja of Satara refused to acknowledge the new titles. Scindhia's ambition, the progressive de-Marathization of his troops, and his but distant connection with the Maratha people further alarmed Nana Fadnis and induced the latter to intensify his hold both on the Peshwa and the Raja, whom he feared Scindhia would try to employ as an instrument to overthrow the brahman government.[44] When Madhav Rao Narayan died in 1796, all the great Maratha sardars, the Bhonsle Raja of Nagpur, Scindhia, Holkar, and the jagirdars of the Deccan assembled at Poona for the last time and, as Elphinstone described it, 'a scene of factions, violence and intrigue ensued, at the conclusion of which Baji Rao, the rightful heir but the representative of the unpopular and proscribed house of Raghunath Rao, was elevated to the masnad by the military power of Scindhia'.[45] Baji Rao II first remained a puppet in the hands of Scindhia. The threat of a second change of dynasty became quite acute but it was prevented perhaps by the dread of interference by the British.[46] Scindhia also had to withdraw to Hindustan as his authority there had begun to be undermined by his prolonged absence.

Scindhia's fear of British intervention, if he had any such fear, would by no means have been out of place. In 1802 Holkar invaded the Deccan and this further threat led the Peshwa to conclude with the British the Treaty of Bassein, resulting in the permanent establishment of a British subsidiary force in Poona, for the protection by which the Peshwa sacrificed his independence and which Scindhia anticipated might soon affect his own. The Treaty of Bassein was the first fruit of a 'subsidiary system' devised by Wellesley, which constituted – this was acknowledged by some contemporaries – 'a novel system of encroachment' that 'threat-

44 Grant Duff, *History*, 2, pp. 181, 205.

45 M. Elphinstone, *Report on the Territories Conquered from the Peshwa* (1809) (Delhi, 1973), p. 16.

46 *Ibid.*

ened the subversion of the Marathas as effectually as their establishment of cauth and sardeśmukhī had overwhelmed the empire of the Mughals'.[47] The pivot of British policy was to treat each important sardar as an independent sovereign. As Palmer wrote in 1801

The power of the great constituted members of the Maratha empire to form separate political engagements was not only understood, but had often been acted upon by the British Government in treaties concluded and executed with various chieftains of his state, several of which are still in force, without objection or interference from the supreme authority.[48]

To a certain extent this was analogous to the traditional policy of the Mughals and the Nizam. But they, like the British themselves in an earlier stage, had always particularly tried to exploit the endemic brahman–Maratha schism. Lord Wellesley appears to have been unaware of the existence of the Raja of Satara.[49] He referred to the Peshwa as a 'sovereign' and, like Palmer in the above quotation, spoke of a 'Maratha Empire', and he attributed to this a 'constitution' under which Scindhia, Holkar, Gaikwar, and the Bhonsle of Nagpur held positions like he himself and his peers held under the British constitution.[50] Part of the explanation is perhaps that under Nana Fadnis the relationship of the Peshwa and the Raja had, even in its ceremonial aspect, more than ever before approached one of equality.[51] But this encroachment on established custom existed only during the time of Nana Fadnis, when brahman power went unchallenged, and the British did become aware of the King in the period which followed. In 1810 again considerable attention was drawn by the fact that Baji Rao II observed

the same forms of external respect towards the Raja that were observed when the Raja was the efficient sovereign of the state, and the Peshwa only his minister. The change that has taken place in the relative power and consequence of the Raja and the Peshwa has produced none in their personal behaviour towards each other. The Raja maintains in the ceremonials of his court all the state of a real sovereign; and the Peshwa approaches and treats him with the same marks of respect that are paid by the most dutiful subject to the person of the most despotic prince.[52]

47 Grant Duff, *History*, 2, p. 269.
48 *PRC*, 6, no. 431 (20 November 1801).
49 Thompson, *Indian Princes*, p. 8.
50 *Ibid.*
51 Cf. H. Russell to Gov. Gen., 30 June 1810, *PRC*, 7, p. 472.
52 *Ibid.*

These 'ceremonials' not only emphasize the Peshwa's subordination to the King, but equally give pride of place to the *mānkarīs* as the 'ancient military tenants of the Mughal Empire'.[53] Yet all treaties with the British were concluded by the Peshwa alone.[54] They were considered valid without the confirmation by the Raja of Satara. It was in this way denied, as H. Russell wrote to the Governor-General in 1810, that the Raja of Satara was then 'the real head of the Maratha State'.[55] After the Second Anglo-Maratha War in 1803 the Peshwa, relying still on British 'protection', attempted to regain control over his sardars, the nearly-independent chiefs like Gaikwar, Scindhia, Holkar, and the Bhonsle Raja of Nagpur, and especially also over his recalcitrant jagirdars in the southern Maratha country. In the Deccan a large number of the smaller assignments were resumed by the Peshwa acting on his own account. In other cases of more crucial importance only British arbitration could effect a settlement. At the same time claims were revived to sovereignty and *cauth* and *sardeśmukhī* in Hindustan and against the Nizam. The almost century-old rivalry with the Pratinidhi finally ended in the Peshwa's favour in the period 1807–11 when the former began to 'create *fitvā*' after declaring himself a 'servant of the Raja of Satara', then 'went over from the *svarājya* to

[53] Cf. *ibid.*, pp. 473–4: 'When the Peshwa approaches Satara, the Raja sends some person to the distance of two or three miles to meet him. This person conducts him to the Raja's palace in the town. Upon his arrival at the gate of the palace, he is met by some of the Raja's Huzrats (personal troops) who go through the form of tying his hands slightly together with a handkerchief in the posture of respect and introduce him in that way to the Raja's presence. . . . The Raja in addressing the Peshwa calls him merely by his name "Baji Rao", or frequently with greater kindness and familiarity simply "Bajiba". In public the Peshwa never sits in the Raja's presence; and even in private he sits only when the Raja desires him to do so. If the Peshwa is accompanied to Satara by the Raja of Berar or any of the other Maratha chieftains, who nominally hold directly of the Raja of Satara, they are received with him into the Raja's presence, with forms generally resembling those observed by the Peshwa, but varying in some degree according to their different gradations of rank. If the Peshwa is accompanied by Holkar or Scindhia or any of the chieftains who hold of the Peshwa and not of the Raja, they are none of them entitled to the honour of being admitted to the Raja's presence. The Mankaris who are the ancient military tenants of the Mughal Empire, are upon all occasions entitled to be received into the Raja's presence; and although the Peshwa himself does not sit before the Raja in public, the Mankaris do. . . . In all external forms and ceremonies of respect, the Mankaris still preserve a superiority above the Peshwa. Whenever a Mankari meets the Peshwa, the Peshwa makes the first Salam (greeting); and if any personal intercourse takes place between them upon the arrival of a Mankari at Poona, the Peshwa must pay the first visit.'

[54] H. Russell to Gov. Gen., 1 September 1810, *ibid.*, p. 489.

[55] *Ibid.*, p. 490.

the *pararājya*' and denied any obligation towards the Pant Pradhan.[56] In the conflict which ensued the Pratinidhi was taken prisoner and confined in Poona; his extensive jagir between the Nira and the Varna was sequestrated. But the British had already decided that Baji Rao would have to 'resign both the name and power of a sovereign'.[57] His claims to the *cauth* in the remote areas of Hindustan they considered 'antiquated'.[58] When once in 1812 a minister of Baji Rao began a long discourse with Elphinstone on the Peshwa's right to sovereignty over the Raja of Nagpur, Scindhia, Holkar and many other chiefs elsewhere in India, pointing out that to see the justice of these claims he would only have to examine the sanads under which they held their lands, Elphinstone, as he himself reported to the Governor-General, 'remonstrated against the renewal of those absurd claims . . . and said that the minister's observation would lead to a question by whose sanads the Peshwa held his country, and whether we ought not to assist the King of Delhi in recovering this part of his former dominions?'.[59] The minister replied that 'whatever sanads the Peshwa might have from Delhi, he held his country of God alone', on which Elphinstone told him that 'if that were the case, his right was extinguished when Providence was pleased to resume its gift'. The Peshwa was made to understand that the alliance with the British, while it had fortified and secured his 'just and legitimate authority' in his own dominions, left no ground at all for 'the visionary hope of re-establishing the feudal superiority of the state of Poona over the other branches of the Maratha Empire'.[60]

An outbreak of hostility led to the Third Anglo-Maratha War, the expulsion of the Peshwa in 1818, and the conquest and annexation of the entire Deccan. Much care was taken, however, to reconcile the Citpavan brahmans by recognizing the privileges and exemptions which they had acquired during more than half a century of Peshwa rule.[61] As counterpoise to their remaining

56 Cf. pp. 328–9

57 Malcolm, quoted in Thompson, *Indian Princes*, p. 258.

58 Elphinstone to Vice President, 18 August 1811, *PRC*, 12, p. 61.

59 Elphinstone to Gov. Gen., 27 June 1812, *ibid.*, p. 171.

60 Gov. Gen. to H.H. the Peshwa, 20 January 1816, *PRC*, 13, p. 17.

61 Similar privileges and exemptions operated in 1817 against the annexation of the Southern Konkan; as is stated in a Dispatch from the Marquis of Hastings to the Court of Directors of 4 September of that year: ' . . . it was found expedient not to press the cession of the Southern Konkan, the possession of which would have been a very valuable acquisition to the honourable Company, as completing our command of the sea coast, and being itself a fertile country full of strong military

influence and to balance the Maratha interests the Chatrapati was set up by Elphinstone in a small sovereignty under British paramountcy around Satara.[62] Scindhia, Holkar, Gaikwar, the Pawars, and the Bhonsle of Nagpur were also established as Princes with sovereignties qualified only by British paramountcy. The other sardars were divided into three classes: the old hereditary jagirdars known as *mānkarīs* retained all their lands under unchanged titles as 'jagirdars of the first class'; similarly the old commanders and officials of the Raja of Satara, 'jagirdars of the second class', were given or continued in hereditary jagirs, or, as some of them chose, were placed under the government of the Raja of Satara; of the 'sardars of the third class', all raised by the Peshwas, only some of the oldest were given hereditary titles, while the others received titles for life. What remained of the supremacy of the Mughal Emperor at the time of this settlement was nothing concrete. Lord Wellesley had still sought his support as giving 'greater stability and

positions: it is, however, the native country of the Peshwa, and of almost all the principal brahman families connected with the Poona government. The great majority of the inhabitants is composed of brahmans who enjoy peculiar privileges and are naturally attached to a Hindu government, which favours their order. These circumstances operated so powerfully against urging the cession of the Konkan, that Mr Elphinstone desisted' (Dispatch from the Marquis of Hastings to the Court of Directors, 4 September 1817, *Parliamentary Papers*, 1818, 11, 369, no. 9, p. 47, art. 7th). In Elphinstone's own words: 'I could not take the lower Konkan without giving great pain to the Peshwa, and what is worse, great disgust to every man about the Government. I have therefore contented myself with the part North of the road to Bombay . . . ' (M. E. to Napean, 7 June 1817, *Bombay Secret Consultations*, 25 June 1817). The Peshwa being a brahman created, as Colebrooke saw it, 'another source of danger which we have not experienced in any former conquest in the East, at least as regards the Hindus; and that was religion' (T. E. Colebrooke, *Life of the Honourable Mountstuart Elphinstone*, 2 vols (London, 1884), 2, p. 74). On this account Elphinstone also wrote: 'The preservation of religious establishments is always necessary in a conquered country; but more particularly so in one where the brahmans have so long possessed the temporal power' (quoted in G. W. Forrest, *Selections from the Minutes and other Official Writings of the Honourable Mountstuart Elphinstone, Governor of Bombay* (London, 1884), pp. 59–60).

62 Elphinstone to J. Grant, 8 April 1818, *Bengal Secret and Political Consultations*, 31 July 1818 (Pt. 2), no. 131; Forrest, *Selections*, 2, p. 57; J. Adam, Secretary to Gov., to Elphinstone, Resident, 15 December 1817, *PRC*, 13, p. 271; Elphinstone to Gov. Gen., 18 June 1818, *ibid.*, p. 396. The Raja was, from the outset, strongly curtailed: 'A minister to be appointed to act in his name. The head revenue and judicial authorities to receive their appointments from him, and their orders from the proper minister, who is to receive his instructions exclusively from the Political Agent' (*IOL: MSS, Eur. F.88*, Box 14H, 17, undated letter (from E.?) in pack of papers called 'Miscellaneous Papers and relative letters (1) Rajah of Satara').

strength' to the British dominion.[63] Under the guardianship of Lake he had been given the new title of King and retained a small kingdom around Delhi, in the administration of which, however, he was not to interfere.[64] The Nawab of Awadh was then, in return for a loan to the Company, also allowed to style himself 'King of Awadh'. The nominal suzerainty of the King of Delhi over British dominions was evident until 1835 in the coins which continued to be issued in his name. The last relic of the Empire vanished after the Mutiny. From then onwards the Nizam of Hyderabad remained as its only representative. Until the end he refused the title of King.

b. The Deccan

After the fall of Rajgarh in 1689 the widow of the late king Sambhaji and their son Shahu, the prospective heir to the throne, were taken as prisoners into the imperial camp. With Rajaram a junior branch of the Bhonsle family then inherited the Maratha kingship. Not until 1705, five years after Rajaram's death, did Aurangzeb adopt the plan of releasing Shahu. In that year he gave him the districts of Akulkot, Indapur, Supa, and Nevasa in jagir. But the plan of releasing him did not materialize during Aurangzeb's lifetime, and even after the Emperor's death in 1707 Shahu remained for a while in the camp of prince Azam Shah.[65] Khafi Khan writes that towards the end of Aurangzeb's reign Rani Tarabai, the widow of Rajaram, continued to oppose the Emperor for a number of years after her husband's death but then offered to submit to him upon the condition of receiving a grant of the *sardeśmukhī* of the six Mughal subhas of the Deccan at the rate of 9%.[66] Aurangzeb rejected her proposal 'for the honour of Islam, and for other reasons'.[67] When after Aurangzeb's death the succession dispute broke out among the Emperor's three sons, Shahu was carried to the north, beyond the Narmada, with Azam Shah and the Mughal Deccan army. At that stage Zulfiqar Khan, in reaction to Maratha pressure, succeeded in persuading Azam Shah to set Shahu at liberty.[68] Shahu's family were to be held as hostages while

[63] Thompson, *Indian Princes*, p. 59. [64] *Ibid.*, p. 142.
[65] Grant Duff, *History*, 1, pp. 225, 230.
[66] Elliot and Dowson, *History of India*, 7, pp. 409, 465; Grant Duff (*History*, 1, p. 225) and M. G. Ranade (*Rise of the Maratha Power* (Bombay, 1900), p. 226) hold that Aurangzeb was in 1705 prepared to grant 10% of the revenue of the Mughal Deccan as *sardeśmukhī* to Shahu.
[67] Elliot and Dowson, *History of India*, 7, p. 465. [68] *Ibid.*, p. 395.

he himself was given the promise that if he would be able to establish his authority and if he remained loyal to the Empire, he would receive the districts conquered by his grandfather Shivaji from Bijapur with an additional tract between the Bhima and the Godavari.[69] Well before this promise was made, Tarabai, fearing that Shahu's release would reduce her own influence, had petitioned to Azam Shah for a farman of the Bhonsle's *zamīndārī*, but the Son of the Protector of the Islamdharma (as Azam Shah styled himself) chose to ignore her request. In June 1707 the prince declared that the Maratha *zamīndārī-rājya* in what he refers to as 'our country' was to be hereditarily given to Shahu.[70] Many Maratha sardars who had joined the widow of Rajaram now came over to Shahu.[71] 'Having collected a large army, Shahu proceeded to the neighbourhood of Ahmadnagar, and then, according to a contemporary report, he put off his journey and went to the place where Aurangzeb [had] died. He paid a mourning visit to the place, and distributed money and food to the poor. Then, with his large army, which numbered nearly 20,000 Maratha horse, he marched [on] with the intention of showing his respect to the tomb of Aurangzeb, near Daulatabad, at a place now called Khuldabad.'[72] Tarabai, on her part, did not give up her pretensions to Mughal recognition of the Maratha sovereignty on her son's behalf and accused Shahu of *fitvā*.[73] The argument she put forward was that after Shivaji had completed the conquest of his kingdom it was lost by his son Sambhaji, but Rajaram had regained it and had established a new *rājya* by his own efforts. Secondly, and somewhat inconsistently, she argued that it had been Shivaji's wish that Rajaram, and not Sambhaji, should succeed him.[74] This carried little conviction since Rajaram, on his accession in 1689, had publicly declared that he received the kingship only on behalf of his nephew Shahu (then six years of age) and because the precedence of the senior branch of the family was an established right. Shahu

[69] Grant Duff, *History*, 1, p. 231.

[70] Letter from Azam Shah to Shahu, *MIS*, 8,. no. 56: '*kāraṇ kīṇ āmce mulakāṇtīl rājya va zamīdārī tumhāṇkaḍe asāvī āṇi tumhi āple vaḍilāṇpramāṇeṇ tetheṇ kāyam rahāveṇ*'.

[71] Elliot and Dowson, *History of India*, 7, p. 395; Grant Duff, *History*, 1, p. 231.

[72] Khafi Khan, in: Elliot and Dowson, *History of India*, 7, p. 395.

[73] Cf. p. 102.

[74] See the letter from Shivaji II, the son of Tarabai, of 17 September 1707 to Somnaik Desai, in: G. S. Sardesai, *Marāṭhī Riyāsat*, Puṇyaśloka Śāhū, 1 Peśva Bāḷājī Viśvanāth (1701–1720) (Bombay, 1942), p. 35.

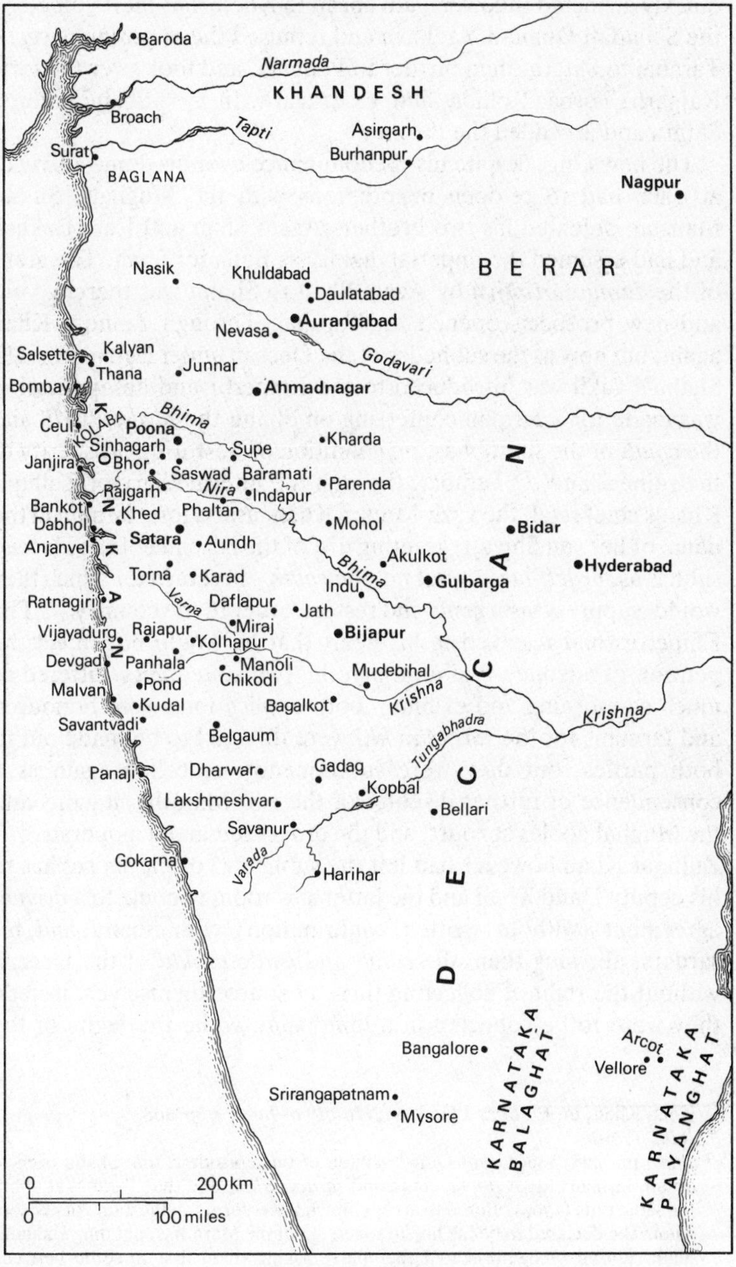
Baroda
Narmada
KHANDESH
Broach
Tapti
Asirgarh
Surat
Burhanpur
BAGLANA
Nagpur
BERAR
Nasik
Khuldabad
Daulatabad
Aurangabad
Nevasa
Godavari
Salsette
Kalyan
Thana
Junnar
Bombay
Ahmadnagar
KONKAN
KOLABA
Bhima
Ceul
Poona
Sinhagarh
Kharda
Supe
Janjira
Bhor
Saswad
Baramati
Parenda
Nira
Rajgarh
Indapur
Bankot
Khed
Phaltan
Dabhol
Mohol
Bidar
Anjanvel
Satara
Aundh
Akulkot
Hyderabad
Bhima
Torna
Karad
Gulbarga
Indu
Ratnagiri
Varna
Daflapur
Jath
Miraj
Vijayadurg
Rajapur
Bijapur
Kolhapur
Devgad
Panhala
Manoli
Mudebihal
Chikodi
Malvan
Pond
Krishna
Kudal
Bagalkot
Krishna
Savantvadi
Tungabhadra
Belgaum
Panaji
Dharwar
Gadag
Kopbal
Lakshmeshvar
Bellari
Savanur
Varada
Gokarna
Harihar
DECCAN
Bangalore
Arcot
Vellore
KARNATAKA BALAGHAT
KARNATAKA PAYANGHAT
Srirangapatnam
Mysore
0
200 km
0
100 miles

The Deccan

quickly attracted followers, advanced to Khed, was there joined by the Senapati Dhanaji Yadhava and repulsed the opposing party of Tarabai to Satara, then further to Panhala, and took over the forts Rajgarh, Torna, Rohida, and Vicitragarh. In 1708 Shahu entered Satara and ascended the throne.

The new king, despite his predominance over his domestic rival, at once had to re-open negotiations with the Mughals. Sultan Mauzam defeated his two brothers Azam Shah and Kam Bakhsh and had assumed the imperial dignity as Bahadur Shah. The grant of the *zamīndārī-rājya* by Azam Shah to Shahu was thereby void and new prospects opened for Tarabai. Through Zulfiqar Khan again, but now as the subhedar of the Deccan under Bahadur Shah, Shahu's vakil was introduced to the Emperor and an application was made for a farman conferring on Shahu the *sardeśmukhī* and the *cauth* of the six subhas, on condition of 'restoring prosperity to the ruined land'.[75] Tarabai, through the intermediary of Zulfiqar Khan's chief rival, the vazir Munim Khan, asked for a farman in the name of her son Shivaji, granting 9% of the revenue of the Deccan subhas as *sardeśmukhī* – but not the *cauth* – in return for which they would 'suppress insurgents and restore order in the country'.[76] The Emperor 'had resolved in his heart that he would not reject the petition of anyone', and although the two statements 'differed as much as morning and evening' both applications were honoured and farmans for the *sardeśmukhī* were directed to be made out to both parties, but they were subsequently cancelled again as a consequence of further disputes of the two Maratha litigants and the Mughal nobles at court, and the orders remained inoperative.[77] Zulfiqar Khan however had left the subhedari of the six subhas to his deputy Daud Khan and the latter saw room to come to a private agreement (without written confirmation) with Shahu and his sardars, allowing them the *cauth* and *sardeśmukhī* of the Deccan without the right of collecting these at source themselves; instead they were to be collected in a lump sum, while the jagirs of the

75 Khafi Khan, in: Elliot and Dowson, *History of India*, 7, p. 408.

76 *Ibid.*

77 *Ibid.*, pp. 408, 466. Grant Duff's version of this episode is that Shahu tried to obtain farmans for *svarājya*, *cauth* and *sardeśmukhī*, and that Tarabai at about the same time (1709) offered to accept 'much lower terms' in the name of her son, whom she declared to be the lawful sovereign of the Marathas, but that 'Bahadur Shah refused recognition to either party asking them first to settle between themselves as to whom he should deliver the goods' (*History*, 1, p. 234).

princes and the highest nobles were to be exempted.[78] This arrangement appears to have been put into practice from 1709 until 1713, when Daud Khan was removed to Gujarat and the subhedari of the Deccan was assigned to Nizam-al-Mulk, the other great rival of Zulfiqar Khan. At the change of government it was immediately dissolved. Shahu's Senapati Candrasen Yadhava was sent out with an army to levy the *cauth*, the *sardeśmukhī*, and *ghāsdāṇā* ('grass and grain' for the horses) in the old style. But the Senapati soon defected to the Nizam, from whom he received a large jagir near Palki.[79]

In the intervening time a rival throne had been maintained by Tarabai and her son Shivaji at Kolhapur, but she herself was set aside by her Amatya Ramcandra Pant when her son died of smallpox, and Sambhaji, a son of a younger widow of Rajaram, was installed.[80] With regard to Kolhapur, Shahu was secure in his position only as long as Daud Khan's government was maintained. Nizam-al-Mulk tried to take advantage of the dissensions amongst the Marathas to divert their pressure and consolidate his own position and he favoured the Kolhapur party. In contrast also to his rival predecessor, Nizam-al-Mulk, after being appointed to the Deccan subhedari, came down to Aurangabad in person. Khafi Khan says that 'the fame of the sword of this renowned noble put a stop to the ravaging of the country and the plundering of the caravans which the forces of the Marathas practised every year, without his having to fight with either the army of Raja Shahu or that of Tarabai'.[81] The same writer however admits that the Maratha collectors were entrenched everywhere and that Nizam-al-Mulk was able to put a stop to their interference only in a few places in the neighbourhood of Aurangabad.[82] In this period Shahu nevertheless suffered from many defections: the Pratinidhi, Thorat, Krishna Rao, and most important Angria, all went over to Kolhapur. The process was reversed again with the entry into Maratha politics of Balaji Vishvanath and especially when in March 1713 the new Mughal Emperor Farrukhsiyar, soon after he succeeded Bahadur Shah, raised Shahu to a *mansab* of 10,000/10,000

78 Chandra, *Parties and Politics*, p. 48. Grant Duff (*History*, 1, p. 235) states that only the *cauth* was allowed, without the 'right of collecting' and 'with certain reservations'.

79 Grant Duff, *History*, 1, p. 240.

80 *Ibid.*, p. 237.

81 Elliot and Dowson, *History of India*, 7, p. 450. Khafi Khan appears here to have been ignorant of the changes at the Kolhapur court.

82 *Ibid.*, p. 451.

and asked him to send his vakil to court.[83] This concession seems to have balanced Nizam-al-Mulk's support to Kolhapur and Maratha *fitna* was contained for some time. But in May 1715 Nizam-al-Mulk was recalled to Delhi and Husain Ali Khan, the younger of the two Saiyid brothers, was appointed to replace him in the Deccan subhedari. The latter initially tried to continue the hardline policy of the Nizam, but intrigues at his court and the subsequent extension of Maratha encroachments induced him to resume negotiations with Shahu. Through the Peshwa a proposal was made to the effect that Shahu's agents were to collect from the Mughal revenue-officials in the parganas a quarter, called *cauth*, of the total revenues of the lands belonging to the government and jagirdars.[84] In addition there was to be collected 10% of the revenue as *sardeśmukhī* directly from the rayats.[85] This amounted to 35% of the total collections including the *abwāb* or extra 'cesses' exhibited in the government rent-roll and the *rahdārī* or 'road duties'. According to Khafi Khan the Mughal subhedar acceded to this proposal and accordingly Maratha collectors, regularly equipped with horsemen and footsoldiers, were stationed everywhere.[86] Husain Ali wrote for a confirmatory *farmān* to the Emperor, but 'several well-wishers of the state urged that it was not well to admit the vile enemy to be overbearing partners in matters of revenue and government, and so Farrukhsiyar rejected the treaty'.[87]

An official imperial farman settling the terms of Maratha subservience in the Deccan was not obtained before 1719. Up to that time several draft agreements with fluctuating and often imprecise terms appear to have been drawn up. An undated document which purports to contain stipulations given by Shahu to Shankarji Mulhar to be observed in his negotiations with Husain Ali promises 'to have cultivated and populated all districts between the Narmada and Rameshvara which belong to the King' if all forts in these districts are brought under his own direct control.[88] The *Śāhū Caritra* also describes draft stipulations to be negotiated by Shankarji Mulhar.[89] The demands here are that the entire *svarājya* with all the forts and *ṭhāṇas* which Shivaji held under the sanction of Raja Jai Singh would have to be restored to Shahu, that the *cauth* and *sardeśmukhī* of the six subhas of the Deccan were to be paid to

83 Unpublished Persian letter kept in the historical museum of the Deccan College, Poona.

84 Elliot and Dowson, *History of India*, 7, pp. 466–7.

85 *Ibid.*, p. 467.

86 *Ibid.*

87 *Ibid.*

88 *SPD*, 7, no. 28.

89 Hervadkar, *Śāhū Caritra*, pp. 54–8.

him, and that Shahu's family be released from Mughal confinement. In return for this the Marathas were to serve the Mughal Emperor with 50,000 horse. A *yādī* attached to this draft specifies the sardars selected for service with the Mughals and their daily allowances and further stipulates that 'in payment of the *sardeśmukhī* one village in each mahal must be held revenue-free [in *inām*]' and that 'the *cauth* and *sardeśmukhī* are to be received not only in the six subhas, but also in Gujarat and Malwa'.[90] The draft terms as given by Grant Duff show a slightly greater exactness and seem to represent the final stage in the negotiations with Husain Ali Khan.[91] The number of horse to be maintained by Shahu in the service of the Emperor is now reduced to 15,000; for their support and payment the *cauth* of the six subhas was to be granted. In return for the right to levy the *sardeśmukhī* in the six Mughal subhas of the Deccan, Shahu was to provide service in the form of 'protection' of the country and the 'suppression and punishment of robbers'. The demands for both the *cauth* and the *sardeśmukhī* also encompassed the entire Karnataka – an area which was subsumed under the subhas of Bijapur and Hyderabad – and the tributary kingdoms of Mysore, Tiruchchirappalli and Thanjavur. From the demand of *svarājya* Shivaji's former possessions in Khandesh were excluded and substituted by holdings adjoining the old districts as far east as Pandharpur. Again different *svarājya* claims are set forth in a *jābtā svarājya* or 'statement of *svarājya*' drawn up in September 1718 by Shankarji Mulhar himself (partly in Persian, partly in Marathi/moḍi).[92] This equally purports to be a specification of the districts which were conquered by Shivaji: over these districts, making up a total of 127 *tālukās* or 'divisions' and 145 forts (of which 89 are already under Maratha control), full control is demanded and all Mughal *ṭhāṇas* to be removed.

The stipulations of Shankarji Mulhar – whatever may have been their exact final terms – with regard to the Deccan (not the claims on Gujarat and Malwa) were accepted by Husain Ali Khan but the Emperor again refused to ratify the agreement.[93] In Delhi however all power temporarily passed to the Saiyid brothers when early in 1719 Husain Ali, supported by his Maratha allies, deposed and put to death the Emperor and succeeded in setting up two puppet Emperors, Rafi-ad-Darjat and Rafi-ad-Daula, each of whom lasted

90 *Ibid.*, p. 58. 91 Grant Duff, *History*, I, pp. 248–9.
92 P. V. Mawji, 'Shivaji's Swarajya', *JBBRAS*, o.s. 22 (1908), pp. 30–42.
93 *Ibid.*, p. 32; Grant Duff, *History*, I, p. 252.

no longer than seven months. The agreement between Raja Shahu and Husain Ali was formally sanctioned by Rafi-ad-Darjat and imperial farmans were given for the *cauth*, *sardeśmukhī* and *svarājya* on 13 and 24 March 1719. With these farmans and with the Raja's family Balaji Vishvanath returned to Rajgarh in May of the same year. The original documents were still in the possession of the Raja of Satara in the early nineteenth century when Grant Duff was Political Agent at his court, but they were made out in the name of the Emperor Muhammad Shah in what is called the first year of his reign.[94] In fact Muhammad Shah did not become Emperor before 1720, but his name was substituted for that of either one of the two ciphers advanced by the Saiyids on these and on many Mughal records, just as they were to be eliminated from the seals of the later Emperors. In addition to Grant Duff's description of the 'corrected' originals (which are now no longer extant) we have a few Marathi documents which give a summary of the original terms of service and there are the Marathi sanads which are allegedly replicas of the original Persian farmans. They run closely parallel to the originals as described by Grant Duff but they contain the name of Rafi-ad-Darjat.[95] There is no indication that Muhammad Shah ever sanctioned the same farmans as were issued under pressure of the Saiyid brothers whose faction was overthrown a year afterwards by the Turanis when they brought the new Emperor to the throne.[96] The Marathi copies of the Persian farmans were definitely made after 1720. One document in effect says that 'the *cauth* of the six subhas of the Deccan is given to Raja Shahu for the maintenance of 15,000 troops, with which he has to serve the subhedar Nizam-al-Mulk'. This was in accordance with the terms of the draft of the time of Husain Ali, but Nizam-al-Mulk was reappointed to the Deccan subhedari by Muhammad Shah. We also learn from the same set of documents that 'the *khidmat* ['post of service'] of *sardeśmukhī* of the six subhas of the Deccan is confirmed to our *yajmān* ['master'] in accordance with the farman given during the reign of the venerable Rafi-ad-Darjat and the sanads in his divan's office; ... the *yajmān* is reminded that he should remain prepared for this service with an armed force, that

94 Grant Duff, *History*, I, *loc. cit.*

95 For Grant Duff's summary description of the originals, see *History*, I, pp. 532–3; for the Marathi translations, see *P.A.: Selected Rumals, no. 9*, section 4, 5301–4; Vad, Mawji and Parasnis, *Treaties*, pp. 1–9.

96 Saiyid Husain Ali Khan was murdered in 1720, his brother Saiyid Abdullah Khan in 1722.

he should attend to the settlement of the rayats, and punish robbers and marauders for the *sarkār* [here, the 'government' of the Mughal Emperor]'. Shahu is also enjoined to 'work in co-operation with the rayats, restore desolate villages within three years time, cause them no trouble, punish thieves and restitute the property taken by them'. Another sanad says that 'in accordance with the petition made by Raja Shahu's vakil it is agreed with our *yajmān* that, since marauders have been disturbing the country of the Deccan for a long time and consequently it has fallen waste, he will take up the service of *sardeśmukhī* of the Deccan for an emolument (*rusūm*) of 10% of its revenues; he will punish for His Majesty the Badshah disturbers [of peace] and populate the country, keep marauders beyond the borders and prevent them from harassing the rayats'. Finally, the districts of the 'old kingdom (*rājya*)' of Shivaji are enumerated and it is said that they are restored on condition that the present Maratha king 'serves loyally'. Further details are in accordance with the draft treaty as described by Grant Duff. No new items are added in any other surviving Marathi documents of 1719; they speak of the restitution of *svarājya* and the grant of *cauth* and *sardeśmukhī* in terms tantamount to the above, referring to the receiving of original farmans from the Mughal Badshah, whose role of 'Protector of Islam' is reiterated.[97] Conspicuously absent are any suggestions of an imperial recognition of the right to *cauth* and *sardeśmukhī* in Gujarat and Malwa, both of which had been included in an earlier draft. Grant Duff thought that 'some very indefinite verbal promise' might have been made on this account and that Balaji Vishvanath left his vakil Hingane in Delhi with instructions to obtain the sanads for the recognition of these claimed rights.[98] But no deeds extenuating the *cauth* and *sardeśmukhī* beyond the Deccan appear to have been issued at this time by the Emperor or any of his nobles, although later this was generally pretended by the Marathas.

In the Deccan, as we have seen now, the *fitna* of the Maratha 'marauders' was formally transformed into *zamīndārī* service to a nominally still universal Emperor. The Maratha king, whose independent sovereignty was thus denied, became the *sardeśmukh* of the entire Deccan, including the Karnataka. The 10% of its revenues became the king's hereditary *vatan* right; this was also referred to as his *rusūm*, which under the Mughals was a technical term to denote the part of the land-revenue which *zamīndārs* were

97 Cf. *MIS*, 8, no. 77–8. 98 *History*, 1, p. 252.

allowed to retain in their districts as remuneration for their service. The *cauth* and *svarājya* grants were also made in payment of 'service' and, like that of the *sardeśmukhī*, were thought of as hereditary rights – a fact which is also underscored in the accompanying payments of *peśkaś*. The sanads exhibit in extreme detail, in rupees, anas and paisas, the assessed amounts of the total revenue and the *sardeśmukhī* in the six subhas:[99]

	jamā or 'valuation'	
Aurangabad	12,376,042	1/2.3.3
Berar	11,523,508	3/4.3.3
Bidar	7,491,879	3/4.0.1
Bijapur	78,508,560	3/4.2.1
Hyderabad	64,867,483	.0.0
Khandesh	5,749,819	.0.3
	180,517,294	1/4.2.3
Sardeśmukhī (10%)	18,051,730	

These valuations are based on measurements or estimates of agricultural proceeds and other income but do not show actual collections. The extreme precision moreover seems to be no more than a formality concomitant with the Mughal pretension to universality. This pretension made it unavoidable to express the Maratha–Mughal relationship in a purely monetized and quantitatively and territorially defined form. Money – not honour or *fitna* – is here the 'substance' of universal dominion. The monetized figures, especially the subha-specific aggregates, could hardly have fulfilled any practical function. In fact, in the period following 1719, the only Maratha right which was in principle no longer disputed was their *svarājya* over the districts which had originally been conquered by Shivaji. Even here there were no precise boundaries but continually fluctuating and interspersed holdings of different sovereigns. The collections of *cauth* and *sardeśmukhī* in the Mughal Deccan were never stabilized. In 1720 Nizam-al-Mulk, then subhedar of Malwa, was the first to resist successfully the Saiyids who had been instrumental in securing imperial recognition for the Maratha claims, and, after bringing Muhammad Shah to the throne, availed himself of the support of some powerful Maratha sardars dis-

99 Vad, Mawji and Parasnis, *Treaties*, pp. 3–4.

affected with Shahu and possessed himself of the Deccan subhas. The grateful Emperor not only confirmed him in the subhedaris of Malwa and the Deccan but also bestowed on him the vazirate of the Empire. The Nizam at once began to oppose the *cauth* and *sardeśmukhī* collections of the Marathas and, as he had done during his first term of office in the Deccan (1713–15), colluded with Sambhaji of Kolhapur. Only a protracted contest between Shahu and the Nizam, which continued for more than a decade and finally tailed off into squabbles and disputes extending over the remainder of the eighteenth century, could settle the Maratha claims in the Mughal Deccan and Karnataka.[100] Encouraged by the Nizam, the jagirdars and revenue officials first began to obstruct the Maratha collections but before anything decisive could happen the Nizam left for Delhi, in October 1721, to take charge of the vazirate. Under the Nizam's deputy Mubariz Khan opposition continued but could not prevent the Marathas from making their exactions widely felt. Nizam-al-Mulk held the vazirate only until December 1723. He aroused suspicion at court when he added the subha of Gujarat to his charge and this led him to withdraw to the Deccan. When the Nizam reached Ujjain early in 1724, the Emperor had however already reclaimed the six Deccan subhas and Malwa (and Gujarat) from him. Nizam-al-Mulk then saw himself forced to conciliate Peshwa Baji Rao and with his aid he overcame in May 1724 Mubariz Khan, his former deputy who had been appointed subhedar of the Deccan in his stead. In return for the Peshwa's assistance the Nizam acknowledged the Maratha claims of *cauth* and *sardeśmukhī* and awarded him with a mansab of 7,000/7,000.[101] After this the Nizam was able to reduce Mubariz Khan's son and take possession of Hyderabad in the beginning of 1725.

From this period is commonly dated the Nizam's virtual independence from Delhi and the foundation of the state of Hyderabad.[102]

[100] Cf. Z. Malik, 'Documents relating the Chauth Collection in the Subah of Hyderabad, 1726–1748', *Proceedings of the 32nd Session of the Indian History Congress* (Jabalpur, 1970), vol. 1, pp. 336–52; V. G. Dighe, *Nizam-ul-Mulk Asaf Jah I and the Marathas, 1721–1728* (Paper read at the public meeting of the 14th session of the Indian Historical Records Commission held at Lahore in December 1937) (Simla, 1938).

[101] *SPD*, 10, no. 27; Malik, 'Chauth Collection in Hyderabad', p. 338; Dighe, *Peshwa Baji Rao I*, p. 10.

[102] W. Irvine, *Later Mughals* (Delhi, 1971), pt. 2, p. 154; Grant Duff, *History*, 1, p. 266; Thompson, *Indian Princes*, p. 14; Z. Malik, 'Documents relating to Pargana Administration in the Deccan under Asaf Jah I', in: *Medieval India: A Miscellany*, vol. 3 (Asia Publishing House, 1975), p. 152.

The Nizam did not repudiate his nominal subordination to the Emperor but no revenue or tribute was ever again transmitted to the imperial treasury from the country south of the Narmada. Offices, jagirs, grants of land, and mansabs were freely given without reference to the Emperor's court. Apart from the repudiation of any royal title, the other attributes of sovereignty which the Nizam did not arrogate to himself were the recitation of the Friday prayer in his own name, the issuance of coins with his own inscription, and the use of a throne.[103] The Deccan capital was removed from Aurangabad to Hyderabad. According to Khafi Khan, 'it was so arranged that instead of the *cauth* of the subha of Hyderabad, a sum of money should be paid from his treasury and that the *sardeśmukhī* which was levied from the rayats at the rate of 10% should be abandoned'.[104] In effect the Hyderabad *subhā* – or at least a part of it around the capital – appears to have enjoyed exemption from Maratha interference, while commutation of the *cauth* and *sardeśmukhī* took the form of assignments of jagirs next to direct payments from the treasury.[105] In the other directly administered subhas of the Nizam the Marathas made their own collections and increased their demands or gave incidental exemptions, as they saw fit.[106]

The *entente* between the Nizam and the Peshwa was lost when the latter undertook in 1725–6 a large-scale invasion of the Karnataka, allegedly to enforce legitimate claims to tribute of *cauth* which were in arrears from Mysore and elsewhere. The Nizam once more turned to Kolhapur, setting himself up – still in the capacity of subhedar of the Mughal Emperor – as the arbiter of the Maratha succession dispute. As was a regular procedure in the case of disputed *zamīndārī* rights, the *cauth* and *sardeśmukhī* of the six Mughal subhas were formally sequestrated. For a time many of the collectors of Shahu and the Peshwa appear to have been actually

103 Irvine, *Later Mughals*, *loc. cit.*; Malik, 'Pargana Administration under Asaf Jah I', *loc. cit.*

104 Elliot and Dowson, *History of India*, 7, p. 530.

105 *Poona Akhbars*, vol. 2 (Hyderabad, 1954), no. 156 of 21st September 1781; Hervadkar, *Śāhū Caritra*, p. 80; Grant Duff, *History*, 1, p. 277; Dighe, *Peshwa Bajirao I*, *loc. cit.* There is an interesting parallel here with the 'protection-rent' called *rakhī* which the Sikhs imposed as a levy of 4 or 5% of the assessed land-revenue on their neighbours; Scindhia's treaty with the Sikhs of May 1785 stipulated in a similar way an exemption from it in the circuit of his palace and in his *khāsgī* or 'private' holdings. Yet in this case no compensation was provided for (*PRC*, 1, p. 161; and see *ibid.*, pp. 25–6).

106 Cf. Elliot and Dowson, *History of India*, 7, p. 530; Hervadkar, *Śāhū Caritra*, pp. 80–1; Grant Duff, *History*, 1, p. 276.

removed and replaced by those of Sambhaji of Kolhapur.[107] The Nizam also succeeded in luring away some Maratha sardars who felt threatened by the increasing power of the Peshwa. His most important ally, apart from Sambhaji of Kolhapur, thus became Trimbak Rao Dabhade, whose position in Gujarat was being severely undermined by the brahman minister. The Nizam however suffered a strategic defeat at the hands of the Peshwa at Palkhed in 1728. This was followed by a convention at Mungi Shevgaon where the Nizam again had to acknowledge the legitimacy of, and promise to comply with, the collection of 'the dues of *cauth* and *sardeśmukhī* as formerly conceded to Raja Shahu, with the co-operation of the rayats, and through the *sardeśmukh* of the kingdom and his collectors'.[108] New sanads were given not only for the *cauth* and *sardeśmukhī* but also for the *svarājya*, and the Nizam agreed 'not to support the Kolhapur Raja'. The Marathas bound themselves 'to populate and settle the country' and 'not to take more than is exhibited in the rent-roll (*jamābaṇḍī*)'.

These concessions were made not merely in acknowledgement of Maratha political strength but also to gain more support against the Emperor – a support which earlier had allowed the Nizam to set himself up as a quasi-independent sovereign in the Deccan. For his part, Shahu allowed his cousin Sambhaji a portion of the *cauth* and *sardeśmukhī* of the subha of Bijapur beyond the Krishna.[109] After his defeat at Palkhed, the Nizam no longer conspired with Sambhaji but he did unite once again with the Senapati Dabhade, exploiting for his own purpose the increasing antagonism between the latter and the Peshwa. Only when the Senapati was reduced in 1731, did the Nizam think it expedient to make a further secret compact with the Peshwa to back each other's positions and allowing himself to expand to the south and the Peshwa to the north.[110] The remaining issue between the Peshwa and the Nizam was now merely the *manner* in which the *cauth* and *sardeśmukhī* were to be collected from the Mughal Deccan. Nominally, 75% of

107 Malik, 'Chauth Collection in Hyderabad', p. 338; Grant Duff, *History*, 1, p. 277; Chandra, *Parties and Politics*, pp. 194–5.

108 *P.A.: Selected Rumals*, *loc. cit.*; *SPD*, 15, no. 86 (pp. 83–5). Malik, on the evidence of a Persian source, holds that at Mungi Shevgaon it was again stipulated to exempt the subha of Hyderabad from direct Maratha interference ('Chauth Collection in Hyderabad', p. 339).

109 *SPD*, 15, no. 86 (p. 91).

110 *MIS*, 3, no. 97; *SPD*, 30, nos 90–1; *BISMQ*, 26, 1–3 (1946), pp. 11–13; Grant Duff, *History*, 1, p. 284; M. Elphinstone, *The History of India* (Hindu and Mohammedan Periods) (London, 1874), p. 687.

the total amount of the land-revenue and additional cesses exhibited in the rent-roll was left to the Nizam; in the Maratha accounts this share continued throughout the eighteenth century to be referred to as the *moṇglāī*. The remaining 25% was to be collected by the Marathas as *cauth*, while the 10% *sardeśmukhī* was levied in addition to it, nominally without affecting the amount of the land-revenue demand. In the districts which were shared with the Nizam (i.e., all directly administered districts except the subha of Hyderabad) the Maratha collectors realized their dues in juxtaposition to the Mughal officials.[111] Disputes over the divisions of the revenue were of course rife, particularly also over additional levies which were highly variable. In fact the Marathas appear to have increased their demands constantly. Appeals from the Nizam to the Emperor to help curtail the Maratha collectors were of no avail. On the contrary the Emperor did not miss an opportunity to strike out at the Deccan subhedar. After Malwa was overrun and most of the country south of the Chambal occupied by the Marathas, the Peshwa applied to the Emperor for the assignment of Malwa in jagir and concomitant with it, as an imperial testimony of his increased power at home, the hereditary *vatan* right of *sardeśpāṇḍe* or 'head-district-accountant' of the Deccan.[112] Only this latter request was acceded to (in return again for a large *peśkaś*). Obviously the Emperor lost nothing by an arrangement of which the practical implications fell entirely on the Deccan. The grant was analogous to that of the *sardeśmukhī*, except that it was made to the brahman minister (and not to Shahu) and that the *rusūm* consisted of only half of the emoluments of the *sardeśmukhī*, hence a nominal 5% of the total revenues of the Mughal Deccan.[113] The Maratha encroachments upon Malwa and Hindustan nevertheless caused the Emperor shortly afterwards in 1737 to prevail upon the Nizam to return to Delhi and to restore to him the subhedaris of Malwa and Gujarat. This was on the condition that he would drive the Marathas out of these provinces. A new conflict with Baji Rao ensued. The Nizam was again strategically defeated at Bhopal in 1738 and had to promise the Peshwa to make over to Baji Rao the subhedaris of Malwa and his other rights over the territories

111 Malik, 'Chauth Collection in Hyderabad'; *idem*, 'Pargana Administration under Asaf Jah I'.

112 *SPD*, 15, no. 86 (p. 95); Grant Duff, *History*, 1, pp. 294–6.

113 These figures faithfully correspond to the normal proportions of the emoluments of the *deśmukh* and *deśpāṇḍe* in the Deccan. But in the accounts this is never brought up as an item separate from the *sardeśmukhī*.

between the Narmada and Chambal, and to have these confirmed by the Emperor with an additional payment of 52 lacs of rupees as war-indemnification.[114]

There were still at this date a number of Maratha sardars around Shahu who insisted – in accordance with the original proposal of the Pratinidhi, but contrary to the secret compact between the Peshwa and the Nizam – on invading the south and abandoning the northern conquests. The recent successes against the Nizam, his not keeping his promises, and possibly an invitation from Mir Asad, the divan of Safdar Ali, the Nizam's subhedar of the Karnataka, were sufficient motivation for Shahu to send an army under Raghuji Bhonsle and Fattesingh Bhonsle into the Karnataka in 1740–1.[115] They entered into an alliance with Safdar Ali for the collection of *cauth*.[116] The subhedar imposed it on the Karnataka Payanghat but Canda Saheb, the son-in-law of the Nawab of Arcot who had taken unauthorized possession of Tiruchchirappalli, refused to pay it. Raghuji Bhonsle invaded his territory, captured Canda Saheb, but then suddenly returned to Satara without consolidating his conquests and left merely a garrison. The Karnataka Balaghat was in this period fragmented into a large number of small chiefdoms which were all subjected to the payment of the *cauth* either directly to the Marathas or indirectly through the local Mughal government.[117] Thanjavur was itself a Maratha state, ruled by the descendants of Shivaji's brother Venkoji, who founded it between 1666 and 1675. Shivaji had left it in his brother's hands and consequently it was cut off from the Maratha *rājya* in the Western Deccan. In the eighteenth century it diminished in importance and remained in a position of isolation. Raghuji Bhonsle's invasion of the Karnataka Payanghat did not result in an alliance with the internally divided Thanjavur Marathas.[118] Raghuji, after his departure from the Karnataka, became involved in Bengal and Eastern India, and the south was left to itself until the rise of Hyder Ali. Here the Nizam re-established his sovereignty in 1743.

In the Mughal Deccan subhas there was a renewal of disputes

114 *SPD*, 15, no. 86 (pp. 86 ff); Grant Duff, *History*, 1, pp. 302–3.
115 Cf. Grant Duff, *History*, 1, pp. 309, 314, 545.
116 Malik, 'Chauth Collection in Hyderabad', p. 341.
117 *Ibid.*; Grant Duff, *History*, 1, p. 315; Ranade, *Rise of Maratha Power*, p. 249.
118 For the history of the Marathas in the Karnataka and of the Thanjavur principality, see Ranade, *Rise of Maratha Power*, pp. 238–54. The early exploits of Shahaji Bhonsle in the Karnataka are best described in Sardesai, *New History*, 1, pp. 234–53.

about *cauth* and *sardeśmukhī* with the accession of the new Nizam Salabat Jang. He was brought in dire straits by the Peshwa and all his districts in Khandesh – until then merely burdened with *cauth* and *sardeśmukhī* – were annexed by the Marathas under a treaty. Sanction from the Emperor came twelve years later in the form of an assignment to the Peshwa's sardar Malharji Holkar of the whole subha in Jagir.[119] In this way the annexation was not openly allowed but the six Mughal subhas of the Deccan were effectively reduced to five. Disputes over jagirs and arrears of payments culminated in an even more serious set-back of the Nizam in 1759–60.[120] A number of his forts were taken: Asirgarh, Daulatabad, Ahmadnagar, and Bijapur, while he had to give up holdings in the subhas of Aurangabad, Bijapur, and Bidar to the annual value of 62 lacs of rupees. From 1753 to 1760 the Peshwa – by then supreme in the Maratha government – organized a number of campaigns into the Karnataka to enforce payment of the *cauth*: to Srirangapatnam in 1753, to Bagalkot, Savanur and Harihar in 1754, to Bednur in 1755, to Savanur again in 1756, and to Srirangapatnam again in 1757. Maratha agents were expelled by the Mysore government almost immediately after the retreat of the army. Elsewhere in the Karnataka some districts were annexed and large sums were taken as *cauth* but the arrangements always kept changing. Maratha sovereignty in the south remained much more fragile and limited than in the north, or even in the Mughal Deccan subhas proper. In three consecutive campaigns the Marathas conquered the districts of Bijapur, Belgaum and Dharwar from the Savanur Nawab, the local representative of the Nizam. Afterwards the Marathas extended the conquests as far as the Tungabhadra but they remained in perpetual contest with Hyder Ali and Tipu Sultan of Mysore. The latter state was once briefly allied with the Poona government in Nana Fadnis' coalition of 1780 against the British; it was also among the first Indian states to be brought under Wellesley's subsidiary system. The Marathas exacted tribute from Mysore as early as 1726. (It was demanded earlier.) After 1776 Hyder Ali began to intrude into the Maratha territories in the Krishna–Tungabhadra Doab, thus forming a menace which precipitated an alliance of the Peshwa with the Nizam in 1784. This alliance was dissolved with the defeat of Tipu.

119 V. V. Thakur, *Hoḷkarśāhīcā Itihāsācīṇ Sādhaneṇ*, 2 vols (Indore, 1944–5), I, no. 118.

120 *SPD*, 25, nos 179–84; *MIS*, I, nos 73–119.

The Marathas then began to urge for outstanding balances of *cauth* and *sardeśmukhī* from the Nizam.

From the comparison of Malet it appeared clearly that in the 1790s the Nizam was not equal to the contest with the Marathas, but had, as the Mughal representative, retained superiority over the Peshwa merely in the protocol of address.[121] Three-quarters of a century of *cauth* and *sardeśmukhī* payments had drained his resources and reduced him to a condition of 'weakness and subjection'.[122] The Nizam could not evade the demands. In March 1795 his troops for the last time dodged the arbitrament of a battle against the assembled Maratha sardars at Kharda. A treaty was forced upon him a month later, stipulating the cession of *moṇglāī* holdings of over 35 lacs of rupees in Parenda and Daulatabad to the Peshwa, of 2.5 lacs of rupees to Nana Fadnis and others, an indemnity of 1 crore, and another crore for arrears of *cauth* etc., plus some payments and cessions to Raghuji Bhonsle and Daulat Rao Scindhia.[123] The political reversal at Poona occurring after the death of Peshwa Madhav Rao Narayan gave the Nizam some respite from enforcement of these stipulations. Nana subsequently restored some cessions and tribute to him to secure his support in installing Baji Rao II. Their secret compact was ratified by Baji Rao after he had become Peshwa. The Nizam was thus saved from a final débâcle but thought it safer nevertheless, as early as 1798, to enter into a subsidiary alliance with the British. During the nineteenth century and part of the twentieth the Nizam's dynasty survived as sovereigns of the largest Princely State under British paramountcy.[124]

c. Kolhapur

The argument with which after Rajaram's death in 1700 his widow Tarabai claimed the Maratha throne for her son Shivaji and opposed the elder branch of the Bhonsle family was a spurious one, for, as we have seen, Rajaram had personally declared he assumed

[121] Cf. p. 41.
[122] C. W. Malet to W. Kirkpatrick, 2 August 1794, *PRC*, 4, p. 118.
[123] 'Account of the sums to be paid and the territorial cessions to be made by the Nizam to the Marathas, conformably to the convention of Khurdah, officially communicated to the British Resident by order of His Highness', *ibid.*, pp. 307–13; *IS*, 6, 7–8–9 (1915), 'Peśve Daftarāṇtīl Sanadāpatrāṇtīl Māhitī', pp. 76–7.
[124] Thompson, *Indian Princes*, pp. 13, 15, 200, 278.

the kingship only 'on behalf of' Shahu.[125] The case of Kolhapur illustrates however the way in which a matrix of marginal conditions can be brought to interfere with dynastic succession. Moving from fort to fort and supported by the Senapati Dhanaji Yadhava and Rajaram's former representatives in the west Ramcandra Pant Amatya and Shankarji Narayan Saciv, she was for seven years the self-proclaimed regent for her son, the Chatrapati and sole sovereign of the Marathas until Shahu was released from the Mughal camp and re-established the Satara throne in 1708. Already before his royal consecration Shahu had won over Dhanaji Yadhava with most of the army which had been sent by Tarabai to oppose him at Khed. Immediately afterwards negotiations for a division of rights appear to have begun. Thus a *tahnāmā* or 'treaty document' was written by Shahu less than a month after he ascended the throne which proposes 'not to take on each other's disloyal servants', the cession of all revenue, *ṭhāṇas* and forts to the south of the Varna and Krishna up to the Tungabhadra, the cession of the Konkan from Salsi up to the Panc Mahal, and the restoration of the districts of Miraj and Bijapur.[126] Tarabai was not willing to accept these terms and Shahu had to drive her further back from Panhala to Rangna. From here she continued her attempts to draw local landed chiefs and *zamīndārs* to her side by outbidding Shahu, whom she accused of *fitvā* and 'causing disturbances in the kingdom'.[127] Many servants of both sovereigns crossed to the other side several times in rapid succession, each time demanding additional concessions from the rival contestant for their allegiance.[128] Others like Candrasen Yadhava or Rambhuji Nimbalkar first left Shahu for Tarabai, then accepted service under the Mughals.[129] Daud

125 *MIS*, 15, no. 286. And cf. p. 87.

126 *MIS*, 20, no. 282.

127 E.g. Tarabai's letter to Khem Savant, the sardesai of Kudal, of 19 February 1708: 'Now Raja Shahu's *fitvā* took place and this caused disturbances in the kingdom. Some of our servants disregarded us and went over to him. These we no longer rely on; but you remained loyal to the Svami ... you did not join Shahu, [and] the Svami is pleased to send an order to continue to you the districts of Kudal, Banve, Dicoli, Sankhli, Maneri, and Pedne ... as your *vatan*' ('*sāṃprat rājśrī śāhurāje yāṇcā fitvā nirmāṇ hoūn rājyāṇt ḍohṇā jāhālā kitek sevak lokīṇ avakrīyā karūn jāūn tyāṇs milon ansārikhī vartṇūk āraṃbhilī āhe* ...&c.'; K.G. Sabnis (ed.), *Paṇt Amātya Bāvḍā Daftar*, vol. 1 (Kolhapur, 1937), no. 71).

128 *Ibid.*, no. 70; W. Courtney and J.W. Auld, 'Memoir of the Sawunt Waree State', *BGS*, n.s. n. 10 (Bombay, 1855), p. 2; *Sardesai Gharāṇyācī Itihās* (n.p., n.d.), no. 74; B. Kishore, *Tarabai and her Times* (Asia Publishing House, 1963), p. 81.

129 Kishore, *Tarabai*, pp. 117, 120, 126, 142–3; Pawar, *Tarabai Papers*, p. xiii and nos 10, 21, 137; *P.A.: List 13, Ru. 75, File 1044*, pp. 14–15.

Khan, the deputy of the Mughal subhedar Zulfiqar Khan, succeeded in drawing away other sardars directly from Shahu but eventually greatly strengthened the latter's position by recognizing his claims to the *cauth* and *sardeśmukhī* of the six subhas. Shahu's successes fluctuated but on the whole his following gradually increased. The two disputing Maratha sovereigns each found supporters among the two factions which opposed each other at Delhi: while Shahu allied himself with the Iranis and the Saiyid brothers (in particular with Husain Ali Khan), Tarabai and her son were allied with the Turanis and Nizam-al-Mulk. When Nizam-al-Mulk became subhedar of the Deccan in 1713 he patronized the weaker party of Tarabai from the outset. But Shahu was relieved by Balaji Vishvanath winning over Angria and thereby depriving Tarabai of her main supporter, after which they appealed successfully to a large number of other sardars.

After Shivaji's death in 1714, Sambhaji, the second son of Rajaram by a younger wife, was brought to the Kolhapur throne through the combined support of the Amatya Ramcandra Pant and Nizam-al-Mulk.[130] In this way the Amatya attempted to regain some of the authority which he had held during Rajaram's stay in Jinji, when he was his *Hukmatpanhā* or 'lieutenant', but which he had gradually lost under Tarabai. Shahu had offered him the post of Amatya in his own government in 1708 but the conditions of office had apparently not satisfied him and he continued to serve Tarabai. A list of the revenue assignments, hereditary rights, and other possessions which he held in 1713 still shows him as formally the Amatya of the Kolhapur Chatrapati Shivaji.[131] Under Sambhaji he was reinvested with the *Hukmatpanhā* authority but not before first attempting to strike the same deal with Shahu. His list of demands to which Shahu appears to have been prepared to accede mentions not only the post of *Hukmatpanhā* with precedence over the other ministers in all state affairs, but also large additions in revenue rights, the control over a number of forts, the post of *Amātya* for his eldest son and an assignment of revenue for his second son.[132] But it was the Kolhapur King who in 1714 granted him an almost identical list with the *Hukmatpanhā* auth-

130 Pawar, *Tarabai Papers*, nos 8, 12–13.

131 *BISMQ*, 21, 2 (1940), pp. 240–1.

132 A. Pawar, 'Palace Revolution at Kolhapur 1714 A.D.', in: M. S. Mate and G. T. Kulkarni (eds), *Studies in Indology & Medieval History* (Prof. G. H. Khare Felicitation Volume) (Poona, 1974), p. 166; *idem*, 'An Episode in the life of Ramchandra Pant Amatya', *BISMQ*, 28, 1–2 (1947), pp. 73–85; *TKKP*, 1, no. 274.

ority.[133] It seems a reasonable guess that the negotiations with Shahu were cut short by the intervention of the Peshwa.

When Nizam-al-Mulk came to the Deccan for the second time, in 1720, Sambhaji became practically a tool in his hands.[134] Shahu again attempted to reach a settlement with his cousin in 1725 when the Nizam began to meddle further with their dispute by setting himself up as 'arbiter'. The proposals of Shahu now comprised not only the territories, forts, and thanas of the earlier *tahnāmā* of 1708 and the stipulation not to take on each other's servants, but also a plan to extend in a combined effort the Maratha kingdom and to share on an equal basis the tributes levied and new conquests made in the Mughal districts of the Deccan and Karnataka.[135] No agreement was reached before the Nizam was defeated in 1728 and Shahu's sovereignty was recognized by him with the additional rights of *cauth* and *sardeśmukhī*. The Kolhapuris became completely isolated and were forced in 1731 to accept the Treaty of Varna.[136] The Kolhapur Raja obtained an independent sovereignty – in conformity, with some modifications and additions, with the *tahnāmā* of 1708 – within the wider Maratha *svarājya*. To the *cauth* and *sardeśmukhī* Kolhapur was entitled only to a portion of the subha of Bijapur beyond the Krishna.[137] The Raja of Kolhapur afterwards showed little interest in expansion into the Karnataka and did not take part in any of the campaigns nor claimed a share in any of the conquests made by the Raja of Satara and the Peshwa.[138] Like Thanjavur he isolated himself more and more. When Sambhaji visited Satara – every year from 1732 to 1736 and again in 1740 – it was to discuss minor adjustments of holdings. Military aid was sometimes asked for from Satara, but during Shahu's reign it was never given. With the Peshwa the relationship was one of animosity. Still, the Kolhapur state remained formally independent and it retained an *aṣṭapradhān* council similar to the one which was first introduced by the Chatrapati of Satara, but with hereditary posts remunerated with hereditary jagirs.[139] Many of the subordinates of Kolhapur continued to have landed rights on sanads of the Mughal Emperor, the Nizam or the Raja of Satara outside the territory (of

133 *TKKP*, 1, no. 291; Pawar, 'Episode'. 134 Pawar, *Tarabai Papers*, nos 13 ff.

135 Sardesai, Kale and Vakaskar, *Aitihāsik Patreṇ*, no. 14 (p. 39); Vad, Mawji and Parasnis, *Treaties*, p. 44 (tahnama 1).

136 Vad, Mawji and Parasnis, *Treaties*, p. 44 (tahnama 2); Pawar, *Tarabai Papers*, nos 50, 122, 173; *TKKP*, no. 83.

137 Cf. p. 97. 138 Elphinstone, *Report*, p. 16.

139 D. C. Graham, 'Statistical Report on the Principality of Kolhapoor', *BGS*, n.s. no. 8 (Bombay, 1854), p. 493; *TKKP*, 2, no. 128.

an odd 4000 square miles (10,000 square kilometres)) which the British in the nineteenth century thought to constitute Kolhapur proper.[140]

There were attempts to reintegrate the two sovereignties into one. When Balaji Baji Rao came to Satara in 1740 to be invested as Peshwa, he had a meeting with the Kolhapur Raja and the two made a secret pact to unite, after Shahu's death, under the sovereign head of Kolhapur while reserving the position of prime minister for the incumbent Peshwa.[141] This plan never materialized. The childless Satara King declared that he would adopt Sambhaji but on the condition that he had issue and as this was not the case a grandson of Tarabai was adopted instead. The Peshwa acquiesced and kept silent about the agreement he had made with Sambhaji. He visited the Kolhapur Raja twice – first in 1754 and again in 1759 – to conciliate him and conclude agreements about military and financial aid.[142] The Kolhapur Raja was still childless when he died in 1760 and thus provided the Peshwa with an occasion to attempt to bring the kingdom under his own sovereignty. The queen Jijabai prevented this by adopting a boy from the putatively related house of the Khanwat Bhonsles of Indapur and installing him as Shivaji II with herself as regent. The king took over the government personally in 1762 and reigned until 1812, in which period his state became virtually closed in on all sides by the Peshwa's assignment-holders: the Patwardhans, Rastias, Gokhales, and others. Continuous conflicts were the result, leading to British intervention in 1812. On several occasions nevertheless, the Peshwa provided aid to restore Kolhapur's sovereign authority over jagirdars who allied themselves with outside powers. After 1764 the main bone of contention between the Peshwa and the Raja of Kolhapur became the two southern talukas of Chikodi and Manoli. These were mortgaged to bankers (*sāhukārs*) who made over their revenues to the Patwardhans in lieu of a payment of 7 lacs of rupees for military assistance provided by them against Hyder Ali. The sardars of Kolhapur also repeatedly undertook campaigns into the Peshwa's dominions. In this they were soon to be encouraged by Hyder Ali. Mahadaji Scindhia was sent down in 1778 to prevent a possible liaison between the two states. From 1781 to 1793 a relative stability prevailed in the east, but a conflict broke out with the Savants of Wadi when Laksmibai, the wife of Khem

140 *BGS*, n.s. no. 8, p. 492.
141 Sardesai, Kale and Vakaskar, *Aitihāsik Patreṇ*, no. 246.
142 *TKKP*, 3, no. 136; Vad, Mawji and Parasnis, *Treaties*, pp. 45–8.

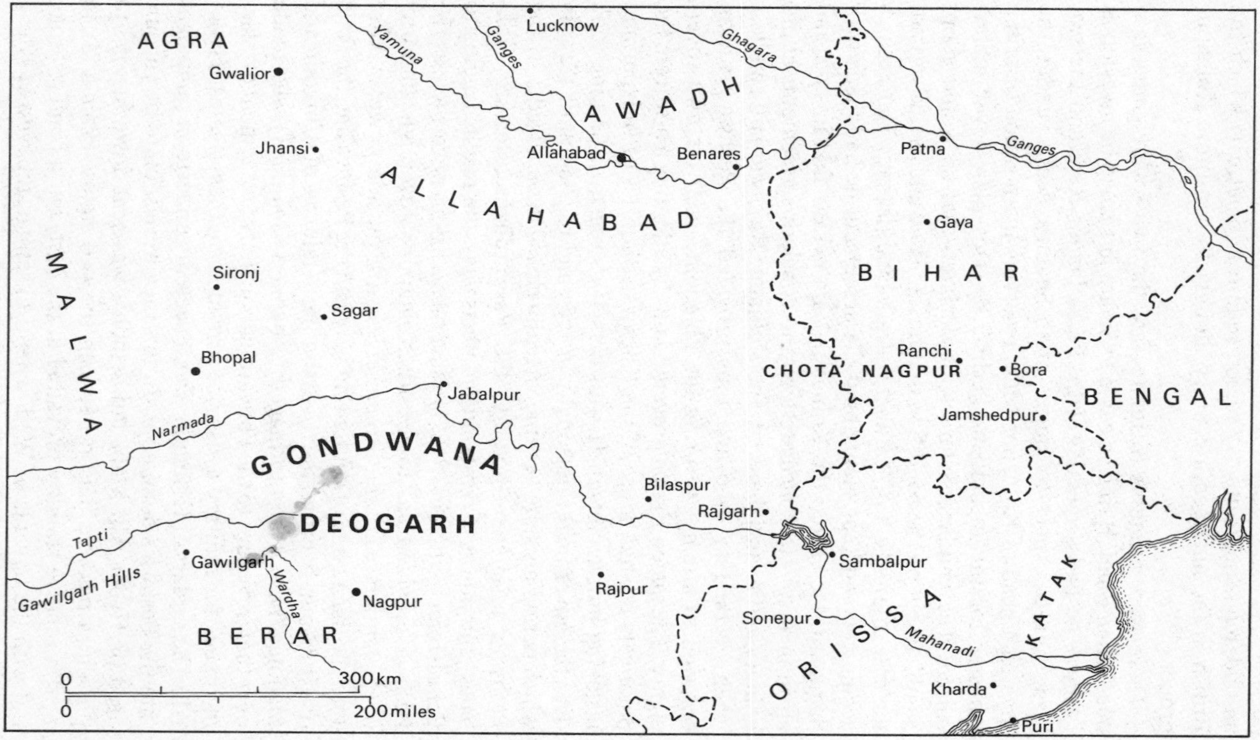

Berar, Bihar and Orissa

Savant and a half-sister of Mahadaji Scindhia, obtained for her husband the title of Raja Bahadur and some other emblems of royalty from the Mughal Emperor.[143] In 1778 the Kolhapur Raja, envious of the distinctions conferred on the Wadi sardesai, overran his country and captured some of his forts. These forts were not restored until 1793 through Mahadaji Scindhia's influence. But Khem Savant remained embroiled with Kolhapur for the greater part of his life, which ended in 1803. Conflicts with the Patwardhans broke out anew in 1793 with the recovery by Kolhapur of Chikodi and Manoli. These talukas were brought back under the sovereignty of the Peshwa in 1808 by Appa Desai. In 1811 the Raja solicited British arbitration. Issues which had never been very clear – and were not supposed to be so – now had to be decided unambiguously. The British were most of all at pains to find out whether the Peshwa had either ever possessed any claims to sovereignty over the Kolhapur Raja, or whether he was 'nominally dependent' on the Raja of Satara, or should be considered as 'a foreign power'.[144] It was at any rate certain that the governments of Poona and Kolhapur had rival pretensions over the districts of Chikodi and Manoli. Elphinstone declared them in 1812 to belong to the Peshwa exclusively.[145] To the Raja of Kolhapur the British became a guarantee against 'foreign aggression'. When the Third Anglo-Maratha War broke out in 1817 he immediately espoused the British. His sovereignty was thereafter maintained and demarcated under British paramountcy and Chikodi and Manoli were restored to it.

d. Berar, Bihar, Bengal and Orissa

The first Maratha conquests and *cauth* levies in the north-eastern direction were made, independently of the Peshwa, by Parsoji Bhonsle, a descendant of a family of *pāṭīls* or 'headmen' of the village of Hingni in the district of Poona claiming kinship with the Chatrapatis of Satara through a younger branch of the same family.[146] Not a single contemporary document relating to Parsoji

143 *BGS*, n.s. no. 10, pp. 3–4.

144 M. Elphinstone to chief Secretary Edmonstone, 16 October 1811, *PRC*, 12, p. 86; *idem*, to Gov. Gen., 27 June 1812, *ibid.*, pp. 170–1.

145 Extract from Manson's Report of 1 May 1853, *BGS*, o.s. no. 12 (Bombay, 1853), p. i.

146 In the nineteenth century this family of Bhonsles, known as the 'Bhonsles of Nagpur' or 'Bhonsles of Berar' after the capital and the region where they set themselves up in the eighteenth century, did not pretend to trace their origin further back than Mudhoji, the great-grandfather of Parsoji, and their preten-

has so far been discovered.[147] He appears to have been one of the first sardars to have joined Shahu after the latter's return from the Mughal camp in 1707. In recognition of this Shahu confirmed him in his conquests in Berar and the title of *Senā Sāheb Subhā*, which he held since the time of Rajaram. Parsoji died in 1710 and was succeeded in the same title by his son Kanhoji.[148] Under Balaji Vishvanath's expansion scheme the *Senā Sāheb Subhā* again received the Satara King's sanction of his exclusive right to Berar, Gondwana, Katak, and 'some mahals in Hindustan'.[149] It was professed that an imperial grant was received sanctioning the conquests and collections of *cauth* made in this region simultaneously with the grant of *svarājya*, *cauth* and *sardeśmukhī* in 1719.[150] In actual fact this latter grant covered the Mughal *subhā* of Berar, i.e., only the southern part of a much wider region which was known under the same name. Directly, the Bhonsles made their collections to the north of the Mughal subha under the title of a *fauj-saraṇjām* or 'military assignment' with delegated sovereign powers of *śikkekaṭyār* from the Raja of Satara.[151] All their further conquests, whether they led to the establishment of full sovereignty or merely the levying of *cauth*, were added to their assignment, always through the mediation of the Raja of Satara or the Peshwa. Kanhoji neither paid the shares of revenue which were formally due from him to the Raja nor did he obey the latter's orders regarding allowances to be paid to his uncle Ranoji and nephew Raghuji. In 1726–7 Shahu ordered a division of the *saraṇjām*: 2/3 of the portion assigned by the Peshwa, and 3/4 of the portion assigned by the Raja, were to be retained by the Senā Sāheb Subhā, while the rest was to be disposed of by Ranoji and Raghuji.[152] It was also stipulated that 3/4 of the tributes (*khaṇḍaṇī*) levied from the *paramulūkh* was to be divided among Kanhoji and Ranoji proportionately to the size of their respective armies (the remaining 1/4 being transferred to Satara), while Raghuji hereditarily received the district of Malkapur revenue-free in *inām*. Exasperated by such far-reaching interference, Kanhoji offered his service to the Nizam

sions to a defined relationship with the first Maratha king had either fallen into oblivion or were not seriously believed (Jenkins, *Nagpur*, p. 54).

147 *SPD*, 20, 'Introduction', p. 1.

148 Hervadkar, *Śāhū Caritra*, p. 94.

149 Cf. p. 72.

150 Hervadkar, *Śāhū Caritra*, p. 62.

151 *SSRPD*, 4, nos 226, 231; Vad, Mawji and Parasnis, *Treaties*, p. 141; K. N. Sane (ed.), *Kāvyetihās Saṃgraha* (n.p., n.d.), 'Nāgpurkar Bhoṇslyāṇcyā Saṃ baṇdāce Kāgadpatre', no. 8.

152 *SPD*, 20, nos 5, 7; *SSRPD*, 1, no. 163.

but Shahu had him imprisoned at Satara immediately afterwards.[153] Kanhoji's nephew Raghuji, a favourite companion of Shahu on his hunting expeditions, was then appointed as Senā Sāheb Subhā and Shahu had him married to the sister of one of his own wives (of the Shirke family), which is, probably, the only direct familial connection that can be traced between the Bhonsles of Berar and those of Satara.[154]

When Raghuji received the title of Senā Sāheb Subhā and the sanads for Berar he pledged himself to keep up a body of cavalry of 5,000 (to be increased to 10,000 if necessary) in the service of Shahu and his Peshwa, and to pay annually a sum of 9 lacs of rupees and half of all tributes and contributions (except *ghāsdāṇā*) levied.[155] In continuation of a practice which was to some extent already followed under Kanhoji and which was of common occurrence in all Maratha revenue assignments, a number of officials and auditors called *darakdārs* were hereditarily appointed from Satara to check the totals of the revenue receipts *in situ* and to serve as informing agents.[156] The Peshwas, after the mid century, employed the same officials; in the disputes that often arose between the different members of the Bhonsle family they always upheld the party which was favoured at Poona.[157] The Bhonsle Raja of Berar (as he came to be called) was thus not a sovereign king like the Bhonsle Raja of Kolhapur: instead of having an *aṣṭapradhān* or similar council of ministers he was provided with officials or clerks like a *muzumdār*, a *diwān*, and a *faḍṇīs*, originating from the central *huzūr*.[158]

In the 1720s and 1730s the town of Nagpur was still the capital of Deogarh, the Gond kingdom of Cand Sultan, whose dominions had been subjected to the *cauth* by Kanhoji but were not yet fully conquered.[159] Upon the death of Cand Sultan in 1735, one of his illegitimate sons usurped the throne and Raghuji Bhonsle was called in by the widow of the former ruler to help expel the usurper and secure the kingdom for her own two sons Akbar Shah and Burhan Shah.[160] Raghuji thus came to Nagpur in 1738 on invitation and he did set up the legitimate sons of Cand Sultan after putting to death the usurper Wali Shah. For this aid he received a reward of 11 lacs of rupees and an assignment on the revenues of several districts

153 *SPD*, 10, no. 73; 20, nos 10, 14.
154 Hervadkar, *Śāhū Caritra*, p. 52; Grant Duff, *History*, 1, p. 289.
155 Grant Duff, *History*, 1, *loc. cit.*
156 *SPD*, 20, nos 10–11; Jenkins, *Nagpur*, p. 77.
157 Jenkins, *Nagpur*, *loc. cit.* 158 *Ibid.*, p. 79. 159 *Ibid.*, p. 54.
160 *Ibid.*

but he returned for the present to Berar. In 1743 however the Marathas were called in again when dissensions broke out among Burhan Shah and Akbar Shah. They now supported the former and forced the latter to flee to Hyderabad. Raghuji then became the guardian of the Gond King and finally established himself at Nagpur, which he made his own capital and from where he gradually brought the whole of Deogarh under his sovereignty.[161] Burhan Shah's authority was maintained in form. The Marathas always allowed the Gond princes the title of Raja and the privilege of receiving and collecting their share of the revenue through their own officials.[162] A kind of formal pre-eminence was assigned to the Gond Raja by requesting him to give the *ṭīkā* mark of royalty to each successive Bhonsle ruler upon his accession and by making him entitled to put his seal on certain revenue documents. As a result the Bhonsle dynasty could found its right to the government of Deogarh on the consensus of the original rulers of the region. This nominal division of the sovereignty could distract nothing from its practical implications but underscored a qualified autonomy on the part of the Bhonsles with regard to the Satara Raja and particularly the Peshwa. It perhaps also reinforced their claim to superiority over the other Maratha sardars elevated by the Peshwa – a claim which they originally derived from their putative or real relationship with the dynasty of Shivaji. On account of such pretensions the Peshwas could usually only with much difficulty extort the Bhonsles' compliance. After first providing the mainstay for the Peshwa's coup, the Bhonsle Raja became apprehensive of the brahman government and began to consider himself accountable only to the Raja of Satara. In effect this meant that he was almost as much connected with the Nizam as with the Peshwa.[163]

The first open conflict with the Peshwa Balaji Baji Rao broke out in Bengal in 1742 and had to be settled by Shahu in the year following. The Mughal subha of Bengal, Bihar and Orissa had been appropriated by Ali Vardi Khan in 1740, shortly after the invasion of Nadir Shah. A relation of the then murdered subhedar, Sarfaraz Khan, solicited the intervention of Raghuji Bhonsle, while Ali Vardi Khan sought assistance from the Peshwa who aspired to establish the claims of *cauth* and *sardeśmukhī* over these provinces in his own name. The Emperor could only think of granting these rights to Shahu. Ali Vardi Khan first promised the *cauth* to the Peshwa, a prospect which tempted the latter to drive Raghuji's

[161] *Ibid.*, p. 55. [162] *Ibid.*, p. 75. [163] Elphinstone, *Report*, p. 16.

army from the province in 1743. On Raghuji's appeal however Shahu assigned in one sweeping resolution all rights to *cauth* and *sardeśmukhī* in Bihar, Bengal and Orissa as well as in Berar and Awadh to the Senā Sāheb Subhā.[164] Excepted were a mere 12 lacs of rupees from the *cauth* and *sardeśmukhī* of Bihar and some 'detached assignments' (*fūṭmokāsā*) in Berar, tributes from chieftains, etc.; these were added to the earlier sanctioned rights of the Peshwa in Northern and Central India, which on the occasion were specified as the 'campaigning right' (*svārī amal*) of Malwa, Ajmer, Agra, and Allahabad (Prayag or Antarvedi without Awadh) and the '*svarājya* of the *cauth* and *sardeśmukhī* of those provinces'.[165] The contestants were ordered not to interfere in each other's collections and to exempt the sacred cities. In an attempt to put a stop to the Maratha presence in Bengal and Bihar and thus to prevent the Nawab Ali Vardi Khan from building up closer ties with the Bhonsle Raja, the Emperor Muhammad Shah proposed early in 1746 to arrange for a lump sum payment of 25 lacs of rupees for the *cauth* of Bengal and of 10 lacs for that of Bihar, to be transmitted annually by the subhedar to Delhi, where it was to be handed over to the agents of the King of Satara.[166] Such an arrangement does not seem to have taken actual effect. Another treaty was concluded in 1751 directly with the Nawab to have paid an annual tribute of 12 lacs of rupees in lieu of the *cauth* of Bengal and Bihar, and stipulating the cession of a portion of the revenue of Orissa to the Bhonsle Raja of Nagpur.[167] The province of Orissa was divided into two parts, of which the northern part remained under the full sovereignty of Ali Vardi, while the southern, thinly populated part was given in jagir to the Marathas, with the intention of it being governed by Mughal officials.[168] But this fiscal right was gradually transformed into Maratha sovereignty over that part of the province which was called Mughalbandi (i.e., *Mughulbaṇdī*, 'obstacle to Mughal rule') comprising a large number of

[164] G. S. Sardesai, K. P. Kulkarni and Y. M. Kale (eds), *Aitihāsik Patravyavahār* (Poona, 1933), no. 35; *SPD*, 20, no. 31; Hervadkar, *Śāhū Caritra*, pp. 121–2; Grant Duff, *History*, 1, p. 327.

[165] We have seen in Chapter I–III–a (p. 72) that in 1719 the Peshwa was formally allowed to make collections of *cauth* and *sardeśmukhī* in Khandesh, Malwa and perhaps Baglana.

[166] J. Sarkar, *Fall of the Mughal Empire*, 4 vols (Bombay, Calcutta, etc., 1971), 1, p. 79.

[167] *Ibid.*, pp. 101–2; *PRC*, 5, 'Foreword' by Y. M. Kale, p. iii.

[168] Sarkar, *Fall*, 1, p. 104.

small tributary states or chiefdoms.[169] The chiefs, living in small forts surrounded by jungle, managed their own revenues and maintained armies but began to acknowledge the suzerainty of the Raja of Nagpur, paying him an irregular *peśkaś* in return for his effective support and arbitration in disputes. The most powerful of the chiefs, the Raja of Kharda, was a descendant of the Orissa royal family and the Marathas allowed him the royal privilege of conferring titles on the smaller chiefs throughout Mughalbandi and also in Garjat, the Mughal part of the province. The Kharda domain itself, like many of the other tributary chieftaincies, was parcelled out among 'jagirdars' bound to render service to the Raja and pay him a quit-rent in cowries or in kind.

After the death of Shahu, Raghuji Bhonsle was the Peshwa's crucial supporter despite the overtures made to him by Ramraja and his sister and Tarabai with the prospect of large additional assignments to prevent through him 'the Peshwa making a *brāhmaṇ rājya*'.[170] Raghuji acknowledged the Peshwa as 'equal in authority to Shahu'.[171] The Peshwa, after obtaining *de facto* supremacy, first saw himself obliged to issue new sanads to him for Berar, Deogarh, Bengal, Bihar, and Orissa and some more assignments adjoining Berar, but he soon began to feel uneasy about the Bhonsle's vast, compact and remote dominion, and from then onwards always tried to obstruct and curtail him. When in 1755 Raghuji died, the Peshwa could take advantage of a succession dispute among his four sons and divide the *saraṇjām* in three parts, while giving the title of Senā Sāheb Subhā to the eldest son Janoji.[172] This division, greatly weakening the joint power of the Bhonsles, was given effect in 1757 and persisted until the termination of Janoji's lineage.[173] Raghuji's four sons remained embroiled in domestic dissensions and consequently also began to question the Peshwa's right to intervene in their affairs, and they attempted to substitute the Peshwa's revenue claims in Berar for a lump sum with the right of collection reserved.[174] Military contingents from Nagpur took part in every campaign of the Nizam against the Peshwa but were absent

169 Shejwalkar, *Nagpur Affairs*, 2; B. C. Ray, 'Maratha Policy in Orissa', *Maratha History Seminar*, pp. 307–15.
170 *SPD*, 6, nos 19, 23, 50, 151; 20, nos 57–9, 65, 88.
171 '*jyāpramānen rāje śāhū hote tyājpramāṇeṇ peśve āhet*' (*SPD*, 20, no. 72).
172 The dispute arose on account of the juniority of Janoji's mother.
173 Jenkins, *Nagpur*, p. 76; Shejwalkar, *Nagpur Affairs*, 1, p. xii and nos 1–2 of the letters.
174 *SPD*, 20, nos 107, 114, 118.

at Panipat.[175] In 1762 Janoji conspired with Raghunath Rao in an attempt to overthrow the Peshwa; as a reward for his support he was promised the Satara throne, but the attempt failed. The year after, Janoji overtly joined the Nizam ('went under *pararājya*') and all rights and assignments which he held from the Peshwa were nominally sequestrated.[176] They were restored when Janoji again submitted to the Peshwa, which he did not without first receiving an additional assignment valuated at more than 3 lacs of rupees.[177] In 1766 the province of Berar was again temporarily sequestrated (nominally it appears) for Janoji's failing to take part in a campaign against Hyder Ali.[178] In 1768 Janoji was again involved in an abortive plot against the Peshwa with Raghunath Rao. The Peshwa now retaliated by organizing a campaign to Nagpur and enforcing restrictive demands: an annual tribute of 5 lacs of rupees, regular service to the Peshwa with 5,000 troops, a prohibition to increase the army, 'not to negotiate without the Peshwa's permission with the *pararājya*', 'not to engage in *fitvā*' and the cession of holdings worth 8 lacs of rupees.[179] After these dictates were made, a certain complaisance was evident on the part of Janoji and his successors Sabaji (1772–5), Mudhoji (1775–88), and under Raghuji II (1788–1816), until the dependence of the dynasty of Nagpur on the Peshwa was formally dissolved by the Treaty of Bassein with the British in 1803, but active service was never rendered.[180]

As Edward Thompson put it, the Bhonsle Rajas 'sat loose to the Maratha confederacy', and they were therefore 'easily detached' by the British.[181] Janoji Bhonsle had first come into direct contact with the East India Company after it had obtained the diwani of Bengal, Bihar and Orissa from the Emperor in 1765, and he had begun making attempts to recover, through the British Company, arrears of *cauth* to which he thought himself entitled according to the treaty of 1751.[182]

Clive offered to pay annually the 12 lacs and make up for three years of arrears in exchange for the cession of Orissa, but this offer was turned down.[183] Warren Hastings made another unsuccessful

175 *Ibid.*, no. 120; *PRC*, 5, 'Foreword', p. i.
176 *SPD*, 20, nos 136–7, 139; *SSRPD*, 9, no. 147.
177 *SSRPD*, 9, no. 148. 178 *SPD*, 20, nos 165, 168.
179 Sardesai, Kulkarni and Kale, *Aitihāsik Patravyavahār*, nos 116–20; Vad, Mawji and Parasnis, *Treaties*, pp. 135–40.
180 *SPD*, 20, no. 285; *PRC*, 5, *loc. cit.* 181 *Indian Princes*, pp. 57–8.
182 *PRC*, 5, *ibid.*, p. x; Sarkar, *Fall*, 1, pp. 107–9.
183 Sarkar, *Fall*, 1, pp. 108–9.

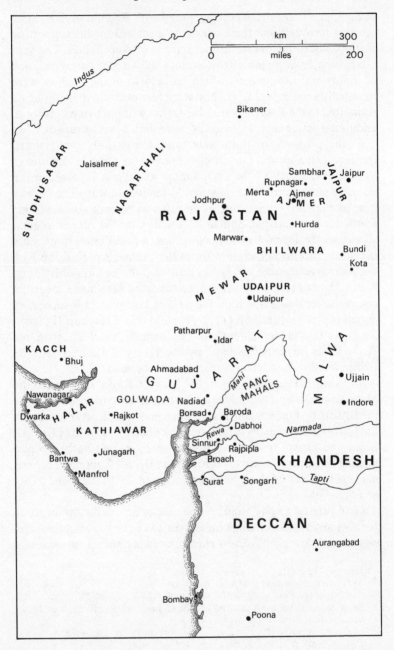

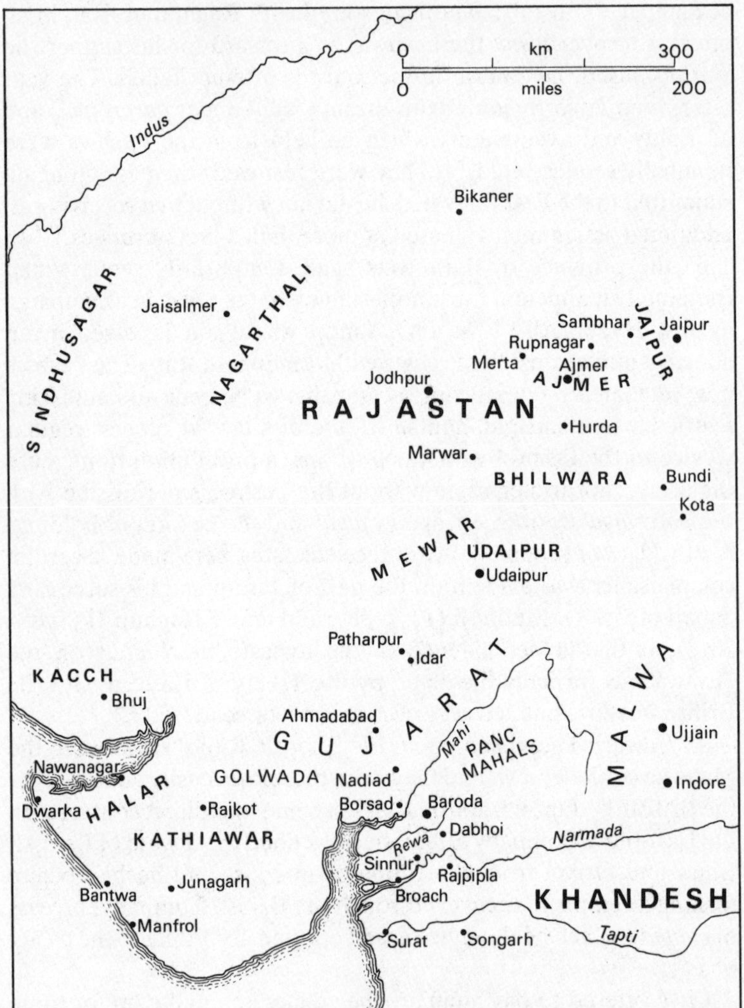

Gujarat and Rajastan

attempt to rent a tract of coast of Orissa. This same Governor-General also intended to raise Mudhoji Bhonsle to the Satara kingship after the death of Ramraja in 1777, in the hope of strengthening the Maratha Raj into a stable barrier against the French.[184] In 1781, when the Peshwa was at war with the British, the Raja of Berar concluded a separate treaty with the Governor-General and his Council, which stipulated that he would give no assistance against him to the Peshwa.[185] The first British Resident was posted at Nagpur in 1788 but the succession of permanent Residents did not begin before 1804, the year after the Treaties of Bassein and Deogaon were concluded. After this Elphinstone thought the Raja of Berar 'no more entitled to claim the Peshwa's assistance than he was bound to yield him obedience'.[186] By the Treaty of Deogaon the Raja was deprived of Orissa and the districts west of the Wardha and south of the Narmada and the Gawilgarh hills. Under Raghuji's successor Appa Saheb a subsidiary alliance with the British was concluded but after a year the Raja tried to break away from it and was sent into exile. A puppet was then set up until 1853, when the Princely State of Nagpur was annexed to British India proper for want of an heir.

e. Gujarat

After Shivaji's expeditions of 1664 and 1670 to Surat the Marathas did not reappear in the Mughal subha of Gujarat until 1702 when again *cauth* was collected from the same city. Three years later a large cavalry force crossed the Narmada and spread into Malwa and Berar, while a detachment of 15,000 penetrated further into Gujarat.[187] From 1705 up to the accession of Muhammad Shah in 1720 no other large-scale invasions took place but the Marathas made piecemeal collections of *cauth* in wide areas of Gujarat in annually organized *mulūkhgirī* campaigns of (for the Mughal armies) a highly elusive nature and under the command of an ill-co-ordinated number of sardars.[188] When Balaji Vishvanath went to Delhi to receive the imperial farmans for *svarājya* and the *cauth* and *sardeśmukhī* of the Deccan, Shahu had instructed him to try to obtain concomitantly the sanction of the *cauth* of Malwa and

184 Athavale, 'Restoration of the Chhatrapati', p.229.
185 *PRC*, 6, 'Palmer's Embassy', no. 431, 20 November 1801, p. 673.
186 Elphinstone to the Vice-President, 18 August 1811, *PRC*, 12, p. 60.
187 Irvine, *Later Mughals*, pt. 2, p. 165; Grant Duff, *History*, 1, p. 224.
188 Irvine, *Later Mughals*, *loc. cit.*; Dighe, *Peshwa Bajirao I*, p. 22.

Gujarat on the plea that if he could derive his authority from the Emperor he would be able to restrain his sardars in the until then unregulated collection of their 'established' tribute.[189] Such an expectation indeed, together with the need to build up local alliances against his own rival intent on replacing him, motivated the subhedar of Gujarat to give this sanction, but this was not before 1727 and lacked imperial endorsement. The draft of the Maratha–Mughal agreement of 1719 had included these concessions and the Marathas asserted that they were recognized. In fact, Shahu could only attempt to impose his own scheme of demarcations on the Maratha expansion to the north and for the time being had to make do without imperial or even subhedari acknowledgement. In this scheme the collections of *cauth* in the area of Gujarat, Ahmadabad and Kathiawar were assigned to the Senapati Dabhade, with careful provisions to remit stipulated amounts of revenue to the *huzūr* and submit accounts of the receipts and expenditure.[190] But other Maratha sardars continued entering the same area and probably did so without the prior authorization of Shahu. Dabhade had been active in Gujarat from the very beginning of the eighteenth century and this could have given him a right of precedence. The earliest document in the Peshwa Daftar relating to this family is a list of 1716 enumerating the holdings of Khande Rao, the first of the Dabhades who rose to greatness.[191] It shows that Khande Rao was then still titled *Āsnākhāskhel* and that he was the collector of the *cauth* of a large portion of Gujarat, consisting of fifty-four districts on both sides of the Mahi. The first recorded member of the Dabhade family, Yaspatil bin Bajpatil, was one of Shivaji's domestic adherents, who in remuneration for his services obtained from him the villages Talegaon, Uril and Dhamve (all near Poona) in *inām*.[192] He accompanied Rajaram to Jinji and was one of the first Maratha sardars to make incursions beyond the Deccan into Gujarat. After his death he was succeeded by his son Khande Rao who received many additional hereditary grants and assignments both within and beyond the Deccan and was eventually promoted by Shahu to the position of *Senāpati*, with the

189 Cf. p. 72.

190 Cf. *ibid.* The *Śāhū Caritra* says that 'from the revenue of this (area) he had to deduct the monthly payments and the *huzūr* expenditure, keep up the army, assign 6 mahals to the *huzūr khazgi*, give an account of the receipts and expenditure and exhibit any deficiency in the government's tribute' (p. 53).

191 *P.A.: List 13, Ru. 73, File 1025*, no. 960 of 1859.

192 *Ibid., Ru. 75, File 1044*, pp. 13–14.

command of 5,000 cavalry, in November 1716 when Candrasen Yadhava forfeited this title by joining the Nizam.[193] At the same time Khande Rao's son Trimbak Rao became *Senākhāskhel*.

The Dabhades soon delegated their campaigns in Gujarat to an especially distinguished lieutenant, Damaji Gaikwar, and after the latter's death in 1721, to his nephew Pilaji. These leaders who, like the Dabhades themselves, were only one or two generations away from village-headmen, were confirmed by Shahu as second-in-command in Gujarat under the Senapati with the title of *Saṃsār Bahādūr*.[194] Of the other sardars which in this period collected *cauth* in Gujarat it is not clear to what extent they worked in concord with each other or whether and when they received authorizations from Shahu. Kanthaji Kadam Bande and Udaji Pawar were the most prominent among them. The former carried out expeditions into Gujarat and Malwa from Khandesh. The latter appears to have worked in the same provinces, from 1722 onwards, on behalf of the Peshwa who had then obtained the right to collect half of the *cauth* of Gujarat and sub-assigned half of the *mokāsā* to Pawar to collect it.[195] Pilaji Gaikwar was at this stage able to acquire a *pied-à-terre* in Gujarat by conciliating local zamindars and the Bhils and Kolis at Songarh and allying himself with the Raja of Rajpipla. From these entrenchments he could easily organize *mulūkhgirī* into Northern Gujarat, repel (in 1723) the governor of Surat, and then begin the regular collection of *cauth* in Surat Athavisi.

We have seen that in 1723 Nizam-al-Mulk seized the subhedari of Gujarat after he had been appointed vazir of the Empire and subhedar of the six Deccan subhas and Malwa.[196] The Emperor on this occasion formally resumed all his charges but the Nizam refused to comply and, as in the Deccan, sought to make himself strong in Gujarat by an alliance with the Marathas. Nizam-al-Mulk had appointed his uncle Hamid Khan as his deputy for Gujarat. When the Emperor called him back to court and appointed Sarbuland Khan as the new subhedar, with Shujat Khan as his deputy, the Nizam persuaded his uncle to appeal to the Marathas and offer them the *cauth* and *sardeśmukhī* of the province for their

193 *Ibid., Ru. 73, loc. cit.*; *SPD*, 12, 'Introduction', p. 1.
194 *P.A.: List 13, Ru. 73, loc. cit.*; *SPD*, 30, no. 349; Irvine, *Later Mughals*, pt. 2, pt. 166; Grant Duff, *History*, 1, p. 262; Dighe, *Peshwa Bajirao I*, p. 26.
195 K. K. Lele and S. K. Oak (eds), *Dhār Saṃsthāṇcā Itihās*, 2 vols (Dhar, 1934), 2, pp. 10–11.
196 Cf. p. 95.

support against Sarbuland Khan. Hamid Khan was thus joined by Kanthaji Kadam Bande with 15 or 20,000 Maratha horsemen and drove back the deputy Shujat Khan. Bande was assigned the *cauth* and *sardeśmukhī* of all parganas to the west of the Mahi. At the same time all revenue remittances from Gujarat to the Mughal court at Delhi were for ever brought to a stop.[197] What followed was now merely a tussle among the Mughals for Maratha support through further concessions of what nominally continued to be referred to as *cauth* and *sardeśmukhī* but what in fact gradually and almost imperceptibly led to the establishment of full Maratha sovereignty and the eventual Mughal retreat from the province by the mid century. To oust Hamid Khan the Emperor first sent Rustam Ali Khan to Ahmadabad, the Mughal provincial capital of Gujarat. This noble tried to secure the assistance of Pilaji Gaikwar on a promise of a payment of 2 lacs of rupees, but the latter chose to co-operate with Hamid Khan, who offered him an equal share of *cauth* and *sardeśmukhī* as was assigned to Bande.[198] The Mughal overtures in the meantime drew still larger numbers of Marathas from the Deccan to Gujarat, until they exceeded 70 to 80,000. Rustam Ali Khan was killed and Hamid Khan could re-enter the subhedar's palace.[199] The Maratha collectors with their troops spread everywhere: in the districts to the west (on the Ahmadabad side) of the Mahi, which were assigned to Bande, and to the east (Baroda, Surat) of that river, the part assigned to Gaikwar. No permanent thanas were as yet set up; the Marathas returned after each rainy season from the Deccan. Hamid Khan's demarcations and authorization of the *cauth* collections of course could not avert all friction amongst the Marathas, the more so as his decisions to an extent ran counter to those of Shahu. Bande looked down on Gaikwar as merely an agent of Dabhade, yet Dabhade was considered the superior authority in Gujarat.[200] There was also the Peshwa's representative Udaji Pawar, who at this time appears to have been forced back into a more marginal position as the collector of the *cauth* in merely a number of parganas bordering on Malwa.[201]

In 1726 Sarbuland Khan, responding to a request of the Emperor, took the subhedari of Gujarat back in his own hands and

197 Irvine, *Later Mughals*, pt. 2, pp. 172–3.
198 *Ibid.*, pp. 176–7; Grant Duff, *History*, 1, p. 273.
199 Irvine, *Later Mughals*, pt. 2, pp. 179–83.
200 *Ibid.*, p. 184; Grant Duff, *History*, 1, *loc. cit.*
201 *SPD*, 30, no. 312.

succeeded in driving Hamid Khan out of the province to the Deccan. The new governor continued his predecessor's assignment of the *cauth* and *sardeśmukhī* of the districts to the west of the Mahi to Kanthaji Bande with only a futile change, that of exempting the *havelī* pargana around the capital Ahmadabad which he held as a private assignment.[202] On the east side of the Mahi however the Peshwa's general Udaji Pawar began to contend for the *cauth* with Pilaji Gaikwar. The latter was now present in Gujarat on behalf of Trimbak Rao Dabhade who had succeeded his father as *Senāpati* and whose efforts to increase his power the Peshwa intended to thwart by all means. When Bande joined Gaikwar, the Peshwa sent his brother Chimnaji Ballal into the province. Sarbuland Khan then chose to conclude a further, direct agreement about the *cauth* and *sardeśmukhī* with an envoy of the Peshwa for the whole of Gujarat (and Malwa), stipulating that the *bābtī* or 25% share of the Raja of Satara was to be transmitted as usual, while the rest was to be equally divided between the Peshwa and Dabhade.[203] A year later, in 1727, Sarbuland Khan issued two new sanads directly to Raja Shahu.[204] One was for the *sardeśmukhī* of 10% of the land-revenue of the whole of Gujarat – valued with the same 'universalist' precision as in the Deccan, which here too stands in such marked contrast with the fluidity of the actual political situation, at 413,080 rupees and 13 anas – to be given to Raja Shahu on payment of a *nazar* and to be transmitted to his treasury through his own collectors (*kamāvīsdārs*). In return for this the Maratha king had to 'serve the Badshah, punish marauders, repress thieves, and populate the country', while the Maratha collectors had to 'give assistance at the collection of the government's revenue in the crown mahals (*khālsā*) as well as that of the jagirdars'. The second sanad says that 'the *cauth* of the subha of Gujarat is given to Raja Shahu in *saraṇjām* (assignment) for the upkeep of 2,500 horsemen [whose task is] to punish marauders and populate and protect the country – in conformity with the petition of Peshwa Baji Rao'. For the *cauth* too a *nazar* was to be paid and a stipulation was added that it was to be collected by Maratha officials: two or three *kamāvīsdārs* in each pargana, working in accord with the collectors of the Mughal government and jagirdars.

There is no evidence of any imperial ratification of this agreement, in which the 'marauders' are presumably Gaikwar and his

202 Irvine, *Later Mughals*, pt. 2, p. 193.
203 *SSRPD*, 1, no. 105.
204 *SPD*, 15, no. 86 (pp. 84–5).

Bhils and Kolis, and Bande. Shahu was experiencing great difficulty in taking account of the growing antagonism between the Peshwa and Dabhade, the latter having become the focus of resistance against the brahman minister and enjoying the support not only of Pilaji Gaikwar and Kanthaji Bande but now also of an increasingly jealous Udaji Pawar, Kanhoji Bhonsle, and, at court, the Pratinidhi and the Sumant. Dabhade still claimed the whole of Gujarat as his province under Shahu's sanction. Shahu's attempt to placate Dabhade by assigning him in 1728 an equal share of the *cauth* of Gujarat with Chimnaji Ballal could therefore not prevent Dabhade, after the Peshwa's victory over the Nizam in the same year, from making proposals for an alliance with the Mughal subhedar of the Deccan.[205] Faced with this threat, the Raja decided to give precedence to the Peshwa and assigned to him the entire *cauth* collection of Gujarat and consented to have Gaikwar, Dabhade and Bande expelled from the subha.[206] This decision was made known to Sarbuland Khan and his officials; in 1731 it was followed up by a private pact between the Peshwa and Sarbuland Khan's successor Abhay Singh to the same effect.

Despite the support received from the Nizam, from Gaikwar and from others who were opposed to the Peshwa, the power of the Dabhades was considerably weakened when Trimbak Rao was killed by a stray shot at Dabhoi in 1731. From that moment the decline of the family began, eventually leading to its near annihilation. For the Peshwa Trimbak Rao's death was a crucial event in his rise to supremacy. Trimbak Rao's son Yaswant Rao made some attempts to re-establish the family's fading fortunes, but was for some time imprisoned by the Peshwa and he and his descendants, although still recognized by the designation of *Senāpati*, did not partake any longer in high politics.[207] For the present the Dabhades

205 Cf. Sane, *Kāvyetihās Saṃgraha*, 'Senāpati Dābhāḍe va Gāykvāḍ yāṇcī Hakīgat', p. 8: 'Peshwa Baji Rao Ballal . . . communicated to the Senapati that he would give half of the mahals in Gujarat to him and put him at the head of the Malwa conquests and himself take half of the mahals.' To this Dabhade answered that 'the Maharaja formerly assigned the conquest of Malwa to you and that of Gujarat to us: you take your province, we take ours and don't want to share'. See for the assignment by Shahu, *SSRPD*, 1, no. 159; *SPD*, 30, no. 317 (p. 299); Dighe, *Peshwa Bajirao I*, pp. 36–7 (referring to *Surat Factory Diary*). For the overtures of Dabhade to the Nizam, see *SPD*, 10, nos 59–73.

206 *SPD*, 15, no. 86 (p. 82); 12, no. 39.

207 *P.A.: List 13, Ru. 75, File 1044*, pp. 13–14. The Peshwa Diary (*ghaḍṇī* ledger) shows Yaswant Rao to have been the *Senāpati* in 1732–3 and his youngest brother Babu Rao the *Senākhaskhel*, and not Pilaji Gaikwar, as Grant Duff states (*History*, 1, p. 285).

however were continued in the possession of their jagirs and they were restored in the half share of the *cauth* and *sardeśmukhī* of Gujarat, while Shahu maintained them to some further extent as a counterpoise to the Peshwa by arranging that the latter's share of the revenue of Gujarat was to be paid to him through Yaswant Rao.[208]

Baroda and a large part of Eastern Gujarat were brought under full Maratha sovereignty by Mahadaji Gaikwar, after the murder of his brother Pilaji by the new Mughal subhedar Abhay Singh in 1732 had unnerved the Bhils and Kolis all over the country. In 1735 the same Gaikwar expelled Bande from Northern Gujarat. Damaji Gaikwar, the son and successor of Pilaji, was again allied with the succeeding subhedars Mumin Khan and Fakhir-ad-Daula from 1737 till 1743 and later. He was conceded half the city of Ahmadabad and the whole revenue of a considerable number of additional districts (amongst which Borsad and Nadiad) in return for his support.[209] From Trimbak Rao Dabhade's death in 1731 until Shahu's death in 1749, Damaji Gaikwar is described in the Daftar documents as a subordinate of Dabhade. Although the Gaikwar's rise to independent status in Gujarat began from around 1731 (or even before that), it was still not possible to detach himself from the Senapati. As late as 1747 Yaswant Rao Dabhade gave clear proof of this dependence by conferring on Damaji Gaikwar the title of *Saṃsār Bahādūr*.[210] When after the death of Shahu in November 1749 the Peshwa assumed sovereign power, the last vestiges of Mughal rule in Gujarat were about to disappear. The Peshwa, without any alteration of the conventional formula, first issued new sanads for 'half the *cauth* and *sardeśmukhī*' of Gujarat to Dabhade. Only when Gaikwar protested and, in conjunction with Tarabai, became a threat to the Peshwa's position, a proposal was made to him to hold half of the Gujarat revenue on his own account, but subordinate to the Peshwa, while leaving the other half to the Peshwa himself.[211] Gaikwar now 'returned the *śikkekaṭyār*, laid down his sword, and resigned from Dabhade's service'.[212] Further intrigues with Tarabai then led to the temporary confinement of both Dabhade and Gaikwar.

208 Grant Duff, *History*, I, *loc. cit.*
209 F. A. H. Elliot, *The Rulers of Baroda* (Bombay, 1934), p. 32.
210 Elphinstone to Secretary Warden, Bombay, 24 March 1816, *PRC*, 13, p. 29.
211 *Ibid.*
212 *Historical Selections from Baroda State Records*, 5 vols (Baroda, 1934–9), I, no. 40.

A transfer entry in the Peshwa's Diary of 15 May 1751 shows that nine sanads were issued on that date for the sequestration of Dabhade's holdings in the districts of Poona and Khandesh, and in Ahmadnagar and other districts of the Nizam.[213] Another entry of the Diary of 18 May 1751 shows that the Satara Raja had in the same year ordered Yaswant Rao Dabhade Senapati and his son Trimbak Rao Senakhaskhel to give up to the Peshwa half the provinces of Surat and Gujarat on both sides of the Mahi.[214] But instead of obeying this order they had protested against it, saying that they had lately agreed to pay a sum of 25 lacs of rupees as the revenue of the Peshwa's half share of these provinces of that year. In case they would fail to pay this amount, they would turn over to the Peshwa the whole of their Gujarat assignments from the following year onwards, with all the fortified places, etc., under the condition that the Peshwa was to retain them no longer than until the sum of 25 lacs was recovered, after which they were to be restored to Dabhade.

There is also in the Daftar a *vāṇṭṇīpatra* or 'deed of division' of Gujarat of the same year.[215] It specifies the component parts of the two above-mentioned shares, one of which is however termed as being that of Gaikwar, while the other as that of the Peshwa, who is termed the *sarkār*, i.e., the 'government' or 'superior'.[216] After some negotiating the Gaikwar appears to have agreed to pay to the Peshwa 25 lacs of rupees as arrears, to maintain 10,000 cavalry in his service and to pay an annual *peśkaś* of 525,000 rupees and a sum for the maintenance of the Senapati and finally to part with half of his new conquests. By the same arrangement the Peshwa obtained an annual assessed revenue in Gujarat of 2,468,700 rupees and the Gaikwar one of 2,372,500 rupees. Another *vāṇṭṇīpatra* exists, of 21 March 1752, in which the Gaikwar's share in the districts of Surat Athavisi and those between the Rewa and the Mahi and beyond is specified, with an additional provision that future conquests in the tract from Golwada to Dwarka and in Kacch Bhuj, Sindhusagar and Nagarthali were to be equally shared.[217] The Gaikwar's share

213 *P.A.: Peśve Rozkīrd, Ghaḍṇī Ledger*, 18 Jamādilākhar ihide khamsain.

214 *Ibid.*, 21 Jamādilākhar ihide khamsain.

215 *P.A.: List 13, Ru. 73, File 1025*, no. 960 of 1859; and see Elliot, *Rulers of Baroda*, App. IV: 'Territories obtained by the Gaikvad or the "Partition of Gujarat"'.

216 Compare 'Peśvyāṇcī Bakhar', *MIS*, 4, p. 46: '*gujrāthece mahāl nimme sarkārāṇt gheūn nimme gāykvāḍākaḍe dilhe āṇ damājī gāikvāḍ yācī beḍī toḍūn vastreṇ dilīṇ*'.

217 *Historical Selections from Baroda State Records*, 1, no. 56 (pp. 52–5).

in these districts which was looked upon by the two parties as already in his possession (including 12 *zortalabī* or 'unsubdued' mahals) was valued at 2,773,000 rupees. The collectors of the Peshwa appear to have been introduced in many of the districts comprising his share. Raghunath Rao again went on expedition into Gujarat after the rainy season of 1752 and took Ahmadabad, thus bringing into the Peshwa's hands the capital of Gujarat and expelling the last Mughal governor.[218] After it was taken, the city was divided between the Peshwa and the Gaikwar in a manner which subsisted up to the British conquest.[219] The Gaikwar made Baroda his capital. The districts of Surat, Halar, Golwada, and Kathiawar were also divided at this time, the Peshwa receiving as his share lands with a total assessed value of 2,259,000 rupees. The districts which were to be jointly managed were also specified and both parties bound themselves not to draw away from the other his *rayats*, *zamīndārs* and *mavāsī* chiefs, and to share equally new conquests of *zortalabī*.[220]

It cannot be ascertained when the Dabhades were released, but their holdings in the Deccan are recorded to have been restored to them in 1752.[221] Damaji Gaikwar ceased to be described as a dependant of Dabhade from the time of his own release, which occurred immediately after the partition. It is thus evident that Damaji was permitted to usurp the rights in Gujarat of Yaswant Rao Dabhade, the son of his patron Trimbak Rao, on the condition of his acknowledging the Peshwa's supremacy. The Peshwa in tacitly sanctioning this course, which was in fact similar to the one he had himself recently followed, not only effectually weakened forever his rival, the hereditary Commander-in-Chief of the Raja of Satara, but safeguarded for himself half of the Maratha conquests in Gujarat and secured the aid of a powerful leader, who, having become unpopular as an usurper and deprived of half of his resources, could no longer cause great annoyance to the Peshwa as an opponent. Yaswant Rao Dabhade's son Trimbak Rao, who on the death of his father in 1753 succeeded to his Deccan lands and to his title of Senapati (now an empty honour) in addition to his own title of Senakhaskhel which he held as heir apparent, again joined the Nizam and Janoji Bhonsle in 1761–2 in the unsuccessful attempt

218 *SSRPD*, 3, no. 63.
219 Elphinstone to Warden, 24 March 1816, *PRC*, 13, p. 30.
220 Vad, Mawji and Parasnis, *Treaties*, pp. 164–9; *Historical Selections from Baroda State Records*, 1, no. 56 (pp. 55–8). For the term *mavāsī*, see p. 196.
221 *P.A.: List 13, Ru. 73, loc. cit.*

made after the Battle of Panipat to subvert the brahman sovereignty in the Deccan. His family was therefore detained in the fort of Sinhagarh and all his possessions were sequestrated in the same year. In the following year the title of Senakhaskhel was conferred upon Damaji Gaikwar (on payment of a nazar of 500,000 rupees), and the sequestrated holdings of Dabhade were turned over to him in trust (*tasalmāt*).[222]

In Gujarat, throughout the second half of the eighteenth century, the Gaikwar dynasty exercised sovereign rights in what they knew to be their *daulat* or 'dominion', but they did so in subordination to the Peshwa and the Raja of Satara. Like the Bhonsles of Nagpur they formally enjoyed merely the status of *saraṇjāmdārs* or *jāgirdārs*, i.e., of 'assignment-holders', not of kings, and there were auditors and other supervisory officials resident in Baroda with similar titles as in Nagpur (*diwān*, *muzumdār*, *faḍṇīs*, etc.) and in the same way directly appointed from Poona.[223] Damaji Gaikwar regularly performed active service for the Peshwa and was present at the Battle of Panipat. He supported Raghunath Rao in the contest for the Peshwaship with his nephew Madhav Rao, on which occasion Raghunath received from Damaji a cession of six districts near Surat as a compensation for some deficiency in the Peshwa's share at the original partition. These districts – valued at 254,000 rupees – are often mentioned in later disputes.[224] After Raghunath's defeat and imprisonment in 1768, Damaji atoned for his disloyalty to the Peshwa and for his non-attendance of one year by the payment of a *nazar* of 2,325,001 rupees.[225] It was then also determined that Damaji was three years in arrears with the tribute payments which were due from him at 525,000 rupees per year, and moreover that this annual tribute was to be increased to 779,000 rupees per year from 1769 onwards in accordance with an agreement which was allegedly made during the reign of Peshwa Balaji Baji Rao. The contingent of cavalry troops which the Gaikwar was bound to supply was reduced from a nominal 10,000 to 3,000 (4,000 in emergency). Before this time the

222 P. M. Joshi (ed.), *Selections from the Peshwa Daftar* (New Series), 3 vols (Bombay, 1957–62), 3, no. 210; *Historical Selections from Baroda State Records*, 1, no. 100; *SSRPD*, 9, no. 143; *P.A.: List 13, Ru. 73, loc. cit.*

223 *MITSA*, 1, no. 13 (pp. 115, 117); Vad, Mawji and Parasnis, *Treaties*, p. 187; *Historical Selections from Baroda State Records*, 1, nos 60, 78; *SSRPD*, 4, no. 217.

224 *PRC*, 13, p. 30.

225 *P.A.: List 13, Ru. 73, loc. cit.*; Vad, Mawji and Parasnis, *Treaties*, pp. 167–9.

Gaikwar does not appear to have paid a regular tribute and to have served with whatever he could assemble.

Upon his death in the same year 1768, Damaji left the succession disputed between his eldest son by his second wife, Sayaji Rao, and his second son by his first wife, Govind Rao. After long investigations the Poona pandits decided for the second son by the first wife. Govind Rao succeeded to the *saraṇjām* in Gujarat and the other landed estates as well as the title of Senakhaskhel, on the condition of his fulfilling the terms of the last agreement made with his father and his paying a *nazar* of 2,100,000 rupees, and turning over to the Peshwa one-half of the districts conquered by Damaji from the Babi Raja of Patharpur. The sanad of recognition is entered in the Peshwa Diary on 21 September 1768. However, from Damaji's death up to that time, Fattesingh, the youngest son of Damaji, appears to have held the *saraṇjām* in charge for Sayaji, who himself was unfit for governing.[226] Fattesingh did not comply with the succession of Govind Rao and succeeded in having the decision revoked by the Peshwa and Sayaji's right confirmed with himself as *mutālīk* or 'deputy'. The family titles of *Saṃsār Bahādūr* and *Senākhāskhel* were also in 1769 conferred upon Sayaji, as appears from entries in the Diary of 10 and 11 October, but the usual honorary dress was presented to Fattesingh, who also paid the *nazar*. Govind Rao was set aside with a *saraṇjām* of a mere 3 lacs worth. It was now decided that the military service could be commuted into a payment of 675,000 rupees for each year of non-attendance.[227] This new facility was made use of in 1772–3 for the first time.[228] After the death of Peshwa Madhav Rao, followed by the murder of his brother and successor Narayan Rao, their uncle Raghunath Rao took over the Peshwaship and issued sanads on 13 December 1773 which reinstated Govind Rao in his paternal rights. But on the success of the party which was formed in favour of the infant Peshwa, the posthumous offspring of the murdered Narayan Rao, orders were issued for the sequestration of the whole assignment and all hereditary rights of the Gaikwar in Gujarat.[229] These orders are entered in the Diary on 29 March 1775.[230] Shortly afterwards in the same year the office of Senakhaskhel with the Gujarat assignment was conferred on Sayaji Rao Gaikwar and

226 Elphinstone to Warden, 24 March 1816, *PRC*, 13, p. 31. 227 *Ibid.*
228 *P.A.: List 13, Ru. 73, loc. cit.*
229 *SSRPD*, 4, nos 209–10, 212–13.
230 *P.A.: Peśve Rozkīrd, Ghaḍṇī Ledger*, 26 Muḥarram khamas sabain.

orders were issued to an official of the Peshwa at Ahmadabad to prepare seals bearing Sayaji Rao's name and to send them to him.[231] But these appear to have been revoked almost immediately. Still in the same year the sequestrated *inām* and *vatan* holdings of Govind Rao were restored to Fattesingh. After Raghunath's surrender in 1777, the latter was also confirmed in the Gujarat *saraṇjām* and in the rank of Senakhaskhel. Sanads for this are registered in the Diary on 23 October 1777.[232] Fattesingh agreed to pay a *nazar* of 500,000 rupees and an equal sum on account of arrears. Honorary dresses were presented to Fattesingh and to his principal dependants, among whom Sayaji Gaikwar is now mentioned.

In 1778 Fattesingh formed an alliance with the British through which he hoped to obtain the Peshwa's share of Gujarat to the north of the Mahi. In exchange for this he proposed to give up his share of the districts of Surat Athavisi, Broach and Sinnur to the British and serve them instead of the Peshwa with 3,000 cavalry. For lack of funds to continue a war with the Peshwa the Company however had to conclude the Treaty of Salbai in 1782, of which article VIII makes the Gaikwar their protégé and could but avert an impending sequestration of his Gujarat domains; as it stipulated 'the territory which has long been the jagir of Sayaji and Fattesingh Gaikwar, shall forever hereafter remain on the usual footing in his possession; and the said Fattesingh shall pay for the future to the Peshwa the tribute as usual previous to the present war, and shall perform such services and be subject to such obedience as have long been established and customary. No claim shall be made on the said Fattesingh by the Peshwa for the period that is past.'[233]

On the death of Fattesingh, his brother Manaji Rao was recognized as his successor by a sanad of the Peshwa, registered in the Diary on 18 May 1791.[234] He had on this occasion agreed to pay a *nazar* of 3,313,001 rupees and 3,687,000 rupees as the amount of arrears of tribute and commutation for the non-attendance of the contingent for three years. The name of Sayaji is mentioned amongst the dependants of Manaji, to whom the honorary dresses were presented. The Peshwa's records show that Manaji having

231 *SSRPD*, 4, no. 211.
232 *P.A.: Peśve Rozkīrd, Ghaḍṇī Ledger*, 20 Ramazān samān sabain; and see *SSRPD*, 4, no. 216.
233 C. U. Aitchison, *A Collection of Treaties, Engagements and Sunnuds relating to India and Neighbouring Countries*, 7 vols (Calcutta, 1862–76), 3, p. 52.
234 *P.A.: Peśve Rozkīrd, Ghaḍṇī Ledger*, 14 Ramazān ihide tisain.

failed to pay the stipulated nazar and other sums, his elder brother next to Sayaji, Govind Rao, was by a resolution of the Peshwa, dated 7 December 1792, permitted to take his place, on payment of a nazar of 5,638,001 rupees and arrears of tribute and non-attendance commutation of 4,362,000 rupees and giving up lands of the estimated value of 639,000 rupees to make a provision for Sayaji, Manaji and Malhar Rao Gaikwar, and on condition of conforming to all the terms dictated to him in 1768 by Peshwa Madhav Rao.[235] Manaji dying soon after, the terms described above, which do not appear to have been carried into force, were modified in so far that the amount to be paid was increased to 12,000,000 rupees, while the cession of land was reduced to a single district. The reason for Manaji's supersession by Govind Rao and for the modifications of the terms granted to the latter cannot be ascertained from the Peshwa's records. The modified terms granted to Govind Rao are dated 4 November 1793. Subsequent to this date there is nothing in the Peshwa's records to show that any succession in the Gaikwar family was recognized by the Peshwa's government before its close in 1818.

While the Treaty of Salbai of 1782 made the Gaikwar a protégé of the British, he was not yet disengaged from Poona. Nana Fadnis could still secure his co-operation in the Kharda campaign of 1795 against the Nizam. In 1799 the British annexed Surat and the Gaikwar was asked to hand over an adjacent district with it, a cession for which the Gaikwar affected to require the Peshwa's permission. In 1800 however the British had to settle the succession of Govind Rao by Bhagwant Rao Gaikwar. The latter accepted a subsidiary force in 1802, while the British Resident Walker became the *de facto* ruler in Baroda.[236] On the request of Peshwa Baji Rao II, after the death of Nana Fadnis in 1800, Govind Rao Gaikwar ejected Nana's agent Abu Shalukar from Ahmadabad and he took the Peshwa's share of the Ahmadabad revenue (the city, the Panc Mahals and the *mulūkhgirī* tribute from Kathiawar) in farm for five years.[237] This brought a temporary end to the system of divided government in the region.[238] On the instigation of the British Resident at Poona the farm was renewed in 1804 for another ten years in the name of Bhagwant Rao Gaikwar. The British favoured

[235] *Ibid.*, 22 Rabilākhar salās tisain; Vad, Mawji and Parasnis, *Treaties*, pp. 179–84; Elphinstone to Mr Secretary Adam, 21 September 1813, *PRC*, 12, pp. 277–82.
[236] Thompson, *Indian Princes*, pp. 16–17.
[237] See also pp. 366–7.
[238] Cf. Elphinstone to Francis Warden, Chief Secretary, 12 July 1814, *PRC*, 12, p. 333.

not only territorial consolidation of holdings and considered divided government an evil, but by the renewal they also expected to facilitate the severance of the relations between the Gaikwar and the Peshwa considerably. The Treaty of Bassein of 1803 between the Peshwa and the East India Company had acknowledged the subsidiary alliance between the Company and the Gaikwar and directed an adjustment of the Peshwa's claims on the latter to be adjusted by the British. But Baji Rao II could not be prevented from resuming the Ahmadabad farm in 1813, when he also renewed his claims to arrears of tribute.[239] A letter from the Supreme Government of 15 December 1802 expressly admitted the Peshwa's right to grant investiture to the Gaikwar and declared this right 'to be nowise incompatible' with its treaty with the Gaikwar.[240] Elphinstone at the time still denied the British 'a right of interfering in the domestic concerns of the Gaikwar'.[241] But in 1813 Elphinstone wrote to the Secretary at Bombay that with relation to the Gaikwar the Peshwa had made 'a formal call for our arbitration'.[242] The question to what extent there still was a connection between the two governments now became acute. Elphinstone thought the Gaikwar's treaty with the British 'by no means consistent with his ancient allegiance to the Peshwa', but at the same time observed 'that the article of the Treaty of Bassein in which the Peshwa acknowledged the treaty, declares that the said treaty was mediated and executed without any intention that it should infringe any of the just rights or claims of His Highness Rao Pandit Pradhan Bahadur (the Peshwa) affecting the Sarkar of the said Raja (the Gaikwar)'.[243] The legitimacy of the Peshwa's financial claims was not yet disputed in principle by the Gaikwar himself, who admitted the Peshwa's right to tribute, military service, and a *nazar* on his investiture, but he brought forward counterclaims to remissions and deductions.[244] The total amount claimed by the Poona government was 34,076,790 rupees. A vakil, Gangadhar Shastri, sent to Poona by the Gaikwar to adjust these claims and counterclaims,

239 Elphinstone to Mr Secretary Adam, 21 September 1813, *PRC*, 12, pp. 275–92; Elphinstone to the Earl of Moira, 5 November 1813, *ibid.*, pp. 301–3; F. Warden, Chief Secretary, to Elphinstone, 10 November 1813, *ibid.*, pp. 303–4; J. R. Carnac, Resident at Baroda, to Francis Warden, Chief Secretary to Government, Bombay, 31 October 1813, *ibid.*, pp. 304–6; Elphinstone to Warden, 5 January 1814, *ibid.*, pp. 308–10; Elphinstone to Gov. Gen., 11 May 1814, *ibid.*, pp. 324–6.

240 Elphinstone to Warden, 11 May 1815, *ibid.*, p. 370.

241 *Ibid.*, pp. 370–1.

242 *Ibid.*, p. 276.

243 Elphinstone to Warden, 24 March 1816, *PRC*, 13, p. 35.

244 *PRC*, 12, pp. 277–92; Vad, Mawji and Parasnis, *Treaties*, pp. 179–84.

was murdered (probably) on order of a confident of the Peshwa, Trimbakji Dainglia, and the British consequently held the Gaikwar's government absolved from all claims by the Poona court. The Gaikwar became henceforward a subordinate ally of the British and later achieved Princely status under their Paramountcy.

f. Malwa

The subha of Malwa, bordering on the Rajastan desert and Gujarat in the west and Gondwana and Bundelkhand in the east, was for the Mughals the political and commerical nexus between Hindustan and the Deccan. For the Marathas the conquest of this province was equally important as it enabled them to round off their northern possessions and made it possible to penetrate further into the heart of the Empire. The earliest accounts of Maratha invasions of the plateau are still vague.[245] Bhimsen says that from the times of the early sultans until 1699 the Marathas had never crossed the Narmada, but that in this year Krishna Savant, Hindu Rao Ghorpade and other Maratha sardars crossed the Narmada with 15,000 cavalry, 'entered the imperial dominions with wicked intentions' and 'collected a vast *saraṇjām* ("booty") by robbery'.[246] In 1703–4 the Marathas were near Ujjain.[247] The year after, Nima Scindhia crossed the Narmada and, supported by Chatrasal Bundela, entered the province as far as Sironj.[248] He then 'wished to go to the Ganga-Bhagirathi and Benares, but the local *zamīndārs* barred his path'.[249] After that incursions were not resumed until 1710.[250] A large-scale invasion of 30,000 troops took place in 1713 under Gangaram and Kanhoji Bhonsle, who marched into Malwa as far as Ujjain. In 1715 the Mughal subhedar Jai Singh scattered a Maratha force engaged in the collection of *cauth* and *sardeśmukhī* in the south-west. In 1716 the first Maratha outposts were permanently established on the Narmada and in 1717 Khande Rao Dabhade again levied contributions in Ashta, Deogarh, Sohoni, and in co-operation with Santaji Bhonsle repulsed the imperial troops.[251]

245 J. Malcolm, *Central India*, 1, p. 58.
246 Khobrekar, *Tarikh-i-Dilkasha*, p. 216.
247 J. Sarkar, *History of Aurangzib*, 5 vols (Bombay, Calcutta, etc., 1972–4), 5, p. 295.
248 Cf. Khobrekar, *Tarikh-i-Dilkasha*, p. 243.
249 *Ibid.*, p. 245.
250 Dighe, *Peshwa Baji Rao I*, p. 89.
251 *Ibid.*, pp. 90–1.

The claim to the *cauth* of the whole of Malwa was for the first time submitted to the Emperor in the same year and it was, with that of Gujarat, included in the draft treaty of 1718 but rejected. The Marathas however pretended that it was conceded and Shahu included Malwa in the assignment of the Peshwa as if it had been granted by the Emperor.[252] The Raja thus authorized his brahman minister to levy the *cauth* and *sardeśmukhī* in this province at the exclusion of other sardars. The Peshwa himself soon afterwards proposed to the Senapati Dabhade to exchange half of their respective charges in Gujarat and Malwa, but the latter refused the offer, and for the time being 'both acted upon the Maharaja's order'.[253]

After 1719 claims to both the *cauth* and the *sardeśmukhī* of Malwa were again put forward in 1724 when the Nizam established his practical independence in the six subhas of the Deccan, and both he and the Emperor sought Maratha support. Still, neither of them appears to have been hard-pressed enough to recognize these fargoing claims.[254] Meanwhile however, in Malwa as in the other Mughal subhas, the actual advance of the Marathas under the co-ordinating command of the Peshwa was strongly facilitated by the concurrence of interests of and aid received from the local Rajput chiefs and *zamīndārs*. The various Maratha leaders could insert themselves into the system of rights at various levels by becoming the supporter of one of the parties in a dispute in exchange for the payment of *cauth* and *sardeśmukhī*.[255] Of crucial importance for the Marathas was the co-operation they secured from Nandalal Mandaloi, the caudhari of Indore, who enjoyed wide influence among the *zamīndārs* in the region.[256] Wherever they established their sovereignty the Marathas took care to offer conciliating terms rather than press their revenue demands.[257]

From the year of his appointment onwards Baji Rao annually sent his troops from Khandesh into Malwa, but he did not enter the

252 Grant Duff, *History*, I, p. 250; Hervadkar, *Śāhū Caritra*, pp. 53, 57–8; S. N. Gordon, 'The Slow Conquest: Administrative Integration of Malwa into the Maratha Empire, 1720–1760', *MAS*, 11, 1 (1977), p. 12

253 Sane, *Kāvyetihās Saṃgraha*, 'Dābhāḍe Hakīgat', p. 8. And see note 205.

254 Chandra, *Parties and Politics*, p. 196; Gordon, 'Slow Conquest', p. 12.

255 Malcolm, *Central India*, I, p. 61; Sarkar, *Fall*, I, pp. 145–73; Gordon, 'Slow Conquest', p. 7; Irvine, *Later Mughals*, pt. 2, p. 244, note by Sarkar; Chandra, *Parties and Politics*, p. 203.

256 G. S. Sardesai, *Marāṭhī Riyāsat*, Pt. II, vol. 2 (Bombay, 1920), pp. 363–71.

257 S. N. Gordon, 'Scarf and sword: Thugs, Marauders, and State-Formation in 18th Century Malwa', *IESHR*, 6, 4 (1969), p. 423.

province in person until 1723. That year he collected *cauth* in the south. Another expedition led by the Peshwa took place in 1724. But then Nizam-al-Mulk was deprived of the governorship and replaced by the uncompromising Girdhar Bahadur, whose policy was successful in reducing Maratha influence in Malwa in the period 1724–8. The Peshwa was at that time embroiled with the Nizam in the Deccan and left behind in Malwa his sardars Pawar, Scindhia and Holkar to levy the *cauth* and *sardeśmukhī* where they could. It was determined that of these dues – which they termed the *svarājya* share – they would retain half of the *mokāsā*, while the other half was remitted to the Peshwa.[258] During the Peshwa's absence in the Deccan his sardars remained occupied in factional disputes among the Rajputs in western Malwa and the old rivals Dabhade and Bande took the opportunity to start encroachments upon the province and for some time threatened to form a coalition with the Mughal subhedar. Immediately after Palkhed the Peshwa's brother Chimnaji Appa invaded Malwa, defeated the Mughal forces, and overran most of the country. The Mughal subhedar was killed in the campaign, his administration broke up, and the Emperor appealed to the subhedar's son and successor Bhavani Ram to defend the province against 'the infidels'.[259] The Peshwa gave out new assignments of the *cauth* to his sardars.[260]

Mughal policy kept alternating between appeasement and resistance. In 1729 Sawai Jai Singh was appointed subhedar and he, during his first year of government, proposed to secure immunity from Maratha interference by granting Raja Shahu a jagir in Malwa of a value of 10 lacs of rupees.[261] The Mughal court quickly grew suspicious of his intentions and replaced him for two or three years by the Turani Muhammad Khan Bangash, but then re-appointed Jai Singh up to 1737. Amongst the Maratha sardars also the Peshwa redistributed the collections. Udaji Pawar lost the right to the half of the half-*mokāsā* of the province which he had received in 1722 and was substituted by his brother Yaswant Rao, taking a minor position next to Holkar and Scindhia. The nominal shares of *mokāsā* given out as military assignment which defined these sardars' positions relative to each other were now: 31% to the Peshwa, 30% to Scindhia, 30% to Holkar, and 9% to Pawar. These

[258] Sardesai, *Marāṭhī Riyāsat*, Pt. II, vol. 2, p. 375.
[259] Irvine, *Later Mughals*, pt. 2, p. 245.
[260] Lele and Oak, *Dhār*, 2, p. 25; *SPD*, 30, no. 316; Joshi, *Selections*, 1, no. 6.
[261] Dighe, *Peshwa Baji Rao I*, p. 102.

were immediately afterwards modified to the following: 45% to the Peshwa, 22.5% to Scindhia, 22.5% to Holkar, and 10% to Pawar.[262]

The Marathas were by this time in Malwa with about a hundred thousand cavalry.[263] At the head of another army the Peshwa had also entered Bundelkhand; this he did on the request of Raja Chatrasal who was then plagued by the Mughal governor of Allahabad, the same Muhammad Khan Bangash who later became governor of Malwa. In return for his support in expelling Bangash the Peshwa received a jagir from Chatrasal's sons Hirdesa and Jagat Raj of the value of 2.4 lacs of rupees and the promise of aid in Hindustan. The jagir was enlarged to 5 lacs soon after.[264] The incursions in Malwa itself were also extended, and the Maratha leaders further consolidated their contacts and tributary agreements with the zamindars. Sawai Jai Singh's policy of appeasement, leading to new concessions, only encouraged greater presumptions. In 1733 the subhedar's army had to extricate itself by a payment of 6 lacs of rupees in addition to the *cauth* of 28 parganas.[265] Again in 1735 the Mughal army had to buy forbearance from the Marathas with a *cauth* payment of 22 lacs of rupees.[266] These payments were nevertheless not sufficient to prevent Baji Rao accumulating very large debts – one reason why he began to apply through Jai Singh for the formal cession of the province in *jāgīr*.[267] The Peshwa himself was at the head of a large force marching into Malwa after the rains of 1735. An appeal was made to all Hindu rulers to unite

262 *SPD*, 13, nos 54–6; 30, no. 318; Lele and Oak, *Dhār*, 2, pp. 10–11.

263 Irvine, *Later Mughals*, *loc. cit.*

264 B. D. Gupta, 'Maratha–Bundela Relations', in: *Maratha History Seminar*, pp. 127–36; R. K. Jain, 'Kingship, Territory and Property in the Native States of Pre-British Bundelkhand, Northern Madhya Pradesh' (Paper contributed to the Fifth European Conference on Modern South Asian Studies, Leiden, 1976). Chatrasal declared Baji Rao his adopted son and first promised him a third of his kingdom. The correspondence between the Peshwa and the two sons of Chatrasal, Hirdesa, the Raja of Panna, and Jagat Raj, the Raja of Jaitpur, continues to acknowledge a sentiment of brotherhood. In proportion to his share of Chatrasal's estate the Peshwa agreed to pay a third of the cost of building the royal cenotaph (*chatrī*) for Chatrasal, as a real son would have done. The actual transfer of the 1/3 of the kingdom was indefinitely postponed. In 1731 Chatrasal's two sons handed over jagirs of 2 lacs and a quarter to the Peshwa's agents. In 1732 Chimnaji Appa came to Bundelkhand to secure the partition and realize tribute. It was again postponed. But in 1738 the receipt of jagirs to the value of 5 lacs was acknowledged (*SPD*, 14, no. 9).

265 *SPD*, 14, no. 2.

266 Dighe, *Peshwa Baji Rao I*, p. 118; Irvine, *Later Mughals*, pt. 2, p. 280.

267 Grant Duff, *History*, 1, p. 295.

under his banner for a demonstration of force which was intended to discourage the Turani opposition at the court in Delhi.[268] At the same time a detachment of the Peshwa's force invaded the realm of Abhay Singh of Marwar, a prince who strongly resented Maratha expansion and had allied himself with the Turanis.

Through his vakil Dhondo Mahadeo Purandare the Peshwa pressed the Emperor for the *subhedārī* of Malwa and the whole subha in *jāgīr*, including the Emperor's forts but excepting the existing *ināms* and chiefdoms.[269] A host of smaller demands of mansabs, jagirs, indemnifications and the demand of the *sardeśpāṇḍgirī* of the Deccan, as well as a '*vatan* in Hindustan', went with it. All were promised but none were immediately acceded to. The demands then appear to have been raised; added were a 2 lacs reward to the Peshwa's brother for his 'service to the sarkar (the Badshah)', the right to levy specified amounts of tribute from a number of rajas and zamindars of Malwa, a jagir of 50 lacs in Khandesh, Aurangabad and Bijapur, the fort Shivner, some *inām* villages, and for Shahu the kingdom of Thanjavur.[270] Later demands comprised also the relinquishment of forts commanding the passes into Malwa from the south to the Peshwa 'to keep his family in', the assignment of Allahabad, Benares, Gaya, and Mathura in jagir to the Peshwa, the districts up to the Chambal river also in jagir to the Peshwa, the Emperor's aid in expelling the Rohilla chiefs Yar Muhammad Khan and Ijat Khan from Bhopal, further pecuniary payments, and permission 'to meet the Emperor during a horse-ride, while being given leave immediately afterwards'.[271]

The demands thus became more and more excessive and in the end all that Jai Singh could persuade the Emperor to relinquish was the *vatan* of *sardeśpāṇḍgirī* of the Deccan. In 1736 Muhammad Shah issued a farman confirming to Baji Rao this *vatan* with its 'rights and perquisites (*hakrāī*)' and some *jāgīrs* and a *mansab* on condition of 'loyal service to the *sarkār*'.[272] In the same year a private agreement was reached between Jai Singh and the Peshwa

268 Joshi, *Selections*, I, no. 27.
269 *SPD*, 15, no. 86 (pp. 92–3).
270 *Ibid.*, (pp. 93–5).
271 *Ibid.* (p. 95). For Yar Muhammad Khan, see S. N. Gordon, 'Legitimacy and Loyalty in some Successor States of the Eighteenth Century', in: J. F. Richards (ed.), *Kingship and Authority in South Asia* (Madison, Wisc., 1978), pp. 286–303.
272 *SPD*, 15, no. 86 (p. 86). Sarkar, *Fall*, I, p. 171 says that the mansab was of 7,000 and that the Peshwa on the occasion was invited to visit the Emperor. The Marathi sources omit this.

for the latter to become the deputy-*subhedār* of Malwa under the former, but this as yet had to go without the authorization of the Emperor.[273] The other claims remained undecided during Baji Rao's lifetime. Jai Singh again incited the Peshwa to invade Malwa and urged him to push on to Delhi. In response the Emperor in 1737 re-appointed Nizam-al-Mulk to the subhedari of Malwa and Agra – now in the name of his eldest son Ghazi-ad-Din and on condition that he would drive the Marathas back beyond the Narmada.[274] The Nizam was given the 'supreme command' (*kul-yekhtiyār*) of the Empire.[275] He did not, however, have the slightest success in holding back the Marathas and had to sign a humiliating treaty with Baji Rao in 1738 at Daroha Sarai, near Bhopal, under which he promised to turn over to the Peshwa the *jāgīr* and *subhedārī* of the whole of Malwa and the tributes levied by him from all the rajas in the districts between the Narmada and Chambal, as well as the remittances that were sent to him from the Emperor, and to secure the latter's sanction for all this.[276]

The Mughals made no further attempts to retake Malwa. Shortly after the invasion of Nadir Shah, when the Peshwa again expressed his submission to the Emperor, the latter in his turn confirmed him (on payment of a *nazar*) in his rank, jagirs, and other rights, but still not in the *subhedārī* of Malwa, although this post was now considered disposable.[277] On the death of Baji Rao it was nominally given out to Azim Ulla Khan.[278] In 1741 however, Muhammad Shah, on the advice of Jai Singh, issued a farman bestowing on the Peshwa the *niyābat subhedārī* or 'deputy governorship' of Malwa under the Emperor's son Prince Ahmad, with the duty 'to punish marauders and resettle the rayats'.[279] In a *karārnāmā* or 'deed of agreement' Balaji Pant Pradhan agreed 'not to allow any other Maratha army (than his own) to cross the Narmada, . . . not to ask for additional sums of money, . . . not to invade any province outside of Malwa, . . . to serve the Emperor with 4,500 cavalry, . . . not to demand more than the established *nazars* and tributes from the zamindars south of the Chambal, . . . and to punish refractory zamindars (*zamīndār muṣasat*)'.[280] The four principal Maratha

[273] Irvine, *Later Mughals*, pt. 2, p. 284.
[274] *Ibid.*, p. 301; Grant Duff, *History*, 1, p. 300; *SPD*, 15, no. 53.
[275] *SPD*, 15, *loc. cit.* [276] Parasnis, *Brahmendrasvāmī*, no. 35.
[277] Sarkar, *Fall*, 1, pp. 169–70; Grant Duff, *History*, 1, p. 308.
[278] Grant Duff, *History*, 1, p. 321. [279] *SPD*, 15, no. 86 (p. 86).
[280] *Ibid.* (pp. 97–8). A Persian document, no. 18 in G. H. Khare, *Aitihāsik Fārsī Sāhitya*, vol. 4 (Poona, 1949), dated 12 May 1741, makes explicit that the

sardars working under the Peshwa, Ranoji Scindhia, Malharji Holkar, Yaswant Rao Pawar, and Pilaji Yadhava stood surety for the Peshwa's observing these terms on sanction of leaving his service.[281] A subsequently concluded pact with the Emperor was to withhold the Peshwa from forming alliances with the Nizam.[282] The Peshwa's government in Malwa was re-authorized by the Raja of Satara in 1744 when he settled his dispute with Raghuji Bhonsle.[283] From about this time the Marathas collected the entire revenue of Malwa without any participation by the Mughal Emperor. Only the eastern part of the province – about one-half of the whole – was directly administered by the Peshwa; in the west were located vast hereditary *saraṇjāms* of Holkar, Scindhia, Pawar and various smaller sardars.[284]

Of the three mentioned who built up hereditary dynasties but acquired royal status only under the British, the Pawars were one of the oldest and most distinguished Maratha families and were associated from the earliest times with the house of Bhonsle, on which account they considered themselves superior in rank to the Holkars and Scindhias who were promoted by the Peshwa. Udaji Pawar was also one of the first sardars – almost a decade before Baji Rao – to levy *cauth* and *sardeśmukhī* in Malwa and Gujarat and neither he nor his descendants ever reconciled themselves with the Peshwa's pre-eminence in the province. This was no doubt the main reason for their lapse into relative obscurity.[285] Udaji first established himself at Dhar but was forced to evacuate the place when Girdhar Bahadur was appointed subhedar. The Pawars however made secret overtures to Sawai Jai Singh to oppose Scindhia and Holkar in their claims.[286] After offending the Peshwa by uniting

agreement was arrived at through the mediation of Nizam-al-Mulk and with the consent of Azam Shah and Muhammad Saiyid Khan, i.e., with the approval of both the Turani and Irani parties. The terms mentioned in this Persian document are substantially the same, but the 'deputy-governorship' here comprises both Malwa and the districts between the Chambal and Yamuna, and service with 12,000 horse of which 4,000 were not to be held at the expense of the Emperor. A 'Peśvyāṇcī Śakavalī' (in *MIS*, 2, pp. 95–6) says: 'The Badshah was pleased to assign to his servants (*nokar*) Balaji Rao and Chimnaji Rao the task of *subhā* (004*subhedārī*) of Malwa; ... they will not make incursions into any other district ... no other Maratha sardars will cross the Narmada into Upper Hindustan ... they will remain loyal in the Badshah's service, etc.'

281 *MIS*, 2, p. 96; Khare, *Aitihāsik Fārsī Sāhitya*, 4, no. 19.

282 Khare, *Aitihāsik Fārsī Sāhitya*, 4, no. 20.

283 Cf. pp. 110–11. 284 Gordon, 'Slow Conquest', p. 39.

285 M. Malgonkar, *Puars of Dewas Senior* (Orient Longmans, 1963), p. 36; Grant Duff, *History*, 1, p. 267; Malcolm, *Central India*, 1, p. 98.

286 *SPD*, 14, no. 2.

with Dabhade, Udaji was replaced as head of the family by his younger brother Anand Rao. It was the latter who was commonly considered the founder of the principality of Dhar.[287] Anand Rao was the first to hold the district of Dhar with adjoining parganas and receive the tribute of some neighbouring Rajputs. The estate was once sequestrated when Khande Rao Pawar joined with Raghunath Rao. The deed of restoration of Madhav Rao specifically mentions it to be a *saraṇjām*.[288] Another branch of the family settled in Dewas, where they held a similar *saraṇjām*, equally under supervision of *huzūr kārkūns* of Poona, but of smaller extent and partitioned among two brothers and their descendants.[289] The Pawars held assignments and hereditary lands in the Deccan and Khandesh as well. For some time they were also entitled to receive 23% of the tributes levied in Hindustan; later, from 1788–9 onwards, this became 12% of the levies of 'newly conquered country'.[290] Holkar and Scindhia, with whom they shared the newly conquered country, were the chief direct cause of the ruin of the estates of the Pawars in Malwa after 1797, but even they continued to acknowledge the Pawars' superior rank.

The Holkars were, like the Scindhias, Dabhades and Gaikwars, village *vatandārs* of recent origin. The father of the first prominent military leader among them, Malhar Rao, was still a *caugulā* or assistant-headman (of the Dhangar or shepherd caste) in the village of Hol, near Jejuri on the Nira, whence they took their name. Up to 1721 Malhar Rao was a *śiledār* commanding his own horsemen in the service of Kanthaji Kadam Bande.[291] After this date he was always in the immediate service of the Peshwa, whose *mutālīk* Purandare appears first to have taken notice of him. He received his first *saraṇjāms* upon the *cauth* collection in districts north of the Narmada (Malwa, Gujarat) and Khandesh in 1727.[292] Additional assignments (perhaps seventy districts) were made over to him in 1728 and 1731, when he was also appointed *subhedār* of the collections of the whole province of Malwa, in association with Scindhia. This was probably designed to check Udaji Pawar and it may further explain the latter's constant search for allies amongst the Mughals and Mughal partisans against Holkar

287 Malcolm, *Central India*, I, p. 100. 288 *Ibid.*, pp. 102–3.
289 *Ibid.*, p. 112; M. V. Gujar, *Pavār Gharāṇyācyā Itihāsācīṇ Sādhaneṇ* (Poona, 1940), nos 124, 221.
290 *SSRPD*, 4, no. 250; 9, no. 155. 291 Thakur, *Holkarśāhī*, I, no. 6.
292 *Ibid.*, no. 10; Joshi, *Selections*, I, no. 6; Malcolm, *Central India*, I, p. 146 note.

and Scindhia.[293] It seems that at this time Muhammad Khan Bangash granted Holkar the *cauth* of the province for a year. In practice, in and after 1731 the *cauth* collection was divided between Holkar, Scindhia and Pawar. In 1733 Holkar was assigned the district of Indore. This grew into the hereditary dominion or *daulat* of the Holkars, while technically it remained a military assignment or *saraṇjām* for the support of troops with *darakdārs* appointed from Poona and the obligation to render annual accounts of the revenue – an obligation which was still fulfilled in the reign of Ahalyabai, late in the eighteenth century.[294] Holkar remained loyal to the Peshwa even at the height of his power and we find his conquests and acquisitions added to his *saraṇjām* under the same title, in Malwa, as in Hindustan, the Deccan and in Khandesh.[295] At times the Holkars were assigned lands by the Rajput Raja of Bundi, or more commonly, by the Mughal Emperor (Khandesh in jagir for example) whom they served through the Peshwa.[296] Malhar Rao Holkar survived by five years the Battle of Panipat. The *saraṇjām* was then passed on to his grandson Male Rao, but not without a thorough inspection of all the accounts.[297] Male Rao died within a year, the administration falling into the hands of Ahalyabai, the widow of Khande Rao.[298] She appears to have shared her authority with Tukoji Holkar, an official of the late Male Rao who adopted him. The succession *nazar* was paid by Tukoji. The latter attempted to gain full control of the *saraṇjām* but he was effectively opposed by the lady.[299] The division of authority was maintained for more than thirty years with Tukoji at the head of the military department and Ahalyabai at that of the revenue and civil administration.[300] Under the rule of Ahalyabai the Holkar state attained an unprecedented prosperity but the dynasty greatly lagged behind Scindhia in expansion.[301] The establishment of Maratha sovereignty in Hindustan was mainly due to the latter. In the period 1788–93 there were constant clashes between the two

293 Malcolm, *Central India*, 1, p. 146; *SPD*, 30, pp. 285, 292, 300, 304; Thakur, *Holkarśāhī*, 1, no. 23.
294 Malcolm, *Central India*, 1, p. 148; D. V. Apte (ed.), *Caṇdracūḍ Daftar* (Poona, 1920); *SSRPD*, 4, no. 266; Thakur, *Holkarśāhī*, 1, no. 50.
295 Thakur, *Holkarśāhī*, 1, nos 40, 50, 86, 90, 150, 244; *SSRPD*, 9, no. 162.
296 Cf. Thakur, *Holkarśāhī*, 1, nos 113, 118, 125.
297 *Ibid.*, no. 256. 298 *Ibid.*, pp. 158 ff.
299 *SSRPD*, 9, nos 172, 176; G. S. Sardesai (ed.), *Historical Papers relating to Mahadji Sindhia* (Gwalior, 1937), nos 215, 274.
300 *Poona Akhbars*, 2, nos 135, 138, 142, 147.
301 Thakur, *Holkarśāhī*, 1, nos 226, 287; Malcolm, *Central India*, 1, pp. 174–7.

sardars. There were also constant complaints from Tukoji to Ahalyabai about the manner in which newly acquired country (*navā mulūkh*) was distributed by Mahadaji Scindhia; what remained for them, after the deductions were made for Scindhia, the Peshwa and the Emperor, was nothing but 'waste land' (*mulūkh ujāḍ*).[302] Tukoji Holkar supplied a force of 10,000 and a vast number of Pindharis in the campaign against the Nizam in 1795, one year before his death and one year after that of Ahalyabai. Under his successor Yaswant Rao in Malwa the so-called 'period of trouble' or *gardī kā vakt* (1800–18) began. Yaswant Rao also invaded the Deccan in 1802 to support his demands for a cession of the new conquests in Hindustan. After this the Peshwa entered the subsidiary alliance with the British, who declared war on Holkar in 1804, simultaneously in Hindustan, Malwa and the Deccan, and soon broke his power. By the Treaty of Rajpur Ghat of 1805 the British acknowledged Yaswant Rao as the legal heir to the Holkar estates in Central India. The Treaty of Bassein had left Holkar, Scindhia and the Bhonsle of Nagpur each in the control of lands which did not exceed the value of 60 lacs of rupees.[303] Colonel Close maintained that by the arrangements of the Treaty of Bassein both Scindhia and Holkar were to be regarded as the heads of independent governments; this position however was still denied to them.[304] In 1811 Elphinstone wrote to Yaswant Rao Holkar that he 'had now for many years exercised all the functions of sovereignty without any reference to His Highness the Peshwa' and concluded that he stood in no need of a *khilāt* of investiture on the part of any state.[305] The British government thought an investiture of Yaswant Rao's successor Malhar Rao in 1811 to be 'fundamentally inconsistent with the whole system arising from the Treaty of Bassein', considering that it implied a practical recognition of a form of constitution the dissolution of which was the primary object of its policy.[306] By the Treaty of Mandasar in 1818 Holkar gave up all his claims in Rajputana, Khandesh and Bundelkhand and had to reduce his cavalry to 3,000, while accepting a subsidiary force from the British.

302 Thakur, *Holkarśāhī*, 1, nos 229, 233–4, 236, 241, 247, 249, 250.

303 Grant Duff, *History*, 2, p. 327.

304 N. B. Edmonstone, Chief Secretary, to Elphinstone, Resident at Poona, 31 May 1811, *PRC*, 12, p. 22.

305 Elphinstone to Edmonstone, 22 June 1811, *ibid.*, pp. 35–6.

306 Edmonstone to C. J. Metcalfe, Resident at Delhi, 2 August 1811, *ibid.*, p. 51; Elphinstone to the Earl of Moira, 5 November 1813, *ibid.*, p. 302; Elphinstone to the Secretary to Gov., Fort William, 4 October 1817, *ibid.*, p. 217.

Scindhia's power, as we noticed, in the later eighteenth century gravitated more and more towards Hindustan but the family rose to prominence in Malwa. The first Scindhia we hear from after Nemaji is Ranoji, a member of a Maratha family of *pāṭīls* of the village Kunnerkhar in Satara. Ambition induced him to enter the service of Balaji Vishvanath as slipper-bearer; once noticed by the powerful man his rise was spectacular.[307] First he was appointed to a commanding position in the Peshwa's body-guard. He soon afterwards led military campaigns into Malwa, where he received his first *saraṇjām* in 1729. In 1731 he came to share equally in the collections of the province with Holkar and received the Peshwa's seal.[308] In the British period Scindhia's name was associated with Gwalior, but actually Gwalior had not belonged to Scindhia until the last quarter of the eighteenth century, when he conquered it from the Raja of Gohad, then lost it to the British, but quickly recaptured it and obtained authorization for its possession from the Mughal Emperor.[309] Before that Scindhia's headquarters in Malwa were Ujjain. The Scindhia *saraṇjām* or *jāgīr* was worth about 65 lacs of rupees when Jayappa succeeded Ranoji in 1745. It was quite insufficient to pay for his ceaseless campaigning and made repeated borrowing from Holkar unavoidable. With Holkar he took to the field in 1751 against Abdali and the Rohillas. This they did as servants of the Peshwa, who himself avowed to serve the Emperor. Scindhia was a hereditary *saraṇjāmdār* exactly like Holkar and he equally held directly from the Peshwa (with the nominal confirmation of the Raja of Satara). The Peshwa regulated and authorized their successions, received their *nazars*, and sent his auditors or *darakdārs* from Poona to the *daulat*.[310] Despite their growing power they formally remained submissive – often demonstratively so – to the brahman government which was accredited with the sovereign rights over all their conquests, which they themselves merely held as assignments. Countless were the additions thus assigned by the Peshwas, in Malwa as well as in Hindustan, the Deccan and elsewhere.

Jayappa was succeeded in 1755 by his son Jankoji. In 1761

[307] See for the Scindhia family Malcolm, *Central India*, 1, pp. 116–41; Grant Duff, *History*, 1, p. 267.

[308] *SPD*, 30, no. 318.

[309] Thompson, *Indian Princes*, pp. 7, 95.

[310] Cf. *SSRPD*, 9, nos 159–60, 165, 167–8, 179; A. B. Phalke (ed.), *Śiṇdeśāhīcā Itihāsācīṇ Sādhaneṇ*, vol. 1 (Gwalior, 1929), nos 241, 244, 247; *MIS*, 13, no. 59. In 1756 the Peshwa demanded seven years' accounts when irregularities were discovered (Sardesai, Kale and Vakaskar, *Aitihāsik Patreṇ*, no. 148).

Scindhia's contingent was annihilated at Panipat, but Jankoji's son Mahadaji escaped from the battlefield and quickly re-established the family's power in Malwa after the death of Malhar Rao Holkar and then became the *de facto* sovereign of Hindustan. In opposition to Raghunath Rao, who favoured another member of the family, Mahadaji was confirmed in his rights in 1767 by Peshwa Madhav Rao.[311] His regular army not only subsisted on the revenues of his assignments but also on the tributes which it collected from the rajas in Rajastan. When the *gardī kā vakt* began in 1795, Scindhia was ejected from the Doab and the Deccan and was thus thrown back on Malwa by the Treaty of Sarje Anjangaon of 1803 with the British. At the same time his hold on Rajastan was weakened. In compensation his remaining possessions in Malwa were guaranteed to him independently of the Peshwa.[312] Daulat Rao accepted a subsidiary force in 1804 and survived the British victory over the Peshwa as a Prince. The *gardī kā vakt* and the devastations caused in Malwa by roaming bands of Pindharis were brought to an end by Hasting's Pindhari campaign, which merged into the Third Anglo-Maratha War and the subsequent Malwa Settlement by Malcolm in 1817–18.

g. Rajastan

The Marathas reached the outskirts of Rajastan via Malwa shortly after the appointment to the *peśvāī* of Baji Rao in the early 1720s.[313] *Cauth* was realized in Mewar in 1726.[314] Here Baji Rao took his tribute directly from the subordinate chiefs – until Shahu issued an order in 1728 not to invade the Mewar country.

Internal disputes among the Rajputs however soon provided new opportunities for interference. During the second quarter of the eighteenth century there were three main centres where Maratha assistance was sought: Bundi, Jaipur (Mewar) and Marwar.[315] After a while all three split, in true *fitna* fashion, into two united camps, each inviting the Marathas to decide the outcome of their dispute. This was repeated almost every year and made it easy for the invading Marathas to establish more permanent links in the province. In 1734, on the initiative of Jai Singh, the leading Rajput

311 *MIS*, 13, nos 59–60. 312 Thompson, *Indian Princes*, p. 92.

313 R. Sinha, 'Rajput–Maratha Relations', in: *Maratha History Seminar*, p. 255; K. S. Gupta, *Mewar and the Maratha Relations (1735–1818 A.D.)* (New Delhi, 1971), p. 21.

314 Gupta, *Mewar*, p. 23. 315 Sarkar, *Fall*, 1, pp. 142, 155–6.

princes met at Hurda in an attempt to confederate against the Marathas, while seeking support from the Mughals.[316] Such a unison of the Rajputs had not been achieved or even attempted since 1527 and it is not surprising therefore that nothing came out of the conference.[317] In 1735 Baji Rao personally set out on a mission to obtain sanads for *cauth* payments from the principal Rajputs. One result of this was an agreement with Mewar for ten years concerning an annual contribution of 160,000 rupees; this remained in force during the stipulated period but the amounts actually paid varied.[318] From 1735–6 onwards Holkar and Scindhia continued to make expeditions to Jaipur, Kota and Bundi as well as to Udaipur, Ajmer, Rupnagar, Merta and Mewar. Baji Rao's visit nevertheless forms a watershed in the relations with Rajastan: before this visit the small states paid the *cauth*, afterwards even the biggest like Udaipur and Mewar.[319]

The invasion of Nadir Shah in 1739 and the concomitant collapse of Mughal authority in Rajastan, the acquisition of the 'deputy-governorship' of Malwa by the successor of Baji Rao in 1741, then the death of Jai Singh in 1743 which was followed by the deaths of the other imperial Rajputs (Abhay Singh in 1749, and Ishwari Singh in 1750), the continuing succession disputes – all this allowed the Marathas to intensify their hold on the province and increase their demands for tribute. Now they also took to demanding succession fees or *nazars* expressive of their claim to a form of suzerainty over the Rajput states.[320] In contrast with Malwa and Gujarat, the Marathas did not establish any regular direct administration in Rajastan. In some cases, like Jaipur and Bundi, they succeeded in setting up their own nominees. Elsewhere, like in Marwar, a claimant at times still acquired his throne without their aid.[321] As in Orissa no collection could be made without the threat of applying military force. The repercussions of Panipat were felt in Rajastan but led to a neglect of the tribute collections only for a few years.[322] It fell to Holkar to restore Maratha influence in Rajastan.[323] With the resumption of Rajput internecine quarrels the

316 Sinha, 'Rajput–Maratha Relations', p. 264; Sarkar, *Fall*, 1, pp. 156–7.
317 Gupta, *Mewar*, p. 41.
318 *Ibid.*, pp. 43–5. 319 *Ibid.*, p. 47.
320 Sinha, 'Rajput–Maratha Relations', p. 266.
321 Sarkar, *Fall*, 2, p. 120. 322 *Ibid.*, pp. 359–66.
323 R. K. Saxena, *Maratha Relations with the Major States of Rajputana (1761–1818 A.D.)* (New Delhi, 1973); S. K. Bhatt, 'Holkar–Rajput Relations', in: *Maratha History Seminar*, pp. 197–203.

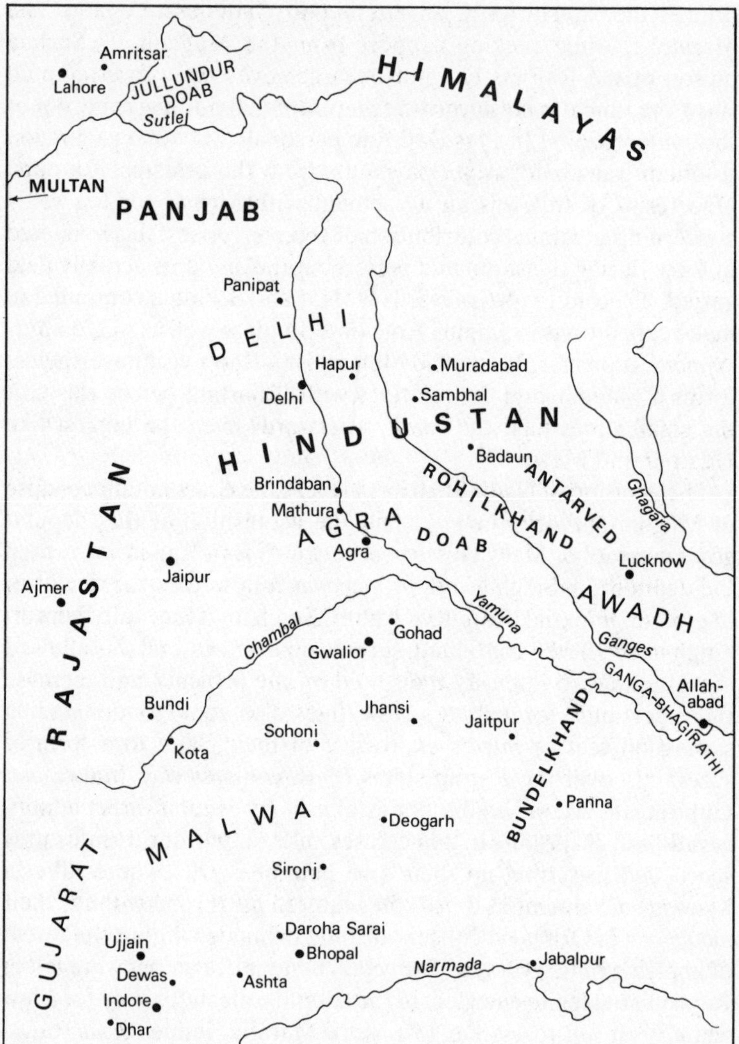

Malwa and Hindustan

Marathas again gained opportunities for interference. Predictably the rulers whom they provided with support commonly turned against their Maratha benefactors almost immediately after succeeding in their aim. After the death of Malhar Rao Holkar the collections from Rajastan – still essentially of tribute only – were mostly made by Scindhia, who with his Europeanized contingents quickly acquired a decisive superiority over the Rajputs. Holkar was expelled from all dominions to the north of Jaipur. For Scindhia Rajastan became an important source of income and a compensation for his unlucrative acquisitions in Hindustan. Scindhia obtained his tribute from the Rajput chiefs under direct sanction of the Emperor, but, like in Hindustan, he also claimed it in the name of the Peshwa.

h. Hindustan

The first important edict of the Raja of Satara concerning Hindustan proper[324] dates from 1744, the year in which he effected a division of the rights to *cauth* and *sardeśmukhī* between the Peshwa and Raghuji Bhonsle in Allahabad, Agra, Ajmer and Bengal and Bihar.[325] After conquering Malwa and establishing his hegemony in Rajastan the Peshwa undertook to support the Emperor against Ahmad Shah Abdali, the Afghan successor of Nadir Shah who had begun to invade Hindustan from 1747–8 onwards. As a consequence of these invasions – of which there were seven in the period 1748–67 – there was a general recuperation of Afghan power in the settlements of Rohilkhand, Allahabad, Darbaga, Sylket, and Orissa, signalling a come-back after being ousted by the Mughals in 1556. This eventually resulted in a contest with the Marathas for the control of the Mughal throne and the sovereignty of Hindustan – the remains of the Empire – in the Emperor's name.

After the death of Nadir Shah, Ahmad Shah Abdali claimed the Panjab as part of his inheritance and seized Lahore in 1748, but he was forced to retreat by the advancing Mughal forces under Prince Ahmad. After the Emperor's death, which occurred in the same year, power temporarily passed to the Vazir and Mir Atish Safdar Jang. The latter entered upon a two-year campaign against the

324 It is not uncommon to define Hindustan as 'that part of India which lies between the rivers Sutlej and Narmada' (E.g., Thompson, *Indian Princes*, p. 69). But the Marathi documents usually exclude Malwa and Gujarat from it, and it is in this sense that the term is used here.

325 Cf. pp. 110–11.

Rohillas and saw himself forced to call Scindhia and Holkar to his assistance. Their alliance brought a victory over the Rohillas in 1752, but the Afghans called on Abdali again to invade Hindustan and set aside the Vazir. The latter was now asked by the Emperor to attempt to conciliate the Rohillas through their representative at court Najib-ad-Daula. Abdali entered India for the third time in 1752 and annexed the two provinces of Lahore and Multan. Faced with this menace, the Emperor Ahmad Shah was at last persuaded to solicit Maratha assistance to break the Rohilla–Afghan axis and to secure 'the welfare of the Sultanate' of the Mughals.

In the characteristic universalist idiom, the *farmān* which was given on this occasion to the Peshwa and his sardars Malhar Rao Holkar and Jayappa Scindhia has taken the form of a reply by the Emperor to a petition of the Marathas in which they propose to serve him, 'punish the Emperor's enemies', in exchange for the *cauth* and a large number of *subhedārīs* and other such rights in Hindustan.[326] In the following year 1753 Safdar Jang was evicted

[326] Cf. *MIS*, 1, no. 1: 'Copy of a *farmān* to Balaji Baji Rao: An *ahadnāmā* is made with Malhar Rao Holkar and Jayaji (Jayappa) Rao Scindhia to the effect that they will wholeheartedly execute our orders and punish our enemies, whether these be Abdali or any other raja or big or small *zamīndār* and whoever does not submit to us, but do nothing more than this order implies. Accordingly they have to protect the welfare of the kingdom (*khairīyat sultanat*) and our dynasty itself. Our friends will be your friends and our enemies will be yours. Of a total sum of 50 lacs of rupees 30 lacs are given to you to redress Abdali. Of the subhas and faujdaris of Multan, Panjab, Thata, and Bhakar [in present-day Sindh] and of the Carmahal [?] and of the faujdari of Badaun and of Hisar, Sambal, Muradabad [in Antarved and Rohilkhand] the *cauth* is given to you to be applied to the expenditure of your army. And also given up to you are the subhedari of Ajmer subha and the faujdari and the mutaliki of Narnol [in Antarved] and Sambhar [in North Rajastan], as well as the subhedari of Akbarabad (Agra) and the faujdari and mutaliki of Mathura etc., and another great number of subhedaris and faujdaris with their nazars. You will make your own settlement of these subhas and faujdaris. And if someone seizes by force a prant which belonged of old to the Badshah or one of his nobles, then you shall take it back from him and give half of it to the sarkar and apply the other half of it to the maintenance of your army. And if you, on the occasion of making a prant *khālsā* or on the occasion of putting down an insurrection, shall have to employ extra forces, it is agreed between us that their expenses will be paid by the huzur. You will not bring under your power those places which were until now under the huzur itself. You will bring under government control the assignments of those jagirdars who do not perform government service, and you will take your *cauth* from them. Do not obstruct the revenue-officials of the Badshah. Punish robbers and rebellious killedars who obstruct the road and molest travellers [etc.]' (abbreviated translation). In a footnote the editor V. K. Rajvade says that the document (which is undated) is probably of 1750. It should however be 1752. The original *ahadnāmā* is in two parts. In the first of these the petition ('allow us') is made; in the second part the answer to the petition ('you will') is given.

from Delhi and compelled to retreat to Awadh. In 1754 the Emperor Ahmad Shah was deposed and with the aid of the Marathas Imad-al-Mulk was installed in the Vazirate. It was thus in 1756 the turn of the Emperor Alamgir II and Najib-ad-Daula to call Abdali to their assistance and have the latter installed as Mir Bakhshi or 'Commander-in-Chief'. Najib however was set aside again by the Marathas immediately after Abdali's departure. A new agreement was arrived at with Imad-al-Mulk for 'removing the government from Abdali and bringing it in the power of the Peshwa' in return for half of the revenue of the Mughal subhas in Hindustan.[327] Six subhas from Lahore to Attock were left to Abdali, who appointed here his son Timur Shah as governor to contend with the widow of the late Panjab subhedar of the Mughals, Mughlani Begam, and with the Sikhs. On the invitation of the latter and of Adina Beg, the governor of the Jullundar Doab, the Marathas for the first time invaded the Panjab in 1758. Timur Shah was driven back and replaced by Adina Beg, who agreed to pay a tribute to the Marathas. After the death of Adina Beg the Marathas were again in the Panjab in the year 1759, now acting as representatives of the Emperor. Abdali then invaded the province for the fifth time and again with the aid of his ally Najib-ad-Daula re-established his authority in Lahore. When the Vazir Gazi-ad-Din also joined with Abdali, Alamgir II resolved to give the 'plenipotentiary power' (*mukhtyārī*; Persian, *mu<u>kh</u>tār*) of the Empire to the Peshwa with the order to protect it with his army and assign to a suitable person the Vazirate and the Mir Bakhshigiri.[328] Nana Saheb Peshwa put the Raja of Satara in this combined position.[329]

Such was the constellation of ranks and powers on the eve of the Battle of Panipat. Despite the fact that in 1761 he virtually annihilated the Maratha army, Abdali retreated from Hindustan,

The document which is reproduced by Rajvade is a rambling translation of the original Persian for the perusal of the Marathas. In fact only the verbs are Marathi. Even the inflection of the nouns is done in the Persian manner. As Rajvade points out, no ruler in Hindustan could at this time conclude a *karārnāmā* or 'agreement' with the Emperor of Delhi on terms of equality, and this is why, according to the same author, it was given the form of a petition. Rajvade says further that 'by this sanad the Emperor of Delhi renounced the whole of Hindustan to the Peshwa, as Baji Rao (II) gave his whole state to the English'. It thus holds pride of place as the first document in the famous series *MIS*, the editor of which was a Citpavan brahman himself and perceptively remarks that the name of the Maharaja of Satara does not occur in it.

327 *SPD*, 2, no. 84. 328 *Ibid.* 329 *BISMQ*, 1, 1 (1920), pp. 41–4.

demanding merely an annual tribute to be paid to him and the recognition of Shah Alam as Emperor and to have Imad reinstalled as Vazir with Najib as Mir Bakhshi. For nine years the Rohilla leader remained master of Delhi and Hindustan. In 1770 Najib-ad-Daula allied himself with the Marathas in an attempt to save the Emperor from British tutelage. Scindhia brought the Emperor back from his exile in Allahabad to Delhi and installed him as a Maratha protégé in 1772 after the death of Najib. This event marked the return of the Marathas to Hindustan after the Battle of Panipat.[330]

Mahadaji Scindhia had recovered from the disaster most quickly and in 1767 he obtained the Peshwa's sanction for his succession to the *jāgīr* with the injunction 'to set off into Hindustan'.[331] Scindhia's acquisitions were all made in the name of the Peshwa, who himself acted as a servant of the Emperor. But the disproportionate power he accumulated in Hindustan gave rise to a life-long antagonism between Scindhia and the Peshwa's regent Nana Fadnis.[332] The share of the revenues accredited to the Peshwa in the newly obtained districts was nominal and Scindhia, on top of this, did not hesitate to make exactions in the Peshwa's country north of the Narmada.[333] Still, after 1775 Scindhia was the principal supporter of the Peshwa against his opponent Raghunath Rao and the British. The latter, after Raghunath's surrender, agreed under the Treaty of Salbai not to interfere with Scindhia's affairs in Hindustan and declared Mahadaji an independent sovereign. But Scindhia himself continued to pay the most scrupulous attention to the forms of submission in his relation with Poona.[334] Under the regency of Nana Fadnis all Scindhia's possessions to the south of the Chambal were brought under his direct authority but to the north of this river the Peshwa's name continued to be used and two agents from Poona attended him as supervisors.[335] The Peshwa also attempted to play Scindhia off against Holkar but the two became so hostile to each other that Holkar had to evacuate the area. In the second stage of Scindhia's career, which may be dated from 1784, his

[330] J. Sarkar (ed. and transl.), *Persian Records of Maratha History* (News-letters from Parasnis' Collection), 2 vols (Bombay, 1953–4), I.

[331] *MIS*, 13, nos 59–60.

[332] Cf. G. S. Sardesai, *The Main Currents of Maratha History* (Bombay, 1949), ch. 6.

[333] Malcolm, *Central India*, I, pp. 121–2.

[334] *Ibid.*, p. 122.

[335] *Ibid.*, p. 123; *SSRPD*, no. 406; Sardesai, *Historical Papers relating to Mahadji Sindhia*, no. 594.

pre-eminence became more firmly founded on his European military technique while his reputation was enhanced by his rescuing the Emperor from the hands of Ghulam Qadir. In all practical matters the Peshwa's sanction could only reinforce Scindhia's independence. To the same purpose Scindhia filled nearly all his key administrative and military positions with Gaud Saraswat or Shenavi brahmans who were opposed to the subcaste of Citpavans which were in power at Poona.[336]

The Emperor's power was for some time wielded by a Persian noble Mirza Nazaf Khan. After the latter's death Shah Alam invited Scindhia to take over the Mughal administration on his behalf.[337] Nana urged him to accept the responsibility but Scindhia's answer was that he needed time to make preparations and required more resources from Poona to keep the English at bay.[338] It appears that early in 1784 the office of *Amīr-al-Umarā* was offered to Scindhia by the Emperor, but that he had declined this offer as 'incompatible with the obedience he owed to the Peshwa'.[339] Later in the same year Mahadaji wrote to the Peshwa of a visit he had made to the Emperor on which he obtained for Nana and the Peshwa the *Bakhshīgirī* and the post of *Nā'ib-i-manāb* ('deputy'), while the superior office of *Vakīl-i-muṭlaq* or 'regent' was bestowed on Mahadaji himself despite his requesting the latter office to be bestowed on the Peshwa.[340] At the same time the provinces of Delhi and Agra were turned over to Scindhia's management and a monthly allowance was fixed for the Emperor of 1 lac and 30,000 rupees.[341] Nana's envoy Sadashiv Dinkar protested to Mahadaji for having secured a higher title for himself than for the Peshwa.[342] The Poona court did not accept Scindhia's explanation and refused to accept the lower dignities.[343] Scindhia then tried the argument that as *Vakīl-i-muṭlaq* he was only the servant of the Peshwa, but he again met with refusal.[344] The Poona

336 N. K. Wagle, 'The History and Social Organization of the Gauḍa Sāraswata Brāhmaṇas of the West Coast of India', *Journal of Indian History*, XLVIII, pts I and II (1970), p. 22; Sardesai, *Historical Papers relating to Mahadji Sindhia*, no. 358; Grant Duff, *History*, 2, pp. 144, 228, 246; *MITSA*, 1, no. 12 (p. 103).

337 Sarkar, *Persian Records*, 1.

338 Sardesai, *Historical Papers relating to Mahadji Sindhia*, nos 250, 297, 312, 318, 335, 339.

339 J. Anderson to W. Hastings, Gov. Gen., 25 November 1784, *PRC*, 1, p. 15.

340 Sardesai, *Historical Papers relating to Mahadji Sindhia*, nos 342–3, 359; Anderson to Hastings, 2 December 1784, *PRC*, 1, p. 17.

341 Sardesai, *Historical Papers relating to Mahadji Sindhia*, no. 411.

342 *Ibid.*, no. 371.

343 *Ibid.*, nos 372, 374, 377–8.

344 *Ibid.*, nos 391, 398.

court objected to accepting the titles as long as they were conditional upon Scindhia's being appointed *Vakīl-i-muṭlaq* directly to the Emperor; it wanted them without this condition.[345] Scindhia became impatient and sent messages to Poona that his authority in Delhi was being undermined by this attitude and he continued to urge the acceptance of the titles, arguing again that the Emperor would object to issuing them exclusively in the Peshwa's name.[346] It seems that eventually Scindhia was invested with the title of *Nā'ib-vakīl-i-muṭlaq* or 'deputy-regent' by the Emperor, second to the Peshwa who became *Vakīl-i-muṭlaq*.[347] Scindhia adopted a new Persian seal with the name of the Peshwa minister appearing on it as that of his master.[348] So it happened that on first entering Hindustan some grants were made in the Peshwa's name only, but when the latter became *Vakīl-i-muṭlaq* these were recalled and new sanads were given in the name of the Emperor with the seal of the Peshwa and Scindhia as his deputy.[349] Scindhia's relations with Nana Fadnis as well as with Holkar remained troubled on this titular question. It soon became clear however that Scindhia derived little or no profit from his new power. The newly acquired districts were mostly held by Mughal chiefs or *jāgirdārs* admitting a but nominal submission to the Emperor.[350] To keep the Sikhs at bay in the north Scindhia needed to increase his army but Nana, despite his ambition to intensify Maratha control over Hindustan, refused to supply funds. The only way out for Scindhia was thus the dispossession of the Mughal jagirdars or imposing heavy fines on them for non-attendance and press his demands of *cauth* from the Rajputs.[351] Scindhia's acute financial problems, coupled with a deteriorating relationship with the Emperor personally, were brought to the attention of Nana and were entirely confirmed by Sadashiv Dinkar in his dispatches to Poona.[352] But at times he finds it difficult to make an estimate of Scindhia's new revenues.[353] In particular there were disputes between Scindhia and the Emperor

345 *Ibid.*, no. 399. 346 *Ibid.*, nos 400, 403.

347 *PRC*, I, 'Introduction', p. ix. The date which is given here (1784) probably should be corrected as 1785 (cf. Sardesai, *Historical Papers relating to Mahadji Sindhia*, no. 404).

348 Sardesai, *Historical Papers relating to Mahadji Sindhia*, nos 411, 567, 577.

349 Malcolm, *Central India*, I, p. 123.

350 Sarkar, *Persian Records*, 2; Anderson to Cornwallis, Gov. Gen., 13 December 1786, *PRC*, I, p. 85.

351 Sardesai, *Historical Papers relating to Mahadji Sindhia*, nos 351–2.

352 *Ibid.*, no. 358. 353 *Ibid.*, no. 360.

about the management of the *khāzgī* or private demesne of the latter.[354] In 1785 Dinkar seemed sure that the new districts that Mahadaji was administering for the Emperor were all desolate.[355] British observers also reported in the same year that 'hitherto the measures of Scindhia in this quarter have involved him in much additional expense without yielding him any substantial advantages in return'.[356] It was commented that Scindhia had not yet seized the jagirs of the Mughal nobles, but that it was clear that since the greatest part of the country was parcelled out amongst them 'Scindhia without a resumption of them would never derive any benefit from his situation here'.[357] Scindhia had already abandoned the plan to possess himself of the jagirs of the Mughal princes and substitute these by cash equivalents – the reaction of the Emperor was too violent. It was apprehended that the other jagirdars had entered into secret negotiations with the Sikhs for an eventual junction with them in the case of resumption of their jagirs.[358] Scindhia probably intended to order the Mughal jagirdars to join the army of the Peshwa, in the expectation of meeting with their refusal and on that ground to resume their jagirs which he calculated to bring a profit of 60 or 70 lacs of rupees.[359] He was already facing then the discontent of all the zamindars and small rajas in the region, which he attempted to reduce through his own officials.[360] The jagirdars who owned their own forts were – in confederation – ready to throw off their dependence on Scindhia, and Scindhia gave up his plan to dismiss them for fear that he would thereby increase the power of his enemies.[361] From the Rajputs he claimed payments of arrears both for the Peshwa and the Emperor.

The British diplomat Anderson thought that Scindhia had at first undertaken his project in Hindustan in the expectation of treasure but that 'his views opened and enlarged themselves with the favorable events which afterwards fell out'.[362] His object, according to Anderson, almost certainly changed to 'connecting his own provinces of Malwa and Ajmer with those of Agra and Delhi to erect an independent Empire of his own and to shake off all subjection to the Peshwa'.[363] It remains improbable that Nana ever

354 *Ibid.*, no. 363. 355 *Ibid.*, nos 406, 607.
356 Anderson to John Macpherson, Gov. Gen., 23 March 1785, *PRC*, I, p. 20.
357 *Ibid.* 358 *Ibid.*
359 Anderson to Macpherson, Gov. Gen., 20 June 1786, *PRC*, I, pp. 69–70; Anderson to Cornwallis, Gov. Gen., 13 November 1786, *ibid.*, p. 85.
360 Anderson to Macpherson, Gov. Gen., 6 August 1786, *ibid.*, pp. 74, 88.
361 *Ibid.*, pp. 85–6. 362 *Ibid.*, p. 88. 363 *Ibid.*

derived any pecuniary advantage from Scindhia's activities in Hindustan and without doubt no remittances have been made to the Peshwa.[364] Scindhia indeed gave out to have greatly suffered in his private fortune by the service in which he was engaged.[365] He affected to be willing to abandon his acquisitions in Hindustan to Tukoji Holkar and came to Poona in person in order to give an account of his administration and to apply for a jagir in the Deccan as reimbursement for the enormous sums he had expended in establishing Maratha power in Hindustan.[366] In 1788 he explained to Sadashiv Dinkar that he had made the task at Delhi quite easy for his successor and asked him to request the Poona Darbar to transfer his charge to the Nizam Ali Bahadur.[367] Repeated requests followed. The intention of the Poona minister however was to supersede Scindhia altogether and to place the Maratha interests in Delhi in the hands of Holkar under the nominal authority of the Nizam Ali Bahadur. But Scindhia managed to bring Nana to his side and severed the connection between Holkar and Ali Bahadur.[368]

In 1788 Scindhia's detrimental preoccupations with the Rajputs allowed the Emperor to fall into the hands of the Rohillas, by whose chief Ghulam Qadir he was deposed after being forced to give him the titles of *Amīr-al-Umarā* and *Mīr Bakhshī*. Mahadaji reinstated the Emperor in his capital and even before the end of 1788 Shah Alam had renewed the title of *Vakīl-i-muṭlaq* to the Peshwa and that of his deputy to Scindhia.[369] It took some time to bring the zamindars and jagirdars back into submission but then the imperial administration and the disposition of the revenue reverted to Scindhia as completely as before. Ali Bahadur became a mere puppet and Holkar was soon to be expelled from Hindustan.[370] In 1790 the Emperor made the Peshwa's titles hereditary and inalienable; they remained conditional however upon Scindhia being appointed as his hereditary deputy.[371] In effect, the entire administration remained in the hands of Scindhia.[372] There were other

364 W. Kirkpatrick to Cornwallis, Gov. Gen., 26 April 1787, *ibid.*, pp. 178–9.
365 Kirkpatrick to Cornwallis, Gov. Gen., 26 April 1787, *ibid.*, pp. 180–1.
366 *Ibid.*, p. 180.
367 Sardesai, *Historical Papers relating to Mahadji Sindhia*, no. 535.
368 W. Palmer to Earl Cornwallis, Gov. Gen., 6 December 1788, *PRC*, 1, p. 326.
369 Grant Duff, *History*, 2, p. 148.
370 Palmer to Cornwallis, Gov. Gen., 15 December 1788, *PRC*, 1, p. 329; E. O. H. Ives to C. W. Malet, 10 January 1789, *ibid.*, p. 324.
371 Grant Duff, *History*, 2, p. 175.
372 Malet to the Chairman of the Hon. The Court of Directors, 16 December 1792, *PRC*, 2, pp. 253–5; *SSRPD*, 4, no. 117; Palmer to Cornwallis, Gov. Gen., 11 August 1790, *PRC*,. 1, p. 371.

farmans granting in perpetuity to the Peshwa the holy places of Mathura and Brindaban and prohibiting the slaughter of horned cattle throughout the assumed extent of the Mughal Empire.[373] Grant Duff thought it certain that Scindhia now aimed at replacing the brahman court and setting up his own authority at Poona.[374] When Scindhia marched southward to the Deccan this was ostensibly to deliver the farmans and insignia of the imperial office to the Peshwa. He arrived at Poona in 1792 and remained there until his sudden death in 1794, apparently not without settling the disputes with Nana and Holkar concerning the revenues and administration of Hindustan. But Nana did his utmost to prevent the Peshwa from accepting the new imperial titles, fearing that this would draw the Peshwa too close to Scindhia. Nana in particular thought the concomitant appellation of *Mahārāja Ādirāja* an improper arrogation on the part of the Peshwa *vis-à-vis* the Raja of Satara.[375] Scindhia had little difficulty in making the Raja comply.[376] The Peshwa was formally invested as hereditary *Vakīl-i-muṭlaq* of the Emperor with Scindhia as his hereditary deputy and both titles were – now for the first time – confirmed by the Raja of Satara.[377] Scindhia died at the height of his power when his vakils were stationed all over India and those of the Peshwa and Tipu Sultan were dismissed from Delhi; the *Pāṭīlbāva* was in the position to proclaim all imperial orders even at the court of Hyderabad and impress them with the Emperor's seal.[378]

The Treaty of Salbai was effected through the mediation of Mahadaji Scindhia. His death removed a major obstacle to British expansion in Hindustan. Mahadaji was childless but he adopted

373 *PRC*, 2, p. 254; Grant Duff, *History*, 2, p. 176; G. S. Sardesai, *Musalmānī Riyāsat*, vol. 2 (Poona, 1928), p. 432.

374 *History*, 2, p. 175.

375 Grant Duff, *History*, 2, p. 176; Sen, *Administrative System*, p. 117.

376 Grant Duff, *History*, 2, pp. 176–8; Sen, *Administrative System*, *loc. cit.*; *SSRPD*, 4, no. 275; Malcolm, *Central India*, 1, p. 123; *IS*, 6, 7–8–9 (1915), 'Peśve Daftarāṇtīl Sanadāpatrāṇtīl Māhitī', pp. 74–5.

377 On this occasion, according to Grant Duff (*History*, 2, p. 177), 'the pomp and grandeur displayed was beyond anything the inhabitants of Poona had ever seen'. The Mankaris and the old officials of the Raja of Satara refused to enter the imperial tents and withheld their *nazars* from the *Vakīl-i-muṭlaq*. The confirmatory *ājñāpatra* of the Raja of Satara (*IS*, 6, *loc. cit.*) recalls how Ghulam Qadir, a servant of the Badshah, 'rebelled' (*foṇḍ karūn*) and 'did much injustice' against him and put him in prison, but that 'then Mahadaji Scindhia came and punished Ghulam Qadir and his followers, settled the imperial country, released the Badshah and restored him on the throne.'

378 Sir John Shore's Minute on the death of Mahadaji Scindhia, 7 April 1794, *PRC*, 1, pp. 399–406; Sardesai, *Historical Papers relating to Mahadji Sindhia*, no. 429; Thakur, *Holkarśāhī*, 1, no. 294.

Daulat Rao, the son of his youngest nephew. This adoption was acknowledged by Nana and his court in 1794 and Daulat Rao thus became the heir to all the Scindhia estates in Malwa, the Deccan and Khandesh as well as to the deputyship of the post of *Vakīl-i-muṭlaq* and *Amīr-al-Umarā*.[379] The Peshwa attempted to use the opportunity for regaining some of his lost influence by introducing certain ceremonial limitations at Daulat Rao's nomination.[380] When the *khilāt* was conferred on Daulat Rao the Darbar for some time reserved the *śikkekaṭyār* and *jarīpaṭkā*, the specific insignia of the delegation of the Peshwa's authority, on the pretext of something inauspicious in the planets.[381] The complacence that Mahadaji had still shown on many occasions was not to be expected from his successor, who, raised in Hindustan amongst the Muslims and Rajputs and the British and from the outset in the possession of an army superior to that of any other Indian ruler, considered himself 'more the principal sovereign of India than a member of the Maratha confederacy'.[382] The first step the Peshwa took was to remove Scindhia's (and Nana's) nominee to the post of *Kulmukhtyārī* of the revenue management of Hindustan and substitute him by an agent of his own, Baloba Pagnis.[383] This, says a contemporary document, led to 'the ruin of the Sultanate'.[384] Daulat Rao's support of Baji Rao II signalled the end of Nana Fadnis' regency in Poona. As we saw, the fear of British intervention was one of the major reasons which made him return to Hindustan. Back in the north he again clashed with Holkar and ignored the Treaty of Bassein. The British declared war, destroyed his army, and dictated the Treaty of Sarje Anjangaon in 1803. Scindhia ceded the country between the Yamuna and Ganges and that to the north of Jaipur, Jodhpur and Gohad, the forts and districts of Ahmadnagar and Broach and the districts between the Ajanta Ghat and the Godavari. He also gave up all claims on behalf of the Mughal Emperor, the British government, the Peshwa, the Nizam, and the Gaikwar. Scindhia was thus cut loose from a web of political relationships which by their very delicacy had constituted the foundation of his power, and the year after he accepted a subsidiary force.

379 *SSRPD*, 4, no. 281. 380 *PRC*, 1, p. 400.

381 Malet to J. Shore, 7 March 1794, *PRC*, 2, pp. 336–8; J. Uhthoff, Ass. Resident, to J. Shore, 12 May 1794, *ibid.*, pp. 358–60.

382 Malcolm, *Central India*, 1, p. 132.

383 *IS*, 5, 4–5–6 (1914), 'Dillī yethīl Marāṭhyāṇcīṇ Rājkārāṇeṇ', no. 121.

384 *Ibid.*

IV Conclusion and summary

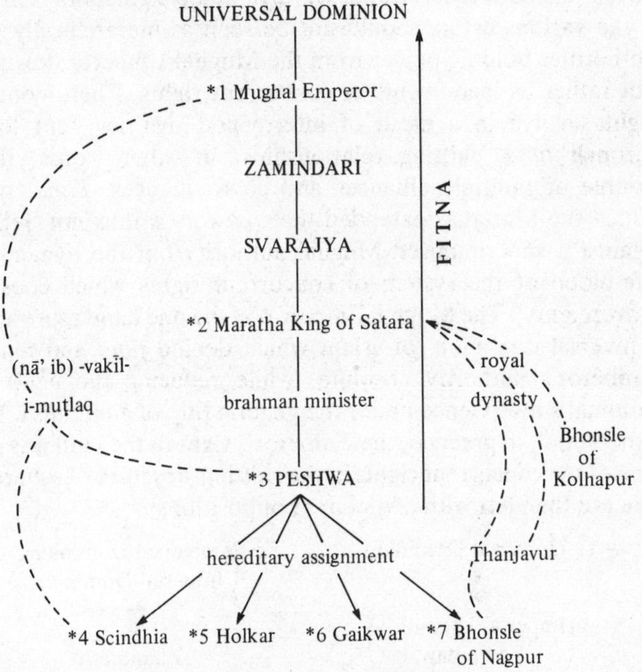

Paradigm of Maratha sovereignty in the eighteenth century

*1 *Mughal Emperors*	AD
Babar	1526
Humayun	1530
Akbar	1556
Jahangir	1605
Shah Jahan	1628
Aurangzeb	1658
Bahadur Shah	1707
Jahandar Shah	1712
Farrukhsiyar	1713
Rafi-ad-Darjat	1719
Rafi-ad-Daula	1719
Muhammad Shah	1720
Ahmad Shah	1748
Alamgir II	1754
Shah Jahan III	1759
Shah Alam II	1759
Akbar Shah II	1806
Bahadur Shah II	1837–58

*2 *Satara Kings*	AD
Shivaji	1674
Sambhaji	1680
Rajaram	1689
Tarabai	1700
Shahu	1708
Ramraja	1749
Shahu II	1777
Pratap Singh	1810

*3 *Peshwas*	AD
Balaji Vishvanath	1714
Baji Rao I	1720
Balaji Baji Rao	1740
Madhav Rao I	1761
Narayan Rao	1772
Raghunath Rao	1773
Madhav Rao Narayan	1774
Baji Rao II	1796–1818

*4 *Scindhias*	AD
Jayappa	1745
Jankoji	1755
Mahadaji	1761
Daulat Rao	1794
Jankoji Rao	1827

*5 *Holkars*	AD
Malhar Rao	1728
Ahalyabai	1765
Tukoji	1795
Yaswant Rao	1798
Malhar Rao II	1811

*6 *Gaikwars*	AD
Pilaji	1721
Damaji	1732
Govind Rao	1768
Sayaji Rao	1771
Fattesingh	1771
Manaji	1789
Govind Rao	1793
Anand Rao	1800
Sayaji Rao II	1818

*7 *Bhonsles of Nagpur*	AD
Kanhoji	1710
Raghuji	1727
Janoji	1755
Sabaji	1772
Mudhoji	1775
Raghuji II	1788
Appa Saheb	1816–53

In this paradigm an attempt is made to visualize the inward development of the Maratha *svarājya* in the eighteenth century. In it the various actors should not be seen as hierarchically graded authorities holding power from the Mughal Emperor downwards, but rather as incumbents of concurrent rights. These concurrent rights evolve in a mesh of intertwined rivalries kept together through *fitna*, shifting relationships, in other words, through double or multiple alliances and cross-alliances. *Fitna*, through which the Marathas extended their power, is thus not 'rebellion' against a superimposed Mughal authority but the dynamics and life-blood of the system of concurrent rights which constituted 'sovereignty'. The Mughal Emperor on the one hand represents the 'universal dominion' of Islam which denied *fitna* and made the Emperor's authority absolute, while reducing the gentry to a nominal subservience under the generic title of *zamīndārī*. On the other hand, in practice, the Emperor's right to the land was merely one of the concurrent rights in the shifting structure of sovereignty. We are then left with a system of oppositions:

1.	2.
Universal Dominion	(Universal Dominion / Imperial Dominion)
↕	↕
(Imperial Dominion / Zamindari)	Zamindari

The rise of the Marathas in the eighteenth century and earlier can be seen as a result of the logic of the mechanism of *fitna*, and what is called the 'decline' of the Mughal Empire is merely the other side of this process. The Maratha leaders were of relatively low origin, recruited from the autochthonous Hindu *zamīndārī* gentry of the Western Deccan, and, while the Maratha *svarājya* compounded universal dominion and the conflict-cum-*fitna* order, it remained in form a *zamīndārī* tenure encompassed by the Mughal Empire so that the Marathas allegedly were there to execute the humble tasks of *zamīndārs*, 'to populate and settle the country'. In fact the *svarājya* also represented the core of an eighteenth-century 'gentrified' structure of sovereignty in its own right. The Mughal centre was progressively pushed upward while its shares of revenue became available for localized agrarian expansion, leading to an intensification of rights and thus of conflicts. Mughal expansion had generated schismatic conflict at court and through the intensification of conflict which occurred in its wake among the *zamīndārs*, Marathas as well as Rajputs, Bundelas, Rohillas, Sikhs and others who were all tied up in the same processes of *fitna*, it led to a general involution of imperial dominion in the eighteenth century. For more than forty years in that century a crucial mediatorial role was played by the Maratha king Shahu (the most Persianized *zamīndār* of the period) until another schismatic conflict – that between Marathas and Citpavan brahmans – brought the Peshwa to the fore. All this establishes a direct continuity between Mughal expansion and the expansion of Maratha sovereignty, or we may say that the latter was an outgrowth of the former. A radical historical break occurred only under the impact of the British when they, after the initial stage of the 'open frontier' in which they had still been partners in the pan-Indian *fitna* tussle, began to make attempts at territorial consolidation and set out to dissolve the system of alliances and rivalries by replacing it with isolated units, each tied separately to the universal sovereignty of the British themselves and now without the potential of dissidence which had been, in the context of the eighteenth century, rather a strength than a weakness to it.

2
The co-sharers of the realm

I Sovereignty, vested rights and sedition

In the first chapter we have followed and disentangled the processes of *fitna* whereby the Marathas – originating from the gentry of the Western Deccan – through alliance-building or 'conquest on invitation' gradually established their *svarājya* in various parts of India. We have demonstrated that the concept of 'sovereignty' in this context should be stripped of its modern connotations of autonomous unity and abstract territory. Further, that the old notion of 'despotism' or unmitigated sovereignty is of no value to understand the mechanics of Mughal politics and its incorporative, assimilative methods of expansion. Intermediate structures took form within the Mughal polity but these were different from the European feudal structure of sovereignty on account of the subsistence base of the latter and the absence in it of a generalized pattern of royal taxation. We find a closer approximation in the continental Polity of Estates (the German *Ständestaat* or Dutch *standenstaat*) in which such a taxation pattern evolved out of the feudal idea of 'aid' (*auxilium*) and where the Estates saw themselves as the 'people of the land' and in this capacity could strengthen or weaken the claims to rule of one dynasty against another. In India sovereignty from the political point of view was the direct result of 'sedition', of *fitna*, but from the religious point of view it had to be universal since the religious universality attributed to it should make the result of sedition legitimate power. On this issue the historical Indian sources not infrequently speak in a quasi modern-sounding idiom of centralist and unitary state-power which abhors all particularism on the local level as it is underpinned by the universalist religious ideologies of Muslim or Brahmanic origin. This universalism should not be dismissed as 'idealistic', for we have seen that the state needed to expand in order to survive and that 'world-conquest' was an understandable and a logical political imperative. But the result is that our texts often meet us halfway in our modernity in their moral rejection of local self-affirmation as 'rebellion' or 'disloyalty'. At court it was of course standard protocol to use the most abject terms for 'refractory zamindars'. Still, a moral rejection should not interfere with our analysis of a political mechanism.

Such local self-affirmation became a particularly acute problem in the Mughal Empire of the eighteenth century when there was no longer an expanding outer frontier and when in the wake of expansion a multiplicity of power centres was established which offered new scope to the autochthonous gentry, to the *zamīndārs*. This problem of *fitna* on the level of the gentry also existed in the heyday of Mughal power, but could be contained. 'It is the general custom of the *zamīndārs* of Hindustan', wrote Abul Fazl in the *Akbarnāma*, 'to leave wrongfully the path of single-mindedness and to have an eye to every side, and to join anyone who is triumphant or making commotion'.[1] Although it cannot be denied that the sovereign put certain limits to the power of zamindars generally, it appears nevertheless that sovereignty should not be seen, with regard to the zamindars, as simply the result of a brutal imposition of superior force. Here too conflict and *fitna* played the key role. If we can say that an empire existed, it 'existed' on the local level. The eighteenth century abundantly demonstrates that it is possible to see the entire fabric of vested gentry rights and privileges, although at odds with generalized and uniform royal taxation, as but an extension of sovereign power. Elements of such a view have already been advanced somewhat piecemeal for smaller states in South India.[2] Mughal historiography however is still

[1] '*ki rasm-i-beśtarī az zamīndārān-i-hindūstān ān satt ki rāh-i-yakjihatī guzāśta hama ṭarafrā nigāhbānī mīkanand wa har ki ghalib-o-śor afzā bāśad bā-o-hamrāhī mīnamāyand*' (Abul Fazl, *Akbarnāma*, 2, fol.63) For an example of *fitna* amongst the Ujjainiya Rajput zamindars during the reign of Shah Jahan, see Khwaja Kamgar Husaini, *Ma'āṣir-i-Jahāngirī*, pp. 129–31.

[2] Thus D. Shulman sees the South Indian polity as 'founded on the principle of inherent internal conflict' with a king who is 'the focus of a delicate balance' ('On South Indian Bandits and Kings', *IESHR*, 17, 3, (1980), pp. 283–306). A. Appadurai and C. Appadurai Breckenridge concluded that the sovereign deity – the paradigm of royal authority – is the ruler 'not so much of a domain, as of a *process*, a redistributive process' ('The south Indian temple: authority, honour and redistribution', *CIS*, n.s. 10, 2 (1976), pp. 187–211). G. W. Spencer has emphasized that in South India royal patronage of temples is better understood as a 'system-maintaining mechanism of a weakly organized polity' than as the 'self-glorification of a

dominated by the conception of a unitary, despotic and parasitic state of a peripatetic noble composition superimposed on a 'fatally divided' gentry, the *zamīndārs*, who by themselves were incapable of creating an empire.[3] The *fitna* mechanism has not gone entirely unnoticed but its operation is thought to be limited to incidental succession disputes about the Imperial throne and restricted to the peripatetic nobility, or it is seen as a phenomenon of the external frontier only.[4] Satish Chandra, for instance, noted that 'a civil war among the princes usually provided the nobles an opportunity for securing concessions of various types from the rival contestants'.[5] And Irfan Habib remarks that it was customary 'that officers supporting the vanquished side of the war of succession were all pardoned and retained in service'.[6] This fact is mentioned in passing, which is indicative of the degree to which conflict is seen as marginal to the state. That 'sedition' among the nobility occurred on a grand scale in the Mughal Deccan campaigns is well demonstrated by M. Athar Ali.[7] But in the latter's analysis we still get the picture of the state as a monolithic body *integrating* other states' nobilities while the function of expansion is not accounted for at all.

despotic ruler' ('Royal Initiative under Rajaraja I', *IESHR*, 7, 4 (1970), pp. 431–43; 'Religious Networks and Royal Influence in Eleventh Century South India', *JESHO*, 12 (1969), pp. 42–56). In the latter case it seems unwarranted however that 'despotism' is replaced by a model which verges on the 'soft state'. For the Benares region in the eighteenth century see also Cohn, 'Political Systems', p. 315.

3 Cf. Habib, *Agrarian System*, p. 169.

4 J. F. Richards, in some places, empirically shows the relationship between Mughal state and *zamīndārs* to have been one of complementarity and of intervention in local conflicts, the 'exploitation of rivalries' or 'exploitation of disunity' (*Golconda*, pp. 113–15, 128–9, 134, 312–13). He also suggests that 'an alliance between imperial administration and *zamindars* (i.e., *nayaks*), based on a mutual interest in stability and order, is seldom considered an important feature of the Mughal system. Perhaps too much attention has been paid to the tension between the administration and the local aristocracy, and not enough to the possible congruence of interest between the two – especially when long-established *zamindari* houses were threatened by new and aggressive elements in the local society' (*ibid.*, p. 252). The flaw in this suggestion in my opinion does not lie in the 'possible congruence of interest' but in the conception of 'stability and order' in modern terms of an internally pacified realm in which conflict is seen as a disturbance (cf. pp. 6–7). For the use of the term *fitna* in the context of Mughal succession struggles, see Hardy, 'Force and Violence', pp. 174, 188.

5 *Parties and Politics*, p. 10.

6 'An examination of Wittfogel's Theory of "Oriental Despotism"', in: *Studies in Asian History* (Proceedings of the Asian History Congress 1961; London, 1969), p. 391. See also M. N. Pearson, 'Shivaji and the Decline of the Mughal Empire', *JAS*, 35, 2 (1976), pp. 226, 234.

7 *Mughal Nobility*, pp. 102–10.

The Maratha texts demonstrate that *fitna* was not exclusively or even primarily a matter of conquering military élites but operated far more diffusely on the more fundamental level of hereditary vested rights in land.[8] A sovereign, or a potential sovereign, to be successful in conquest, first had to 'entrench' himself within the structure of *zamīndārī* and other hereditary rights such as are called *vatan* in the Deccan. *Fitna* by intervention in the conflictive structure of vested rights was essential in state-expansion as it was the gentry whose co-operation was needed to gain access to the agrarian resource-base without which no state could survive. Without it not even an army could maintain itself in the field. *Fitna* and generalized taxation were the foundations of sovereignty in India, and the two are related in such a way that purely technical parameters involved in a land-revenue settlement cannot account for the working of the fiscal system. This is because the fiscal system is intimately bound up with the vested rights of the *zamīndārs*. It is difficult to recognize this if we limit ourselves – as does most of the existing scholarly literature – to being informed by the Mughal documentation or by nineteenth-century British official reports. Both suffer from a centralist bias generating artificial views such as that of H. J. S. Maine, who holds that the first 'civil act' following upon 'conquest' is always 'to effect a settlement of the land revenue; that is, to determine the amount of that relatively large share of the produce of the soil, or of its value, which is demanded by the sovereign in all Oriental States, and out of which all the main expenses of government are defrayed'.[9] In reality conquest is 'drawing' *zamīndārs*. As it is put by the *Ājñāpatra*, the Maratha treatise on politics which was written in the wake of the Mughal invasions:

> When a foreign invasion (*paracakra*) has come, with the hope of a hereditary *vatan* right they [i.e. the zamindars] first make peace, meet personally the invader and, making use of dissension (*bheda*) on both sides, they then let the enemy enter the kingdom and become mischievous to it and hard to control.[10]

8 As will be seen later, it operated also directly on the cultivating *rayats* (cf. pp. 287–8).

9 *Village-Communities in the East and West* (London, 1876), p. 149.

10 Banhatti, *Ājñāpatra*, ch. 6. Contrast this description with that of the early Muslim chronicler Ahmad Yadgar of the universal conqueror Babar: 'When the King's camp reached Lahore, Mirza Kamran was honoured by admission to the presence, and he brought the *zamīndārs* of the country to kiss the feet of the Conqueror of the World' (Elliot and Dowson, *History of India*, 5, p. 40).

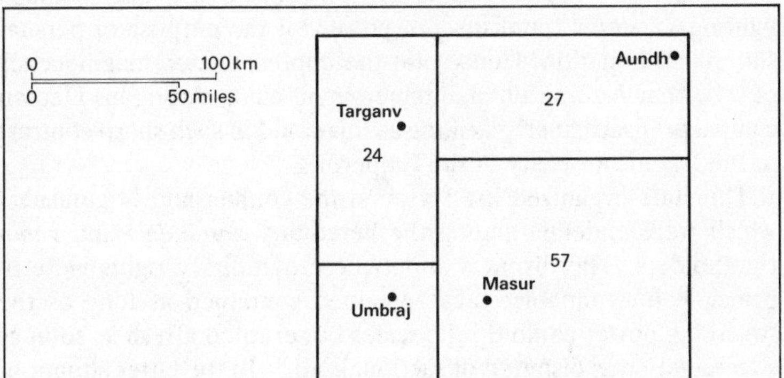

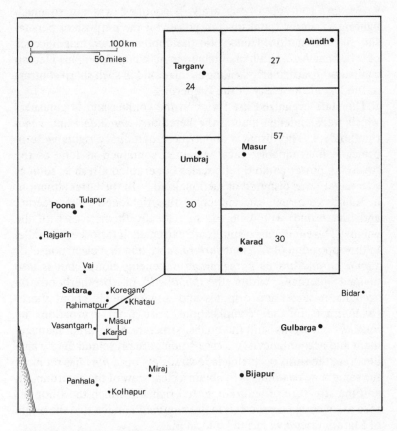

The Western Deccan and Tarf Karad

Thus sedition was the means of establishing sovereignty. Unlike the anonymous national war, *fitna* or *bheda* was a personalized political contest. By implication territory cannot be seen as a primary constituent of the Indian state. Instead we find a people-cum-territory or *janapada*, shot through with vested rights. These vested rights again are shot through with conflict and it is this which constituted the point of impact of sovereign power. It was a matter of political arithmetic: a conquering power needed 'local knowledge' to be able to wedge itself into the conflictuous structure of vested rights, while for the holders of these rights, the *zamīndārs* or *vatandārs*, it was a problem of measuring or estimating the chances of success of the conquering power against those of the established sovereign. The role of the army in conquest was not so much fighting as simply the display of power for the purpose of persuasion or intimidation. Hence also the unprecedented magnificence of style that Aurangzeb maintained in his camp during his Deccan campaign – particularly striking as this stood in such sharp contrast to the Islamic austerity of the Emperor.

The state organized itself around the conflict and litigiousness which were endemic among the hereditary *zamīndārī* and *vatan* rightholders. The disputes about these hereditary rights were in principle interminable; they remained contained as long as the sovereign power could tip the scales but erupted afresh as soon as sovereignty was disputed or factionalized.[11] In the latter situation, in Kautilya's terms, 'the enraged', 'the frightened', 'the greedy', and 'the proud' would be the first to ally themselves with the enemy. The *zamīndārī* disputes are extremely interlocked. Parallel to the opposition of *sva-* and *para-rājya* we find that each 'house' or *zamīngharaṇa* has its *paragharaṇa* or 'enemy house' but is also divided internally within the *bhāūbaṇd* or 'brotherhood' on account of succession disputes and disagreements about shares (*bhāūhisās*). Further complications arise from usurpations by *mutālīks* or 'agents' and the dualist structure of agrarian management and accountancy. Two case-studies are presented here which illustrate the shifts occurring in local society once *fitna* has set in, at the same time enabling us to obtain a clear view of the environment and the structure of agrarian vested rights in which the Bhonsles rose to sovereign power. It is in this *zamīndārī* milieu that the origin of Maratha *svarājya* has to be located.

Case-study 1: The Jagdale déśmukh of Masur[12]

The available documents describing the history of the Jagdale deśmukhi of the tappa of Masur were all written in the lifetime of Mahadaji Rao in the late seventeenth and early eighteenth century, the period in which Maratha sovereignty was re-established in the region in which it is situated. Some of the documents are *hakīkats*

[11] Cf. Grant Duff, *History*, 1, pp. 176, 194, 197, 277, 441; 2, p. 296; *EIP*, 4, pp. 229, 250, 269, 299; Malcolm, *Central India*, 2, p. 58; Gordon, 'Slow Conquest', pp. 8, 13; *idem*, 'Legitimacy and Loyalty', p. 291; M. Alam, 'The Zamindars and Mughal Power in the Deccan, 1685–1712', *IESHR*, 11, 1 (1974), p. 91; *TKKP*, 1, no. 80; *SCS*, 7, p. 5.

[12] *MIS*, 15, nos 1–61; *TKKP*, 1, nos 39, 41, 43, 47–8, 60, 63–5, 67, 139–40, 143, 176–8, 322, 361; *SCS*, 5, no. 779; *BISMQ*, 23, 3 (1943), nos 33, 35.

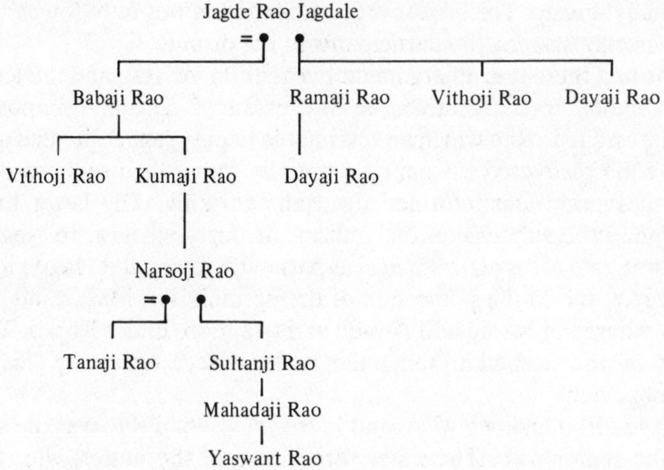

or historical accounts submitted by Mahadaji to the Bijapur court or the early Maratha kings of Satara. There are also orders and sanads received by him from the various kings then contesting with each other for the control of the Western Deccan. Finally there are also some letters from the major rivals of the Jagdales, the Yadhavas. A narrative can thus be pieced together which shows not merely the intricate development of a dispute over hereditary gentry rights in land which was continued from the fifteenth or perhaps the late fourteenth to the early eigheenth century but, more especially, how such a dispute becomes a point of impact for the establishment of Maratha sovereignty.

Mahadaji Jagdale's *hakīkats* cover five generations tracing their ancestry to Jagde Rao Jagdale who was deśmukh of the tarf Karad under the Bahmani dynasty (1347–1526). This *deśmukhī* or *zamīndārī* right seems to have comprised 168 villages, in several of which also *pāṭilkī* or 'headmanship' rights were held. In which way these rights were originally acquired is not mentioned. The only subdivision we meet with from the beginning is that of the tappa of Masur, containing fifty-seven villages, the management of which Jagde Rao had delegated to his younger brother. The other subdivisions of Umbraj, Targanv and Aundh perhaps date from a later period. The subdivision of Aundh is sometimes referred to as a *karyāt*, which implies that it was composed out of other mahals or units of more ancient existence. In the documents the old name Karad is sometimes used when only one or more of its subdivisions is actually meant. This is a source of confusion not only for us but apparently also for the participants in the dispute.

At first there was an argument between Jagde Rao and the local government representative, the Naib of Karad. The latter imposed a fine on Jagde Rao which he was unable to pay. Jagde Rao fled and the Naib recovered it from his estate by force, then sequestrated the deśmukhi and informed the Bahmani king. The latter then assigned the subdivision of Umbraj, of thirty villages, to Negoji Thorat, one of his high officials, as part of his jagir, while Jagde Rao was restored in the possession of the deśmukhi of Masur and the two villages of Karad and Aundh and two more under Karad. The rest of the deśmukhi remained under direct crown or *khālsā* management.

Jagde Rao had two wives and four sons. Babaji Rao was the son of the senior wife. The other three were of the junior wife: the eldest of these was Ramaji Rao the second Vithoji Rao, and the youngest Dayaji Rao. When their father became old the sons started to quarrel about the inheritance. Jagde Rao then divided the patrimony as follows: to the eldest Babaji Rao he gave the deśmukhi and patilki of Masur and to Ramaji Rao he gave the other four villages. Ramaji Rao was not satisfied and complained to the Badshah, bringing forth a hakikat of the deśmukhi. The Badshah then decided to restore to him the sequestrated portion of Karad but demanded for this the exorbitant *peśkaś* of 10,000 hons. To obtain the money to pay the *peśkaś* Ramaji Rao had to sell the division Aundh of twenty-seven villages to Lukhaji Yadhava, a mansabdar of the Badshah. In this way he regained the deśmukhi of Targanv, Umbraj, and the subdivision of thirty villages of Karad. In some part of this vatan he appointed agents. But these agents, in co-operation with the *mokāsadār* or 'assignee' of the district, began to embezzle revenues which were due to the government. Together they set out to kill the three brothers Ramaji Rao, Vithoji Rao and Dayaji Rao. Only Vithoji Rao could save his life and took refuge at the court of the Badshah in Bidar. There he managed to collect supporters with whom he returned to Karad and in his turn killed the agents.

Babaji Rao, the deśmukh of the fifty-seven villages of Masur, became very old but in his old age he ran into similar difficulties as his brother with agents which he had appointed. The aged zamindar had two sons, Vithoji Rao the elder and Kumaji Rao the younger, who were 4 and 1½ years old when he appointed his mali (garden-keeper) and one of his dhangars (shepherds) to the management of his household and vatan. These two made common cause with some sweepers of a mosque and decided to murder Babaji Rao and his two sons. Babaji Rao and his eldest son were killed by them but Babaji Rao's wife saved the younger son Kumaji. This son lived until he was 10 or 12 years old as a dhangar, tending sheep in the village of Citali. One day another dhangar informed him about the murders of his father and his brother. Kumaji Rao then collected fifty men and set out to take revenge but the sweepers of the mosque captured him in the ensuing fight and locked him up in a fort. There he remained for three years. Afterwards he was liberated and stayed for some time with the patil of Koreganv.

This episode must have taken place around the 1530s. A hakikat says that it was in this period that 'the Badshah came to Gulbarga [Kilbarga]' and that he built three domes (gumaṭ) there and that then the country came under the rule of the Bijapur Badshah. The new king started the construction of a fort and summoned the zamindars to his aid, in return for which he increased their remunerations (*hak*). Kumaji Rao also wanted to go to Bijapur but he had become too weak. His son Narsoji Rao, then about eleven years old, went in his place and for three years served the king as the commander of his father's Mavali footsoldiers. The Bijapuri queen eventually brought him to the attention of the Sultan. The latter heard his account and demanded mahzars to be drawn up by local assemblies (*gota*) to establish the justice of his claim to the deśmukhi of Masur. An ordeal was also held when further disputes arose. In the end Narsoji was proven to be the rightful incumbent and was restored in his deśmukhi.

Who by this time was in the possession of the deśmukhi of Karad is not clear. It may have been Vithoji Rao or one of his sons – if he had any – but it may also have been Narsoji Rao or someone else. It is clear however that the Yadhavas still held on to the deśmukhi of Aundh which they had obtained by purchase from Jagdale. Possibly they had taken possession of Karad as well. During the reign of Ibrahim Adil Shah they concluded an agreement about the paying of a tribute (*khaṇḍaṇī*) with a '*zabardastī* marauder', Vangoji Nimbalkar, while at the same time suspending their payments to the Bijapur government. Jagdale's account says that the Yadhavas joined Nimbalkar in his 'plundering raids' but the Yadhavas themselves later represented that they merely 'made an agreement with him to have the villages settled'. It seems evident that by the agreement with Nimbalkar the Yadhavas in the first place aimed at the preservation and extension of their deśmukhi of the Aundh karyat. The result was however that not only Aundh but also the entire tarf of Karad, including Masur, was sequestrated by the Bijapur king. This was due to the complicity of the Yadhavas in the 'maraudings' of Nimbalkar and also to a dispute which had broken out beween them and the Jagdales. The exact background of this dispute is not given but it may be guessed that the Yadhavas had encroached upon the rights of Jagdale through the support they received from Nimbalkar. The government sequestrated the rights of both parties involved but the settlement and investigation of the claims was delayed by the Yadhavas' refusal to attend at court in Bijapur. The deśmukhi of Karad was held in assignment by twelve vazirs in succession (of whom no names are given), then by a noble Randulla Khan, and finally passed into the hands of Shahaji Bhonsle.

Shahaji Bhonsle had come from the extinct Nizam Shahi to Bijapur in 1636, where he was given a high mansab by the king. This was a fortunate turn of events for the Yadhavas since members of their *bhāūbaṇd* were servants of Shahaji. They now approached him for the deśmukhi of Karad, stating that there were no descendants of the Jagdale family left and asking him to turn over the deśmukhi to them. Most probably this statement was partially true; there is no mention in the documents of any descendants of Ramaji Rao Jagdale or of any of his two brothers Vithoji Rao and Dayaji Rao. But Narsoji Rao was still alive. It is possible that he was actually running the deśmukhi of Masur as it was later represented by Mahadaji Rao, which however would have been in spite of the sequestration. Shahaji Bhonsle brought the request of the Yadhavas before the Bijapur king and 'on the authority of his rank' managed to have the Yadhavas installed in the deśmukhi of Karad and Masur. Narsoji Jagdale was murdered by Shahaji and the Yadhavas when after hearing this news he had gone to Bangalore to visit Shahaji with the intention of submitting to him a hakikat of the deśmukhi. It seems that this event induced Shahaji to effect some changes in the management of the deśmukhi. The headmanship of Masur was separated off and given to a Maratha servant of the Badshah called Pisal and the pargana of Masur, although in the hands of the Yadhavas, was formally subsumed by Shahaji in his *jāgīr*. Shahaji now also put his own garrison in the fort of Masur. But shortly later when Dadaji Kondadeo became Shahaji's subhedar in his jagir a gota was assembled of the havaldar (a government district official) and patils, artisans and others in Masur which decided that the deśmukhi of this pargana and the patilki of the kasba belonged to Jagdale. The old deeds were brought forward. Pisal admitted that he had been put in his position only as a servant of Shahaji Bhonsle and wrote an *ajitpatra* or 'deed of relinquishment'. Accordingly the havaldar gave out a mahzar to witnesses in the neighbourhood of the right (*hakkjavār*). Narsoji Rao's son Tanaji Rao went to the court of Sultan Mahmud and secured from him a confirmatory farman. A *takīdpatra* or 'deed of injunction' was also sent to the fort-commander (*killedār*) of Panhala.

The Bhonsle, defying the Bijapur authority, refused to give up the deśmukhi. More soldiers were moved into the thana of Masur. Tanaji Rao was killed. But while the deśmukhi remained in the hands of Shahaji and the Yadhavas, Pisal was dismissed and the patilki of Masur restored to Sultanji Rao Jagdale. The latter appears first to have collaborated with Shahaji's son Shivaji in his *fitna* against the Bijapur king in the years 1644 and after, when Shahaji himself was with the Bijapur army in the Karnataka. But Sultanji Rao probably left Shivaji's side when Afzal Khan approached. For him this turned out to have been a miscalculation. After Afzal Khan was murdered a Maratha army 'came down from Vasantgarh, seized the thanas and took Sultanji Rao prisoner to Vasantgarh where he was beheaded'. At two places his son Mahadaji Rao writes that when this happened he himself was still a child and ignorant about it. But we also read that he was still 'in the womb of his mother'. In any case Mahadaji's mother sought protection at Satara and from there went to Rajgarh to visit Jijai, the mother of Shivaji to whom she protested that the family's vatan had been taken and that three of them had been murdered and that her son had to be given a deed of assurance (*kaul*). After she gave an expression of her loyalty she received both the deśmukhi and the patilki of Masur from Shivaji. But Shahaji had earlier made indecisive arrangements with the Yadhavas for the deśmukhi of Karad. The part of Umbraj–Targanv–Aundh was given to Dhanaji Yadhava and a number of villages of Masur was also wrongly appropriated in it. Dhanaji Yadhava's brothers Padaji and Piraji took charge of it with the sword. They joined the Bijapur Sultan's army with their forces while Padaji's two sons Ekoji and Kusaji served the Mughals with a force of 500 horsemen and started taking levies in the Bijapur territory. With the money brought back from these raids they again reinforced the troops of Padaji and Piraji who could thus successfully obstruct Jagdale's claims. The Yadhavas sent their horsemen and footsoldiers into the country threatening to kill anybody who would give support to the zamindar Jagdale. In this way Dhanaji Yadhava's brothers set up their power and took written agreements from the rayats. Mahadaji Jagdale then returned again to the Bijapur court to have his vatan released, asking for the testimony of a *gota* proclaiming Yadhava a *nasardār*, or 'despoiler'.

But the Bijapur power had already become ineffective and no response seems to have come to Jagdale's request. Bijapur was conquered by the Mughals in 1686, Golconda in 1687, and the Mughals began the invasion of the Maratha country. After executing Sambhaji they took the Maratha capital Rajgarh in 1689 and Rajaram had to set up his provisional government at Jinji. Mahadaji Jagdale now turned to the Mughals. He writes that he 'went to Vai to meet the Mughal nawab Nyahar Khan and received from him fifty horsemen and fifty footsoldiers and added to these some horsemen and footsoldiers of his own and seized the thana of Masur'. This was at the time when Aurangzeb's son Azam Shah was campaigning against Panhala. On his petition Mahadaji obtained from him a farman of his deśmukhi. The nawab Rohilla Khan also gave his *parvānā*. Mahadaji again made a petition in Aurangzeb's camp at Tulapur where Jansar Khan, the faujdar of prant Khatau, issued another order on his behalf. After that Sarja Khan took over the siege of Satara. The garrison at Vai of Nyahar Khan was dismissed and those of Masur and Rahimatpur were also replaced. Mahadaji Jagdale however obtained an equal number of horsemen and footsoldiers from Sarja Khan as he had held under Nyahar Khan. But subsequently the Maratha generals Santaji Ghorpade and Dhanaji Yadhava succeeded in lifting the siege of Satara and drove out Sarja Khan. The Mughals had to abandon Masur as well and 'withdrew its garrison at night'. They also gave up the thanas of Vai, Budh and Khatau and the fort of Asira, thus leaving the Jagdales without support. After the capture of Asira it took the Marathas eight days to bring the villages under their control by means of the distribution of *kauls*. Mahadaji Jagdale's son was taken prisoner into the fort of Vasantgarh. Mahadaji himself went to Jinji to make a petition to Rajaram for the release of his son and the restoration of his deśmukhi.

From Jinji a whole series of documents were issued by the Maratha king on Mahadaji's behalf in the period 1691–4. These not only effected the release of his son but also restored to him the deśmukhi of Masur and his patilki of the kasba. They recall that the enjoyment of the vatan was interrupted for many days and stipulate that for its restitution a fee (*śerṇī*) of 2,000 hons was to be paid to the huzur to make up for arrears of payments. Mahadaji Jagdale is blamed for having gone over to the side of Aurangzeb and taking a farman from him for his deśmukhi. It is on the other hand expressly admitted that 'in this way he could regain his vatan'. With the Mughal farman Jagdale was allowed to enter the service of the Maratha king. His offence of joining the Mughals was pardoned but he was warned that he would be regarded as a 'transgressor' (*gunegār*) if he would again take a sanad from the enemy. Farmans of the Bidar Badshah, of Ibrahim Adil Shah, and of Sultan Muhammad Shah and other documents were brought forward as evidence of the justice of Mahadaji's claim to the vatan. Some Marathas were questioned about it. Another fee (*śerṇī*) of 750 hons was demanded for the confirmation of all rights and *ināms* of the vatan which were accorded in the old farmans. The Maratha subhedar of Satara, the officers of the fort of Vasantgarh and Rajaram's Amatya were all informed about the restoration.

It appears that Mahadaji had to go to Jinji twice. After its restoration to Jagdale the vatan of Masur was again contested by Sunder Tukdeu, a subordinate of Raja Karna, an illegitimate son of Rajaram. Sunder Tukdeu claimed that the deśmukhi of Karad had been given to him and that it included the deśmukhi of the tappa of Masur. At this stage it seems to have become a matter of doubt what the deśmukhi of Karad actually comprised. After investigations it was eventually determined that Karad was no longer the old tarf of 168 villages which once entirely belonged to the Jagdales and that the new subdivision of Karad which had been given (probably temporarily) to Sunder Tukdeu was exclusive of the 57 villages of Masur, the 30 villages of Umbraj, the 24 villages of Targanv, and the 27 villages of Aundh.

Of the latter three subdivisions the deśmukhi was still in the hands of the Yadhavas. Documents issued by Rajaram at Jinji state that the mahal of Umbraj–Targanv–Aundh had been given by Shahaji Bhonsle to the Yadhavas. But no sanad had been given either by Shahaji or Shivaji. It was not found out before 1716 that the Yadhavas too had taken a sanad for their deśmukhi from

Aurangzeb. Whether this was before Rajaram returned from Jinji is not clear but Rajaram confirmed the Yadhavas' possession of the deśmukhi of Umbraj–Targanv–Aundh while he was in Jinji. Almost immediately a new dispute broke out with the Jagdales. Now the issue was that when Jagdale came back from the Mughals into the service of the Maratha Svami he had been unable to produce the farman of the first Ibrahim Adil Shah according to which, as Jagdale had stated, the tappa of Masur contained 57 villages but he had merely shown a farman of the later Adil Shahi which showed only 37 villages, while 20 villages were shown to be 'detached' from the former tappa as *fuṭgāṇv* or 'loose villages'. Rajaram affirmed however that originally Mahadaji's branch of the Jagdale family had possessed the deśmukhi of 57 villages under Masur and that when Shivaji conquered the country the 20 villages were situated in Umbraj and Targanv but that they were excluded from the mahal of Umbraj–Targanv–Aundh which was given to the Yadhavas. The testimony of a gota which Jagdale and Yadhava had agreed to assemble established that the 20 villages belonged to Masur. Such a testimony had to be made once again by another public assembly before the possession of the whole of Masur was finally, in 1694, confirmed to Jagdale. On payment of a fee (*śerṇī*) of 2,000 hons the Yadhavas now for the first time received sanads for their mahal, which it is said 'formerly belonged to the King himself'.

In 1698 the Mughals are back in the area. Girjoji Yadhava represented to Rajaram that Mahadaji Jagdale in unison with the Mughals 'obstructed his vatan'. Again Rajaram had to intervene to establish the claims of the Yadhavas. Mahadaji Jagdale however again approached a Mughal nawab Haminuddin Khan. According to Jagdale's hakikat Dhanaji Yadhava's dependants Padaji Yadhava and Piraji Yadhava's sons were servants of 1,000 and 5,000 *savār* (cavalry) of the Mughals and obstructed the Jagdale vatan together with Dhanaji Yadhava. Again a Mughal garrison was stationed in the fort of Masur. Then Aurangzeb came to Miraj and on his march to Satara he took Vasantgarh. Jagdale and the other *zamīndārs* in the area received parvanas from the Mughals and were given *śisādi mansabs* (spurious Rajput status) and the rank of 100 *savār*.

The Mughal army then moved further to the north. Rajaram died in 1700 and the Yadhavas again got the upper hand in their dispute with Jagdale through their connection with the Senapati Dhanaji

Yadhava who now supported Rajaram's widow Tarabai as the regent of her son Shivaji II. According to Mahadaji Jagdale's account Shivaji, the son of Rajaram, gave out an order to Dhanaji Yadhava stating that the deśmukhi of Karad had been made *khālsā* by the Bhonsles and that now Padaji and Piraji Yadhava were to take possession of it. Accordingly they did so with the support of Dhanaji Yadhava to whom they gave a part of the money which they realized from it. Meanwhile some members of the Yadhava *bhāūbaṇd* were still serving the Mughals, as of old employing the spoils of their campaigns and detaching horsemen from the army of the Emperor to assert themselves in Karad in opposition to Jagdale. Again Ranoji Ghorpade expelled the Mughal garrison from Masur and installed several hundreds of horsemen and footmen of his own for 2½ months. These were thrown out again by Dhanaji Yadhava's brother Shivaji with the aid of Lingoji Mane. These then occupied the thana but there was great scarcity and they could not pay the soldiery. They received, however, financial assistance from some Mughal officers and thus managed to hold on to the deśmukhi of Karad and seem to have been able to set aside Jagdale almost completely. Dhanaji gave 15,000 rupees to the *deśpāṇḍe* of Karad for his support. Shivaji II confirmed the Yadhavas in the possession of the entire tarf Karad, disregarding the claims submitted by Jagdale to Rajaram in Jinji as 'false representations' (*gairvākā*). The names of Sunder Tukdeu and Raja Karna, the illegitimate son of Rajaram, are not mentioned again.

Shahu was released from the Mughal camp in 1707. He was almost immediately joined by the Senapati Dhanaji Yadhava who left the party of Tarabai. In 1708 Shahu ascended the throne and in that same year issued a deed in which he stated that the dispute between Mahadaji Jagdale and the Yadhavas had not been settled with justice. The Senapati, as the documents say, had attempted to persuade him to give the deśmukhi of Karad to the Yadhavas and Shahu had allowed 'out of respect for his Senapati' a draft of a sanad to be drawn up in which the fifty-seven villages of the Masur pargana were subsumed under Karad. Then Yaswant Rao, the son of Mahadaji Jagdale, had come to the Chatrapati with the old farmans of the Adil Shahi and the recent documents of Rajaram and the deeds of the *gotas* and claimed that the deśmukhi of Masur belonged to him and that the Senapati had done injustice to him. Shahu restored Mahadaji in his deśmukhi and gave some remissions on account of the bad state of the cultivation in the pargana caused by the passing of the armies.

In 1709 the Jagdales were holding the deśmukhi of Masur under a sanad of Shahu but the Mughals are still there. The Mughal nawab Rohilla Khan imposed a *peśkaś* or 'tribute' on the pargana of 4,000 hons. Jagdale, as the deśmukh of the pargana, represented to him that the pargana had fallen waste and asked for a remission. Out of the 4,000 hons 2,500 were remitted; the remainder was directed to be turned over to 'the Badshah's servant Nagoji Mane'. This is accompanied with an order to 'populate and cultivate the villages'. Dual government was continued for a few years more. In 1711 it was reported to Shahu that Mahadaji Jagdale by giving kauls to the villages 'made the pargana populous and made government gainful (*kifāyat sarkār*)'

Case-study 2: The Jedhe deśmukh of Bhor[13]

The Jedhes were one of the deśmukh families of the Twelve Mavals, the range of hill-valleys to the south and east of Poona. They had their residence in the village Kari, about ten miles from the town of Bhor. In contrast with Jagdale, we do have some information on how the Jedhe *vatan* was originally acquired under the Bahmani dynasty of Bidar. The earliest members of the Jedhe family we meet with during that period are Kheloji Jedhe and his younger brother Baji Naik Jedhe who were commanding a body of troops in the service of the Badshah. The *Jedhe Kariṇā* describes how at that time the village Ambavade was still a hamlet of Kolis in the midst of a forest. These Kolis allegedly terrorized the surrounding countryside and due to them much land had fallen waste. Complaints reached the Bahmani Badshah and he sent the Jedhe brothers with some troops from Bidar to subdue the Kolis and settle the area. This they did and Baji Jedhe requested the Badshah to grant him the *deśmukhī vatan* of Rohidkhore as reward. So it was granted to him after an investigation had established that as yet there was no other deśmukh in this tappa. Baji Jedhe received a

[13] *MIS*, 15, nos 281, 283–5, 325–65; *MIS*, 16, no. 1; *SCS*, 2, nos 198–239; *SCS*, 3, nos 576–609; *SCS*, 5, nos 761–2, 769–70, 787–8; *BISMQ*, 7, 1–4 (1926–7), no. 29; *BISMQ*, 8, 1–2 (1927), pp. 94–7; *BISMQ*, 11, 4 (1932), pp. 38–40; *BISM-Caturth Sammelan Vṛtt* (1910), 'Jedhe Śakavalī', pp. 175–207; Sarkar, *House of Shivaji*, pp. 73–4; Apte and Kelkar, *Sivcaritra Pradīpa*, pp. 39–48; *Śrī Rāmdās āṇi Rāmdāsī Granthamālā: Śrī Rāmdāsīcīṇ Aitihāsik Kāgadpatreṇ*, 1, 'Kārī va Āṃbavaḍe-Jedhe Deśmukh' (Dhulia, 1930).

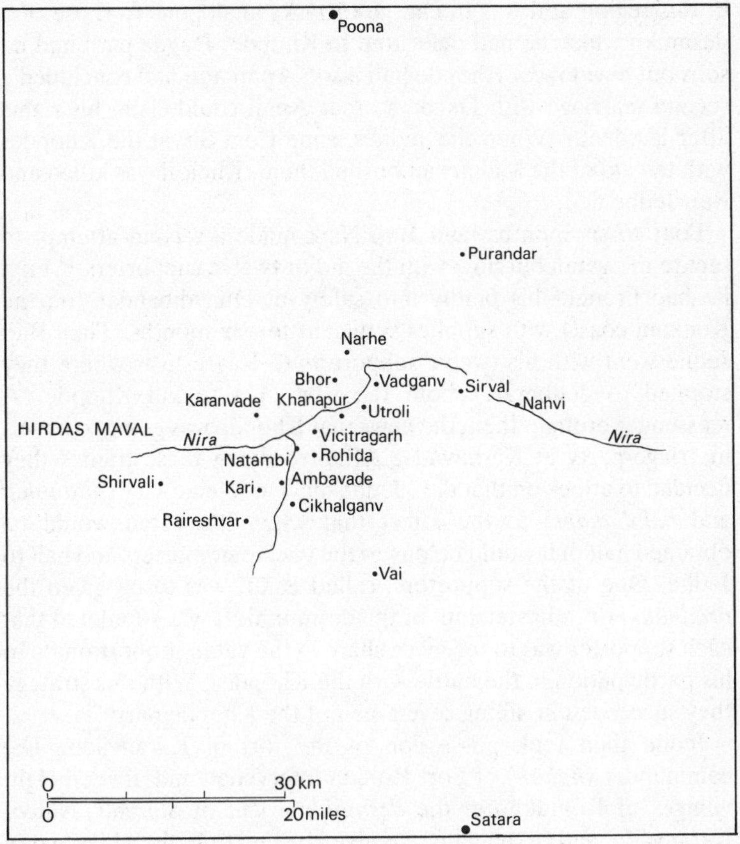

Bhor

farman and confirmatory letters were sent to the thana of Sirval and the fort of Rohida.

When Baji Naik and Kheloji arrived at Sirval with the Badshah's farman to take possession of their deśmukhi they were however violently resisted by a family called Khopde who worked in alliance with the local Mahars and Kolis and claimed a prior right to the deśmukhi of Bhor which they thought to comprise Rohidkhore as well. The Khopdes appear to have come to Bhor from Vai at about the time of the dissolution of the Bahmani Sultanate and when the conflict with Jedhe broke out we are probably about to enter the Nizam Shahi era. The Khopdes were staying at Bhor as collateral relations of Dagde, the patil of the town who enjoyed much power in this region and was in charge of tasks analogous to those of a deśmukh which he had delegated to Khopde. Dagde patil had no sons but a widow of Khopde had a son Apaji and had concluded a second marriage with Dagde so that Apaji could claim his rights after his death. When the Jedhes came from Sirval the Khopdes with the aid of the Mahars ambushed them. Kheloji was killed and Baji Jedhe fled.

Four to six months later Baji Naik made a second attempt to secure the vatan but now with the aid of twelve supporters.[14] First he had brought his family into safety at Dhavdibandar (on the Konkani coast) with supplies sufficient for six months. Then Baji Jedhe went with his twelve supporters to Rayreshvar where they stopped to deliberate about the best plan to kill Khopde. A messenger brought them the news that Khopde was going to have a marriage-party at Karanvade. After verifying these tidings they decided to attack on that day. Jedhe made a solemn vow (*dūdhbhāt* and *belbhaṇḍār*) to the effect that when the vatan would be obtained half of it would belong to the twelve supporters and half to Jedhe. One of the supporters, called Raut, was to be given the *pradhānki* or 'ministership' of the deśmukhi. It was stipulated that each supporter was to receive a share in the vatan proportionate to his participation in the battle with the Khopdes. With this strategy they succeeded in killing seven men of the Khopde party.

Jedhe then took possession of the fort of Karanvade. The commander (*hakīm*) of Fort Rohida intervened and divided eight villages of Rohidkhore: the *deśmukhī vatan* of Shirvali, Nahvi, Karanvade, and Cikhalganv was given by him to Jedhe while that of Vadganv, Khanapur, Narhe, and Pale was given to Khopde. Afterwards Baji Naik's son Kanhoji obtained in addition to the original four villages sixteen others which together came to constitute the tarf Bhor. Out of these the village Kari was given revenue-free (*izāfat*) to the twelve supporters and Ambavade was held revenue-free by the deśmukh Jedhe himself. Some scattered *inām* fields were also given to the supporters. There thus appears to have been divided up a mahal called Rohidkhore in two equal shares – or 'plates' as it is said (*don tarfā don ṭhai*) – of twenty villages each, one called Bhor which was granted to Jedhe and

[14] The number is not to be taken literally – there were in fact fifteen – but as the standard requisite of a complete village-establishment (cf. L. Dumont, 'The "Village Community" from Munro to Maine', in: *idem.*, *Religion, Politics and History*, pp. 117–18).

another called Utroli granted to Khopde. The former is to the west of the hill of fort Rohida, the latter to its east. The Khopde residence was first Narhe but then their *inām* village Ambavade.

In the *Jedhe Kariṇā* we read that now Kanhoji Naik Jedhe and his seven sons received a *varāt* or 'order' from Rohida demanding from them the transfer of 4,000 taka as revenue from their mahal. When *varatdārs* came to collect this amount Kanhoji became furious and, after consulting his mother, sent them away. The *varatdārs* went back to the fort Rohida and returned with troops. But Kanhoji and his retinue and family had in the meantime moved to Kari where 'the troops could not go'. These went back to Rohida. After a short time the seven sons of the deśmukh came to the fort repentant of the offence which they had given to the varatdars. The *hakīm* was approached and Kanhoji's son Naikji said to him: 'We are honourable servants. You are the master (*dhaṇī hakīm*), the parents of us *zamīndārs* (*āmce zamīndārāce māyabāp*).[15] Our offence to you is like an offence to our mother. Pardon us our mistake'. With that and the transfer of the revenue the hakim was satisfied and he announced that all *vatans* and the *deśmukhī* would be maintained as formerly. Naikji was selected as the most suitable person to hold the seniority rights of the *zamīndārī* with the seal. From then onwards Naikji Jedhe began to manage the désmukhi but Naikji's elder brothers were not satisfied with the arrangement and one day they all came together and killed him. Then, again, the twelve supporters asked Raut, the *pradhān* of the deśmukhi, to take revenge for Naikji's death by killing Sonaji and Bhivaji Jedhe whom they held to be responsible. But Raut and one of the other supporters called Gholap said that they would not violently lay hands on Jedhe. A relative of Gholap was then called from Junnar and he agreed to unite with the supporters and kill Sonaji and Bhivaji. The *pradhānki* was taken away from Raut and handed over to Gholap. After that the twelve supporters together went to the hakim and informed him of the death of Naikji Jedhe. They asked for instructions as to who was now to manage the deśmukhi and to whom the seal had to be given. The hakim ordered that Anasava, the widow of Naikji who was five months pregnant, had to take over the management. If no son was born she was to manage the deśmukhi for her lifetime. But four months later she gave birth to a son who was called Kanhoji. The child was put in the hands of a

15 In this way commonly the Rajputs or 'kings' sons' spoke of their king as a paternal patron (cf. Kolff, *Armed Peasantry*, pp. 80, 83).

nurse and raised by the supporters. Raut and Gholap kept Anasava under their safeguard but could not prevent the four remaining sons of Kanhoji from murdering Anasava and her nurse. The young Kanhoji however managed to escape and went into hiding. The hakim, when he learned about these events, brought a part of the deśmukhi under sequestration. Kanhoji returned to Kari in his thirteenth year and appears to have been restored in the seniority of the deśmukhi of Bhor.

After the extinction of the Nizam Shahi the Mavals passed to Bijapur in 1636. At first the vatan of Jedhe was somehow given to the daughter of a kazi but Jedhe received it back almost immediately afterwards, apparently through the mediation of Randulla Khan. With the latter the Jedhes were part of the retinue of Shahaji Bhonsle. The sovereignty of the Bijapur Sultan however was not immediately recognized by all 'sharers of the Mavals'. Krishnaji Naik Bandal, the deśmukh of the neighbouring Hirdas Maval made attempts to extend his holdings by force. This appears to have been a continuation of a boundary dispute with the Jedhes which had started much earlier but was for a time suspended. Now, shortly after the change of sovereignty, it came to an open conflict involving, according to the *Jedhe Kariṇā*, almost 2,000 armed retainers on both sides and leading to a slaughter of 300 of them in a single day. But this settled the dispute. Bandal resigned to accept his old share and acknowledged the former boundary. In 1639 we find Kanhoji Jedhe in the possession of his deśmukhi of twenty villages, of which now four: Ambavade, Kari, Cikhalganv and Natambi were held by him in *inām*. Of the latter Cikhalganv was still disputed by the daughter of the kazi but the Adil Shah again decided in favour of Jedhe. The extra *inām* villages were given as a recognition of Jedhe's loyalty to Shahaji Bhonsle who had to establish his authority in the Mavals in opposition to the Khopdes.

In 1644 Sultan Muhammad Adil Shah wrote to Kanhoji Jedhe that Shahaji Bhonsle had 'become a rebel' but that Khandoji and Baji Khopde had not joined him and stayed loyal to the Sultan's ministers and that Jedhe should do the same. Shivaji took the fort of Rohida in 1645 but the Adil Shah continued to grant *inām* lands to Jedhe until as late as 1649. But in 1652 Kanhoji Jedhe joined the Bhonsle. By doing this he seems to have been able to hold out against Krishnaji Naik Bandal who was again attempting to seize lands from him. Shivaji wrote to Jedhe: 'we did not allow Krishnaji Naik a share in your tappa'.

Kedarji Khopde, the son of Narsoji, remained loyal to the Badshah of Bijapur on account of his old dispute with Jedhe. He received another *inām* village from the Bijapur general Afzal Khan in 1659 when the latter came to the Mavals on his punitive expedition against Shivaji. Afzal Khan also promised a reward to Jedhe for leaving the side of Shivaji but in spite of this, and in spite of Shivaji's admonitions that his vatan was in danger, he remained loyal to him. As the *Jedhe Śakavalī* says, 'he placed his vatan at the feet of the Saheb' after which Shivaji asked him to resign from the Bijapur service by pouring water over his hand. The entire Jedhe family then took refuge in Talegaon.

After Afzal Khan's death Khopde was imprisoned for a while but in 1661 Shivaji restored him in his deśmukhi, reclaiming only the deductions of revenue payments which had been granted by Afzal Khan. Kanhoji Jedhe's deśmukhi of Bhor 'which was with the Saheb' was immediately given back to him. In 1668 the sons of Kanhoji Jedhe, Sarje Rao, Sivaji, Candji, Naikji, Rayaji, and Sambhaji fell into a dispute in their bhauband concerning the division of the vatan. Shivaji ordered this to be done according to the decision of their father. In 1669 Sivaji and Naikji took over the 'prime share' (*vaṭ pāhilī*) and a new dispute ensued. It was again settled with reference to their father's wishes.

Later, under Shivaji still, a system of crop-sharing (*baṭāī*) was introduced and as a consequence ¾ of the government revenue or *rājbhāg* of Jedhe's formerly revenue-exempt *inām* villages was claimed by the government which temporarily substituted the vatandars' remuneration by cash payments from the treasury. Jedhe, like the other vatandars, was gravely upset by this measure. There was 'shortage of food and clothes'. This was still the situation when Aurangzeb invaded the Deccan and set up his camp in Tulapur. The Emperor's son came to Sirval and took Rohida. Khopde immediately took deeds for the confirmation of his vatan from him. Sarje Rao did not come over to the Mughals until his brother Sivaji had done so. Rajaram wrote a reproachful letter to him – the senior son of Kanhoji Jedhe – in 1685, complaining that 'in spite of having eaten the food of the Svami for a long time' he had followed his brother to the Mughals and warning him that the Mughals were losing out and that he could be cut off with the enemy. In 1690 the Marathas began to gain ground again. Sarje Rao proved his loyalty to the Maratha king and brought the lands of his vatan back under cultivation. The cash payments (*moīn*) which they received since Shivaji's time were stopped and the old rights and revenue-free tenures were restored. In 1686 Sarje Rao's going over to the Mughals was formally pardoned. The vatan was restored 'because resources were failing'.

These two case-studies give a detailed view of the beginnings of Maratha *fitna* against Muslim overlordship, of the origins of *svarājya* in the agrarian society of the Western Deccan, and of the ways that sovereign power was interwoven with vested *zamīndārī* rights and that both parties were dependent on mutual support against omnipresent rivals. 'What is the strength of the enemy worth', wrote Rajaram in a letter to the Jedhe deśmukh, 'if people like you remain loyal to us? You acted like the enemy. If you had offered resistance Aurangzeb would not have conquered the *rājya*'.[16] Starting from the late Bahmani rule in the accounts of Jagdale and Jedhe we passed through the Nizam Shahi and Adil Shahi, witnessed the rise of the Bhonsles, the invasion of the Mughals, the Maratha succession dispute between the Satara and Kolhapur branches of the Bhonsle dynasty, and finally the establishment of dual Maratha–Mughal government. Among the *zamīndārs* it was always the party which stood to gain most that first went over to the rival sovereign who intervened in the disputes and attempted to re-shuffle and guarantee the existing rights in such a way that loyalty was assured.

The sovereign was dependent on *fitna*, competition for local influence with a rival sovereign. We find another telling example of this in the Hyderabad Karnataka where Aurangzeb gave orders to destroy certain temples but where the local *zamīndārs* rose to defend them, forcing the retreat of the Mughals and precipitating an alliance under Telugu leadership with the Marathas.[17] Compare also the following statement of the Desai of Lakshmeshvar: 'when estate-holders like us remain loyal to the Chatrapati, this place cannot fall into the hands of the Mughals'.[18] It was in the same way that *zamīndārs* stood in *fitvā* between Shahu and Tarabai[19] and that the Marathas gained access to Malwa through the influential

16 '*ganīmācā hisāb kāy āhe tumhī lok jevhā manāvarī dharitāṇ tevhā ganīm to kāy āhe ganīmsā tumhī lokī kelā āhe te tumhī c lok yā rājyācī poṭatiḍīk dharitāṇ tevhāṇ avraṇgzebācā hisāb dharīt nāhī*' (*MIS*, 15, no.347).

17 J. F. Richards, 'The Hyderabad Karnatik, 1687–1707', *MAS*, 9, 2 (1975), p. 246.

18 '*tumhāṇāmhāṇsārikhe vṛtīvaṇt māhārāj rājśrī chatrapatī svāmīsīn yekaniṣṭ astāṇ sthal tāṃbravaś hoū naye mhaṇūn*' (*SCS*, 6, p. 52).

19 Cf. p. 102.

Nandalal Mandaloi.[20] In Gujarat it was the Rajpipla zamindar who supported Gaikwar with his Kolis.[21] Bhimsen writes that when Scindhia crossed the Narmada in 1705 and wanted to go to the Ganga-Bhagirathi and Benares 'local zamindars barred his path'.[22] But wherever the Maratha campaigns were successful they appear to have been so not only because they found allies among Mughal mansabdars but also because they had been able to draw the zamindars to their side. This first happened in the Deccan when, according to Bhimsen, 'the zamindars . . . assumed strength, joined the Marathas, enlisted armies, and laid the hand of oppression on the country'.[23] But also in Khandesh and Berar the Marathas 'joined by the zamindars of that side gathered about 60,000 troopers and made ready to fight Nusrat Jang'.[24] Maratha intrusions were made possible by the co-operation of local zamindars as far as Bundelkhand.[25] Zamindars also played a central role in the Maratha contest with Hyder Ali and Tipu Sultan of Mysore[26] and, finally, in the conflicts with the British.[27]

The picture we get of the role of the zamindars is a composite one. There is the military and strategic involvement in the setting up of thanas, in campaigns, in the siege of forts, and, most importantly, in the divulging of local information. In addition the zamindars' co-operation was indispensable to gain access to the agrarian resource-base, to 'make government gainful'. We saw that the process of conquest almost always passed through a transitory stage of dual government. It is essential however to note that there is nothing like a 'conquest' or the establishment of sovereignty – partial or complete – which was immediately followed up by a land-revenue settlement (as conceived by Maine). Conquest meant first of all the consolidation of sovereignty through the integration of local zamindars. This took the form of the issuance of *kauls* and 'proclamations of safety' and sanads or other documents confirming as well as delimiting their rights against those of local rivals. To the phase of consolidation also belongs the guaranteeing of religious alienations.[28] An actual land survey could only be undertaken in areas which had been consolidated in this way for at least a

[20] Cf. p. 130. [21] Cf. p. 117. [22] Khobrekar, *Tarikh-i-Dilkasha*, p. 245.
[23] *Ibid.*, p. 230. [24] *Ibid.*, p. 228. [25] Cf. Grant Duff, *History*, 2, p. 301.
[26] *SSRPD*, 4, no. 12.
[27] Cf. 'Invitation to the feudatories of the Bhonsle (Raja of Sambalpur, Sonepur and Bona) to come under British protection and throw off their allegiance to the Marathas, 13 December 1803', *PRC*, 5, pp. 149–50.
[28] Cf. *SSRPD*, 3, no.49; Gordon, 'Slow Conquest', p. 27.

number of years for otherwise the danger of *fitna* would be too imminent. With such respite, surveys based on measurement and designed to determine the productivity of the land and to assess the *rājbhāg* or 'king's share' were made by Murshid Quli Khan in many areas of the Mughal Deccan in the 1650s and by Shivaji in much of his *svarājya* after he returned from Agra.[29] Under the latter settlement the general sequestration of *vatans* which is referred to in the accounts of Jedhe took place and they were then mostly substituted by cash allowances from the treasury. This policy outdid itself but was officially reversed only under pressure of Mughal *fitna* much later. Land-revenue surveys did not always follow the consolidation of sovereignty. The Marathas were often satisfied to continue to use the pre-existing assessment schemes. This was the case in most of the districts newly conquered by them beyond the Deccan in the eighteenth century. In the Western Deccan itself no new general survey was made after Shivaji's until the beginning of the Peshwa régime.

Fitna by an invading power then was motivated by the aim to integrate *zamīndārs* under these two aspects – the military or strategic and the agrarian – and to achieve it the conqueror-to-be exploited their conflicts through his sovereign power of arbitration and guaranteeing of vested rights. In the process of *fitna* which led to the establishment of Maratha sovereignty in the Western Deccan we can discern three stages. There was first the original *zabardastī* or 'rebellion' of the Bhonsles against Bijapur. This was primarily the result of the political fragmentation of the Deccan Sultanates caused by Mughal intervention. Through a policy of shifting alliances similar to the one to which the Deccan Sultans owed their own rise to independence the Maratha *zamīndārs* established *svarājya* under Shivaji.[30] Sovereignty in the area around Poona had been disputed since Malik Ambar had in 1607 entered into an alliance with the Mughals against the Adil Shah. From then on Nizam Shahi and Adil Shahi nobles competed for influence in the region, both sides indulging in *fitna*, until Shahaji Bhonsle obtained the Poona district in *mokāsā* from the Nizam Shah for his aid in ousting the Adil Shahis.[31] From then until Shivaji's consecration the Bhonsles kept changing sides with this assignment and all through this period

29 See Chapter 3.
30 *SCS*, 4, nos 712, 714; 5, nos 757, 844; 6, pp. 31–58; 7, p. 32; Khobrekar, *Shivaji Period*, nos 76 ff, 97–104.
31 *SCS*, 1, nos 9–21.

they were busy strengthening their position by *fitna* against the Bijapur nobles, who in their turn set up 'a campaign for drawing off people from allegiance to Shivaji Bhonsle to the Badshah'.[32] The Bijapur stage gradually merged into a second stage in which the Mughals predominated.[33] After the conquests of Golconda and Bijapur Aurangzeb fixed his camp (*mukam*) at Tulapur, near Poona, in March 1689. From there mansabs, inams, jagirs, honorary robes, kettledrums, and pecuniary rewards were handed out with unprecedented liberality. Particularly the Mughal *mansabs* introduced a new element of glamour in this part of the Deccan. They varied from 7,000/7,000 of the great sardars to 300 savar of small zamindars.[34] Local zamindars on occasion rose as high as 1,500/600.[35] Conversions to Islam were encouraged, perhaps occasionally forced, and the *jiziya* appears to have been imposed, although unsystematically. In spite of this Aurangzeb initially had much success in winning Maratha loyalties due to a pervasive undercurrent of discontent among the *vatandārs* against Shivaji's sequestration policy. An undated note explains: 'Shivaji sequestrated all *vatans* and gave cash allowances instead. Then Aurangzeb Badshah made his camp in Tulapur in prant Poona. All *vatandārs* of the Nizam Shahi, the Adil Shahi and the Kutup Shahi came to him'.[36] This is confirmed by the accounts of Jagdale and Jedhe and a number of other zamindari accounts referring to decisions and confirmations made by Aurangzeb at Tulapur.[37] 'The Badshah made his camp in this zilha . . . and the zamindars of the Deccan assembled there.'[38] Aurangzeb not only gave them their vatans back but he added to them and at places strengthened the zamindars' positions locally by giving them the semblance of *peśkaś* or 'tributary' zamindars.[39] Such 'political arithmetic' had its counterpart on the other side. The Maratha king Sambhaji still could write a reproachful letter to Sarje Rao Jedhe in 1685 in which

32 '*sivājī bhoslece fitaratīmadhe pādśāhī maslahat*' (*SCS*, nos 712, 714). The term *fitaratī* is a corruption of *fitūr* or *fiturī* and seems to occur here as a synonym of *fitna*.

33 Khobrekar, *Shivaji Period*, nos 41–2, 49.

34 See the Jagdale case-study; and Sarkar, Ma'āṣir-i-'Ālamgirī, pp. 135, 141, 143, 158, 166, 181.

35 S. M. Pagadi, *Studies in Maratha History*, vol. 2 (Kolhapur, 1971), p. 37.

36 '*rājśrī svāmīnīṇ kulvatandārāṇcīṇ vataneṇ amānat karūn moinī karūn didhlī tyāvarī tulāpur pr.puṇeṇ yetheṇ avraṇgzeb pādśahā yāc mukām jālā tetheṇ nizām-śāhī va adilśāhī va kutupśāhī yaise kulvataṇdār jamā jāle*' (*MITSA*, 2, no. 488).

37 Cf. *SPD*, 31, nos 185, 191.

38 *Ibid.*, no. 185.

39 Alam, 'Zamindars and Mughal Power', pp. 74–80.

he stated that 'the Mughals cannot remain here for more than a short period, and yet you have gone over to them'.[40] But in a letter of October 1686 Mahadaji Nimbalkar, then a servant of the Mughal, writes to Khem Savant that 'the Badshah of Delhi is very powerful' and that 'there is nobody equal to him'.[41] This is followed by an admonition to join the Mughals without delay in order to derive all the benefits and it is calculated that Sambhaji was going to meet the same fate as the Bijapur and Golconda sultans.

However, in the early 1690s a third stage set in when the Marathas began to 'gain back their kingdom'. Maratha expansion became possible through the exploitation of scissions amongst the Mughal nobility which followed in the wake of the stalemate reached in the southern expansion of the Empire. At Jinji, Rajaram reversed Shivaji's policy and restored under his own sanads the *vatans* and *ināms* in the Western Deccan while it was still occupied by the Mughal forces. By the end of the seventeenth century we find 'double government' (*dutarfā kasālā*) established.[42] This remained the general pattern in varying proportion, until the Mughals pulled out some time around 1718. The justification which Rajaram gave for the restoration of the vatans was not *fitna* but the argument that 'the country had fallen waste because of the Mughal disturbances which took place in our kingdom for thirty years'.[43] The Maratha vatandars rallied around their king declaring themselves his 'loyal servants' and requesting their rights to be restored for the reason that 'on account of the devastations by the enemy and famine the rayats had gone away or died, while the few remaining had nothing to eat and no clothes to wear'. The rayats 'needed to be reassured and given assistance with the cultivation'. 'If the vatandars are not given their rights', decided Rajaram, 'with these troubles the country cannot be settled as they have no stake in it, and therefore the vatans and inams have to be sanctioned.'[44] There are quite a few of such sanads, emphasizing the agrarian service-relationship, 'the stake in the country', which is appealed to for the settlement.[45] The

[40] S. N. Joshi (ed.), *Saṃbhājīkālīn Patrasārsaṃgraha* (Poona, 1949), no.162 of 5 October 1685.

[41] *SCS*, 13, no.8. [42] Cf. *ibid.* [43] *MIS*, 16, no.28. [44] *Ibid.*

[45] Cf. *IS*, 2, 5, pp. 17–30, 22–3; *MIS*, 17, no.21. For 'a stake in the country' the texts have *mulakhāṇci jaftaraft*, the latter term being a compound of the Marathi *rafat*, Arabic *rabṭ*, practice, customary performance or action, constant intercourse with, and Persian/Arabic *juft*, couple, yoke, pair.

process of vatan restoration was continued until 1706 or later.[46] Great was the confusion in the period preceding the Mughal retreat. Special councils were set up to adjudicate and enforce the sanads given by Rajaram from his exile.[47]

II The king's co-sharers

The Indo-Persian term *zamīndār* means 'holder of land'. But in the Mughal idiom it covered a wide range of local landed rights varying from those of village-headmen to those of semi-autonomous chiefs or rajas. It was a generic concept for the indigenous Indian gentry and liable moreover (in some cases) to be stretched considerably in order to perpetuate the fiction of universal Mughal dominion. This, as we saw, occurred in the eighteenth century, when the Marathas established *svarājya* over the larger part of India but nominally did so in the capacity of *zamīndārs*.

South of the Narmada the use of the term *zamīndār* related in particular to the hereditary district 'officials' which were called *deśmukhs* or *desāīs* in Marathi, literally 'heads of country', in practice a kind of country squire. Maratha documents may also employ the term more loosely, either without explication, or explicitly embracing *deśmukhs, deśpāṇḍes* (district-accountants), *pāṭīls* (village-headmen), *kuḷkarṇīs* (village-accountants), and the like.[1] These, in effect, were the most common *vatan-dārs* or 'holders of hereditary office'. We find the equation of '*zamīndārs* of the Deccan' with '*vatandārs*' but this is not quite correct since vatandars do not necessarily have a direct connection with land-control, as zamindars always do. More importantly, as distinct from *zamīndār* the term *vatandār* normally refers to such tenures only which are found in 'regulation territory'. It carries a pronounced emphasis on the aspect of regular service to the state, on allegiance therefore, while *zamīndār* is unspecific in this respect and more elastic in both Mughal and Maratha usage. *Vatan* is associated with regulation, but regulation was not a structure out of which conflict was eliminated but rather one of 'management by conflict'. As the 'regulation tract' under Maratha sovereignty we may define that area where the structure of landed *vatan* showed an effective dualism of *deśmukh/deśpāṇḍe* and *pāṭīl/kuḷkarṇī*, collecting and managing the land-revenue on the basis of a measurement survey.

46 *SPD*, 31, no.191. 47 *MIS*, 8, no.52.

1 *SSRPD*, 3, no.495; 4, no.253; 7, no.482.

'Regulation' and 'non-regulation' are relative to political and economic circumstances, varying in space and time. *Zamīndārs* are ubiquitous but their tenures were diverse: those of the regulation tract were *vatandārs* in the Deccan, while those of the non-regulation tract were just *zamīndārs*, or chiefs called *saṃsthāniks* or *nāyaks* or *mavās* (especially in Gujarat and parts of Malwa), enjoying autonomy in the internal management of their estates.[2] During periods of agrarian or financial and administrative crisis, regulation could be relaxed and zamindars could acquire a temporary autonomy under a system of revenue farming.[3] From the point of view of the state their position would then no longer be that of vatandars but more akin to that of tributary chiefs.

It is important to recognize that the designation of the autochthonous Indian gentry by either of the terms *zamīndār* or *vatandār* is an introduction of Muslim rule.[4] The actual origin of their rights, which the Muslims called 'patrimonial' (*mirās*), is lost in an obscure past. In some instances they can be traced back to colonization and agricultural settlement under Muslim rule. Or they were obtained by purchase. But most often they preceded the Muslim régimes, and what the Muslims did was in the first place the imposing of a new bureaucratic grid on a resilient pattern of old and vested rights.[5] The district- and village-zamindars came in the possession of commissions of the Emperors of Delhi or the Deccan Sultans but rarely owed their rights to appointment by the state. All that can be said is that they had historically arisen out of the agrarian function of colonization and settlement – a function which had a military and political character as well.[6] No descriptions are found of the nature

2 Cf. B. R. Grover, 'Nature of Dehat-i-Taaluqa (Zamindari Villages) and the evolution of the Taaluqdari system during the Mughal Age', *IESHR*, 2, 2 (1965), pp. 166–77, and 2, 3 (1966), pp. 259–89; N. A. Siddiqi, 'The Classification of Villages under the Mughals', *IESHR*, 1, 3 (1964), pp. 73–83; S. Nurul Hasan, 'Zamindars under the Mughals', in: R. E. Frykenberg (ed.), *Land Control and Social Structure in Indian History* (Madison, Milwaukee and London, 1969), pp. 17–31.

3 Cf. Chapter 4–IV.

4 Both terms are Arabic–Persian compounds. According to Habib, *Agrarian System* p. 136, the term *zamīndār* 'was probably coined in India as early as the 14th century'. Nurul Hasan thinks that the term *zamīndār* gained currency during the Mughal period ('Zamindars under the Mughals', p. 18).

5 Cf. N. A. Siddiqi, *Land Revenue Administration under the Mughals (1700–1750)* (Bombay, 1970), p. 21; B. H. Baden-Powell, 'A Study of the Dakhan Villages', *Journal of the Royal Asiatic Society* (April 1897), p. 251; Habib, *Agrarian System*, pp. 159, 162; *EIP*, 4, p. 667; Chandra, *Parties and Politics*, p. xix; Malcolm, *Central India*, 2, pp. 9–12; Gordon, 'Slow Conquest', p. 3.

6 *SCS*, 7, p. 4; Baden-Powell, 'Dakhan Villages', p. 253.

of *vatan* in the Deccan before the arrival of the Muslims.[7] Many deśmukhs and deśpandes adorned their story by saying that they owed their rights originally to 'the favour of the Badshah'. This was of course considered as the honourable recognition of settling a pargana. In fact only the *sardeśmukhs* or 'head-deśmukhs' owed their title and rights to royal favour. These were influential sardars of renowned families who did important service under the Muslim or early Maratha kings. The principal sardeśmukhs in the Western Deccan were Shirke, Sardesai and Bhonsle, all of whom obtained their vatans under the Muslims. They were regarded as far superior to ordinary district-zamindars, whose military operations and political influence were of a comparatively petty order and linked to revenue collection.[8] As far as is known systematic state-sponsored migrations of whole groups of zamindari settlers occurred only outside the Deccan. For instance in Malwa a process of Rajput immigration started sometime in the fourteenth century and was greatly stimulated by the sovereigns until as late as Aurangzeb to create a collaborating élite.[9] Similar but less massive migrations of zamindars occurred apparently from the Yamuna–Ganges Doab to the eastern distichts of Nagpur.[10] Historical evidence on such early settlements is extremely scarce. The main sources of information are Muslim court chronicles.[11] In the administrative manuals of the Mughals the zamindars are hardly acknowledged.[12] The official ideal being direct contact with the rayats, the zamindar of the regulation area was at best seen as an 'intermediary', holding a *khidmat* or 'post of service' in the state's revenue administration.[13] The zamindar's vested right is not emphasized.

Given this singular lack of counter-evidence – it will be recalled that the same *rayatvāri* ideal prevailed in the Sanskrit literature[14] – the opinion easily gained ground that India knew no old allodial

[7] *SCS*, 7, p. 2.
[8] See for instance the Jedhe case-study; and *SPD*, 31, no. 1.
[9] Gordon, 'Slow Conquest', pp. 3–5. [10] Jenkins, *Nagpur*, p. 133.
[11] Gordon, 'Slow Conquest', p. 3.
[12] Habib, *Agrarian System*, p. 169. [13] *Ibid.*, p. 173.
[14] Cf. pp. 18–19. An author like Śabara makes a point of explaining that not only the sovereign king or *sarvabhaum* has a right over the earth but others as well: the *sarvabhaum* is entitled to a share of the crops produced on the earth since he is the protector of the people but all other persons walk on it, produce crops on it, get their sustenance from it and therefore they also have rights over it and there is no real difference between the Emperor and others as regards rights over the earth (Kane, *History of Dharmaśāstra*, 2, p. 866). This is hardly more a concession than Kautilya's *puruṣavaddhi rājyam*, the 'peopled realm', which is in essence a kingdom of docile, tax-paying cultivators (*Arthaśāstra*, 7.11.25).

aristocracy.[15] Thus it was either considered as prebendal (following Weber) or held to be absent, more in line with Marx's or Bernier's view that the sovereign in India concentrated all 'property' of land in his own hands. Earlier, Machiavelli and Montesquieu had seen the absence of a vested aristocracy as the crucial difference between East and West.[16] The theory of Oriental Despotism also served British imperialist needs to explain away the eighteenth-century Maratha nobility as entirely *parvenu*.[17] This conception, with its corollary that the state exacted the whole of the 'surplus produce' of the land from the cultivators, is still dominant. A tidal wave of administrative records generated by the Peshwa régime could not wash it away, as most of these records are highly schematic centralist accounts of income/expenditure analysis exhibiting the zamindars in neat categories on the side of the latter together with the salaries of state-officials. Moreover, in the period immediately preceding British conquest their position had become less visible and they had in fact been pushed to the background (not without attempts to create a substitute) under the then prevailing system of revenue farming.[18] The *Ājñāpatra* however makes perfectly explicit what the Muslim and Sanskrit works strive to pass over. It says:

> The vatandārs in the kingdom, the deśmukhs and deśkulkarnīs, the pātīls et cetera, they may be called 'office-holders', but this is only a term of convention. They are in fact very small but self-sufficient chiefs. They are not strong on their own, but they succeed in keeping up their power by allying themselves with the 'lord of all land', the *sarvabhaum*. Yet it must not be thought that their interests coincide with that of the latter. These people are in reality the *co-sharers* (*dāyadā*) of the kingdom.[19]

The interests of the vatandars do not 'coincide' with that of the sovereign: the text employs here the word *sādhāraṇa*, a derivative of the Sanskrit compound *sa-ādhāra*, which means literally 'having

15 Cf. T. B. Jervis, *Geographical and Statistical Memoir of the Konkan* (Calcutta, 1840), p. 122; B. H. Baden-Powell, *The Land Systems of British India*, 3 vols (Oxford, 1892), I, pp. 127–9; *idem, The Origin and Growth of Village Communities in India* (London and New York, 1970), pp. 99, 129–30.

16 Machiavelli, *Il Principe*, Cap. IV; C. L. de Secondat de Montesquieu, *De l'Esprit des Lois* (Paris, 1868), Livre XVIII, ch. XX.

17 Cf. Thompson, *Indian Princes*.

18 Cf. Chapter 4–IV.

19 '*rājyāṇtīl vatandār deśmukh va deśkuḷkarṇī pātīl ādikarūn yāṇsī vatandār mhaṇon mhaṇāveṇ hī prākṛt paribhāṣa mātr āhe te svalpac paraṇtu svataṇtra deśanāyakac āhet sārvabhaumāpāsūn balnyūnateneṇ utaratī paraṃparā baḷivaṇt rākhon durbal vartatac āhet paraṇtu tyāṇs sādhāraṇa gaṇāveṇ yaiseṇ nāhī he lok mhaṇje rājyāce dāyādac āhet*' (Banhatti ed., ch. 6).

the same basis'. It is the same term which is used in the *Arthaśāstra* to explain that 'the *janapada* is shared with the enemy'.[20] It was the ever-present danger of external encroachment which gave all vested rights a kind of double basis. The *Ājñāpatra* explains further that the vatandars are never satisfied with the vatan they possess and don't have the intention 'to remain loyal to the lord of all land, the raja'. Their ambition is always to become stronger by encroaching upon each other and creating 'sedition' (*dāve darvaḍe*).[21] Anticipating the king's punishment they first collect a retinue, fortify themselves, obstruct the roads, ransom the country and ally themselves with the foreign invader.[22] They then threaten to get out of hand. But to avert this danger – a consequence of what is admitted to be the 'natural' faults of vatandars – the text enjoins a policy of moderation in their treatment. To bring the vatan to a stop is dangerous; at the same time, allowing them complete freedom of movement will 'make manifest their peculiar nature'. These two extremes the king has to avoid. The right way to assure their loyalty is to keep them positively 'in between friendship and suppression'. This means that the vatans should be continued as of old but that no new and unauthorized rights and immunities should be allowed and that the vatandars' power over the cultivators should be reduced to as little as possible. The king should also try to prevent large brotherhoods to get absorbed jointly in any particular vatan. In short, there are established usages of vatandari policy which should not be deviated from. The king may take refuge to extra levies only if a vatandar becomes too overbearing. Loyal vatandars are to be flattered – but they are very hard to find. A vatandar of reliability is 'like a gold-glower emitting good smell'.[23]

Thus the *Ājñāpatra* regards the zamindars from a completely different angle. No longer are they seen as mere office-holders at the mercy of the king, but they become his partners, his co-sharers, his *dāyadā*. In the current usage of the Deccan this term referred to all holders of vested interests on an inheritance or joint family asset. These were the male members of a patrilineage who had a birthright to the property. Birthright, as we saw, has been defined by the eleventh-century jurist Vijñāneśvara as the conception of

[20] Cf. p. 14.

[21] Banhatti, *Ājñāpatra*, ch. 6. The term *dāve darvaḍe* is a corrupted form of *dāvā darfaḍā*, a compound of *dāvā* (Arabic *da'wā*), 'opposition' and *fāṇḍā*, 'bifurcation', 'digression', which also occurs in the generic term *fitvāfāṇḍā*, 'seditious risings' (cf. p. 33).

[22] *Ibid.* [23] *Ibid.*

property 'known to the world'.[24] Such interest or *dāya* arising at birth by consanguinity alone was the very antithesis of the orthodox Brahmanical and Islamic conceptions, which favoured partition at death – not sharing – and had an individualistic basis. In a way which is analogous to Vijñāneśvara's rejection of these individualistic or atomistic conceptions as 'alien to the world' the *Ājñāpatra* opposes the *vatandār* to the *dāyadā* as but a convention – the convention, we might say, of universal dominion and universal religion as opposed to co-sharing and the politics of *fitna*.[25] In this way too Ibn Khaldun considered the support given to the king by his agnatic co-sharers (*shurakā'hu-l-amr*) as an inevitable 'dualism' or *shirk* in society which was linked to *fitna*, and ultimately meant 'polytheism', 'giving partners to God'.[26]

If *svarājya* then was a replica of *vatan* it will cause no surprise to find an autochthonous royal dynasty like the Bhonsles rooted in their realm as incumbents of a variety of *vatans* independently of their sovereignty. This phenomenon has its parallels in *ancien régime* Europe, e.g., in France where the king received in addition to tax also some seigneurial rents and proprietorial rents and perhaps even tithes from vacant bishoprics.[27] In India it is absent under Mughal imperial dominion[28] but it flourished under the Marathas. Thus the Rajas of Satara clung to their zamindari rights in Indapur and elsewhere which dated back to the period from before their rise to sovereign power.[29] The northern Maratha sardars Gaikwar, Holkar and Scindhia we meet again as incumbents of village headmanships and the like in Khandesh and the Deccan.[30] These rights were either transmitted to them from ancestry or were conferred on them by the Peshwas. It is well known how in particular Mahadaji Scindhia prided himself upon the hereditary village honours and rights which he retained in the Deccan. All great Maratha commanders as well as the brahmans

[24] Cf. p. 18.

[25] The term *dāyadā* corrupted to *dāīj* is also often used to describe the coparceners of a *vatan* (e.g. *SCS*, 3, no.578; 7, no.14); or it may be said that a certain deśmukh's *bhāūbaṇd* are *daite* of the Twelve Mavals (*Śrī Rāmdāsīcīṇ Aitihāsik Kāgadpatreṇ*, 1, nos 19, 31; and cf. p. 176).

[26] Wafi, *Muqaddima*, 2, p. 677.

[27] P. Goubert, *L'Ancien Régime*, 2 vols (Paris, 1973), 1, p. 135.

[28] Under Jahangir however the custom developed of granting nobles their birthplace in *altamghā jāgīr*, a permanent tenure under 'red seal'.

[29] Cf. *TKKP*, 1, no.42; *SSRPD*, 9, no.76; Grant Duff, *History*, 1, pp. 74, 163; *P.A.: List 13, Ru. 8, File 134*, no.1997.

[30] See esp. *Historical Selections from Baroda State Records*, 1, nos 8, 31–2; *SSRPD*, 1, no.169; Thakur, *Holkarśāhī*, 1, no.358.

were eager to possess a *vatan* or *inām* in their native villages. The Peshwas themselves and Nana Fadnis held deśmukhis, patilkis, kulkarnis, inams, and shares of ½ or ⅓ of vatans, by grant from Shahu or through purchase, commonly in the Southern Konkan, which was their homeland.[31] The possession of such *vatans*, like the possession of *śerī* or 'government land' or a piece of *kuraṇ* (meadow) was not merely an investment opportunity but also a point of honour. Similar rights were also bought by the Peshwas, sometimes at the request of the earlier incumbents, after disturbances.[32] In such cases the exact rights of the bought vatan or share of vatan were carefully specified and it was determined who was to hold the seniority rights. The share bought by the Peshwa became 'crown domain' (*khāsgī*) if it was not granted away again. Neither the Peshwas nor any other sardars with sovereign attributes could lay claim to any rights or privileges in virtue of these estates which were not enjoyed by other persons holding lands on similar tenures. We never hear for example of Scindhia or Holkar making attempts to encroach upon the local jurisdiction of the Peshwas and arrogate to themselves an independent jurisdiction in their possessions and assignments in the Poona districts.[33] In practice of course their vatans were always managed by appointed agents (*mutālīk, gumāstā*). Such stations could be declared hereditary, as happened in the case of the Satara Raja's *désmukhī vatan* of Indapur which was held as a *gumāstā deśmukhī vatan* hereditarily in one family 'for as long as the Raja's dynasty should exist'.[34] The vatan was then held on a salary, but this was nominal for there were constantly extra appropriations being made. Yet the deference to the time-hallowed structure of vested rights is significant in its own way as it shows that sovereign power had to accommodate itself within this structure and could never impose itself despotically upon it.[35]

Instead of centralized despotism and a uniform pattern of taxation we found a territory which was parcelled out amongst co-sharers with vested rights, partly defined as 'offices' and partly as 'chiefdoms' but everywhere at odds with arbitrary rule. The king's

31 *BISMQ*, 19, 4 (1939), pp. 113–26; 20, 1 (1939), pp. 121–6; 21, 3 (1941), pp. 265–9; *SSRPD*, 9, no.92.

32 Cf. *SSRPD*, 3, no.520 and preceding note.

33 *P.A.: List 13, Ru. 67, File 891*, no.361 of 1854.

34 *Ibid., Ru. 8, File 134*, no.1997.

35 Cf. F. Perlin, 'Space and order looked at critically. Non-comparability and procedural substantivism in history and the social sciences' (revised paper presented to the Colloquium on Bifurcation Theory, Erasmus University Rotterdam, January 1982), pp. 25–6.

co-sharers were his allies and his counterpoise, his 'dissident allies'. As the *Ājñāpatra* says there was no essential difference between *vatandārs* or 'office-holders' and 'very small but self-sufficient chiefs'.

The Indian territory did not really have any fixed boundaries except the natural ones of the subcontinental profile. Only to a limited extent did the area of non-regulation, the *mamāliki ghair-a'īn*, of pseudo-autonomous chiefs and turbulent tribes – which we may call the 'inner frontier'[36] of Mughal dominion – coincide with natural frontiers within the subcontinent. Regulation and non-regulation must not be seen as absolute opposites but as ends of a continuum. At both extremes of this continuum the fundamental principle of sovereignty remained that of management through conflict. Sovereignty was dependent on the measure that *fitna* could be institutionalized. Fiscal docility was usually more a feature of the plains and of settled agriculture but this was by no means a pacified or demilitarized zone free of conflict. Here too the zamindars had a considerable number of armed retainers and the cultivators themselves could easily produce arms and horses and were always apt to offer resistance to the government and indulge in internecine strife.[37] The inhabitants of the hill-ranges and the interstitial valleys, on the other hand, while less docile, were not exempted from agricultural and non-agricultural imposts of their own chiefs. Hills, jungles and ravines however were *mughulbaṇdī*, a natural obstacle to direct Mughal dominion at all times. For this reason the early seventeenth-century Dutch traveller Pelsaert could call the Mughal Emperor Jahangir the 'king of the plains or the open roads only'.[38] There were quite many tiny states and tribal chiefdoms in such inaccessible hill and mountain regions – often in clusters – all over India, over which neither the Mughals nor even the Marathas could establish more than a perfunctory kind of paramountcy. As Pelsaert describes it:

[36] Cf. J. C. Heesterman, 'Was there an Indian Reaction? Western expansion in Indian perspective', in: H. Wesseling (ed.), *Expansion and Reaction: Essays in European Expansion and Reactions in Asia and Africa* (Leiden, 1978), pp. 31–58.

[37] Cf. Khobrekar, *Tarikh-i-Dilkasha*, p. 231; H. W. Van Santen, *De Verenigde Oost-Indische Compagnie in Gujarat en Hindustan, 1600–1660* (Leiden, 1982), p. 179.

[38] W. H. Moreland and P. Geyl (eds and translators), *Jahangir's India: The Remonstrantie of Francisco Pelsaert* (Cambridge, 1925), p. 58; for the Dutch text see D. H. A. Kolff and H. W. Van Santen (eds), *De Geschriften van Francisco Pelsaert over Mughal Indië: 1627 Kroniek en Remonstrantie* (The Hague, 1979), p. 307.

The whole country is enclosed and broken up by many mountains, and the people who live in, on, or beyond the mountains know nothing of any king, or of Jahangir; they recognize only their Rajas, who are very numerous, and to whom the country is apportioned in many small fragments by old tradition. Jahangir, whose name implies that he grasps the whole world, must therefore be regarded as ruling no more than half the dominions which he claims, since there are nearly as many rebels as subjects.[39]

The exact number of chiefdoms beyond the pale of Mughal regulation can only be a matter of speculation. Pelsaert's estimate of 'one-half of the country which knows nothing of any king' is certainly a gross exaggeration. Manucci wrote in a later period that the great and petty rajas and zamindars living in the midst of jungle exceeded 5,000 in number.[40] It may be presumed that the process of agrarian expansion and settlement in the course of time considerably reduced their number or pushed them further back into the hills.[41] Almost nothing can be said about this process in general (particularly in quantitative terms) except that it had not yet entirely come to a stop in our period.

In Marathi the generic name for all autonomous or semi-autonomous chiefs, rajas, nayaks or zamindars was *saṃsthānik*, 'one who possesses a *saṃsthān*, a royal abode'. The actual reference of the term, although always to a royal residence, could vary widely. A *saṃsthān* was sometimes as small as a single village.[42] Usually it would denote a small chiefdom or state under Maratha suzerainty but it could also refer to an independent state or rival sovereign, like the state of Mysore which was identified by its capital as *saṃsthān śriraṅgapaṭhaṇ*.[43] Thus, unlike the term *zamīndār* in its Mughal usage, the Marathi term *saṃsthānik* did not necessarily entail Maratha suzerainty or a fictional 'universal dominion'.[44] It conferred a status which did not derive from submission but rather from a free-standing right. This status was one of an often petty

39 Moreland and Geyl, *Jahangir's India*, pp. 58–9; Kolff and Van Santen, *Pelsaert*, pp. 307–8.

40 W. Irvine (ed. and translator), *Storia Do Mogor by Niccolao Manucci*, 4 vols (Calcutta, 1965–6), 2, p. 444.

41 See for instance the case-study of Jedhe.

42 *BGS*, o.s. no.4, p. 5. The word *saṃsthān*, lit. 'one's own place', is also sometimes used for religious foundations (*SSRPD*, 6, no.797). No rigid distinction can be made between *inām* and *saṃsthān*. The Savants of Vadi in fact held their *saṃsthān* under an *ināmpatra* (*BGS*, n.s. no.10, p. 2).

43 *SSRPD*, 4, no.378. See also *ibid.*, 3, no.229; 4, no.9; 7, no.457.

44 If however they were under Maratha suzerainty *saṃsthāniks* would be addressed through *tākīdpatras* or 'deeds of injunction' which, by definition, were never on terms of equality.

royal dignity which however always warranted an administrative autonomy even after formal submission. Given their internal autonomy in revenue administration the *saṃsthāns* were not brought under the surveys. If they were not independently remodelled on the revenue system of the Peshwas they continued to operate under their own 'archaic' systems.[45] The numerous references to them in the Peshwa Diaries are concerned with little else than the payment of tribute (*khaṇḍaṇī*).[46] They show that the height of demand usually ranged from 15,000 to 30,000 rupees per year, or in a few cases ran as high as several lacs, and always had a portion of about 10% separated off as *darbārkharc* or *aṇtastha*, a 'secret payment' to the Peshwa himself. The actual payment of tribute was usually in arrears and fluctuated much, sometimes even leading to the cession of land.

The height of the tribute demand was, in contrast with the land-revenue demand in the regulation provinces, not determined on the basis of an assessment of the *saṃsthān*'s resources but rather in proportion to its power of resistance. The weaker chiefs always paid more than the stronger who considered it a point of honour not to pay unless forced to do so.[47] The tribute represented a simple aggregate sum imposed as a recognition of sovereignty and in payment of support or protection against internal or neighbouring rivals. Most of these rajas were brought under Maratha sovereignty when the Mughal recession offered scope for intervention in and arbitration of succession and financial disputes, or preserving a dynasty from 'falling from royal status' (*rajyabhraṣṭ*). In many regions the Marathas supported one of the most powerful chiefs to keep the rest in check and to be able to hold him responsible for the depredations that were carried out in the plains.[48] Regular succession was often a problem and acknowledgement by a suzerain power was eagerly sought for. This entailed the payment of a *nazar* or recognition-fee in any case, and if the stakes were high it could result in a true financial blood-letting or be accompanied by the cession of large holdings to the Maratha government. The Peshwa was sometimes explicitly made responsible for 'protection against

45 For an example of the first see Y. V. Khare, 'Lakṣmeśvar Pargaṇyācī Jhaḍatī', BISMQ, 18, 2 (1937), pp. 25–31; for a description of an archaic system see *BGS*, n.s. no.10, p. 2.

46 *SSRPD*, 3, pp. 202–45; 9, pp. 269–314. See also Jenkins, *Nagpur*, pp. 131–42.

47 Cf. S. Prakash, 'Gujarat in 1857' (Mimeograph, Centre of South Asian Studies, University of Cambridge, 30 January 1985); Wafi, *Muqaddima*, 2, p. 613.

48 Jenkins, *Nagpur*, pp. 131–42.

invaders'.[49] As a suzerain power the Maratha government also retained certain prerogatives in the field of criminal justice.[50] Apart from the payment of tribute, or discountable from it, the *saṃsthāniks* in their turn were liable to the performance of military service for the Peshwa.[51] Their military service was primarily directed locally against recalcitrant neighbouring chiefs or zamindars but at times was also integrated on a wider and more regular basis in armies of composite recruitment.[52] In the same way tribals armed with bows and arrows issuing from the chieftaincies in the hills were enlisted as village guards in the plains or as watchmen and protectors (not the least against their own kind) of roads, or as animal-hunters, or as foot-soldiers in the army as the Mavalis already were under the Bijapur Sultanate. Brigandage and policing were two edges of the same sword, a sensitive insurance system for unmolested passage which is of ancient inspiration in India.[53] We find it recommended for instance in the *Kāmandakīya* with respect to the Bedar living between the Krishna and the Tungabhadra.[54] In the course of centuries such tribes could become more and more drawn into the life of the plains, sometimes becoming agriculturalists as well. Thus the Bedar reached a fairly high social status in the seventeenth and eighteenth centuries. The Mavalis of the Ghat-Mahta and the Hetkaris of the Konkan became instrumental in the establishment of the power of the Bhonsles. Ramoshis policed the villages and roads throughout Maharashtra; Bhils and Kolis did the same in Khandesh, along the Sahyadri range north of Junnar, in the greater part of Gujarat and north of the Narmada. But from being in charge of *caukīs* as *vatandārs* it always remained an extremely easy step back to 'unlawful' brigandage or blackmail.[55] This occurred constantly with the complicity of the chiefs or *zamīndārs*, in particular when some guns could be procured. All the Maratha

49 E.g. *SSRPD*, 9, no. 314, where a tribute of 150,001 rupees is demanded from Soma Shelhar Naik Rohasappa of Harapanhali with the stipulation that 'his country should be protected by the (Maratha) government against attacks by Haiderkhan'.

50 *P.A.: List 12, File 569*, no.597 of 1865.

51 Cf. Gordon, 'Scarf and Sword', p. 421.

52 *TKKP*, 1, nos 5–6, 9–10, 13–17; *MIS*, 15, nos 1–2; *SSRPD*, 9, no.54; *SPD*, 31, no.1; Richards, 'Hyderabad Karnatik', p. 243; Habib, *Agrarian System*, pp. 141, 163–8.

53 Cf. pp. 45–6; Cohn, 'Political Systems', p. 319.

54 Cf. Derrett, *Hoysalas*, p. 9; Shulman, 'South Indian Bandits', p. 286.

55 *SSRPD*, 3, nos 249–51; 4, no.128; 6, no.646, 657–8; 9, nos 323–32; M. Elphinstone to J. Briggs, *Bengal Secret and Political Consultations*, vol.301, 31 July 1818, pt. 1, no.89; *P.A.: List 13, Ru. 27, File 530*.

government could do in such a situation was to sequestrate their vatans and attempt to withhold their emoluments, send a regiment to chase them out of their *haṭīs*, the fortified residences which they built in the wilds, and then try to induce them to stick to their official police-duties (*jaṇgal*) and make them wear a packet bearing the government's seal around their necks.[56] Other tribal groups, such as the Pindharis living on the borders of Maharashtra and in the Karnataka, or the Beldar, did not lose their predatory character at all and were employed in hordes in the Maratha *mulūkhgirī* armies as plunder specialists.[57] In principle, the Maratha policy of recruiting marauders to make levies in foreign country is not different, except in scale, from what the *saṃsthāniks* did when they descended into the plains or raided their neighbours. It was always the incorporation of disorder, or rather the complementarity of order and disorder, which made possible the establishment of sovereignty.

Variations in the political situation of hill- and jungle-chiefs derived from topographical differences as well as from the vicissitudes of state-development at large and the occurrence of cluster formation or the development of pockets of tiny states allying with each other against outside interference. The two most notorious of such clusters developed in the Southern Maratha Country, and in Gujarat, in the *mavāsī* part beyond the Mahi river. This was due not merely to the advantages of the natural habitat but also to the perpetually continuing rival claims to sovereignty over these areas. In the Southern Maratha Country, the later British-Indian districts of Dharwar and Belgaum, there were many *zamīndārs* who constituted themselves into *saṃsthāniks, pāḷegārs* or *peśkaś zamīndārs* ('tributaries') around the middle of the seventeenth century in the wake of Bijapuri expansion.[58] The rivalries of successive sovereigns, the Mughals, the Nizam, the Nawabs of Savanur, the Peshwas, the Kolhapur Rajas, Hyder Ali and Tipu Sultan made it possible for them to retain their position of tributaries. In parts of these districts where rival pretensions to sovereignty became permanent the *peśkaś zamīndārs* or *saṃsthāniks* could become tributary to both of the rivals. Such was for instance the case in the districts of Chikodi and Manoli where most zamindars were held by

[56] *SSRPD*, 6, nos 656, 658. [57] *SSRPD*, 9, nos 350–1.

[58] G. Wingate, 'Reports on the revenue survey settlements of the Hoobullee, Nuwulgoond, Kode, and Dharwar Talookas of the Dharwar collectorate', *BGS*, o.s. no. 12 (Bombay, 1853), pp. 4–5 and 'Extract from Manson's Report', *ibid.*, pp. i, vii; *BG*, XXII, pp. 442–6.

both the governments of Poona and Kolhapur to be tributary to them and to have to furnish military aid throughout the second half of the eighteenth century. What became a permanent situation here was only a transitory phase in many areas in Hindustan when the Marathas started levying their *cauth*. In the north many zamindars first acquired tributary status by exploiting Mughal–Maratha rivalry, then started to pay one-quarter of the tribute to the Marathas, and after that paid the whole tribute to the Marathas alone, to be brought back under regulation eventually by the Marathas.[59] In the Southern Maratha Country the position of *peśkaś zamīndārs* could become so strong that they began to withhold their payments indefinitely until forced by military threat.[60] As under the Mughals these were called *zortalab zamīndārs*. Again, in those areas of the Southern Maratha Country and Northern Gujarat where the zamindars could not achieve the position of tributaries they greatly enlarged their emoluments by appropriating *inām* lands.[61] With the zamindars becoming more and more independent *puṇḍa* broke out, a kind of protection-racketeering or 'sub-infeudation' leading to regular tribute payments and alienations of land by chiefs and their armed retainers (*śetsanadīs*) of tribes of Berads, etc., amongst each other.[62] In parts of Gujarat – notably Kathiawar – a whole network of tributary relationships arose by a process of commendation of smaller to bigger chiefs. By far the largest receivers of tribute remained here the Peshwa and the Gaikwar but on various occasions Junagarh, Bantwa, Manfrol and Nawanagar in Kathiawar and Idar in Mahi Kantha also made smaller tributary demands on their weaker neighbours in return for assistance against the Maratha *mulūkhgirī* army.[63]

In Kaira and Ahmadabad, the two districts of Gujarat beyond the Mahi, we find most of the *mavāsī* villages situated in hilly or

59 *MIS*, I, no.I.

60 G. R. Gleig, *The Life of Sir Thomas Munro*, 3 vols (London, 1830), 2, p. 274.

61 *B.A.: R.D.*, vol. 5/549 of 1834, p. 86; T. Marshall, *Statistical Reports on the Pergunnahs of Padshapoor, Belgam, Kalaniddee and Chandgarh, Khanapoor, Bagulkot and Badamy, and Hoondgoond, in the Southern Maratha Country, etc.* (Bombay, 1822), pp. 22–3; A. T. Etheridge, 'Narrative of the Bombay Inam Commission', *BGS*, n.s. no.132 (Poona, 1873), p. 19.

62 Cf. Marshall, *Statistical Reports*, pp. 22–3, 173. Marshall opposes *puṇḍa* to *kāṭika*: while the latter is plunder and robbery and possibly pure destruction, *puṇḍa* is the levying of contributions by means of an armed force and will rather protect than destroy resources in order to be able to make a second draft.

63 I. Copland, *The British Raj and the Indian Princes: Paramountcy in Western India, 1857–1930* (Bombay, 1982), p. 19.

broken ground surrounded with ravines and jungles and difficult of access.[64] *Mavāsī* is a Muslim appellation introduced as early as the twelfth century, deriving from the Arabic *ma'ṣiya*, 'to oppose, to rebel'.[65] The villages so called were held by aboriginal Kolis and Bhils or by pre-Muslim immigrant *girāśī* chiefs or Rajputs. Under the Muslim rulers the latter retained a larger part of their talukas and villages than the aboriginal tribes. Also they later recovered much of the land which they first lost, when in 1573 the districts were transferred to the Mughals and particularly in the period 1720–50 when they were the scene of almost unceasing conflicts between the Marathas and the Muslim viceroys and nobles. Under the shared government of the Gaikwar and the Peshwa the *mavāsīs* paid a tribute which could be increased when the government gained strength. They also levied a tribute themselves, called *girās*, from their weaker neighbours. It was not usual to interfere with the internal management of their villages or to examine the state of their receipts.

As the above examples show the inner frontier was a structural feature of sovereignty but not a static one. It could expand or contract to some extent. Damaji Gaikwar writes in a letter of 1761 that 'due to the news of the Panipat disaster, the Muslims, Koli chiefs and *mavāsīs* have grown insubordinate.'[66] This also demonstrates quite clearly that these supposedly isolated hill-chiefs were capable of responding without delay to a shift in the political balance-system of the subcontinent at large and that, in other words, they can be seen as an integral part of this balance-system. Furthermore, this inner frontier was not so much anarchy as just another form of dissidence around which the state organized itself through *fitna*. Manucci says that 'usually there is some rebellion of the rajas and zamindars going on in the Mughal kingdom' and that in response the king issues orders to 'destroy the rebels and send their heads to court' or 'the rebel to be sent in alive or dead'.[67] It is an established fact that the Bahmani Muhammad Shah and later the Mughal Emperors occasionally massacred 'robbers' and immor-

64 *EIP*, 3, pp. 677–97, 701–6.

65 *Indian Antiquary* (Bombay, 1872–1923), 4, pp. 74, 76; F. Steingass, *A Comprehensive Persian–English Dictionary* (London, Henley and Boston, 1977), s.v.; K. P. Kulkarni, *Marathi Etymological Dictionary* (Poona, 1964), s.v. The appelation of *mawāsāt* was applied under the Delhi Sultans to regions stretching from the Doab as far as Awadh and Bihar (Raychaudhuri and Habib, *Cambridge Economic History of India*, 1, p. 60).

66 *Historical Selections from Baroda State Records*, 1, no.80.

67 Irvine, *Storia Do Mogor*, 2, p. 462.

tared thousands of heads in pillars along the roadsides.[68] But in this practice (which is perhaps Central-Asian in origin) the intention of a demonstration effect is obvious, and it has drawn an inordinate amount of attention even in modern historiography. Force was no doubt applied, but always within the context of *fitna*, i.e., in a politic way. The Peshwa Diaries are full of reports of 'disturbances' created by gangs of Kolis issuing from *saṃsthāns* or by *mavāsīs*.[69] These appear to have been a regular feature in certain areas and show a remarkably obstinate continuity over long periods of time. In particular trade-routes and commercial centres attracted 'marauders' from the hills. 'Near Ahmadabad, Burhanpur, Agra, Delhi, Lahore, and many other cities, thieves and robbers come in force by night or day like open enemies', writes Pelsaert.[70] In his time, at Surat the forces of the Rajpipla Raja came 'pillaging up to, or inside, the city, murdering the people, and burning the villages'.[71] The latter Raja, who apparently visited the Dutch lodge, lived about a hundred kilometres north-east of the city in the jungle-fort Songarh where he enjoyed vast influence among the numerous tribes of Bhils and Kolis. He is first mentioned by Pelsaert but we meet him again in the early eighteenth century when the Mughals appointed some officials in his zamindari.[72] The appointment of these officials was resented by the Raja and he had the principal of them killed. This led to a military action against Rajpipla. The Raja was not killed however, but compelled to pay an indemnity. To exterminate him would, we may presume, have been too dangerous as he kept in check large numbers of tribals. For the Maratha general Pilaji Gaikwar the Rajpipla Raja was first an easy ally who greatly facilitated *mulūkhgirī* raids into Northern Gujarat and the defeat in 1723 of the Mughal governor of Surat.[73] In the Peshwa Diary the chiefs of Rajpipla and surrounding places, with their Bhils and Kolis, turn up again in the years 1754–6, 'carrying off cattle and committing *mavāsgirī* and levying tribute (*girāspaṭṭī*)'.[74] But the Peshwa's government, instead of suppressing these 'plunderings', imposed

68 V. A. Smith, *The Oxford History of India* (third ed. by P. Spear, Oxford, 1958), p. 282; R. C. Temple (ed.), *The Travels of Peter Mundy in Europe and Asia, 1608–1667*, 5 vols (London, 1914–24), 2, pp. 90, 185–6.

69 E.g. *SSRPD*, 4, no.9; 6, no.664; 9, nos 269, 289.

70 Moreland and Geyl, *Jahangir's India*, pp. 58–9; Kolff and Van Santen, *Pelsaert*, pp. 307–8.

71 *Ibid.*

72 Siddiqi, *Land Revenue Administration*, p. 24.

73 Cf. p. 117.

74 *SSRPD*, 3, nos 226, 234.

cesses on the chiefs and thus indirectly participated in their spoils.[75]

Another example may be given to illustrate further the inefficacy of brute force. At the turn of the seventeenth century the *zamīndār* of Ramnagar, a region also adjacent to the port of Surat, was in imperial service with a mansab of 1,500 zat and 600 savar. At this time the local Mughal governor Matabar Khan was confronted with unremitting Maratha incursions. The zamindar served the Mughals with 100 cavalry and 500 infantry and had a considerable population of Kolis and Bhils attached to him with which he was also involved in the security maintenance of four forts and the highways in his region. Owing to the death of the zamindar the Kolis and Bhils became unnerved. His fourteen-year old son is then put forward, and he is assured of the same imperial favours as his father enjoyed. Additional lands are even assigned to him to enable him to keep his troops intact and pay off his father's debts. The governor, in a letter to his superiors, expresses his fear that if the zamindar 'gets a small mansab and the jagirs are not given to him it is possible that the Kolis may continue to create disturbances and join the Marathas'.[76]

In this way the potential of dissidence was exploited to establish sovereign power. The zamindars not only needed their own armed forces and their fortifications for the collection of revenue and to keep the roads under protection but they also commonly made up the core of the hereditary garrisons of the forts under direct royal patronage.[77] The Maratha hill-forts, many of which were built by Shivaji, were practically unconquerable by force. They continued to give protection until about the period after the Battle of Panipat, when the Marathas began to rely more on mercenaries and Scindhia introduced a European type of infantry and artillery which made the hill-forts useless.[78] The *Ājñāpatra* still asserts that 'the essence of the whole kingdom is forts'.[79] The forts however, being

75 The latter appears to have been a general proceeding (cf. Cohn, 'Political Systems', p. 319; W. H. Moreland, *From Akbar to Aurangzeb* (New Delhi, 1972), p. 288).

76 Pagadi, *Studies in Maratha History*, 2, no.22.

77 Habib, *Agrarian System*, pp. 164–5; Grant Duff, *History*, 1, pp. 125, 240; Gordon, 'Slow Conquest', p. 4; *idem*, 'Scarf and Sword', p. 421; *idem*, 'Forts and Social Control in the Maratha State', *MAS*, 13, 1 (1979), p. 16; Banhatti, *Ājñāpatra*, ch.8; Vakaskar, *Sabhasadācī Bakhar*, pp. 30, 72; Gleig, *Life of Munro*, 2, p. 268; Marshall, *Statistical Reports*, pp. 80 ff; *P.A.: List 13, Ru. 1, File 1*, Proc. no. 1014; *ibid., Ru. 3, File 28*, no. 181 of 1849.

78 M. G. Ranade, 'Introduction to the Peshwa's Diaries', *JBBRAS*, XX (reprint 1969), p. 459; Gordon, 'Scarf and Sword', p. 426.

79 Banhatti ed., ch.8.

practically unassailable, could be (and often were) captured through *fitna*, in which case their strength was merely one of the determinants of the price of surrender.[80] To counter this the Marathas could do no more than attempt to maintain, as they did everywhere, a system of management by conflict in each fort through appointing three officials of conjoint authority.[81] For the same reason the *Ājñāpatra* warns against the appointment in fort garrisons of 'deśmukhs and deśpāṇḍes, pāṭīls, kuḷkarṇīs, caugulās, and other hereditary vatandārs from the neighbourhood of the fort'.[82] The treatise is apprehensive that they would rather surrender the fort than have their lands ravaged by the enemy. In practice no fort could do without at least a subsidiary garrison of the local tribal militia under the command of its own zamindars, enjoying service lands all around. Ramoshis, Mahars, Kolis, etc., were furthermore always of great importance particularly in the intelligence service. In some areas, like in the Southern Maratha Country, the local country militia provided even the main body of the military garrison.

Coming to the realm of settled agriculture, the area of direct administration or 'regulation', we find that rivalry and conflict among the co-sharing *zamīndārs* provided the organizational principle of sovereignty in the same way as it did in the complementary tribal realm of 'non-regulation'. In the settled areas 'regulation' however implied that the *zamīndārs* were not left with internal administrative autonomy in their estates as the *peśkaś zamīndārs* or *saṃsthāniks* always were. Regulation, as we defined it, was a dualist system of revenue management and accountancy and it presupposed the sovereign's interference through a land-survey, an assessment of the agricultural productivity of the land. Complementary to non-regulation, the extent of regulation varied inversely with it. The Mughals sometimes attempted to make an assessment of the land even of *peśkaś zamīndārs* or, in other words, to change tribute into land-revenue.[83] On the other hand the Mughals also attempted, as in the eastern Deccan under Aurangzeb, to give to land-revenue-paying *zamīndārs* the semblance of *peśkaś zamīndārs* in order to secure their loyalty and active service.[84] Under the Maratha and Indo-Muslim kings regulation

80 Cf. p. 33.
81 S. N. Sen, *The Military System of the Marathas* (Calcutta, 1979), pp. 81–2.
82 Banhatti ed., ch.8.
83 Nural Hasan, 'Zamindars under the Mughals', p. 22.
84 Cf. p. 181.

could also temporarily make place for revenue farming or contract tenure which dispensed to a varying degree with accountancy and the kind of dualism and supervision which it made possible.[85]

Only with these reservations can we designate the agricultural plains and lower hill regions as the 'regulation area'. It was an area which was parcelled out among *vatandārs* in rather ill-defined, historically shifting units which were unsystematically called *parganā, karyāt, tālukā, sammat, tappā*, or *tarf*. One such unit made up the *vilāyat* or 'domain' of one *deśmukh/deśpāṇḍe* combination and comprised a number of villages ranging from 10 (e.g. *karyāt* Sasvad of the Jagtap deśmukh) to 200 (e.g. *parganā* Vai of the Pisal deśmukh), and on the average was perhaps 40–80.[86] In the *vilāyat* in which he 'had a stake', in which he was 'rooted through customary practice' (*jaftaraft*), the deśmukh had to do the *gastī* or 'patrolling' and the *lāvṇīsāṇcṇī*, the 'settlement of leases and rents'.[87] Like the *pāṭīl* on the village level, in the latter task he was assisted and checked by a brahman accountant or registrar, the *deśkuḷkarṇī* or *deśpāṇḍe* who kept all records. In the Deccan it is common to find the vatans of *deśmukh* and *deśpāṇḍe* united with respectively those of *pāṭīl* and village *kuḷkarṇī* in one or a few villages within the vilāyat.[88] Mergers of the offices of *deśmukh* and *deśpāṇḍe* were rare but if they occurred were completely at odds with dualist management, which was normally easily achieved also because the accountants virtually always belonged to the brahman caste while the patils and deśmukhs were Marathas, i.e. non-brahmans. An example is found in the town of Ahmadnagar where a brahman was ⅓ deśmukh and at the same time patil and kulkarni.[89]

In whatever ways they were entangled with each other, the vatandars were the medium through which the sovereign had to gain access to local resources and secure the adhesion of the tax-paying rayats.[90] The more difficulties with the agrarian *mise en valeur* had arisen the more pronounced their role usually became. With their aid only could the government's rent-roll or *jamābaṇḍī*,

[85] Cf. Chapter 4–IV. [86] *SCS*, 7, p. 5.

[87] *SCS*, 2, no. 197; Malcolm, *Central India*, 2, p. 9.

[88] An illustration of this is provided by the Jagdale deśmukh. See also R. D. Choksey, *Ratnagiri Collectorate (1821–1829)* (Poona, 1958), p. 142.

[89] W. H. Sykes, 'On the Land Tenures of the Dekkan', *Journal of the Royal Asiatic Society*, 2 (1835), p. 220.

[90] Cf. *SCS*, 7, p. 6; Siddiqi, *Land Revenue Administration*, p. 35; Nurul Hasan, 'Zamindars under the Mughals', p. 26; Malcolm, *Central India*, 2, p. 9; Gordon, 'Slow Conquest', p. 4; Jenkins, *Nagpur*, p. 95; Habib, *Agrarian System*, p. 167.

which was based on a survey made once for all, be adjusted annually to the prevailing conditions.[91] Remissions, loans, higher or lower assessment rates or extra cesses were always given effect by local government officials through their agency. In all cases *vatan* was a hereditary office associated with a package of dispersed rights and privileges (*haklājimā*) of a material nature and of honours and honorific presents (*tasrīfatī, mānpān*) to the least of which the incumbent clung with extreme tenacity.[92] When speaking of a *vatandār* we should normally not think of an individual incumbent but of a brotherhood (*bhāūbaṇd*) of patrilineal relatives with a certain number of non-related clients sharing the vatan, and with one member – usually the eldest – holding the seniority right (*vaḍīlpān*) with the seal (*śikā nagar*). Moreover a vatan could be broken up into even more shares through sale to outsiders.[93] The resulting, often quite complicated repartition schemes we leave out of consideration for the present and treat *vatan* as a single executive office and a single *hak* or 'right'. In concrete terms this *hak* of deśmukhs, deśpandes, patils and kulkarnis was composed of three elements: 1. *haklājimā*, 'rights and perquisites', 'dues' (including honours) contributed directly by the cultivators as the zamindar's 'salary' (*muśāhirā*) or *hak* in the strict sense; 2. *rusūm*, a customary share in the government's land-revenue; 3. *ināms*, revenue-exempt lands and villages.[94]

By *haklājimā* or *hak* in the strict sense the Marathas denoted what under the Mughals was generally referred to as *haq-i-zamīndārī*, a miscellany of fractional charges made upon the gross produce of the rayats in both kind and cash, varying regionally and from village to village according to customary practice.[95] Under the Marathas the amount and nature of these dues also showed great variations, and in some places certain types of hereditary holdings, *mirās* land or *ināms* or *kuraṇ* pasture, were exempted from the *haks* of either village- or district-vatandars, or of both, or of some of them. Kulkarnis and deśpandes were entitled to similar haks as the patils and deśmukhs but these were commonly 25% to 75% lower.[96] Village artisans and servants who were not counted as

[91] *EIP*, 4, pp. 628–31. [92] *MIS*, 20, nos 13, 89; *SPD*, 31, no. 85.
[93] See Chapter 2–III.
[94] See esp. *SSRPD*, 3, no. 495; 4, no. 253; 7, no. 482.
[95] *MIS*, 17, no. 30; *BGS*, o.s. no. 4; Malcolm, *Central India*, 2, p. 7; Sykes, 'Land Tenures of the Dekkan', p. 220; Grover, 'Dehat-i-Taaluqa', 1, pp. 166–77, 259–61.
[96] Sykes, 'Land Tenures of the Dekkan', p. 233.

zamīndārs but as *balutedārs* were also recipients of *haks* which were however of still much smaller amount. Under the Deccan Sultans and the Marathas the zamindars and balutedars were always permitted to collect their *haks* themselves.[97] These permanent dues however were not received on a rayatvari basis but out of a village-pool called the *grām kharc* or *gāṇv kharc*. This village-pool covered not only the *haks* of the village- and district-vatandars and the balutedars but also the so-called 'contingent expenses' (*sādilvārī*) of the village which were of a fluctuating and incidental nature, comprising such items as allowances to temples, the expenses of religious festivals, nazars, etc. The dues of the vatandars and balutedars which were paid directly out of the *grām kharc* were designated as *parbhārā haks*, as they were levied 'with the pretermission of the government'. This does not mean that they could be charged *ad libitum*. The government sanctioned a certain customary practice or could demand an increase or decrease of the haks. For instance, 'a new hak on account of the rayats' consisting of 2 man of grain and 5 taka in cash per village was given hereditarily to the Silimbkhar deśmukh of Gunjanmaval in 1703, allegedly because he had so many coparceners (*vārisdār*) that he could not maintain himself.[98] Or, to take another example, the Bijapur Sultan increased the haks of the deśmukhs and patils as a reward for the assistance they gave him in the construction of the Bijapur fort.[99] The government's power to keep the haks under control must have varied considerably and was certainly never complete. The *Ājñāpatra* expressly warns against 'the imposition of additional haks on the rayats', which, it says, 'causes extreme hardship'.[100] We can perhaps also infer from this that the imposition of an extra hak was not normally accompanied by a corresponding deduction from the government's land-revenue demand (*rājbhāg*). The *grām kharc*, although it always left room for contingent charges, was relatively circumscribed under the Peshwas in the second half of the eighteenth century when the haks had a place in the village *jamābaṇḍī* of the government, until about twenty years before the British take-over. The haks were nominally fixed and the patil's power to redistribute the sadilvari was limited. Even then, it has been estimated, the total village expenses were never less than 25% of the gross revenue. At times when the powers of the village- and district-zamindars increased due to a

97 *EIP*, 4, p. 667. 98 *MIS*, 17, no.30. 99 *MIS*, 15, no.2; cf. p. 165.
100 Banhatti ed., ch.7.

change in the wider political constellation, the *grām kharc* could amount to double or treble the acknowledged government demand.[101] Under Shivaji the zamindars were strongly curtailed when their vatans, with the *haklājimā*, were held under sequestration and the incumbents were paid by means of annual cash allowances from the treasury.[102] Even during that period the collection of haks was not entirely stopped in practice.

The vatandars always enjoyed an authority over the rayats which was to a large extent beyond the control of the government and irreducible by centralizing efforts of the sovereign. They were co-sharers of sovereignty and *ipso facto* co-sharers of the land's produce. It should further be emphasized that, whether the haks were 'surreptitiously' enlarged or not, they were always a charge additional to the land-revenue demand or 'king's share' (*rājbhāg*) and the cesses siphoned off by the government on its own behalf. From the latter however the vatandars also received a 'salary' (*muśāhirā*) directly. This was in the first place the *rusūm*, a customary payment of a share of the government's land-revenue which was paid to district-zamindars under Indo-Muslim and Maratha sovereignty generally.[103] In the Mughal regulation districts this share nominally ranged from perhaps 2.5% to 10% of the assessed land-revenue and was either deducted from the government collections or collected directly by the zamindars from the rayats.[104] Under the Marathas it was in practice usually more, but generalized estimates are in the nature of things impossible to give. Under the name of *rusūm* the Maratha king received 10% of the assessed revenue of the six Mughal subhas of the Deccan as *sardeśmukh*, while the Peshwa received 5% of the same as *sardeśpāṇḍe*.[105] These figures again had only a distant bearing on actual collections made under the title. The Maratha king's *cauth* is not formally subsumed under *rusūm* but in principle it is also a share deducted on the zamindars' behalf from the government land-revenue. The 'one-quarter' remuneration of zamindari still survived at some places in the eighteenth century: as *mālikāna* and *do-biswī* in Northern India, as *vāṇṭā* in Gujarat.[106] Under the latter tenure one-quarter of the village lands was set apart for the

101 *EIP*, 4, pp. 715–6. 102 Cf. pp. 269–70.

103 Cf. Alam, 'Zamindars and Mughal Power', p. 77; Grover, 'Dehat-i-Taaluqa', p. 260.

104 *Ibid.* 105 Cf. pp. 93–4, 98, 203–4.

106 Habib, *Agrarian System*, pp. 148–50; *EIP*, 3, p. 708; *P.A.: List 11, Kaira Volumes*, no. 7 of 1864.

zamindars and it may therefore with perhaps more justice be called a revenue-free tenure than a share in the land-revenue. Under the Marathas the deśmukh of Phaltan also still claimed one-quarter of the whole revenue of his district.[107] Patils in Deogarh and Chanda claimed a quarter of the government demand in money or in rent-free land.[108] Bhils in Khandesh still had a right to *cauth*.[109] An interesting survival is also found in taluka Kalanudi in the Southern Maratha Country, where the aggregate body of zamindars together claimed a prescriptive right to one-fourth of the revenue of all the land.[110] Here the district-officials desai, deśpande and nadgaunda were united with the properly local functionaries patil, kulkarni, caugula, gurav, and even the dhers in the interior subdivision of the fourth or *cauthāī vatan*. There seems to have been no uniform rule for proportioning the shares of the several officials, but in some villages one office was endowed with the largest portion and in some another. At or near the residence of the families of the desais or deśpandes they themselves had become the greatest sharers, but in many of the distant villages the patil stood at the head of them. *Cauth* perquisites such as these are perhaps best seen as appropriate to a form of semi-regulation. In any case it is far in excess of normal *rusūm* deductions made under the Maratha government, even in the eighteenth century. Under Maratha regulation the *rusūm* of deśmukhs fluctuated between 1 and 10% and on the average reached about 5% of the assessed nett revenue and customs charges, while the *rusūm* of deśpandes was about half as large.[111]

Finally, in the regulation tracts the zamindars were always supported by revenue-free villages and lands (*inām*), the amounts of which varied according to the size of the districts and the magnitude of their tasks as well as on account of political reasons.[112] *Izāfat* or 'additional' villages were sometimes given permanently in *inām* to deśmukhs and deśpandes over and above the *inām* villages already in their possession if they did additional work. A deśmukh had some 1 to 4 villages in *inām* and service lands

107 Elphinstone, *Report*, App. p. 125 (Extract of a letter from Capt. Grant, Political Agent at Satara to the Hon. M. Elphinstone, 17 August 1819).

108 Jenkins, *Nagpur*, p. 84.

109 *SSRPD*, 3, no.250.

110 Marshall, *Statistical Reports*, p. 76.

111 Jenkins, *Nagpur*, p. 95; Malcolm, *Central India*, 2, p. 7; Gordon, 'Slow Conquest', p. 4; *TKKP*, 1, no.23; Sykes, 'Land Tenures of the Dekkan', pp. 220–1; *P.A.: List 14, Ru. 1, File 9*, no.703 of 1828.

112 Cf. esp. Malcolm, *Central India*, 2, pp. 7–8.

scattered in many villages of his pargana; a deśpande considerably less. The service lands of the deśmukhs could in some instances reach a great number. At Mohol for instance the two sharers of the office of deśmukh each had 600 bighas of revenue-free land.[113] At Parnair the three sharers of the office and the kulkarni and one or two gosavis had over 1,004 bighas. The deśpandes had 25–50% less. Patils, kulkarnis, and mahars (or dhers) etc. had lands in *inām* but never whole villages. In general, if the proceeds of a pargana increased the remuneration of the zamindars in terms of shares of land-revenue and exempted lands increased with them; their remuneration also decreased if the proceeds decreased. In this respect too the vatandars remained co-sharers of sovereignty rather than servants of a despotic king engaged in the collection of the 'surplus produce' of the land.

III Patrilineage and coparcenary

The vatans, zamindaris or chieftaincies of the king's 'co-sharers' were held by vested right and descended in patrilineal inheritance. With regard to succession, semi-autonomous chieftains of royal or pseudo-royal status – no matter how petty – generally observed the rule of primogeniture.[1] Indian rules of succession however were never absolute and, apart from the exclusive rights in the male line, succession to kingship would be a matter of a scale of priorities. Thus the claims of sons had priority over those of brothers, elder brothers over younger brothers, and natural sons over adopted sons.[2] Such a unitary *rāj* was the zamindari of the dynasty of Bhonsle, until a split into a Satara and a Kolhapur branch became unavoidable.

For all tenures under regulation the evidence is again very strong of the general custom of genealogical sharing, but no uniform rule was observed in dividing the shares of inams, vatans, or miras lands among brothers.[3] The strict Hindu custom dictated that all sons and grandsons in patrilineal succession should inherit equal shares, while Muslims also allowed for a share to females. The division of a vatan or inam into shares did not imply a partition of the actual land but only a division of the proceeds, rights, privileges, and duties

113 Sykes, 'Land Tenures of the Dekkan', p. 220.

1 Siddiqi, *Land Revenue Administration*, p. 24; Habib, *Agrarian System*, pp. 183–4; Gordon, 'Legitimacy and Loyalty', p. 291.

2 Cf. Burling, quoted by Gordon, 'Legitimacy and Loyalty', p. 291.

3 *EIP*, 3, pp. 816–18.

amongst the members of an essentially undivided family.[4] The eldest male member of the family often received a larger share of the proceeds on account of his function of general manager (*mālik zamīndār*). While the coparceners sharing an estate could rise to an enormous number, partition of the land was much more checked and rarely led to the creation of more than two, three, or perhaps four independent units. Even so, the definition of such units as fractions (½, ⅓, or ¼) of an original single zamindari shows a continuing recognition of its unity.[5] And if fractionalization of a vatan took place on account of sale or any other reason, the 'seniority rights' (*vaḍilpan*) and the seal (*śikā nagar*) of the entire vatan were reserved to a single individual.

This situation has conflict, so to speak, built in and we did notice in effect that disputes about vatans and other hereditary rights were rife. Problems of succession commonly played a large role in these. If the zamindar's task of agrarian management became jeopardized by such a dispute, the government would sequestrate the estate and temporarily appoint an agent of its own to do the work. The problem could then be decided by ordering a formal partition, or by ordering the vatan to be enjoyed alternately by two different branches of the family, or by imposing a certain division of shares in conformity with the dictates of Vijñāneśvara's joint family law in consultation with a brahmasabhā or 'brahman committee'.[6] The joint or 'extended' family was a characteristic form of hereditary property enjoyment in India in general and particularly in the Deccan and the south.[7] This was so even when the eldest lineal heir ostensibly appeared as the sole proprietor and his name was recorded in all deeds as that of the vatandar or inamdar.[8] The incumbent of a vatan or inam was always a *bhāūbaṇd* or 'brotherhood', the members of which are referred to as 'co-sharers' or 'coparceners' of the vatan, as *dāīj* – a corruption of the term *dāyadā* which the Ājñāpatra uses to describe the zamindars as

4 *BG*, XVII, p. 556; XIX, p. 327; XX, p. 365; XXIII, p. 456; A. Steele, *The Law and Custom of Hindoo Castes within the Dekhun Provinces subject to the Presidency of Bombay* (London, 1868), p. 209; Cohn, 'Political Systems', p. 316; *TKKP*, 2, no. 19; *P.A.: List 13, Ru. 90*, Report no. 42.

5 Cf. also Habib, *Agrarian System*, p. 157.

6 *P.A.: List 13, Ru, 1, File 2*, Proceedings 43A, 815B (nivāḍpatra, moḍi document 7 in *Inam Commission Rumals*, no. 5); *ibid.*, Proc. 681C; *ibid., File 1*, Proc. 776B; *MIS*, 20, no. 126.

7 Derrett, 'Development of the Concept of Property', p. 57.

8 *P.A.: List 13, Ru. 1, File 131 of 1831.*

'co-sharers' of the king and which is also central to Vijñāneśvara's conception of the joint family.[9] These coparceners were the *vārīs-dārs*, the agnatically related kin and a certain number of clients or supporters holding a patrimonial estate (*vārīs*).[10]

The legal foundation of joint property does not lie in religious (whether Hindu or Muslim) law but rather in customary practice. The *dharmaśāstra* endorses separation and denies birthright in property, while the only form of collective property known to it is the religious endowment. 'Property destined for pious uses and sacrifices is not to be partitioned'.[11] This is not a particularity of Brahmanical law only. Max Weber pointed out that the definition of the legal status of the endowment (the *Anstalt* or *Stiftung* of German legal literature; the 'charitable trust' in Maitland's rendering) reflected the interests of priests or religious intellectuals everywhere in the world.[12] In our view it is more an issue of 'universal dominion'. The *waqf* or *ḥabs* of Islamic law typically developed out of the Byzantine monastic foundations in which the management and revenue rights were reserved for the family of the founder in perpetuity. *Waqf* is an Arabic verbal noun which means 'to prevent', 'to restrain'. In the Sharia it denotes the 'tying up' of property in perpetuity in order to prevent it from becoming the property of a third person. The historical development of the *waqf* endowment, like that of the Byzantine prototype, received its impetus from strictly mundane considerations: to secure family property, obtain tax-exemptions, and most of all to prevent property becoming fragmented under the Islamic law of inheritance. The Sharia postulated, in a manner resembling that of the *dharmaśāstra* and that of the Christian canonical law in Medieval

9 Cf. pp. 18, 186–8; *SCS*, 3, no.578; 7, no.14; *Śrī Rāmdāsīcīṇ Aitihāsik Kāgadpatreṇ*, 1, nos 19, 31.

10 *MIS*, 17, no.30.

11 '*yogakṣemaṃ na vibhājyaṃ*' (Manu 9.219; Gautama 28.46–47; Vishnu 18.44). Cf. H. T. Colebrooke, *The Law of Inheritance from the Mitacshara* (Calcutta, 1896), p. 39. The prohibition of alienation of the *nibandha* or 'religious foundation' is found in the *Kātyāyanasmṛtiḥ on Vyavahāra*, 882–4 (P. V. Kane ed., Poona, n.d., p. 107 with comments on pp. 311–13). In practice many gifts of lands or villages were made to brahmans jointly: thus the *brahmadeya* villages of South India were held on the *gaṇa bhogam* tenure (cf. T. V. Mahalingam, *South Indian Polity* (Madras, 1967), pp. 182, 370; G. D. Sontheimer, 'Religious Endowments in India: The Juristic Personality of Hindu Deities', *Zeitschrift für vergleichende Rechtswissenschaft*, Bd.67, Heft 1 (1965), pp. 69–71).

12 *Economy and Society*, 2 vols (Berkeley, Los Angeles and London, 1978), 2, pp. 707, 713 and note 116.

Europe,[13] a strictly individual freehold title to property. Bypassing all the normal restrictions of customary or tribal conceptions of property (especially of property in land), this title not only allowed for free commercial transactions but also for the transformation of the property into a legal *waqf*.[14] In consequence of this transformation (technically not a donation[15]) the property is declared sacrosanct: as a permanent endowment it becomes inalienable and is taken out of the domain of the law of inheritance which demands partition in equal shares among all (male and female) descendants. The importance of this institution as a means to evade the rigid application of the Islamic law of inheritance and its consequent uneconomic fragmentation of landed estates and other forms of wealth cannot be doubted when one sees the often spectacular proportions of agricultural land which were held under the title of *waqf*, in the Ottoman Empire (perhaps 75%), and in the other traditionally Islamic lands.[16] Whereas in Islamic countries the *waqf* provided an easy and legal solution to the problem of fragmentation, in India neither the Islamic nor the Hindu code historically had such effect as to necessitate a proliferation of the *waqf* system. The theory that such fragmentation actually occurred seems to have been derived, again, from the uncritically accepted notion of Oriental Despotism which linked the absence of entail and primogeniture to the political structure of the state and declared the prevalence of these features the distinctive characteristics of Western European society, stabilizing and preserving noble estates which were them-

13 For the latter see M. Bloch, *Feudal Society*, 2 vols (London and Henley, 1978), 1, pp. 132–3; P. Vinogradoff, *Roman Law in Medieval Europe* (London and New York, 1909), p. 26; J. Goody, *Death, Property and the Ancestors* (London, 1962), pp. 295, 297; *idem*, 'Inheritance, property and women: some comparative considerations', in J. Goody, J. Thirsk and E. P. Thompson (eds), *Family and Inheritance: Rural Society in Western Europe, 1200–1800* (London, 1976), p. 24.

14 The antagonism with customary law in Indonesia comes out particularly clearly in K. Atmadja, *De Mohammedaansche Vrome Stichtingen in Indië* (The Hague, 1922), p. 13.

15 E. Clavel, *Le Wakf ou Habous*, 2 vols (Cairo, 1896), 1, p. 37.

16 H. A. R. Gibb and J. H. Kramers (eds), *Shorter Encyclopaedia of Islam* (Leiden, 1953), p. 627; J. N. D. Anderson, *Islamic Law in the Modern World* (London, 1959), p. 78; Clavel, *Wakf*, 1, pp. 6, 8, 91; *idem, Du Statut Personel et des Successions*, 2 vols (Paris, 1895); G. Baer, 'The Evolution of Private Landownership in Egypt and the fertile Crescent', in: C. Issawi (ed.), *The Economic History of the Middle East, 1800–1914* (Chicago, 1966), p. 88; S. K. Rashid, *Wakf Administration in India* (New Delhi, 1978), pp. 127–30. In some measure *ijāra* or sub-farming also made it possible to evade the principles of the inalienability of waqfs (cf. *Encyclopaedia of Islam*, s.v. idjāra).

selves essential to true monarchy.[17] In India, *waqf* and 'divine protection' under Brahmanical endowment never fulfilled a similar function on a scale even approaching that of the Islamic Near East. The structure of co-sharing accounted for this. The sovereign first of all was a *dāyadā* of all property by his *adhikāra* or 'right' of taxation; this made it necessary to obtain his co-operation in constituting endowments. The gift of land for religious purposes, as for any other, remained in principle a prerogative of the king and this created a situation which was exactly the reverse of what was normally the case in Islamic states where any property-owner could constitute a *waqf*, except the sovereign in power.[18] Moreover, in India the patrilineal coparcenary appears to have remained too strong to allow much scope to the application of either the Muslim or Hindu code of inheritance and checked the splitting up of landed property and alienations to brahmans or outsiders in general. Rather than that in the Near East, the situation in India resembles that in China, where from the eleventh century onwards charitable estates – modelled on the permanent endowments of Buddhist monastic communities – were instituted as a means to preserve the unity of property on a but limited scale, since the still powerful rights of objection and pre-emption of the immediate family continued in most cases to counteract the fragmentation of land.[19]

The double operation of a religious law initiating private ownership and thereby facilitating the transference to the clergy (or to its institutions) of the property, then declaring it sacrosanct after this has taken place, is also enacted in the *dharmaśāstra*. The *dharmaśāstra* equally insist on a purely individualistic conception of ownership (*svatva*) which makes land freely transferable and favours partition at death.[20] Vijñāneśvara, providing the legal foundation of the joint ownership of the extended family in his *Mitākṣara on Yājñavalkya*, observed that this conception was

17 Cf. J. Cooper, 'Patterns of inheritance and settlement by great landowners from the fifteenth to the eighteenth centuries', in: Goody, Thirsk and Thompson, *Family and Inheritance*, pp. 192 ff.

18 Clavel, *Wakf*, I, p. 115.

19 Cf. H. J. Beattie, *Land and Lineage in China: A Study of T'ung-Ch'eng County, Anhwei, in the Ming and Chi'ing Dynasties* (Cambridge, 1979), p. 8; D. Twitchett, 'The Fan Clan's Charitable Estate, 1050–1760', in: D. S. Nivison and A. F. Wright (eds), *Confucianism in Action* (Stanford, 1959), pp. 97, 102; *idem*, 'Documents on Clan Administration: I. The Rules of Administration of the Charitable Estate of the Fan Clan', *Asia Major*, 8 (1960–1), pp. 1–35.

20 Cf. p. 18; for Kovalevski's view on this subject see D. Thorner, 'Feudalism in India', in: *The Shaping of Modern India*, p. 284.

designed merely to arrive at a definition of 'property' fit for sacrificial and donational purposes. He opposed against it that male patrilineal descendants had a right by mere relationship in the *sva* of their male lineal ancestors, this being the normal or 'worldly' custom.[21] Among the possible sources of acquisition of property listed by the *śāstra* birth is not mentioned. Vijñāneśvara, asserting that *svatva* does not exclusively exist for religious or sacrificial purposes, attempted to introduce established custom into the canonical (*smṛti*) texts and, significantly, his *Mitākṣara* also quotes a verse forbidding the sale of land.[22] The *Mitākṣara* concept of *dāya* expressed a vested interest on an inheritance or joint family property or a share in such property. It became irreconcilably opposed to the orthodox Brahmanical conception represented by the *Dāyabhāga* school of Jīmūtavāhana. The interpretation of Vijñāneśvara has the strongest etymological foundation of the two, since *dāya* originally derives from the root *dā*, 'to share' and not, as Jīmūtavāhana suggests, from the root *dā*, 'to give'. Hence the more ancient view appears to be that the *dāyāda*, i.e., sons and other 'takers of *dāya*', in one way or another participated in the property by relationship alone, rather than acquiring a share at the death of the proprietor–ancestor who during his lifetime was unencumbered by them.[23] Thus in the *Mitākṣara* conception any person's property is pictured as being enclosed in a series of concentric circles representing the rights (*adhikāras*) of 'relations', from the sons to the king, which all curtail the free disposal of the property. The inner circle is occupied by the agnatic kin to the fourth degree, while the king's rights to taxation and escheat belong more in the outer circles. In principle every vested right resting on property had its circle but there were many which were of little consequence in comparison with those of the agnatic kin and that of the king.

The Muslims found in the Deccan and elsewhere in India a variety of hereditary rights implying joint ownership conceived along these lines. What they called *mirās* were mostly the estates of brotherhoods of cultivators or *jathās* organized in patrilineages called *kūḷas*.[24] Probably the entire settled Deccan had originally

21 Derrett, *Concept of Property*, p. 7.

22 2.114. One other *smṛti* text prohibiting the sale of land is Medhātithi on Manu 11.61.

23 Derrett, 'Development of the Concept of Property', p. 53.

24 R. S. V. N. Mandlik, 'Preliminary observations on a Document giving an Account of the Establishment of a New Village named Muruḍa, in Southern

been held by such lineages and clans which ritually demarcated their fields by stones representing their tutelary deities. If a member of a *jathā* died without an heir, his fields were divided among the surviving members of the family. No part of the patrimony was permitted to pass out of the *jathā* by sale if another member was willing to buy it. If sale to an outsider did take place the formalities concomitant with it included incorporation in the brotherhood. The *mirāsdārs* of the Muslim and Maratha periods were either descendants of the original families which had settled the land or purchasers of land of which the original cultivators had become extinct and which were called *gatkūḷ*. These were redistributed without governmental interference. The government participated only in the redistribution of the superior vested rights of patils, deśmukhs, etc., which the Muslims categorized as *vatan*. But these too were held in joint ownership: the incumbent families called them their *bāproṭī* or 'father's bread',[25] which was 'eaten' by them in as many 'plates' as there were portions into which they were partitioned.[26]

The right to sell any hereditary estate, whether *mirās* or *vatan* or *inām*, was recognized in principle, the main exceptions being religious *ināms* held by maths and temples.[27] But the right of a person to alienate a hereditary estate or land was regarded as possibly affecting the interests of other parties, principally those of the heirs on whom the land was entailed and the government. In the case of *mirās* land the only documentary attestation of a transfer was a copy of a deed of sale (*mirāspatra*) kept by the village kulkarni in his dafter.[28] This deed was also testified to by the village-officers and artisans and sometimes by the district-zamindars and the mirasdars of the surrounding fields as well. Under the Marathas all of these received small fees for their attestation in the form of a percentage of the purchase money. These exactions however did not appear in any account of the

Konkaṇa', *JBBRAS*, 8 (1865), pp. 1–48 (with text); Sykes, 'Land Tenures of the Dekkan', pp. 208–9, 212, 215.

25 *MIS*, 20, no.34.

26 *SCS*, no.623; 7, no.38; *P.A.: Inam Commission Rumals*, no.142; and see F. Perlin, 'To identify change in an old regime polity: agrarian transaction and institutional mutation in 17th to early 19th century Maharashtra', in: M. Gaborieau and A. Thorner (eds), *Asie du Sud: Traditions et Changements* (Colloques Internationaux du C.N.R.S.) (Paris, 1979), pp. 197–204.

27 *P.A.: List 13, Ru. 1, File* 7, nos 41, 177, 317, 417, 558 of 1831; *List 12, File 753*; Steele, *Law and Custom of Hindoo Castes*, pp. 435–41.

28 *EIP*, 4, p. 763.

government, nor did anything similar reach the government treasury. The Maratha government on the other hand inserted formal entries in its accounts of the particulars of all old and new *inām* and *vatan* grants as deductions from the revenues of a district, and in the case of a purchaser *dumālapatras* or 'title-deeds' were issued in his name and a corresponding alteration was made.[29] The government explicitly had to sanction the sale of all *ināms* and *vatans* of any importance beforehand. And for this attestation, which came in the form of a rājpatra from Satara or a sanad from the Peshwa, a fee (*śerṇī, harkī, nazar*) was exacted of a discretionary and indefinite amount.[30] Such fees were not usually taken on direct inheritance or succession of zamindars and inamdars as this right was implied by the terms of their tenure but it was taken on sales, adoptions, restorations, and partitions. In all such cases the average amount levied was perhaps one-half of the annual value of the estate. In addition to this considerable fees had to be paid to village and district zamindars.[31] These levies greatly discouraged partition but they were only one cause of the small number of transfers. The other was the circumstance that the assent first had to be obtained of all the coparceners of the inam or vatan before it could be alienated, while moreover all members had a right of pre-emption.[32] In this way all male relations were the 'owners' of the land according to their respective shares, while with Muslims females had a right as well.[33] With a vatan or inam thus unipartite no individual could sell his share out of the family without their consent before a formal partition was first effected. Still after partition the right of pre-emption persisted. Every member of the family was entitled to a preference, according to the order of their relationship, at the same price that might be offered by an outsider. This went with the maxim that every person was entitled to dispose freely only of what he had acquired himself.

29 *P.A.: List 13, Ru. 1, File 7*, no.558 of 1831.

30 *SSRPD*, 3, nos 482, 484, 583; 7, no.661; 9, no.40; *TKKP*, 1, nos 224–7, 234; 'Minutes of Evidence taken before the Select Committee on the Affairs of the East India Company', III (1832) *Parliamentary Papers*, 1831–2, 11, pp. 535–6; *EIP*, 3, pp. 814–15; Steele, *Law and Custom of Hindoo Castes*, pp. 277–8; *SCS*, 1, no.34; Choksey, *Ratnagiri*, pp. 26–36. If the sale was transacted in a village which was held in inam the fee was paid to the inamdar, who gave his attestations (*SSRPD*, 6, no.764).

31 E.g. *MIS*, 15, no.10½.

32 *P.A.: List 13, Ru. 1, File 7*, nos 64, 417 of 1831; Habib, *Agrarian System*, pp. 154–8.

33 *P.A.: List 13, Ru. 1, File 7*, nos 131, 558 of 1831.

Thus no vatan could be sold before '[the rights of] the coparceners (*dāīj*) and family (*gotra*) were suspended'.[34] Potential purchasers first made sure that there were no objections from the *bhāūbaṇd*, sometimes even of the neighbours, and so did the government before it gave its sanction.[35] As sales were usually an accompaniment of crisis and depopulation it was not always easy to determine the chances of a possible return of any surviving relatives. This could create interminable disputes, particularly when a family resorted to adoption on the presumption that it would otherwise become extinct. For adoption the same rules prevailed as for sale: government sanction had to be given previously and whatever members of a bhauband there were had to assent.[36] The reverse side of these coparcenary rights was a very high degree of penal solidarity. Commonly children and other relations of a managing vatandar were held liable for the payment of debts made by him, and they could be imprisoned on this account.[37] Debts and the threat of starvation were practically the only reasons which could lead to the extreme step of sale of a part or the whole of a vatan.[38] After each major famine or agrarian crisis – the *durgādevī* of 1396, the *sorat* of 1628, and the one in the early eighteenth century – there was widespread confusion due to vagrancy and high mortality of vatandars.[39] Sales were particularly abundant in these periods, when prices dropped extremely low. Buyers appear to have been fellow vatandars of neighbouring villages or districts, the

34 *SCS*, 7, no.14. *Gotra* in this context may also refer to neighbours.

35 *MIS*, 3, no.560; 15, no.10½; *TKKP*, 2, nos 81, 169, 191; 3, no.159; *SSRPD*, 3, no.486; 5, no.195.

36 'Correspondence illustrative of the practice of the Peshwa's government regarding adoptions, and the circumstances under which adopted sons could succeed to property held from the state', *BGS*, n.s. no.28 (Bombay, 1856), pp. 1, 37–8 and Statement C, pp. 53–5; *SSRPD*, 7, nos 506–7, 554; *P.A.: List 12, File 753*. The practice with regard to adoptions was uniform in all Maratha territories. Sometimes the sovereign carried his interference so far as to forbid the very ceremony of adoption. There were specific cases where adoptions were disallowed and inams resumed on the recorded grounds that they had not been made with the sanction of the Peshwa.

37 R. B. G. C. Vad, P. V. Mawji and D. B. Parasnis (eds), *Decisions from the Shahu and Peshwa Daftars* (Bombay, 1909), p. 34; *SSRPD*, 2, nos 1, 83, 115, 174, 176; 7, no.661.

38 *MIS*, 3, no.560; 15, no.10½, 414; 20, no.34; *SCS*, 7, nos 41, 49; Vad, Mawji and Parasnis, *Decisions*, p. 34; *SSRPD*, 1, nos 283, 289; *TKKP*, 3, no.94; Elphinstone, *Report*, App. pp. 107–12.

39 *P.A.: Selected Rumals*, no.52, 23523, 23444, 23512, 23889, 23756–60, 23885; *SCS*, 7, nos 14, 23, 44; Moreland, *Akbar to Aurangzeb*, p. 212; Van Santen, *Verenigde Oost-Indische Compagnie*, pp. 174–5, 177; Perlin, 'To Identify Change'.

government itself, or powerful jagirdars for whom this provided lucrative investment opportunities.[40] Violent feuds often ensued when vagrant vatandars returned, sometimes after a decade or more, to find their rights sold without their consent.[41] A claim could then still be derived from 'hereditary investment' (*mavsāricī kuvāt*), but whether this was honoured depended on the arbitration of the government and the terms of the transaction. In the case of a vatan or inam falling vacant it automatically escheated to the sovereign. This reversionary right in case of extinction of male offspring was, next to taxation, one of the adhikaras which was of old associated with Indian kingship.[42] This is also what ultimately constituted the difference between a grant of land and a grant of money to which the donor lost his right forever.[43] When a family became extinct and no adoption or sale took place vatans and inams and other property, also *saṃsthāns*, lapsed to the government (*sarkārāṇt japt ahe, s.amānat ahe*) but widows were given maintenance for life. The vatans were ordinarily regranted to other families.[44] Not much distinction was made in general between Muslims and Hindus but it is interesting to observe that the lands given to religious brahmans were – in conformity with the classical Sanskrit texts – not held liable to escheat and were conferred on other brahmans, and with omission of the payment of a nazar as was taken from vatans.[45]

IV Grants of land

The implication of a 'grant of land' or *bhūmi-dān* was basically no more than a formally sanctioned permanent exemption from royal taxation. There were two categories of such exemptions according to incumbent: firstly, those held *ex-officio*, as an appurtenance of vatan; and secondly, free gifts on account of religion and personal sinecures. While both were called *inām* or 'gift' tenures the

40 Perlin, 'To Identify Change', pp. 198–200 assigns an 'almost monopolistic role' in the purchase of patilki in the early eighteenth century to the military and administrative élites. Estimates are however lacking. K. V. Purandare in *SCS*, 7, pp. 3–4 holds that it was almost always village-vatandars who were buyers of patilki.

41 *SCS*, 7, no.44.

42 Derrett, *Hoysalas*, p. 185.

43 *P.A.: List 13, Ru. 73, File 1030*, no.3026 of 1850.

44 *SSRPD*, 5, no.157; 7, nos 560, 670; 8, no.1043; *TKKP*, 3, nos 8, 39, 41, 102; *P.A.: List 13, Ru. 90*, Report 206; *Ru. 54, File 726*.

45 *Arthaśāstra*, 3.5.28–9; *Mānava Dharmaśāstra* 9.189; *P.A.: List 13, File 452*, Proc. 653.

difference was that the first category of grants involved a kind of reciprocity between the donor and the donee in the form of ongoing service and the second did not. The first were given in payment of service (*deṇgī, badal muśāhirā*) to village- and district-vatandars and to balutedars as well as to a variety of professionals (physicians, perfumers, acrobats, etc.).[1] In virtually all such cases the grants of land were part of a package of rights and privileges associated with the office. Very common denominations of this kind of tenure were *pāṣodī* held by patils, *vaveli* held by balutedars (in the Mavals), *hāḍolā*, *haḍkī* and *ṭomṇī* held by Mahars, and *inām-izāfat* held by deśmukhs and deśpandes. Outside the Deccan again different denominations occurred, like in Gujarat where all land held revenue-free by village- and district-officials was referred to as *pasāetuṇ*. These names, referring to incumbents, were meaningless in themselves and the variety need not detain us. They were all exemptions enjoyed conditionally upon active service to the sovereign. In contrast, the sinecure tenures were *bin cakarī*, 'without the stipulation of service', given to 'respectable persons' (*saṃbhāvit*) as *zat* or 'personal' *inām ex post facto*: to the relations of someone who had died in battle; for performing *satī* (self-immolation on the pyre of the husband); for bringing wasteland under cultivation or for populating villages and bazaars, or for any other work of utility or special service performed in the past.[2] While these latter tenures are always classified as *kherīj muśāhirā* or *kherīj taināt*, i.e., 'extra to salary', the religious grants of land (as well as of cash) are held *badal dharmādāya* or *khairāt*, as a charitable or religious endowment 'in the service of the dharma'.[3] Under the Marathas such religious grants were made both to Muslims and Hindus. The Muslim lands served the upkeep of mosques, mausoleums and religious institutions of all sorts; very few were *waqfs* dating back to the sultanates.[4] The grants to religious brahmans, bhats, shastris, joshis, pandits and puraniks became quite numerous under Shahu and even more so under the Peshwas. *Devasthān ināms* also abounded – lands given in support of gods and temples, comprising at least several whole villages in the case of temples of celebrity or popular shrines. There were also numerous grants made to *maths*, monastic establishments of various sects of gosavis who provided

1 *Deṇgī* is more generally a 'reward for exhibiting a skill'. *Badal muśāhirā* may also refer to temporary assignments of land for the maintenance of troops (cf. Jervis, *Konkan*, p. 314; *P.A.: List 13, Ru. 3, File 28*, no. 181 of 1849).

2 *P.A.: List 13, passim*. 3 *Ibid*. 4 E.g. *BISMQ*, 15, 3 (1934), no. 19.

free food to religious pilgrims. These lands were held in charge by the guru or by the pujari, the officiating priest, and whatever part of the produce was not directly used was sold by them and the money appropriated for the ordinary daily expenses of the establishment, for clothes, food, red paint, oil, utensils, etc.

Additional grants of land or villages to established *vatandārs* commonly served the mechanism of *fitna* or the consolidation of sovereign power, although such motivations are never made explicit in the deeds. Instead we find an emphasis on 'loyal service' and 'virtue'. The danger of *fitna* for the sovereign was of course an excessively great permanent loss of land-revenue. The *Ājñāpatra* therefore discourages the granting of land.[5] It says that any great service should as much as possible be rewarded with money, horses, elephants, clothes, or ornaments, and in suitable cases with the assignment of new honourable tasks. If an exemption from the land-revenue is given, the revenue accruing to the sovereign will decrease hereditarily by that amount, and the diminishing of the revenue 'sets off the decay of the kingdom'. The royal family must be especially watchful against giving away land under the influence of flattery.[6] A king who is over-generous with the granting of land becomes 'his own enemy'; he can no longer be called 'lord of the land' (*bhūpati*) because he is giving it away. Special tasks will always remain to be executed but salaries are a greater inducement to loyal service than hereditary grants, which lead to indolence especially in the succeeding generations. The king will then be responsible for supporting these successors' wickedness by grants of land, but yet to resume them would be sinful since they were given hereditarily.

The grants of lands and villages in *inām* were of a permanent nature under the Marathas, and as such the latter treated in principle the grants which were made or sanctioned under this title by preceding Muslim sovereigns. The revenue-exempt tenures that we find under the eighteenth-century Maratha régime were for a very large part ancient holdings which originated perhaps at the founding of a village or at the time of the settlement of a pargana during or before Muslim rule.[7] The small holdings in the possession of village-officials and artisans were simply deducted as exempt land in the government rent-roll (*jamābaṇḍī*) drawn up for each

[5] Banhatti ed., ch. 7. [6] An example of this occurs in *MIS*, 15, no. 3.
[7] *P.A.: Selected Rumals*, no. 52, section 2, 23424, 23444; *List 13, Ru. 5, File 45*; Mandlik, 'Muruḍa'.

village under the so-called *tankhā* or standard measurement surveys which were executed in the Mughal regulation districts in Hindustan by Todar Mal in the late sixteenth century and by Malik Ambar, the Mughal divan Murshid Quli Khan, and Shivaji in the Deccan in the seventeenth century. Thus in the eighteenth-century Maratha village accounts the tiny *ināms* of the balutedars (tanners, barbers, smiths, carpenters, etc.), priests, and also those of kulkarnis and patils are mostly classified as *kadīm* or 'ancient', rarely as *jadīd* or 'new'. If they were *jadīd*, they were religious grants or service lands of patils, kulkarnis, and district-zamindars or personal inams given to outsiders of the village under sanads of the Maratha kings or the Peshwas. Numerous new grants of land as well as of whole villages were made particularly by Shahu, but there was a steady increase throughout the eighteenth century. Many new grants – but always small ones – came to be held as *gāṇv nisbat inām* or '*inām* on charge of the village', i.e., without government sanction and without being deducted from the total village *jamā*. These were nothing but an internal village repartition of the revenue burden. Taken together with the new village *ināms* given out by the sovereign (in the village accounts these are rarely differentiated), the total proportion of exempted land increased from the late seventeenth to the early nineteenth century from about 5–10% to about 15%, at most 25%, in the villages in the Maratha core districts around Poona.[8] There was always a temporary scramble for village *ināms* during times of disputed sovereignty, especially at the turn of the seventeenth and in the early nineteenth century. But such ināms often disappear from the village records again after a decade or so. In areas like the Southern Maratha Country and Gujarat where the zamindars were much more powerful – approaching the situation of non-regulation – a large proportion of village *ināms* were held without sanads of the central huzur. This could increase to one-half, even to as much as 90% of the total cultivated land of a village.[9] Here the government collections were correspondingly reduced to a minimum.

Grants of land with exemption from royal taxation were known in India from a very ancient date. Before the arrival of the Muslims however tax-exempt lands were merely designated by terms

[8] These estimates are based on samples of villages from: *P.A.: Poona Jamav, Rumals 1, 324, 1321, 989, 310, 247, 125, 1107*; *Satara Jamav, Rumal 227*; *Nagar Jamav, Rumal 12*. All of these give fairly complete chronological series.

[9] Marshall, *Statistical Reports*, pp. 25–6.

denoting the function of the recipient of the grant or signifying the purpose to which they were directed. In the Deccan the term *inām* was, with *vatan* and *mirās*, one of the concepts of the new bureaucratic grid superimposed on the pattern of vested rights by the Muslim conquerors. While many of the old, more specific, designations continued to be used, *inām* became the generic term for all exempt tenures. This generic usage of the term was introduced in wide areas beyond the Deccan by the Marathas which they conquered from the Mughals, probably everywhere in the *svarājya*. But with the Mughals *inām* had been only a minor category of exempted land and was not always of a hereditary nature.[10]

The Marathi term *inām* derives from the Persian *in'ām*, originally an Arabic word which stood for 'favour' or 'beneficence', essentially denoting financial awards or robes of honour given to troops and commanders in particular as a means of forestalling mutinies.[11] In the Mughal Empire, before it expanded into the Deccan, *in'ām* could denote hereditary or non-hereditary grants of revenue-exempt land as well as incidental or annually repeated financial awards out of the government treasury.[12] In its Deccan usage – under the Sultanates, but later also under the Mughals and the Marathas – the term very rarely denoted cash grants made directly from the treasury.[13] Here almost always an *inām* was a hereditary grant defined in terms of land. The *Rājyavyavahāra Kośa*, an administrative dictionary in Sanskrit written in Thanjavur in the seventeenth century, equates *inām* with *vṛtti*.[14] But *vṛtti* as it is often found in Marathi documents has the more general meaning of a hereditary 'estate' or 'source of maintenance' and, although this often included *inām* land, it seems to come closer to *vatan*. No indigenous generic term existed for exempted land as such and this is what the borrowed Persian word *inām* came to mean in Marathi: a grant of land which was permanently 'exempt from taxation' (*dastībād*, *māf* or *pālak*[15]) regardless of such a grant being part of a service tenure (*vatan*) or not.

To be exempt from taxation meant in practice to be exempt from

10 Habib, *Agrarian System*, pp. 258–9, 283 note 54, 312.
11 *Encyclopaedia of Islam*, s.v.
12 Cf. note 10; *P.A.: List 11, Ahmadabad Volumes*, no. 5 Ahmadabad Kothlisanth Vol., no. 782 of 1886; *SSRPD*, 3, no. 63.
13 *SPD*, 15, p. 97; *MIS*, 2, p. 95; Khare, *Aitihāsik Fārsī Sāhitya*, 4, no. 180; *P.A.: List 13, Ru. 1, File* 7, no. 358 of 1831; *SSRPD*, 3, no. 102; *MIS*, 18, no. 25; 20, no. 254.
14 '*inamo vṛttināmakaḥ*' (Hyderabad ed., 1956, no. 312–b).
15 E.g. *SCS*, 2, no. 203; *MIS*, 20, no. 85.

the payment of the assessed land-revenue and sometimes from the payment of all or some additional cesses levied in the name of the king. But the exemption could of course only be expressed in terms of land when the land was assessed. In all other situations it was expressed in terms of produce. Thus for instance in the case of newly laid-out plantations it is said in a document of 1619 that 'of ten newly planted trees one is *inām*, while of the other trees the *king's share* is to be one-third [of the produce]'.[16] In Gujarat, when the system of crop-sharing (*bhāgbaṭāī*) obtained, the revenue-exempt land was referred to as *bāher-khalī*, i.e., '[land of which the produce remained] outside the granary [of the government]'.[17] After an assessment was made this term could only survive as an anachronism. In the eighteenth century a grant in *inām* was commonly made either of a delimited piece of land or of a fraction or the whole of one or more villages. In no case what was granted in *inām* amounted to more than the right to collect the 'king's share' or *rājbhāg* as assessed under the survey. In districts under dual sovereignty only the *rājbhāg yektarfā*, 'the king's share of one side', was granted.[18] Under the system of multiple fractionation which was introduced by the Peshwas it became very common to grant *amals* or percentages of the aggregate *rājbhāg* in *inām* to different parties, some of them also being assigned in temporary tenure.[19] The Peshwa's repartition scheme was mostly applied village-wise or *mauzevār*. If all *amals* of the land-revenue and the extra cesses levied from a village by the government were alienated to a single party, that party was said to hold the village as *sarv inām* or 'wholly inām'. Excluded from the grant were then only the *haks* of village-servants and zamindars and the pre-existing village-inams. Grants of plots of land were, apart from extra cesses, commonly wholly *inām* since the intra-village repartition of the aggregate revenue-burden was usually not carried out by the government or its assignees and since such plots were usually granted out of the village wasteland or fallow land which was unoccupied at the time of the grant. With whole villages it was more often the case than not that the sovereign did not grant in inam all amals to a single party. If a village was not someone's *sarv inām*, that is, if one or more *amals* were reserved by the government for itself or for others, it was

16 *MIS*, 15, no. 330.

17 E. G. Fawcett, 'Report on the Collectorate of Ahmadabad', *BGS*, n.s. no. 5 (Bombay, 1854), pp. 11–13.

18 S. V. Avalaskar (ed.), *Aitihāsik Sādhaneṇ* (Bombay, 1963), no. 39.

19 Cf. pp. 71–2 and Chapter 4–II–a.

called *sarakatī* or 'held in partnership'. But even in *sarakatī* villages the entire revenue management was frequently in the hands of the *ināmdār*. If not, the government would make an agreement with the *ināmdār* for a partition of the management.[20] If the government afterwards imposed some cesses on a *sarv inām* village this would not thereby become a *sarakatī* village. To become so a definite *amal* of the land-revenue would have to be alienated to another *ināmdār* or be held in assignment by someone else. In addition to lands and villages, on occasion entire districts were given as *sarv inām*, sometimes comprising as many as 200 villages in all.[21] These grants were as usual made with the explicit exception of the *haks* and pre-existing *ināms* (lands and villages). They were in fact small chiefdoms, differing from *saṃsthāns* only by their originating in a grant and by the absence of a tributary relationship with the sovereign.[22]

The king could only grant his own legitimate share. All other rightholders or co-sharers maintained their claims. Nor did a grant in *inām* affect existing tenancy relations. If the *ināmdār* of a village 'oppressed' the rayats or transgressed the assessed *rājbhāg*, the government could be called on to intervene.[23] Many inam lands, even those which were at the date of granting explicitly exempted from 'all cesses present and future', in course of time became *apūrṇ māfī zamīn* or 'incompletely exempted land'.[24] Thus *ināmdārs*, while not liable to pay *nazars* on succession, were often made to pay quit-rents: *inām nimāī*, *inām tizāī* or *inām cauthāī*, respectively 1/2, 1/3 and 1/4 of the annual proceeds. These were irregularly levied next to other incidental levies like *karjpaṭṭī*, *eksālī paṭṭi*, *dahakpaṭṭī*, etc., which were taken on almost any pretext and often acquired surreptitiously the character of a permanent annual imposition.[25] Quit-rents and other impositions were commonly introduced within districts, or at least for a number of villages simultaneously.[26] In the Peshwa Diaries there are references to the imposition of *karjpaṭṭī* simultaneously in a large number of parganas in Gujarat, Khandesh, Gangathari, Miraj, Konkan, and the

20 *P.A.: List 13, Ru. 1, File 1*, Report no. 477 of 1856.
21 *SSRPD*, 9, no. 164; *TKKP*, 1, no. 50.
22 Some small chiefdoms were confirmed under *ināmpatras* (cf. *BGS*, n.s. no. 10, p. 2; no. 8, p. 2).
23 E.g. *SSRPD*, 9, no. 650.
24 On this see esp. Goldsmith, quoted in *BG*, XVI, p. 209.
25 Cf. Chapter 3–III.
26 *P.A.: List 13, Ru. 1, File 1*, Proc. 1045B–1051B; *Ru. 77, File 1063*, no. 47 of 1855.

Deccan Desh, on all zamindars, of an amount equal to one year of their emoluments of haks, rusum, and inams.[27] It appears to have been a general rule that religious inams were not burdened with cesses of any kind.[28] In many areas a dichotomy was thus made between such religious inams and others which were 'entirely exempt' as *sarvmānya* and those which regularly paid pattis, called *joḍimānya*.[29] Where the proportion of inam land became very excessive quit-rents and other levies became heavier or refuge was taken to indirect taxation by increasing the assessment rates of the non-alienated land or by imposing a tax on rayats who cultivated inam lands on lower terms.[30]

In the Maratha districts with very high proportions of inam there was a pressure on labour rather than on land because inam lands were mostly granted from *gatkūḷ* land which had no occupant and was lying fallow.[31] If the lands granted in inam were not arable waste, they were most often made out of the *śerī*, land which did not properly belong to any village corporation but to the government itself and was cultivated by 'government rayats'.[32] It could happen however that a grant was made out of village lands which were already under cultivation. Such lands would be deducted from the village assessment or *tankhā* as were the old village inams under the measurement surveys when they were first made or whenever they were rescheduled.[33] Inam lands, whether granted out of waste or out of cultivated land, were 'not entered in the *jamābaṇḍī*', i.e., they were excluded from the government rent-roll or, more precisely, they were 'deducted (*vajā*) from the *jamābaṇḍī*'. Parallel to this, inam villages were deducted from the pargana rent-roll in their entirety.[34] But in this way the lands granted were nevertheless registered as *inām*, which forms a contrast with those tenures which

27 *SSRPD*, 3, no. 495; 4, no. 253; 6, no. 807; 7, no. 482.
28 *SSRPD*, 6, no. 797. There were exceptions; cf. *P.A.: List 13, Ru. 90*, Rep. 42.
29 *P.A.: Poona Jamav, Rumal 1321.*
30 Cf. Chapter 3–III; *P.A.: List 13, Ru. 90*, Reports 38–9.
31 *EIP*, 4, p. 544. To grant revenue-free tenures from arable waste was no speciality of the Marathas. For comparative evidence see R. Burghart, 'Regional Circles and the Central Overseer of the Vaishnavite Sect in the Kingdom of Nepal' (Mimeograph), p. 7; D. Singh, 'Local and Land Revenue Administration of the State of Jaipur (c. 1750–1800)' (Thesis, Jawaharlal Nehru University, New Delhi, 1975), p. 39; Habib, *Agrarian System*, p. 302; Nurul Hasan. 'Zamindars under the Mughals', p. 27
32 *P.A.: List 13, Ru. 1, File 2*, Proc. 17A, 18A, 28A–31A, 39A. On *śerī* see further p. 282.
33 *SSRPD*, 3, no. 154; *BISMQ*, 24, 3 (1944), no. 57.
34 *SCS*, 5, nos 792, 797; *MIS*, 15, no. 182; *P.A.: Prant Ajmas, passim.*

were never brought to account, being granted by the village or by zamindars without the sanction of the central huzur. These unregistered tenures were called *ajīṇ vajā* or 'altogether deducted'.[35] Whether they resulted in a loss of revenue for the government depended on political circumstances; it was not necessarily so. In no case did they enjoy the sanctity which was inherent to a government grant under sanad and registered in the accounts. The only kind of unregistered inams which were overlooked as a matter of course by the government, even when it had the power to resume them, were the so-called *ghair dākhlā ināms*, tiny plots of flower garden held revenue-free by village fakirs or gosains which from the point of view of the state were unproductive but which were treated with circumspection as the incumbents possessed vast influence in the villages.[36] All inams not *ghair dākhlā* and given out by the sovereign power were registered in the Huzur Daftar. For this a registration-fee was paid by the *ināmdār*. At the time of the original grant, moreover, four separate sanads were made out: 1. To the grantee; 2. To the village-headman and village community; 3. To the district-zamindars; 4. To the government revenue officials and clerks 'of the present and the future'. Under the Maratha Rajas and Peshwas the deed issued to a recipient of *inām* was called *ināmpatra* or *dānpatra* ('deed of gift', in the case of a 'free gift') or *rājpatra* in the case of a royal deed but more often simply *sanad* as the other deeds were called which were issued to the village, the zamindars and the government officials. The issuance of *farmāns* appears to have been a prerogative of Mughal and Sultanate rule; documents of such title – which even under the Muslims served often as only an ultimate confirmation of what was called a 'draft document' (*sanad*, *hujat*, *khurdkhat*) issued by some high official or a jagirdar – were never used by the Maratha sovereigns.

After the original grant was made, new *sanads* and *tākīdpatras* or 'deeds of injunction' (also called *ājñāpatras* or 'orders') were issued on any occasion of interference in the collection of the revenue of the *inām*. The sovereign, in his role of arbiter, had to safeguard the undisturbed enjoyment of the land and regulated the succession to it by making this subject to his confirmation (*makhalāhisaṇe*). Complaints made at court by inamdars were commonly directed

35 *P.A.: List 13, Ru. 1, File 1*, Proc. 1085B; *Ru. 73 File 1025*, Extract paras 27 to 32 from the Inam Committee's report to Government d.d. 20th July 1844: Ajmas extract appointment of T. Dainglia as sarsubhedar of the Karnataka 1812/13.

36 *P.A.: List 13, Ru. 3, File 28*, Proc. 552B; *Ru. 75, File 1042*, no. 2013 of 1838.

against encroachments by military assignment-holders, or against individual *amaldārs*, zamindars, army officers and soldiers encamped nearby, garrisons of forts, or against village-officials not fully respecting the exemption specified in the original deed. Such annoyances would generate at least a few dozen of 'deeds of injunction' in the case of any substantial inam grant in the course of the eighteenth century and even more in the case of grants made to defenceless religious people.[37] Often the threats contained in the *tākīdpatras* were not backed by immediate assistance, especially in areas at some distance from the government thanas. Often *tākīdpatras* had to be repeatedly issued over a number of years before a 'despoiler' withdrew. The renewal, continuation or sale of an inam also had to be announced to all parties concerned.[38] Each new invader wrote out his *abhaypatras* or *kaulnamas*, 'assurance-deeds', to bring the local vatandars, inamdars and rayats to his side. *Fitna* and the extension and legitimation of sovereign power were the *raison d'être* of the grants of land; the giving of exemptions, privileges, and the safeguarding of vested rights the mechanisms of the annexation of territory by a sovereign. 'The wise king', as Manu said, 'after gaining victory, should show honour to the gods and the virtuous brahmans, and grant exemptions and cause promises of safety to be proclaimed'.[39]

Documentary evidence

Since the grant of land primarily concerned exemption from the payment of the 'king's share' it could in principle only be made by the king in power. At the very least it required his compliance and sanction. If a village-headman or zamindar or a government revenue official made a grant in inam without such sanction he would have to screen the exemption in his own accounts and in one way or another compensate for the deduction. Such grants were not 'real' inams, but they were often made and sometimes were passed on hereditarily. The issuance of a document called a *sanad* or *ināmpatra* was not a sovereign monopoly. Only the *rājpatra* (and the *farmān* under the Muslims) was specific about the donor. Of *sanads* there were three categories: those issued by mahal officials (*mahāl sanads*), those issued by provincial governors (*subhā*

[37] *P.A.: List 13, Ru. 1, File 1*, Proc. 232B, 595B; *Ru. 55, File 751*, Report C 16.
[38] *P.A.: List 12, File 569*, no. 597 of 1865; *BGS*, n.s. no. 28, Statement B, pp. 49–52.
[39] *Mānava Dharmaśāstra*, 7.201.

sanads), and those issued by the central court (*huzūr sanads*). An *ināmpatra* could be issued by any authority, even by village officials and zamindars. But only a *huzūr sanad* or *rājpatra* could in the final resort exempt land from royal taxation.[40]

The vast number of grants made under Maratha *huzūr sanads* almost all over India in the eighteenth century were all drawn up in a standard format.[41] To a varying degree this also provided the model for grants by lower authorities and semi-autonomous chieftains but the seal made recognition of the source easy. Copper plates were rarely used, but almost always ordinary paper. The text was in Marathi (moḍi script), except in the case of *agrahāra* grants of whole villages to communities of brahmans which were in Sanskrit and a few grants made in the Maratha districts by the Mughal Emperor in the eighteenth century under *farmāns* in Persian.[42] A deed of grant always identifies the donor at the outset, the Raja or the Peshwa or a *sardār* with sovereign attributes (like Scindhia or Holkar) and then the donee and the donee's status. Whoever the latter might be, he is said to be a 'loyal servant' of the donor, 'an old servant of the svami', while in the case of free gifts to brahmans the donees are described as being of such conduct as 'brings prosperity to the svami and the rajya'.[43] The date of the grant is given in years, months and days, in several eras, of which some date back to Muslim rule (*faslī*, *hijrī*) and of which the *rājyabhiṣeka śaka* became mandatory after the coronation of Shivaji in 1674. It was customary to add a sentence at the end of the grant to the effect that the original document was intended to last and that 'no copy should be made of it every year'. The original deed – of which a copy was kept by the huzur – appears to have been preserved by inamdars with the utmost care and rarely got lost except in a conflagration.[44] They were however not uncommonly pretended to be lost to cover up encroachments. But this was

[40] Cf. Chapter 2–v.

[41] Countless examples occur in the publications of the *BISM*.

[42] The use of Marathi in deeds of grants was already in vogue, next to Persian, under the Deccan Sultans.

[43] Common expressions with regard to servants are: *tumhī gharāṇdār svāmīce purātan sevak yekaniṣṭpaṇeṇ vartan āhā*; *āpaṇ svāmīce purātan vaḍīl vaḍilāṇ pāsūn seva niṣṭheneṇ karīt alo*; *āpaṇ svāmīcī sevā niṣṭheneṇ karit āhoṇ va puḍheṇ anyatra avalaṃb na dharitaṇ sarv prakāre sevā karāvī yaisā niscaye kelā āhe*; *tumhī svāmīcyā pāyāṇsī suddāṇtaḥkarṇeṇ karūn niṣṭheneṇ vartāve*. With regard to brahmans: *svāmīs va svāmīcyā rājyas kalyāṇ ciṇtun sukhrūp rāhṇe*; *yāstav tumce cālavilyā śreyaskar jāṇūṇ*; *rājyopayogī manuṣya*; *rājyās abhiṣṭ ciṇtan karīt āhoṇ*; *rājśrī svāmīṇs va svāmıṇsce rājyas śreyaskar*.

[44] Marshall, *Statistical Reports*, p. 79.

difficult; to establish the correctness of a claim there were many other documents which could be adduced, for instance the village *jamābaṇḍī* or district estimate (*prāṇt ajmās*) of the government or the *taināt jābtā* of military assignments from which the inam was regularly deducted at a certain amount.[45] If necessary local assemblies were convoked to decide about a claim.

When a sanad was renewed – by the established ruler or by a new sovereign – the usual practice was to issue the new sanad with the date of the renewal upon it; to make a copy of the old sanad with the dates and seal of the original was exceptional, but it was always briefly reiterated under which former sovereigns the grant had been held.[46] After the date, the place of issue is mentioned. This could be Satara or Poona or one of the provincial capitals of the Northern Maratha sardars, or a 'temporary residence' (*mukām*) such as Jinji was for Rajaram or Tulapur for Aurangzeb; or it could be anywhere, since the Maratha sovereigns, like their Mughal predecessors and contemporaries, exercised their function in a peripatetic style during a part of the year.[47] Finally, the body of the grant specifies in as much detail as is needed the amount and location of the lands or villages given and the amals which are made *dumālā*, 'alienated', or literally, brought 'under double sovereignty', i.e., 'excluded from the *khālsā*'.[48] Only sometimes the exemption explicitly includes 'the present and future cesses' (*hālīpaṭṭī va pestarpaṭṭī*) or 'all cesses and dues' (*kulbāb kulkānū*) and corvée labour demands (*veṭh begār*); such was generally the case with religious grants. Almost always the *ināmpatra* qualifies the enjoyment of the grant by the clause *kherīj hakdār va (kadīm) ināmdār karūn*, i.e., 'with the exclusion of the [rights of] the hakdars and the [old] inamdars'.[49] A shorter version of this clause, *kherīj hakdār karūn*, was used when there were no inams in existence prior to the grant in question within its boundaries, as was usual with grants of plots of land but never with grants of whole villages.[50] By *hakdārs*, we recall, were meant the village- and district-officials and servants who were entitled to the so-called *parbhārā* or 'intermediate' haks of varying amount, proportionate shares of the produce of each

45 *P.A.: List 13, Ru. 1*, Proc. 996, no. 678 of 1860.
46 *SSRPD*, 1, no. 347.
47 *SSRPD*, 7, pp. 383–446; for the Mughals see Blake, 'Patrimonial-Bureaucratic Empire', p. 92.
48 Cf. especially *P.A.: List 13, Ru. 54, File 726*, no. 122 of 1874.
49 E.g. *MIS*, 10, no. 277.
50 In some cases of grants of plots of land the haks are included (*hakkāṇsah*, *hakkāṇsuddhām*).

field, paid in kind or cash. The actual consequence of the exclusion of these haks from the inam grant was that these servants' dues were paid by the inamdar. The principle of excluding *kadīm ināms* also extended to assignments of land-revenue for the maintenance of troops. In parallel forms it is found in India from very early times both under the Hindu and Muslim sovereigns.[51] In particular, military assignees, were, on account of their quick transfers, often tempted to encroach upon revenue-free tenures. Still then, in this formula the ambition is evident of the sovereign power to separate potentially conflicting rights and to define and delimit these rights *vis-à-vis* each other. And since boundary disputes were rife it was also no luxury to make a special provision in the grant for the exact determination of the four boundaries, *catussīmā pūrvak*, a formula of which parallels are also often found in ancient inscriptions relating to donations of land to brahmans and temples and which is also dictated by the smṛtis.[52] Apart from an occasional free-floating inam specified in rupees to be deducted from the *jamā* of the village, the exemptions were given in measured plots of land but they were measured very often with a longer stick than khalsa land, thus resulting in an additional privilege for the inamdar.[53] Measurement was dispensed with in the case of inams of especially venerated religious personages.[54]

Never absent in an authentic Maratha *ināmpatra* was an inheritability clause.[55] Most often, also in grants to women, it is stated that the grant was to be held *putrpautrādi vaṃsaparaṃpareneṇ* or 'hereditarily unto the sons and grandsons'.[56] Often recurring alternative expressions are *pīḍh dar pīḍh*, 'generation after generation', and *kārkīrdī dar kārkīrdī*, 'lifetime after lifetime'.[57] The property and inams of maths descended *śiṣyaparaṃpareneṇ*, 'hereditarily to the pupils', i.e., 'hereditarily to the spiritual descendants'. In deeds of grants to Muslims the word *putrpautrādi* is not common; instead *avlād va aflād* is used, 'to the sons and

51 Cf. *Śatapatha Brāhmaṇa*, 13.7.1.13 and 13.6.2.18; Moreland, *Agrarian System*, p. 72; *P.A.: List 13, Ru. 1, File 1*, no. 3350 of 1851.

52 Kane, *History of Dharmaśāstra*, 2, p. 861.

53 Marshall, *Statistical Reports*, p. 79; *SSRPD*, 4, no. 93; *TKKP*, 1, nos 223, 256, 268. See also Chapter 3–IV.

54 *Śrīsaṃpradāyācīṇ Kāgadpatreṇ* (Dhulia, 1915), nos 21–2.

55 In parts of Scindhia's districts in Central India however *inām* could be given for life only, as under the Muslim sovereigns (cf. *P.A.: List 12, File 753*, no. 223 of 1845).

56 E.g. Sabnis, *Paṇt Amātya Bāvḍā Daftar*, 1, nos 29–31.

57 *SSRPD*, 4, no. 344 has *pust dar pust*.

daughters'.[58] Pure matrilineal inheritance occurred only among the Mahars and other low castes, holding service tenures for professional prostitution.[59] Every stipulation making a grant inheritable – whether in the male or female line or in both, or through disciples – implied as we saw earlier a reversionary right of the sovereign in the case of extinction of heirs. The practice of escheat differentiated, ultimately, grants of land from hereditary grants of money from the central or district treasuries of the state.[60] The question of escheat further introduced a difference between certain religious grants and service tenures. The communities of brahmans, although they were never organized as a college or in a hierarchy under a pontiff,[61] held the right of escheat to the lands of which the incumbents became extinct. A sect like the Ramdasis, which was widespread in Maharashtra, also differed in its organization with regard to inheritance and escheat.[62] Of old its members avowed celibacy and all grants made to them were held *śiṣyaparaṃparenen̩*.[63] Later however many Ramdasis began to marry and the successive disciples were sons. To regulate such successions the Raja of Satara in 1725 gave out a sanad to the head of the chief math at Chafal which allowed him far-reaching discretionary power to interfere in inam disputes of the sectarians, declaring that any of them disregarding his orders would forfeit his lands to him.

On the side of the dynasty of the sovereign donor the hereditary right of the inamdar to his land had its counterpart in the duty to uphold the grant's permanency. Such a duty was also felt to be incumbent on succeeding dynasties, although in such cases *fitna* could lead to the suspension of grants. The grants are usually declared 'forever imperishable' (*ajarāmarhāmati*)[64] and 'absolutely certain' (*bilākusūr*)[65] or to last 'as long as the moon and sun endure' (*ācandrark*) in conformity with the ancient protocol of the

58 *MIS*, 20, nos 66–7, 89–90, 111; *P.A.: List 13, Ru. 9*, no. 3066; *SSRPD*, 9, no. 498. The *Rājyavyavahara Kośa* explains: *avlādaḥ putrasaṇtānamaflāda duhitṛ saṇtatiḥ* (255–b).

59 *P.A.: List 13, Ru. 80, File 1112*.

60 *P.A.: List 13, Ru. 73, File 1030*, no. 3026 of 1850; *List 14, Ru. 1, File 13*; *List 11, Nasik Records, vol. 3*, no. 239 of 1871, etc.

61 Max Weber stressed this often.

62 Compare the Vaishnavite sect in Nepal: Burghart, 'Vaishnavite Sect', pp. 2, 4.

63 *P.A.: List 13, Ru. 56*, no. 1491 of 1861; *Ru. 87, File 1204*, no. 79 of September 1857; *Ru. 2, File 20*, Report no. 410 and no. 985 of 1857; *List 12, File 533*.

64 E.g. *MIS*, 15, no. 392.

65 On which see *Rāj. Kośa*, 236–a: *niḥsaṇdeho bilākusūr*.

Hindus.[66] Particularly in religious grants warnings are often included against resumption of or interference in the grant, for example: 'if any Muslim obstructs or stops it, he breaks an oath on the Prophet of God, the Quran, and Mecca, and if any Hindu obstructs or stops it, he is bound by the oath on Harihar, the Veda, the Shastra and his parents, and it will be tantamount to killing a cow at Kasi (Benares)'.[67] Often in Maratha inampatras passages are inserted in the original Sanskrit from the *dharmaśāstra* containing the most fanciful threats against the resumption of grants and eternal rewards for their continuation. Of frequent occurrence in Maratha inampatras of all sorts is also the enumeration of the seven (formerly eight) *bhogas* giving rights over the subsoil, also known from copperplate and ancient stone-edicts, *jalataru-tṛṇa-kāṣṭha-pāṣāṇa-nidhinikṣepa*: water, trees, grass, wood, stones, treasure-trove, and deposits.[68]

Religious grants

In grants of land to pious brahmans we often find the Shastric maxim of the offering of 'gold and water' or just 'water'.[69] The pouring of water intimated the relinquishment of the right to the land by the donor, while the offering of a piece of gold was originally meant as an inducement to a brahman to accept the grant.[70] Such an inducement was necessary on account of the Brahmanic ideal of the 'free gift' – the gift which was made to serve the dharma and denied any reciprocity between donor and donee. Ideally the brahman stood apart from society and royal power in order to be able to provide a transcendent legitimation, that is, to transcend *fitna* by representing the universalist dharma.[71] The ideal brahman therefore was autonomous and in himself complete; he was *ṣaṭkarma*, combining within himself three pairs of complemen-

[66] *P.A.: List 11, Surat Volumes, no.* 27, no. 3842 of 1858; *BGS*, n.s. no. 10, pp. 251–65.

[67] Vad, Mawji and Parasnis, *Sanadāpatreṇ*, p. 25.

[68] Cf. Steele, *Law and Custom of Hindoo Castes*, p. 284; *BISM-Vārṣik Itivṛtt* (1916), p. 131; Kane, *History of Dharmaśāstra*, 2, p. 865.

[69] *MITSA*, 2, no. 216; 3, no. 807; Vad, Mawji and Parasnis, *Sanadāpatreṇ*, pp. 209, 215–17; *MIS*, 8, p. 190; 20, no. 27; *BISM-Vārṣik Itivṛtt* (1916), p. 131; *SPD*, 31, no. 122; *SSRPD*, 3, no. 154; Kane, *History of Dharmaśāstra*, 2, pp. 854–5; 3, p. 497.

[70] Cf. M. Biardeau and Ch. Malamoud, *Le Sacrifice dans l'Inde Ancienne* (Paris, 1976), pp. 155 ff.

[71] Cf. Chapter I–1–c.

tary 'duties': patronage and priesthood of the ritual (*yājan/yajan*); learning and teaching of the Veda (*adhyayan/adhyāpan*); and the giving and receiving of gifts (*dān/pratigrahaḥ*). By contrast, the *kṣatriya* and the *vaiśya* were merely *trikarma*, i.e., they were qualified only for patronage of ritual, learning of the Veda, and the giving of gifts.[72] We have seen that the condominium of king and brahman on which legitimate sovereignty in India was founded was fraught as a result of this with a contradiction between universalism and *fitna* or political sovereignty. The brahman was always in danger of losing his transcendence by entering into formal relations with the king and the king needed him in his transcendent capacity to legitimize his universal dominion. The introduction of the fiction of the 'unseen' purpose which the brahman derived from the *pratigrahaḥ* or 'acceptance' of gifts was hence necessary to preserve the Brahmanic ideals of extra-social exclusiveness and independence which otherwise could not but lead to the refusal of the king's donations.[73]

Still, political association with the court and the acceptance of grants of land for non-religious services normally lowered a brahman's status. This was for instance expressed in the relatively low ritual rank of the Citpavans in Maharashtra next to the Deshastha brahmans who were politically of much less consequence. Traditionally it came out clearly in the low position of the *purohita* or 'court chaplain' in the brahman hierarchy. The so-called Rajput Bhats of the Deccan and Gujarat also owed their degradation to the adoption of a kshatriya way of life and the acceptance of grants of land for services.[74] As did Islam and early Buddhism, the universalist *dharma* required political aloofness and religious ascetism from its priesthood or interpreters. The Islamic *waqf* was technically not a donation to the ulama but rather 'wealth brought under divine protection'; members of the Buddhist Samgha could only accept grants of land under the fiction that these were not given to them but to the Samgha. From the standpoint of universalist, ascetic religion all *fitna* was the corruption of power and 'seduction'. Refusals of grants of land are, however, not often heard of, except in hagiographies. But it is always clear when *fitna* irrupts in the universalist purity. A particularly instructive example of this is

72 Cf. Sabnis, *Paṇt Amātya Bāvḍā Daftar*, I, no. 71.

73 At times this did occur; an interesting case is described in V. Das, *Structure and Cognition: Aspects of Hindu Caste and Ritual* (New Delhi, 1977), pp. 18 ff.

74 R. E. Enthoven, *The Tribes and Castes of Bombay*, 3 vols (Bombay, 1920–2), I, p. 125.

provided in R. M. Eaton's study of the Sufis of Bijapur.[75] Eaton describes how the Sufis, in order to become the recipients of revenue-exempt villages or lands, had to enter into a formal relationship with the court, an association which was initially suspect to them. Their accepting of *inām* lands presupposed their coming into line with the ulama orthodoxy and their unquestioning adhesion to the Bijapur government. In the early stage we indeed find some of them refusing the Sultan's grants. But from about the mid seventeenth century onwards grants of land became a widespread institutional arrangement for the Sufi tombs, reflecting a closer liaison with the government. It was at this period that the Marathas began to rise to power and that their relations with the Bijapur court became strained. There is evidence that landed Sufis participated in the conflict by giving it the sanction of *jihād* or 'holy war'.

In spite of the ultimately renunciatory quality of brahman universalism the vast collections of stone-tablet and copperplate edicts from all over the Indian subcontinent show the brahmans as the most common recipients of donations of hereditary revenue-exempt lands, in fact monopolizing them up to the tenth century.[76] Max Weber thought that 'the social and economic privileges of the brahmans were unsurpassed by those of any other priesthood'.[77] Brahmanical exemptions and privileges were maintained as a matter of sound policy by most Muslim sovereigns in India – to an extent even by those who reimposed the *jiziya* or poll-tax on non-Muslims – although most of them favoured their own religion more strongly.[78] Shivaji, while referring to his kingdom as a *hiṇdvī*

75 R. M. Eaton, *Sufis of Bijapur, 1300–1700* (Princeton, 1978); see also *idem*, 'The Court and the Dargah in the Seventeenth Century Deccan', *IESHR*, 10, 1 (1973), pp. 50–63.

76 Cf. D. D. Kosambi, *An Introduction to the Study of Indian History* (Bombay, 1975), p. 363.

77 *Religionssoziologie*, II, p. 62.

78 The early Delhi Sultans introduced the jiziya on Hindu and other non-Muslim subjects in India. Like the Deccan Sultans later they were often openly partial to Muslims. Brahmans were exempted from the jiziya by the early Sultans, but Firuz Tughluq imposed it on them as well; later he reduced the amount to be paid by the brahmans (S. C. Raychaudhary, *Social, Cultural and Economic History of India (Medieval Age)* (Delhi, 1978), p. 5). Akbar abolished the jiziya and started a policy more favourable to the Hindus. The tide turned again with Aurangzeb who was the first to introduce an element of religious discrimination into the fiscal system of the Deccan of the seventeenth century. There is no contemporary evidence that the jiziya was ever imposed on the Hindu subjects by Muhammad Adil Shah (cf. J. A. Ghauri, 'Kingship in the Sultanates of Bijapur and Golconda', *Islamic Culture*, 46, 1 (1972), p. 50). Aurangzeb revived the jiziya in 1679

svarājya[79] and to himself as a 'protector of cows and brahmans', does not appear to have been biased in any way against the Muslims in his realm. Under his sovereignty the inams of both communities were sequestrated but shrines and places of worship and religious personages of either were scrupulously maintained by allowances 'according to their importance'.[80] There are many examples from Shivaji's early reign of new grants of land made by him to mosques and Muslim saints as well as to brahmans, temples and gosavis.[81] After the Mughal invasion the Maratha kings Rajaram and Shahu were particularly generous to brahmans.[82] The Maratha kingdom became known, already before the rise of the Peshwas, as 'the rājya

(Sarkar, *Ma'āṣir-i-'Ālamgirī*, pp. 181, 315; *idem*, *History of Aurangzib*, pp. 268 ff); he remitted for an unknown period up to 1668 the *zakāt* of the Muslims, maintaining it to the full for the Hindus ('English Factory Records of 1667 and 1668', in *SKPSS*, nos 1187, 1202; Athar Ali, *Mughal Nobility*, p. 98, note 1). Under Aurangzeb exemptions from the jiziya to brahmans were sometimes granted with the provision that they 'pray for the Emperor's health and prosperity' (B. R. Bhalerao, 'Exemption from the Jazia Tax secured by Brahmins of Ujjain', *Proceedings of the 15th Session of the Indian History Congress* (Gwalior, 1952), p. 385). Brahmans were also sometimes exempted from the jiziya in the Mughal Deccan. Grant Duff, *History*, 1, p. 180 says that the jiziya was 'to be as strictly exacted in the Deccan as in the Northern part of the empire'. Evidence for the imposition of the jiziya in the Western Deccan is found in: *SCS*, 4, nos 694, 704; 5, pp. 7–8, 69–81; *BISM-Aitihāsik Saṃkīrṇa Sāhitya*, 1, nos 9, 13; Khobrekar, *Tarikh-i-Dilkasha*, p. 231. In the Deccan too brahmans appealed to the Emperor for exemption, but it is not known whether such exemptions were granted (cf. A. R. Kulkarni, 'Social Relations in the Maratha Country in the Medieval Period', *Proceedings of the 32nd Session of the Indian History Congress* (Jabalpur, 1970), Presidential Address, Medieval India Section, p. 256). In the Mughal Deccan the jiziya was in fact levied rather haphazardly, sometimes also from Muslims (*SCS*, 5, no. 763). Immediately after the revival of the jiziya Shivaji wrote a letter to Aurangzeb, protesting against its imposition (*BISM-Vārṣik Itivṛtt* (1915), pp. 166–8; Sarkar, *History of Aurangzib*, 3, pp. 285–9). In 1704, allegedly on account of the distress caused by famine and the Maratha war, Aurangzeb saw himself forced to remit the jiziya throughout the Deccan for the period of the war, which meant in practice until his death (Habib, *Agrarian System*, p. 245). With grants of land Aurangzeb was much less selective: there are numerous instances of brahmans and Hindu saints receiving confirmations from him for their inams and agraharas (cf. Athar Ali, *Mughal Nobility*, pp. 98–9, note 1). The jiziya continued to be imposed in isolated instances until at least 1752 (*P.A.: Peśve Hindustan Rumal 179*, jamābaṇḍī of 1742 mahāl sarkār t.prāṇt Namad, accrediting Rs 86 as 'jizhiya'; *Rumal 178*, terīj tāḷebaṇd sarkār udaipur gives Rs 13,426 on account of 'jizhiya' in 1752). The Marathas also imposed jiziya in the early eighteenth century (see *SPD*, 30, no. 21 of 1719 for a government order to the deśmukhs and deśpandes of the district of Candvad to give in all accounts of the cesses imposed by them and desist from exacting the jiziya in the future).

79 *MIS*, 15, no. 269. 80 Vakaskar, *Sabhāsadācī Bakhar*, pp. 30–1.

81 Kulkarni, 'Social Relations', pp. 231–68.

82 Grant Duff, *History*, 1, pp. 245–6.

which is beneficent to gods and brahmans'.[83] The *Ājñāpatra* says that 'to make a grant of land for the purpose of [spreading] dharma is an act of eternal merit', and among the functions of the king it counts 'the inquiry into the prevalence of dharma and adharma, timely grants (*dan*), . . . the gaining of the favour of gods and good brahmans devoted to gods, and the destruction of irreligious tendencies, the propagation of the duties of religion, the acquisition of merit for the eternal world.'[84] While enjoining religious grants of land the same text dictates that such should not be made to 'those who wander from place to place for alms, nor to those who themselves or whose descendants are or can become wicked and promotors of evil ways, nor to those who are the enemies of dharma or who are heterodox (*svadharmavirodhī pāṣaṇḍī*)'.[85] In conformity with this, most deeds of grants of land to brahmans in effect describe the recipients as 'family-men' (*kuṭuṃbvatsal*), 'very well versed in the Veda and Shastra', and as being of 'perfect behaviour'. Many of the grants were – also in accordance with an injunction found in the *Ājñāpatra* – made at auspicious times such as sun- or moon-eclipses. But the criterion of orthodoxy was in practice quite elastic. It was at no time in the eighteenth century uncommon to make grants to Muslim religious establishments or even to Christian churches.

When under the Peshwas, from the reign of Balaji Baji Rao onwards, the Citpavan brahmans became the governing class, *fitna* and *brāhmaṇapratipālana*, 'the protection of brahmans', became compounded to an unprecedented degree. Particularly the last Peshwa, Baji Rao II, appears to have been extremely liberal in the patronage of religious brahmans and sacred institutions. Throughout the second half of the eighteenth century all categories of brahmans enjoyed, apart from land-revenue remissions, also exemption from customs, ferry charges, house-taxes, purchase-taxes, forced labour, death penalty, and enslavement.[86] As in the

83 *Śrīsaṃpradāyācīṇ Kāgadpatreṇ*, nos 106, 371.

84 Banhatti, *Ājñāpatra*, chs 4 and 7.

85 *Ibid.*, ch. 5.

86 *SSRPD*, 1, nos 240, 253, 263, 379; 2, no. 328; 3, nos 79, 341, 446, 452; 6, no. 738; 7, no. 692; Ranade, 'Introduction', pp. 455–6, 473; Sen, *Administrative System*, pp. 176, 190; *SCS*, 2, no. 242; *SPD*, 18, no. 36; 32, nos 74, 177, 183, 186, 190–2, 199; 43, no. 168; Vad, Mawji and Parasnis, *Sanadāpatreṇ*, p. 176; *EIP*, 4, pp. 227, 231, 271–3, 281–2, 580; Choksey, *Ratnagiri*, p. 171; *P.A.: List 13, Ru. 79, File 1081*, no. 701 of 1856; H. Fukazawa, 'Some Aspects of Slavery in the Eighteenth Century Maratha Kingdom', *The Journal of Intercultural Studies* (Inaugural

preceding period, under the Peshwas religious grants to brahmans were strictly the prerogative of those who were qualified as *ṣaṭkarmī*.[87] It was commonly reiterated in the inampatra that the recipient brahman was *ṣaṭkarmadhikāri* and qualified for *dānpratigraha*.[88] Under the Citpavan dominance however political considerations again began to affect the question of caste-purity. An example of this is the famous dispute about the subcaste of 'fish-eating' brahmans called *śeṇavī macchāharī* or *gauḍa sāraswata*.[89] To the other brahman subcastes their credentials had always been suspect, but we find the Shenavis holding *inām* and *agrahara* grants from as early as the fourteenth century.[90] They were definitely *ṣaṭkarmī* in the early seventeenth century and Shivaji seems to have guaranteed this status to them.[91] Under Shahu and up to about the death of Madhav Rao I the Shenavis were confirmed in the possession of religious *ināms* and were exempted from the death penalty like full brahmans.[92] In 1788 the question of the Shenavis' brahmanhood was brought before a board of pandits in Benares, who, however, confirmed it.[93] During Madhav Rao I's reign the dispute had erupted afresh in Poona on the occasion of the grant of the *agrahara* village of Malkhed to an assembly of fifty-four brahmans of the four Vedic denominations of Deshasthas, Citpavans, Karhads, and Shenavis.[94] A special court was convoked at Poona to investigate the ritual purity (food and living-habits) of the Shenavis but like the pandits in Benares later it decided in their favour. Later in the eighteenth century however

Number, 1974), p. 12; V. K. Bhave, *Peśvekālīn Mahārāṣṭra* (Poona, 1935), p. 370.

87 Bhave, *Peśvekālīn Mahārāṣṭra*, p. 367.

88 Vad, Mawji and Parasnis, *Sanadāpatreṇ*, pp. 138–9, 164–5; *SSRPD*, 2, no. 175; 3, no. 165; 4, no. 86; *MIS*, 11, no. 113; 13, no. 29; 15, no. 426; 20, no. 193; *MITSA*, 2, nos 205, 334; *TKKP*, 1, no. 82; 2, no. 235; 3, nos 126, 147; *SCS*, 5, no. 759; *SPD*, 7, no. 22; *BISM-Vārṣik Itivṛtt* (1913), p. 234; etc.

89 *IS*, 5, 12 (1909), p. 37. There were also Prabhus whose *ṣaṭkarmī* brahman status was disputed (cf. A. Rayrikar, '"Gramaniyas" (caste disputes) under the Satara state (1825–1838)' (Paper presented to a seminar on the 16–20th-century history of Gujarat and Maharashtra held at the M. S. University of Baroda, 19–21 March 1982), p. 4). For the Saraswats see G. R. Sharma, *Sāraswata Bhūṣaṇa* (Bombay, 1950), p. 528; R. B. Gunjikar, *Sāraswatīmaṇḍaḷa* (Bombay, 1884), pp. 180–8; Wagle, 'Gauḍa Sāraswata Brāhmaṇas'; F. F. Conlon, *A Caste in a Changing World: The Chitrapur Saraswat Brahmans, 1700–1935* (Berkeley, 1977).

90 Sharma, *Sāraswata Bhūṣaṇa*, pp. 503–4.

91 *SCS*, 5, no. 759; Gunjikar, *Sāraswatīmaṇḍaḷa*, p. 181.

92 Gunjikar, *Sāraswatīmaṇḍaḷa*, p. 181; Sharma, *Sāraswata Bhūṣaṇa*, pp. 509–10, 528–9, 535; *SSRPD*, 3, no. 42; 8, nos 115, 866, 983.

93 Sharma, *Sāraswata Bhūṣaṇa*, pp. 564–6, 569, 590.

94 *IS*, 5, 12 (1909), p. 37.

the Shenavis obtained more and more political power in the Northern Maratha states of Baroda, Indore, Nagpur, and Gwalior. Mahadaji Scindhia gave virtually all the key positions in his government to them. When Scindhia began to challenge the Citpavan power at Poona, the Shenavis under the leadership of Baloji Tatya for some time wielded much influence in the Peshwa's capital as the opponents of Nana Fadnis. With the support of Scindhia and the Shenavis, Madhav Rao Narayan was made Peshwa in 1794; but he was ousted a few years later by Baji Rao. The latter had a number of Shenavis executed to clear the field of opposition, but since they were still regarded as full brahmans the Peshwa set out to excuse his offence by establishing that the Shenavis were *trikarmī* brahmans. This also made it possible for him to resume most of the religious lands of the Shenavis around Poona on the pretext that they had no right to receive them.

Religious grants were thus supportive of the sovereign's power either by the fact that they served the universalist *dharma* or by being implicated in the political tussle itself on the level of *fitna*. Shrines, temples and religious endowments multiplied in and around Poona, while in areas like the Southern Maratha Country or Gujarat beyond the Mahi the *zamīndārs* and *mavās* left little scope for them.[95] In the latter districts, grants of land by the Poona huzur were quite moderate but it often occurred that local zamindars turned *puṇḍa* or that they became devotees and then frittered away their estates among the brahmans without even the pretence of authorization from Poona.[96] State-sponsored religious grants were, as we saw, made with the most solemn declarations of permanency as fully defined and delimited, but they were vulnerable on account of the unmilitary character of the recipients.[97] Like the Islamic *waqfs*, the religious establishments of maths, temples, mosques, and brahmans, with their tax-exemptions, were threatened to the degree that the 'co-sharers' of the king, of the sovereign donor, had the power to interfere in them.[98] From an early date there is

95 The last portion of *SSRPD* gives a list of about 250 temples in and around Poona which were of sufficient importance to receive the Peshwa's direct support in 1810–11. For Gujarat see *EIP*, 3, pp. 677–97; for the Southern Maratha Country see Marshall, *Statistical Reports*, pp. 23–4, 157.

96 Cf. Marshall, *Statistical Reports*, p. 758; *BGS*, n.s. no. 132, p. 11.

97 It is therefore only in a limited sense that Baden-Powell's assertion that 'the religious and charitable inams were always among the most stable' holds true ('Dakhan Villages', p. 274).

98 For the waqfs see C. H. Becker, 'Zur Kulturgeschichte Nord-Syriens im Zeitalter der Mamluken', in *Islamstudien*, 1 (Leipzig, 1924), pp. 268–9: 'Die Emire

evidence in India of village-headmen and gentry objecting to the government's converting their villages into *agraharas*.[99] Frequently there are references to plunderings of maths by passing armies, *saṃsthāniks* or *puṇḍa zamīndārs*.[100] Quite a few brahmans' grants were also usurped by agents which they had appointed temporarily as managers before going on pilgrimage to Benares.[101] If not plundered, the religious establishments of brahmans and gosavis were skimmed incessantly by virtually everybody around. A typical case in point is the Sadanand math at Nimb in pargana Vai, which we can follow closely over the years 1635–1773.[102] Like other religious centres of importance the math accumulated in this period a large number of *inām* villages and lands, orchards, gardens, and periodic or daily grants of produce and cash from many (at least eighty) different villages in its neighbourhood under the sanction of the successive sovereigns. But hardly a single year passed without a report or complaint of some obstruction: karkuns refusing to part with the proceeds of the inams; water-canals being closed off by the patils; *paṭṭīs* and *bābs* being levied by karkuns, patils, zamindars, and army-officers; or mokasadars not recognizing the grants; *kuṃbhārs* (potters) claiming their rights to dig up clay in the inam fields; cattle being stolen; various *amals* of the revenue taken by assignment-holders; ghasdana being levied by the army; molestations by hunting parties; conflicts over cultivators, etc. So common was this kind of obstruction that it can be taken for granted that a large part of the expenditure exhibited in the government Daftar for the support of religious foundations never reached its assigned destination.[103]

drängen sich überall hinein zwischen die Wakfbauern und die Rentner der Wakfs, so dass letztere noch von Glück sagen können, wenn ihnen ein Zehntel ihrer Rente zufliesst. . . . Das Wakf war also in vielen Hinsichten bedroht'. Comparison with documents describing religious institutions elsewhere in India shows that the obstruction of rent-free lands and other sources of income, which is constantly referred to in the Marathi documents, is far from atypical (e.g., see B. N. Goswamy and J. S. Grewal, *The Mughal and Sikh Rulers and the Vaishnavas of Pindori* (Simla, 1966)).

99 Cf. Derrett, *Hoysalas*, p. 181.

100 *SSRPD*, 7, no. 687; *TKKP*, 1, nos 358, 365; Sharma, *Sāraswata Bhūṣaṇa*, pp. 528–9; Khare, *Aitikhāsik Lekh Saṃgraha*, 4, p. 2458.

101 E.g. *SCS*, 7, no. 49.

102 *MIS*, 15, nos 62–265; 20, nos 161, 165, 167, 173. Similar cases: *BISM-Vārṣik Itivṛtt* (1915), no. 178 (pp. 313–18); *P.A.: List 13, Ru. 3, File 30.*

103 See for this also H. D. Robertson to M. Elphinstone, 31 October 1818, in: R. D. Choksey (ed.), *Early British Administration, 1817–1836* (Selections from the Peshwa Daftar, Deccan Commissioner's Files and Pre-Mutiny Records on Gujarat) (Poona, 1964), p. 40.

Next to this 'skimming' of the religious funds there was the problem of their application. Heirs of private grantors of large sums of money to a temple usually obtained a right of superintendence if they demanded it.[104] An account of Gopalnaik Tambvekar, one of the greatest bankers under Madhav Rao I describes such a situation: how he gave a few lacs of rupees in support of a great temple in Gujarat and how this fell into disorder, then was reorganized by the government of the Gaikwar and how the banker afterwards appointed a hereditary superintendent from his family (who in 1909 was still in charge).[105] In other cases, normally, if the devasthan was large, a karkun on the part of the sarkar would superintend the revenue and expenditure.[106] In small temples the pujari superintended the expenses and the mamlatdar of the district would occasionally send a karkun to examine the accounts.[107] Baji Rao II appointed a committee of four persons to superintend the disbursement of the sums made over by him from his private treasury to temples at Nasik.[108] Detailed accounts were kept of the receipts and expenditure by the committee and submitted to Poona, where regular *tāḷebaṇds* were prepared by the Peshwa's Daftar establishment. In general however – in the case of religious grants as everywhere – more effective than such methods of centralized auditing was the system of management by conflict. Wherever villages or lands were allotted to maintain religious institutions the mutual supervision and control of the officiating brahmans or the coparceners of the grant were the best check on peculation.[109] In the same light should be seen the governmental interventions in disputes originating in the distribution of religious resources. It would be wrong to envisage such intervention as the forcible intrusion of the sovereign's power from above. It was always brought about on the request of one or more of the parties involved in the dispute. This form of arbitration was merely one other way in which the sovereign could extend his influence through the utilization of pre-existing conflict.[110]

104 Steele, *Law and Custom of Hindoo Castes*, p. 206.
105 *IS*, 5, 12, (1909), p. 37.
106 Steele, *Law and Custom of Hindoo Castes*, p. 206. 107 *Ibid.*
108 *P.A.: List 11, Nasik Records, vol. 1*, no. 1100 of 1861.
109 *EIP*, 4, p. 303.
110 Cf. also L. W. Preston, 'Subregional Religious Centres in the History of Maharashtra: The Sites Sacred to Ganesh', in: N. K. Wagle (ed.), *Images of Maharashtra: A Regional Profile of India* (London and Dublin, 1980), pp. 102–28; Spencer, 'Rajaraja I', pp. 439–41.

V The grant of land as act of sovereignty

While the levying of the land-revenue or *rājbhāg* was postulated as the royal prerogative, to exempt land from the payment of land-revenue was the act of sovereignty *par excellence*. Vijñāneśvara states that 'the king is the "lord of the land" because only he has the right to make a grant of land or an endowment, and not a provincial governor'.[1] Since the establishment of sovereignty was the result of successful *bheda* or *fitna*, it becomes nearly a tautology to say that the sovereign, the 'lord of the land' (*bhūpati*), was he who sanctioned grants of and vested rights in land. The real question must be: who should be considered as the sovereign at a particular time and place? This is virtually tantamount to asking: who made grants of land and who guaranteed the hereditary vested rights and exemptions?

The Mughal government was uniform in its operations and great accuracy appears to have been maintained in the keeping of records, especially of those relating to grants of land, either for a limited or unlimited period, for service performed or expected, or as free gifts to religious personages or institutions. No deed was valid unless sanctioned by a farman from the Emperor accompanied by a parvana from the subhedar of the province. At all events, it was stated in the body of the parvana that the grant was made with the permission of the Emperor. It was during the distractions incident upon the incursions of the Marathas, resulting in frequent changes of subhedars, that innovations began to prevail. The formerly essential requisite of obtaining a farman from Delhi or Agra to accompany the subhedar's parvana was disregarded and it was often merely written in the body of the grant that it was made 'by the order of the Emperor'. On the fall or recall of a subhedar his followers forfeited the lands and privileges which were granted to them for supporting his interests when he was a successful powerholder.[2]

In the Deccan the Nizam felt strong enough to arrogate to himself the sovereign attribute to grant rent-free lands in 1725 and he exercised it from then on, while keeping up other conventional symbols of sovereignty – the striking of coins, the reading of the *khuṭba* – in the name of the Emperor. The Marathas by that time

1 '*pārthivo bhūpatiḥ; anena bhūpatereva bhūmidāne nibandhadāne vā'dhikāro na bhogapateriti darśitam*' (Parvatiya (ed.), *Mit. on Yājñ.*, I, 318).

2 *P.A.: List 13, Ru. 73, File 1025*, no.1 of 1822; *SPD*, 31, no.77.

had already successfully terminated their contest for the sovereignty of the Western Deccan and were beginning to expand northward. Shahaji Bhonsle, as well as his immediate ancestors, gave out *ināms* in the capacity of jagirdars of the Ahmadnagar and Bijapur Sultans under *hujats* which were often confirmed by royal *farmāns* later.[3] Shivaji was the first to alienate land without reference to the Muslim powers of Hindustan or the Deccan. The legitimacy for this was emphasized by the *abhiṣeka* ceremony in 1674. Shivaji's successors continued to act on the same footing to counteract Mughal *fitna* at the turn of the seventeenth century. After retreating from the Western Deccan, the Mughal Emperors went on to grant incidentally lands and villages or shares of revenue in inam in the Maratha country, even close to Poona. Such grants are recorded until as late as 1770.[4] They, as also a few grants of the Nizam, were respected and confirmed by the Maratha Rajas and Peshwas.[5] Throughout the eighteenth century we also find confirmations and continuations by Mughal Emperors and the Nizams in Maratha districts of grants – mostly to Muslims – made by the earlier Emperors in the seventeenth century or by the Deccan Sultans.[6] These were simultaneously upheld by Maratha *tākīdpatras*. The eighteenth-century Mughal Emperors still thought it opportune sometimes to confirm a grant newly made by the Maratha King or Peshwa.[7] From their side the Marathas generally respected grants made by the Mughal Emperor in the districts which they conquered from him, but resumed some of the Nizam's in districts ceded by the latter.[8]

Under the Maratha *svarājya*, the granting of land and confirming of vested privilege was also at first strictly a royal prerogative or at least the king's sanction was required to do so. In the *aṣṭapradhān* council under Shivaji there existed the office of *Paṇḍit Rāo*, whose

[3] *MIS*, 15, nos 372, 385, 400; *P.A.: List 13, Ru. 2, File 17*, proc. 696B.

[4] *SSRPD*, 3, no.195; *P.A.: List 13, Ru. 13, File 380*, proc. 585C; *File 268*, proc. 875B; *Ru. 4, File 35*, proc. 563C; *Ru. 55, File 75*, Report C-16. The last case is a grant to the vakil Hingane of 1742 of which it is impossible to ascertain whether it was enjoyed until 1751. In the taleband of Nasik for 1752 the amal in question was first excluded from the list of authorized alienations because the sanads were not forthcoming: hence it was entered as *ghair sanadī*. The Peshwa however subsequently admitted the validity of the grant (*App. Inam Commission Rumal*, no. 142).

[5] *P.A.: List 13, Ru. 75, File 1049*, pp. 18–19.

[6] *Ibid., Ru. 1, File 1*, proc. 43C, 77, 73B; *File 6*, proc. 137A; *File 8*, Report 12A; *Ru. 3, File 28*, proc. 201.

[7] *Ibid., Ru. 1*, proc. 595B.

[8] *Ibid., Ru. 13, File 332*, no.477 of 1856.

function was that of *Dānādhyakṣa* or 'Superintendent of [religious] Gifts'.[9] This office may be compared with that of the *Ṣadr* in the Mughal Empire, the difference being however that the latter was at times authorized to make small grants of land as *madad-i-ma'āsh* or give out stipends (*vazīfa*) independently of the Emperor, while the former was merely advisory.[10] The office of *Dānādhyakṣa* was soon obliterated. Shivaji's son Sambhaji entrusted the 'plenipotentiary power' (*kārbārācā yekhtīyār*) of his administration to a favourite, Kavi Kailash.[11] It cannot be ascertained if this implied the right to make land-grants but it seems likely. During Aurangzeb's Deccan invasion Rajaram wrote from Jinji to the vatandars in the Western Deccan that the 'plenipotentiary power of the kingdom' (*rājyācā kāryabāg, yekhtiyār, rājyabhār, kārbārācā makhtīyār, kul akhtiyār*, etc.) with the seal of the king (*svāmīcī mudrā*) was given to Shankarji Narayan Pandit Saciv and Ramcandra Pant Amatya, the Hukmatpanha. The former had this authority in the districts beyond Karad, the Upper Ghats to the East of Rajgarh and the Konkan up to Gokarna; the rest of the districts was under the authority of the latter. With this division of territory went, as we have seen, a division of the army. The vatandars were ordered by Rajaram to obey the orders and submit to the decisions of these delegates and treat their sanads 'as if they were the sanads of the King [himself]'.[12] It was also stated then that this delegation of power was to last only until the time that the country and the forts would again be completely under Maratha control.

Thus when Shahu was released from the Mughal camp he became the sovereign or granting authority, but he had to contend in *fitna* with his cousin. In the period when the succession dispute remained undecided the Kolhapur Raja still made grants in the

[9] *IS*, 6, 10-11-12 (1915), 'Bhoṇslyāṇce Kulācār', p. 66; Vad, Mawji and Parasnis, *Sanadāpatreṇ*, pp. 122 ff, 157; Sardesai, Kale and Vakaskar, *Aitihāsik Pareṇ*, no.2; Hervadkar, *Saptaprakaraṇātmak Caritra*, p. 229.

[10] I. Hasan, *The Central Structure of the Mughal Empire* (Lahore, etc., 1967), pp. 254–88; *SCS*, 2, nos 236, 241.

[11] *TKKP*, 1, no.143.

[12] *SPD*, 31, no.51; *IS*, 2, 5 (1909), p. 26; *TKKP*, 1, no.65; *MIS*, 15, no.349; *SCS*, 2, no.225; *SCS*, 5, no.846; K. V. Purandare (ed.), *Purandare Daftar*, vol. 1, no.3; V. S. Bendre (ed.), *Rājārāmcaritam* (Poona, 1931), I, 43–5 and IV, 11–12; Khobrekar, *Shivaji Period*, no.107; *BISMQ*, 2, 1–4 (1922), p. 26; *ibid.*, 9, 4 (1928), pp. 65–7; Sabnis, *Paṇt Amātya Bāvḍā Daftar*, 1, no.52; P. S. Joshi, 'Ch. Rājārām mahārāja (1688–1700) hyāṇca vataneṇ deṇyācā nirṇay', *Bhāratīya Itihās āṇi Saṃskṛti Quarterly*, 7 (1970), pp. 41–6; Sarkar, *History of Aurangzib*, 5, p. 194.

Poona district.[13] Later he had the authority to do so only in his own dominion around Kolhapur where he did not need the sanction of the Raja of Satara or the Peshwa.[14] There were a number of sardars who held lands from both branches of the Bhonsle family, while in some districts (such as Chikodi and Manoli) where the governments of Poona and Kolhapur had rival pretensions to sovereignty, grants of exempted land continued to be made by both throughout the eighteenth century.[15]

In the early period the Peshwa had no independent granting power. There are letters of injunction, enjoining the continuation of grants, extant from him from 1718 onwards. Grants made by the Peshwa in 1725–6 still needed a confirmatory sanad from Shahu.[16] By 1743 this appears to have been no longer the case. A *dehajhāḍā* of Junnar of that year divides the exempted villages of this district in *huzūrce sanadece dehe* and *sarkārce sanadece dehe*; this means that there were at this time two independent sources of exemption: the *huzūr* or Raja of Satara and the *sarkār* or Peshwa.[17] After 1750 the successors of Shahu were nominally treated by the Peshwa with all the respect due to royalty, but in fact they were kept as state prisoners in the Fort of Satara while the Peshwa's court became both *huzūr* and *sarkār*. Each of the successors (Tarabai, aunt of Shahu from 1750–61; Ramraja, the adopted son of Shahu from 1750–77; Shahu Raja from 1778–1808) seems to have exercised less power than his predecessor.[18] No grants are found to have been made by the second Shahu's sons subsequent to 1808 and prior to their elevation by the British government. In the period 1750–1808 it is evident that neither the Raja nor any member of the Raja's family could have issued a sanad without the cognizance of the Peshwa's official (*māmlatdār*) who was in charge of his *daulat* or 'household'.[19] This person was one of the high officials who held the *mutālik* seal and could issue orders in the name of the Peshwa. All grants made by the Raja of Satara in the second half of the

13 *P.A.: List 13, Ru. 1, File 1*, proc. 232B, 234, 941B.

14 *TKKP*, 3, nos 8, 39, 41; 2, no.76; V. G. Khobrekar and S. S. Shinde (eds), *Selections from Kolhapur Records: Source Material for the History of Konkan (1692–1828)* (Bombay, 1971), nos 105, 141, 169; *MIS*, 8, no.122.

15 'Extract from Manson's Report 1853', *BGS*, n.s. no.12.

16 *P.A.: List 13, Ru. 1, File 6*, proc. 405C. The first grant by Balaji Vishvanath was made at least as early as 1719 (*ibid., Ru. 3, file 31*, Report 204).

17 *Ibid., Ru. 1, File 7*, proc. 749B; *Ru. 2, file 7*, no. 130 of 1852. The *dehajhāḍā* of Junnar is found in *P.A.: Prant Ajmas, Rumal 151*.

18 *P.A.: List 13, Ru. 1, File 1222*, no.237 of August 1858.

19 *Ibid.*, no.379 of 3 March 1859; *Ru. 90*, Report 188.

eighteenth century were entered by this official in the Peshwa's accounts, but not all of them were confirmed by a sanad on the Peshwa's part. Those which were not confirmed were mostly made from the holdings – villages, śeri lands, gardens, pastures, etc., in the vicinity of Satara – which the Rajas, their mothers, and their wives held from the Peshwa under the title of *saraṇjām* or 'assignment'.[20] In a few cases however the Raja's title-deeds are only forthcoming for grants which were made in the Peshwa's villages.[21] Except in rare instances, the Peshwa does not appear to have interfered with these. But again, the Peshwa not uncommonly wrote to his *daul māmlatdār* at Satara to obtain *rājpatras* for grants made by himself.[22] Although the Raja was in custody of the Peshwa, a title-deed sealed by him was considered of extra importance. Still, by far the largest number of grants made after 1750 by the Peshwa was not confirmed by the Raja.

Members of the Peshwa's bureaucracy and the Peshwa's military assignees typically were not classified on the basis of distinct, clearly demarcated spheres of competence associated with particular ranks, but rather on the basis of personal influence. The sovereign attribute of the granting of land was shared, in effect, with a number of individuals who held the *śikkekaṭyār* or *mutālik* seal. Among these were first of all the great sardars like Holkar, Scindhia, Gaikwar, Bhonsle of Nagpur, or Angria of Kolaba, who were technically *saraṇjāmdārs* commanding stipulated quota of troops in the service of the Maratha king, but who were equipped with sovereign power in their own assigned districts or when campaigning 'in the *pararājya*'. Other military commanders were sometimes temporarily given the delegatory *śikka* on *ad hoc* commissions. Ultimately the delegation of authority implied by it derived from the Raja of Satara who continued to give a similar emblem and seal to the Peshwa himself. When the Peshwa then further delegated the insignia, Holkar, Scindhia, Gaikwar, and the Raja of Nagpur became sovereign in the areas to the north of the Narmada and all of them (except the Gaikwar) had their own subordinate officials holding the *mutālik* seal from them with the

20 *Ibid., Ru. 1, File 2*, proc. 27A-29A, 31A, 39A; *Ru. 88, File 1222*, no.650 of 24 March 1859; *Ru. 90, File 1271*, Report 410.

21 *Ibid., Ru. 90, File 1263*, Report 20; *File 1268*, Report 206; *TKKP*, 3, no.147; *SSRPD*, 2, no.211; *SSRPD*, 7, no.695.

22 *P.A.: List 13, Ru. 90, File 1268*, Report 188; *File 1271*, Reports 6, 68; *File 1263*, Report 210; *Ru. 3, File 28*, proc. 360; *SSRPD*, 1, no.352.

authorization to make grants of land.[23] As has been seen, on first entering Hindustan some grants were made in the Peshwa's name only, but when the latter became *Vakīl-i-muṭlaq* these were recalled and new sanads were given in the name of the Emperor with the seal of the Peshwa and Scindhia as his deputy.[24] Permanent alienations by Holkar and Scindhia in the Deccan districts under the Peshwa's immediate authority or even in the Peshwa's frontier districts, required the Peshwa's confirmation but did not always have it when they were made from the saranjams which they held in the Deccan.[25] In the Deccan, grants made by ordinary (i.e., temporary) saranjamdars or jagirdars were numerous, but while they were always irregularly paid and often discontinued even by the assignment-holders themselves, they almost invariably ceased on the resumption by the Peshwa of the assignment or amals from which they were rendered payable.[26] Normally any grants made by a holder of a military assignment were understood by all parties to be made for, at the utmost, the term of his tenure.[27] In the early eighteenth century even if an amal like the sardeśmukhi was permanently alienated as *vatan*, the subgrant in *inām* of a territorial section of it by the amaldar needed confirmation by the Raja.[28] But the Raja, or later the Peshwa, could always take land out of an assignment in order to give it in *inām* or he could order an assignment-holder (not without compensating him) to make a grant out of his assignment.[29] Apart from the northern sardars, a small number of old jagirdars of rank were also occupying a rather different position. This was the case apparently with some members of the former *aṣṭapradhān* council. In the first half of the century we find many grants made by the Pratinidhi and the Saciv from their jagirs confirmed by the Raja.[30] The Pratinidhi appears to have lost his granting power later; in a minute of the Peshwa of 1779/80 he was distinctly prohibited from ordering any alienation or assignment.[31] Amrat Rao, the family of Raste, Nana Fadnis, Vinchurkar and Purandare were no doubt entitled to make

23 *EIP*, 3, p. 827; *P.A.: List 13, Ru. 73, File 1025*, nos 1272–9 of 1821, 46 of 1821, 73 of 1821.
24 Cf. p. 148.
25 *P.A.: List 13, Ru. 21, File 407*, no.216 of 1850; *Ru. 17, File 322*, no.16 of 1851.
26 *P.A.: List 11, Khandesh Volumes, no.1.*
27 *P.A.: List 13, Ru. 73, File 1025*, no.15 of 1855.
28 *TKKP*, 1, nos 157–9, 169, 256, 258.
29 *SSRPD*, 1, no.106; *P.A.: List 13, Ru. 1, File 1*, proc. 680C.
30 *P.A.: List 13, Ru. 90, File 1263*, Reports 39, 88; *Ru. 1, File 2*, proc. 848.
31 *Ibid., Ru. 90, File 1267*, Report 116.

grants of land in their jagirs on account of their influence and power.[32] Shahu's brother Fattesingh Bhonsle could make grants before 1750; after that only with the sanction of the Peshwa.[33] Under the Peshwas the position of all these sardars became similar in this respect to that of the Raja of Satara.

Individual provincial governors might have the *mutālik śikka* but only with regard to their own districts and often only temporarily: thus the *sarsubhedār* of the Konkan; the *subhedārs* of Poona and Junnar; the gaikwar as *sarsubhedār* in the Peshwa's districts to the north of the Mahi during the period that he held them in farm; and at times the *subhedār* of the Peshwa in Ahmadabad.[34] There were other instances of *subhā sanads* which have been respected but they were not considered to confer a full and complete title and if they were not set aside by succeeding subhedars they were generally held by brahmans or religious institutions so that the donee of the grant rather than the authority conferring it seems to have procured it respect.[35] The power to make grants of revenue-exempt land was not inherent in the office of sarsubhedar or that of subhedar. The sarsubhedars of the Karnataka never possessed it, except in the case of Patwardhan and Phadke, who did not have this power however by virtue of being sarsubhedars but as high officials who were allowed for special reasons to hold the *mutālik* seal for several years.[36] Normally, in the *ajmās* of every sarsubhedar (as well as in that of mamlatdars and other inferior officials) special instructions were given to inquire about existing alienations and to establish if there was satisfactory proof of their validity, but no authority to give new inams was implied beyond the recognition by the huzur of their accounts in which such grants were registered.[37] Grants made by government revenue officials without an order from the court were not recognized and only registered by the mujumdar of the pargana.[38] Under Baji Rao II an immense

32 *Ibid., Ru. 73, File 1025*, nos 15 of 1855, 73 of 1821.

33 *Ibid., Ru. 12, File 228*, nos 394 of 1840, 35 of 1853, 1510 of 1859.

34 Cf. Chapter 4-IV-g; App. B, section V of Lumsden's report on the judicial administration of the Peshwas d.d. 6 September 1819, in V. T. Gune, *The Judicial System of the Marathas* (Poona, 1953), pp. 373–84 and *ibid.*, p. 117.

35 *P.A.: List 13, Ru. 73, File 1025*, nos 1272–9 of 1821.

36 *Ibid., File 1025*, 'Extracts being para 6 of Government letter to Inam Committee no.3329 d.d. 28 September 1844'; Vad, Mawji and Parasnis, *Kaifiyats, Yadis*, pp. 147–8.

37 *P.A.: List 13, Ru. 73, File 1025*, 'Extract paras 27 to 32 from the Inam Committee's report to gov. d.d. 20th July 1844.'

38 *Ibid., Ru. 73, File 1025*, no.1 of 1822; *SSRPD*, 7, no.660.

number of alienations was also made by revenue farmers of the mahals or districts under *mahāl sanads*. These were never officially acknowledged by the huzur and generally set aside by succeeding farmers, while the British did not admit most of the alienations made after 1803, the period of maximal revenue farming.[39]

In all other cases too, the delegatory power was strictly circumscribed according to time and place. Nana Fadnis, the Vinchurkars, Raste and Parashuram Bhau, for instance, held the *mutālik* seal in particular provinces for periods varying from six months to fifteen years.[40] Whenever the Peshwa's darbar went on tour, a regent was appointed to Poona for the time, and he received the *mutālik śikka* from the Raja.[41] Of all sanads and kauls issued under the mutalik śikka or 'under orders of the huzur' (*parvāngi huzūr*), copies were filed in the Peshwa's Diaries, where also exact registration was maintained of the issuance of the seal itself.[42] This careful supervision and registration of all *huzūr* and *mutālik* grants, combined with the registration in the district and village accounts and proofs of occupancy, made it virtually impossible to err on their authenticity, although it was technically not difficult to forge a grant's seal. From time to time inquiries (*caukśī*) were ordered to be made into the land-titles with the purpose to sift out the *ghairsanadī* from the *sanadī* grants. Such inquiries were analogous to the operations of the British Inam Commission which took place in the nineteenth century and which were basically made on the same evidence and criteria, but the Peshwas never made investigations on a similar exhaustive scale; they worked pargana-wise or on incidental cases. Rajaram however upon his return from Jinji to Maharashtra in 1699 ordered his Nyayadish Konher Pandit to investigate all vatan and inam claims in the svarajya country.[43] He writes that 'army people' had taken certain kinds of evidence of the grants when he was at Jinji and that disputes had arisen about them, and he therefore demanded the genuine deeds to be brought to the inspection of Konher Pandit but distinctly prohibited the latter to give out new grants to anyone. A year later this was revised and a new order was given, stating: 'The Maharaja Chatrapati Saheb

39 Cf. p. 371. 40 *P.A.: List 14, Ru. 1, File 3*, pp. 2–4.
41 Lumsden's report, *loc. cit.*
42 *P.A.: List 13, Ru. 90, File 1268*, Report 188; *Ru. 73*, nos 420 d.d. 21 December 1854, 15 of 1855, Reports 39–40.
43 *SSRPD*, 7, no. 518; 8, nos 1042–3; *B.A.: R.D.*, vo. 5/549 of 1834, p. 86; Gleig, *Life of Munro*, 2, pp. 279–80; Gordon, 'Slow Conquest', p. 27; *P.A.: Selected Rumals, no.52*, section 4, 23649; *MIS*, 3, no. 144.

[Rajaram] gave *dharmādāya, ināms, izāfats*, and new *vatans* from his temporary residence at Jinji. But those sanads were given when the kingdom was unsettled. They must be given effect conform to the decisions of Tarabai and the whole *rājmaṇḍal*'.[44] Here, in contrast to the British operations, the motive was control of conflict rather than counteracting alienations.

By sanctioning grants of land and arbitration of disputes about hereditary titles the sovereign was able to check *fitna*. Thus anyone who was prohibited from making grants of land or sanctioning vested rights was debarred from indulging in it. On the other hand, anyone who did have the delegated or otherwise effective power to sanction grants of land participated in sovereignty to the extent that he could 'create *fitna*'. It was only in those areas which enjoyed fiscal and a certain degree of administrative autonomy that hereditary exemptions could be legitimately given independently of the paramount sovereign power. These comprised, firstly, the areas under 'non-regulation' of most of the chiefs, small rajas, grassias, or samsthaniks.[45] Secondly they comprised the lands and villages held by inamdars.[46] In both cases sub-grants could be allowed to be made without any financial loss to the paramount government. As has been described, in almost all villages – also in those under 'regulation' – the village servants or balutedars as well as village-temples and brahmans also held small pieces of land in inam. These were registered as such in the seventeenth- and eighteenth-century village records, but not in the central government daftar or the district accounts. When, in the mid nineteenth century, the Bombay Inam Commission started to investigate their titles almost all claimants stated that the original grantor was unknown to them. Only very rarely was a sanad produced from Shahu or some jagirdar. Many said that their ancestors had received them '250 or 500 years ago'. Sometimes however it was admitted what was really the case, namely that they had been granted by the village headmen and by the village-community itself. Such inams, granted by the village-authorities, were commonly *begutā* or 'held by long uninterrupted possession' and were classified as *ināmparbhāra*, i.e., *inām* taken directly, not received from the sarkar. Under the tankha settlements they were deduced from the *jamābaṇdī* or village rent-

44 *MIS*, 8, no.52. See also Khobrekar, *Shivaji Period*, no.50.

45 *EIP*, 3, p.827; *P.A.: List 11, Surat Volumes, no.27*, no.3841 of 1858; *List 13, Ru. 73, File 1025*, nos 1 of 1821, 73 of 1821.

46 *P.A.: List 13, Ru. 1, File 1*, proc. 1002B; *File 7*, proc. 824B.

roll. The Inam Commission also respected them if they were registered in the village accounts. They thus continued to receive a kind of overt recognition from the time that the villages were first brought under a standard measurement survey. For this reason they are not classifed as *gāṇv nisbat inām* or '*inām* on charge of the village' in the strict sense. By that term were understood, in the eighteenth century, inams granted by patils, mokadams, or other village officials, the village community as a whole or by the hereditary district zamindars, in payment of debts incurred by the village to an individual money-lender or banker. Such inams became numerous but were usually very small, and most of them were increased, diminished or entirely discontinued by the grantors at will.[47] They normally had no sanad from the government, which had nothing to do with them and did not allow a deduction for them in the village jamabandi. Under these circumstances they were a common source of profit to their grantors, although the latter had to make up gradually for them from the payments of the other tenants or from the village funds. Since they lacked governmental sanction their vulnerability was evident. As a means to circumvent this to some extent the grants were sometimes disguised as religious alienations (*dharmādāya*), although they were equally intended to pay off debts.[48] To the same category of village alienations we may reckon the *pasāetuṇ*, village service-lands in Gujarat, which are of two main types: *vecāṇyā*, lands sold by village officials or zamindars; *girānyā*, land mortgaged; and perhaps the *valatdāṇya*, lands set apart by the representatives of the village community for the benefit of a moneyed man who had agreed to stand surety, *manotidār*, for the payment of the state's revenue demand. The purpose of these alienations was similarly the payment of debts incurred by the village; in the case of a mortgage, the land was held revenue-free until the loan was redeemed, while the cultivators made up the deficit. In Gujarat these tenures were much more numerous than in the Deccan, but like the Deccan *gāṇv nisbat inām* they originated in times of overassessment – often when the village was farmed – in order to be able to pay the revenue demand or demands of tribute or to make up for occasional expenses for repairs of the village walls or to pay śibandis for protection in times

47 Baden-Powell, 'Dakhan Villages', p. 274; *P.A.: List 13, Ru. 87, File 1210*, no.59 of 1857.

48 *P.A.: List 13, Ru. 1, File 1*, proc. 796B.

of trouble.[49] Instead of in land the grants could be made out of the village *sādilvārī* fund, but then were called *inām* nevertheless.[50] The same outward forms were observed as with regular government inams by drawing up an *ināmpatra* or alternatively a *kharedīpatra* or 'deed of sale'. For example, in 1804 the mokadam and the entire village community (*samast dahijān*) of the village of Parganv in tarf Karepathar in prant Poona addressed an *ināmpatra* to the astrologer–accountant of the village Khalad and thirteen other villages, stating that on account of Holkar's invasion the villagers had become *parāgaṇḍā*, and that after they returned the Pindharis started to levy forced tribute (*manasvī khaṇḍaṇī*) from them, while the government revenue farmers also demanded irregular contributions; in this way a debt was incurred with a banker (*sāvkār*) which could not be repaid because of further troubles: 'we approached you, a fellow vatandar and a kulkarni, and took 201 rupees from you to pay the sarkar and the banker ... we gave you in exchange 30 bighas in inam ... and determined its boundaries ... the land is exempt from all taxes, forced labour, cesses present and future, haks of the balute and kulkarni ... it is hereditary.'[51]

Lands alienated in this way were only in rare cases ratified by a sanad from the Raja or Peshwa.[52] This could be done to give security to the title in cases where much money was involved (this could exceed 10,000 rupees) or if the banker giving the loan was at the same time an important government lender.[53] A government-sanctioned *gāṇv nisbat inām* would be *sanadī inām* but was not exempted by the government. The government merely backed the lender in his claim against the village. This is also clear in the case of cash *varṣāsans* given out of the sadilvari of the mahal or village, which were more commonly confirmed by sanads of the Peshwa or holders of the mutalik seal. Apart from confirmation we also find the sovereign power attempting to put a stop to the practice of the

49 *IS*, 7, 4-5-6 (1915–16), 'Peśve Daftarāṇtīl Sanadāpatrāṇtīl Māhitī', pp. 283–4; *P.A.: List 14, Ru. 1, File 9*, pp. 19–28, App. 1; R. D. Choksey, *Economic Life in the Bombay Gujarat (1800–1939)* (Bombay, etc., 1968), p. 66.

50 *P.A.: List 13, Ru. 39*; Elphinstone, *Report*, p. 26.

51 *IS, loc. cit.*; *P.A.: List 13, Ru. 9, File 147*, proc. 101 describes a very similar case.

52 R. D. Choksey, *The Aftermath (1818–1826)* (Bombay, n.d.), p. 33; *P.A.: List 13, Ru. 1, File 1*, proc. 765B; *SSRPD*, 3, no.487.

53 *Vaidya Daftarāṇtūn Nivaḍlele Kāgad*, 4 vols (Poona, 1944–9), 1, no.19; 4, nos 38, 41; *P.A.: List 13, Ru. 1, File 8*, proc. 749B; *Ru. 3, File 28*, proc. 614B; *File 13*, Report 455.

villages or village-headmen alienating lands at their own debit, particularly in Gujarat.[54]

What remains to be considered, finally, is the question of the resumption and sequestration of grants of land and vested rights. It is obvious in the case of *ancien régime* Europe that the kings, although absolute, never attempted or even proposed to abolish privileges as such.[55] But in this respect European absolutist states are often put in sharp contrast (even in modern historiography) with Asian 'tyrannic' or 'despotic' régimes coeval with them.[56] Now, as Max Weber pointed out, the fact that certain rights are 'vested' frequently means no more than that they are not liable to expropriation without compensation.[57] In this sense we can certainly speak of a *vatan-cum-inām* as a vested right not essentially different from those known in early modern Europe. When under Shivaji these vested rights were sequestrated *en masse* (cf. pp. 269–70) they were compensated by cash equivalents paid annually from the royal treasury. The sequestrations moreover were of a temporary nature, being part of a scheme designed to determine the agrarian potential of the state under a standard measurement survey. They were without exception restored to their former incumbents shortly afterwards under succeeding sovereigns of the Bhonsle dynasty. In the eighteenth century no measures of this sort were taken again, and certainly there were no attempts to abolish vatans and fiscal immunities anywhere. What was effected at times was at most a restructuring of rights and privileges. This was always motivated by *fitna* rather than by a caprice of the stereotype Oriental Despot. The power of resumption or sequestration was thus exercised but not in an arbitrary manner. Arbitrary resumption of hereditary rights and privileges was impolitic and was also denounced in moral terms. The *Ājñapatra* says: 'It is a great sin to cancel *vṛttis (vṛttilop)*, small or great, which exist from ancient times. Nobody's vṛtti should be given to someone else nor should the king himself take it. If a vṛtti-holder commits an offence he must be punished in conformity with the prescriptions of the śāstra. But it is not ordained [in the śāstra] that the vṛtti should be seized. Only for great offences the vṛtti has to be

54 *P.A.: List 13, Ru. 73, File 1025*, no.1 of 1822; *SSRPD*, 6, nos 758, 765.

55 Goubert, *Ancien Régime*, 2, p. 25.

56 E.g. Anderson, *Lineages of the Absolutist State*, p. 51: 'No Absolutist state could ever dispose at will of the liberty or landed property of the nobility itself, or the bourgeoisie, in the fashion of the Asian tyrannies coeval with them'.

57 Weber, *Economy and Society*, 2, p. 642.

seized, but even then the śāstra have to be consulted before action is taken'.[58] Religion, moral rectitude and 'proper service' are always brought up as the patent justification for the granting as well as the resumption of land. *Fitna* was, in this way, generally covert, disguised in appeals to the universalist dharma. Thus Rajaram gave out inams and vatans posing as the 'upholder of the dharma', when the covert purpose was to draw vatandars away from the Mughals. And in the same way Baji Rao II resumed the Shenavi lands around Poona under the pretext that the holders of these were not full *ṣaṭkarmī* brahmans, while the real purpose was to reinforce the position of, and his alliance with, his own subcaste of Citpavan brahmans. It is significant that no difference was observed in the wording of orders directing temporary sequestrations or attachments and final resumptions; both were called *japtī* or *amānat*.[59] This meant, in effect, that there were no irreversible resumptions or that they could always be undone if the formation of a faction or an interest at court demanded it. The Peshwa Diaries and other records give the following reasons as the most common grounds for resumption or sequestration of inam land: disloyalty or 'non-service' (*sarkārcā sī rujū nāhī, vartṇūk yathāsthīt nāhī, vartṇūk ṭhīk nāhī, pararājyāṇt jāṇūn*, etc., for example joining the impostor Sadashiv Bhau or serving with Raghunath Rao); encroachments; 'misconduct' (*aṇtar*); debauchery (in the case of religious grants); non-payment of cesses or fines; liquidation of a debt to a banker; disputes among members of the incumbent brotherhood.[60] Disputes (about succession to, or division or management of estates) and 'disloyalty' and hence *fitna* were, as we saw earlier in this chapter, directly linked to each other; if not because an estate being disputed led to its neglect and hence to 'non-service' then because disputes were the most strategic point of impact for *fitna* by rivals of the sovereign in power. Of course the sequestrations effected on account of offences, non-service, or breaks of loyalty, were not accompanied by financial compensation. The proceeds of the vatan or inam were in such a case accredited to the government or the

58 Banhatti, *Ājñāpatra*, ch.7.

59 *P.A.: List 13, Ru. 90, File 1267*, Report 141. Sometimes the word *dūr* is used (apparently with the implication of a final resumption) in the very beginning of the eighteenth century in the ledgers of the Shahu Daftar (e.g., *Rumal 26*, pudke 1). This appears to refer to the resumption of grants in inam which were considered unauthentic.

60 *BGS*, n.s. no.28, p.. 34; *ibid.*, Statement A (pp. 43–8); *TKKP*, 1, no.32; *P.A.: List 13, Ru. 9, File 143*, no.692 of 1850; *TKKP*, 3, no.43; *SSRPD*, 7, nos 535–44.

jagirdar of the district, either of whom sent agents to manage it (in the first situation as *khālsā*), or to a third party who held the right 'in trust' (*tasalmatīs*) for the period that the sequestration lasted.[61] The attachment was always cancelled (*mokaḷī karūn*) whenever a vatandar came back into service. This provides a further reason why we should not interpret the succumbing to *fitna* as a form of 'treason', at least not in its modern sense which makes it an unpardonable crime. It is on the contrary the pivotal element in the political system of the period.

[61] In the Ajmas records, income from sequestrated vatans and inams is credited to the government under the heading of *japtī* or *amānat*. For a vatan given 'in trust', see *SSRPD*, 9, no.143. A case of a regrant to a brother of the incumbent: Sabnis, *Paṇt Amātya Bāvḍā Daftar*, 1, no.120. Houses, fields, cattle, etc., were also sequestrated (*TKKP*, 1, no.32). A case of a sequestrated deśmukhi vatan given to the jagirdar: *P.A.: List 13, Ru. 17, File 329*, no. 253 of 1856.

3
The king's share

I Land and taxation

The conception of a 'king's share' (*rājbhāg, rājvāṇṭā* or *rājhisā*) as a uniform and generalized right *sui generis* is perhaps the most typical expression of the ideology of universal dominion which we find in the revenue records. Such a conception can not be dissociated from the artificialist postulate of the king as the 'guardian of order' who receives a 'salary' for the execution of his task, rather than as a co-sharer and arbiter who is himself caught up in the immanency of political sovereignty. Thus the 'king's share' is defined with great precision as a permanent imposition on all agricultural land, as the exact complement of the 'subject's share' (*prajbhāg, prajvāṇṭā* or *prajhisā*), and it maintains the rigidity and unambiguousness of the universalist grid when it is granted permanently in *inām*: the king only granted away what was legally his.

The uniform imposition of the king's share in practice served the important function of providing a reference point for the regulation of the collections of the land-revenue, but the consequence of its introduction as a regulatory principle was that any encroachment on this permanently fixed share became inevitably a form of *fitna* or *fasād*, 'rebellion' or 'corruption', or was stigmatized as *zulūm* or *zabardastī*, 'oppression'. From this derive the deceptive but stereotype repudiations of everything which was somehow at odds with regulation: *zamīndārs* extending their power at the cost of the sovereign, the exuberant overgrowth of customary localized cesses, the 'unregulated' entrepreneurial activities of revenue farmers, the 'drawing away' (*fitāviṇeṇ*) of cultivators. Of course, in each specific case it is hardly possible to determine where 'oppression' of the rayats – the real assessees – in our sense of an infringement of 'basic human rights', or in the sense of 'oppressive exploitation' by the ruling class, really began. To identify the uniformly imposed king's share which our records adhere to as the reference point for 'legitimate' centralized sovereignty by no means excludes the possibility of 'oppression' in the latter sense by any of the incumbents of superior rights in land, whether this be the sovereign or any of the 'co-sharers of sovereignty'. What seems crucial in this regard is that the definition of a permanent king's share of the agricultural proceeds in each locality was brought up as the index of legitimate sovereignty for its own sake – and this to a large degree without a direct correlation to the conditions of agriculture and cultivators. The magnitude of the king's share was nominally not a function of political considerations but entirely of technical parameters and it was justified, if at all, by an appeal to ancient conventions. Indeed, generalized royal taxation was postulated in India from early times and, unlike in Western Europe, it did not represent a novel claim of the sovereign who theoretically had to live off his own domain.[1] It was not 'extraordinary' but permanent, at least in the areas where direct dominion was established under a dualist managerial–bureaucratic administration and which were not under indirect tributary arrangements.

Our understanding of Indian taxation has been largely shaped by documentary evidence which was generated by the central governments' administrations – often the only type of evidence which survived – and since this always tenaciously clings to the mould of centralist regulation we have come to perceive government and sovereignty as the fountain of 'order' in an agrarian 'society' which was dubbed chaotic, anarchic, or at best 'bafflingly complex'. The universalist idiom confirmed modern preconceptions in many respects; but one serious consequence was that modern historiography took the moral condemnations of this idiom (in India and in most of the Islamic world) for economic evaluations even where it was not warranted to speak of economic decline on quantitative evidence. We will see again in the present and following chapter that the categoric charge of *fitna* or *zulūm* meant in principle nothing more than a loss in terms of resources, manpower or political loyalties for one sovereign to the extent that it meant a gain for another or to the extent that it implied a resurgence of particularist power. In the present chapter we shall address essentially only the question of the assessment of the king's share,

[1] See in particular Goubert, *Ancien Régime*, 2, pp. 22, 135, 139–41.

leaving for chapter 4 the questions of its monetization and collection.

Concerning the question of assessment, we have seen earlier that Maine considered the first 'civil act' following upon the conquest of an area 'to effect a settlement of the land-revenue' and that he equated this with the determination of 'that relatively large share of the produce of the soil, or of its value, which is demanded by the sovereign in all Oriental states' (p. 160). We pointed out that in the Indian context conquest was not primarily a military venture (as opposed to a 'civil act') but a process of *fitna* and the sovereign's intervention in the conflict-ridden structure of vested gentry rights. A land-revenue settlement or land-revenue survey as understood by Maine was an essential part of bringing land under 'regulation', of institutionalizing *fitna* (even though it was not effected in all areas conquered). It implied an assessment of the agricultural potential and the determination of the king's share and it became a feature of the 'regulation area' while in the 'non-regulation area' there was no such determination of the paramount sovereign's share but merely a realization of an aggregate (*peśkaś, khaṇḍaṇī, maktā*). Chieftaincies were not brought under the surveys but retained their own 'archaic' systems or were independently remodelled. Thus it was only in the regulation area that the king's share was collected with reference to an assessment (*dast*) of the land or of the produce (then called crop-sharing, *baṭāī* or *gallā*). And here it put the king before a political problem: regulation was fraught with the danger of *fitna*, but without regulation – without determining the king's share and setting a limit to the king's revenue claims – sovereignty was illegitimate and remained *zabardastī* or 'tyranny'. The only alternative solution to a survey was then to continue the assessment rates of the preceding sovereign; this implied at least a tacit recognition of the legitimacy of the preceding sovereign's rule and in the case of the Marathas in effect it happened most often that they dispensed with a new survey and levied revenue as the nominal servants of the Mughal Emperor, with reference to pre-established Mughal assessment rates.

Instead of opposing 'conquest' and 'settlement' as 'military' and 'civil' acts it appears more accurate to interpret the latter as an institutionalization of the former, as an institutionalization of *fitna* therefore. As the wording of the *rāj/praj* ratio already indicates, under regulation the official ideal was always to have direct contact with the 'subjects' and make a separate assessment of the holdings of each cultivator.[2] But settlement was not synonymous with an increase of 'centralization'. We see this quite clearly in the Deccan, when under pressure of the Mughals from the north, standard measurement-surveys were introduced – following the example of a settlement effected by Akbar in Hindustan – to increase revenue but at the same time 'to keep the rayats content in their homes' by vesting them with hereditary rights and, furthermore, to maximize the number of cultivators. The competition for cultivators which was concomitant with 'settlement' was also designated as *fitna*. A survey was necessary to be able to institutionalize conflict or 'management by conflict', a dualist administration of accountancy and management which allowed the king to keep interests overlapping but distinct. Here we should again highlight the difference from the type of expansionism which existed in the European Absolutist age. In Absolutist Europe expansion of the state's realm was primarily a military venture and it was concomitant with centralization, the formation of standing armies and the introduction of national taxation. By contrast, the result of Mughal involvement in the Deccan (as elsewhere) was intensified competition, *fitna*, a tightening of the ties with the autochthonous Hindu gentry, expansion-cum-rebellion, and 'settlement' of rayats. In this way expansion ultimately inverted centralization and the 'rationalization' of royal taxation involved no break with the past as it did in Europe.

To be sure, the magnitude of the king's share was not rationally founded but an *a priori* convention. As says Abul Fazl: 'Throughout the whole extent of Hindustan where at all times so many enlightened monarchs have reigned, one-sixth of the produce was exacted; in the Turkish empire, Iran and Turan a fifth, a sixth, and a tenth respectively'.[3] Hindu law-books generally refer to a one-sixth proportion of the gross produce as the king's share, while the Islamic land-tax or *kharāj* should (according to different jurists) be something in between one-tenth and one-half.[4] However the king's share may be nominally defined, it can safely be stated that in general in the East the land-revenue made up a proportionately much larger share of the state budget than in Absolutist Europe. This is why Maine can speak with justification of 'a

[2] Cf. p. 185.

[3] H. S. Jarrett (transl.), *The Ā'īn-i Akbarī of Abul Fazl*, vol. 2 (New Delhi, 1978), p. 58.

[4] M. Wilks, *Historical Sketches of the South of India*, vol. 1 (Madras, 1891), p. 78; *Encyclopaedia of Islam*, s.v.

relatively large share of the produce of the soil'. But the reason for this divergence is not so much a more 'despotic' character of the Oriental sovereigns but the simple fact that in the European states there was a (progressively) more important reliance on indirect taxes due to an ever higher level of commercial activity and the extension of an exchange economy as well as advances in agricultural and industrial production.[5] In Europe too the most important direct tax on land, the so-called *tithe* (French: *la dîme*) which was defined as a 'percentage of the harvest' was criticized by the economists as detrimental to capital investment in agriculture.[6] It was argued that the *tithe*, and by extrapolation all other similar levies on the gross produce such as the Islamic *kharāj* and the Indian *rājbhāg* seemed to represent, discouraged any capital investment of which the nett benefit was lower than the imposed tax and hence encouraged economy in methods of cultivation rather than increased production. This criticism is still brought up with reference to Third World countries by contemporary development economists. The same criticism (originating from the Enlightenment) of the *tithe* however is hardly relevant for the question of agricultural rent in the Islamic East and India. The *rājbhāg*, as we will see, was a paper construction. It was commonly converted into a permanent assessment of entire villages which retained to a very substantial degree a customary (*rivāj*) autonomy in the internal repartition of taxation. Agricultural development and restoration were linked up with contract tenures on the village or supra-village level and with revenue farming which allocated generated surpluses to the contractors or farmers as an inducement to 'enterprise'. This again cut across universalist regulation, or, to put it otherwise, we touch here the internal frontier again, a frontier which skirts the interface of agriculture and wasteland.

II The standard assessment

'Assessment' of the land implied firstly that the respective shares in its proceeds of the king on the one hand and of the cultivators on the other were determined according to a fixed ratio; and secondly

5 G. Ardant, 'Financial Policy and Economic Infrastructure of Modern States and Nations', in: Ch. Tilly (ed.), *The Formation of National States in Western Europe* (Princeton, 1975), pp. 165, 186, 193, 199; Goubert, *Ancien Régime*, 2, p. 142.

6 Ardant, 'Financial Policy', p. 183; *idem, Histoire de l'Impôt*, 1, pp. 112, 335, 337, 387–90; D. Thorner, 'The Relevance of Entrepreneurial Economics to Production by Peasant Households', in: *The Shaping of Modern India*, pp. 292–309.

that the first of these shares was converted in a rate or amount per given quantity of land. There was another system called 'crop-sharing' under which the *rājbhāg* was fixed, but not with reference to a given quantity of land. As a method of revenue collection, consisting of a division of the grain-heap on the threshing floor or by a calculation based on a sample estimate called *nimtānā*, it could dispense with assessment. As such it was employed in conditions of exceptional distress, when no assessment could be made, or to end disputes about the amount of revenue to be levied from a village. Under the Marathas, in the eighteenth century, crop-sharing was the usual arrangement on fields described as *śerī* (or *kamat*), which were excluded from the village rent-roll (*jamābaṇdī*) and which were managed directly by the government on account of their being sequestrated because of interminable disputes or the disappearance of the original proprietor. In the Deccan (and perhaps also in Hindustan) crop-sharing was temporarily resorted to on a very extended scale as a means to help determine new assessment rates per standard bigha on the introduction of the 'standard' or *tankhā* settlements in the eighteenth century.

Not all assessments were standard assessments. The earliest assessment schemes we know of are non-standardized, not based on standard surface measures. And the fact that they were not based on standard land measures is about all that is known of these early schemes. The records describing the system of land assessment and revenue collection employed under the Bahmani Sultanate and under the Nizam Shahi up to the end of the sixteenth century define the *rājbhāg* as a one-third proportion of the gross proceeds of the cultivated land of each village, designating the remaining two-thirds as the *prajbhāg*.[1] The same proportion was normally claimed under the Adil Shahi until 1669, while in the Southern Konkan (which fell to Bijapur in 1502) the *rājbhāg* is found to have been one-sixth under this government, with another one-sixth assigned to charitable and religious foundations, two-thirds again being *prajbhāg*.[2] The lands were not yet measured but were divided into large estates – perhaps one for each original settler – of which the different fields were identifiable by names.[3] The productive capacity of these estates were either expressed by the amount of seed required to sow them, as in the Southern

[1] *SCS*, 7, no.67; *P.A.: Selected Rumals, no.*52, section 1, 233383.
[2] Jervis, *Konkan*, p. 94; *BISM-Vārṣik Itivṛtt* (1913), p. 320.
[3] Mandlik, 'Muruḍa'; *BG*, XVI, p. 108.

Konkan where they were called *dhārā* or *kamāl* (meaning the 'whole' or 'total' amount), or by an average over a number of years of the amounts of grain they produced, the system found in the Northern Konkan and the Deccan where they were referred to as *dheṃp, ṭoka, huṇda*, etc., all terms meaning 'lump', and were later divided into shares or *bighās* in the original sense of the term, indicating a measure varying according to the qualities of the soil.[4] They were assessed for the one-third king's share with reference to this capacity, according to an ocular inspection (*nazar pāhāṇī*) of the standing crop which took into account the state of agriculture of the year.[5] Or, where the system of lump assessment did not obtain, as sometimes in the hills and on recently cleared jungle, assessment was made per plough, i.e., per amount of land that could be ploughed with one plough; or crop-sharing was employed, which in the Deccan usually implied an equal division of the nett produce of agricultural land and a 1:2 division of garden produce between the government and the rayats after deducting the *haks* or dues of village servants, headmen, zamindars, and others.[6] This latter mode of collection was commonly used by the Bijapur government when *jāgīrs* and *ināms* were held under sequestration.[7] Ordinarily, under these early schemes the collection of the king's share was leased out per mahal to revenue farmers for whom the rates of assessment were only an index (if they were not entirely nominal) and who added to them an indefinite amount of extra cesses on their own account, interfering in the village management as much probably as they thought necessary.[8]

The method of assessment according to the actual state of cultivation of a fixed proportion of the produce of unmeasured estates in the Southern Konkan was inherited by the Bijapur government from Vijayanagar, and it was continued throughout the period of its rule, for 149 years, after which it was soon set aside under the Marathas when Anaji Datto introduced here his measurement survey and fixed a permanent standard assessment for each village. In the Deccan it was abolished by the Ahmadnagar regent Malik Ambar and the vazir Haibat Khan, but in a part of the Ahmadnagar lands in the Northern Konkan (in Thana particularly) it was maintained; and here it remained the prevalent system until late in the eighteenth century. To the south-east, in the districts

4 Jervis, *Konkan*, pp. 81–2. 5 *BISM-Vārṣik Itivṛtt* (1913), *loc. cit.*
6 Jervis, *Konkan*, p. 81; *EIP*, 4, p. 747.
7 *B.A.: R.D.*, vol. 5/549 of 1834, p. 97. 8 Cf. Chapter 4-IV.

south of the Krishna that the British later referred to as the Southern Maratha Country, the foundation of the system of assessment employed by the successive governments of Bijapur (1573–1686), the Nawab of Savanur under the Mughals (1686–1752), and the Peshwas (1752–1807), was laid by the Vijayanagar king Krishnaraja in the first half of the sixteenth century.[9] From him originated the *rāya rekhā* or 'royal line' measurement and the assessment associated with it. This also was not applied everywhere: the dry land was assessed either on a measurement of its actual extent by the *rāya rekhā*, or in the western parganas bordering on the malnad (wet-land) villages, by some local measure; or it was estimated by the quantity of land to which the payment of a certain sum was attached, while gardens were estimated by the space occupied by certain numbers of trees and divided in *thals*, and the wet lands were estimated under the *bījvārī* or 'seed' system.[10] The latter resembled the *dhārā* or *kamāl* lump assessment of the Southern Konkan, except that in the Southern Maratha Country the assessment was not arrived at by an annual inspection of the crops but by taking the rent in kind for a series of years: the dues of village and district officials and other expenses being deducted from the grain on the threshing floor, the residue was divided into equal shares of which the rayat was allowed to take his choice; the average proceeds of the sarkar, commuted in money, determined the permanent assessment on the quantity of land required for the seed producing the whole.[11] In all these modes of measurement the measures varied in extent with reference to the qualities of the soil, while the sum assessed on it was always the same, the supposed equivalent of one-third. This was also the case under the *bījvārī* system, but there the lands were further subdivided into classes paying different rates. The measures were maintained in the Southern Maratha Country by the Bijapur Sultans, but to the original share or *raqam* which was continued as the basis of the new assessment extra cesses were added under the farming system.[12]

As *standard* land-revenue assessment schemes we can designate all those systems which in Maratha and Mughal parlance are referred to as *tankhā* (P. *tan<u>kh</u>wa*).[13] In effect these were settlements

[9] *B.A.: R.D.*, vol. 5/549 of 1834, pp. 94 ff. [10] *Ibid.*, pp. 95–6.
[11] *Ibid.*, p. 96.
[12] *Ibid.*
[13] The following sections on the Deccan *tankhā* settlements were earlier published in a slightly adapted form as an article, 'The Settlement of the Deccan, c.1600–1680', *BISMQ*, 60, 1–4 (1981), pp. 47–65.

which in different regions of India were executed at different times, sometimes superseding the 'standard' of the preceding sovereign, but had in common that they, after defining the king's share as a proportion of the total proceeds, converted this proportion into fixed and invariable rates of assessment per *uniformly* measured unit of land of each quality. Such a standard measurement survey or *tankhā* rent-roll was first introduced in Northern India by Todar Mal in the late sixteenth century, under Akbar. After measuring and classifying the cultivated land, Todar Mal assessed it per bigha according to a uniform standard for each class, the rates presumably representing the equivalant of one-fourth of the total produce. This northern standard assessment penetrated into a part of Khandesh and of Gujarat,[14] but to the south of these districts the *tankhā* settlements are of a later date and are associated with the names of the Ahmadnagar regent Malik Ambar, the Mughal divan Murshid Quli Khan, and the brahman pradhans of Shivaji, Moro Trimbak and Anaji Datto. The evidence which is extant on the Deccan *tankhā* settlements is, although incomplete, far more detailed than that on the northern one. It can be made out clearly that in the Deccan they were invariably permanent village settlements; the elaborate operations of measurement and classification of all the arable land of each village appear to have been undertaken merely to have on record a near approximation of what each village could yield and the assessment rates employed for this purpose were in no way designed to supersede the old customary or *rivāj* rates or to become the standard of assessment of individuals or of particular estates.[15] In this subchapter we shall not describe in detail the different modes of classification and measurement and the scales of assessment rates that were employed in these settlements in the different regions of the Deccan, but merely attempt to bring out their main principles and the stages in which they were executed. In this context we shall have occasion, more specifically, to focus attention on the system of *baṭāī* or 'crop-sharing' that appears to have been a characteristic transitional and preparatory measure in each of them. In the Deccan we find that a prepostulated king's share (*rājbhāg*) of the produce – differing sometimes according to the quality of the soil and the method of irrigation – was converted into uniform rates of assessment applied to uniformly measured areas of land of which the production capacity was

[14] *EIP*, 4, pp. 341, 426, 688; Habib, *Agrarian System*, p. 262.
[15] Cf. *B.A.: R.D.*, vol. 10/94 of 1824, pp. 247–8.

estimated on the basis of data acquired by means of *baṭāī*.[16] The sum total of these became the permanent *tankhā* or standard assessment of the village as exhibited in the village *jamābaṇdī* or rent-roll.

Malik Ambar

The earliest *tankhā* settlement in any part of the Deccan was effected by Malik Ambar and his delegate Haibat Khan between 1605 and 1626 throughout most of the old and new possessions of the Nizam Shahi Sultanate.[17] This territory extended southward as far as the Bankot river in the Konkan, it comprised the Poona District which became the jagir of the Bhonsles early in the seventeenth century, and to the north it included the greater part of Berar and what became the subha of Aurangabad under the Mughals after they had conquered the kingdom in 1636 (when they annexed the northern part of it, the southern part falling to Bijapur), and, finally, some districts in Khandesh. Certainly not all areas were affected by it. As under the other *tankhā* settlements, in many of the hilly tracts (particularly in the Northern Konkan) the older archaic system of lump assessment was left intact,[18] while elsewhere assessment per plough was sometimes continued.[19] But in most of the districts of Ahmadnagar, as says one of the sources, 'the ancient mode of assessment' was abolished by Malik Ambar and Haibat Khan.[20]

Some British authorities of the early nineteenth century assert that prior to Malik Ambar the revenues were farmed by interme-

16 There is some evidence that a similar procedure was followed by Todar Mal in the north; cf. Wilks, *The South of India*, 1, p. 103, referring to two Persian authorities which state that Todar Mal applied an equal division of the crop between the government and the cultivators and called this *baṭāī*.

17 *EIP*, 4, p. 409.

18 Jervis, *Konkan*, pp. 100–1; 'Papers relating to revised rates of assessment for thirteen different Talookas of the Tanna collectorate', *BGS*, n.s. no.96 (Bombay, 1866), pp. 2–3.

19 Jervis, *Konkan*, p. 96.

20 Quoted by Robertson, *EIP*, 4, p. 417. Haibat Khan was the court title of a brahman whose family name was Vithal Jagde Rao (*SCS*, 6, p. 65). He is called a *vazīr* or *hukmatvazīr* (*P.A.: Selected Rumals, no.5*, section 1, 23383). Malik Ambar was an ex-slave of Abyssinian origin who became the regent of Sultan Murtaza Nizam Shah (1599–1631). The latter's name is usually substituted by that of Malik Ambar in the farmans issued during his reign. Grants of land made by Haibat Khan are often confirmed by Malik Ambar, which implies that the former was a subordinate of the latter.

diaries, but that he brought this to an end.[21] What really seems to have happened is that Malik Ambar, while fixing his demand permanently on the village, brought farming down from the intermediary to the village level. And this brought with it two important changes. Firstly, the extra cesses and forced labour demands that could multiply freely under the old system when the collection of the land-revenue – nominally a one-third share of the total proceeds[22] – was farmed by an intermediary agent, were now abolished, and the state settled the amount of revenue to be paid by concluding a contract or *maktā* directly with the cultivators.[23] Evidence for this we find in a document of 1731, describing the history of Ceul.

In the third year [of the reign of the Nizam Shah in Ceul] a survey (*rakamālā*) for the settlement of the *jamābaṇḍī* was made in conformity with Malik Ambar's plan as adopted in the other territories. The revenue capacity of the villages, fields, gardens and saltpans was calculated in consultation with the rayats and the zamindars. There was no need to make an inspection (*pāhāṇī*) and settlement of the leases and groundtaxes (*saṇcṇī*) every year. The rayats paid a fixed amount settled by contract [*makṣtā*; read *maktā*]. The rayats remained 'content in their homes'. They were not disturbed by additional cesses (*jyāj farmāvīs*) and impositions of forced labour (*veṭh begār*).[24]

Thus, secondly, the settlement appears to have been a permanent village settlement, for it is said that 'there was no need to make an inspection and settlement of the leases and groundtaxes every year'. But the height of the assessment, the amount of the contract, was calculated on a knowledge of the land's productivity and the condition of the rayats when the survey was made. With the rayats, at that time, mostly consisting of hereditary inhabitants or *mirāsdārs* of the village, they must either have discharged their obligation collectively or entrusted the revenue collection of the village to the headman. The *pāṭīl* was therefore either to be seen as an agent of the government, bound to discharge a fixed sum from a corporate body of cultivators which in joint liability could demand from each member the contribution of his share proportionate to

21 Cf. Grant Duff, *History*, 1, pp. 38, 47; Jervis, *Konkan*, p. 66.

22 *P.A.: Selected Rumals, no.*52, section 1, 23383; *EIP*, 4, p. 417.

23 *Maktā* is the term most commonly used for a 'revenue farm' or a 'contract' in general (cf. p. 344).

24 *BISMQ*, 28, 3–4 (1947–8), p. 1. (The date of this document is wrongly transcribed as AD 1631.) For the prohibition of cesses and forced labour by Malik Ambar see also the account of Ceul of 1644 in *BISMQ*, 3, 1 (1922), pp. 15–16.

the quality and extent of his land (whether he cultivated it or not), or he was a contractor for the village, merely bound to raise a certain fixed sum from it.[25] Given the nature of the tenure of *mirāsdārs* (cf. Chapter 3-IV) there could however not have been much difference between these two positions.

The principle of giving out the land on *maktā*, on 'contract', fixing the limit of demand, would not only induce agricultural improvements but also served to secure new cultivators from neighbouring states, while preventing their emigration. An influx of new rayats did not affect the rate of the standard assessment of the village but it did diminish the proportionate share of the total *tankhā* that each rayat had to contribute individually, whereas the benefits of improvements went entirely to the cultivators or zamindars themselves and not to government officials, assignees or district farmers. By bringing to a stop in this way the leakage of revenue which occurred under revenue farming on the district level (which in the earlier stage must have been indispensable however to promote capital circulation and investment), Malik Ambar could increase his resources, yet ensure the stability of his collections, and keep his rayats 'content in their homes'. It is possible, and even likely, that he had planned to increase the amount of the *tankhā* when at a later date a further increase of cultivation would have made this feasible. But, as it happened, revisions of this sort were undertaken only by succeeding governments.[26]

Now the reverse side of the whole scheme was inevitably that the rayats were obliged to pay their revenue even if the land was not cultivated and, furthermore, had to bear all conceivable risks of harvest failures and destructions. Although it was designed under Mughal pressure to raise resources and keep the rayats on the land, it overoptimistically presupposed almost perfect agricultural conditions and an uninterrupted political stability. But when the Mughals again started invading the Ahmadnagar districts 'fixed rents' could no longer be levied. A *maksūdnāmā*, submitted just after such an invasion in 1629, to the diwan of Nevase by the mokadams and other vatandars of Kasba Sonai was replied to as follows:

> [you stated in the maksudnama] that in the past year the Mughals came and caused utter destruction all around. The rayats of the jagir of the Bhonsles were molested badly. People became *parāgaṇdā* ('fugitive'). As the

25 Cf. *EIP*, 4, p. 419.

26 A case in point is the *kamāl* settlement of the Peshwas (cf. Chapter 3-III).

land-revenue [demand] was fixed permanently the amounts the cultivators could pay fell short of the *maktā* and therefore the *maktā* was remitted (*māf karūn*) and *kauls* had to be given. Give a remission of one-half to the cultivators who come to the kasba.[27]

Here an attempt is made to 'appease' or to bring back the rayats through concessions, necessitated by the destructions and *fitna* caused by the Mughals. The economic situation of a large part of the Deccan deteriorated further on account of a famine in 1630. It remained in a severely damaged condition until twenty years afterwards, when Murshid Quli Khan introduced a new settlement in those parts – including the northern division of the former Ahmadnagar territory – which had then temporarily come under Mughal sovereignty.[28] Malik Ambar's fixed rates perhaps nowhere survived their author for very long. In the districts which on the division of Ahmadnagar had been ceded to Bijapur, the revenue collection was generally farmed by zamindars at the time Shivaji first settled a part of them. It appears from the account of Sabhasad that not a trace was left of a permanent village settlement; extra cesses prevailed everywhere.[29] The bakhar of Chitnis relates that in the same area, shortly before its cession to Bijapur, already the Mughals had resorted to farming.[30] It seems probable then that in the Northern Ahmadnagar territory the practice of farming had also spread during the unsettled period preceding Murshid Quli Khan's reform.

Nevertheless, despite the short span of time that it was operative, Malik Ambar's settlement led to a great increase in the central government collections.[31] Only a small portion of this increase can be accounted for by a formal increase of the *rājbhāg*;[32] the rest must

27 *SCS*, 4 (*BISMQ*, 12, 1–4 (1931–2), no.691. 28 See the following section.

29 Vakaskar, *Sabhāsadācī Bakhar*, p. 30.

30 Hervadkar, *Saptaprakaraṇātmak Caritra*, p. 30.

31 According to a Maratha legend it is supposed to have doubled by 1618 (*EIP*, 4, p. 408).

32 What exact share was claimed by Malik Ambar's government is not certain. Two-fifths is often suggested as the most likely proportion when levied in kind, and one-third if commuted in money (cf. *EIP*, 4, p. 463; R. Shyam, *The Kingdom of Ahmadnagar* (Delhi, 1966), p. 284). Robertson thought it was probably the same as Todar Mal's rate (*EIP*, 4, p. 418). Graham held it to be two-fifths everywhere (*BGS*, n.s. no.8, p. 69); Jervis one-third (*Konkan*, pp. 93–4). With the later settlements on Malik Ambar's model there is a similar uncertainty about the king's share. In one mid-seventeenth-century document I found Malik Ambar's *rāj:praj* ratio given as 1:3 for *bagāīt* or garden-land (*P.A.: Selected Rumals, no.49*, section 8, 22046). In another document of the same period the

have been collected at the cost of the former revenue farmers (and also no doubt represented the benefits of their investments) and perhaps of the hereditary district zamindars, who, it must be presumed, under the old dispensation had also arrogated farming rights to themselves, but who were now checked by a settlement made directly with the village and what for all practical purposes became a form of 'group assessment'.[33] An inspection took place in 1617–18 of all titles to alienated lands, but if this proved them to be held under an authentic *farmān* of one of the former Nizam Shahs, of Malik Ambar himself, or under a *khurdkhat* or *hujat* of Haibat Khan or one of the big jagirdars, they were always confirmed with the *vatans*, never sequestrated or resumed.[34] There is no evidence to show that the *ināms* were assessed and revalued according to the new rates in use on non-alienated lands. That the standard assessment was not restricted to the *khālsā* lands but was also (as far as it went) introduced in the *jāgīrs* is already evident from the *maksūd-nāmā* of 1629 (quoted on p. 262), stating that the land-revenue demand in the *jāgīr* of the Bhonsle family was 'fixed permanently'. In this case we will see that a part of it – the Mavals in the western hillrange of the Poona District – was still unsettled territory, and it may be surmised that one implicit aim of assigning this area in jagir was to have it settled by the jagirdar, which is what eventually happened.[35]

With regard to the method of ascertaining the amount of produce reaped on the different qualities of land in a particular village, Robertson mentions that according to a tradition Malik Ambar founded his calculations on the results of a procedure called *nimtānā*, and that with him this was the first operation of a system of *baṭāī*.[36] *Nimtānā* consisted of the counting of the sheaves of grain produced on a field – the extent of which was not necessarily known – and then selecting from them one of the best, one of a middling, and one of the poorest quality, in order to discover the quantity of grain they contained; the average of the three selected sheaves was then applied to the entire number, and thus the whole produce was estimated.[37] This supposition that Malik Ambar had employed the

rāj:praj ratio under his *baṭāī* system on *jīrāīt* was 1:2 on the nett produce, i.e., after deducting the dues of village servants, etc. (*ibid.*, 22043).

33 Moreland employs this term for *nasaq*. This was a form of settlement which was expressly prohibited under Akbar, except in the case of land newly brought under cultivation (*Agrarian System*, pp. 15, 112).

34 *MIS*, 20, nos 400–2; *SCS*, 4, no.675; *Sahāvicār*, vol.1, no.4, pp. 169–70ff.

35 See the section on Shivaji. 36 *EIP*, 4, p. 420. 37 *Ibid.*

method of *nimtānā* Robertson thought 'by no means improbable'.[38] The less so since he was also informed that Dadaji Kondadeo imitated it from him when he resettled the *dhārā* (assessment) of the Poona jagir of Shahaji Bhonsle.[39] A recently published document from the Poona Jamav, of the year 1667–8, confirms this when it states that during the settlement of the village of Bahuli in tarf Muthekhore of prant Maval, Shivaji's minister Moro Trimbak 'applied *baṭāī* after taking into account the results of *nimtānā*', and adds that this, as well as the final *bighāvṇī* assessment following upon it, was effected 'in conformity with Malik Ambar's plan'.[40] Malik Ambar's first step, following upon *baṭāī*, seems always to have been the fixing of the quantity of grain payable by a village, and the next (which was not always taken) the valuing of this quantity in money. For the latter purpose a commutation price (*tasar*) was adopted and fixed once for all conforming to the market rates of grain at that time.[41] In Robertson's account, of the 290 villages of Poona District 110 received a fixed assessment in money from Malik Ambar; these became 'money villages', while the rest remained 'grain villages'.[42] Some of the 'grain villages' again appear to have remained largely '*baṭāī* villages'. But most commonly *baṭāī*, with *nimtānā*, was only employed in preparing the measurement survey. Next to *nimtānā*, Malik Ambar may have used the more cursory method of *nazar pāhāṇī* or 'ocular inspection' in some of the less accessible areas. Hill-lands, if measured at all, were always classified in a more general way than the normal garden (*bāgāīt*) or agricultural (*jīrāīt*) lands.[43]

Murshid Quli Khan

About twenty years after the fall of Ahmadnagar (1636) a new standard assessment was introduced in the territories of what was then the 'Mughal Deccan'. How this relates to the Mughal settlement of the Eastern Deccan of 1689–90 is a question which is still hard to answer.[44] In Golconda there appears to have been a standard measurement survey preceded by *baṭāī*, while in Bijapur there was apparently a *tankhā* effected by Ali Adil Shah II which

38 *Ibid.* 39 *Ibid.*, pp. 420–1. 40 Khobrekar, *Shivaji Period*, no.25.
41 Jervis, *Konkan*, p. 66.
42 *EIP*, 4, p. 419.
43 *EIP*, 4, p. 415; *P.A.: Selected Rumals, no.49*, section 8, 22045.
44 Cf. also p. 272.

was adopted by the Mughals as the basis of their assessment.[45] Detailed guidelines of the first Mughal land-revenue settlement by Murshid Quli Khan to the south of the Narmada have been preserved in the Poona Archives in a series of *dastūrammals* or 'assessment regulations' relating to Haveli Ahmadnagar, a pargana of eighteen villages in the district of Ahmadnagar of the subha of Aurangabad, all of the period 1651–7.[46] In one of these documents it is explicitly mentioned that at this time the Mughal settlement (*amal pātśāhi*) superseded the one of Malik Ambar.[47] They thus point to the systems of measurement and *baṭāī* as antedating the advent of the Mughal diwans Dyan Khan and (his successor) Murshid Quli Khan, but no mention is made of 'assessment per plough', a method which is said to have prevailed in other regions of the Mughal Deccan and sometimes to have been continued under the new settlement.[48] It is stated that under Dyan Khan and the diwans before him, an assessment system of cash rates per bigha (*bighoṭī*) co-existed with *baṭāī* at a *rāj:praj* ratio of 1:3 on *bāgāīt* or garden land up to the year 1651.[49] And on this land the *dhārā* of Dyan Khan was maintained by Murshid Quli Khan during the years 1652 and 1653.[50] After that, in 1654, the latter brought into force a *differential baṭāī* on all *bāgāīt* land with shares as follows: 1:2 for *moṭsthaḷ* (land irrigated from a draw-well), 2:3 for *pāṭsthaḷ* (land irrigated by a channel), and 1:1 for *barāṇi* (land watered by rain only), in all cases to be applied to the nett revenue, i.e., after deduction of the haks of the village servants (*baḷute*) and mokadam.[51] The mokadam and village servants are also registered as 'revenue-exempt' (*pāḷṇūk, māfik*), and a number of *aīmadārs* (holders of *aīma*, land on a low quit-rent) is enumerated, while the

45 For the first see Richards, *Golconda*, p. 171, note 1; for the second *B.A.: R.D.*, vol 5/549 of 1834, p. 98.

46 *P.A.: Selected Rumals, no.49*, sections 4 and 8.

47 *Ibid.*, section 8, 22045, describing successively the *amaldakṣaṇī kārkirdī malik aṃbar* and the *amal pātśāhi*.

48 According to a Persian account discussed in Moreland, *Agrarian System*, pp. 184–5, neither sharing nor measurement had been practised in the Deccan up to the time of Murshid Quli Khan, but assessment was always per plough. Moreland admits that this statement cannot be applied to the territory settled by Malik Ambar, but he infers from it that 'plough-rents' were then 'the prevailing system in a large part of the Deccan' (p. 185). Crop-sharing was reintroduced on a wide scale by the Mughals even before Murshid Quli Khan (cf. *B.A.: R.D.*, vol.7/117 of 1825, p. 486).

49 *P.A.: Selected Rumals, no.49*, section 8, 22045.

50 *Ibid.*, 22046, 22010.

51 *Ibid.*, 22009, 22011–2, 22036, 22049–50, 28056, 22097, 21544.

deśpāṇḍe of the pargana is seen to be in the enjoyment of an *inām* garden.[52] The differential *baṭāī* however appears to have been too heavy a burden for the rayats and cultivation deteriorated. It is recorded that soon afterwards '*baṭāī* was abolished and the *amīns* and *jāgīrdārs* made a measurement survey (*jarīb*) introducing a *bighoṭī* assessment with new rates (*rāye*), under abandonment of the old measurement rope (*dorī*), replacing it with the daulatabād gaz'.[53] But with this the process had not come to an end: the *bighoṭī* again lasted only up to 1657, when the rayats once more became 'dispirited' and again began to neglect cultivation; the old *dorī* is then reapplied and yet another *dhārā* is made.[54]

For the *jīrāīt* land separate dasturammals are extant which again demonstrate that both the *khālsā* and the *jāgīrs* were settled in the same manner, although not always simultaneously.[55] *Baṭāī* – already widely used (on perhaps an equal share basis)[56] – was applied everywhere, as on the *bāgāīt* land, with differential rates, *viz.* 1:1 on *polīj* or continuously cultivated land, 1:2 on *causāl*, 1:3 on *tīsāl*, 1:4 on *dusāl*, i.e. land lying fallow one in respectively four, three and two years, and 1:5 in *baṇjar* or cultivable wasteland.[57] On the agricultural land the *amal baṭāī* – referring as always to the nett produce – was in force from 1654 to 1655 only and after that substituted again by cash rates per bigha.[58]

On what ratio, if different from the *baṭāī* ratios, the cash rates were determined is nowhere stated;[59] as commutation price the current market rate for agricultural produce appears to have been employed.[60] It is certain that the differential system of *baṭāī* was not retained as a permanent method of revenue collection, and it seems most likely therefore to have served only as an aid to determine the *rāye* for the different crops to be used under *jarīb*.[61] The *jarīb* or

52 *Ibid.*, 22012, 22049.

53 *Ibid.*, 21544, 22011, 22036, 22050, 22097.

54 *Ibid.*, 22050, 22037.

55 *Ibid.*, 22038. Here it is mentioned that *baṭāī* was retained for some time longer in a *jāgīr* of Mirza Khan, after it had been abolished in the *khālsā*.

56 See note 48 *supra*.

57 *P.A.: Selected Rumals, no.49*, section 8, 22009.

58 *Ibid.*, 22038.

59 According to Moreland however the standard or maximum government claim was one-fourth of the total produce (*Agrarian System*, p. 185).

60 *P.A.: Selected Rumals, no.49*, section 8, 22009.

61 A similar conclusion is arrived at by Habib in *Agrarian System*, p. 228: 'It would seem, therefore, that the major result of Murshid Quli Khan's reform was the introduction of measurement and that crop-sharing was only employed at the

measurement survey, known as 'the *dhārā* of Murshid Quli Khan' became the prevalent system in the Mughal Deccan. And in a large part of it which was later conquered by the Marathas, this remained the single general standard settlement executed in pre-British times. Under the Marathas it acquired the function of a permanent village settlement and was referred to as the *tankhā*. The original rent-roll on which basis it was fixed lost its relevance entirely and the *tankhā* itself became of mere nominal value and was again soon overgrown with 'extra cesses'.[62]

Shivaji

As we have seen Shivaji's father held an extensive *jāgīr* from the Bijapur Sultan. This comprised Junnar, Chakan, Poona, Supa, Baramati, Indapur, the Twelve Mavals, and possibly Vai and Sirval. Under the Adil Shahi it had been a common practice that when *jāgīrs* and *ināms* were held under sequestration, *baṭāī* was introduced along with it, this being considered the most suitable means to prevent embezzlement of the revenue.[63] This twin measure of *baṭāī*-cum-sequestration we find applied on a systematic scale under the settlements of Shahaji's agent Dadaji Kondadeo within the above-mentioned jagir and under those of Shivaji shortly afterwards. With the first it was, most likely, limited to the districts of Poona and Supa, with the second it extended throughout the *svarājya*.

When Shahaji entrusted the management of his jagir to Dadaji Kondadeo, Poona and the surrounding country had been suffering greatly from the conflicts with the Mughals and the preceding famine of 1630. Chitnis describes how Dadaji gave out *kauls*, recollected the zamindars of the Mavals, extirpated wolves, re-peopled and restored the land, and then 'made a *nimtānā* and fixed

beginning to help in fixing workable *rai's* for the different crops.' This author also suggests a possible parallel with Malik Ambar (*ibid.*, note 51).

62 Cf. *EIP*, 4, p. 644; Grant Duff, *History*, 1, p. 63; Jenkins, *Nagpur*, pp. 93–4. Jenkins states that the last measurement and classification of the lands in the territories of Nagpur had been made by Murshid Quli Khan and that these had served to fix the assessment permanently, but he adds that 'the scheme totally failed here, as indeed it seems to have uniformly done elsewhere'. The reason for this contention was that the measurements and assessment rates *of the fields* in later times deviated greatly from those fixed and recorded by Murshid Quli Khan. But this, it should be clear, cannot be an index for the failure of the settlement.

63 *B.A.: R.D.*, vol.5/549 of 1834, p. 97.

the *dhārā*'.[64] Only a part of this account is corroborated by contemporary documents, which mention that 'Dadapant gave a *kaul* to the whole country' or that 'he gave a *tākīd* to deśmukhs and deśkulkarnis'.[65] But we referred earlier to the testimony of informants of Robertson, according to which Dadaji Kondadeo imitated Malik Ambar in employing the system of *nimtānā* and *baṭāī* before settling his *dhārā*.[66] If there was this parallel, there was also a contrast: while under Malik Ambar *ināms* were 'inspected', under Shahaji orders were issued to put all inams of Poona and Supa under sequestration (*amānat*).[67] This measure was taken in the years 1650–1 and kept up for an unknown duration.

After the Mughals invaded the country, Poona became the headquarters of their army and the conflict with Shivaji, which ended in his capitulation at Purandar in 1665, was again ruinous to the territory around it. When the Mughal army marched southward to Bijapur the district was placed in charge of Shafi Khan, who, in order to restore cultivation, started granting *kauls*, charging a 1/10 share of the nett produce in the first year and increasing the amount yearly until half of the crop was paid to the Mughal government in the fifth year.[68] At the same time that *baṭāī* was employed in the area, the Mughals drew up records for all villages in which the local measurements were converted into standard *cāvars* and *bighās*.[69] From this we may conclude that here too crop-sharing was only intended to be employed as a temporary expedient to precede a new standard settlement, where the old one had become obsolete or useless. This program was cut short when Shivaji recovered the country in 1666; and it was left to him to effect such a settlement.[70]

In other parts of his jagir and everywhere in his later conquests, Shivaji put all the *vṛttis, ināms, izāfats* and *vatans* with their 'rights and perquisites' (*haklājima*) under sequestration, indemnifying the incumbents with annual cash allowances (*moīn, muśāhira*, in the case of brahmans sometimes *dharmādāya*).[71] In the different

64 Hervadkar, *Saptaprakaraṇātmak Caritra*, p. 30.

65 *SKPSS*, 3, no. 2429; *SCS*, 2, nos 95–6.

66 Cf. p. 265. 67 *SCS*, 2, no. 122; *MIS*, 20, no. 13. 68 *EIP*, 4, p. 421.

69 Some of these records, or early eighteenth-century copies of them (which are entirely in moḍi), can still be found in the Poona Archives (e.g. *Poona Jamav, Rumals, 1, 201, 247*). See for the conversion of measurements also *EIP*, 4, p. 421 and *B.A.: R.D.*, vol. 7/117 of 1825, pp. 486–7.

70 *B.A.: R.D.*, vol. 7/117 of 1825, pp. 487–9.

71 *MITSA*, 3, nos 187, 211, 214, 216, 488; *MIS*, 15, no. 283; 16, no. 28; 17, no. 21; *SCS*, 2, nos 220, 243–4, 253–4; 3, nos 666, 668; 6, nos 114, 121; 9, no. 75; Avalaskar, *Aitihāsik Sādhaneṇ*, nos 25, 63; *Śrīrāmdāsicīṇ Aitihāsik Kāgadpatreṇ*,

regions of the *svarājya* this occurred at different times, in the newly conquered areas not immediately upon conquest but usually after a respite in which the vatandars and inamdars were given assurance deeds (*kauls*). The earliest evidence on this sequestration policy comes from Indapur and the Northern Konkan, and dates from before 1660. But elsewhere it was not given effect before 1671. In almost all cases these vatans and inams were not formally restored until the late seventeenth and early eighteenth century when Rajaram and Sambhaji II (of Kolhapur), under pressure of the Mughals, were forced to do so as a price of the loyalty of their holders.[72]

Simultaneously with the sequestration of the hereditary estates Shivaji introduced *baṭāī*.[73] In effect this implied that the cash allowances of the former vatandars were now paid from a government-sold portion of the *rājbhāg* of *baṭāī*. With this latter fixed at a half share of the *gross* produce,[74] the introduction of crop-sharing was accompanied by a prohibition of all 'contingent cesses' (*sādilvārpaṭṭīs*); these were abolished or, by exception, substituted by a payment in kind from the *rājbhāg*.[75] As with Malik Ambar and the Mughals, the main function of *baṭāī* appears to have been to supply data about the productivity of the land needed to fix the assessment. Thus one document explained later:

> the late great Svami [Shivaji] introduced *baṭāī* in the *svarājya*. On that occasion an inspection (*pāhāṇī*) was made of the land and its assessment (*dast*) was determined.[76]

It seems that the lands held under sequestration were in the same

1 nos 23–4, 60; *IS*, 2, 5 (1909), pp. 17–30; *SKPSS*, 1, nos 857, 887; *BISM-Vārṣik Itivṛtt* (1916), pp. 139–56; *Ibid*. (1913), no.56; Khobrekar, *Shivaji Period*, no.44; Vad, Mawji and Parasnis, *Sanadāpatreṇ*, pp. 136–9, 155; *TKKP*, 2, no.10; 3, no.89.

72 Most of the information (listed in note 71 *supra*) on Shivaji's sequestrations is obtained from such restoration grants by Rajaram and Sambhaji II.

73 Cf. *SCS*, 3, no.434: 'the late Svami (Shivaji) introduced *baṭāī* in the country and sequestrated all *ināms* on that occasion'; Vad, Mawji and Parasnis, *Sanadāpatreṇ*, pp .143–4: 'in the time of the Maharaja, the late great Svami [Shivaji], *baṭāī* was introduced in Prant Maval [and] the vatandars were given a salary'. In *SCS*, 4, p. 12 mention is made of '*baṭāī* country' (*baṭāīcī mulūk*). I take this to mean that other districts were (at that time) not yet under this system of collection, or had already been emancipated from it, not that the application of *baṭāī* was regionally restricted.

74 *SCS*, 4, p. 16; *MIS*, 15, no.340.

75 Cf. *SCS*, 4, pp. 11–12, 16.

76 Vad, Mawji and Parasnis, *Sanadāpatreṇ*, p. 155.

way 'inspected and assessed'.[77] After several seasons *baṭāī* was set aside – in different areas at different times.[78] – while the sequestrations were continued. In a part of the Mavals, and in the Desh, Moro Trimbak drew up the *jamābaṇdī* for each village, fixing the assessment for the different qualities of land in cash per bigha.[79] This, we saw before, was a reproduction of Malik Ambar's settlement, with rates derived from estimates 'based on *baṭāī* and *nimtānā*'.[80] Malik Ambar's model was also followed in the settlement of Poona after 1666 and it is likely that the same minister was responsible for it.[81] In the other regions, comprising the Konkan, Satara and another part of the Mavals, *baṭāī* was set aside by Anaji Datto. A *kaulnāmā*, issued by him in 1678, recalls this:

> in the past year 1677 *baṭāī* was [still] made at [a rate of] ½ [of the produce]. Then, in the same year, the land was measured in *bighās* and according to the *nimtānā* a settlement (*tah*) was ordered to be made.[82]

Concluding remarks

It is perhaps regrettable that not a single *jamābaṇdī* of any of the Deccan *tankhā* settlements has survived up to the present. On the other hand, if there had, it would be of theoretical value merely and of no use to understand the intra-village distribution of the assessment. The *tankhā* was a village settlement and was never intended to supersede the village customary or *rivāj* rates. These latter rates were of course affected by it, but, as was generally the case in the Islamic world as well as in early Europe, the land-tax was not directly levied from individual cultivators but repartitioned by the community of the inhabitants of the village.[83] It was only the aggregate assessment that interested the government: this represented the full revenue capacity of the village as a whole. This was

77 As an exception it is found that under Anaji Datto the *ināms* of the Math of Chafal, founded by Shivaji's guru Ramdas, were to be 'exempted from measurement or inspection' (*Śrīsaṃpradāyācī Kāgadpatreṇ*, nos 21–2). These were, obviously, also not held under sequestration.

78 Cf. *SCS*, 3, no.434; 4, p. 12; Vad, Mawji and Parasnis, *Sanadāpatreṇ*, pp. 143–4.

79 *MIS*, 20, nos 55–6; Khobrekar, *Shivaji Period*, no.25.

80 Khobrekar, *Shivaji Period, loc. cit.*

81 *B.A.: R.D.*, vol.7/117 of 1825, pp. 478, 489.

82 *MIS*, 15, no.340. For Anaji Datto's *bighāvṇī* settlement of the Konkan, cf. *BISM-Vārṣik Itivṛtt* (1913), pp. 323–6; Choksey, *Ratnagiri*, p. 132. For Satara, cf. *Śrīsaṃpradāyācī Kagadpatreṇ*, nos 21–2.

83 *Encyclopaedia of Islam*, s.v.; A. K. S. Lambton, *Landlord and Peasant in Persia* (London, 1953), p. 6; Goubert, *Ancien Régime*, 2, p. 9.

also the contradiction of the *tankhā*: that it was first introduced as a contract concluded once for all, but that the repeated interventions of the Mughals were to nullify it and necessitated re-settlement after re-settlement. In all cases these re-settlements were preceded – as was the 'model' settlement of Malik Ambar – by a period of *baṭāī*, a system of collection in kind which not only allowed the king to know exactly the amount of produce yielded by each village while it was still unsettled, but also simultaneously helped him to prepare new estimates for the planned re-settlement. In its final form the Deccan system probably differed very little from the northern settlement of Todar Mal, which was repeated each year and took into account the state of cultivation of that year.[84] In the eighteenth century, in the Deccan, a large number of cesses was added to the *tankhā* but no general revision took place until the Peshwas introduced the *kamāl* settlement in the 1750s and 1760s in a large region. Until then, the *tankhā* was nominally maintained, and any remission of the total sum – whether this was fixed by, or (wrongly or rightly) attributed to, Malik Ambar, Murshid Quli Khan or Shivaji – had the appearance at least of being an 'act of grace' of the sovereign who reiterated his right to the whole amount. In practice however this must have come to much the same thing as a settlement based on an inspection of the state of cultivation, repeated each year.

III Adjustments of the standard assessment

In the eighteenth century, in most of the Mughal and Maratha regulation territories, the standard assessment rates arrived at in the preceding period were repeated in the revenue documents and manuals without change, but actual collections were never identical to the amounts representing the standard king's share.[1] Under the Peshwas the *tankhā* still served as a baseline for the determination of the height of the annual demand. At that time, as is stated in a prant ajmas of the district of Poona of 1775, 'of the *tankhā* the *jamābaṇḍī* is no longer extant'.[2] This was due to the fact that the *tankhā* was a village assessment and that its internal distribution

[84] *EIP*, 4, pp. 410, 418, 426, 463.

[1] Cf. S. Chandra, *Medieval India: Society, the Jagirdari Crisis and the Village* (Delhi, etc., 1982), p. 8; M. A. Nayeem, 'Mughal Documents Relating to Land Revenue of the Andhra Districts of Northern Sarkars (1700–1765 AD)', *Itihas-Journal of the Andhra Pradesh State Archives*, VIII, 2 (1980), pp. 73–4.

[2] *P.A.: Prant Ajmas Poona, Rumal* 29, dumāljhāḍā prāṇt puṇe vagaire, 1775.

was left to the patil and the village managers and zamindars. These did not need the detailed rent-roll which had allowed the government to determine the *tankhā* but resorted to their own measurements and *rivāj* rates.

From the death of Shivaji until the late 1750s and 60s when the *kamāl* or 'completion' settlement was made in parts of the Western Deccan, the *tankhā* rates were nominally maintained everywhere but in various ways temporary and permanent adjustments were introduced on a local basis. Records of the years 1718 and 1720 show that the land-revenue demand was then not directly determined according to the (much reduced) state of cultivation, but indirectly through remissions assessed on the total amount of the *tankhā*.[3] In practice of course this was not different from exacting an amount according to the ability to pay; in the records however the right of the sovereign to the whole amount continued to be reiterated.[4] The *tankhā* also was the amount which served as a mark of the full assessment to which a village could be restored.[5]

In addition to the regular land-revenue or *ain jamā*, the government now began to impose a number of extra collections in the form of *paṭṭīs*. These came to constitute the 'extra collections' or *śivāy jamā* (which the Mughals called *sā'ir*) and were in essence of the same nature as the cesses that the *tankhā* had sought to set aside. These dues were imposed on the cultivators as well as on other inhabitants and varied extremely in the different districts and even in different villages.[6] They had a systematic bias towards the privileged and office-holding groups, especially brahmans, who were also exempted from forced labour.[7] British observers – probably with the European development in mind but not without justification – sometimes saw in these impositions an attempt to compensate for the devaluation of money which allegedly occurred after the fixing of the standard assessment due to the influx of precious metals from America.[8] At any rate, one consequence of the introduction of the numerous new cesses was an increasingly intricate accounting system which made the rayats more dependent

[3] *EIP*, 4, p. 425. [4] *Ibid.* [5] *MIS*, 15, no. 283.
[6] Elphinstone, *Report*, pp. 36–7.
[7] Malcolm, *Central India*, 2, p. 48; Jervis, *Konkan*, p. 112; *B.A.: R.D.*, vol. 59/746 of 1836, p. 218; *SSRPD*, 2, no. 446; 3, nos 341, 452; etc.
[8] Cf. *EIP*, 4, p. 426; *B.A.: R.D.*, vol. 5/549 of 1834, p. 101; Jervis, *Konkan*, pp. 83–4; A. Hasan, 'L'Historie sauf l'Europe, En Inde aux XVIe et XVIIe siècles: Trésors Américains, Monnaie d'Argent et Prix dans l'Empire Mogol', *Annales ESC*, 24, 4 (1969), p. 835; J. S. Deyell, 'Numismatic methodology in the estimation of Mughal currency output', *IESHR*, 13, 3 (1976), pp. 393–401.

on the brahman kulkarni and the village- and district-officials.[9] Often the cesses were first introduced as special and temporary (like the European 'extraordinary levies', 'subsidies' or 'subventions') and became permanent after being continued for a number of years. Such were in particular the *jāstī paṭṭīs* or *eksālī paṭṭīs*, which however until the introduction of revenue farming by Baji Rao II were fairly rare in the central districts around Poona.[10] In the Deccan the list of additional taxes imposed under the Peshwas (and to a large degree already before them) further included such items as: *dahakpaṭṭī*, a tax of one year's revenue in ten on the exempt lands of zamindars; *hak cauthāī*, a fourth of the village fees levied every year; *mau mahārkī*, a tax on the inams of the Mahars; *mirāspaṭṭī*, a tax levied once in three years from mirasdars; *inām paṭṭīs*, occasional and fixed levies (of one-fourth, one-third, or one-half or discretionary amounts) from inams; *mohatarfā*, taxes on shopkeepers; *balute*, a tax on the village servants; *gharpaṭṭī* or *ambar sari*, house-taxes; *faḍfarmās*, occasional contributions in kind; as well as miscellaneous payments in commutation of service.[11] Under the *śivāy jamā* fell also: *kamāvīs gunhegārī*, fines and forfeitures; *amānat*, money derived from sequestrations; *betanmāl*, escheats; *masālā*, legal fees; forced labour demands in a great variety. Besides these, and extra to the *gāṇv kharc* or village fund, there were dues to defray the *mahāl sādilvārī* or district expenses and *aṇtastha* or 'secret payments' which were not provided for by the government and in which were also included many of the personal expenses of the revenue collectors.[12] One extra impost of 10% or 12½% on the *ain jamā* or *tankhā* which stood apart but which was not included in the *śivāy jamā* was the Maratha king's special prerogative of *sardeśmukhī*. After the introduction of the *kamāl* rates this latter became part of the new standard, the *ajtankhā* assessment; next to *ajtankhā* we then find an *ain tankhā* or '*tankhā* without sardeśmukhi'.[13]

The imposition of cesses as described above was typical of the Deccan districts which were administered directly by the Peshwas

9 Cf. Jervis, *Konkan*, p. 115.

10 Elphinstone, *Report*, p. 37; Jenkins, *Nagpur*, p. 88; *B.A.: R.D.*, vol. 5/549 of 1834, p. 98. *Eksālī* means 'for one year'; *jāstī* is 'additional'.

11 'List of principal pattis or extra cesses levied beyond the regular assessment ... etc.', *EIP*, 4, pp. 622–4; M. Elphinstone to Col. Montressor, 26 January 1812, *PRC*, 12, p. 138; Elphinstone, *Report*, pp. 36–7.

12 For the *aṇtastha* payments see also Chapter 4–IV–h.

13 *P.A.: Prant Ajmas, passim.* Equivalents of *ajtankhā* are *tankhā dekhīl sardeśmukhī* and *tankhā sardeśmukhīsuddhām*.

or their immediate jagirdars. But a similar development took place in Kolhapur.[14] In Gujarat the extra cesses were called *veras*.[15] In Nagpur the Marathas increased the collections by superinducing *bargans* or percentages on the *ain jamābaṇḍī*, the nett revenue taken from the districts, which, when they took possession of them, already greatly deviated from the original *ain jamābaṇḍī* fixed by Murshid Quli Khan on account of cesses added to it by the preceding government of the Gonds.[16] Many of the *bargans* were imposed on the whole country generally, some on particular parganas only. Those of the first Raghuji Bhonsle, from 1743 to 1755, amounted to 80% of the *ain jamābaṇḍī*; those of Janoji, from 1755 to 1772, to 96%; those of Sabaji, between 1772 and 1775, to 32%; of Mudhoji, in 13 years, to 35%; and those of Raghuji II, imposed between 1792 and 1816, amounted to 130%.[17] In Malwa and Central India the *ain jamā* was brought to account under the headings *māl* and *abwāb*.[18] The former included the collections of land-revenue and customs, taxes on liquor, etc.; the latter accounted for the difference of the exchange rate between that of the market and the fixed rate at which the revenue of the district was paid, casual assistance to government officials, and various other contributions to feasts, marriages of the princes, etc. As elsewhere, all other extra charges like house-taxes and fines were accounted for under *śivāy jamā*.

In the Konkan, a few years after Shivaji's death, Kavi Kailash imposed a number of cesses on the original *tankhā*.[19] Whole districts were then put up to farm. This lasted until 1689, when both Sambhaji and Kavi Kailash were executed by Aurangzeb. In 1699 the Sidi of Janjira possessed himself – under a farman of the Mughal Emperor – of Suvarnadurg and Anjanvel and the forts of Rajpuri and Raigarh. He retained authority over these territories until 1734 and imposed a few new cesses on garden-land, bullocks, as house-tax, and so on. The Sidi also collected from the rayats the *haks* of the former *sardeśkuḷkarṇī* Anaji Datto, one-fortieth of the grain rental, which under Shivaji used to be defrayed from the

[14] *BGS*, n.s. no. 8, p. 69.

[15] *EIP*, 3, p. 697; J. Khaur Dhot, 'The Pattern of Taxation and Economy of North Gujarat in the Second Half of the 18th and early 19th century: A Case Study of the Pargana of Nadiad' (Paper submitted to a seminar on the 16th-20th-century history of Gujarat and Maharashtra held at the M. S. University of Baroda, 19–21 March 1982), pp. 2–7.

[16] Jenkins, *Nagpur*, p. 88. [17] *Ibid.*

[18] Malcolm, *Central India*, 2, pp. 48–9.

[19] *BISM-Vārṣik Itivṛtt* (1913), pp. 328 ff.

treasury. Further exactions were made on the money commutation or *tasar* of the produce, produce sold by weight, etc. Only eleven mahals of the Rajpuri taluka were retained in shared administration by the Sidi after 1736 under a *tahnāmā* with the Peshwa, and these he continued to hold throughout the eighteenth and through part of the nineteenth century.[20] In 1744 Angria took possession of the districts included in the old Dabhol subhedari and held them until he was expelled by Clive in 1756. Angria imposed new cesses again: taxes on trees, laden bullocks, cattle, fishermen, an impost to compensate for the losses by vermin, and others. To pay for his fleet Angria demanded a proportion of each rayat's produce at a price below the market rate of the day. Changes were made in the proportion of the produce to be commuted into a money payment, rates were altered. Afterwards, from 1756 till 1818, the Konkan, with the exception of Bombay and Salsette, the Portuguese territory and the small chieftaincies of Angria and the Jowar Raja, the Sidi, and the Savant, was under the Peshwas. New taxes and imposts on tribes again swelled the *jamā*. *Kārsaī*, a tax levied for the repair and maintenance of hill forts, became a more general exaction in every part of the Konkan, covering almost everything that any government official might require. *Aṇtastha* or *darbarkhārc*, like in the Deccan (where they were subsumed under the *mahāl sādilvār-paṭṭīs*), were levies made to enable the darakdars to attend at the huzur and to meet expenses of the mamlatdars; these were instituted on all levels, from the mamlatdar down to the lowest official in each district. With the additional cesses the collections amounted to about 70 or 80% of the gross produce as determined under the *tankhā* settlement on the line of coast from Bassein to Dumar.[21] Not all of these cesses were however collected by the government directly; in the Konkan often *khots* were responsible for them, or other revenue farmers.[22] Of all cesses, in Thana, the number well exceeded 150, and most of these had their origin from the death of the second Peshwa Balaji Rao.[23] The latter was succeeded in 1761, by Madhav Rao, who left even more to the discretion of temporary revenue farmers who indemnified themselves by making exactions over and above the established rates or, at times, attempted to increase or otherwise adjust the nett assessment (*ain dhārā*).[24] In the three southern talukas of Thana

20 Cf. p. 73. 21 *B.A.: R.D.*, vol. 16/16 of 1821, p. 518.
22 *Ibid.*, vol. 59/746 of 1836, pp. 195 ff.
23 *Ibid.*, pp. 196–7. 24 *Ibid.*, p. 197.

bābtīs and *paṭṭīs* were laid on to the amount of 50%.[25] In the Southern Maratha Country this was often higher. Here every addition made to the *tankhā* by the Nawab of Savanur between 1686 and 1752 in the form of extra cesses was continued under the general heading of *izāfa taufir*.[26] The Peshwa's sarsubhedar Ichalkaranjikar raised the *jamā* by introducing a *māmūl paṭṭī* or 'customary cess', and *jāstī* cesses, which together doubled or trebled the original standard.[27] The *māmūl* bore a definite proportion to the standard and was levied mostly from the *cālī* or fully assessed land.[28] This *paṭṭī* (like many others) was always omitted from the cultivation accounts.[29]

We thus see the cesses varying in all possible ways, but the *ain* rate being nominally maintained. This was also generally the case under the village revenue farmers called *khots*, but under farming on the district level it could be increased, or equalized without reference to the different qualities of land, or it could be lowered by the farmer as a matter of favouritism.[30] Such a proceeding always required more interference in village affairs than was usual.

Until after the mid eighteenth century, as we have stated, no general revision of the standard assessment took place. But, apart from new cesses being added everywhere to the *ain jamā*, local settlements or re-assessments were given effect in the Deccan[31] and in Kolhapur;[32] while in the Konkan the Peshwa's officials attempted a survey of the hill-lands, which was attended with very little success however and these lands continued for the most part to be estimated by ocular survey or by the plough.[33] Changes were also effected in the commutation rates of the grain rental, or the portions to be received in cash and grain were adjusted. Under Nana Fadnis a new general survey of the Konkan was begun in about 1780, but it never extended further south than Kalyan.[34] Here an assessment in money was introduced by the sarsubhedar Sadashiv Keshav according to the bighas cultivated of each quality of land.[35] This was a revision of an earlier survey conducted in 1771–2 by the mamlatdar Trimbak Vinayak.[36] Sadashiv Keshav fixed the king's share at the money value of one-third of the

25 *Ibid.* 26 *Ibid.*, vol. 5/549 of 1834, p. 98. 27 *Ibid.*, p. 99.
28 *Ibid.*; *BGS*, n.s. no. 12, p. 5.
29 *EIP*, 4, p. 469; *B.A.: R.D.*, vol. 5/549 of 1834, pp. 101, 103.
30 Cf. *BGS*, n.s. no. 8, p. 72; *BG*, XI, p. 173.
31 Jervis, *Konkan*, p. 124. 32 *BGS*, n.s. no. 12, p. 69.
33 Jervis, *Konkan*, p. 119.
34 *Ibid.*, p. 125. 35 *Ibid.* 36 *BG*, XIII, pt. II, p. 558.

average produce.[37] But this settlement remained in use only for a few years; soon after the death of Nana Fadnis farming by talukas set in on a nearly universal scale. New surveys in the Southern Konkan, made in the years 1788–1802 by the two mamlatdars Parasharam Ramcandra Paranjape and Raghunath Trimbak Barve – all attempts to reproduce Anaji Datto's system – probably suffered the same fate.[38] As distinct from Anaji Datto's fixed village settlement, these latter surveys allowed for periodical revision and adjustment of the commutation rates.

Since under the *tankhā* settlements the commutation price of grain was fixed with reference to the market price current at the time they were given effect, in the 'money villages' the devaluation of money must have occasioned a reduction of the land-revenue and the resources accruing to the sovereign. This effect may have been one reason for the imposition of some of the cesses which we have described. The same cause and the expansion of agriculture and increase of prosperity led in some districts to a more general adjustment of the standard assessment itself through the form of a *kamāl* settlement. In the districts of Poona, Junnar and Ahmadnagar this took place between the years 1758 and 1769.[39] The *kamāl* here was made up of a new assessment based on measurement and classification of qualities of the land actually under cultivation.[40] The *rājbhāg* under it appears to have been only one-sixth, and hence was lower than that of the *tankhā*.[41] But while under the *tankhā* extra cesses were at the outset prohibited, under these new settlements the *śivāy jamā* was included in the *kamāl*.[42]

Like the *tankhā*, the *kamāl* employed standardised measures and assessment rates, and again these served merely to arrive at a total for each village.[43] The steps by which it was attained were the

37 *Ibid.*, p. 559; *B.A.: R.D.*, vol. 13/700 of 1836, p. 150.

38 Cf. *BG*, x, p. 217.

39 *EIP*, 4, pp. 426, 731; *B.A.: R.D.*, vol. 5/692 of 1836, p. 33.

40 *Ibid.*

41 *EIP*, 4, pp. 434, 493; *B.A.: R.D.*, vol. 7/717 of 1825, p. 493.

42 *EIP*, 4, p. 426. The *haks* of village officials, etc. were excluded from the *kamāl* (*ibid.*, pp. 433–4; *B.A.: R.D.*, vol. 7/117 of 1825, p. 498).

43 Cf. *EIP*, 4, p. 548; *B.A.: R.D.*, vol. 10/94 of 1824, pp. 246, 250; *R.D.*, 7/117 of 1825, pp. 490–3. R. Kumar, *Western India in the Nineteenth Century* (London and Toronto, 1968), p. 19, argues the contrary: 'Prior to the 1760's, once the tax to be paid by a village had been settled through negotiations between the *patil* and the *mamlatdar*, the internal distribution of this tax was left to the *jathas* of the village, and was accomplished on the basis of the *rivaj* or customary rates of the community. After the disastrous defeat of Panipat, however, since the revenues of Maharashtra stood in desperate need of augmentation, Madhav Rao Peshwa

means, not the ends of the survey. They enabled the government to know its current resources and fixed a limit to the demand; but 'extra taxation' was not abolished and was even resorted to on a wider scale than before the settlement of the *kamāl*.[44] Extra taxation came to comprise the expenses of collection and of direct management independently of the *kamāl*, which was left undiminished.[45] If necessary, remissions were given as a lump sum to the village and were then distributed by the patil, or, if cultivation increased further, extra demands were made while the *kamāl* remained nominally the assessment of legitimate demand.[46] Only if the collector could not get the *mauzevār kamāl* did he proceed to make a settlement in more detail by sending an agent to do the work of the patil for that year.[47] The *kamāl* was always an index of the value of the village and was not intended to supersede the village *rivāj*: not even in the year that it was made does the *kamāl* form the groundwork of assessing individuals, or *jathā* lineages, or estates.[48] The single tendency towards further centralization that became evident at about the same time is that the headmen's privilege of drawing on the village *sādilvārī* fund was brought under stricter control and entered in the *jamābaṇḍī* accounts of the government.[49]

The term *kamāl* (Arabic) by itself means nothing more than 'total' or 'completion', and in the seventeenth- and eighteenth-century revenue documentation it was applied constantly with no further implication than this. The *kamāl* settlement discussed above can be understood as a specification of the general meaning

introduced the *kamal* survey, which anticipated the ryotwari survey of Sir Thomas Munro, and attempted to undermine the autonomy of the *jathas* by replacing the *rivaj* rates with a new scale of assessment, and by obliging the *kunbis* to pay their dues directly to the state.' The author of this refers to a letter of R. H. Pringle to H. R. D. Robertson of 20 November 1823 in *B.A.: R.D.*, vol. 10/94 of 1823. This volume I have not been able to trace, and I was informed that it does not exist. There is however a vol. 10/94 of 1824 containing a long letter from Robertson to Pringle (pp. 237–76) in which it is explicated that the kunbis or rayats did not pay the revenue directly to the state at any time. In doing so Robertson corrected earlier statements made by himself on this question which Kumar seems to have adopted (cf. note 44 *infra*).

44 *B.A.: R.D.*, vol. 7/117 of 1825, pp. 496–7; here too Robertson corrects his earlier views published in *EIP*, 4, pp. 426 ff., esp. that under the *kamāl* there was 'no limit to demand left'. See also *ibid.*, p. 731.

45 *B.A.: R.D.*, vol. 7/117 of 1825, p. 498.

46 Cf. *EIP*, 4, p. 547; *B.A.: R.D.*, vol. 7/117 of 1825, p. 494.

47 *EIP*, 4, pp. 547–8.

48 *B.A.: R.D.*, vol. 10/94 of 1824, pp. 248–9. Cf. note 43 *supra*.

49 *EIP*, 4, pp. 552–3; *P.A.: Prant Ajmas*, *passim*.

of the term: it 'completed' the *tankhā* assessment by systematically taking into account the land newly brought into cultivation and admitting the *śivāy jamā* as part of the regular collections. The *kamāl-ākār* was the total amount of revenue raised from the village. A *kamāl* settlement was not effected everywhere in the Maratha territories, but then we might understand by *kamāl* 'the highest rent ever levied' under a specific settlement.[50] This of course is also an implication of the fact that the *kamāl* formed the 'limit of demand'. The terms *tankhā* and *kamāl* can also be used as synonyms. This is understandable if it is kept in mind that the *tankhā*, or 'standard' in origin, was supposed to be the 'full' or *kamāl* assessment of a village; on the other hand, when a *kamāl* settlement was made (as in Poona) the new 'total' became the standard or *tankhā* assessment of the village for the future.[51] In general, from the mid eighteenth century onwards, we find that land newly brought into cultivation was brought under assessment, or accounted for by cesses, and that this and all other accretions (like for instance pasture land) were subsumed under the general heading *kamāl*.[52]

Only in some of the provinces around Poona a nominally permanent *tankhā* or *kamāl* continued to be adhered to. In most places it was openly looked at as but a reference point. Everywhere in the Deccan, Southern Maratha Country, Gujarat, Central India, and Nagpur, in the late eighteenth century, a village settlement was made annually according to the state of cultivation and taking into account local constellations of political power. A 'closed' or 'permanent' village settlement had evolved, by a gradual process which may have started with the beginning of Peshwa rule (in the mid eighteenth century) or perhaps earlier, into an 'open' village settlement. The assessment of each village rose or fell with the increase or decrease of cultivation each year, or remained stable if

[50] *EIP*, 4, pp. 318–19, 644, 688, 799; Grant Duff, *History*, 1, p. 40. In the Southern talukas of the Southern Maratha Country the settlement of Hatim Khan, a minister of the Savanur Nawab, of about 1748, is referred to as the *kamāl* (*EIP*, 4, p. 779; *B.A.: R.D.*, vol. 5/549 of 1834, p. 98). In neighbouring talukas other local settlements of about the same period had the same designation (*EIP*, 4, p. 98). In the Konkan the totals of each village determined by Sadashiv Keshav are termed *kamāl* (*B.A.: BGS, MS* 1828–31, p. 773). Sometimes also the measurement and assessment of the Bijapur government, effected perhaps at the end of the sixteenth century, is called *kamāl* (*EIP*, 4, pp. 318–19, 644, 646, 731).

[51] The term *tankhā* is used in this double meaning in for instance the source mentioned in note 2 *supra*.

[52] See e.g. *P.A.: Prant Ajmas, Rumal 56*, tāḷebaṇd mauze murtī p.supeṇ of 1813. One other meaning of the term which we already encountered was that of 'lump assessment' in the Konkan (cf. pp. 257–8).

no change had occurred, but the *kūḷvār* or individual distribution of this assessment was made by the patil and kulkarni, not by the government's mamlatdar.[53] In settling the *jamābaṇḍī* of a village cultivation accounts were rendered which – if it was considered necessary – were checked by a *pāhāṇī*; then the amount of the *jamā* of the village was fixed by the mamlatdar.[54] Only by exception – if the collector suspected the village of concealing resources, or if the rayats were not under the authority of the patil – was the individual distribution interfered with.[55] Normally the collector, after examining the accounts of the patil and kulkarni, gave out a *paṭṭā* or lease of the village to the patil, from whom a *kabulāyat* or written agreement was taken to pay the sum then fixed.[56] After this the mamlatdar or kamavisdar did not interfere in the village until the next year. Whatever profit arose from new cultivation or the goodness of the season went to the patil, and he was to bear all losses arising from opposite causes. The kamavisdar, however, attended to the complaints of rayats who were forced to pay too much. In the Konkan the Peshwas' system differed in so far as surveys of the new state of cultivation were made once in seven years.[57] As in the Deccan each year, newly cultivated land was then assessed and perhaps improved land might be brought into a higher class and consequently be brought to bear a higher rate of assessment; the rates of each class remained fixed.[58] Late in the eighteenth century in the Konkan, these surveys were no longer carried out and instead more *caḍhs* were imposed.

The above held for lands or districts under the immediate management of the government. If land was assigned for the maintenance of military contingents, the *saraṇjāmdār* had the authority to settle the village *jamābaṇḍī* himself under the supervision of government agents.[59] When the revenues were farmed, the farmers not uncommonly made, if possible, separate agreements with the individual cultivators.[60]

IV Tenancy relations

We shall look more closely now at the intra-village distribution of the land-revenue demand, the imposed king's share and additional

53 Cf. *EIP*, 3, pp. 661, 680; 4, pp. 455, 632, 788; Malcolm, *Central India*, 2, p. 31; Jenkins, *Nagpur*, pp. 84, 88.

54 *EIP*, 4, pp. 631, 635. 55 *Ibid.*, pp. 455, 632. 56 *Ibid.*, p. 720.

57 *B.A.: R.D.*, vol. 16/16 of 1821, pp. 517–18.

58 *Ibid.* 59 Cf. Chapter 4–II–b. 60 Cf. Chapter 4–IV–e.

cesses. This was a matter of customary arrangements, patronage and communal relationships which allow for little systematic classification. One distinction however which is recurrent is that of 'hereditary' or 'resident' cultivators and 'temporary' ones. From the North-Indian literaure these are best known as respectively the *khud-kāśt* and *pāhī-kāśt* cultivators.[1] In the Deccan they were commonly referred to as *mirāsdārs* and *uparīs*. According to tradition, when the *tankhā* settlements were made the lands were with very rare exception cultivated by *mirāsdārs* or 'hereditary holders'.[2] *Mirāsdārs* were found to the north as far as Khandesh, but only in the mahals which were originally settled by Malik Ambar.[3] In the Konkan they were called *dhārekarīs*, and all cultivators were of this single description when the lump assessment was in use (the villages being *kuḷārag*), while the later, often vaguely defined, less secure tenures of a more temporary nature (*ardhelī, baṇdhekarī*) were largely the product of the encroachments of *khots*, the village revenue farmers who were introduced by the Bijapur and succeeding governments from 1502 onwards.[4] In the Deccan the greater part of the lands cultivated by *uparīs* or 'temporary cultivators' were, at the beginning of British rule, recorded in the village accounts as being *gatkūḷ*, belonging to absent, extinct or emigrated *mirāsdārs*.[5] There was a third title, called *śerī* in the Deccan and *kamat* in the Southern Maratha Country, which comprised lands which were entirely the property of the state and were not considered to belong to any village.[6] This was not necessarily *khālsā* or 'crown dominion'; possession of *śerī* land was often a prestige object with high officials or saranjamdars who obtained it by usurpation or by grant. It neither paid revenue nor *haks* of the patil and kulkarni.[7] The latter characteristic, and the fact that this land was almost always cultivated by private servants on the basis of a one-half or, in the case of garden land, one-third share of the crop, distinguish it from *inām* land proper.[8] *Inām* land could be cultivated by *vāṇṭekarīs* or 'sharecroppers', but

1 Cf. Chandra, *Medieval India*, pp. 29–45: 'The Structure of Village Society in Northern India: The Khud-Kasht and Pahi-Kasht'.

2 Elphinstone, *Report*, p. 25; *EIP*, 4, pp. 419, 720. In Poona the mirasdars were also called *thaḷkarīs*.

3 *EIP*, 4, p. 477. 4 Cf. Chapter 4-IV-f. 5 Elphinstone, *Report*, p. 25.

6 *EIP*, 4, p. 782; *P.A.: List 13, Ru. 3, File 30*, no. 310 of 1860.

7 But the *haks* of balutedars, who did the same services for the holders of śerī land, were discharged from these lands (*EIP*, 4, pp. 739–40).

8 *EIP*, 4, p. 739. *Śerī* sometimes signified the same thing as *baṭāī* (cf. H. H. Wilson, *A Glossary of Judicial and Revenue Terms* (Delhi, 1968), s.v.).

just as well by *uparīs* or *mirāsdārs*; it paid no revenue, and was, like the *śerī*, deducted from the village rent-roll, but it commonly remained burdened with the *haks* of the village officials. *Śerī* had its origin either as *gatkūḷ*, like the *uparī* tenures of the Deccan, or as land sequestrated on account of interminable conflicts.[9] It was everywhere a very minor category.

In some of the Maratha territories *mirās* occupation did not exist. This was the case in Nagpur, where the cultivators held their land on annual leases granted them by the patil, and none of them was entitled to cultivate the same fields hereditarily.[10] In the Southern Maratha Country and Gujarat there was a more complicated system, and it was rare in Kolhapur.[11] The British estimated the proportions of *mirāsdārs* and *uparīs* as 1:6 in Khandesh, 3:1 in Satara and Poona, and 1:1 in Ahmadnagar.[12] Such figures do not say much about the proportions of land held by mirasdars and uparis respectively. Moreover, they conceal the fact that mirasdars of one village were often at the same time uparis in another or even the same village.[13]

Through the mediation of the village headmen the extra cesses which we discussed in the preceding subchapter were commonly laid both on mirasdars and uparis, but a mirasdar had many advantages over an upari.[14] He had a voice in all village affairs, was often exempted from the *ghugrī* dues to the patil, and sometimes (as in the Mavals) from marriage fees or house-tax.[15] Once a rayat had acquired hereditary right of occupancy he could never be dispossessed as long as he paid his tax, and he was entitled to dispose of his land by sale, gift or mortgage without previously obtaining the permission of the government.[16] A mirasdar who declined to cultivate his fields or pay tax could be compelled to give a written deed of renunciation.[17] Miras land was formally forfeited (like all property) in the case of open *fitna* or 'rebellion'.[18] The government or the village disposed of miras after long absence of the holder, but the latter had a right of reclaiming his estate for at least thirty years.[19] Mirasdars, however, were made to pay considerably more

9 *EIP*, 4, p. 739. 10 Jenkins, *Nagpur*, p. 85. 11 *BGS*, n.s. no.8, p. 69.
12 *EIP*, 4, pp. 477, 694.
13 Cf. *BG*, XIX, p. 324; F. Perlin, 'Of White Whale and Countrymen in the Eighteenth-century Maratha Deccan. Extended Class Relations, Rights, and the Problem of Rural Autonomy under the Old Regime', *The Journal of Peasant Studies*, 5, 2 (1978), pp. 185–7.
14 *EIP*, 4, pp. 466, 662. 15 *Ibid.*, pp. 466, 475, 662. 16 *Ibid.*, pp. 474, 662.
17 *Ibid.*, p. 475. 18 Cf. *ibid.* 19 *Ibid.*, pp. 475, 662.

than uparis. This was partly justified by the fact that their lands were often more productive due to improvements which uparis, not being ensured of continued occupancy, normally did not make at their own expense.[20] But the extra profit arising from improved miras land was not always left entirely in the hands of the mirasdar. If dry land was converted into irrigated garden, in some areas an additional tax was imposed of four or five rupees for each well, or the assessment of the land was upgraded into a higher class of rates.[21]

Uparis, temporary residents or residents from neighbouring villages, but also sometimes mirasdars from the same village, paid lighter rates especially agreed upon with the patil and other local zamindars and fixed by a temporary contract (*maktā* or *khaṇḍmaktā*).[22] The *uparīs* (or *uparwāriā* in Gujarat; *parasthaḷ* or *harsot* in the Southern Maratha Country) held a lease on the expiration of which their claims and obligations also expired. When they practised shifting cultivation, their lease was called *ulṭā*.[23] Otherwise their contract was mostly a mere verbal agreement (*ukte*).[24] They could also cultivate on *istāvā* or *kaul* lease, with increasing rates, to bring waste under cultivation. Never were they entitled to interfere in the management of village affairs (unless of course as mirasdars) and sometimes they also were not allowed to cultivate *inām* lands. They could not dispose of their land in any way, and they could easily be replaced by a better tenant or one who offered to pay more.[25] Some of the uparis paid as high an assessment as mirasdars and these could become mirasdars in the long term.[26] The village headmen could assign the gatkul (or other upari land) to mirasdars to enable them to pay for their highly assessed land. In general, the internal distribution of different rates was entirely an affair of the village and the patil with which the government had no direct concern. Local power and privilege always interfered with technical determinants.

This was also the situation under the more complicated systems of tenancy found in the Southern Maratha Country and Gujarat. In the former territory tenures were divided into five classes, none of which bore any relation to the quality of land. The possibility of unequal distribution by the patil was here still greater. *Cālī* was the highest assessed land; this chiefly carried the additional cesses and

[20] *Ibid.*, p. 474. [21] *Ibid.*, p. 476. [22] Cf. Chapter 4-IV-a.
[23] Jarvis, *Konkan*, pp. 80–2.
[24] *Ibid.* [25] Cf. *BG*, XIX, p. 324. [26] *Ibid.*

the 'customary cess' or *māmūl paṭṭī*.[27] It was cultivated by the *cālikars*, the core inhabitants of the village who were held responsible for the realization of the revenue of the village and the management of it.[28] The sums levied from this land were very high, its cultivation obligatory. If a calikar declined his piece of cali land he automatically lost all his rights in the village.[29] In reality the sums taken from it were not as high as they appeared to be, for the measure of cali was generally double of what it professed to be, and if it bordered on the waste it was still more extended on that side.[30] Moreover, only the calikars, and not the temporary cultivators (*harsot, parasthaḷ*), could hold tenures on *inām* land on lighter terms, *kaul* or *istāvā* to cultivate waste, or *kuttgutkā* land which generally paid one-half of the cali ratio, and some other tenures on contract (*gutkā, maktā, khaṇḍmaktā*) for which they made a bargain with the patil.[31] Under these latter tenures cultivation was usually optional, but in some hard-pressed places *kuttgutkā* was obligatory as well.[32] Like *mirās, cālī* was always an object of ambition and a temporary cultivator could become a *cālikar* in the same way as elsewhere he could become a *mirāsdār*.[33] Other privileges concomitant with his position included better housing and precedence in village festivals.

The 'customary' or *cālī* system prevailing in the districts between the Krishna and the Bhima differed from the above described. Here the village headman and his brotherhood were almost the only calikars and they held a certain quantity of *inām* land proportionate to the amount of *cālī*.[34] These calikars of Indu and Mudebihal resembled the 'shareholding' or *bhāgdār pāṭīls* of Gujarat, while the first described or southern system of cali was more like that prevailing in many communities of the Karnataka where the village concerns were regulated by the body of inhabitants collectively.[35] In its two varieties, the *cālī* system of the Southern Maratha Country was a complication of the system found in the Deccan generally, where *cālī* was synonymous with *sasthī* and indicated the highly assessed land of the *mirāsdārs*.[36] Everywhere the patils had

27 *EIP*, 4, p. 469; *BGS*, n.s. no. 12, p. 5; *B.A.: R.D.*, vol. 5/549 of 1834, pp. 97, 101.
28 *B.A.: R.D.*, vol. 5/549 of 1834, *loc. cit.*
29 Marshall, *Statistical Reports*, p. 159. 30 *Ibid.*
31 *B.A.: R.D.*, vol. 5/549 of 1834, pp. 97, 103; Marshall, *Statistical Reports*, pp. 159–60; *EIP*, 4, p. 782; *BGS*, n.s. no. 12, p. 5. See also chapter 4-IV-a.
32 Marshall, *Statistical Reports, loc. cit.*
33 *B.A.: R.D.*, vol. 5/549 of 1834, p. 102.
34 *Ibid.*, p. 104. 35 *Ibid* 36 *EIP*, 4, pp. 651–2, 739.

it in their power to grant tenures and hand out alienated lands on lighter terms to assist its holders in the discharging of their burden.[37]

In Gujarat we find a situation similarly complicated as in the Southern Maratha Country. In Kaira there was the system called *khatābaṇdī*.[38] Under this tenure a rayat received a permanent lease of *vaita* which was very highly assessed and carried most of the cesses; along with it he received other land at a more favourable rate, proportionate to the extent of *vaita*, and he could also cultivate alienated lands on much lighter terms.[39] If a rayat gave up his *vaita* he would not be allowed to cultivate alienated lands or even lands belonging to another village as *uparwāriā*. Again, it might happen that the alienated land was taxed indirectly by the imposition of a *swadde* on the rayats who cultivated these lands.[40] In Broach almost all the alienated lands were taxed either directly or indirectly; the cultivators of it held it on terms which always assisted them materially in enabling them to pay their portion of the government demands.[41] In some parganas, like in Jambusur and Ahmud, where the claims to alienated lands were much higher than elsewhere, the demand on the government land was equally disproportionate, reaching as much as 90 rupees per bigha.[42] The British were cautious about making a rayatvari settlement in these regions.[43] Government land was let at half the rate of *uparwāriā* of adjoining villages, while alienated lands in the form of *vāṇṭā* (grassias' land), *waẓifa* (given for past service), or *pasāetuṇ* (service lands) were invariably let at a much lower rate than government lands normally.[44] The holders of these alienated lands often received no more than a small quit-rent.[45] Unauthorized

[37] *EIP*, 4, pp. 651, 678, 739, 801. Brahman and Muslim *ināmdārs* were often forced to allow the retinue and relatives of the patil and kulkarni to cultivate their *ināms* at a reduced rate. If they attempted to let them out to other rayats, the latter could be prohibited by the village officials from accepting them.

[38] *EIP*, 3, p. 678.

[39] *Ibid.*, pp. 692–3. [40] *Ibid.*, p. 679.

[41] *Ibid.*, p. 661; M. Monier Williams, *Memoir of the Zilla of Baroche* (London, 1825), pp. 52ff.

[42] *Parliamentary Papers*, 1831–2, 11, 'Minutes of Evidence taken before the Select Committee on the Affairs of the East India Company', III (1832), pp. 553–5 (Minute by the Governor, M. Elphinstone, 25 April 1821, p. 554); J. Cruikshank, 'Report on the Pitlad Pergunna and the Nepar Tuppa, in the Kaira Collectorate', *BGS*, o.s. no. 11 (Bombay, 1835), p. 91.

[43] *BGS*, o.s. no. 11, p. 91; Monier Williams, *Baroche, loc. cit.*

[44] T. Marshall, 'A Statistical Account of the Pergunna of Jumboosur', *Transactions of the Literary Society of Bombay*, vol. 3 (London, 1823), p. 364.

[45] Monier Williams, *Baroche*, p. 61.

alienations by the patil, mostly originating in years of over-assessment and granted to pay off a loan to enable the village to satisfy the revenue demand, had the same function of compensation, but were, like the *gāṇv nisbat inām* in the Deccan, not allowed to affect the *jamābaṇdī*.[46] If the patil failed to screen the moneylender, the alienated land would have to be assessed again.[47] In the *bhāgdārī* or *narwādarī*, i.e. 'sharehold' villages, everywhere in Gujarat, the same circumstance was taken into account while the village community apportioned the shares. Here too the alienated lands not actually cultivated by the proprietors themselves (which comprised the greater part) paid an indirect revenue to the government by being let out at a low rent to established cultivators.[48]

Inām lands were assessed once by the government before they were made *dumālā* or 'brought under double sovereignty', and were then let out by the *ināmdār* – if he did not personally cultivate the lands – to tenants at rates chosen by himself. While the grant in *inām* did not normally effect the occupancy rights of existing *mirāsdārs*, the *ināmdār* generally had the liberty to offer lower terms to his tenants than those which were customary on non-alienated lands. Thus it is found that almost everywhere the *ināmdārs* of whole or half villages had entered in competition for tenants with the government. To counter the loss of revenue resulting from this 'drawing away' or *fitvā* of cultivators the assessment on revenue-paying land had to be increased; and where the amounts of alienations were excessively high there was usually an increase of the assessment on the non-alienated land proportionate to it. This was particularly striking in Gujarat and the Southern Maratha Country, as well as in Kolhapur, where the inamdars offered their excessive amounts of alienated land to the rayats for cultivation at a rate which was much lower than rates in force on government land.[49] *Fitvā*, the competition for cultivating tenants, among the government and the *ināmdārs* or *jāgīrdārs* and chiefs or neighbouring polities, also operated as a safety-mechanism against over-assessment. For the rayats this meant migration and a kind of non-violent 'tax revolt'. To take an example: it is recorded in the Peshwa's Diary that in 1764 two cultivator families of tarf Khed in prant Dabhol of the Konkan had

[46] Choksey, *Aftermath*, p. 33. [47] *EIP*, 3, p. 661.

[48] H. Fukazawa, 'Structure and Change of the "Sharehold Village" (*Bhagdari* or *Narwadari* Village) in the Nineteenth Century British Gujarat', *Hitotsubashi Journal of Economics*, 14, 2 (1974), p. 34.

[49] *BGS*, n.s. no.8, p. 76.

gone to reside in the *inām* village Anjani; the government collector of the prant therefore tried to levy 132 rupees extra from this village on account of these immigrant cultivators, but an order was sent from the Peshwa's court prohibiting this imposition and directing the collector to 'persuade them to return' (*fitāviṇeṇ*).[50]

The occurrence of *fitvā*, resulting in temporary or permanent exoduses, vagrancy of 'uprooted' (*parāgaṇḍā*) rayats (particularly during invasions and famines, but also frequently in times of tranquillity) was common, and under the Peshwas rights of hereditary precedence inherent in sedentary agriculture were probably the major restraint on this process. To be sure, Muslim theory tied the peasants to the soil as *glebae adscripti* in strict accordance with its universalist ethos, which emphasized fiscal docility and denied *fitna*.[51] It still has to be established however what were the practical implications of this sovereign postulate in the Muslim empires. Under the Marathas it was hardly acknowledged at all and there does not even seem to have been a recognized 'right of pursuit'.[52] Only sometimes were special arrangements made which necessitated interference in the village, like the *swadde* in Gujarat which was imposed on government rayats who went to cultivate *inām* lands, or where quit-rents (e.g. *salāmī*) were imposed on these lands, or the village averted the danger by establishing a system like *khatābaṇḍī* or *cālī*. Many treaties made express stipulations to this effect; for instance, when in 1751 Gujarat was divided between the Gaikwar and the Peshwa, the *vāṇṭṇīpatra* or 'division deed' stipulated that in the mahals which were held in joint administration 'each party shall not accommodate the other's grassias, talukdars, zamindars, mavasis, and rayats'.[53] In the Rajpuri taluka under the Peshwa's government, a practice prevailed by which, if a cultivator left his village to reside in another within the taluka, his *dhārā* or land-revenue was written off from the *jamā* of the village which he had deserted, and added to that to which he resorted, although the land remained in the hands of the khot of his original village. This

50 *SSRPD*, 7, no.649.

51 In the Mughal Empire the village officials bound themselves according to the official doctrine 'not to allow any cultivator to leave his place' (Habib, *Agrarian System*, p. 116). Under Ottoman rule a principle of the same kind obtained that the peasant could not leave his land (*Encyclopaedia of Islam*, pp. 906–7). In the ancient Indian literature little mention is made of 'absconding peasants'. In the *Arthaśāstra* (8.1.34) there is the line *deśāntaritānāmutsāhanaṃ* which may be rendered perhaps as 'incitement of those away from the land'.

52 See esp. *SSRPD*, 6, no.774; also *EIP*, 4, p. 469.

53 Vad, Mawji and Parasnis, *Treaties*, p. 166.

practice had become a perfect system under the denomination of *dhārābād*, and was extended to all descriptions of land. The Rajpuri taluka consisted originally of eleven mahals or tarfs and was held conjointly by the Peshwa and the Sidi of Janjira. In the year 1736 an arrangement was concluded between these governments by which each was to hold possession of 5½ mahals, but the accounts were to be adjusted annually between the parties. It was found after the division of the district that the rayats of the villages of the Peshwa's mahals deserted to those of the Sidi and vice versa, and on this account it was determined that the revenue due from the deserting rayats should be added to that of the village to which they retired. This appears to have given rise to the system which afterwards was gradually extended so as to affect rayats going from one village to another, even when both were situated within the mahals of one party.[54] The practice of *dhārābād* was also found in the districts of Suvarnadurg and Anjanvel. In the latter it affected only the hill lands or *varkas*. In Suvarnadurg it first extended, as in Rajpuri, to all descriptions of land, until 1805–6, when the mamlatdar abolished it in regard to the rice lands, while continuing it on the *varkas*. In both these districts the *varkas* land was not actually divided, but each rayat was rated at the quantity he happened to occupy at the time of survey, no matter whether afterwards he cultivated more or less. The fields were not fixed, and the prior occupation for the season conferred the temporary right to the use of the land. So in this case the *dhārā* appeared more to be attached to the individual than to the land, and this may give some reason to the practice of transferring the *dhārā* with the individual. But under its extended form the practice was opposed to the interests of the rayats, for not only was it usual to transfer the rent of the land which they cultivated for a khot with them but also the khot could claim a remission of his revenue on the desertion of one of his rayats, and hence he felt no interest in conciliating his tenants or in rendering their position easy.[55]

V Conclusion

It seems useless to attempt to penetrate deeper into the village *rivāj*. Apart from the complications which the non-technical, political parameters introduced in the system, both the customary

[54] *B.A.: R.D.*, vol.5/211 of 1828, pp. 172–3.
[55] *Ibid.*, pp. 190–1.

measurements and the assessment rates show a bewildering variety throughout the eighteenth century. Only under the *tankhā* and *kamāl* surveys were the same quantities of land of different qualities rated at standard values. But these were rates of theory. The internal distribution of the village assessment (*tankhā* or *kamāl*), once determined, was almost entirely left to the patil and the village itself. By the old custom of the villages equal quantities of land could be – and usually were – rated at different values in a non-standardized way. Plots of ground measured in bighas were almost everywhere entered on a nominal standard of productiveness, varying in the different parganas, with the bigha of good land or garden land being smaller than the bigha of bad land, or, again, the bigha varying with the nature of the soil might be representing a 'share' of a large unmeasured estate or of units assessed by the plough.[1] Only in a few places the assessment was fixed upon bighas of a uniform measure, higher or lower according to the various classes into which the land was divided with reference to its productiveness or to the expense or difficulty of cultivating it.[2] In most areas great partiality was shown in the measurement to favoured individuals or brotherhoods, and the *inām* lands were also quite often measured with another bigha than the sarkar's lands.[3] Next to the bigha a large number of other measures was in use, differing in every district and often in every village, none of them having reference to any fixed length.[4]

At times, where custom dictated it, brahman and other privileged landholders (zamindars, village grassias and pattidars in Gujarat) were permitted to hold lands on lighter terms on account of their having to employ labourers for cultivation or for other reasons.[5] Thus in a memorandum which bears the seal of Nana Fadnis and which was dispatched to Sadashiv Keshav on his being appointed as mamlatdar in Kalyan Bhivandi in 1788–9, the latter is enjoined to conform to the practice of former mamlatdars who 'allowed brahmans, zamindars and others to cultivate lands on lighter assessment than the kunbis on the plea that it is in conformity to the *brāhmaṇ śerista*'.[6] This *brāhmaṇ śerista* or

[1] *P.A.: Jamav, passim*; *EIP*, 3, p. 805; 4, pp. 319, 464–6; *BGS*, n.s. no. 8, p. 76; Malcolm, *Central India*, 2, pp. 35 ff.
[2] *EIP*, 4, pp. 419, 466. [3] *Ibid.*, p. 390; *BGS*, n.s. no. 8, p. 76.
[4] *EIP*, 4, pp. 320, 343, 389, 465.
[5] *B.A.: R.D.*, vol. 50/203 of 1827, pp. 270, 304, 377; *P.A.: List 11, Kaira Volumes*, no. 16, vol. 1, no. 7 of 1864.
[6] *B.A.: R.D.*, vol. 50/203 of 1827, p. 299.

'brahman custom' seems to have been largely confined to the Konkan, where (at least in many regions) brahmans were also customarily exempted from forced labour and certain taxes on purchases, probably already before the mid eighteenth century.[7] Under Sadashiv Keshav's settlement of 1788–9 the new rates of assessment, though uniformly designed to represent a third share of the produce, remained much in favour of the brahmans and the better class of cultivators.[8] In the Northern Konkan the *pāṇḍharpe-śas*, mostly artisans who represented themselves or their ancestors as the original reclaimers of the land from waste, were allowed to hold their land at especially low rates. Their privileges, which were also said to be enjoyed to make up for the expense they incurred in hiring labour, antedated the Peshwa régime; they retained them under successive governments and were confirmed in them under the surveys made between 1772 and 1793 and even under the farming system of Baji Rao II.[9] In Poona District (under early British rule) the collector Robertson found only in 12 or 14 villages that there were any brahmans who did not pay a full assessment, and this privilege they enjoyed on account of their being wealthy and respectable, not of their poverty or brahmanhood as such.[10] In one subdivision of the Mavals there was a local tenure, called *pālṇūk*, which resembled that of the *pāṇḍharpeśas* of the Northern Konkan, implying exemption from village charges and other payments, and which was granted to hereditary district officials and brahmans generally.[11] Pottinger reported from Ahmadnagar that there too it was not general that any remission of the full rent was allowed to brahmans or Muslims or other high caste people, either in consideration of their poverty or their need to employ labour.[12] Only in the pargana of Sinnur did the brahmans pay a few annas less than the other rayats.

In summary, we may conclude that in the eighteenth century the village *rivāj* remained substantially what it had always been – at odds with the uniformity of the standard surveys – and that the settlements effected under the Peshwas did not lead to a further, more systematic, interference in it in comparison with the seventeenth-century *tankhā* settlements as far as the annual collections of the land-revenue was concerned. We recall that the king's share or assessed land-revenue was by no means the only demand made

7 *SSRPD*, 3, no. 341; 7, nos 413, 419. 8 *B.A.: R.D.*, vol. 13/700 of 1836, p. 150.
9 Cf. Chapter 4-IV-g. 10 *EIP*, 4, p. 580. 11 *BG*, XVIII, pt. II, p. 357.
12 *EIP*, 4, p. 748.

from the rayats. Not only were 'extra cesses' levied by the government or by the government's revenue farmers in ever larger numbers, but there was also the charge called *grām kharc* or *gāṇv kharc*, the 'village expenses'. The latter consisted of two broad categories of payments: the 'dues' of the village officials and district zamindars, the *hakdārs*, who held their allowances hereditarily as 'intermediaries' in the revenue collection, and secondly the *sādilvārī* or *gāṇvsaṃbandhikharc* of the village proper, which were fluctuating and incidental and comprised such items as allowances for temples, payments for religious festivals, alms to beggars, nazars to the government, etc.[13] Under the Peshwas the *gāṇv kharc* was relatively circumscribed and had a place in the village *jamābaṇḍī* of the government, until about twenty years before the British take-over.[14] Until Baji Rao II's reign the allowances were nominally fixed and the patil's power to control the *sādilvārī* was then relatively limited. We have seen that then too the total village expenses were never less than 25% of the gross revenue.[15] When the power of the village- and district-zamindars increased the *gāṇv kharc* could amount to double or treble the acknowledged government demand. Under Shivaji the zamindars were most strongly curtailed when their hereditary rights and *haks* were held under sequestration. Soon after Shivaji's death they regained an authority over the rayats which was to a large extent beyond the control of the government. With the expansion of agriculture in the course of the eighteenth century the shares of revenue which were retained by the zamindars increased independently of the government collections.[16] The actual 'surplus' of agricultural produce collected by the sovereign and his assignees, then, varied greatly according to political and economic circumstances and it could never be equated with the complement of the rayats' subsistence or *prajbhāg*. The king, we conclude finally, despite his universalist claim to a king's share *sui generis*, was in the last resort a co-sharer in the revenue among the other hereditary holders of concurrent vested rights.

13 *P.A.: Prant Ajmas, passim*; *EIP*, 4, pp. 460–1.

14 *B.A.: R.D.*, vol. 11/698 of 1836, p. 45; vol. 13/700 of 1836, pp. 18–19; *EIP*, 4, pp. 701, 715; *P.A.: Prant Ajmas, passim.*

15 Cf. p. 202.

16 See for this also: Nayeem, 'Northern Sarkars', pp. 73–4; Alam, 'Agrarian Disturbances'.

4

Regulation and repartition

1 The brahman bureaucracy

In the foregoing chapters we have noted repeatedly that the ideology of universal dominion which was associated with Indian kingship in both its Hindu and Muslim variants employed an artificial categorial grid which approximated the form of bureaucratic dominion imposed by the modern state. From this fact arose the peculiar danger of an anachronistic misinterpretation of the Indian political system through a seemingly plausible appeal to primary source evidence. The universalist ideology, we also noted, implicitly had to denounce or deny *fitna* and the conflict-ridden underlying structure of patrimonial rights in land-cum-people or 'subsovereignties', while reducing these to service tenures with a clearly defined package of rights and duties. Emphasizing the asymmetrical nature of service relationships, universal dominion postulated a political order in which the king merely had the task of 'protection of cultivators and the *dharma*'. Political reciprocity was thus ruled out and the king only reiterated his general right to taxation.

In its modern connotation the concept of 'bureaucracy' brings to mind an impersonal and formalized delimitation of official jurisdictional areas, hierarchies, channels of appeal, legalistic methods of conflict resolution, and in particular a strict separation of a public and a private domain. Such a scheme of 'perfect' regulation also has its parallel in the Indian law-books, but, as we will see, the Indian administrative bureaucracy was not even remotely of this sort. It was basically no more than an institutional arrangement of the sovereign power to contain *fitna* and to regulate the collection of royal taxation. The principles on which it was founded were a corollary of *fitna* and unrelated to the transcendent norms of universal dominion. Thus in India 'regulation' did not imply the elimination of conflict or *fitna* but rather its integration or institutionalization. As such it could never be 'perfect' but, if properly functioning, it upheld a dynamic tension, an equipoise of rival interests and honours generated by the repartition of the proceeds of revenue.

In the classical Islamic empire the provincial administration had typically been a dualist one of separate politico-military and fiscal-administrative departments.[1] To the former was appointed in each province an *amīr* or 'commander', to the second an *amīn* or fiscal 'superintendent'. These two lieutenants were juxtaposed as mutual checks. Through *fitna* the central authority of the Baghdad Caliphate began to decline in the early Abbasid period when the provincial *amīrs* started building up independent sovereign dynasties for themselves after permanently merging the function of the *amīns* with their own. This was the Islamic parallel to the Western European process of feudalization. The crucial difference is that, while in Europe the military commanders were from the outset provided with landed benefices under hereditary tenure (in response to the very low index of monetization of the contemporary economy), in the Islamic Orient the military commanders surreptitiously forced themselves into a pre-existing fiscal–financial bureaucracy of a highly monetized imperial economy. The high degree of monetization accounts for the fact that in the Islamic world status honours and the assignments of governors or military lieutenants were qualitatively of a much more 'monetized' nature than the feudal relationships of Europe. Hence it is understandable that the official ranks of Muslim nobles were so precisely defined in quantitative terms and that *fitna* in many areas became a question of 'political arithmetic'.[2] In the tenth and early eleventh centuries the military governors still paid a portion of the tax proceeds of their provinces into the central treasury, but under the Seldjuk vazir Nizam-al-Mulk, from about 1087 onwards, this too was abandoned and they ended in a position of mere nominal allegiance to the Caliphate. Practically independent sultanates were thus formed out of the break-away governorships or out of new conquests and these maintained administrative dualism only in their own sub-provinces.

[1] Weber, *Economy and Society*, 2, pp. 1042–4; C. H. Becker, 'Steuerpacht und Lehnswesen', *Islamstudien*, 1, pp. 81–92; C. Cahen, 'L'Évolution de l'Iqta du IX au XIIIe siècle', *Annales ESC*, 8, 1 (1953), p. 35.

[2] Cf. p. 33.

How strictly such dualism could be enforced in the provinces of the Delhi Sultanate is not precisely known. We have one illustration of it from the fourteenth-century account of the Arab traveller Ibn Battuta with reference to the district of Amroha where he noted the existence of a *wālī-al-kharāj* or 'land-revenue collector' juxtaposed to an *amīr*, each exercising his function independently of the other but also operating as mutual checks on behalf of the central government at Delhi.[3] Under the Mughals a similar dualism was very uniformly adhered to in all provinces up to the early eighteenth century, when here too it fell prey to *fitna*. In the Mughal Empire the provincial commander of the military forces was called *niẓām* or *sūbahdar* (earlier also *sipāhsālār*) and he had next to him a *dīwān* or head of the revenue department. Akbar, in his twenty-fourth regnal year (1574), appointed such a set of officials to each of the twelve *sūbahs* into which he divided the Empire.[4] The Emperor also directly appointed military governors called *faujdārs* and revenue supervisors or *dīwāns* on the sub-*sūbah* level. These only differed in the gradation of their rank and had functions similar to those of their counterparts in the provincial capitals. There were always several *faujdārs* in each *sūbah* and they were provided for by an allotment of 25% – a portion called *faujdārī* – of the revenue collected by the *dīwāns* on account of the exchequer (*khāliṣa*) or of jagirdars. The Mughal provincial governors commonly held office for a term not exceeding three years up to the end of the reign of Aurangzeb.[5] And with the same provision the Mughals introduced the dualist regulation system in their newly conquered *sūbahs* of the Deccan. But in the decades following the death of Aurangzeb the Mughal Empire underwent the traditional Islamic process of *fitna*, of 'expansionist disintegration': the subahdars of Hyderabad, Awadh and Bengal styled themselves *nawābs* and arrogated to themselves the revenue administration of the diwans and began to appoint their own officials as faujdars and diwans in the subdistricts, while maintaining a nominal submission to the Emperor at Delhi. Nizam-al-Mulk Asaf Jah I was the first to do this effectively in the Deccan, where from 1724 onwards he became the hereditary and practically independent subahdar. In the same way Saadat Khan in Awadh, and Murshid Quli Khan in

[3] Habib, 'Landed Property', p. 291, note 142.
[4] Cf. Jarrett, *Ā324īn*, 2, pp. 37–8, 41–2.
[5] M. Athar Ali, 'Provincial Governors under Shah Jahan', in: *Medieval India: A Miscellany*, vol. 3 (Bombay, etc.), p. 81.

Bengal abolished the office of Imperial diwan shortly afterwards. Later again, after 1761, Mirza Najaf Khan proceeded to do the same in the central subahs around Delhi.[6] In all cases these autonomist struggles of Mughal subahdars succeeded because they were accompanied by a shift in the balance of power within the provinces towards resurgent zamindari power.

In the period preceding the Mughal conquest, the Deccan had for the most part been under a far less regulated administrative system under the local sultanates. Here, in contrast with the Mughal system, an indigenous brahman element had continued to dominate the revenue collections which were generally farmed.[7] In Bijapur, Ibrahim Adil Shah (1534–57) entrusted his local revenue bureaucracy to brahmans, keeping all accounts in Marathi ('*hiṇdvī*'), not Persian.[8] Marathi was also used in the bureaucracy of Ahmadnagar at the time of Malik Ambar, and probably much earlier. In the latter state brahmans rose to prominent positions already under Burhan Nizam Shah (1508–53), and Malik Ambar effected his revenue settlement in close co-operation with the brahman Haibat Khan.[9] In the Sultanate of Golconda the Telugu brahmans had control of the revenue collection as well as the lower positions in the central bureaucracy, in which at times they rose to the highest positions.[10] The farming system which prevailed in the Deccan was essentially a system of relative non-regulation.[11] Only on the district and provincial levels were there salaried Muslim superintendents or military assignees (*mokāsadars*, *amaldārs*) to check the farmers of revenues. In Ahmadnagar revenue farming was first abolished by Malik Ambar but this was of no lasting effect. Later the Mughals extended their regulation system to their Deccan conquests as far as possible and dispensed with the brahmans on the higher levels of administration, while maintaining them in the local revenue management as accountants.[12] Perhaps the most strongly centralized system of regulation to substitute farming was that instituted by Shivaji in the relatively compact region of the Western Deccan over which he established *svarājya* in

[6] Bayly, *Rulers, Townsmen and Bazaars*, p. 26; Barnett, *North India*, p. 28; Calkins, 'Regionally Oriented Ruling Group in Bengal'; Malik, 'Pargana Administration under Asaf Jah I'.

[7] Cf. p. 68.

[8] J. Briggs (transl.), *History of the Rise of the Mahomedan Power in India, till the year A.D. 1612, by Muhammad Kasim Ferishta*, 4 vols (London, 1910), 3, p. 96.

[9] Cf. p. 260, note 20.

[10] Richards, *Golconda*, pp. 17–18.

[11] Cf. Chapter 4–IV.

[12] Richards, *Golconda*, pp. 64–6.

the second half of the seventeenth century. According to the account of Sabhasad, Shivaji divided his kingdom into three administrative districts or *zilhās* to each of which he appointed a brahman official who was denominated *sarkārkūn*.[13] The country from Kalyan and Bhivandi, including Kolaba up to Salheri, and the country above the Ghats up to Vai, and the Northern Konkan, Lohgad and Junnar with the Twelve Mavals, were placed in the charge of the Peshwa Moro Trimbak. The Konkan from Ceul to Kopal, including Dabhol, Rajapur, Kudal, Bande, and Pond, was entrusted to the Surnis Anaji Datto. The Varghat from Vai to Kopal on the Tungabhadra was placed under the Vaknis Dattaji Pant. As they are described by Sabhasad these three brahman *sarkārkūns* had no autonomy or undivided authority in their districts. The Raja personally appointed the *killedārs* in each of the 262 forts of the whole region, as well as the *kārkūns* of each subdistrict. The *sarkārkūns* moreover had to station their *mutāliks* or 'representatives' at the court, where they personally had to give in annual accounts of the revenue of their *zilhā*. The local revenue bureaucracy, we learn from the *Saptaprakaraṇātmak Caritra*, was in the hands of brahman *kamāvīsdārs* who had to keep accounts in co-operation with hereditary local government officials known as *darakdārs* (specified are a *majumdār*, a *ciṭṇis*, a *faḍṇīs*, and a *daftardār*) and which also had to be approved of by the zamindars of the area.[14] Possibly there were also officials called *māmlatdārs* or *subhedārs* appointed in the larger subdivisions, as Grant Duff writes.[15] Sabhasad's Bakhar mentions the presence of brahman *subhedārs* only in the Mughal territories, where they collected *cauth* under the supervision of the Peshwa.[16] As a rule – to which exceptions appeared possible – all officials under Shivaji regularly rotated at short intervals from one location to another.[17] It is a moot point whether Shivaji managed to dispense with the system of military assignments as it was in universal use in his time elsewhere. Perhaps he temporarily sequestrated many of them (like in Northern India Alauddin Khalji and Akbar[18]), replacing them, as

13 Vakaskar, *Sabhāsadācī Bakhar*, pp. 80–1.
14 Hervadkar ed., p. 107.
15 *History*, 1, p. 125.
16 Vakaskar, *Sabhāsadācī Bakhar*, p. 80.
17 B. V. Bhat, 'Svarājyāṇtīl Deśādhikārī', *BISM-Tṛtīya Saṃmelan Vṛtt* (1915), pp. 127–31. As an exception we may mention that the post of royal Citnis was given as hereditary *vatan* (*MITSA*, 2, no. 134; *SKPSS*, no. 1654).
18 Moreland, *Agrarian System*, pp. 33–4, 39, 92, 97; *idem*, *Akbar to Aurangzeb*, pp. 235, 247, 249.

he had done with the *vatans* and *ināms*, with direct payments from the treasury or by *varāts* or 'drafts' on the district revenues which were collected by his own agents.[19]

In contrast with the eighteenth-century Mughal Nawabs, the Peshwas nowhere maintained the Mughal geographical divisions and gradations of officials, although to a limited extent they did retain the Mughal administrative nomenclature. Their administrative officials and collectors were commonly designated as *kamāvīs-dārs* or *māmlatdārs* (more rarely: *vahivāṭdārs*). It is often supposed that, of these, the mamlatdars held the bigger divisions of territory, the kamavisdars the smaller. This is a simplification. In fact, the general jurisdiction of whole provinces – called *subhās* like the Mughal provinces, but much smaller, not exceeding a few hundred villages – was always in the hands of mamlatdars, who held it as an *appurtenance* of their duties as the principal collector of government revenue of the province. Such *māmlatdārs* might be more specifically designated as *subhedārs*. The *kamāvīsdārs* always held smaller charges of revenue within the jurisdiction of a mamlatdar or subhedar; they were appointed independently either by the central huzur or by a holder of a military assignment (*saraṇjāmdār*,

[19] There is no contemporary evidence on the prevalence or absence of jagirs in Shivaji's *svarājya*. The supposition that he abolished the system of direct assignments of land-revenue is based on a single passage in Sabhasad's Bakhar which has been often accepted as historical evidence by Maharashtrian writers on the subject. Sabhasad in effect says that under Shivaji the *sarnobat*, a commander of 7,000 troops, as well as the karkuns and the Raja's personal attendants were given *tankhe varāts*, i.e. 'drafts' on the revenue collected in the huzur- or district-treasuries as their support and remuneration (Vakaskar, *Sabhāsadācī Bakhar*, p. 28). In the sequel, the same chronicle appears to be strongly preoccupied with the ideal of universal dominion: 'Assignments (*mokāsā*) of mahals and villages were not at all to be made to army-men, to the militia (*hâsam*) and to forts. All payments were to be made by means of *varāts* or cash payments from the treasury. Only the karkuns had authority over the land. All payments to the army, the militia and the forts were to be made by them [only]. By making assignments of *mokāsā* the rayats would become refractory and grow strong. The collections of revenue would no longer be orderly made. If the rayats would become strong they would start to create disturbances in their territories. The assignment-holders (*mokāsadārs*) would unite with the *zamīndārs* and become disobedient. Therefore assignments should not be made to anyone' (*op. cit.*). Grant Duff writes that Shivaji confirmed many assignments or *jāgīrs* but that he seldom gave out new ones (except to his forts) since he did not 'approve' of the *jāgīr* system (*History*, I, p. 124). In the nineteenth century the British found in Kolhapur some large *jāgīrs* which were alleged to date back to Shivaji's time (cf. *BGS*, n.s., no. 8, pp. 294–6). And even Sabhasad mentions that on occasion Shivaji assigned *mokāsā* villages to his officials and relatives (*op. cit.*, p. 23; and cf. pp. 24, 58). The evidence of later times is thus fragmentary and contradictory and it seems unavoidable to leave the question open.

mokāsadār, *jāgīrdār*) to collect and allocate separate divisions of revenue. Provincial governors called *subhedārs* we find not only in the provinces of the Peshwa in the Deccan and elsewhere, but also under the great northern sardars, Pawar, Holkar, Scindhia, Gaikwar, and the Bhonsle of Nagpur, where they were appointed without the intervention of the Poona court; sometimes we find them here in the capacity of collectors of tribute from the Rajput states.[20] These sardars, as we noted, were technically *saraṇjāmdārs* but their vast dominions brought them closer to patrimonial sovereigns than to mere assignment-holders. The administrative systems established in the northern saranjam states were in principle copies of that of the Peshwa. The prime difference was that they had *dīwāns* and other auditing and supervisory officials imposed on their central administration from Poona. The same sardars also held scattered small assignments and inams and vatans in the Deccan which fell under the direct jurisdiction of the Peshwa's subhedars. Again, in the Deccan and the Southern Maratha Country there were a number of other very large saranjams of a pseudo-hereditary nature, supervised by the Poona officials stationed in them but without interference in their local and district administration. Such saranjams exceeded three or four times the normal number of villages grouped together in a Maratha *subhā*. In some of the remoter territories of the Peshwa, such as Khandesh, Gujarat, the Karnataka, and in the Konkan there was another official interposed between the central court and the mamlatdars who was called *sarsubhedār*.[21] The latter's powers and duties varied in the various regions. In the Karnataka he was responsible for the revenue collections of the government and appointed his own mamlatdars, but in for instance Khandesh he was only a general superintendent and the mamlatdars were directly appointed by the Peshwa and they handed in their own accounts directly and paid the revenue to the central court. Elsewhere, as in the territory between the Godavari and the Krishna, a distinct sarsubhedar was appointed for a limited period under Balaji Baji Rao I to effect a local administrative overhaul, after which the post was resumed under Madhav Rao.[22]

The provincial governorships under the Maratha régime were associated with a diffuse administrative and judicial authority,

20 Broughton, *Letters from a Mahratta Camp*, p. 160.
21 Elphinstone, *Report*, p. 31; Grant Duff, *History*, I, p. 410; *SSRPD*, *passim*.
22 Grant Duff, *History*, I, pp. 453–4.

which was bound primarily by customary tradition and extended or diminished to a large degree commensurate with an incumbent's influence and position at court. The judicial power of the sarsubhedars usually comprised the power of life and death; this they held in common with the greatest saranjamdars but not with mamlatdars or subhedars and smaller assignment-holders who remained dependent in this respect on the central huzur or on the sarsubhedars.[23] While the Mughals juxtaposed to each subahdar a diwan, the Maratha subhedars were in charge of both the revenue bureaucracy and the military checkpoints or *ṭhāṇas* with śibandi or police forces which they employed to enforce governmental demands, if necessary, and to maintain regulation.[24] At times they were given extra forces to counter plundering raids by tribals or external enemies.[25] Hill-forts however were, as under Shivaji, managed independently of them, under direct supervision of the central huzur.[26] For the tasks of revenue administration each mamlatdar and kamavisdar could appoint his own staff or assessment officials and clerks who were known as *tarfdārs* and *śekhdārs*.[27] The most commonly applied check on the kamavisdars' and mamlatdars' transactions was a *behaḍā* or estimate of their income and expenditure, audited by independently appointed *darakdārs* and associated karkuns, who formed a fixed *subhā* establishment founded on that of Shivaji.[28] Normally, at the end of the year, the kamavisdar or mamlatdar had to submit his accounts of the collections, confirmed by the accounts of the zamindars, and a statement of the income and expenditure in his office (*behaḍā*) drawn up by the *faḍṇīs* and countersigned by the other darakdars.[29] It was thus ordered that they had to submit *kaccā hiśeb* or 'detailed accounts' to the huzur annually.[30] Orders to employ these karkuns and darakdars to settle the jamabandi with reference to the standard assessments and, if necessary, measure the land and prepare detailed registers of it, and submit accounts to the government, always accompanied the assignments of land-revenue of kamavisdars and mamlatdars, and *mutatis mutandis* those of *zakāt*

[23] *Ibid.*, p. 456; *EIP*, 4, pp. 214, 218, 223–4, 247, 262, 268, 276, 292, 300, 308.
[24] *SSRPD*, 7, nos 438, 444, 447, 456; 9, nos. 12, 150. [25] Cf. *SSRPD*, 3, no. 77.
[26] *BGS*, in n.s. no. 8, p. 494; Gordon, 'Forts and Social Control', pp. 4–13.
[27] Elphinstone, *Report*, p. 31
[28] Grant Duff, *History*, 1, p. 453; *EIP* 4, pp. 625–8.
[29] Cf. esp. B. Breloer, *Kauṭalīya Studien* (Osnabrück, 1973), pp. 33–5.
[30] *SSRPD*, 7, nos 438–9; 9, nos 210–12.

or 'customs'.[31] The darakdārs were, at least in the Peshwa period, generally hereditary officials, appointed (on the acquisition of new territory) and continued and paid (for the most part) by the huzur, and they were obliged to give information about possible malpractices of the collectors.[32] Darakdars and karkuns were maintained in all districts, also generally in military assignments and forts. They were called *darakdārs* or 'feemen' because their payment included, in addition to the salary or small assignment from the huzur, a *darak* or 'fee' from the villages under their charge.[33] The establishment was not uniformly the same: both the number and pay of the different classes were smaller in proportion to the size of the districts. Rarely was the full complement of twelve imposed.[34] In many documents describing regular kamavis assignments the list of darakdars mentions merely a fadnis and a majumdar. Sometimes, as in Malwa, there was only a travelling auditor, called majumdar, under a sanad from the central government periodically checking the accounts.[35] The darakdars were only removable (temporarily or permanently) for misconduct by order from the huzur, and the kamavisdars and mamlatdars were obliged to employ them in the tasks which were prescribed for each of them.[36]

Apart from the auditing officials there was a further check on the subhedars and other collectors, but one less universally applied. This was the system of paying in advance a portion or the whole of the expected revenue (*rasad*) of the district. It served not only as a *cautionnement* but also as a means to supply a government hard-pressed for funds with money.[37] Interest was paid on it of 1–1½%.[38] In the territories of Scindhia and Holkar the government demanding advance payments of the revenues from kamavisdars and mamlatdars – of one year and sometimes of two years – was a relatively late development. But in the Peshwa's portion of Malwa this had been the practice from the start.[39] In Nagpur it seems to have become customary only after 1792.[40] In some districts, such as

31 *Ibid.*, 3, no. 118; 6, no. 777; 7, nos 436, 438–9, 441–3; 9, no. 222; Thakur, *Holkarśāhī*, 1, nos 21, 44, 68, 285; etc.

32 Breloer, *Kauṭalīya Studien*, pp. 33–5; Elphinstone, *Report*, pp. 31–2.

33 They also received a share of the *darbārkharc* or *aṇtastha* (*EIP*, 4, pp. 625–6, 8).

34 Twelve was only the traditional round number that we often meet in the local setting of village establishments (cf. p. 174, note 14).

35 Gordon, 'Slow Conquest', p. 23.

36 *EIP*, 4, p. 625.

37 *SSRPD*, 7, no. 445; Sen, *Administrative System*, p. 158.

38 Cf. p. 334.

39 Gordon, 'Slow Conquest', p. 22.

40 When the revenue was already generally farmed (Jenkins, *Nagpur*, p. 96).

Thana, it never became the usual practice.[41] In principle a subhedar or collector was appointed for the year but in practice the rotation pattern varied greatly and this could have a correlation with the system of advances. In any case, when removed the officials were given a bond for the amount of advance paid by them to the government with the interest.[42] But many were, in the later eighteenth century, not removed for several years, and quite often we find them retaining office for thirty or forty years, to be succeeded by their sons.[43] Or a subhedari might be guaranteed for life.[44] However, when held on farming terms the tenures were often short and advance payments were usually demanded.[45] This at least was the case under forms of revenue farming which dispensed with the regulation by auditing and *darakdār* supervision.

With their sanad of appointment, and again at the beginning of every year, the mamlatdars received a separate account or *ajmās* of the assets and expenses of the mahals under their charge.[46] This ajmas ascertained at the same time what collections had remained outstanding from the preceding year. It stated what was the expected amount of revenue, what were the authorized salaries, varats, permanent and temporary allowances of cash, food, clothes of darakdars and other officials, śibandi soldiers, religious institutions, as well as those of the mamlatdar himself; it furthermore gave instructions about authorized remissions, the improvement of the state of agriculture and other changes of any kind; most importantly, it contained a very minute account of the existing scheme of direct repartition of the land-revenue as well as the extra collections of *śivāy jamā*: thus recording all saranjams, inams, farms of revenue and their exact locations, as well as nazars, income from sequestrated vatans, etc. The issuance of such a document was always accompanied by a number of additional sanads directed to persons in charge of forts and to zamindars in the mahals concerned informing them of the appointment. In the course of the year the mamlatdar then kept his own accounts of the collections and payments made, in co-operation with the zamindars and the darakdars. These were submitted in a finalized form at the

41 *BG*, XIII, pt. II, pp. 560–1. 42 *SSRPD*, 7, nos 439, 449.

43 Grant Duff, *History*, I, p. 454; *EIP*, 4, p. 634.

44 Cf. Broughton, *Letters from a Mahratta Camp*, p. 184. 45 Cf. Chapter 4–IV.

46 These *ajmās* documents, with the *tāḷebaṇds* (cf. *infra*), make up the most voluminous sections of the Daftar in Poona as well as the central *huzūr daftars* of the northern saranjam states.

end of the year to the *huzūr kārkūns* who compared them with the *ajmās* given out at the beginning of the year. From this comparison they then drew up a *tāḷebaṇd* giving an explanatory detail of the actual receipts and expenditure which were to be authorized by the huzur itself.[47]

Such, in outline, was formally the bureaucratic procedure followed in all territories under full Maratha sovereignty from the period of the first Peshwas Balaji Vishvanath and Baji Rao onwards.[48] The establishment of the bureaucratic apparatus in a complete form evolved gradually after the Mughal retreat from the Western Deccan, after a period of *ad hoc* arrangements of which, in the nature of things, we know little more than that they were based on farming contracts and thus under relative non-regulation. A progressive regulation of the collections took place in the span of a few decades in all newly conquered districts.[49] In the Deccan, as in the northern conquests, the entire bureaucracy was dominated from high to low by the brahmans, Citpavans and later in the north, in particular in Scindhia's territories, also by Shenavis. Everywhere the system at times lapsed into non-regulation in periods of agrarian or financial crisis. The common answer to this was always to put the districts up to farm.

There were also, throughout the eighteenth century, vast regions over which the Marathas had only limited sovereign rights and collected merely their *cauth* and *sardeśmukhī*. Here the situation remained more akin to that which had prevailed in the Western Deccan itself during the Mughal occupation. There was then a double Maratha–Mughal administration and a situation arose which gave great scope to *fitna*, with officials often working for both parties.[50] A similar double bureaucracy became a permanent

47 For a detailed discussion of the contents of the *tāḷebaṇds* of Indapur, see A. R. Kulkarni, 'Source Material for the Study of Village Communities in Maharashtra', *IESHR*, 13, 4 (1976), pp. 513–23. The hundreds of thousands of *ajmās*, *tāḷebaṇds* (or *tankhā jābtās*) stored at Poona give assessments of villages and districts, but of actual collections (*vasūl*) only the portion – of 10 to 20% – which fell to the huzur is given. This often fell short of the assessment. We do not know from these central government records how much was collected in the way of alienations and assignments. Equally significant is that these records do not exhibit what happened to the part of agricultural proceeds which was not siphoned off as government revenue, but left to the rayats and the zamindars. Lastly, the entire 'black circuit' of *aṇtastha* payments is left out of consideration.

48 The administrative documentation does not become really massive before the period 1750–60.

49 Cf. the description of this process in Gordon, 'Slow Conquest', pp. 6–15.

50 Cf. Grant Duff, *History*, 1, p. 224; Khobrekar, *Tarikh-i-Dilkasha*, p. 230.

feature throughout the territories of the Nizam in the eighteenth century.[51] In every subdistrict there were two collectors of the Maratha government; one was called the *kamāvīsdār* and was in charge of the *cauth*, the other was the *gumāstā* in charge of the *sardeśmukhī*. Besides these there were two separate collectors of the *rahdārī* road duties in each subdistrict. All of these operated with their own parties of horsemen and footmen stationed at the thanas, contending with the faujdars and jagirdars and officials of the Nizam. The cauth was generally levied through the mediation of the Nizam's local officials, while the sardeśmukhi was taken directly from the rayats. Nominally this came to a 35% of the assessed land-revenue and the abwab (cesses). The Maratha collectors however commonly farmed these revenues, and constant disputes occurred with resulting complaints reaching the Peshwa. Equally common were petitions sent by jagirdars to secure exemptions. It never became customary to make payments of cauth and sardeśmukhi in any place other than where they were due. The Nizam only obtained acquiescence to have the cauth and sardeśmukhi of the subha of Hyderabad levied in a lump sum from his treasury, while being allowed to make his own arrangements to collect them without the interference of the Marathas.

II Repartition and assignment of the king's share

a. The repartition scheme

Next to the regulative checks built into the bureaucracy proper, the procedure of revenue repartition deserves attention as a device to maintain a unity of interests by keeping them divided. We met with the term *jamā* in the sense of 'assessment' or 'valuation' of land, in other words as a quantitative measure. But the hard line of the repartition procedure of this *jamā*, as it was sanctioned by the sovereign power, should not be seen only in quantitative terms but as much in terms of 'monetized honours'. The *jamā* was the sum total of the legitimate collections which the sovereign set out to regulate by fixing them proportionately with reference to the king's share. As such the repartition schemes of the *jamā* are a kind of blueprint of the king's universal dominion and do not refer to actual collections.

51 Elliot and Dowson, *History of India*, 7, pp. 466–8; Th. Sydenham to Col. Close, 20 May 1805, *PRC*, 7, p. 221; Malik, 'Chauth Collection in Hyderabad', pp. 336–7.

Table 1

name of district	*jama in rupees*
Akluj Mahal	500,311
Belganv	1,324,389
Dabhol	1,691,084
Manjipur	931,970
Torgal	1,671,126
Bankapur	1,000,172
Miraj	55,910
Raybag	982,673
Panhala	596,104
Kalyan	207,000
Ramgiri	782,844
Yetgiri	134,365
Akalkot	480,000
Taklikhed	114,568
	13,266,636

Table 2

name of subha	*jama in rupees*
Delhi	28,658,375
Agra	24,546,995
Ajmer	13,759,000
Allahabad	9,401,515
Berar	9,518,250
Ayodhya	6,613,500
Orissa	10,262,500
Bengal	11,572,500
Ahmadabad	14,524,750
Sindh	2,374,250
Multan	6,116,375
Lahore	22,334,250
Kashmir	3,157,125
Kabul	3,163,000
Malwa	19,226,750
Kedar	3,865,000
Aurangabad	12,743,502
Burhanpur	5,704,023
Bidar	7,504,565
Ilajpur (Varadh)	11,250,000
Bijapur	46,976,651.02
Hyderabad	57,736,526.10
	331,009,412.12

What we have left of Shivaji's reign are merely aggregate figures of the standard assessments of the various districts (Table 1). These amount to a total *jamā* or valuation of 13,266,635 rupees for the whole *svarājya*, exclusive of cauth and sardeśmukhi collections from adjacent polities.[1]

A comparison with a *jamābaṇḍī* of the late reign of Aurangzeb (Table 2), showing similar valuations for the twenty-two Mughal *subhās* which then covered the entire Indian subcontinent, reveals that Shivaji's *svarājya* represented hardly more than a quarter of the total assessed income of the single *subhā* of Bijapur.[2]

It is obvious that the small extent of the *svarājya* of Shivaji allowed for a far greater degree of centralization than the later *svarājya* of the eighteenth century which was about ten times that size. According to a calculation made by General Wellesley on the basis of the above figures of Aurangzeb the total *jamā* of India in 1803 was allotted to the following sovereigns:

Peshwa	124,220,916
Nizam of Hyderabad	34,673,304.7
British Company	123,578,709.1
Abdali (Afghans)	16,301,500
Sikhs and others	32,234,983.4
	331,009,412.12

The total sum of 124,220,916 rupees accredited here to the Peshwa is further subdivided into two portions. One is called the *sarkār amal* and comprises the assessed revenue of the following *subhās*:

name of subha	*share of jamā in rupees*
Delhi	8,553,875
Agra	12,173,995
Ajmer	1,300,000
Orissa	1,600,000
Malwa	19,226,750
Ilajpur (Varadh)	6,575,000
Burhanpur	5,538,423
Lahore	3,000,000

[1] V. G. Khobrekar, 'Marāṭhī Rājyāceṇ Kṣetr va Utpanna', *Bhāratīya Itihās āṇi Saṃskṛti Quarterly*, 4, 13 (1967), pp. 79–88.

[2] G. S. Sardesai, Y. M. Kale and V. S. Vakaskar (eds), *Kāvyetihās Saṃgraha* (Poona, 1930), no.475. The *jamā* appears to be the nett assessed land-revenue (a figure closely corresponding to what is called the *ain jamā rasad* in *SPD*, 31, no.33, a document of Shivaji's coronation year, which gives 338,046,231 rupees for the entire subcontinent). Alienations etc. are not yet deducted from it.

name of subha	*share of jamā in rupees*
Bijapur	11,900,601
Ahmadabad	10,798,750
Aurangabad	6,262,522
Bidar	3,000,000
	87,229,916

The remaining amount of 36,991,000 rupees consists of tributes paid by subordinate rajas (*nisbatī rāje*) of the Jats, Rajputs, Bundelas, etc. Both the tributes and the land-revenue collections are further repartitioned by the Peshwa. Slightly over 15% is directly collected by himself as *khālsā*. This amounts to 17,755,702.8 rupees exclusive of nazars and income from his personal vatans. The biggest military assignees are as follows:

	horse	*rupees*
Malhar Rao Holkar	22,000	9,500,000
Anand Rao Pawar	15,000	4,500,000
Daulat Rao Scindhia	22,000	29,500,000
(of which 20,500,000 from districts in the subha of Delhi belonging to the Emperor)		
Raghuji Bhonsle	25,000	10,000,000
Govind Rao Gaikwar	5,000	7,200,000

In one case – that of Scindhia – the total amount of assessed revenue under his charge even exceeds the *khālsā* of the Peshwa.

Evidently, the *khālsā* varied in time in both absolute and proportional terms. Only the absolute difference is striking when we compare the financial position of Shahu almost at the beginning of his reign in 1710–11 with the above figures of 1803. Table 3 exhibits the entire revenue collected under Maratha sovereignty at that time as about 5% of that of the *jamā* of Shivaji and as 0.5% of the *jamā* accredited to the Peshwa in 1803.[3] The proportion of *khālsā* can then be put probably a little above 10%

Precise figures for the *khālsā* collections in the various districts under the Peshwa's government during the eighteenth century can be extracted from the Poona Daftar, but only at the cost of excessive labour. During extended periods it would still be impossible to find evidence for the actual collections in much of the territory when the system of farming obtained, in particular after 1804. The normal system of regulation then broke down,

[3] *SPD*, 45, no.5.

Table 3

	total in rupees	myānmulūk ('home territory')	paramulūk ('foreign territory')
Armies of sardars	355,585	111,085	244,500
Forts	51,750	51,750	–
Huzrāt (Raja's troops)	80,150	70,150	10,000
Kārkūns and āśrit	19,050	16,050	3,000
Haśam (militia) and fleet	2,375	2,375	–
Ināms and devasthāns	3,350	3,350	–
Zilhe Paṇtpradhān	20,200	20,200	–
Zilhe Paṇtsaciv	7,000	7,000	–
Bābtī mahals in charge of Rayaji Malhar	22,000	–	22,000
Bābtī mahals in charge of Cimnaji Damodar	5,000	–	5,000
	568,960	284,460	284,500

obfuscating the repartition in its train. It is also a difficult problem how to estimate with accuracy the proportion of alienated revenue. It is certain that the latter steadily increased during the eighteenth century as a whole. In some areas, like in Kolhapur, the Southern Maratha Country, and in a part of Gujarat it is common to find on average more than half of the *tankhā* alienated in *inām*. But this figure is rather meaningless since in these areas refuge was taken to indirect taxation of the *ināms*, to an extent which is not precisely known but which was usually considerable. Quantitative estimates are equally useless to determine repartition figures in territories which tended to tributary status and where often inordinate proportions of inam were allowed to be perpetuated without the sanction of the central government. The Shahu Daftar ledgers generally give for the regulation area in the first half of the century figures varying between 8–20% of the tankha held in inam; these could rise to 25%.[4] The Prant Ajmas documentation of the second half of the century rarely puts the figure of alienated or mostly-alienated villages below 10%, more usually around 15% or more.[5] Thus the approximate profile of aggregate repartition of the total

[4] *P.A.: Shahu Daftar, Rumals 26–32.*

[5] Cf. *P.A.: Prant Ajmas Poona, Ru. 151*, dehajhāḍā subhā pr. Junnar of 1743; *Prant Ajmas Ahmadnagar, Ru.6*, ajmās p. Nasik of 1797; *ibid., Ru. 199*, tāḷebaṇd mahāl p. Nasik sarkār sangamner of 1761; *Poona Jamav, Ru. 1632*, dehajhāḍā subhā Poona of 1820; *Satara Jamav, Ru. 412*, dehajhāḍā prāṇt Karad of 1728.

revenues collected under the Maratha *svarājya* in the eighteenth century looks somewhat as follows:

10–20% assigned to the khalsa
60-80% assigned to military commanders and others
10–20% alienated in inam

On the local level these aggregates were always broken down into numerous fractions which were scattered and intermixed, not consolidated in unitary and contiguous blocks. The revenue collections made within the jurisdictional area of one subhedar generally went up to the amount of 5 lacs of rupees annually. The subhedar however was directly accountable for the collection of only a small portion of this. Within the territorial boundaries of a subhedar's jurisdiction there were always a number of kamavisdars (or small mamlatdars) and military assignees called *saraṇjāmdārs* who made their own collections which fell outside the *dakhalgirī* or 'responsibility' of the subhedar. In the subhedar's accounts these collections were subsumed, together with the alienations (*inām*), under the rest-category *parbhāre dumālā va kamāvīsine*, i.e., '[charges] beyond the responsibility [of the subhedar] on account of alienations and military assignments (both *dumālā*) and *kamāvīs*'. Both the *parbhāre kamāvīsdārs* and the *dumāladārs* held their assignments and exemptions directly from the central huzur. The provincial governor had a delegated supervisory or regulative power over the repartition of these revenues, but he did not collect them. Hence there was in a Maratha *subhā* not a single collector but always in addition a fairly large number of kamavisdars working either for the central huzur or for some military assignment-holder. These were not sub-collectors of a subhedar but independent assignment-holders whose separate interests operated as reciprocal checks.

The Peshwas added a further complication to this system of management by conflict through splitting up the total *tankhā* (or *kamāl*) of the villages into *amals* or 'fractions' which could be separately assigned or alienated to different parties. Of each village the assessed king's share was in this way divided in what were in effect percentages, varying from 3 to 75%. This had as a result that often in a single village there were a number of different *amaldārs* in charge of the collection.

Max Weber referred to this system of quota repartition under the

Marathas as a 'peculiar Indian development'.[6] However, like administrative dualism – of which it was in fact a refinement – it can already be found in principle under the Islamic governments. For instance, under the Ayyubids and Mamluks the military assignees or *muqṭa'*s likewise did not hold their *iqṭā'*s in a single physically consolidated block, and in practice no single village was dependent on a single assignee.[7] Also under the Mughals there was always a 25% fraction separated off as the *faujdārī*. Yet under no Muslim régime does the principle of subdividing the revenue and appointing separate collectors seem to have been carried as far. The Peshwas applied their elaborate scheme of quota repartition of the *tankhā* everywhere from the period of the return of Balaji Vishvanath from Delhi in 1719.

Of the denominations of the fractions only some reflected the way in which they were acquired. There was first of all the *sardeśmukhī* of 10 or 12½% on the tankha of the six Mughal subhas of the Deccan which was claimed as the Maratha Raja's *vatan*. The remainder of the revenue nominally continued to the same amount, but in the Maratha accounts it was usually referred to as the *aintankhā*. Upon the *aintankhā* the Marathas began to collect their *cauth* as a nominal 25%. From the cauth was deducted 25% as *bābtī* for the Raja. The remainder, representing 75% of the cauth, was referred to as the *mokāsā*. The latter term was a designation which the Marathas adopted from Bijapur, where *mokāsā* meant 'revenue collection', a word which was most probably derived from the Arabic *makasa*, 'to collect taxes' (hence *maks*, plural *mukūs*, tax).[8] Then there was an amal called the *sahotra* or 'six percent' of the *mokāsā*; this was given hereditarily by Shahu to the Pant Saciv, who however had it collected by his own agents (kamavisdars) only in the territory which was completely under Maratha control. The remainder of the mokasa was called the *ainmokāsā*, and this was

[6] 'der indischen Entwicklung eigentümlich' (*Religionssoziologie*, II, p. 71).

[7] Cf. *Encyclopaedia of Islam*, s.v. *iḳṭā'*.

[8] The Arabic seems to go back to the Old Babylonian *miksu* (Ak.), which is described as 'a general tax on increase in value through agricultural or commercial activity' (cf. M. G. Morony, *Iraq after the Muslim Conquest* (Princeton, 1984), pp. 105^{n}, 117–18). The term *mukūs* occurs already in pre-Islamic Arabia and is found in Ibn Khaldun as a general tax or as customs duty. With reference to India the same connotations are evident in the fourteenth century, in Ibn Battuta's *Riḥla* (cf. Z. Islam, 'Zakāt and its connotation in medieval India', *Islamic Culture* (July, 1984), pp. 233–44; *Encyclopaedia of Islam*, s.v. *maks*). The term *mokāsā* was in general use in the seventeenth-century Deccan in the sense of non-hereditary assignment of revenue. It also denoted the top revenue officials under Bijapur.

usually assigned to military sardars. Sometimes another 3% was deducted as *nāḍgauṇḍa* or 'dues of the district chief' (a term adopted from the Kanarese) granted in *inām* or assigned by the Raja to various persons.[9] All in all the *mokāsā* was then reduced to 66% of the *cauth* as the part available for military assignments; the latter was actually the secondary meaning of the term from the outset.

Of the 75% which remained to the Mughals 25%, as has been seen, was named *faujdārī*, while the remaining 50% could be khalsa but much more commonly was held in jagir. These terms were often retained by the Marathas in their revenue documentation of fully conquered territories, which explains why so many exchanges of territory took place throughout the eighteenth century between the Nizam and the Peshwa under the name of *jāgīr*. This designation was then of course merely nominal. Another possibility is that we find the Marathas designating the cauth levied from Mughal territories before these were brought under their own full sovereignty as *svarājya*, while calling the remainder *moṇglāī*. Thus it often happens that in Maratha accounts of different regions a portion of revenue is referred to as *svarājya* despite wide variations in the size of the fraction. For instance, in Kalyan the Mughal governor Matabar Khan started paying ⅓ of the nominal revenue to the Marathas as *cauth* in the year 1700.[10] When after 1719 the province was wholly ceded to the Marathas this ⅓ continued to be referred to as *svarājya*, while in fact the entire revenue was then collected under *svarājya*. In Chakun we find, still in 1733, in the same way 50% of the revenue collected under *svarājya* (exclusive of the *sardeśmukhī*), while the other 50% was accredited to the Nizam as *moṇglāī*.[11] In the village Malkar in pargana Chakun an account was drawn up in 1745 giving a *tankhā* of 1,280 rupees, with a *moṇglāī tankhā* of 640 rupees which is further subdivided in a *jāgīr* of 480 rupees and a *faujdārī* of 160 rupees, while the remainder of 768 rupees is referred to as *svarājya*; of this latter amount 128 rupees is *sardeśmukhī*, 160 rupees *mokāsā*.[12] In Saswad a nominal division existed in 1741 as follows: *svarājya* 1,856 ¼ rupees; *monglāī* 1,856 ¼ rupees; *sardeśmukhī* 412 ½ rupees.[13] In the village Khalad in Karepathar in Poona the revenue continued to be divided as simply half *jāgīr*/half *svarājya*.[14] Most other accounts go into more

9 Cf. *EIP*, 4, p. 653. 10 Pagadi, *Studies in Maratha History*, 2, p. 17.
11 Joshi, *Selections*, 1, no. 16.
12 *Ibid.*, p. 67. 13 *P.A.: Poona Jamav, Ru. 481.*
14 *IS*, 7, 4-5-6 (1915–16), 'Peśve Daftarāṇtīl Sanadāpatrāṇtīl Māhitī', p. 310.

detail, as for example those of the village Cincodi in tarf Kade, pargana Padepedganv, of 1775, which give a *svarājya cauthāī* split up in a mokasa of 17½% and a babti-sahotra amal of 6½%, a jagir of 75% and an additional 10% as sardeśmukhi; these amals are again subdivided in halves (*nime*) assigned to different parties.[15] In pargana Varanganv in 1776 we find a total *tankhā* of 112½% of which 70% is the *hissā* or 'share' of the Nizam, 42½% *svarājya* divided into 30% mokasa and babti, 12½% sardeśmukhi.[16] It is striking that these repartition schemes vary considerably not only pargana-wise but also by village.

Under *svarājya*, in short, were subsumed either all Maratha revenues which were collected, or only a nominal division which reflected a state of affairs of an earlier time which designated merely the *cauth* or both the *cauth* and *sardeśmukhī*. Furthermore, if full *svarājya* was established the original subdivisions of the *cauth* were often transposed on the 100% claim. Then the *mokāsā* would be considered at 75% of the total, the *sahotra* as 6% of the same total, etc.[17] Also then wide discrepancies would occur, making the designations merely nominal. When an *amal* was alienated or assigned it was generally specified in the sanad what percentage was to be levied, or it would mention what local usage was to be followed. If nothing was specified however the original percentages would be adhered to.[18] The sardeśmukhi at some instances was merely 2% instead of 10%, in conformity with a practice which went back to certain grants made by Aurangzeb to some of the mankaris.[19] When later these vatans were sequestrated the sardeśmukhi would rise to a total of 12%.

In one form or another, the repartition scheme was ingrafted on the accounts of every village, even when there were no separate amaldars to collect the specified fraction, which was often the case since commonly two or more amals would be grouped together in an assignment or alienation. There could be however distinct kamavisdars for the babti, the sardeśmukhi, the sahotra of the Pant Saciv, for the nadgaunda, and for the mokasa, or for halves of these and even smaller fractions. In the Shahu Daftar ledgers there are no exhaustive accounts of the repartition of the amals, but there is some information on it for each village. In the Peshwa Daftar of the

[15] *SSRPD*, 6, no.712. [16] *Ibid.*, no.715.

[17] Wilson's *Glossary*, pp. 352–3 gives two explanations, but what happened is that the original meaning was extended to the entire *svarājya*.

[18] *EIP*, 4, p. 654. [19] *Grant Duff, History*, 1, p. 496.

second half of the eighteenth century, particularly after the year 1760 up to Baji Rao II, very detailed accounts become available of the pecuniary sums associated with the amals in all villages together with a complete prosopography recording the minutest changes in assignment and alienation. This precision, again, is of a universalist order and does not relate to actual collections. But the records show that all Maratha sardars had particular claims in the villages or mahals of each other, in a maze of interlocking interests of extreme intricacy. This mode of preserving union through rivalry, co-operation through conflict, was of course completely dependent on the account-keeping of an ubiquitous brahman bureaucracy. Interspersed in many villages were the amals which were to be collected for the huzur by its subhedars and kamavisdars. A subhedar's collection-unit – in contrast with the *subhā* as an administrative unit – cannot be defined in exclusively territorial terms or as a number of villages, but the *amals* must be stated as well. The terms used for a collection assignment of a government official are rather indiscriminate: *māmlat* (or *māmla*), *kamāvīs*, and *amal* may all refer to them, whether they are made up of land-revenue, zakat, or any other charge, of contiguous or non-contiguous territorial divisions or of one or more or all amals.[20] If the largest fraction of a village was assigned in saranjam, the other claimants would normally allow the saranjamdar to collect the whole of the revenue and pay to each his part, the amount of which each would ascertain from the village accounts. But when there was a defalcation each amaldar undertook to collect his own amal and throw the loss on others.[21] The amals, whether they were 'fractions' held in temporary assignment or as hereditary *vatan* or *inām*, were collected *mauzevār* and only in case of insolvable conflict became *rayatvār*. A clear illustration of this is found in a part of the Khatav district in Satara where, in consequence of disputes between numerous amaldars in the villages, the lands and tenants were divided to make up separate amals, accounts of which were kept separately by each amaldar.[22]

[20] *SSRPD*, 3, nos. 431 ff; 6, no.803; 7, nos 441 ff.

[21] Elphinstone, *Report*, p. 30. In one case Peshwa Madhav Rao issued orders on account of a pargana to the effect that the collections should be received in one place at the kaceri of the saranjamdar of the jagir amal and should be distributed among themselves by the parbhare amaldars. The saranjamdars claimed that the holder of the sardeśmukhi amal succeeded by a false representation in having the order revoked by Madhav Rao's successor. He then asked for and obtained re-enforcement (*SSRPD*, 6, nos 729–30).

[22] *P.A.: List 13, Ru. 90*, Report no.40.

b. Assignments

Since in India, in contrast with early Europe, the king had a defined right to tax all the land under cultivation there was no such maxim as that he should 'live off his own demesne'. The theory of sovereignty implied that in principle the land throughout a king's dominion was burdened with the obligation to pay the assessed king's share or *rājbhāg*. It is this theory which is mainly responsible for the widely held view that in India the king 'owned all the land'. In practice the king and his government received only a small fraction of the assessed *rājbhāg*. The problem of *fitna* dictated that about 90% of it or more was either alienated or assigned to the king's agrarian and military supporters. These always nominally collected revenue in the king's name as his 'servants'. From the point of view of universal dominion a repartition of the king's share was simply the means to give material support to the king's servants. This idea postulated the king as the sole rightful collector of taxation and made all other rights conditional upon royal service. The political reality was that repartition was based on reciprocity and assured loyalties; it was constitutive of sovereignty rather than a manifestation of the king's universal or absolute power. The agrarian gentry or zamindars held their patrimonial rights as conditional tenures of vatan and inam with a percentage on the *rājbhāg* assessment in their districts. Yet, as has been seen in Chapter 2, they were not so much the king's 'servants' as the 'co-sharers' of his power. The king's army-commanders form a second category of 'servants' among whom an even larger portion of the proceeds of taxation was repartitioned. Formally these sardars held strictly temporary service assignments of 'fractions' of the royal revenue or tribute levies, and hence, in their tenures, conditionality appears even more pronounced and more unilaterally defined than in the permanent alienations made to the zamindari gentry. But it was commonly found that the largest assignments were rather more like patrimonial states or 'subsovereignties' with their own bureaucracies than assignments conditional upon service. When *fitna* occurred the king had no option but to try to bring back the assignments or alienations concerned – irrespective of their size – under *khālsā* or 'crown' management. And thus a sequestration was always the immediate consequence of 'rebellion'. But this was often purely pro forma since it was in the nature of *fitna* that such a sequestration could not be easily enforced, if at all.

Keeping in mind that a part of it consisted of temporary sequestrations, we can define the *khālsā* or 'crown domain' of the Maratha sovereign as that share of the revenues, defined in terms of *amals* in specific territorial units (such as villages or districts), which is not alienated permanently in *inām* or assigned (in principle temporarily) as *saranjām* (or *jāgīr* or *mokāsā*).[23] The *khālsā* comprised all the revenue collected by the subhedars and by the other mamlatdars and kamavisdars directly appointed by the huzur or one of its sarsubhedars. These government collectors may be called the *khālsā* assignment-holders. The *khālsā* also included a number of *vatans* and *ināms* of the sovereign himself (the king, and later also the Peshwa) as well as all *nazars* or 'honorary gifts' and the proceeds of the *śerī* lands.

Khālsā collections are in no way bound up with regulation. What we know of the *khālsā* does not indicate that it was derived from areas which were easily administrable or particularly fertile. It seems equally to have been derived from the *paramulkī* revenues.[24] The tributes levied from *saṃsthāniks* were also often assigned to the *khālsā*, just as it might happen that an entire chiefdom was brought under *khālsā* when temporarily sequestrated.[25] While the *khālsā* should not be thought of as the king's private demesne, it may be seen as a special assignment to the crown, fluctuating like other assignments in size and likewise transferable from one location to another and differing from them mainly on account of its greater magnitude. After 1751 the crown came to be represented by the Peshwa and after that date the *khālsā* as well was collected by the latter, although always in the name of the King of Satara.

The *khālsā* served to defray the expenses of the government bureaucracy, the maintenance of the regulation system, and the 'private expenses' of the King or Peshwa. The latter expenses were set apart as the *khāsgī* or *huzūr khāsgī*, which constituted the parallel to the Mughal Emperor's *sarf-i-khāṣ*,[26] and which fell under separate sub-collectors who were to deposit it in the

23 The *khālsā* may however be differently defined on different levels of administration. Shares of the revenue of a village may be registered as *dumālā* (alienated or assigned) in a *prānt ajmās* or district estimate, while they are referred to as *khālsā* in the *zamīnjhāḍā* or 'land register' of the village. In the first case the distinction serves to differentiate *dumālā* villages from *khālsā* villages within the district, in the second case it serves to differentiate village *inām* lands from lands which pay revenue, whether this be to the government or a dumaladar.

24 *SPD*, 8, no.1; *SSRPD*, 1, nos 264, 272; Thakur, *Holkarśāhī*, 2, no.27.

25 Cf. *SSRPD*, 1, no.89; Chandra, *Parties and Politics*, p. xlix.

26 For which cf. Siddiqi, *Land Revenue Administration*, p. 103.

treasury.[27] Like the *khālsā* in general, the *khāsgī* consisted of *amals* and only rarely of consolidated clusters of whole villages. The *khāsgī* could also be derived from the *paramulkī*, or from cauth and sardeśmukhi in territory under partial Maratha sovereignty. Under Madhav Rao the *khāsgī* was slightly more than 1% of the *khālsā*: 3 lacs out of an annual 28 million rupees.[28] A similar *khāsgī* domain – likewise including vatans, inams, nazars and śeri from both sides of the Narmada – was held by the great *daulatdārs* Holkar, Gaikwar, Bhonsle and Scindhia, and by others (like the Pratinidhi) who held what were in practice hereditary assignments.[29] Like the *khāsgī* of the Peshwa it was collected by officials or relatives distinct from the normal government officials and it was not entered in the state accounts but in a separate *khāsgī kird*.[30] It was sometimes differentiated or excluded from the *daulat* proper, i.e., from the saranjam collections which were made in the name of the Peshwa and nominally were not at the sardar's own free disposal.[31] The *khāsgī* treasury of the sardars had a special status also in that it could not be claimed in satisfaction of debts.[32] Broughton observed in Scindhia's camp that the *khāsgī* treasury was considered as 'sacred' and that no cash that went into it was ever allowed to come out again except in small sums which on occasion were given to particular favourites, who however had to repay them at stated times at exuberant interest rates.[33]

By far the largest number of non-*khālsā* assignments fell in the class of military assignments or, as they are known in the Weberian terminology, *military prebends*. Such prebends or service assignments were found in the entire Muslim East under the name of *iqṭā*'*s*. Basically the system was a device of the patrimonial bureaucratic state to pay the military at source, without the mediation of the central treasury, and, like the state bureaucracy itself, it

27 *P.A: Shahu Daftar, passim; SPD*, 40, no.28; Hervadkar, *Thorle Śāhū*, p. 53. Next to the *khāsgī* there were special mahals assigned to queens as *darunīmāhāl*.

28 Grant Duff, *History*, 1, p. 457.

29 *P.A.: List 13, Ru. 90*, Report 54; Jenkins, *Nagpur*, p. 102; Malcolm, *Central India*, 2, p. 28.

30 Thakur, *Holkarśāhī*, 1, nos 20, 25, 35; 2, nos 15, 25, 100; Grant Duff, *History*, 1, p. 457; Malcolm, *Central India*, 2, p. 28. In the accounts of Angria's Kolaba estate all revenue proceeds were subsumed in one general *saṃsthān tāḷebaṇd*, but private income from vatans and inams was separately accounted for (*P.A.: List 13, Ru. 54, File 723*, no. 564 of 1864).

31 Broughton, *Letters from a Marhatta Camp*, p. 124; Thakur, *Holkarśāhī*, 2, no.25.

32 Thakur, *Holkarśāhī*, 2, no.28.

33 *Letters from a Marhatta Camp*, p. 124 (and see *ibid.*, p. 133). Grant Duff, *History*, 2, p. 185 seems to point at something similar.

presupposed the existence of a highly monetized economy, the Byzantine and Sassanid heritage in the Near East and Persia.[34] From its earliest conception onwards the prebendal assignment system was determined by the pattern of generalized taxation and the question of loyalty, but the actual measure of regulation maintained by the political centre varied according to circumstances throughout the course of Muslim history. Never absent was a more or less summary or detailed assessment of the anticipated yields of the *kharāj* or land-tax in the districts assigned. Rapid rotation of assignments and assignees had to be abandoned at about the same time that the dualist mode of administration at the provincial level was given up. Still, under the dominance of the Seldjuks the *iqṭā's* remained in essence defined as assignments for service, but they increased in size and number, while the period of tenure not only became longer but even tended to hereditary succession (in particular under pressure of the Crusaders).[35] A closer administrative and financial control over the *iqṭā's* was maintained in Egypt under the Ayyubids and Mamluks until the end of the régime. The Ottoman *tīmār* system, however, later closely repeated the pattern of development of the *iqṭā'* of classical times. Neither in Egypt nor in Ottoman Turkey did anything develop like a feudal hierarchy cemented by oath-bound vassalage; in cases where there was no direct connection between the sultan and the assignees there was at best a form of sub-assignment.

In Hindustan the *iqṭā'* made its entrée under the Delhi Sultans. Here too it was superimposed on an economy already pervaded with bureaucratic techniques of land-revenue collection which had been developed under the patrimonial Hindu kingdoms and which had long made use of comparable systems of military prebendalization. Under the successive dynasties of the Delhi Sultans the frequency with which *iqṭā's* were transferred and the extent to which the other regulative methods of valuation or assessment and auditing of the land-revenue yields and supervision of the quality and expenditure of the troops were employed, all fluctuated. But on the eve of the Mughal invasion, under the Lodis (1451–1526), the revenue assignments were commonly assimilated to extensive administrative powers on a hereditary basis and without any stipulation to remit surplus collections.[36] Such a system continued

34 Cf. Becker, 'Steuerpacht und Lehnswesen', pp. 82–3; Weber, *Religionssoziologie*, II, pp. 70 ff.

35 *Encyclopaedia of Islam*, s.v. *iḳṭā'*.

36 Habib, 'Landed Property', pp. 290–2.

to prevail under the Deccan Sultans, in some cases until the end of their rule, under the name of *jāgīr* or *mokāsā*, forms of prebendalization which made very extensive use of subfarming. The Mughal assignments – *iqṭā'ṣ* but more commonly called *jāgīrs* – on the other hand were characterized by an unprecedented degree of regulation. They were assignments of the right of collection of the land-revenue and were seldom continued to the same person for a period longer than three or four years. Nor did they ever consist of fixed territorial units, and they had no connection with the administrative districts of the Empire to which the official diwans and faujdars were appointed in complete independence of the *jāgīrdārs*. There were, furthermore, permanent local officials of the imperial administration in all territories assigned. Only in the so-called *zor-ṭalab* or 'refractory' areas which were assigned to powerful jagirdars did a greater degree of autonomy prevail. Also outside the regulation area proper were the *vatan jāgīrs* which originated in settlements with the tributary zamindars, chiefs and rajas, especially those of the Rajputs or their subordinates. The hereditary dominions of these chiefs were treated as hereditary jagirs, while the chiefs themselves were given high ranks in the imperial administrative apparatus – a policy dictated by the need to assure their co-operation and loyalty.[37] Under the Mughal system each jagirdar received (directly from the Emperor) a bi-partite rank or *manṣab*: a *zāt* rank, varying between 20 and 20,000, which was the prime determinant of the personal allowance of the jagirdar, and a *suwār* rank which through a series of arithmetical operations was converted into the number of troops stipulated to be maintained and remunerated from the proceeds of the assignment.[38] It was the usual practice that only the very small mansabdars were paid exclusively by means of salaries from the central or provincial treasuries.

Now the Mughal assignment system is thought to have entered a 'crisis' in the last years of Aurangzeb's reign due to the necessity of

[37] Nurul Hasan, 'Zamindars under the Mughals', p. 21; Athar Ali, *Mughal Nobility*, pp. 78–80. The only type of hereditary jagir within the regulation area of the Mughals were the so-called altamgha jagirs. But these were small and were not assigned for military purposes (cf. p. 188, note 28).

[38] On the Mughal mansabdari system see: A. Aziz, *The Mansabdari System and the Mughal Army* (Delhi, 1972), pp. 1–3, 13, 70, 74; Habib, *Agrarian System*, pp. 248, 260, 266, 274, 283, 294; Siddiqi, 'Classification of Villages', p. 76. Mansabs were also given by the Deccan Sultans; according to Grant Duff these corresponded exactly with the number of horse to be maintained (*History*, I, p. 495).

incorporating a vast number of Deccani nobles.[39] This, it is argued, led to a scarcity of resources and an inflation of the ranks of the older nobility with a corresponding decrease in their provisions. Such a view may seem creditable enough if one reads the contemporary documents of the Mughals. The term 'crisis' however, like the terms 'decline' and 'rebellion', has connotations for us which are greatly misleading in the historical context. This is already evident when we read of a jagir 'crisis' of a similar sort in the heyday of Mughal power, under Jahangir.[40] But there is a more fundamental issue at stake here. The Mughal assignment system generated conflict perpetually since it was bound up with loyalty and honour. *Fitna* occurred constantly through the challenge of participation of new groups of nobles and gentry which unleashed major reshuffles in the system of assignments and other rights. The latter system then, since it did not constitute a unitary order, in a sense was in 'permanent crisis'. But this qualification is also misleading because *fitna* was the *raison d'être* of the system. As we have seen, it was only from the viewpoint of Mughal universal dominion that *fitna* constituted a 'crisis' analogous to the sense we give to it. The acknowledgement of Mughal universal dominion nominally reduced all titles to the *jamā* to *vatans* or *ināms* of the hereditary service-gentry or to temporary assignments of army-commanders and governors. In actual fact, the process of *fitna* had a double track: the 'crisis' of the Mughal assignment system was also the rise of *zamīndārī svarājya*. As we have described it in Chapter 1, the autonomist struggles of Mughal mansabdars were successful because they effected stronger alliances with the local gentry. Thus the vatandars or zamindars revealed themselves as the 'co-sharers' of the universal sovereign.

Through *fitna* and alternating alliances with Mughal mansabdars and other aspiring participants in Imperial rule the Marathas established their own system of sovereignty. Under the *svarājya* there soon emerged a new and independent system of assignments. Like that of the Mughals it concerned military assignments of land-revenue (the assessed *tankhā*), but also other income such as tributes, custom fees, etc.[41] The Maratha assignments were either referred to by the old Mughal name of *jāgīr*, or by the Deccan

[39] Cf. Habib, *Agrarian System*, pp. 265, 269; Siddiqi, *Land Revenue Administration*, pp. 104–5; Chandra, *Medieval India*, pp. 46–60.

[40] Siddiqi, *Land Revenue Administration*, pp. 104–5.

[41] *P.A.: List 12*, List of Compilations of the Inam Commissioner Southern Division, no.484 of 1853; *SSRPD*, 3, no.315.

equivalent of *mokāsā*, but most common in the eighteenth century became the term *saraṇjām*.[42] These three terms occur as synonyms throughout the period in all territories conquered. They nearly always designated assignments for military provisions. The full term for *saraṇjāms* of this sort was *fauj-saraṇjām* or 'military assignment', to be distinguished from *zāt* or 'personal' *saraṇjāms*. For the very large military assignments the term *daulat* was often used, as it was in the seventeenth-century Deccan. Formally all Maratha assignments – even the largest – remained wages to be collected at source. As such they were also distinct from an alternative mode of payment by cash assignment or *italākh* from a local government treasury which could be given as a substitute for saranjam or in addition to it, for instance when extra troops had to be raised which were not already provided for or when extra śibandi had to be maintained.[43] Payment by *italākh*, the equivalent of the cash salary paid out to members of the Peshwa's bureaucracy, was much less common throughout the eighteenth century than assignment of land-revenue. After the 1750s however there was a considerable increase in the Maratha armies of foreign mercenaries.[44] These were recruited from the French, Arabs, Abyssinians, Sikhs, Portuguese, and others, and they were constituted into trained battalions or *gardīs* on fixed salaries from the treasury. In Hindustan, Scindhia especially employed many such battalions officered by Europeans. It is estimated that here they outnumbered the old cavalry. Foreign mercenaries were no doubt often a disruptive element; for instance the Gaikwar of Baroda was imprisoned by the Arabs in his palace, and Peshwa Narayan Rao was murdered by mercenaries. But their numerical predominance

42 In the north sometimes the term *jāīdād* was used for an assignment (Broughton, *Letters from a Mahratta Camp*, p. 193). In the seventeenth century, and on rare occasions still in the eighteenth, the term saraṇjām denoted an incidental gift of money or 'bakshish' (cf. *SPD*, 32, no.174; *IS*, 2, 5, (1909), pp. 28–9). In the early period it also meant 'order' (*MIS*, 15, nos 79–80, 113). The *Rājyavyavahāra Kośa* equates *saraṇjāmī* with *ānukūlyam*, 'favour'. Bhimsen has still another sense in mind when he writes that 'Ghorpade ... collected a vast *saraṇjām* by robbery' (Khobrekar, *Tarikh-i-Dilkasha*, p. 216). From the period of Rajaram onwards the term *saraṇjām* generally means an assignment of land-revenue, as distinct from an *italākh nemṇūk* or 'fixed cash payment' (cf. Khobrekar, *Shivaji Period*, nos 61, 112, 114). But in the Shahu Daftar *saraṇjām* is still rarely used; instead we mostly find here *mokāsā*.

43 *IS*, 6, 7-8-9 (1915), 'Peśve Daftarāṇtīl Sanadāpatrāṇtīl Māhitī', p. 189; 7, 1-2-3 (1915), 'Peśve Daftarāṇtīl Nivaḍak Kāgadpatre (Faujsaraṇjāmsaṃbandhī Māhitī)', p. 60; *SSRPD*, 3, no.41.

44 Ranade, 'Introduction', p. 456; Sen, *Military System*, p. xvi.

should on the other hand not be exaggerated. They must have been relatively more visible to contemporaries. Moreover it has become a misleading tenet of Maratha nationalist historians to blame the decline of Maratha power on such gradual replacement of the Maratha military by foreign elements. In a way analogous to Machiavelli in Italy and Ibn Khaldun in the Maghreb, the Maratha journalist S. M. Paranjape (1864–1929) developed a complete theory of imperial decline through the tendency to employ foreign mercenaries.[45] British testimony of the early nineteenth century still points at continued domestic ascendancy in conscription.[46] The Peshwa himself certainly continued to employ *saraṇjāmī silāhdārs*, self-equipped horsemen, on a large scale until the end of his rule, although he did become more and more desirous of dispensing with them and of employing brigades of infantry disciplined by European officers and paid directly from the treasury.[47] Neither in the Deccan nor in Hindustan was the assignment system done away with.[48] The abolition of the system would no doubt have greatly impaired the established code of monetized honours, and mercenaries as we know were not 'honourable'.[49] Farming of the revenue did not really become general before the beginning of the nineteenth century. Nothing indicates even then that this had a direct relationship with mercenary soldiering. As late as 1794 Scindhia started a new practice of making assignments to the Pindharis, a substantial part of his (as well as Holkar's) army which formerly lived chiefly on whatever they could obtain by plunder in the *pararāyja* but who were now, so to speak, 'settled with honour'.[50]

Under the Peshwas there were at least several hundred to perhaps (if we include the very small ones) a thousand saranjamdars holding their assignments under a *taināt jābtā* directly from the central huzur.[51] This was quite a heterogeneous group, comprising

45 Cf. Markovits, 'Nationalisme et Historie', p. 663.
46 Cf. W. H. Sykes (examined), 10 April 1832, *Parliamentary Papers*, 1831–2, 11 (Minutes of Evidence taken before the Select Committee on the Affairs of the East India Company, III, 1832), p. 161; 'The army was constituted principally of cultivators; every Maratha went from his farm to his horse, and returned again to his farm when he was thrown out of employ'.
47 Grant Duff, *History*, 2, p. 349.
48 Cf. Bayly, *Rulers, Townsmen and Bazaars*, p. 14.
49 This is particularly evident in the Ottoman case; see for example B. Lewis, 'Some Reflections on the Decline of the Ottoman Empire', in: C. M. Cipolla (ed.), *The Economic Decline of Empires* (London, 1970), p. 224.
50 Cf. Grant Duff, *History*, 2, p. 332; Broughton, *Letters from a Marhatta Camp*, p. 187.
51 *IS*, 7, 1-2-3 (1915), 'Peśve Daftarāṇtīl Nivaḍak Kāgadpatre', pp. 1–64.

high state councillors, fort commanders, great and minor sardars, samsthaniks, and simple *silāhdārs* or self-equipped cavalry men with their own small following of *pāgā* troops. The *silāhdārs* were generally under the command (*dimat*) of a more powerful sardar, but even then they could hold a saranjam directly from the central court.[52] In addition there were the private household troops or *huzrāt* of the Peshwa (originally the Raja's and until the very end constituted by his immediate dependants) who were likewise provided for by assignments of saranjams.[53] In none of the lists of military saranjams of the Peshwas is there any mention of infantry holding assignments on their own account.[54] In the eighteenth century the infantry lost their prominent position in the army and were retained primarily in the establishments of the forts, except in the hill-ranges where they continued to be of use for local paramilitary tasks. The so-called *bārgīrs* or 'burden-takers', soldiers who rode a horse furnished by the government, are also not found as saranjamdars. The minimum requirement to receive a military assignment appears to have been the status of *silāhdār* or 'equipment-holder'.[55] The *silāhdārs* became the preponderant element in the cavalry from the period of the Mughal invasions onwards. In contrast, in Shivaji's army *bārgīrs* had still prevailed while the infantry of Mavalis and Hetkaris raised in the Ghatmatha and the Konkan were also important.[56]

Like alienation, the assignment of land was in principle a prerogative of sovereignty. Up to the 1750s assignments were made by the Raja of Satara; after that date by the Peshwa, while the Raja became a saranjamdar himself.[57] Maratha sardars often simultaneously held military assignments from the Mughal Emperor and from Rajput kings next to those from their own sovereign. In addition to being military saranjamdars they had, if they were of some importance, a plurality of functions (often further delegated

52 *P.A.: Shahu Daftar, passim; SSRPD*, 9, nos 146, 203.

53 Sen, *Military System*, p. xvi; Grant Duff, *History*, 2, p. 477.

54 Sen, *Military System*, p. 65.

55 *Ibid.*, pp. 4–5; Broughton, *Letters from a Mahratta Camp*, p. 221, note 1. On the fundamental distinction of self-equipment and provisioning by the state see esp. Weber, *Economy and Society*, 1, p.L.

56 Sen, *Military System*, p. 8; Elliot and Dowson, *History of India*, 7, p. 287; Grant Duff, *History*, 1, p. 121; Ranade, 'Introduction', p. 456.

57 A parallel development is shown by the *iqṭā'* in classical Islam with regard to the Caliph (cf. *Encyclopaedia of Islam*, s.v. *iḳṭā'*). When Shahu was still alive the Peshwas were holding a saranjam of a total of at least 745 villages, scattered in small and large clusters, with a third of them in the district of Poona (*P.A.: Shahu Daftar, Ru. 13*, section 2, 16744).

to their own retinue) as subhedar of a province or as kamavisdar and they also invariably held a number of vatans and inams.[58] The greatest pseudo-patrimonial saranjamdars always had a great number of saranjamdars of their own.[59] Also a sub-saranjamdar of for example Scindhia or Holkar might at the same time hold another saranjam from the Peshwa.[60] Saranjamdars of ordinary stature often took refuge to the same expedient of sub-assignment in order to increase their own following or when engaging for loans with bankers demanding a surety. We find however instances of orders in which they are prohibited to do so because of the threat of *fitna* or other difficulties which this practice caused when the saranjam was resumed.[61] In spite of the difference in the length of tenure there was an incongruity in independent sub-assigning which was the same as that in sub-alienation by a saranjamdar. This was especially a problem during conquest or during periods of disputed sovereignty when a particular territory could be given in military assignment by two rival kings leaving it to the assignees to make good their claims through *fitna* for themselves.[62] Assignments to military retainers of unconquered territory or of tribute levies from such territories had accompanied the expansion of the Mughal dominion from the time of Babar, and under the Marathas as well we find this to have been the first step in the extension of their sovereignty from the turn of the seventeenth century. Thus in a letter of Rajaram of 1691 – containing probably the first Maratha design to invade the north – two of his generals are promised saranjams of 2.5 lacs of rupees as rewards for the capture of Delhi and other capitals in the *moṇglāī*.[63] In the account of Shahu of 1710–11 (cf. Table 3 of Chapter 4-II) an almost equal amount of rupees is assigned to sardars in the *paramulūk*. A document of 1734–5 of Peshwa Baji Rao I enumerates a dozen sardars holding in assignment a total amount of 22,204,475 rupees of which only 9,704,475 rupees were derived from the *myānmulūk*, the remainder of 12,500,000 rupees from the *paramulūk*.[64] In such

58 Cf. *PRC*, 7, p. 128.

59 See esp. the list of Holkar in Thakur, *Holkarśāhī*, 1, nos 162, 198.

60 *P.A.: List 13, Ru. 75, File 1044*, pp. 2–4. 61 Cf. p. 329.

62 Cf. for instance Khobrekar, *Tarikh-i-Dilkasha*, p. 321: 'As crown lands have been given in *tankha* to the *jagirdars*, in the same way the Marathas have distributed the same country in *tankha* to their own generals. And thus on one country there have been two jagirdars.'

63 *SCS*, 5, pp. 9–12.

64 D. B. Diskalkar (ed.), *Historical Papers of the Sindhias of Gwalior*, 2 vols (Satara, 1934–40), 2, no.261.

paramulkī saraṇjāms the allocation of the revenue stood under supervision of the central huzur from the outset, even when locally they were still farmed out in small portions under *ad hoc* arrangements beyond the control of the Peshwa. If regulation became more strict this would be a very gradual process.[65] Obviously under frontier conditions the danger that it would be impossible to extricate a saranjamdar was more acute the greater the assignment he held. Conquest, i.e., *fitna*, quickly led to the acquisition of sovereign attributes and patrimonial dominion and a saranjamdar could always attempt to absolve himself to an extent from centrally imposed regulation and to abandon the dualist administrative structure imposed by it. Baji Rao II for instance had the greatest difficulty to keep his southern jagirdars under regulation, after they had so successfully entrenched themselves in the area that the resumption of their assignments would have thrown it into *fitna* which the Peshwa's court-officials would have been unable to reduce.[66]

To some degree however, centralist regulation was inherent to the assignment system. A complete absence of it signals a grave fiscal-administrative crisis and concomitant with it the spread of revenue farming. But even under farming, complete non-regulation only occurred in extreme cases. In an agriculturally stable situation under Maratha sovereignty the *jamā* or 'valuation' of saranjams was normally not subject to bargaining and entrepreneurial speculation but calculated entirely on the basis of estimates of the production capacity of the land. This was derived from the *tankhā* or *kamāl* figures which existed for each village. Sometimes it included zakat and other 'extra collections'. The amount of the *jamā* was always stated at the beginning of the *taināt jābtā*, the document which specified the magnitude of an assignment and the number and pay of the troops which were to be maintained. The assignment was conditional upon active service, but commutation into cash payments was possible and this was frequently resorted to.[67] If no service was provided in failure to respond to mobilization, a sequestration was ordered and this was maintained until an agreement was reached and the *fāzīl* or amount due on account of non-service was determined; this was usually a

65 Cf. *PRC*, 7, pp. 143, 194.

66 Cf. *PRC*, 12, p. 105; for a comparable situation in the Rohilla country see *SSRPD*, 3, no.45.

67 M. Elphinstone to Vice-President in Council, 23 June 1811, *PRC*, 12, p. 87.

weary process because of the many pretences that were brought up.[68] The amounts of assigned *jamā* show, in effect, a wide range of variation. In the early nineteenth century, in about 1811, Gokla was the greatest military saranjamdar in the Peshwa's own territory with an assignment of 1,121,500 rupees for the upkeep of and service with an army of 3,000 cavalry and 2,500 infantry and two guns.[69] Various members of the Patwardhan family together held jagirs amounting to 21 lacs of rupees for 6,000 cavalry.[70] A sizeable number of saranjams exceeded a few lacs. But most were much smaller, frequently not more than a few thousand rupees. These belonged to small paga commanders or silahdars. A number of very small saranjams, up to a few rupees, were also awarded annually for non-military service of karkuns etc., and there were those for personal support which were called *zat saraṇjāms*, also quite small on average.[71] In all cases the valuation of the saranjam was made with meticulous precision and any excess had to be remitted to the government.[72] On the other hand remissions (*majurā*) are found to have been given when the jamabandi could not be made due to disturbances.[73] In the *taināt jābtā* the saranjamdar was further enjoined to increase the revenue of his assignment as much as possible, to populate the villages and to respect the existing alienations and haks, and not to arrogate to himself any of the amals which were not assigned to him.[74] The same document fixed with equal precision the amounts of revenue which were to be allocated to the army (*fauj*) and the karkuns and government officials as well as the part which was assigned as 'personal allowance' (*khudd zat, khāsā zat, zat*, or *khāsgī*) of the saranjamdar himself and sometimes of a number of his relatives and officials. The personal allowances were always a small percentage of the total assignment, varying perhaps from 5 to 10%. All kinds of minute expenses, palanquins, elephants, śibandis, etc. are also

68 Cf. *SSRPD*, 3, no. 282; 9, no.352; *PRC*, 7, p. 128; 12, p. 81.

69 M. Elphinstone to Sir T. Hislop, Commander in Chief, 28 June 1807, *PRC*, 13, p. 209; Elphinstone to Mr Chief Secretary Edmonstone, 26 October 1811, *PRC*, 12, p. 85.

70 *PRC*, 13, p. 209.

71 'Correspondence exhibiting the results of the scrutiny by the Inam Commission of the lists of Deccan Surinjams, etc.', *BGS*, n.s., no.31 (Bombay, 1856), p. 24; *IS*, 7, 1-2-3 (1915), 'Peśve Daftarāṇtīl Nivaḍak Kāgadpatre', yādi 1; Steele, *Law and Custom of Hindoo Castes*, p. 228.

72 Cf. *SSRPD*, 9, no.149.

73 E.g. *SSRPD*, 9, nos 194, 341.

74 *IS*, 7, 1-2-3, 'Peśve Daftarāṇtīl Nivaḍak Kāgadpatre', pp. 55–8, 64, 75–80; *SSRPD*, 9, nos 190, 192, 338, 341; 4, no.299; *PRC*, 12, pp. 90–1; *P.A.: List 13, Ru. 1, File 1*, Proc. no.595–B.

accounted for.[75] The number, description and pay of the troops and the expenses of forts were fixed and were held liable to be mustered at any time. The expenses of collection of the revenue by the assignment-holder's kamavisdars and the costs of protection of the saranjam in normal times were also set apart.

Most often a saranjam was not given for a specific time period determined in advance. Under Shahu the military assignments were resumed and re-assigned to others with very high frequency, often annually or bi-annually. But already by the 1730s a tendency had developed towards longer tenure and hereditary confirmation.[76] In the Peshwa period, although as a rule the saranjams never became formally hereditary, this tendency became more outspoken, as it did with provincial governorships and *kamāvīs* assignments. Still then we rarely find in the sanads a guarantee of continuation for any specified period of time and continuation would normally not have been demanded as a vested right. The saranjam continued to be seen as basically a temporary assignment in lieu of wages in money.[77] Whether a saranjam was resumed or continued depended on political expediency. Resumptions still occurred frequently throughout the second half of the eighteenth century. The Maratha practice in this respect did not deviate from the normal practice which was followed elsewhere in India at that time, for instance in the Nizam's territories and in the Karnataka and in the Rajput states. It was the same in the territories of Scindhia and Holkar and everywhere in Northern India. A number of 554 saranjams are recorded to have been resumed by the Peshwas in the last fifty years of their rule.[78] In particular, Baji Rao II resumed many (even of those which were formerly confirmed hereditarily) in an attempt to break the power of the 'royal circle', the old *rājmaṇḍalkar* sardars. This generated many tensions but the Peshwa succeeded in putting a number of the smaller sardars on cash stipends while introducing his farming system in most of the territory under his direct control.[79] At the time of the British

[75] *PRC*, 12, p. 87; *SSRPD*, 9, nos 190, 192, 209, 341 ff; *BGS*, n.s. no. 31, App. B, pp. 7, 18 ff; *P.A.: List 13, Ru. 75, file 1044*, pp. 10–13.

[76] *P.A.: Shahu Daftar, Rumals 16–32* (documents covering Poona, the Mavals, Supa, Junnar, Khandesh, Konkan, Satara, Kolhapur, Bijapur, Berar, Balaghat, etc. during the period 1706–50).

[77] Cf. *P.A.: List 12*, List of Compilations in the office of the Inam Commissioner Southern Division, no. 484 of 1853.

[78] *BGS*, n.s. no. 31, App. B.

[79] *PRC*, 12, p. 95; Grant Duff, *History*, 2, pp. 345, 351; Vad, Mawji and Parasnis, *Kaifiyats, Yadis*, pp. 58–9, 80, 82, 155, 159.

take-over few military assignments were found to date from before 1714, the year of the appointment of the first Peshwa. Formally hereditary saranjams hardly existed at all.[80] While the length of tenure was not determined in advance, the terms which were used to cancel an assignment, *dūr* or *japtī*, likewise left open whether this was final or merely a temporary sequestration. It could be temporarily assigned in *kamāvīs* and then be 'set free' (*mokaḷī karūn*) and re-assigned as a military saranjam to the same person. Such temporary sequestrations occurred incidentally even with hereditarily continued assignments. An example is the saranjam of Amursingh Shirke which is found in the accounts from before 1714 and in all subsequent years for which they are extant; it was once sequestrated in 1766 because the holder did not appear for service; in the years 1767 and 1772 the Peshwa dispensed with the service and the saranjam was again sequestrated but then re-assigned; later in 1773 it was once again sequestrated because the holder joined Raghunath Rao, but it was again re-assigned afterwards.[81]

The bequest of tenure to heirs was customary with all the very great military saranjamdars who had acquired sovereign attributes and who, as we have seen, were closer to confederate allies than assignment-holders in the strict sense. Scindhia, Holkar, Pawar, Bhonsle, and Gaikwar were formally not hereditary saranjamdars, but since they were continued in their tenure without interruption it becomes extremely difficult to assess whether these were still regarded as conditional assignments or rather as patrimonial states. These saranjams were designated as a sardar's *daulat*, a term which might perhaps be rendered as 'patrimonial dominion'.[82] In Kolhapur, jagirs existed which were said to have been held for more than 194 years uninterruptedly by the same family and which were allegedly originally assigned by Shivaji to members of his Rajmandal or, in one case, by Yusuf Adil Shah.[83] The great jagirdars of the Southern Maratha Country customarily held their assignments in hereditary continuation.[84] A second cluster of patrimonial or pseudo-patrimonial jagirs in the Deccan were the Satara Jagirs,

[80] One odd sanad declares a landed saranjam hereditary to male and female descendants; another makes it hereditary through *barkhurdār* (?) (*BGS*, n.s. no.31, pp. 10, 26–27, 60). Incidentally we also come across a *pustdarpust saranjām*, 'hereditary in the male line' (Vad, Mawji and Parasnis, *Kaifiyats, Yadis*, p. 155) or a *saranjām inām* (*SCS*, 3, nos 405, 408; *SSRPD*, 3, no.102).

[81] *P.A.: List 13, Ru. 44, File 621*. See for another example *SSRPD*, 4, no.201.

[82] *SSRPD*, 3, nos 179–80; 4, nos 220, 248; 9, no.341.

[83] *BGS*, n.s. no.8, pp. 2, 294–6.

[84] *PRC*, 12, p. 87.

those of the Saciv of Bhor, the Pratinidhi of Aundh, the Amatya of Jath, Nimbalkar of Phaltan, and the chiefs of Daflapur and Akalkot, who all received them originally from Shahu.[85] However, in these, as in all other cases, the government had to sanction any direct or collateral succession, as well as partitions and adoptions. These were registered in the sarkar daftar while in return a nazar was stipulated to be paid varying between 2 and 182% of the annual proceeds.[86] Division of a saranjam into shares appears to have been the common practice with inheritance but no general rule was followed in determining the portions.[87] The *mukhtyārī* or 'general authority' was always reserved for a single incumbent (who was not necessarily the eldest); to him solely the *taināt jābtā* was addressed, but not without stipulations concerning the number of troops to be furnished by the other members of the family and the proportions of revenue assigned to these as well as their personal allowances, etc. In determining the shares of a saranjam the government often manipulated intra-family rivalries to create loyalty to itself. Irresolvable disputes were often the ground for effecting a partition of a saranjam among different members of a bhauband. Thus the saranjam of the Bhonsle of Nagpur was partitioned by Shahu; later also those of the Gaikwar, Pawar, and a number of other very large assignments.[88] Disputes and non-service only resulted in a sequestration when they led to *fitna*. We can follow this process quite clearly in the case of what the British called the 'rebellion' of the Pratinidhi. He was one of the old royalist sardars who had been disaffected with the Peshwa from the beginning.[89] In 1807–8 serious quarrels broke out within the Pratinidhi's bhauband.[90] Some of its members started 'creating *fāṇdfitur*', as the document says, by 'going over from *svarājya* to *pararājya*' and making

85 *P.A.: Shahu Daftar, Ru.12*, section 2, 16670, 16672, 16871. In each case these jagirs ran into hundreds of villages.

86 *SSRPD*, 5, no.56; 9, no.141; Vad, Mawji and Parasnis, *Kaifiyats, Yadis*, p.73; Steele, *Law and Custom of Hindoo Castes*, pp.227–8; *IS*, 7, 1-2-3, 'Peśve Daftarāṇtīl Nivaḍak Kāgadpatre', pp.63, 92. The nazar was not always paid at once but in installments. If it was not paid timely the saranjam could be sequestrated. With the dahakpatti or 10% levied in times of emergency the nazar was the only income – if there was not an annual or regular tribute stipulated – which the sarkar derived from the military assignments.

87 *P.A.: List 13, Ru. 75, File 1044*.

88 *SSRPD*, 4, nos 248–9; *IS*, 7, 1–2–3, 'Peśve Daftarāṇtīl Nivaḍak Kāgadpatre', p.82; Vad, Mawji and Parasnis, *Kaifiyats, Yadis*, p.56; *PRC*, 12, pp.81–2; and see Chapter I-III.

89 Cf. Chapter I-III-a.

90 *IS*, 7, 1–2–3, 'Peśve Daftarāṇtīl Nivaḍak Kāgadpatre', pp.54–8.

assignments to 'marauders' (*bakheḍekhor*) and *paradaulatdār* who 'aided them in their plundering (*zulūm*) and *zabardastī*'. The Peshwa at first gave out orders to stop them from attracting more followers. Eventually however, in 1811, when the Pratinidhi declared himself a 'servant of the Raja', the whole of the jagir (of a valuation of 18 lacs of rupees annually) was sequestrated and assigned to Gokla.[91] There are more documents which describe a similar sequence of events: disputes breaking out, a retinue of *svakīya* and *parakīya* sardars is collected, sub-assignments are made, alliance is sought with another sovereign, culminating in *fāṇḍfitur* or *fitna*, after which a sequestration is ordered.[92] *Zabardastī* and *zulūm* in this context indicate no more than that the revenue collections of the assignment are no longer made in conformity with the stipulated regulations and assessments.

It was primarily to prevent the more powerful sardars from slipping out of *svarājya* that virtually all of them were assigned lands scattered over wide distances and intermixed with those of rival sardars. The British saw the Peshwa's success in dispossessing an almost century-old saranjami bhauband like that of the Pratinidhi as due primarily to the latter's disunion with surrounding saranjamdars.[93] It was everywhere the common state of affairs that the various sardars in their dispersed assignments had one or more *amals* excluded from them on account of these being assigned to others.[94] This led to the intricate interlacing of rival interests which served to guarantee 'safety in numbers'.

The saranjamdars made their own collections through officials which were called *kamāvīsdārs*, like government collectors. When a mahal was assigned in saranjam the mamlatdar or subhedar of the province received orders 'not to make the *dakhalgirī*', i.e., not to interfere in the collections of revenue in the assignment.[95] Or a sanad was written with the message that it was 'removed (*dūr*) from the present mamlatdar or amaldars'.[96] The provincial governor was to allow the saranjamdar to collect his revenue after receiving from him an indemnification for expenses made earlier with regard to it and for the amount advanced to the government on account of the mahals in question. At the same time the zamindars received orders

91 M. Elphinstone to the Vice President, 16 June 1811, *PRC*, 12, p. 25.
92 *IS*, 7, 1–2–3, 'Peśve Daftarāṇtīl Nivaḍak Kāgadpatre', pp. 75–80, 93–101.
93 *PRC*, 12, p. 97.
94 *SSRPD*, 3, nos 45, 107; 4, nos 186, 230; 9, nos 105, 158, 190, 199, 209, 346–7; *PRC*, 12, pp. 84–5, 90; 7, p. 219.
95 *SSRPD*, 9, nos 156, 194.
96 *SSRPD*, 4, nos 157, 185, 261.

'to release the amal' (*amal surḷīt deneṇ*).[97] In co-operation with the latter the saranjamdar did his own *dakhalgirī*, i.e., he was allowed to settle the jamabandi and make the collections (*lāvṇī ugavṇī*) of the revenues assigned to him.[98] This however does not mean that his collections were not further supervised or regulated by the huzur.[99] The hereditary local government officials which were known as *darakdārs* belonged not only to the administrative set-up in the *khālsā* but were also employed, in the same way, as a check on the military assignment-holders. The saranjamdars' personal allowances, as well as the number, quality and pay of the troops, as stipulated in the *taināt jābtā*, were permanently under the inspection of the darakdars whose co-operation was required, with that of the zamindars, in submitting annual accounts of a detailed character, *kaccā hiśeb* or *kaccā ākār*, to the Peshwa.[100]

This claim of the Peshwa to have the right to employ darakdars to inspect the saranjam does not seem to have been very much disputed. They are also found with the presumptuous southern jagirdars at the time of Baji Rao II, although not always in the right office.[101] The imposition of darakdars being little disputed may be partly due to the fact (which can hardly be doubted) that an assignment-holder, if necessary, could find the means to make them connive at many of his transgressions. Again, the full complement was not always imposed, and the darakdars did not always meddle with the revenue administration at the local level, particularly if the assignments were very large. The northern saranjamdars had huzur karkuns and darakdars imposed on their administration from Poona, but only at their capitals; these sardars appointed their own darakdars on their own military assignees.[102] In all cases the local darakdars had merely a reporting function. They were to take care that accounts were *kaccā* and that no deviations *(tafāvat)* occurred in the actual payments. Actual interference in the administration was always left to the subhedars and other properly administrative officials. For example, when it

97 *Ibid.*, 9, nos 156, 199–201.
98 Vad, Mawji and Parasnis, *Kaifiyats, Yadis*, pp. 54, 56, 58–9, 73, 78, 105, 135, 141, 159, 166, 169, 178, 185, 196.
99 See esp. *ibid.*, p. 159.
100 M. Elphinstone to Chief Secretary Edmonstone, 26 October 1811, *PRC*, 12, pp. 81, 87; Malcolm, *Central India*, 1, p. 538; *SSRPD*, 4, no.248; 9, nos 190–2, 194, 341, 355, 369; *IS*, 7, 1–2–3, 'Peśve Daftarāṇtīl Nivaḍak Kāgadpatre', pp. 55–8, 61; 7, 7–8–9, pp. 69, 77, 86; 7, 10–11–12, pp. 89, 91, 93–101.
101 *PRC*, 12, p. 87.
102 Cf. Chapter I-III; Gujar, *Pavar*, no.124; *SSRPD*, 3, nos 179–80.

became known in 1748–9 that in the pargana Kade certain villages had suffered from over-assessment by the holders of the jagir, mokasa and the babti-sahotra, the subhedar was ordered to issue a kaul fixing the amount of each amal and to take care that nothing was collected beyond this.[103] Similarly a kaul was issued to the village Mohokal in Junnar when it became known that due to threats of the mokasadar they had left the village and stopped cultivation; this kaul ordered them to return and fixed the amount of revenue due to the mokasadar.[104] Through the same channels a saranjamdar would receive remissions on account of droughts or other disturbances.[105]

III Monetization and the cash-nexus

In the preceding sketch of the regulative system of revenue collection the existence of a monetized economy was largely taken for granted. We noted that from the *tankhā* settlements onwards the land-revenue was usually assessed per village in cash. This at least was the case in the territories under regulation. Large parts of the Deccan in actual fact probably receded to a more composite economy in the late seventeenth and early eighteenth century and the index of monetization did not reach its culmination before the later eighteenth century.[1] The Prant Ajmas tabulations of the Peshwas establish beyond doubt that almost everywhere the government revenue collections were not only assessed but actually converted into cash; only a minor fraction remained in the rubric 'collected in kind' (*ain jinas*).

At this point we should therefore address the problem of how the monetization of the agrarian produce was achieved and how it fitted into the regulation system of land-revenue management. This at present still poses some of the most elusive questions connected with Indian taxation. We know broadly that from at least the thirteenth century in Northern India a progressive monetization took place and that it became an even more dominant feature of the Mughal economy in the sixteenth and seventeenth centuries when

[103] *SSRPD*, 3, no.336. [104] *Ibid.*, no.346. [105] *Ibid.*, no.327.

[1] F. Perlin, 'Money-use in late pre-colonial India and the international trade in currency media' (Contribution to the Mughal Monetary Conference at Duke University, June 1981), pp. 18–20; *idem*, 'The pre-colonial Indian state in history and epistemology. A reconstruction of societal formation in the Western Deccan from the fifteenth to the early nineteenth century', in: H. Claessen and P. Skolnik (eds), *The Study of the State* (The Hague, 1981), p. 284.

it received a great impetus from imports of bullion from Central Asia and through European trade.[2] The vast quantities of imports of New World silver probably played a key role in the land-revenue reforms effected by Akbar in the latter half of the sixteenth century.[3] They may have had a comparable impact on the subsequent reforms in the Deccan. They caused a general inflation of prices in the period 1650–1750. They stimulated internal commerce in general, facilitated Mughal expansion and unification at one stage, while later they must have catalysed *fitna* separatism and local accumulations of wealth.[4] Everywhere the monetization of the economy fostered the development of an intermediary group of financiers and traders between the administration and the cultivating *rayats*.[5] Like the role of the other intermediary group of the agrarian gentry, that of the financiers and merchants is generally underplayed or marginalized in the official representation of the Mughal state, as it was in most agrarian empires. The *Ājñāpatra* again provides a great contrast with this when it refers to merchants or *sāhukārs* as 'the ornament of the kingdom and the glory of the king', adding that through them 'the *rājya* becomes prosperous and well-peopled (*abādān*)'.[6] As with zamindars, a policy of moderation and conciliation is advocated with respect to merchants and the text enjoins the king to induce them to settle in his kingdom.

The monetization of the economy gave rise to a cash-nexus spreading out from market centres linked by trade routes throughout the countryside.[7] At all levels this cash-nexus was controlled by financier–merchants organizing payments and conversions of revenue into cash, transmitting funds and offering credit facilities. Actual transfers of money were, at least in the eighteenth century, in most cases unnecessary because a well-

2 Moreland, *Agrarian System*, p. 204; Habib, *Agrarian System*, pp. 46, 236–9 ff; *idem*, 'Usury in Medieval India', *CSSH*, 6, (1964), p. 393; Bayly, *Rulers, Townsmen and Bazaars*, pp. 46–7, 170, 226.

3 Bayly, *Rulers, Townsmen and Bazaars*, p. 227; J. F. Richards, 'Mughal State Finance and the Premodern World Economy', *CSSH*, 23 (1981), pp. 302, 308.

4 Cf. also Heesterman, 'Was there an Indian Reaction', pp. 43–4; F. Perlin, 'Precolonial South Asia and Western Penetration in the Seventeenth to Nineteenth Centuries: A Problem of Epistemological Status', *Review*, 4, 2 (1980), p. 296.

5 Heesterman, 'Was there an Indian Reaction', pp. 38–9, 43.

6 Banhatti, *Ājñāpatra*, ch. 4. Compare these statements with *Arthaśāstra* 4.1.65 which counts traders among the 'thieves who are not known as thieves'.

7 Heesterman, 'Was there an Indian Reaction', p. 43; Perlin, 'Money-use in late pre-colonial India', p. 24; Richards, 'Mughal State Finance', p. 299.

developed system of bills of exchange or *huṇḍīs* was used by these financiers.[8]

In various ways the cash-nexus with its network of bills of exchange constituted a hinge between regulation and non-regulation and a pivot in *fitna*. First of all it cut across political boundaries. In the eighteenth century hundi transactions covered most parts of India: revenue collections and tribute levies made by the Marathas in distant regions often reached Poona through a chain of hundi dealers.[9] It is not exceptional to find for instance a Poona banker issuing hundis for the amount of tribute received from Hyder Ali and making these payable at Aurangabad.[10] In Maharashtra perhaps no more than a quarter of the land-revenue was paid directly in cash.[11] It was more usually remitted from the villages to the local bankers and moneylenders by *havālā* (Ar. *ḥavala*, 'bill of exchange'). By the latter similar transfers were made to the mamlatdars who took hundis from the district's sahukars or *nāīks* (as they were called when they were brahmans) drawable upon the sahukars in Poona from whom the amount was recovered or by whom it was paid to the huzur at Poona. Occasionally *varāts* (bills of exchange similar to the hundi but issued by the government) were given to individual financiers for advances made by them at Poona and then the amount was collected from those on whom the *varāt* was drawn.[12] To provide surety and to bridge the government's seasonal lack of funds mamlatdars often paid a portion or the whole of the anticipated revenues in advance. This portion, called the *rasad*,[13] was also usually supplied by sahukars by

[8] According to Richards most transfers of official funds were, in the Mughal Empire, carried out by imperial messengers and armed escorts rather than by resort to the private networks of bills of exchange offered by associated groups of money-changers ('Mughal State Finance', p. 297). Leonard objects to this that 'the Mughal state utilized credit facilities of banking firms for short term credit and transmittance of funds in the 16th and 17th centuries' (K. Leonard, 'The "Great Firm" Theory of the Decline of the Mughal Empire', *CSSH*, 21 (1979), p. 311). Habib thinks that 'the total amount transferred via *hundis* on behalf of the Mughal government and officials rivalled, if it did not exceed, the money remitted for purposes of trade' ('Banking in Mughal India', *Contributions to Indian Economic History*, vol. I (Calcutta, 1960), pp. 10–11). Van Santen explains further that actual transfers of money were only undertaken in case of severe imbalance of payments, thus creating a self-regulatory system which expressed itself in increases of exchange rates (Van Santen, *Verenigde Oost-Indische Compagnie*, pp. 122–3).

[9] V. D. Divekar, 'The Emergence of An Indigenous Business Class in Maharashtra in the Eighteenth Century', *MAS*, 16, 3 (1982), p. 432.

[10] *SSRPD*, 4, no. 139. [11] *EIP*, 4, p. 632.

[12] *EIP*, 4, pp. 632, 634; *B.A.: BGS*, no. 160, *MS*, 1828–31, p. 776.

[13] The *rasad* could be the whole of the anticipated revenue (cf. *SSRPD*, 7, no. 445).

means of hundis, indirectly to the mamlatdar or kamavisdar,[14] or directly to the huzur, as in the Maratha territories of Central India where in payment of these loans the bankers would then often receive farms of the land-revenue themselves, which they would in their turn underrent.[15] Interest was paid on the rasad of 1–1.5%.[16] Under the Maratha sardars of Central India and Hindustan, Scindhia, Holkar, the Pawars, and the Bhonsle of Nagpur, to an extent probably also in Gujarat under the Gaikwar, bankers acquired a dominant position at the head of the revenue administration through their control of credit provision.[17] Farming was common and many of the farmers were either bankers themselves or supported by them.[18] Frequently they entered into rayatvari arrangements.[19]

What this shows is that the cash shortages of the government could become so acute that regulation of the collections of land-revenue had to be relaxed to obtain credit and that thus it had to throw the financial side of administration and agrarian development into the hands of private entrepreneurs. In the Deccan too the mediation of bankers was indispensable for the revenue collection but their direct involvement in the agrarian system was, as far as can be made out, more limited. We sometimes find patils borrowing money or obtaining it by sale, on behalf of the whole village, from an individual moneylender or banker who would then take possession of a small part of the village lands on the understanding

[14] *SSRPD*, 3, nos 407, 409; Grant Duff, *History*, 1, p. 455.

[15] Malcolm, *Central India*, 2, p. 50.

[16] *SSRPD*, 3, nos 407, 409, 431. Gordon shows that in Malwa interest rates on *rasad* loans became lower when the districts became more settled, dropping from 2% per month to less than 1% ('Slow Conquest', p. 34). According to Van Santen the differences in interest percentages indicate differences of risk between credit operations in a rural context and the commercial context of the city; 1½% was most common for rural credit (*Verenigde Oost-Indische Compagnie*, pp. 153–4). In Gujarat there was a special bonus stipulated by the money-lender above the current interest, called *manotī* (cf. R. Kumar Hans, 'The Manotidari System in the Agrarian Economy of Eighteenth Century Gujarat' (Paper read at the 43d session of the Indian History Congress, Bodh Gaya, 1981).

[17] Malcolm, *Central India*, 2, p. 50; Broughton, *Letters from a Mahratta Camp*, pp. 122–3; Joshi, *Selections*, 1, no. 27. In Orissa in the second half of the eighteenth century a banker called Chaudhuri seems to have acted as a middleman in the revenue collections; a similar position was held by Lala Harabamsa, a son of Nirderam, the Mughal diwan of Orissa (Shejwalkar, *Nagpur Affairs*, 2). For evidence on the Gaikwar see M. Dharmadhikari, 'Gopal Rao Mairal: A Brief Note on Gaekwad Nobility' (Paper submitted to a seminar on the 16th- to 20th-century history of Gujarat and Maharashtra held at the M. S. University of Baroda, 19–21 March 1982), p. 4.

[18] Malcolm, *Central India*, 2, p. 50. [19] *Ibid.*, p. 31.

that he would hold it revenue-free as *gāṇv nisbat inām*.[20] This practice prevailed more widely in Gujarat, where revenue-free land of this sort was known as *pasāetuṇ*, which was either sold or mortgaged. When the bankers involved were at the same time important government lenders such inams might receive the sanction of government. In the Peshwa's territories in the Deccan the sahukars are only rarely credited with small fractions (of a few hundred or thousand rupees) of the revenue of some parganas. Their active involvement in revenue collection may however be hidden behind the titles of saranjamdars. Military assignees often borrowed money against the future revenues of their assignments.[21] This practice also was at odds with regulation and appears often to have resulted in complications with the resumption of the assignments, and it is no surprise therefore that the practice was at times explicitly forbidden.[22] In general however in the second half of the eighteenth century shortage of cash remained a powerful factor in the Maratha dominions in the Deccan and everywhere in Northern India.[23] All military commanders, and the Peshwas themselves until Baji Rao II's subsidiary alliance with the British, were chronically in debt with the sahukars (chiefly brahmans) and remained continually in want of funds. The Peshwas often attempted to raise loans in the name of the government while at the same time building up their private fortunes.[24] Thus private fortunes could exist side by side with huge indebtedness; as has been seen, the private treasury could be considered as 'sacred'. Debt, even when it was incurred in the name of the government, was always a matter of family credit extending over several generations and the Peshwas were answerable for their fathers' debts.[25] Loans were also taken from merchants under the title of *karjpaṭṭī*; these were never repaid but rather than 'forced loans' they were more in the nature of insurance or 'protection rent'.[26] Whether these

20 Cf. pp. 217.

21 Habib, 'Landed Property', p. 295; *idem*, 'Usury', pp. 408, 410; K. Leonard, 'Banking Firms in Nineteenth-Century Hyderabad Politics', *MAS*, 15, 2 (1981), p. 183; Khare, 'Lakṣmeśvar', pp. 25–31.

22 V. V. Khare, *Aitihāsik Lekh Saṃgraha*, 13 (1926), p. 6901; S. G. Vaidya, *Peshwa Bajirao II and the Downfall of the Maratha Power* (Nagpur, 1976), p. 97; *IS*, 7, 7–8–9, 'Peśve Daftarāṇtīl Nivaḍak Kāgadpatre', p. 79; and cf. p. 323.

23 Cf. Bayly, *Rulers, Townsmen and Bazaars*, p. 227.

24 Vaidya, *Peshwa Bajirao II*, p. 10; *EIP*, 4, p. 228; Grant Duff, *History*, 1, pp. 457–8; Divekar, 'Indigenous Business Class', p. 441.

25 Grant Duff, *History*, 1, p. 320; Bayly, *Rulers, Townsmen and Bazaars*, p. 392.

26 Cf. Bayly, *Rulers, Townsmen and Bazaars*, pp. 391–3.

various forms of reliance on private merchant capital were a new feature of the eighteenth-century polities or already obtained in the Mughal Empire before the Deccan invasions is a much debated question. There seems however to be sufficient evidence to conclude that very often Mughal officials lived in reciprocal dependence with financier–merchants already early in the seventeenth century.[27] In any case, under the Marathas we find them not only at every level in the revenue administration but in a host of other activities: as money-changers, brokers, in construction of dams, providing loans to finance military campaigns and loans to cultivators (*tagāī*), in the minting of coins, etc.[28]

The greatest financier–traders of the eighteenth century controlled extensive all-India networks of transactions and wielded either a considerable amount of direct political power or enjoyed influence at the courts in a more indirect way. This was enhanced by the possibility that they could play off one regional ruler against others. In all cases the financiers also became great patrons of religion and donated large amounts of money for temple construction. Thus for instance Gopal Rao Mairal acquired a very prominent position in Baroda, while he had branches (*peṭhs*) of his banking house in Surat, Bombay, Hyderabad, and Gwalior.[29] Another very wealthy banker was Gopalnaik Tambvekar who under the reign of Madhav Rao 'had his establishments from Kāśi to Rāmeśvara' and became known in particular by his extensive loans to Mahadaji Scindhia.[30] The banking house of Patwardhan at Poona had branches in Nasik, Bombay, Aurangabad, and Bijapur.[31] Most striking is the great political power of bankers under Scindhia, Holkar and the Bhonsle of Nagpur; here they not only stood at the head of the revenue administration but also had a

[27] Richards thinks that until the Deccan campaigns the Empire was self-financing and did not depend on private capital; he sees this as a contrast with the decentralized finances of the eighteenth-century successor polities ('Mughal State Finance', pp. 292–4, 299–300). Leonard on the contrary holds that in the Empire financial intermediaries were always important in the land-revenue ('Indigenous Banking Firms in Mughal India: A Reply', *CSSH*, 23 (1981), pp. 309–13). She quotes authorities to support this thesis. The Dutch VOC material supports her view (Van Santen, *Verenigde Oost-Indische Compagnie*, pp. 19, 119–22, 131–2).

[28] *SSRPD*, 3, nos 180, 212, 232, 244; 4, nos 7, 134, 317, 322; 6, no. 742; 7, nos 530, 562, 732; 9, no. 193; Thakur, *Holkarśāhī*, 1, nos 27, 31, 196; Dharmadhikari, 'Gopal Rao Mairal', p. 1; Grant Duff, *History*, 1, p. 549.

[29] Dharmadhikari, 'Gopal Rao Mairal', pp. 7–8.

[30] *IS*, 1, 12 (1909), p. 37.

[31] G. T. Kulkarni, 'Banking in the 18th Century: A Case Study of a Poona Banker', *Artha Vijñāna*, 15 (1973), pp. 180–200.

place in the councils of state.[32] Gopal Paruk, for instance, a minister of Scindhia, and Tantia Jogh, the regent during the minority of Malhar Rao Holkar, were both bankers.[33] Under the Gaikwar of Baroda there were in addition to the above-mentioned Gopal Rao Mairal several other bankers who became very influential.[34] Such evidence from the Northern Maratha states corroborates Karen Leonard's argument about the 'strategic' position of financial and merchant groups in eighteenth-century India in general, a position which she also links to the spread of revenue farming.[35] To what extent the cash-nexus had been a political factor under the Mughals is less obvious.[36] There is no question however that banking firms which became politically powerful under the Marathas had diverted their resources from the Mughals and thus directly contributed to the Mughal 'decline', as Leonard's theory implies.[37] They were all brahmans who rose with the tide of Maratha expansion from the humble position of village accountant or money-lender.[38] It is not very well known what influence bankers had at the Poona court itself. Native development economists of the Gokhale Institute at Poona, such as D. R. Gadgil and more recently V. D. Divekar, tend to see their role as very limited in policy making in eighteenth-century Maharashtra in general and stress their parasitic relationship with Maratha 'war finance' and advance collection of revenue.[39] Both these authors fail to account for the apparently very different situation under the Maratha sardars in Central India and Hindustan where sahukars not only became politically powerful but often played a restorative role in agriculture as revenue farmers.[40] Moreover, Divekar contradicts himself when he describes the 'merchant prince' Brahmendra Svami of Poona who 'by his timely financial help through loans to the Peshwa and sardars . . . made them remain under his personal obligation' and used this position 'for furthering his influence in

32 Malcolm, *Central India*, 2, p. 50; Jenkins, *Nagpur*, p. 80.

33 Malcolm, *Central India*, 2, p. 50. 34 Grant Duff, *History*, 2, p. 261.

35 'Great Firm Theory', pp. 154, 158–9, 161, 165. For further evidence which supports this, see Bayly, *Rulers, Townsmen and Bazaars*, pp. 46, 164, 169–72, 177, 348, 462–3; Cohn, 'Political Systems', p. 314.

36 Van Santen, *Verenigde Oost-Indische Compagnie*, p. 11; Richards, 'Mughal State Finance', p. 291.

37 'Great Firm Theory', pp. 152, 154.

38 Divekar, 'Indigenous Business Class', pp. 427, 436; Dharmadhikari, 'Gopal Rao Mairal', p. 2; Richards, 'Mughal State Finance', pp. 286, 289.

39 Divekar, 'Indigenous Business Class', pp. 427–43; D. R. Gadgil, *Origins of the Modern Indian Business Class: An Interim Report* (New York, 1959), p. 31.

40 Cf. Chapter 4-IV-e.

political affairs'.[41] Brahmendra Svami in this way appears to have been a great help in Baji Rao II's struggle for power and also seems to have had considerable impact on decisions relating to the Sidis in the Konkan.[42] We also know from Grant Duff that already under Baji Rao I a brahman banker Bapuji Naik of Baramati was the hub of a power struggle at court.[43] He had lent money to Baji Rao which the latter could not repay. Raghuji's faction offered great sums to Shahu to have the banker raised to the office of Peshwa after Baji Rao's death. In the end Balaji Baji Rao was invested in 1740 but since he was answerable for his father's debts Bapuji Naik continued to enforce his demands and put him in dire straits. Balaji Baji Rao eventually was relieved only through the credit received from his diwan Mahadaji Pant Purandare.

We do not find the banking houses of the eighteenth century operating as a defined political interest-group in the strict sense. To be sure, for commercial purposes they were not uncommonly organized into corporations with a certain autonomy and self-regulation, but this did not have the implication of sovereignty or sub-sovereignty.[44] Thus for instance a corporation of bankers existed at Indore under the name of the 'Panc Savkars' or 'Five Bankers'; under this organizational form they would press demands with Ahalyabai Holkar against another corporation called the 'Chatnipur savkars' concerning the proportional distribution of a failing debtor's assets.[45] The corporations were in such a case purely an *ad hoc* consortium and nothing but an extension of mercantile activity. On the other hand, as has been seen, the transitions between banking/trading and landholding or agrarian management were becoming more and more fluid.[46] It can be maintained on this account that the cash-nexus was the locus where a link was forged between the complementary orders of regulation and non-regulation. Organized transport and trade of goods and money were always tied up with irregularly mediatized blackmail/protection payments of cash in country and jungle pathways, giving rise to a 'black circuit' of money.[47] Situations also occurred in which bankers employed military men or 'bandits' to prevent

41 'Indigenous Business Class', p. 440. 42 *Ibid.* 43 *History*, I, p. 320.

44 Cf. Bayly, *Rulers, Townsmen and Bazaars*, pp. 174–88; Leonard, 'Banking Firms', p. 189.

45 Thakur, *Holkarśāhī*, I, no. 242.

46 Cf. further Bayly, *Rulers, Townsmen and Bazaars*, pp. 168–72, 188–9, 384; Divekar, 'Indigenous Business Class', p. 441; Heesterman, 'Was there an Indian Reaction', p. 40.

47 Cf. J. C. Heesterman, 'Boer, Bandiet, Bankier en Heilige' (Paper contributed to the KOTA III conference held in Amsterdam, 12–13 May 1982), pp. 5–6.

government officials by force of arms from resuming assignments of land-revenue in which the bankers were financially involved through sub-farming and credit.[48] Or, to illustrate this complementarity further, we find a banker issuing a *huṇḍī* in the name of a sardesai of Rajapur and Dabhol to pay for the *corpaṭṭī* or 'robber-tax' imposed by a group of 'marauders' from Janjira.[49] In the same way the Maratha invaders of Northern India and Gujarat received bills of payment on account of villages which they subjected to the cauth or to cover tribute levies, sometimes running as high as 50 lacs of rupees.[50] The complementarity of regulation and non-regulation existed on an all-India level, but not beyond it. The incursions of the Persian Emperor Nadir Shah in 1739, the Afghan Ahmad Shah Durrani in 1758–62 and Zeman Shah in 1797–9 always caused immediate financial panic and a recession of the credit networks of the great pan-Indian bankers.[51]

IV Revenue farming*

In Absolutist Europe the administrative device called 'farming' covered at most the collection of customs and a number of other indirect taxes.[1] In contrast we find in India and in many Muslim

[48] Thus the following injunction is found in a *tainät jābtā* (*IS*, 7, 7–8–9, 'Peśve Daftarāṇtīl Nivaḍak Kāgadpatre', p. 79): 'mahals and villages are assigned for the upkeep of an army. Out of these you will not on your own account give mahals or villages in saranjam to anyone nor will you give them out to pay off debts to sahukars. There will be no misgivings about the returning of the mahals and villages to the government (sarkar) after two years. Without objection they will be returned and no trouble will be given on account of payments to be made to soldiers and sahukars.' In another instance a saranjam in the Southern Maratha Country, belonging to Madhav Rao Raste, is farmed out to various banker-mamlatdars who had given loans to Raste against these talukas. We hear of this when in 1801 the bankers, rising up in arms, refuse to surrender the territory to the Peshwa, who had sequestrated the saranjam and assigned it to someone else in *kamāvīs* (Khare, *Aitihāsik Lekh Saṃgraha*, 13, p. 6901; Vaidya, *Peshwa Bajirao II*, p. 97). Leonard describes a similar situation in Hyderabad: 'To collect the revenue, and then to prevent the government from reclaiming the land assignments, the bankers employed military men, predominantly Arab and Pathan mercenaries, who acted as their agents' ('Banking Firms', p. 184).

[49] *SSRPD*, 7, no. 495.

[50] Perlin, 'Money-use in Late Pre-colonial India', pp. 28–9, 33, 121; *idem*, 'Precolonial South Asia and Western Penetration', pp. 291–2; Grant Duff, *History*, I, pp. 218, 351.

[51] Bayly, *Rulers, Townsmen and Bazaars*, p. 68.

* Earlier published in another version as 'Maratha Revenue Farming', *MAS*, 17, 4, (1983), pp. 591–628.

[1] R. J. Bonney, 'The Failure of the French Revenue Farms, 1600–60' *Economic History Review*, 2nd ser. XXXII (1979), pp. 11–31; R. Ashton, 'Revenue Farming under the Early Stuarts', *idem*, 2nd ser. VIII (1956), pp. 310–22; Ardant, *Histoire de*

states that, in addition to customs, indirect taxes, and a wide range of less important miscellaneous items, the land-revenue itself could be farmed as well.[2] It is chiefly with the farming of land-revenue that this sub-chapter is concerned. We will attempt to show that under the Maratha régime a variety of forms of land-revenue farming prevailed not only under the much-discredited Baji Rao II,[3] but was also of regular occurrence under comparatively paternalistic rulers like Madhav Rao I and Nana Fadnis, and in fact throughout the seventeenth and eighteenth centuries. Secondly, it will be argued that revenue farming was either a characteristic response to agrarian and financial crisis, or otherwise occurred only under frontier conditions.

First, it may be pointed out that, during at least a part of the Peshwas' rule, the districts on the frontier of the Nizam of Hyderabad were usually farmed out annually,[4] and that this was often also the case with villages lying within the frontiers of neighbouring states.[5] It also appears to have been a common practice in the eighteenth century to farm out the revenue in territories which were shared by two different administrations.[6] When conquering new territories, or in attempting to retrench their own 'inner frontier', the Peshwas introduced imposts, and these too were usually farmed out on account of the great difficulty and

l'Impôt, 2, p. 295, note 2; D. Dessert, *Argent, Pouvoir et Société au Grand Siècle* (Paris, 1985).

2 For the Muslim régimes, see esp. S. J. Shaw, *The Financial and Administrative Organization and Development of Ottoman Egypt, 1517–1798* (Princeton, 1962), pp. 5, 8, 14, 21–7, 31–5, 38 ff.; F. Løkkegaard, *Islamic Taxation in the Classic Period* (Copenhagen, 1950), ch. IV; *Encyclopaedia of Islam*, s.v. *iḳṭāʿ* and *kharādj*. To understand the importance of land-revenue farming it should be kept in mind that in the East generally the land-revenue made up a proportionately much larger share of the state budget than in *ancien régime* Europe (Ardant, *Histoire de l'Impôt*; *idem*, 'Financial Policy').

3 Much, if not all, of the discredit came from the British. Still, at one place, Elphinstone wrote that Baji Rao II was 'scrupulously just in pecuniary transactions' (Letter to the Governor-General of 1815, quoted in Thompson, *Indian Princes*, p. 201). From the Indian side, an attempt at the Peshwa's rehabilitation was made by S. G. Vaidya in *Peshwa Bajirao II.*

4 *EIP*, 4, p. 630. 5 *EIP*, 4, p. 745.

6 Thus in territories shared with the Sidi of Janjira (Vad, Mawji and Parasnis, *Treaties*, p. 108), in the territories of Broach shared by the Peshwa and Scindhia (Sardesai, *Historical Papers relating to Mahadji Sindhia*, no. 282), and in the Mughal Deccan and Karnataka where the Marathas collected *cauth* and *sardeśmukhī* (Malik, 'Chauth Collection in Hyderabad', p. 340; Grant Duff, *History*, 1, p. 333).

uncertainty of realizing them.[7] Yet, it is not revenue farming on the frontier of states that will be discussed here, but rather revenue farming on the frontier of agriculture and wasteland. We will demonstrate that revenue farming was one of the organizational means of agrarian restoration and expansion, internal as well as external. To bring out the relevance of this observation, it may perhaps be useful to recall that the *communis opinio* on the subject has always been the opposite. W. H. Moreland, for instance, is representative of this when he says that the existence of revenue farming connotes . . . 'two things, obstacles in the way of detailed control, and emphasis on the financial as opposed to the ameliorative side of administration'.[8]

As a response to financial crisis, it is notable that farming of the revenue became general after 1761, the year in which the Maratha army was almost completely annihilated by the Afghans in the Battle of Panipat. Peshwa Madhav Rao I writes in his will of 1772 that both in the Konkan and the Desh the rayats are 'oppressed' due to revenue farming, and he pleads for its abolition and substitution by 'regular management', in order to 'give protection to the subjects'.[9] There can be no doubt that where the degree of 'detailed control' was low, revenue farming could easily become 'oppressive'. In practice, however, the measure of state-control exercised over a farm could vary greatly. In the Indian terminology, a tenure could be held *pakkā* ('unsupervised') or *kaccā*, i.e., with the obligation to render accounts and submit to auditing by the court or *huzūr*.[10] The degree to which a farm was *pakkā* or *kaccā* fluctuated. Control over a farm would increase or decrease inversely with the amount of risk that the state intended to devolve upon

7 E.g. imposts on hill-tribes were farmed out (Jervis, *Konkan*, p. 113), or the tribute collected from zamindars in the early stage of the conquest of Malwa (Gordon, 'Slow Conquest', p. 17).

8 *Akbar to Aurangzeb*, p. 236. As more-or-less articulate exceptions to this view we may mention: Singh, *Jaipur*; Barnett, *North India*; Shaw, *Ottoman Egypt*; Karpat, 'Stages of Ottoman History'; Bayly, *Rulers, Townsmen and Bazaars* (esp. pp. 17, 43, 45–6, 164–7); Richards, *Golconda* (esp. p. 25); Alam, *Mughal Centre* (esp. pp. 27–8, 38, 132–3, 154, 215, 238, 242). The latter studies tend to confirm much of what is proposed here.

9 *IS*, 6, 10–11–12 (1915), 'Aitihāsik Sfuṭ Lekh', p. 97. The spread of revenue farming during the minority of Madhav Rao I is also noted in *B.A.: R.D.*, vol. 59/746 of 1836, p. 195.

10 The terms occur *passim* in the Marathi documentation. Short general discussions of their application can be found in Moreland, *Akbar to Aurangzeb*, p. 235; *idem*, *India at the Death of Akbar* (London, 1920), pp. 31–3; Khaur Dhot, 'Taxation and Economy of North Gujarat'.

the farmer. Thus a *kaccā* tenure could sometimes temporarily become relatively or entirely *pakkā*. This was the case under farming. And so the complete absence of state-supervision can hardly be seen as one of its essential properties. But even in its most unalloyed form, revenue farming did not normally have a destructive effect upon agriculture in either the short or the long term. It would be seen as 'oppressive' where the legitimate king's share (*rājbhāg*) of the agricultural produce no longer represented the limit of a demand which was increased arbitrarily by an uncontrolled revenue farmer imposing extra cesses or raising the assessment rates. Commonly then, farming, as is already evident in the earliest Arabic literature on *kharāj*, was denounced as *fasād*, 'tyranny', or *ẓulm* (Mar.*zulūm*), 'oppression' because it disrupted the universalist order of the unitary state; and since it meant the suspension of dualist management it also meant that 'justice ('*adl*) between men' could be endangered, in other words that the existing order of society could be upset.[11] 'Justice' was a balance between interests which was supervised and had to be maintained by the king. *Ẓulm* or 'oppression' meant literally 'putting a thing in a place not its own' or 'transgressing the proper limit'. And it appears that this refers primarily to the levelling effects that, as will be seen, revenue farming in its more extreme manifestations often had. Yet, even oppression in our sense, as distinct from a restructuring of the old order of rights, could very well coexist with the promotion of agriculture. A prolonged increase in the revenue demand presupposed the stimulation rather than the neglect of cultivation; and only when working under a fixed contract would a local revenue official be directly induced by self-interest to attempt to increase the collections. In 1804, after the invasion by Holkar in 1802, the failure of the rains and the subsequent famine in 1803, which brought ruin from Poona to as far as Berar and Khandesh,[12] Baji Rao II introduced a system of farming by annual auctions to the highest bidders on a nearly universal scale. It operated without the consideration for eventualities or the preventive checks that formerly softened the impact of farming, and it spread to all levels of the administration. Nevertheless, as even the British admitted, in 1818 the state of agriculture had much improved from what it was at

[11] Cf. Abu Yusuf, *Kitāb al-Kharāj* (Cairo, 1887), 'faḍl fī taqbīl . . . etc.'; translation: E. Fagnan, *Le Livre de L'Impôt Foncier* (Paris, 1921), pp. 159–84; Wafi, *Muqaddima*, I, p. 416; Mottahedeh, *Loyalty and Leadership*, p. 179.

[12] Thompson, *Indian Princes*, p. 47; *B.A.: R.D.*, vol. 11/698 of 1836, p. 87; Vaidya, *Peshwa Bajirao II*, pp. 179–80; *BG*, XVIII, pt. II, p. 339.

the beginning of the century. 'Under Baji Rao', wrote R. Shortrede in 1835, 'the assessment appears to have risen in a few years to the full rate, at or beyond which it continued till we got the country'.[13] Elphinstone stated in a Marathi proclamation of February 1818 that 'the farmers which were contracted by Baji Rao levied too much revenue', but 'despite of that, the country became very populous and prosperous'.[14] This prosperity was then ascribed to 'British protection'.[15] While the British, on the one hand, frankly admitted that Wellesley's subsidiary system rendered every Indian ruler who was subjected to it 'cruel and avaricious, by showing him that he has nothing to fear from the hatred of his subjects',[16] they continued to regard the farming of the land-revenue *per se* as the most pernicious system of administration they had ever encountered. Thus the only intentional innovation they initially effected in the Maratha system of revenue management – the abolition of farming – became the first 'blessing' of the new British dominion.

a. Terminology

In order to identify the typical characteristics of farming, we will first, in this section, discuss the terminology which was used to describe it. Then, in the following sections, we will situate farming rights in the context of other rights, like those of village headmen or *pāṭīls* (section b.), *zamīndārs* (section c.), tributary chiefs (section d.), and 'assignees' (section e.). The object of this analysis is to show that the transitions between these different tenurial forms and farming rights proper are very fluid, and that farming as a restorative mechanism pervades the entire system of landed rights.

13 *B.A.: R.D.*, *loc. cit.* This is also acknowledged in Grant Duff, *History*, 2, p. 337.

14 Sardesai, Kale and Vakaskar, *Aitihāsik Patreṇ*, p. 468; 'Substance of a Maratha Proclamation issued on the 11th February 1818 by the Honourable Mountstuart Elphinstone, sole Commissioner for the settlement of the territories conquered from the Paishwa', *PRC*, 13, p. 299.

15 Cf. Governor-General to H. H. the Peshwa, 20 January 1816, *PRC*, 13, p. 17: 'Under the influence of this alliance with the British government the prosperity of your country has increased'; 'Substance of a Mahratta Proclamation', *op. cit.*, p. 300: 'Since then in spite of the farming system and the exactions of Baji Rao's officers, the country has completely recovered through the protection afforded it by the British Government'; *BG*, XVIII, pt. II, p. 341: 'In spite of the exactions of the farmers which reduced almost all the landholders of the district to one level, so great was the advantage of the security ensured by the British protectorate that in the thirteen years before the overthrow of the Peshwa in 1817 the district [i.e., Poona] increased greatly in wealth'.

16 T. Munro to Governor-General, 12 August 1817, quoted in Thompson, *Indian Princes*, p. 23.

The word most commonly used to describe a farm of land-revenue, of customs-duties (*zakāt*), or of any other item, is *maktā* (Ar. *maqṭa*ʻ; corrupt from *makṣtā*). It was applied, in this sense, interchangeably with *ijārā* (Ar. *ijāra*;[17] also *ijāratī*), or with *gutkā* (Mar.; also *guttā* or *gutā*),[18] and, generally in the Konkan, with *khotī* (Mar.). *Maktā* could also indicate the *amount* (*berīj*; of cash and proceeds in kind) which was to be paid for the farm, instead of the farm itself, so that for a certain village we may find for instance the *maktā* specified for a number of years next to the 'profit of the *khotī*' (*khotīcā nafā*), which is specified when the *khotī* is (temporarily or permanently) managed by an agent of the government, but normally left undetermined.[19]

Apart from the usual meaning we found in the seventeenth century, under Malik Ambar's *tankhā* settlement, the same term *maktā* used for a form of 'group assessment', a contract with the body of cultivators of a village as a whole, concluded *permanently* with the same principal aim of encouraging agricultural expansion.[20] This latter contract differs from a farm, firstly, by being permanently fixed from the beginning; secondly, by being concluded directly with the cultivators themselves; and thirdly, by having been concluded with reference only to the assessment of the production capacity of the village, independently of any bargaining. When *maktā*, as in this case, denotes a 'permanent contract', it is always a deviation from its normal use, which implies a limited duration. A similar transition occurs only with the term *khotī*, which could denote specifically a type of 'hereditary farm' occurring in the Southern Konkan. The hereditary *khotī* was however originally obtained through bargaining by an individual (see section f.).

Next, to describe a 'cultivation contract' some of the same terms are used as for a farm. The term *gutkā* we find, in some of the

[17] The *Encyclopaedia of Islam* defines *ijāra* (s.v. *idjāra*) as 'the contract by which one person makes over to someone else the enjoyment, by personal right, of a thing or of an activity, in return for payment'. It adds that the period of the *ijāra* has to be stated, but that no limit is necessarily fixed. In the context of farming, we should not interpret such a 'contract' in the exclusive sense of continental legal theory, which postulates 'sovereignty' as the indivisible attribute of the modern state, and hence regards the acts of its functionaries as the exercise of 'public duties' – and not as obligations deriving from a contract. It should be viewed here rather as 'shared sovereignty'.

[18] Sardesai, *Historical Papers relating to Mahadji Sindhia*,, no. 282; *SPD*, 10, p. 49; *MITSA*, 1, p. 57; *SCS*, 3, no. 465.

[19] *SSRPD*, 3, no. 405. [20] Cf. p. 261.

districts of the Southern Maratha Country, applied to a type of holding of land for which the cultivator made a specific bargain with the *pāṭīl*, the rate fluctuating, with option of tillage, and which was concluded for a limited period only.[21] Here it was one of five tenures under which government land was held, the other four having fixed rates of assessment (i.e., they were not subject to bargaining) and obligatory cultivation (on the most heavily assessed land) or being *istāvā kaul.* This last was also a 'contract' or *maktā* tenure held on a low rate, to be increased each year, until it reached the level of the full assessment for bringing wasteland under cultivation. Elsewhere, like in Kolhapur, a cultivation contract was denoted by the composite term *khaṇḍmaktā*, indicating a tenure under which land was held on an annually changing contract, as opposed to *acalkhaṇḍ*, land held on a contract with a fixed rate; both these contract tenures coexisted with a sharing arrangement (*bhāg zamīn*) and the usual tenures of hereditary (*mirāsī*) and temporary (*uparī*) cultivators with fixed rates of assessment, and with *kaul*.[22] The term *maktā guttā* is found as far north as Khandesh, where it signified a similar contract between tenant and patil on favourable terms.[23] In the Maratha territories of the Deccan generally the temporary cultivators paid lower rates than the hereditary ones and often the agreement by which the former held their tenures from the patil was also called *maktā* or *khaṇḍmaktā*.[24] In the Konkan there were cultivators, called *maktākarīs*, who could bargain for more favourable terms with their *khots*, the village renters.[25] The continuity between the two common meanings of *gutkā* and *maktā* and their compounds lies in the element of bargaining that both a 'cultivation contract' and a 'revenue farm' characteristically involve, and through which the two or more parties concerned arrive at an agreement by which an income or work of variable amount is let for a sum which becomes thus 'fixed' for a specified period of time.[26] A revenue farm differs from a cultivation contract by being always at least at one remove from the soil.

[21] Marshall, *Statistical Reports*, pp. 25–6, 159; *BGS*, o.s. no. 12, p. 5.

[22] Marshall, *Statistical Reports*, pp. 25–6, 159; *BGS*, n.s. no. 8, p. 65.

[23] *EIP*, 4, p. 695. [24] *BG*, XIX, p.324; *EIP*, 4, pp. 468, 651–2.

[25] E. T. Candy, 'Selections, with Notes, from the Records of Government, regarding the Khoti Tenure', *BGS*, n.s. no. 134 (Bombay, 1873), p. 19.

[26] To give out a village in *maktā*, as in *SSRPD*, 3, no. 412, 'from the year ... onwards', is very exceptional. Almost always a *maktā* will be qualified as *eksālā* (one-year), *dosālā* (two-year), *tīsālā* (three-year), *causālā* (four-year), etc.

b. Village headmen

At times the village headmen (*pāṭīls*) could hardly be distinguished from 'village farmers', and were not essentially different from the revenue farmers above them. Normally, however, under the Maratha government, the *pāṭīls* were not the farmers of their villages. In Northern India, Akbar was probably the first to have explicitly forbidden the practice of making a summary settlement under which the headmen contracted to pay a lump sum for their villages.[27] Parallel to this in the Deccan, before the introduction of the *tankhā* or 'permanent village settlement', *pāṭīls* held no regular assignments of either land or money from the government, but remunerated themselves entirely from the surplus revenue of their villages, which they farmed from an intermediary collection agent or subfarmed from the farmer of the district.[28] Under Malik Ambar and Murshid Quli Khan, in the seventeenth century, the patils were still under obligation to raise a certain fixed sum (the *tankhā*) from their villages, and later it was through their agency that 'extra collections' (*śivāy jamā*) were realized. But at this time they held their (hereditary) offices directly from the government and received the proceeds of *inām* land as their remuneration, besides enjoying *haks* or 'dues' from the cultivators, of whom they were the representatives. Since the village was permanently assessed on the basis of measurement and differentiation of the land, bargaining for the amount to be paid was out of the question. At most the patils could contrive to increase their profits through the authority which was left to them to distribute remissions given by the government in case of disturbances or harvest failures. For a long time they enjoyed a considerable latitude to dispose of the fund for 'village expenses' (*sādilvārī*) but this was strongly curtailed under the Peshwas, when these expenses were entered in the regular government rent-roll (*jamābaṇḍī*). Under the Peshwas the settlement remained *mauzevār*, and the patils' scope for manipulation with the internal, individual (*kuḷvār*) distribution of the assessment, and especially with the letting out of *inām* lands, may well have increased during the eighteenth century. This could have happened as the village population became more heterogeneous, no longer mostly consisting of a hereditary core of *mirāsdārs*, but

[27] Moreland, *Akbar to Aurangzeb*, p. 250; *idem*, *Agrarian System*, p. 9; Habib, *Agrarian System*, pp. 232, 234.

[28] Cf. Chapter 3–II.

now for a large part made up of temporary *uparīs*. In the second half of the eighteenth century the assessment of the village had everywhere become subject to annual revisions. These revisions were however based on a calculation of the increase or decrease of cultivation. A *rayatvār* settlement was not uncommonly made by revenue farmers, if they chose to eliminate the patil. But the annual assessment revision did not imply such a settlement, and it was only resorted to if the village was thought to conceal resources or had slipped out of the authority of the patil.

If, in the eighteenth century, we meet with *pāṭilkī* rights held on *ijārā* terms from the government, the origin of these could be twofold. Firstly, the *pāṭilkī* of a deserted and desolate village could be given out in *ijārā* to have it repopulated and brought back under cultivation.[29] Secondly, an *ijāradār-pāṭīl* could be engaged when, through lack of heirs, a *pāṭilkī* had come into the hands of the government. This, according to Jenkins, had become the normal practice under the Maratha government of Nagpur, where formerly a *pāṭīl* without heirs would be allowed to adopt, or else the *pāṭilkī* would be sold by the government.[30] In these two ways – and later, under Baji Rao II, also through subfarming from the district level downwards – the patils could temporarily become revenue farmers. Their bargaining power they then actually derived from being part of the hereditary gentry. As such they were not removable at will, their position resembling that of the *zamīndārs* discussed in the next section.

c. Zamīndārs

In the Mughal Empire, under Akbar and during most of the seventeenth century, revenue farming was discouraged by the court, but it was applied, when occasion demanded, with the intention of restoring to prosperity villages with a considerably reduced *jama*'.[31] This is (prematurely) considered to have been uncommon in most provinces until later in the régime of Aurangzeb and after. In the Deccan Sultanates, on the contrary, we know it to

29 For an example, see *MIS*, 22, no. 21 (of 1792): '*mauze ālaṇd p. zāfarābād yā gāṇvcī pāṭilkī dārkojī nāīk yāṇcī āhe tethīl ijārā āṇkhā pr. ṭharāūn ābādī jhālī*.'
30 Jenkins, *Nagpur*, p. 95.
31 Siddiqi, *Land Revenue Administration*, pp. 43, 95; Habib *Agrarian System*, p. 235; Moreland, *Agrarian System*, p. 112; *idem*, *Death of Akbar*, pp. 31, 33.

have been always very widespread.[32] The Deccan, indeed, was the realm of the *pakkā* tenures.[33] Jagirdars and collectors of the government or farmers of whole districts farmed out the revenues of their territories to the *zamīndārs* who again subfarmed them to the village headmen. In Ahmadnagar, Malik Ambar, by making a settlement directly with the village, temporarily brought this to an end.[34] At the same time an exception was made for the village farmers of the Konkan, *ijāradārs* or *khots*, many of whom were hereditary since the sixteenth century, when they were first introduced as part of an effort to resettle villages which had fallen waste. Under prohibition of extra cesses and forced labour demands,[35] these *khotī* tenures, of usually one or a few villages,[36] fairly easily fell in line with the *tankhā* settlement of Malik Ambar and the later settlements along similar lines of Murshid Quli Khan and Shivaji.[37]

According to T. B. Jervis, Malik Ambar brought 'the intermediate revenue agency which had been gradually usurping the character of the farming system' to terms with a definite assignment in money and a percentage of the collections.[38] It is however abundantly clear now, that this latter change was made only under the later settlement of the Marathas, when the hereditary rights or *vatans* of the zamindars were put under sequestration. Under the Ahmadnagar system the hereditary district revenue agents were continued in the enjoyment of revenue-exempt lands and villages and *haks*.[39] Prior to Malik Ambar's reform, the *deśmukhs* and *deśpāṇḍes*, in their capacity of revenue farmers, had already arrogated to themselves all kinds of immunities in the form of *inām*, etc.; after this reform they ceased to be farmers, but were not dispossessed of their *ināms*. When the conflict with the Mughals regained intensity, the old conditions reimposed themselves, and already two years after Malik Ambar's death we find evidence of zamindars holding their districts in farm on *istāvā* leases.[40] One of the bakhars also states that the Mughals had resorted to farming in

32 Moreland, *Akbar to Aurangzeb*, pp. 239, 243, 245; idem, *Agrarian System*, p. 187; *EIP*, 4, p. 667. Alam, *Mughal Centre*, contends that revenue farming was also a widespread practice under the Mughals in the seventeenth century (p. 133).

33 Moreland, *Death of Akbar*, pp. 31–3.

34 Cf. Chapter 3–II.

35 *BISMQ*, 28, 3–4 (1948), p. 1.

36 Only later, in the eighteenth century, are whole parganas sometimes given out on the *khotī* tenure (*SSRPD*, 3, no. 408).

37 Their continued existence into the eighteenth century testifies to this, but it is also made explicit in the documents (*BISMQ*, 21, 1 (1940), pp. 179–80; B. P. Oak, *Oak Gharāṇyācā Itihās* (Poona, 1973), pp. 251–3.

38 *Konkan*, p. 66.

39 Cf. Chapter 3–II.

40 *SCS*, 4, no. 751.

some of the districts which had been given in jagir to Shahaji Bhonsle.[41] And Sabhasad describes as follows the accomplishments of Shivaji:

The Adil Shahi, the Nizam Shahi, and the Mughal Desh were conquered [by Shivaji]. In the Desh all the rayats were in the power of local patils and kulkarnis and deśmukhs. By them the collections (*kamāvisī*) used to be made; and extra cesses (*mogham ṭakkā*) used to be given to them. If in a village the mirasdars [read: *zamīndārs*] took one to two thousand, they used to give two or three hundred as *khaṇḍmaktā* to the government. . . . But Shivaji left nothing in the power of the mirasdars. And he sequestrated (*amānat karūn*) everything that the mirasdars used to take of their own will as *inām* or *ijāratī*, and he fixed the dues in grain and cash for the *zamī(n)dārs*, as well as the rights and perquisites (*hakk*) of the deśmukhs, the deśkulkarnis, and the patils and kulkarnis, according to the capacity of the villages.[42]

Significant in this passage is the use of the term *khaṇḍmaktā* for the payment these *zamīndār–ijāradārs* used to make to the government. The amount of this 'fixed sum' was a function of the zamindars' bargaining power in their relation with that government; as says Sabhasad, 'if the government ordered them to pay more, they stood up in resistance'.[43]

Such a situation, in which the zamindars obtained farming, or similar, rights was typical of all 'marginally subdued' territory.[44] Shivaji's arrangements did not outlast the Mughal invasion at the turn of the seventeenth century. And even before that time, in parts of the Deccan and the Central Konkan, revenue farming was reintroduced under his son Sambhaji in 1683.[45] It is not unlikely that farming became yet more general during the subsequent Mughal campaign and Rajaram's absence at Jinji.[46] After the campaign, and already in the last decade of the seventeenth century, the position of the hereditary *zamīndārs* (or *mirāsdārs* as they were often called in the early period) was regulated under Rajaram and Shahu by means of grants or restitutions of *ināms*. If their tasks of administration and the settling of the leases and

41 Hervadkar, *Saptaprakaraṇātmak Caritra*, p. 30.
42 Vakaskar, *Sabhāsadācī Bakhar*, p. 30.
43 *Ibid.*
44 See on this also Gordon, 'Slow Conquest', pp. 16–17; Grant Duff, *History*, 1, pp. 66, 70.
45 Jervis, *Konkan*, p. 108; Grant Duff, *History*, 1, pp. 174–5; *SCS*, 3, no. 422; Ranade, *Rise of Maratha Power*, p. 176.
46 Cf. Grant Duff, *History*, 1, pp. 233–4.

ground-taxes necessitated bigger inputs of time and money they might receive *izāfat* or 'additional' villages. These were, like the *ināms*, always hereditary and rent-free, and, with them and the haks and a small percentage of the government collections, constituted their official remuneration. Like the patils, they were no longer farmers of the revenues of their villages or talukas. Again like the patils, they could later be transformed into farmers again,[47] but it seems to have been particularly this class of hereditary zamindars which suffered badly at the hands of the Peshwas' farmers, especially those of Baji Rao II.[48]

d. Tributary chiefs

Everywhere in the Maratha dominions, and most of all in the outlying regions, there were numerous *saṃsthāniks* or quasi-independent chiefs with titles like *rājā*, *nāīk*, etc., who were liable to pay a tribute – usually called *khaṇḍaṇī* or *peśkaś* – but who were left with the internal revenue management of their territories.[49] 'From the purely fiscal standpoint', as Moreland put the case of their counterparts in the Mughal Empire, their status approached that of revenue farmers.[50] The term *peśkaś* could be used in an Adil Shahi sanad to denote the payment due to the state from a *khot*, when stating that the khotship had been transferred to someone else in consideration of a higher '*peśkaś*';[51] but in the Southern Maratha Country the same word commonly described the 'tribute' which the Marathas levied in a lump sum from many of the local *pāḷegārs*, whose revenue affairs were not interfered with. *Peśkaś* was also paid by the great and small Rajput princes in Malwa and Central India.[52] Elsewhere in this region the initial administrative arrangements of the Marathas had mostly consisted of agreements about the payment of *khaṇḍaṇī* with the large zamindars.[53] *Khaṇḍaṇī* was a lump-payment due each year and came into use following an earlier stage when military campaigns brought in plunder or resulted in the levying of *rakhvālī*, 'protection money'

47 This appears to have been the case, for instance, with the *desāīs* in Surat (*BG*, II, p. 214).

48 See the statement by Marriott, 14 August 1820, quoted in *BG*, XIII, pt. II, p. 555; *BG*, XVIII, pt. II, pp. 340–1; and section g.

49 The tribute included about 10% *darbārkharc* or *aṇtastha*, i.e., 'secret payments' (cf. section h.). Numerous examples occur in *SSRPD*, 9, pp. 245–92.

50 Moreland, *Agrarian System*, p. 10; *idem*, *Akbar to Aurangzeb*, p. 236.

51 Choksey, *Ratnagiri*, p. 139.

52 Malcolm, *Central India*, 2, p. 60.

53 Gordon, 'Slow Conquest', pp. 15–16.

paid incidentally for support or as the price for exemption from devastation.[54] It was not until a later stage that the collections were beginning to be made to conform to an assessment of agricultural potential. The fixing of the amount of the tribute, as well as later fluctuations in it, would always be the result of a process of negotiation, reflecting the unequal strength of the parties involved. Thus, after the capture of Ahmadabad in 1753, the chiefs in the outlying parts of the province were left in the free possession of their lands, and they retained that position until their transfer to the British in 1803, as long as they did not become openly hostile. But the tribute they had to pay was gradually *raised* when the power of the Maratha government to enforce its demands increased. Similar to this was the position of the *udhaḍ* or 'lump sum' villages, mostly owned by *mavāsī* chiefs in Gujarat; and that of the so-called *malikī* villages in Kaira which were originally rent-free and for more than 200 years continued to be so, but were early in the eighteenth century subjected to the payment of a fixed lump-assessment or *udhaḍ jamābaṇdī* by the Marathas. In the latter case, the *maliks* could immediately raise their claims on their tenants by imposing a new cess.

It appears from the documents that some of the *saṃsthāniks* were granted remission of a part of their tribute, when their territory had been laid waste by an enemy during an attack, under which they had remained loyal.[55] Such consideration could be shown under farming conditions but was certainly atypical of revenue farming in its 'hard' form. And while the collections from tributary chiefs were generally in arrears and formed the most continually fluctuating source of income of the government,[56] farming always led to a stabilization of the collections. Then, many (if not all) *saṃsthāniks* had to perform military service and supply troops, provisions, and ammunitions when called upon,[57] an aspect of their tenure which brought them closer to military assignees (*fauj-saraṇjāmdārs* or *mokāsadārs*) than to revenue farmers. A still more fundamental difference between these tributary chieftains and revenue farmers as such lies in the fact that the former, like the patils and zamindars, normally held their lands hereditarily for an indefinite period, while the latter held them temporarily, for a definite, and usually much shorter, period. This difference is clearly brought out in the

54 *Ibid.* 55 *SSRPD*, 9, nos 272, 277.
56 Malcolm, *Central India*, 2, p. 60; Gordon, 'Slow Conquest', p. 17.
57 *SSRPD*, 9, nos 294, 299.

Peshwa's objections to British proposals in 1813 to renew the *ten-year* Ahmadabad farm to the Gaikwar of Baroda, when he states that 'if he was to go on from ten years to ten years, renewing the lease, he might as well give up the place once for all, securing only a regular tribute'.[58] In eighteenth-century Bengal (and Awadh) a whole class of hereditary zamindars – often called *rājās* or *mahārājas* – and talukdars developed out of revenue farming by officials and bankers, who replaced, after outbidding them, the older zamindars.[59] Under the Marathas a comparable development took place, or rather continued, in a systematic way only in the Southern Konkan where many of the *khots* assumed the place of hereditary chieftains, but – in contrast with Bengal – essentially on the village level.

e. 'Revenue assignments' and 'revenue farms'

The payment of the government officials which were called *kamāvīsdārs* and *māmlatdārs* could take different forms. It could be fixed as a percentage of the revenue under their charge, often of the revenue which they paid in advance as *rasad*, or as a stipulated sum, but it could also be left undetermined under a farming contract (*maktā*). The latter condition, as we will see, characterised attempts to restore or expand cultivation over a relatively wide area and always entailed a process of bidding and competition on the part of the kamavisdars and mamlatdars. In the first two cases the amount of revenue to be realized was, like the *jamā* or 'valuation' of the assignments of *saraṇjāmdārs*, normally not subject to bargaining, and calculated entirely on the basis of estimates of the production capacity of the land. Yet we do find, already in the early 1760s, a *kamāvīsdār* on a fixed payment asking the government for a promise that his *māmlat* would not be taken from him in the current year, but would be continued during the next, if he agreed to the terms that might be offered by others; and that, in case it was transferred to another incumbent, he would be allowed to collect the arrears (of the revenue paid in advance) due to him. The huzur then informed him that he would not lose his *māmlat* in this year if he continued to serve without committing fraud, and if he rendered

[58] M. Elphinstone to the Earl of Moira, 5 November 1813, *PRC*, 12, p. 301.
[59] J. *Sarkar, The History of Bengal: Muslim Period, 1200–1757* (Patna, 1973), p. 409; Siddiqi, *Land Revenue Administration*, pp. 98–99; Alam, *Mughal Centre*, p. 238.

accounts.[60] This shows that bargaining for a *kamāvīs* assignment did take place, at least sometimes.[61] But in general the assignments in the strict sense were completely *kaccā*. As is stated in a contemporary 'Account of the revenue management of the Peshwa's territory during the administration of Nana Fadnis', they were 'conferred on persons of trust without reference to any special agreement in respect to the amount of the revenue proposed to be drawn from the districts'.[62]

These officials, then, not being primarily speculators, were remunerated in principally two ways. The first was by means of a salary (*vetan*, *muśahira* or *muśāra*). This may be given as 4 or 5% of the *rasad*, the part of the revenue paid in advance,[63] but the rate of the salary was never directly correlated to the revenue actually realized, so that an increase of the revenue due to extra efforts on the part of the *kamāvīsdār* would not automatically result in an increase in his salary. Nor would a smaller revenue imply a decrease of it. Under these circumstances the fluctuations of the revenue were primarily the concern of the huzur itself, and not of the officials. The huzur took the risks *and* the extra profits of the assignment. Some sanads explicate that 'if the *rasad* is not collected from the mahal, it will be returned (to the kamavisdar) with the interest'.[64] Inducements to a kamavisdar were given out separately in the sanad. It may be put to him for instance that

> if at the end of the year the amin [the chief assessment official] communicates [to the huzur] that the rayats have prospered and the government profited by the management of these parganas, the *kamāvīsdār* will be given an addition to his salary (*vetan*).[65]

In general the amounts of the allowances (and of unauthorized income) of the officials must have varied greatly and were not uniformly standardized.[66] The *rasad*, as we have seen, was usually advanced by bankers (*sāhukārs*) by means of an exchange-bill (*huṇḍīpatra*), indirectly to the kamavisdars or directly to the huzur

60 *SSRPD*, 7, no. 441.

61 Similar implications seem to have *ibid.*, nos 443, 445 and *ibid.*, 3, nos 340, 431. See also Broughton, *Letters from a Marhatta Camp*, p. 147.

62 *EIP*, 4, p. 624.

63 *SSRPD*, 3, nos 407, 409, 420. According to Gordon, in Malwa, in the period 1740–60, the Peshwa's kamavisdars received 4% of the *rasad*, which varied from 1/3 to 1/2, and was as low as 1/10 in the early period of administration ('Slow Conquest', pp. 22, 32).

64 *SSRPD*, 3, no. 407; nearly identical formulas in *ibid.*, nos 409, 420.

65 *Ibid.*, no. 431.

66 Cf. *EIP*, 4, p. 745.

as in Central India where the bankers would then often become farmers of the land-revenue themselves.[67]

The second method of remuneration was by giving the *kamāvīs* or *māmlat* in farm. Regular references to this practice occur in the Peshwas' Diaries throughout the second half of the eighteenth century. The holder of such a *kamāvīs* or *māmlat* might be designated as *maktedār* or *ijāradār*, but he could also continue to be referred to as *kamāvīsdār* or *māmlatdār*; and this was the case even under Baji Rao II's system.[68] Yet there were material differences between the earlier forms of farming of *kamāvīs* and the system of farming of the last Peshwa. One of these lay in the method of recruiting the farmer–assignees. But there were others as well.

When in 1764 the *kamāvīs* of pargana Bose is given in farm (*maktā*), a yearly increasing amount of revenue is stipulated for a term of five years (*pāṇcsālā istāviyācī berīj*), ranging from 40,000 rupees in the first year to 50,001 rupees in the fifth.[69] Part of this had to be paid in advance as *rasad*, against the interest of 1%. It is stated in the sanad that 'in conformity with the *istāvā* the loss or profit [resulting from the farm] is the kamavisdar's (*istāvā kelā āhe yāṇmadhyeṇ toṭā nafā kamāvīsdārācā*)'. Such *istāvā* farms, either of whole tarfs or of a single kasba or a number of villages, are frequent in this period: during four or five years increasing amounts of revenue are to be paid; these are fixed for each year in the sanad, which usually contains the injunction that the increase in the amounts should not be made good by undue exactions from the rayats, but by increasing the revenue by the extension of cultivation. The renewal of the farm to the same incumbent may even be made conditional on this extension of the cultivated area. In nearly all cases accounts are demanded from the farmer–kamavisdar and it is stipulated that he should employ karkuns, like a *faḍṇīs* or 'deputy auditor' and a *majumdār* or 'accountant', appointed directly by the huzur under a sanad, for the clerical work. Finally, he may be ordered to measure the cultivated lands and to fix rates per bigha.[70] With salaried kamavisdars it was the standard practice to include in their sanads the injunction to extend the cultivation by giving *istāvā* leases to the cultivators.[71] But these farms were the means to restore areas which had fallen behind their normal

[67] Cf. p. 334.
[68] Cf. *P.A.: List 11, Nasik Records*, vol. 1, no. 161 of 1850, ff.
[69] *SSRPD*, 3, no. 447. [70] *Ibid.*, nos 410, 414, 425, 427, 430.
[71] *SSRPD*, 3, nos 431 ff, 456.

productivity, yet were not totally ruined. In the Peshwa's dominions in Malwa, in 1751, out of the regularly administered revenue of 2.1 million rupees about 1.5 million were collected under *istāvā maktā*.[72] Here we see clearly how this caused the collections in a large newly conquered area to become more predictable and also how it necessitated the farmers to come to a *rayatvāri* settlement.[73] In comparison with the salaried kamavisdar, the farmer probably had some more room to levy extra cesses from the cultivators. He also bore more risk, and his income was more liable to fluctuations. A *pāhāṇī* or 'inspection' of the land would be a provisional determinant of the height of the *maktā*; bargaining, within limits, could alter it.[74]

In other cases, where the amount of revenue to be drawn from the *maktā* or *ijārā* is maintained on the same level throughout the stipulated period, similar injunctions are found 'not to over-assess the rayats',[75] and remissions (*majurā*, *sūṭ*) are given or promised on account of invasions or plunderings.[76] Such recompense *together with* all forms of accounting by government-appointed clerks was to be abandoned under Baji Rao II. But the instances of farming in the eighteenth century show dissimilarities as well as similarities with the later system. When in 1750 the seven-year *maktā* of tarf Nane Maval comes to an end and a karkun is sent by the government to inspect, in co-operation with the zamindars, the lands and fix the assessment (*ākār*) which has to serve as an index for the incoming *māmlatdār* who is taking over the revenue collection on non-farming terms in the next year, this change of management is stated to be effected 'at the request of the rayats'.[77] This fact is doubly significant as it shows firstly that the farmer was left sufficient freedom in the management of his farm to be able to upset his rayats and secondly that the rayats' complaint was met by a response from the huzur. The combination of these two features was characteristic of farming in the eighteenth century. However, under Baji Rao II complaints by the rayats were no longer listened to.

One document of 1760 contains a particularly clear description of changes concomitant with the transformation of a farm into an ordinary *kamāvīs* assignment.[78] Here it is written that the *māmlat*

[72] Gordon, 'Slow Conquest', p. 33. [73] *Ibid.*, pp. 30–1.
[74] *SSRPD*, 7, nos 416–17.
[75] *Ibid.*, 1, no. 279; 7, no. 416; 8, no. 1155 ff. [76] *Ibid.*, 3, no. 411; 7, no. 473.
[77] *Ibid.*, 3, no. 340. [78] *Ibid.*, no. 431.

of the two parganas of Van and Dindori was held in *maktā* in the preceding year, but that the farmer did not pay the full amount of the revenue *agreed upon*, and did not settle the cultivation. A kamavisdar of another pargana then proposes to have the *māmlat* assigned to him in *kamāvīs*, stating that he would settle the cultivation and would thus ensure a higher revenue than the farmer. Accordingly it is given to him and the villages of the parganas are ordered to be surveyed, the lands to be classified and measured, the assessment to be fixed, and the accountancy to be done by a fadnis and a majumdar. Then the *tankhā* of the assignment is determined, but the usual remissions are ordered to be given (if necessary), and the *kamāvīsdār* is to receive a salary of a fixed amount.

Karkuns are not absent from all farms. As is already evident from some of the examples given above, the huzur could impose them upon an *ijāradār* or maktedār, if it chose to do so.[79] Orders to employ these karkuns or *darakdārs* (singly or together) to settle the jamabandi, and, if necessary, measure the land and prepare detailed registers of it and submit accounts to the government *always* accompanied *kamāvīs* assignments of the land-revenue, and, mutatis mutandis, of *zakāt* or 'customs'.[80] In some documents the darakdars, as well as certain other government servants, are forbidden to hold villages in farm,[81] but it is at the same time evident that this was sometimes tolerated.[82]

Now the darakdars belonged not only to the administrative set-up in the *khālsā* but were also employed, in the same way, as a check on the military assignments or *saraṇjāms*. The *saraṇjāmdār* was, again like the *kamāvīsdār*, not only enjoined to render accounts, but also to increase the revenue of his assignment as much as possible.[83] In contrast with the kamavisdar he never held his tenure on farming terms[84] but he could, like the jagirdars in the Mughal Empire and the *mokāsadārs* in the Deccan Sultanates,[85] farm out to others villages or shares of the revenues entrusted to him. The same motives could be at work here which induced the government to do likewise. One recorded instance of a subfarmed

79 For further examples, see *ibid.*, 7, nos 416–17.

80 Cf. Chapter 4–I.

81 Either in *ijārā* or *khotī* (*SSRPD*, 3, nos 423, 426).

82 *Ibid.*, 8, no. 821.

83 Cf. Chapter 4–II–b.

84 Nor did the *mokāsadār* of the time of Shahu.

85 Cf. Habib, *Agrarian System*, p. 284; B. R. Grover, 'Nature of Land-Rights in Mughal India', *IESHR*, 1, 1 (1963), pp. 9–10; Chandra, *Parties and Politics*, p. xlix; Richards, *Golconda*, p. 13.

military assignment is that of a pargana of forty-two villages which the Peshwa had granted out of his territories in Malwa, first to Laksman Shankar, and then, in 1750, to Malhar Rao Raste.[86] In a letter, the kamavisdar to whom Raste had assigned the management of his saranjam writes to him that out of the total of 42 villages in the pargana 'two are not on record,[87] 40 are desolate, and of these 23 are held in *ijārā* and 17 are *rayatī*'. He further explains that 'in the pargana there are no *mavās* and no big *zamīndārs*, [and therefore] whoever stays here in charge of the administration must be attending to the settlement of cultivation; [a part of the] villages was given in *ijārā* to various people, in others the rayats cultivated under *kaul* and other assurances.'[88] Here again the *ijāradārs*, probably local men of capital, undertake the task of agrarian resettlement which would otherwise have fallen to the zamindars and mavas, in a pargana which had become waste. In a second instance, we have already seen how a *saraṇjām* in the Southern Maratha Country, belonging to Madhav Rao Raste, was farmed out to different mamlatdars who had given loans to Raste against these talukas and how this created difficulties at the resumption of the assignment.[89] We also saw that under the Maratha sardars of Central India and Hindustan, who were technically also *saraṇjāmdārs* (keeping their own accounts but rarely completely exempt from all supervision by the Poona court) bankers commonly acquired great influence through farming.[90] Many of the farmers were either bankers themselves or were supported by them.[91] Here, as usual, they frequently entered into *rayatvāri* arrangements.[92] There is some evidence to suggest that in a farming situation the darakdars would as a rule (but with exceptions as indicated) be altogether dispensed with already in the eighteenth century. This appears in particular from a document of 1781, describing the duties of the *fadṇīs* of the *zakāt* at the fort of Pen, in which the following statement occurs:

86 *BISMQ*, 56, 1–4 (1976), pp. 1–2.

87 Lit. 'their *pāṇḍhrī* [residential area] and *kālīcā ṭhikāṇā* [black soil] are not shown in the records'.

88 '*parganiyāṇt koṇī mavās nāhī zamīdārhī koṇī mātbar nāhī sarkārce tarfene jo rāhīl tyāṇec tartūd lāvṇīcī karāve gāṇv ijārā dyāve kāhī gāṇv rayetīcī niśā karūn kaul karār deūn lāvāve.*'

89 Cf. p. 339, note 48. 90 Cf. p. 334.

91 Malcolm, *Central India*, 1, pp. 31, 38.

92 *Ibid.*, p. 31.

As the *zakāt* used to be held in *ijārā*, the writing-work was not done by a *faḍṇīs*; but as now the *zakāt* is held in *kamāvīs*, all the writing-work, without exception, must be done by a *faḍṇīs*, and the management must always be done in the presence of the *darakdārs*.[93]

Another example in which the transformation of a farm into a *kamāvīs* assignment went together with the introduction of darakdars, a land-survey, and a regular system of accounts, has already been given (pp. 355–6). Relaxation of governmental control in the case of farming is further evident when in 1763 a *māmlā* of thirteen tarfs in Satara is given in farm, with the exception of one tarf, which is given in *kamāvīs*, and only of this latter assignment are detailed accounts ordered to be submitted to the huzur at the end of the year.[94] Lastly, we find it unambiguously expressed in a sanad of 1763, containing instructions from the sarsubhedar of the Konkan, Shankarji Keshav, to five of his subordinates, concerning the taluka of Suvarnadurg, in which it is ordered that:

they should either make an inspection of the proceeds in cash and kind, the agricultural and the garden land, and settle the *jamābaṇḍī, or farm it out.*[95]

Often however the rights of farmers in the eighteenth century were curtailed and supervised to a greater degree than were, as will be seen (section g.), those of the later farmers of Baji Rao II. These rights were also less vulnerable. Under Nana Fadnis on the frontier with the Nizam, says the aforementioned 'Account', 'the contractor had abatements allowed to him to cover the pay of the darakdars', but at the same time 'it was provided, in the event of any great calamity, that he should receive such indulgence as was usual'.[96]

In conclusion, we cannot characterize farming rights in general, as did Moreland, as 'obstacles in the way of detailed control' but we will have to situate them, in each case differently, somewhere on a continuum of possible combinations of *risk-taking* and *regulation*, two variables which always appear to be inversely correlated.[97] Detailed control was not the first issue here, but the furthering of cultivation. To achieve the latter, control could easily be dispensed with if the 'financial side of administration' was

93 *SSRPD*, 6, no. 774. 94 *Ibid.*, 7, no. 436.
95 '*jamābaṇḍī, nakt bāb, ain jinasī, jirāīt bāgāīt pāhaṇī, agar makte*' (*ibid.*, no. 451).
96 *EIP*, 4, p. 630. 97 See the scheme on p. 373.

safeguarded by the farmer. How this worked will be better illustrated in the next section.

f. The *khotī* tenures of the Konkan

The *khots* had their origin in the sixteenth century, when, as local moneyed men (some of them perhaps former revenue officials under the Vijayanagar kings), they were appointed on *kaul* and *istāvā* leases by the Bijapur government of Yusuf Adil Shah to restore desolate villages and reclaim wastelands.[98] They were first introduced in the year 1502, after a long period of trouble (*bhālerāī* or 'rule of the spear'), by the subhedar of Dabhol, a province which extended from the Savitri river to Devgad and which thus included the whole of Ratnagiri except Malwan. In the oldest sanads given to the *khots*, their villages are stated to be granted in *ijārā*.[99] The word *khot*, which is found mainly in the Konkan,[100] can therefore be taken to mean a 'farmer' of revenue, engaged by the government with a clearly ameliorative purpose. Bidding for the *khotīs* took place from the outset, and a *khot* could be removed if he failed to keep up with higher offers made by others; until of course the *khotī* became hereditary. It is unknown what exactly were their rights and duties in the early stage. It probably took two or three generations for them to acquire the power to sell or mortgage their khotships.[101] Most likely many were also continued hereditarily as *vatan* shortly after being given in farm. The *vatan khotīs* being saleable made it possible, in the Peshwa period, for many brahman families to buy themselves in, thereby reducing the older *khotī* families of Marathas and Muslims to a small minority.[102]

In the eighteenth century, under title-deeds of the Mughals, the

[98] *B.A.: R.D.*, vol. 16/16 of 1821, p. 519; *BGS*, n.s. no. 134, p. 5; Jervis, *Konkan*, p. 75; *BISM-Vārṣik Itivṛtt* (1913), p. 320.

[99] *BGS*, n.s. no. 134, p. 13; Choksey, *Ratnagiri*, p. 138; *BG*, I, pt. II, p. 33; *BG*, X, p. 213; *SCS*, 9, no. 24.

[100] There are but traces of *khotī* tenures elsewhere, and mostly in seventeenth-century documents. These speak of *khots*, *khot ijāradārs*, or *khot pāṭīls* in the Deccan. *Khots* appear to have been fairly common in the Mavals until they were suppressed by the farmers of Baji Rao II (*EIP*, 4, p. 468). There were also *khots* under the Delhi Sultans, who imported the term from beyond the Vindhyas, but may have transformed the institution (Tripathi, *Muslim Administration, p. 256, note 193; Raychaudhuri and Habib, Cambridge Economic History of India*, I, pp. 48 ff.

[101] Choksey, *Ratnagiri*, p. 139; *BGS*, n.s. no. 134, p. 13.

[102] A number of brahmans also acquired such rights by grant (*BGS*, n.s. no. 134, p. 1; *B.A.: R.D.*, vol. 16/16 of 1821, p. 518).

Angria, then the Peshwas, and eventually often under deeds of local *subhā*- or *mahāl*-officials (which were held to give less certain rights), the *khots* continued to be associated with agrarian expansion. In a sanad from Peshwa Balaji Baji Rao, for instance, it is related that a three-year farm (*tīsālā maktā*) of a pargana is, on request of the rayats, transferred to another incumbent as *khotī*; the scope of the new contract, likewise for three years, includes 'the inundated, waste, and salty lands, the "bad" villages and the deśmukhi villages, with all rights and cesses'; it is given at an increasing rate and the *khot* is ordered to bring the lands under cultivation, to populate the pargana by bringing in 'new families of cultivators from outside territories (*paramulkī navīṇ kuḷeṇ*)' and to submit a list of the new as well as the old inhabitants to the huzur.[103] In many other sanads it is stated that the lands of a village are almost all waste, and that the few remaining cultivators have petitioned for a *khot*, and that therefore the village is granted as *vatan khotī*.[104] The *khots*, moreover, acquired a right to the unpaid labour of their tenants of one day in eight (*āṭh veṭh*), by means of which they reclaimed many salt marshes and swamps, and constructed a very large area of rice land in Ratnagiri.[105] In Thana and Kolaba, at first, when the districts were lying waste, the *pāṇḍharpeśas* or 'village officers' had taken to the task of cultivation extension, but their assistance was insufficient and from the beginning of Maratha rule revenue farming (by *khots* and others) was introduced.[106] Initially it was mostly confined to villages, under the supervision of salaried mamlatdars, and with leases generally granted for six years. Then, around 1761, during the minority of Madhav Rao I, whole parganas began to be farmed out for one year only, new cesses (*mogham caḍhs*) were levied and the *veṭh begar* or 'corvée' demands were increased. These pressures on the cultivators were intensified and generalized under Baji Rao II. Under the latter's farming system (as later under the English[107]) the rayats are sometimes seen to have preferred a *khot* between themselves and the sarkar.[108] In many ways – by preventing the imposition of higher rates of assessment, by giving loans and assisting with the

103 *SSRPD*, 3, no. 408. (Compare with this *SCS*, 9, no. 81 of AD 1699).
104 *BGS*, n.s. no. 134, p. 5. 105 *BG*, x, p. 206, note 1.
106 *BG*, XIII, pt. II, p. 557.
107 When attempts were being made to introduce *mirās* tenure in the Northern Konkan (*BGS*, n.s. no. 134, p. 19).
108 *Ibid.*

cultivation, etc. – a *khot* could act as a buffer between the rayats and the higher-level revenue farmers.[109]

In the Southern Konkan the 'colonist' *khots* had from an early stage been recognized as *vatandārs*, i.e., as hereditary farmers. There were instances of *vatandār khots*, who, deserting their village during a disturbance, became 'fugitive' (*parāgaṇḍā*) and upon their return resumed their *vatans*, sometimes on payment of a *nazar* or 'recognition'.[110] As in the case of all other *vatans*, a *nazar* would always be paid on succession,[111] at the confirmation by a new ruler,[112] and presumably with alienation. There are also instances of *vatan khotīs* being granted, it being distinctly stated that the former *vatandār khots* were extinct.[113]

There were no *vatandār khots* north of the Savitri or Bankot river – a significant fact perhaps, as this river had originally formed the boundary between the Adil Shahi and Nizam Shahi kingdoms.[114] Yet, many zamindars north of the Bankot arrogated to themselves such titles and the attendant prerogatives, sometimes, as in Raigarh and Rajpuri, calling themselves *sarkhots*.[115] British figures of the late nineteenth century no longer distinguish the *vatandār khots* from the non-hereditary or *sirkārī khots*.[116] All are treated alike as hereditary. In both the Northern and the Southern Konkan the number of *khotī* villages (or *nivaḷkhotī*: purely rented, i.e., not possessing any *dhārekarīs* or 'hereditary cultivators') constituted a little less than one half of the total. And since the British themselves gave out very few new khotis but resumed many, their number at the close of the *peśvāī* must have been even greater. The other villages were classified as *khālsā dhārekarī* or 'peasant-held', *khicaḍī* or 'partly farmed, partly peasant-held', or *inām*. Many of the *inām* villages were farmed (*khotī*) as well, the farmers standing in the same relation to the inamdars in which they would otherwise have stood to the government.[117]

In pre-British times the *vatandār khots* differed from the other *khots* in that they could not be dispossessed by the government. In

109 *Ibid.*, p. 20.
110 In anticipation of the reappearance of the *vatandār khot*, the village could be given out to temporary khots. It was then expressly ordered that it was to be held only up to that time (*BGS*, n.s. no. 134, p. 3).
111 *Ibid.*, p. 2. 112 *SSRPD*, 8, no. 450. 113 *BGS*, n.s. no. 134, p. 3.
114 B.A.: R.D., vol. 12/64 of 1823, p. 248; Jervis, *Konkan*, p. 63.
115 *B.A.: R.D., loc. cit.* 116 *BGS*, n.s. no. 134, p. 2.
117 *BG*, XI, p. 160, X, pp. 202–3.

the Northern Konkan, the designation of 'hereditary contractor' was often ridiculed, since it was thought that, *khotī* only meaning *maktā*, farm or contract, the terms *vatandār* and *khot* were irreconcilable.[118] Except for their origin in the Adil Shahi Sultanate it is not clear why the hereditary *khotīs* only developed in the south. The reasons however why hereditary khotis were so sought after are quite obvious. The *khot*, being engaged in the expansion and restoration of agriculture, often invested a considerable amount of money in his lands. Yet, unless he was protected by a specific grant, he could not be secure in the continued possession of his village. The northern non-hereditary khots, being removable at the will of the government, constantly faced this threat of losing their investments and the further benefits arising from them. In the records they are often called *baṇdhekarī*, which is the opposite of vatandar.[119] The accounts in the Peshwa Daftar show that the former were regularly removed, but there is no instance of a *vatan khotī* being resumed in the south.[120] There it was the object of many khots to obtain a sanad securing a hereditary right, before they undertook the management of a village, or after they had brought it to prosperity.[121] In the case of temporary khotis, however, we find sanads ordering a khot to pay for the embankment constructions made by the preceding incumbent,[122] or in which a khot admits that he is not a *vatandār khot*, but asks the Peshwa not to remove him as he had incurred great expense in improving his village:[123] improvised and uncertain solutions at most of a persistent problem of farming in general.[124] The government probably did not give out sanads confirming the *khotī* in hereditary possession unless it saw no cheaper way to get the village cultivated. It did feel bound to respect such sanads, and was, therefore, all the more averse to hand out new ones. In a letter from the Peshwa to the sarsubhedar of the Konkan it is related that a bhat had acquired the *khotī* of a village during the reign of Tulaji Angria, fifteen or sixteen years before the territory fell to the Peshwa; it was proposed by the sarsubhedar to confirm this khoti to the same bhat, on payment of a nazar of 200 rupees; in reply the Peshwa writes that 'a *khotī* should not be in the hands of one man for many years', and demands an inspection of the papers which the bhat held from Angria, ordering:

118 *B.A.: R.D.*, vol. 16/16 of 1821, p. 321. 119 *BGS*, n.s. no. 134, p. 3.

120 *Ibid.*, pp. 2, 3. They were, probably, resumed on the grounds that any vatan could be resumed, such as 'rebellion', 'oppression' (cf. p. 364), or disputes.

121 *Ibid.*, p. 2. 122 *SSRPD*, 7, no. 450. 123 *BGS*, n.s. no. 134, p. 3.

124 It was a general problem, but only when long-term investments needed to be made, which itself was far from general, or perhaps often optional.

'if it appears that the village has been given as *vatan khotī*, take 200 rupees as nazar and confirm it, but if there is any doubt about it, resume it from the bhat and give it to somebody else'.[125]

The hereditary *khots* of the Southern Konkan differed from the hereditary *pāṭīls* of the Deccan in some of the privileges which were incidental to their position: to a *sanadī vatandār khot* reverted by escheat the lands of even a permanent rayat (*dhāre-karī*) in a mixed (*khicaḍī*) village;[126] they, like the temporary *khots*, enjoyed the right of exacting from their tenants the *āṭh veṭh* corvée, of forcing them to plough for them (*naṇgar veṭh*), and carry their palanquins.[127] In some places in the Konkan there were village headmen called *gāoṇkars*, holding *ināms* from the government, but enjoying likewise some rights to the unpaid services of cultivators.[128] Village establishments like the Deccan *bārā balute* or 'twelve artisans' did not exist anywhere, nor had they ever been known by tradition.[129] Comparatively few villages even possessed a village accountant (*kuḷkarṇī*). In the Konkan former *pāṭīls* and other village officers appear to have been reduced to mere tenants with vague and uncertain, often quite indefinite titles (on a generally longer term than tenants-at-will, however) by the encroachments of the *khots*.[130]

Secondly, the *khots*, both in the Northern and the Southern Konkan, were the farmers of their villages to an extent that the Deccan *pāṭīls* were not. In the Konkan, until the late eighteenth century, the village *jamābaṇḍī* used to be made up under taluka-wise surveys, once in about seven to ten years, while in the Deccan each village was surveyed once a year.[131] The *khot* was answerable for the amount of the jamabandi thus arrived at, until the next survey, and if more land was brought into cultivation or if land had become waste in the intervening period, the *khot* always bore the gain or loss.[132] The situation was essentially similar if the khot held on *istāvā*. Instead of being paid by means of *inām* land, while at the same time being entitled to *haks* from the cultivators, the *khots* were remunerated mainly by the profits they could make out of their farms. This was supposed seldom to be more than

125 *SSRPD*, 7, no. 450.

126 *BGS*, n.s. no. 134, p. 55; *B.A.: R.D.*, vol. 5/211 of 1828, p. 182.

127 The *dhārekarīs* were exempted from all forced labour.

128 *BG*, x, p. 222.

129 *B.A.: R.D.*, vol. 16/16 of 1821, p. 318. There were however the pandharpeśas, who can to some extent be compared with them.

130 *Ibid.*, vol. 5/211 of 1828, pp. 176–8.

131 *BGS*, n.s. no. 134, p. 34.

132 *B.A.: R.D.*, vol. 16/16 of 1821, p. 319.

10%.[133] In letting out the lands the *khot* was not guided by a rent fixed by the government for each rayat's holding but was in practice free to exact whatever he chose, restrained, ultimately, only by the fear that the rayat would throw up his land and take refuge with a milder landlord, or lodge a complaint with the government. The rayat, in his turn, could be ejected if he did not agree to the terms dictated by the *khot.* Sometimes, as we mentioned in section a., the rate could be fixed by a contract concluded on the basis of bargaining. Often, if the khot and the rayats could not agree, a *baṭāī* settlement was made to end the problem, and this implied that half of the produce would be paid to the khot in kind.[134] This plan was also adopted, but more rarely, in the Deccan when no final settlement could be made between a *pāṭīl* and a *māmlatdār*; in such a case, first a special officer was sent to examine the fields and if still no adjustment was made the *māmlatdār* would offer to take one half and leave the other half to the cultivators.[135] A similar practice occurring in Central India is reported on by Malcolm.[136] There it was resorted to only in the poorest districts as sometimes the only settlement a collector could make, taking one-half or two-fifths, on occasion not more than one-quarter. Normally in the Konkan, as in the Deccan and elsewhere, local usage regulated the rates to be paid by the individual rayats. In the Konkan however the government did not know precisely what the rayats together had to pay to the *khot*, nor how much the *khot* might gain or loose by his farm.[137] The government, nevertheless, regularly interfered in the *khotī* villages on behalf of the rayats when they complained to the huzur. If oppression became apparent, it could resume a *khotī* (probably also a *vatan khotī*) and give it to someone else – without taking the khot's *bedavapatra* or 'deed of acquittance'.[138] The same could happen if a village was neglected on account of a *khotī* dispute.[139] In the case of a 'government khoti-village' we hear of rayats being allowed to take over the management after they had become dissatisfied with the agent – against payment of both the *maktā* and the 'profit of the *khotī*' which are both specified for a term of five

133 *Ibid.*, p. 518. The khots were also entitled to some trifling perquisites in kind from the rayats.
134 *BGS*, n.s. no. 134, p. 12.
135 Elphinstone, *Report*, p. 35.
136 *Central India*, 1, p. 34.
137 *BGS*, n.s. no. 134, p. 11.
138 *Ibid.*, pp. 3–4; *SSRPD*, 3, no. 422.
139 It could also be made *dhārekarī* on such occasions (*BGS*, n.s. no. 134, pp. 3–4; *SSRPD*, 7, no. 454).

years.[140] When the government assessment is increased *khots* are often forbidden to increase their demands on the cultivators.[141] This generally high degree of governmental control of the *khotī maktā* is again counterbalanced by some degree of consideration for non-enjoyment in the case of a drastic decline of the harvest proceeds due to disturbances.[142] But the *khots* wrote entirely their own accounts; the rental book kept by them was denominated *boṭkhat*, and this contained their own private schedule.[143] In accounting to the government in a *jhaḍatī*, which they had to hand in every year, the *khots* only exhibited those heads of taxation and such assessment rates as were recognized by the revenue officials. And from the early 1760s onwards the usual seven- to ten-year surveys were less regularly made, the farming of districts became general, and cesses (*bābtīs*, *paṭṭīs*, *aṇtastha*, *mogham*, *nazars*, *caḍhs*, etc.) began to be added (eventually numbering over 167, to the amount of 50% of the nett assessment), which were not accounted for in these *jhaḍatīs*.[144] The *khots* hardly ever attempted to increase the nett assessment (*ain dhārā*) on the land by any amount. This would have been far easier but it would have shown in the accounts and would have given the cultivators a fair ground for complaining. The numerous cesses, on the other hand, not appearing in the accounts, were of a highly particularistic nature, many being confined to particular talukas, or to particular mahals within the talukas, some prevailing only in particular villages, or levied only from particular individuals, but always only from the *kunbīs* (cultivators), the *pāṇḍharpeśas* hardly contributing to a single cess.[145]

g. Revenue farming under Baji Rao II

Peshwa Baji Rao II introduced his system of *pakkā* revenue farming by auction in most of the territories under his immediate control in 1804, after they had been devastated. Elsewhere in the Maratha confederacy it became the universal system somewhat earlier. In Nagpur it started in 1792 and was intensified after the Maratha war of 1802.[146] When in 1803 the districts of Surat and Broach fell to the British, most of their revenue had already been

140 *SSRPD*, 3, no. 405; and see again section a.
141 *SSRPD*, 3, nos 415, 419, 429.
142 *SSRPD*, 6, no. 782.
143 *B.A.: R.D.*, vol. 59/746 of 1836, p. 217.
144 *Ibid.*, pp. 195, 216, 217; vol. 16/16 of 1821, p. 518.
145 *Ibid.*, vol. 59/746 of 1836, p. 217.
146 Jenkins, *Nagpur*, p. 96.

for twenty years in the hands of successive farmers of large districts, known as *desāīs*, mostly Anavla brahmans.[147] Also in Thana the farming of land-revenue had already become universal in 1790.[148]

The farm of the Peshwa's share of the revenue of Ahmadabad, the Panc Mahals, and the *mulūkhgirī* or 'tribute' of Kathiawar, was given for five years to Govind Rao Gaikwar, with whom this district was held in shared authority, after the death of Nana Fadnis in 1800.[149] On the instigation of the British Resident Close the farm was renewed in 1804 for another ten years in the name of Bhagwant Rao Gaikwar, at an annual rent of 4.5 lacs of rupees.[150] Again in 1813 the British exerted themselves – but this time without the desired result – to get the farm renewed in the name of the Gaikwar, or, if necessary, of the British government itself.[151] Elphinstone expressed his doubts about the likelihood of a renewal of the farm in a letter to the Bombay Government as follows:

> The greater part of the revenues of the Peshwa's country is collected by farmers, and the farm of each district is generally assigned to the highest bidder without much regard to the welfare of the country or even the ultimate prosperity of the Government; and it is therefore by no means unlikely that His Highness may prefer putting the Panc Mahals and even Ahmadabad into the hands of farmers, who will pay him a racked rent, to seeing them in the hands of the British Government or the Gaikwar, who will not agree to give more than the country can bear.[152]

The Peshwa, on the other hand, argued that in 1804 the farm had been let at a very reduced rate at a time when the country was very much impoverished but that ten years had since then elapsed and that the condition of the district had so much improved that instead

147 *BG*, II, pp. 213–15; Kumar Hans, 'Manotidari System'.
148 *BG*, XIII, pt. II, p. 555.
149 *Historical Selections from Baroda State Records*, 5, p. 706; cf. p. 127.
150 Elphinstone to the Earl of Moira, 15 Nov. 1813, *PRC*, 12, p. 301.
151 In spite of their opposition to farming in general the British considered the renewal of this farm expedient for the 'consolidation of authority and the exclusion of rival interference' which they thought essential to keep order among the numerous *mavāsīs* in this part of Gujarat (A. Walker to J. Duncan, 2nd Oct. 1808, in: J. H. Gense and D. R. Banaji (eds), *The Gaikwads of Baroda*, 9 vols (Baroda, n.d.), 9, p. 156). The renewal of the farm would, moreover, have facilitated the severance of the relations between the Gaikwar and the Peshwa, another implicit aim of the British which is emphasized by Vaidya, *Peshwa Bajirao II*, p. 228. The Peshwa, as we saw, wanted to protect his own authority by the resumption of the farm (cf. p. 128).
152 Gense and Banaji, *Gaikwads*, 9, p. 1.

of 4.5 lacs of rupees, 6 or 7, or even 8 might now be realized.[153] In accordance with what we take to be the normal aim of farming, the sanad of 1804 had been accompanied with an order to deliver the whole taluka 'in a populous and well-cultivated state' on the commencement of the eleventh year.[154] This is apparently what happened. But, as Elphinstone affirmed in his later proclamation of 1818 (cf. p. 343), this was equally the case in most of the rest of the country. In effect, the difference in Baji Rao II's method of farming did not lie in the results achieved, but in the harshness of the terms with which it was applied – and had to be applied to achieve these results under the prevailing circumstances.

Apart from the land-revenue, customs, and police, Baji Rao II farmed all his expenditure, including such things as 'food-supplies to the palace', to the highest bidder usually, and without consideration for defaulters, who lost their property or were themselves imprisoned.[155] While under Nana Fadnis and Madhav Rao I great attention is said to have been paid to representations of the rayats and patils, the knowledge of which operated to some extent as a restraint on the kamavisdars,[156] no complaints were listened to under Baji Rao II.[157] Apparently all direct intercourse between the government and the cultivators ceased.[158] But we must presume that, given the fractionation of the revenue into *amals*, there still worked the principle of safety in numbers.

It is remarkable that the length of tenure became shorter in comparison with the eighteenth-century farms and particularly with the *kamāvīs* and *saraṇjām* assignments, which in the later part of the century were often allowed to be transmitted hereditarily.[159]

153 Close's report of his conversation with the Peshwa's minister, 31 October 1813, *ibid.*, pp. 2–3.
154 Gense and Banaji, *Gaikwads*, 7, pp. 117–18.
155 Grant Duff, *History*, 2, pp. 354–5; *BG*, XIX, p. 337; XVII, p. 430; *EIP*, 4, pp. 745–51. Torture was also applied to defaulting maktedars (*EIP*, 4, p. 659).
156 *EIP*, 4, p. 745; Grant Duff, *History*, 1, p. 454.
157 Grant Duff, *op. cit.*; Elphinstone, *Report*, pp. 37–8.
158 *BG*, XVIII, pt. II, p. 339.
159 The eighteenth-century farms we examined were generally held by the same person for three to five years, sometimes less, or a few years longer. They might have been renewed, but it does not seem very likely that this occurred on a wide scale. Annual leases were already given under Nana Fadnis in the districts on the Nizam's frontier. The non-hereditary *khotīs* in the Konkan were also farmed out annually or for a short term of years. In Malwa and Central India short-lease farms with often annual changes coexisted for a long time with farms of unusually long leases, sometimes remaining for 70 years in the same family, with under-renters with leases of 30, 40, or 50 years (Malcolm, 154Central India, 1, p. 532, and 2, pp. 38, 40–1, 51). The longer duration and hereditary transmittance of the

This shortness of tenure under *pakkā* farming seems to have worked as a catalyst in the restorative process. The districts were now farmed for one year only, or for two or three,[160] the farmer paying one-third or more of the revenue in advance (with the usual allowance for interest), or having somebody stand surety for him.[161] Sometimes the government renegued on its agreements when a higher offer was made before the lease came to an end.[162] From Baroda it is reported that it was the practice that such an ousted *ijāradār* was given a sum of money from the supplanter, which was held to represent a salary for the period he had managed the district.[163]

First, one of the Peshwa's court-attendants obtained the office of *māmlatdār* on an often risky bid at a public auction,[164] for a fixed sum, which always included a 'secret payment' (*aṇtastha*) to the Peshwa himself.[165] This was then subfarmed to a great number of intermediary agents, all of whom paid some additional charges in order to procure the lease.[166] The farmers were most often new men put forward by the Peshwa, but they could be, like in Thana, the old and experienced government officials as well.[167] Even the latter, if they did not limit themselves to the additional imposition of a large number of cesses – as was the case in some parts – now raised the land-assessment and abandoned the graduated scale based on the different degrees of fertility, adopting a uniform rate for all land.[168] A usual practice of the subordinate revenue farmers in the Konkan was also to threaten the villages from year to year with a new survey, which was then relinquished for a compromised *caḍh*.[169] Characteristic of the system everywhere was the almost complete absence of any form of regular account-keeping.[170] The *huzūr daftar*, the repository in Poona of all government accounts (but not of the private treasury of the Peshwa) concerning the

assignments in the second half of the eighteenth century is demonstrated by innumerable cases everywhere (cf. Chapter 4–I and 4–II–b).

160 *BG*, XIX, p. 337; XVI, p. 210; XVII, p. 430; *EIP*, 4, pp. 697, 746. In the Konkan the length of tenure commonly remained four or five years under Baji Rao II (Jervis, *Konkan*, pp. 120–1, 124; *BG*, XIII, pt. II, p. 559).

161 *EIP*, 4, p. 747.

162 *Ibid.*, p. 769; *B.A.: R.D.*, vol. 13/700 of 1836, p. 156.

163 *BG*, VII, p. 365.

164 Elphinstone, *Report*, pp. 37–8.

165 See section h.

166 Elphinstone, *Report*, p. 38; *EIP*, 3, p. 768.

167 *BG*, XIII, pt. II, pp. 560, 588; *B.A.: R.D.*, vol. 13/700 of 1836, pp. 199–207.

168 *B.A.: R.D.*, *op. cit.*, p. 149; *BGS*, n.s. no. 96, p. 3. There was a bias in the old rates in favour of the pandharpeśas, which was continued by the farmers.

169 Jervis, *Konkan*, p. 124.

170 Marshall, *Statistical Reports*, p. 179; Elphinstone, *Report* p. 139; *BGS*, o.s. n. 12, p. 7; *B.A.: R.D.*, vol. 5/549 of 1834, p. 86.

income and expenditure of the state, kept in great order and with much precision up to the end of the administration of Nana Fadnis, was almost entirely done away with. The rates of assessment of the districts became a distant standard of valuation which served the Peshwa as a baseline when the revenue was put up to auction. District estimates (*prāṇt ajmās*) are extant for some years, but the names of the *māmlatdārs* are not given, as they were formerly. The actual collections are not accounted for. Nor are mentioned the many new cesses which were added everywhere, often as *jāstī paṭṭīs* or *eksālī paṭṭīs*, first introduced as special and temporary, then becoming permanent after having been continued for a number of years.[171]

Turning to the effects which this system of revenue farming had on the different classes of the population, the first outstanding fact seems to be that, with the *darakdārs*, the hereditary *zamīndārs* were mostly set aside and their payments discontinued: they and the other great landholders were its main victims, not the rayats.[172] Such equalizing effects were, however, not universal. The *khots* in the Konkan generally seem to have been able to meet the demands of the farmers.[173] In Thana the *pāṇḍharpeśas* successfully protested against the imposition of a uniform rate of assessment and obtained concessions at the expense of the *kunbīs*, who also paid almost all of the additional cesses.[174] It was not caste-membership which made the farmers continue these largely Brahmanical privileges, for they were members of all castes indiscriminately.[175] In the Southern Konkan many of the principal officials at the Peshwa's court held large estates in their native villages, and these were also less interfered with by the revenue farmers.[176] In some places in the Southern Maratha Country, like in Hungund, the *desāīs* managed to retain sufficient influence to check the rates of taxation of the Peshwa's contractors.[177] Areas in

171 Elphinstone, *Report*, p. 39; *P.A.: Prant Ajmas* for the years 1804–18.
172 Cf. note 15 *supra*; *BG*, XIII, pt. II, pp. 340–1, 556. This seems to have had a parallel under Scindhia (J. Anderson to Governor-General, 13 Nov. 1786, *PRC*, I, p. 88).
173 *BG*, X, p. 218.
174 The privileged position of the *pāṇḍharpeśas* (non-cultivators, mostly brahmans) preceded the Peshwa régime. It was founded on their being the original reclaimers of the land (*B.A.: R.D.*, vol. 50/203 of 1827, p. 270).
175 *Ibid.* 176 Jervis, *Konkan*, p. 126.
177 Here they also participated in the task of agrarian resettlement (*BG*, XXIII, p. 448).

the hands of local chiefs and apt to rise in revolt were also less hard-pressed than areas more completely under the control of the Peshwa.[178]

The districts which became totally unproductive were those of which the inhabitants went over to neighbouring chiefs, whose estates of course greatly benefited from this efflux.[179] Khandesh was for a large part depopulated in this period, but this was not due to revenue farming, but rather to the irretrievable consequences of a number of simultaneously occurring misfortunes.[180] In the Southern Maratha Country, Munro registered a 'decline of the revenue' since the accession of Baji Rao II,[181] but it seems clear that this implied merely a decline of revenue collected by the Peshwa, and that formerly superseded local exploitative networks of protection racketeers had reasserted themselves in his stead, and at his cost.[182] In this march area there was thus an attempt to integrate existing conditions into a 'farming system'. But farming by itself was inevitably more expensive for the government than *kaccā* administration by salaried officials.

The village headmen might, as pointed out earlier, become the farmers of their villages, as happened in Nasik for instance,[183] but they could also be set aside, the district or sub-district contractors then proceeding to make separate agreements with the cultivators individually.[184] If he maintained his position the *pāṭīl* could only ensure his profits by heavier exactions from the rayats.[185] In some places revenue farming destroyed the patils' and other village-officers' privilege to hold *inām* lands: this occurred in the Central Provinces, most notably, and in Badami and Dharwar, where very high quit-rents were levied on these village service lands.[186] The *pāṭīl*, being personally liable for the payment of the revenue, could be forced to sell a share of his *vatan* to raise money, his loss being entered in the village accounts as *pāṭilkī nuksān* or 'patilki loss'.[187]

178 *BG*, XVI, p. 210.

179 *EIP*, 4, p. 269. In the Karnataka a large number of cultivators fled to Mysore (*ibid.*, 4, p. 798; *BGS*, no. 12, p. 51; *B.A.: R.D.*, vol. 5/549 of 1834, p. 86).

180 *BG*, XII, p. 272.

181 Gleig, *Life of Munro*, 2, p. 278.

182 *BGS*, o.s. no. 12, p. 51. A situation which is perhaps broadly similar to the one in Awadh in the first half of the nineteenth century, as described in R. G. Fox, *Kin, Clan, Raja, and Rule: State–Hinterland Relations in Pre-industrial India* (Bombay, 1971), p. 109.

183 *BG*, XVI, p. 210; VII, p. 365.

184 Malcolm, *Central India*, 2, p. 31.

185 *EIP*, 4, p. 672.

186 Baden-Powell, 'Dakhan Villages', p. 253; E. Stokes, *The Peasant and the Raj* (Cambridge, 1980), p. 53.

187 Marshall, *Statistical Reports*, p. 174.

In Bagalkot and Badami, in 1810, the administration of Raste, the *saraṇjāmdār* of these districts, was succeeded by that of the Peshwa's revenue farmers; *pāṭilkīs* which are said to have been sold for eleven years' purchase of their whole emoluments in the time of Raste, were sometimes, out of necessity, sold for one or two in the time of the Peshwa.[188] An immense number of alienations was also made by *ijāradārs* of the mahals or districts under *mahāl sanads* (as opposed to *huzūr sanads*) to suit their convenience or to meet demands. Nevertheless, under Maratha rule, such alienations were never officially recognized, and a farmer of revenue would never have thought of not levying an assessment as was usual from the holders of land which his predecessors might have sold or mortgaged or otherwise freed from liability to taxation.[189] The worst losses under Baji Rao II's farming arrangements were sustained by the gentry, who often saw their privileges and influence dwindle. On the other hand it can be argued that this at the same time cleared the field of the heavy overgrowth of established *zamīndārī* rights. The alienations made by the farmers lacked sanction and remained open to recall. Apparently the developments of the period were not irreversible and moreover produced the desired effect of restoration and extension of cultivation. As we will now ee, even the fiscal losses to the government were to some extent compensated by 'secret payments' from the farmers.

h. 'Secret payments'

When Baji Rao II farmed out a district he stipulated for the payment in advance of a certain amount of money, part of which was to be paid to the state treasury as *rasad*, while another portion of it was to be credited to the Peshwa's private purse (*khāsgī poṭā*) as being the amount payable as *aṇtastha* (Skt. *antaḥstha*, 'what is within' or 'concealed', 'secret payment') by the farmer for the privilege of obtaining the lease.[190] This system was observed by

[188] *Ibid.*, pp. 136, 166.

[189] *P.A.: List no. 11, General Volumes*, vo. 13, no. 92 of 1855. When alienations made by farmers were nevertheless considered legitimate by the *huzūr*, this was because they were made by the farmer *in a different capacity*, which authorized him to do so. For instance alienations made by the Gaikwar in his Ahmadabad farm were valid as he was also considered to be the *sarsubhedār* of the district for the period that he held it in farm (cf. 'List of officers who under the former Governments had power to confer Grants exempting Lands wholly or partially from the Payment of Public Revenue', App. C to Regulation I of 1823, *EIP*, 3, p. 827).

[190] *P.A.: List no. 11, Nasik Records*, vol. 1, no. 1100 of 1861.

previous Peshwas to a certain extent, but it was carried to its highest pitch by Baji Rao II. This Peshwa used to receive the revenues of the mahals let out in farm in two currencies, *viz*. an amount in *śikkā* (or *hallīśikkā*, i.e. 'recently coined') currency, and the remainder in the currency usually received in the government treasury; it was the agio of the former which was termed *khāsgī aṇtastha*, and which was applied for the Peshwa's private use.[191] Part of it served to fill up gaps created by the system of revenue farming itself. Such appears, for example, from *tāḷebaṇds* of 1812/13 and 1813/14 of pargana Kumbhari in Nasik, showing that in those two years out of a sum of 10,800 rupees – being the Peshwa's yearly *khāsgī aṇtastha* on account of the farm of this pargana – an amount of 9, 458 rupees was expended each year on twelve *devasthāns* (also in Nasik), which had become destitute in consequence of Holkar's invasion in 1802 and the famine following upon it.[192] It may be surmised here that Baji Rao's having to spend such a large amount of his *khāsgī aṇtastha* for the restoration of these temples and their not having then recovered was also due to the policy of his contractors of impoverishing the wealthy families.

Like the *khāsgī* revenues of Maratha princes generally, Baji Rao II's *khāsgī aṇtastha* was not entered into the state accounts, but in his own *khāsgī kird*.[193] An idea of their proportionate amount can be gained from the Peshwa's sanad of the Ahmadabad farm of 1804 to the Gaikwar. A summary of that document[194] shows the annual *khāsgī aṇtastha* to have been 6.6% of the stipulated annual rent of 4.5 lacs of rupees. Twice as much as this was the amount subsumed under *darbārkharc*, i.e., similar payments to other dignitaries.

The two terms *aṇtastha* and *darbārkharc* were often used loosely as synonyms. There was thus in each district, as part of the *sādilvārī* or 'contingent' charges levied to pay for expenses not provided for by the government, a fund referred to by either name, which originally was only applied to 'bribe' officials and auditors, but was later indefinitely increased and came to cover many other of the personal expenses of the mamlatdars.[195] In Nana Fadnis' time, and

191 *Ibid.*, no. 117 d.d 2nd April 1850; *SSRPD*, 5, no. 193.
192 *P.A.*, *op. cit.*, no. 161 of 1850.
193 *Ibid.*, no. 1100 of 1861. In Baji Rao II's case these were written in his own hand, on gold- and silver-decorated paper (*P.A.: Peśve Rozkird, Rumals 238–47*). See on such private accounts also p. 316, note 30.
194 In: Gense and Banaji, *Gaikwads*, 7, p. 117.
195 Elphinstone, *Report*, p. 37; *Maharashtra State Gazetteer, History*, pt. III (Bombay, 1967), p. 9; Grant Duff, *History*, 1, p. 454. This fund also enabled the

before that, the *aṇtastha* payments were also secret, in the sense that they were not accounted for by the mamlatdar in the *mahāl jhaḍatī*, but separately in an *aṇtasthacī yādī*.[196] The secret payments were part of all transactions at all levels. Villages used to pay an amount as *aṇtastha* to an outgoing farmer to have him persuade the incoming farmer that their payments in the past year had been less than they actually were.[197] More generally, all heads of taxation invented by revenue farmers to avoid the raising of the land assessment, which before Baji Rao II would have to be accounted for, were *aṇtastha*, which meant that they could be imposed without coming into open conflict with the terms of their contract or with *kaccā* arrangements.[198] Equally, a return to the latter remained possible.

V Conclusion and summary

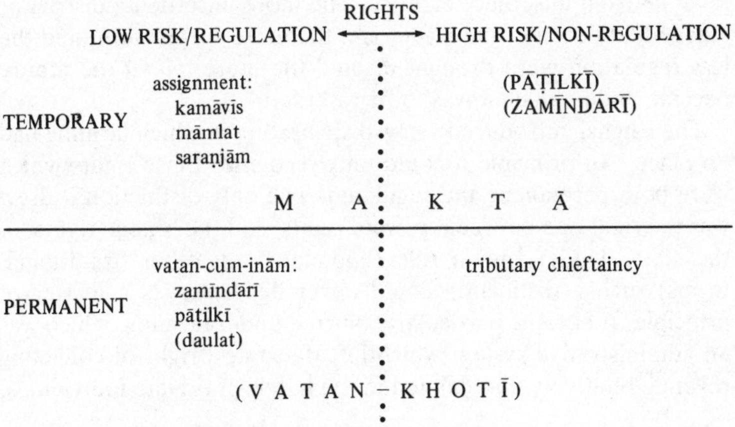

summary graph of land-rights under Maratha sovereignty

This scheme shows the relative positions of the different rights which we have discussed. A continuous dividing line is drawn horizontally in the middle to indicate the abruptness of the transition from temporary to permanent rights: they are either the one or the other. An anomaly in this respect are the pseudo-patrimonial

darakdārs to attend at the huzur and to meet the expenses of complimentary presents (Jervis, *Konkan*, p. 119; *EIP*, 4, pp. 625, 8).

196 See *P.A.: Prant Ajmas*, *passim*; Breloer, *Kauṭalīya Studien*, pp. 47 ff.

197 *BG*, XIX, p. 337.

198 *B.A.: R.D.*, vol. 59/746 of 1836, pp. 216–17; *BGS*, no. 160, *MS*, 1828–31, p. 772.

saranjams of Scindhia, Holkar, etc. These are put as *daulat* in the scheme, with parentheses, under 'permanent'. There is, however, a gradual transition from the condition of LOW RISK/REGULATION to that of HIGH RISK/NON-REGULATION; to indicate this a dotted dividing line is drawn vertically in the middle. Farming rights are written in capital letters. MAKTĀ comprises a variety of differently composed rights (e.g. *istāvā maktā, khotī maktā*) ranging from HIGH RISK/NON-REGULATION to LOW RISK/REGULATION, but is mostly situated on the side of the former. The VATAN KHOTĪ we have situated in an equal measure on both sides; it is put in parentheses since its permanency is atypical of a farming right. For the same reason the PĀṬILKĪ and ZAMĪNDĀRĪ are put in parentheses in the right upper corner: normally such rights are permanent and under regulation, but they become farming rights in a situation of HIGH RISK/NON-REGULATION.

Under Maratha sovereignty these rights merged freely into one another. Farming, we argued, was the means to obtain a settled revenue from unsettled territory. The more unsettled a district or village had become, the more risk, the more speculation, and the less regulation were brought in, and the more *pakkā* the tenure became under which it was to be resettled.

The English introduced a new dispensation in which farming had no place.[1] In principle it could only recognize those rights which were both permanent and regulated. The only distinction it drew was the rigid one between 'private rights' and the 'public rights' of the state. Under Indian rule (and under all other 'traditional' forms) such a distinction could never be drawn as a matter of principle. It became particularly blurred under farming, which was an administrative system which left the state's right of collecting revenue relatively unregulated in the hands of private individuals,

[1] After the conquest of the Peshwa's territories, in 1818, Elphinstone ordered his subordinate Collectors – Robertson in Poona, Briggs in Khandesh, Pottinger in Ahmadnagar – and his Political Agent at Satara, Grant Duff, to 'keep up' the Maratha revenue arrangements but 'to abolish farming at once', and instead make the collections directly from the patils (M. E. to H. D. Robertson, 26 February 1818, in R. D. Choksey (ed.), *The Last Phase* (Bombay, 1948), no.79; M. E. to J. Briggs, 10 March 1818, *Bengal Secret and Political Consultations*, vol. 301, 31 August 1818, pt.I, no.89; M. E. to H. Pottinger, 2 April 1818, *ibid.*, pt.II, no.105; M. E. to J. Grant, 24 April 1818, *ibid.*, no.131. Earlier, in the eighteenth century, the British had still continued the farming of the land-revenue, when they took possession of Salsette and Karanja; this lasted from 1774 up to 1788 (*BG*, XIII, pt.II, p. 562). In the nineteenth century, in British territory only customs were farmed, but in the Maratha (and other) Princely States the land-revenue continued to be put up to auction. The *khotī* tenures were, if not resumed, always treated as hereditary (cf. section f.).

and which thrived on 'secret payments'. The very fact of the prevalence of these payments demonstrates the lack of a watershed between public and private revenues. Hence, criticism of farming, and of the *aṇtastha* payments themselves, can only be *ex post facto* criticism.[2]

[2] See on this problem J. C. Van Leur, *Indonesian Trade and Society* (The Hague and Bandung, 1955), p. 287; W. F. Wertheim, 'Sociological Aspects of Corruption in Southeast Asia', in: R. Bendix *et al.* (eds), *State and Society* (Berkeley, Los Angeles and London, 1968), p. 562; J. Breman, 'The Village on Java and the Early Colonial State', *The Journal of Peasant Studies*, 9, 4 (1982), pp. 207 ff.

EPILOGUE

In the eighteenth century it was left to a French orientalist, A. H. Anquetil Du Perron (1731–1805), to argue that the ideas of oriental despotism and the absence of private property in the East were fictions employed to justify European, particularly British, intervention and conquest.[1] After a stay of nearly six years in India, this *savant* concluded that the country knew only one 'absolute despot': the British Company.[2] Anquetil spoke in terms that the British were apt to reserve for indigenous rulers: 'J'ai vu dans l'Inde entière, le Bengale, les deux Côtes, l'abus énorme qu'une troupe d'Européens, fiers du succès de leurs armes, faisaient de leur nouvelle puissance purement sanguinaire. Le froid des années n'a pas affaibli en moi l'impression que m'a faite, n'a pas diminué l'horreur que m'a causée, il y a 47 ans leur conduite arbitraire opposée à tout droit divin et humain, leurs procédés barbares et atroces.'[3] Such statements were at times criticized even by contemporary Frenchmen as inspired by an excessive 'animosité contre les Anglais'.[4] But Anquetil could quote with approval some British scholars who pioneered the investigation of Asiatic 'customs, manners, language, learning, religion and philosophy' in the eighteenth century. Thus for instance Alexander Dow, also writing 'from experience', that 'the nation of the Marathas, though chiefly composed of Rajputs, or that tribe of Indians whose chief business is war, retain the mildness of their countrymen in their domestic government ... the Marathas who have been represented as

1 A. H. Anquetil Du Perron, *Législation Orientale* (Amsterdam, 1778).

2 *Idem, L'Inde en Rapport avec l'Europe*, 2 vols (Hamburg and Brunswick, 1798), 1, p. vii.

3 *Idem*, 'Observations sur la Propriété Individuelle et Foncière dans l'Inde et en Egypte', in: P. Paulin de S. Barthélemy, *Voyage aux Indes Orientales*, 3 vols (Paris, 1808), 3, p. XL.

4 P. de S. Barthélemy, *Voyage*, 2, p. 161.

barbarians, are a great and rising people, subject to a regular government, the principles of which are founded on virtue'.[5]

Later, in the nineteenth and twentieth centuries, the character of Indian sovereignty was more and more obliterated. It was held as commonplace that before the arrival of the British in India, 'a sharp sword and a bold heart supplant the hereditary laws of descent' and, with increasingly characteristic philistinism, that 'had the average man in India been asked in the eighteenth century to define a sovereign, he would probably have compared such a being to the top dog in a dog fight'.[6] In 1922, F. W. Buckler attempted to propagate a 'radical revision' of the accepted theories of the rise of British power in India, claiming that 'for the last century and a half, Indian history has been represented in Europe almost entirely by the propaganda of the Trading Companies', that 'their much reiterated conclusions have been accepted as axiomatic – even by Indian students – and no effort has been made to examine the biassed judgments of Merchants on the subject of oriental monarchy'.[7]

Such an effort to redress the moral balance sheet has been only a very indirect aim of this book. It is certainly false to see Indian sovereignty as largely a 'parade of vices'. Buckler thought that this was further motivated by the unpopularity of the East India Company in England and to explain and excuse the savage confrontation of arms during the Mutiny of 1857. A dimension of vice can be found probably in all historical political systems. The question is rather whether such vices were inherent in these systems. Here, it has been attempted therefore to go behind the propaganda and counter-propaganda which until recently reflected powerful political interests. And as such this attempt itself may perhaps be seen as due to the passing of Western dominance in the East. History has advanced and so, we tend to think, has the science of history as it becomes ever more detached and attempts to resort to explanation rather than judgment.

Oriental despotism was seen by Europeans as a political order

5 Quoted by Anquetil Du Perron, *Législation Orientale*, p. 232. Cf. also A. Dow, 'A Dissertation concerning the Customs, Manners, Language, Religion and Philosophy of the Hindoos', in: P. J. Marshall (ed.), *The British Discovery of Hinduism in the Eighteenth Century* (Cambridge, 1970), pp. 107–39.

6 D. Dewar and H. L. Garrett, 'A Reply to Mr. F. W. Buckler's *The Political Theory of the Indian Mutiny*', *Transactions of the Royal Historical Society*, 4th series, vol. 7 (London, 1924), p. 152.

7 'Indian Mutiny', p. 73.

which was unlimited in the exercise of power and which, lacking a counter-balancing territorial nobility, was characterized by state monopoly of land. While it had no history of its own it nevertheless contained the potential of a sudden collapse into anarchy. The principles of Islam in effect, expunging the old social organizations and social inequalities, did not endorse hierarchy, caste or aristocracy, and the Islamic empires gave no legal status or an autonomous constituency to any such 'intermediate' structures which European writers considered to be the essential difference between Oriental despotism and West-European feudalism. While, admittedly, Islamic theory emphasizes a static universality, it is proposed here that the different courses of development of the Islamic empires and the European socio-economic structure in the fourteenth to eighteenth centuries should, first of all, be related to the comparative backwardness of Europe. In the Islamic world a pervasive legacy of ancient agrarian civilizations – Byzantine, Roman, Sassanid, Hindu–Buddhist – accounted for a far more sophisticated fiscal system, advanced monetization of the economy, and extensive trade networks which were tapped by complex states with a dualist bureaucracy of separate military and fiscal departments. The prevalence of these features (which developed over millennia) had distinguished Islam as a civilization and their absence reduced Western Europe to a frontier zone until the beginning of the age of European expansion (and in many respects till much later) when Europe could begin to capitalize on the 'advantage of relative backwardness.' In the cosmopolitan Islamic context there was great geographical and social mobility, and, thanks to its highly monetized fiscal economy, its politics evolved around the pivot of an intricate system of almost entirely 'monetized honours' and non-hereditary status gradations which were often expressed in quantitative terms. In comparison with the sturdy tiers of dependence of feudal and post-feudal Europe, Islamic loyalties were fickle and politics was often a question of arithmetic and pecuniary calculation of a sort which to European eyes seems utterly ruthless and corrupt.

On this basis the mechanism of *fitna*, 'sedition' or 'rebellion', became the driving force of Islamic political history. *Fitna* or the threat of it were constantly recurring features in Islamic expansion almost from the beginning. Strongly condemned as *shirk*, 'dualism' or 'idolatry', in the *Qur'ān* and Islamic legal literature, *fitna* broke the monotheistic unity of Islam but explained its dynamic propensity. While *fitna* often had a secretive origin in intrigue, it was all the more effective as a mitigator of despotic, arbitrary or unlimited exercise of power. But the fact that it had no legal or religious sanction set it apart from the feudal *Widerstandrecht* and from the limitations imposed on sovereignty by a parliamentary or estate representation. The context in which *fitna* occurred, the monetized, fiscal, bureaucratic polity is clearly different from feudalism. European feudalism arose on a subsistence base and was characterized by the absence of a generalized system of taxation at the level of the state. In India, since the classical age, generalized royal taxation was postulated as a conventional prerogative at a fixed legitimate rate. In contrast with Western Europe therefore such taxation was not a newly introduced extraordinary levy of the king who theoretically had to live of his own domain and was without the right of permanent taxation of his subjects. In India the course of development can only be reconstructed hypothetically but in the age of incipient Islamic state formation the economy already bore a strong imprint of monetization and bureaucratic techniques of land-revenue management. Here *fitna* occurred. In contrast to feudalization, *fitna* was not a return to a subsistence base. It was always a consequence of further agrarian and political expansion and of an intensification of trade and credit networks, of a condensation of the mesh of intertwined rights and conflicts. More specifically, it was such a process which linked the Indo-Muslim polity throughout its history in a competitive scramble for nobles and retainers with the surrounding polities of Iran and Central Asia, which caused the entry of the Mughals into the late Delhi Sultanate, and which led to the rise of gentry groups – Rajputs, Marathas, Jats, Sikhs – within the expanding Muslim empire and ultimately to its 'gentrification'. Instead of an etiolation of the economy *fitna* represented rather local accumulations of wealth which caused the decline of imperial unity. This was a unity which in retrospect appears to have been possible on the foundation of military superiority but only to the extent that – and for as long as – it represented a balance of conflicting interests of aspiring groups of nobles and gentry which were incorporated in the empire and which thereby enhanced their local strength. Mughal expansion and the successful establishment of a Mughal order created most of the conditions of the rise of autonomous power centres through *fitna*. It was however an old pattern which in India is first described in explicit and general terms in the fourteenth century when the territorial expansion of Islam gained momentum. As Barani writes: 'kings have of old said that wealth and *fitna* and *fitna* and wealth are inseparable from each other'.[8] Normally, Indo-Persian chronicles would ascribe *fitna* in mentalistic terms to faults of character of 'bad Muslims' or the non-Muslim gentry or 'rabble' which are 'seduced' and 'spoiled' by the acquisition of money, horses or elephants.

We have interpreted *fitna* as one of the foundations of the Islamic state: the state owed its origin to *fitna* and it could never really transcend this origin but had to organize itself around it until it built up such impetus that fresh realignments occurred in the polity. The bureaucracy was at best an attempt to institutionalize *fitna* in a dualist structure of management with separate departments and rival personnel, and successfully maintained equilibrium was more of a diplomatic feat than the result of military superiority. In fact the army was usually the most unstable element in the polity, as it was the most calculating and most liable to *fitna*. It was the most dangerous element in the power structure since its loyalties were never certain, not because of its military effectiveness directly but rather as a political element, through the political use of its military power. The notorious Mughal succession struggles bring this out vividly, but it was no less evident in the slow process of Mughal expansion which we have described in some detail in the Deccan. Therefore, whatever weight we might give to superior military organization or striking potential, religious fervour, the 'natural penchant for the raid' of Islamic frontier peoples, to greed or the thirst for booty, *fitna* or 'sedition' provided the link between internal factionalism and the expansive propensity of advanced Islamic polities. This was not primarily a military operation but depended more on collaboration or non-collaboration of disaffected subjects, of soldiery, of autochthonous élites and counter-élites which, amongst each other, were riddled with conflict. As has been long recognized, similar factors operated in European expansion in Asia (and elsewhere), particularly in the late eighteenth and early nineteenth centuries. Thus in India the Great Mutiny (which was also called a *fitna*) of 1857 can perhaps be interpreted historically as the unforeseen climax of a process of intensification of

[8] '*bādśāhān-i-qadīm gufta and kah māl-o-fitna wa fitna-o-māl ya'nī māl-o-fitna mulāzim-i-yakdīgar and*' (*Tārīkh-i-Fīroz Shāhī*, p. 224); cf. also *ibid.*, '*pel-o-māl-i-khāṣṣat kah basyār-o-be-andāza bāśad wāsiṭa' fitna-hāy-i-bazarg ast*'; *ibid.*, p. 343, '*wa māl kah wāsiṭa' fitna' dīnī-o-mulkī ast*'.

conflict and political realignment which occurred in the wake of British expansion.[9] To an extent this may have been comparable to the *fitna* which followed Mughal expansion, but the subsequent restoration of British power represents a fundamental break with the traditional process of proliferating alliance-making and breaking. British power did not brook dissent and replaced *fitna* by the absolute dominion of the single sovereign state.

The historiography of ancient India, of pre-Islamic India, also shows that foreign invaders – the Greeks, Scythians, Parthians and Huns – established themselves most easily and most successfully in areas where Buddhism and republican government had spread in antagonism with more powerful patrimonial, orthodox Hindu kingdoms. Islam, although it eventually gave the death-blow to Buddhism, in its initial expansive move of 711–12 into Sind, had in a parallel way utilized to its benefit the disaffection of the local Buddhist population with the new Brahman ruler Dahir.[10] The *Chachnāma*, which gives a detailed account of this conquest by Muhammad Ibn al-Qasim, clearly exhibits the political means of conciliation, sedition and sowing dissension as principles overriding the application of military force and terror, particularly in the often-repeated conclusion of the so-called *ahd-i-wāṣiq* or 'bond for the fulfilment of mutual promises' with defectors.[11] These political expedients, reminiscent of the 'instigation' policy of Kautilya's *Arthaśāstra*, the exploitation of and intervention in local conflict, also dominated the Mughal campaigns in the Deccan and elsewhere in the sixteenth to eighteenth centuries. Equally, the expansion of the Marathas depended on collusion with *zamīndārs* and Mughal mansabdars in *fitna*, in 'conquest on invitation'. Here, as formerly, the political use rather than the direct application of military power stood out in the expansionist process. The army itself would only fight for money, but when money was made available fighting became unnecessary for the enemy would desert.[12] The application

9 Cf. Bayly, *Rulers, Townsmen and Bazars*, esp. pp. 2 ff; R. Robinson, 'Non-European Foundations of European Imperialism: Sketch for a Theory of Collaboration', in: R. Owen and B. Sutcliffe (eds), *Studies in the Theory of Imperialism* (London, 1972), pp. 118–40; *Descriptive List of Mutiny Papers in the National Archives of India*, 5 vols (New Delhi, 1960–73).

10 A. Schimmel, *Islam in the Indian Subcontinent* (Leiden and Cologne, 1980), p. 4.

11 P. Hardy, 'Is the *Chachnama* intelligible to the historian as political theory?', in: H. Khuhro (ed.), *Sind through the Centuries* (Karachi, 1981), pp. 111–17.

12 Cf. also Mottahedeh, *Loyalty and Leadership*, pp. 81, 83; and see p. 183: 'It is surprising how seldom [this] coercive power [of the army] was actually used'.

of force appears to have been rather a sign of weakness and demoralization.

Especially remarkable were the underlying continuities in the expansion of Islamic states in South Asia from the earliest times to the period of European domination and also the resilience of the frame of reference which the chronicles and histories adduce from the pristine rule of the first four 'rightly guided' Caliphs. It was the transcendent unity of the Muslim Brotherhood against which *fitna* was ultimately set. Beginning in AD 657, a first great *fitna* or 'schism' ripped the Islamic world apart, with in its train a never-ending series of related *fitnas*, leading to lasting and irreconcilable divisions among the Muslims of which those of Shia and Sunni remained the most prominent and articulate. From the first *fitna* onwards, starting with the killing of the third Caliph 'Uthmān at Madina, the Muslims could no longer be governed without the support of one faction against others. Muslim imperial power became anchored in mundane politics instead of being mediated by Islam solely.[13] The transcendent unity of Muslims precluded a worldly foundation of sovereignty, and factionalism and *fitna* were the worst of evils, but these always resurged and in a fundamental sense remained inseparably linked to Muslim domination. *Fitna* became a general term of abuse for sedition or opposition by factions other than one's own. Modern authors consider the role of *fitna* in the Islamic state as paradoxical or, at the least, they explain it by taking refuge in paradox. Concisely put by Patricia Crone, 'the Arabs had to fight one civil war to devise an organization, another to maintain it, and a third to prove it obsolete, all within some eighty years'.[14] Louis Gardet pointed out that the avoidance of *fitna* is one of the principal duties of the Muslim authorities, but yet 'l'histoire événementielle des peuples musulmanes est centrée sur une série de *fitna*(*s*), toujours renaissantes'.[15]

The problem of *fitna* was thus at the core of Muslim politics and religion. It can, however, also be sociologically understood as a concomitant of Muslim state expansion in general, following Ibn Khaldun's analysis of the 'transformation of the Caliphate into

13 Cf. M. G. S. Hodgson, *The Ventury of Islam*, vol. I (Chicago and London, 1974), pp. 215 ff; B. Lewis, 'Islamic Concepts of Revolution', in: P. J. Vatikiotis (ed.), *Revolution in the Middle East* (London, 1972), p. 36; E. L. Peterson, *'Alī and Mu'āwiya in early Arabic Tradition* (Copenhagen, 1964).

14 *Slaves on Horses: The Evolution of the Islamic Polity* (Cambridge, 1980), p. 29.

15 M. Arkoun and L. Gardet, *L'Islam: Hier-Demain* (Paris, 1978), p. 24.

monarchy' (*inqilāb al-khilāfat ilā-l-mulk*).[16] After noting that Islam condemns *'aṣabīya* or political cohesion based on alliances and *esprit de clan* which culminate in monarchy but disrupt the Islamic universality, Khaldun propounded that without a political foundation the religious law could not effectively be upheld and that therefore sovereignty of a worldly ruler became inevitable in Islam. In the earliest period of Islamic history, before the beginning of the period of *fitna* in 35 AH, political sovereignty or monarchy (*mulk*) did not exist in Islam and was considered by Muslims to be a vanity of unbelievers and of the enemies of Islam (*niḥlat yauma'idhin li-ahl al-kafr wa 'a'dā' ad-dīn*). The first four Caliphs up to 'Alī kept themselves aloof from all its manifestations and pomp. In this detachment they were greatly supported by the simplicity and low living standards (*ghaḍāḍa*) of their Bedouin existence in that age; these were initially reinforced by the ascetism (*zuhd*) preached by Islam. 'The Arabs lived away from the fertile plains owned by the Rabī'a and Yamani ... yet they did not envy them for their abundance and often, without objecting, ate scorpions (*'aqārib*) and scarabs (*khanāfis*).' But when later the Companions of the Prophet marched against the Persians and the Byzantines, they amassed great fortunes in land and money. Soon the simplicity of Bedouin life was forgotten and *'aṣabīya* reasserted itself amongst the Arab conquerors and as an inevitable result the monarchy reappeared as well. Monarchy however was of the same order as luxury and wealth, and it was of the same order as *fitna*, seduction and schism. So when *fitna* broke out between 'Alī and Mu'āwiya this was, according to Khaldun, 'a necessary consequence of *'aṣabīya* and both parties were in their right' (*wa limā waqa'at al-fitna baina 'alī wa mu'āwiya wa hiya muqtaḍan al-'aṣabīya kāna ṭarīqhum fī-hā-l-ḥaqq wa-l-ijtihād*). Through political realignments and the resurgence of divisive conflict over the distribution of wealth and conquered territories, the Caliphate lost its unity and was transformed into monarchy. The Caliphate was at first a form of government in which every Muslim was his own sole moderator (*wāzi'*) thanks to the influence of his religion. The principal change which occurred subsequently with the acquisition of landed property and wealth during the conquests was the loss of the moderating influence of Islam and the reappearance of clan and alliance politics as the major factor. *Fitna* then began as a result of the temptations inflicted by God on the Muslim community.

16 Wafi, *Muqaddima*, 2, pp. 708–30.

These developments furnished the paradigm of Muslim sovereignty of all later times, if not explicitly, often implicitly. The Indo-Muslim literature offers ample illustration of this, for example, when it is described in the *Fatāwā-yi-Jahāndārī* how a noble Malik Kafur gains influence over the Sultan Alauddin Khalji and how this may lead to *fitna* in the same way that the ascendancy of the brothers of Caliph 'Uthmān at his court contributed to the first great *fitna* in Islam.[17] Another example is given in the terms of submission dictated by Aurangzeb to the Sultan of Golconda in 1636, stipulating that the Friday prayers should mention the names of the four rightly-guided Caliphs and of the Mughal Emperor instead of the names of the Twelve Shia Imams and the Safavid Emperor of Persia (cf. p. 56). The expansion of the Islamic state and *fitna*, the disruption of its unity, are always described in the religious idiom which stresses the static universal order of 'just' dominion, the essential quality of which (like that of the *dharma* of pre-Islamic India) was the absence of egoistic and political motivation. As Khaldun says: 'all those orders are to be blamed which are merely inspired by political or worldly considerations'.[18] Such a conception of universal justice implies that all obedience and all submission is ultimately obedience and submission to God alone. Without this ideal of religiously sanctioned order the Muslim or Hindu state, no less than their Western counterparts, would have been unthinkable. But the analysis of *fitna* shows a deep rift between the idea of political order and actual political processes because *fitna* is either seen, in the Muslim view, against the background of ideal unity or, in the Western interpretation, of a unitary, pacified state governed by civil law. Hence the apparent contradiction between static 'order' and the 'disorder' of constantly changing factional alignments in the chronicles of Muslim history.

It is against this ideology, with its religious and diplomatic backing, of universal dominion which was associated with kingship in both its Hindu and Muslim variants that sovereignty and *hoc loco* the rise of Maratha power must be understood. Such an ideology is what we find as the counterpart of the classical precedent of Roman law in the Absolutist states of Europe. In the Muslim and Hindu Orient the ideology of imperial or universal dominion employs a deceptively modern-sounding idiom and postulates state monopoly

[17] Cf. Hardy, 'Force and Violence', p. 195.

[18] Wafi, *Muqaddima*, 2, pp. 687–8: '*wa aḥkām as-siyāsa innamā taṭala'a 'ilā muṣāliḥ ad-dunyā faqaṭ*'.

of land and a just but despotic king as the guardian of order, and the absence of a territorial nobility or gentry. It was a desacralized order which was represented by religious experts (ulama or brahmans) who created 'legitimate sovereignty' in a condominium with the king. But while Roman law in post-medieval Europe became the juridical means to effect territorial integration and administrative centralism, in India the ideology equating sovereignty with universal or world dominion did not make of territory a fixed and abstract entity, and territory (*janapada*) in practice remained linked to the vested rights of the indwelling people, the object of a multiplicity of allegiances which was never demarcated by fixed geographical boundaries. Taxation of the land was theoretically the strict prerogative, the 'salary' of kingship for the execution of the royal task of keeping order 'with the rod', but actually the vested rights of the *zamīndārī* gentry constituted the fiscal base of sovereignty, somewhat analogous to the European Estates. In Europe the sovereign gradually had to expand a novel fiscal claim with the aid or co-operation of the Estates under the pressure of international armed conflict. In India there was the postulated right to generalized taxation of the sovereign but this right was at odds with the *fitna* of the agrarian, 'allodial' gentry. The complementary opposition of *fitna* and generalized taxation is what ultimately made sovereignty a limited instead of a despotic function.

This peculiar double-track of 'sovereignty' and 'universal dominion' is evident throughout Indian history. In practice, sovereignty, as in Absolutist Europe, reveals itself as a limited power of arbitration, adjudication and maintenance of contending vested interests in land and associated rights, privileges and duties. Systematically also it reveals an interdependence and interpenetration of public and private domains. Furthermore, we find in India all the tangled complexity, the 'untidiness' and elasticity of form and substance of institutions that are known from pre-modern Europe. The Indian state was a form of institutionalized dissidence, and dissidence was an indispensable 'luxury' of the system until it acquired a potential for 'treason' in modern times. The ideology, the semantic and juridical grid that defined dissidence and the attitudes towards authority and legitimacy, account for the organization of the polity and for the real differences of internal structure that existed with Europe. Sovereignty in India was organized around what the Muslims depreciated as *fitna*: this was a form of 'sedition' (not necessarily armed) which had its own logic in complex shifts in power relations but always with the ideology of universal dominion in the background. About most processes of *fitna* in the Indo-Muslim period we know little more than that they took place, when they took place, and that they resulted from wealth falling into what the chroniclers thought were the 'wrong' hands. About the *fitna* of the Marathas which led to the establishment of *svarājya* in the eighteenth-century Mughal Empire we have come to know much more. The main conclusion which we have drawn from the surviving Maratha documentation is that *fitna* was in no way a pure negation of order, not an anarchic implosion of centralist unity or a return to the state of nature. Such would also have been hard to harmonize with the persistent search for Muslim and Hindu symbols of legitimacy by the Maratha conquerors. We did see, on the contrary, the Marathas being absorbed into the expansionist alliance-building of the Mughals and claiming the 'right to service' from them. Regional development of gentry power and the strengthening of local economies were seen to have led to an intensification of conflict and rapid political change amongst the local élite powerholders rather than to long-term and steady agricultural and economic decline as an overall process. This conclusion, it should be stressed once more, is against the grain of Mughal historiography. Without the Maratha documentation describing, as it were, the other side of the picture, the period in question – the immediate pre-colonial period, that is – would appear to have belonged to that age of medieval South Asian history in which, as Peter Hardy has written, 'the historian today is very much in danger of becoming the prisoner of the historians who have written, or otherwise left evidence relevant to, the study of those periods'.[19] In this respect the conclusion advanced here is likely, if anything, to reinforce the sceptical attitude towards the usefulness of Muslim sources for history which has been a trend in Britain in recent years but which historians of Mughal India have so far not commonly adopted.[20] In the case in point, this does not

19 'Force and Violence', p. 200.

20 Cf. H. Kennedy, 'Review of M. G. Morony, *Iraq after the Muslim Conquest*', *The Times Literary Supplement*, September 7, 1984, p. 999. J. F. Richards, referring to M. C. Pradhan's analysis of Jat documents and chronicles in *The Political System of the Jats of Northern India*, concluded that 'the total impression gained of the Jats and of Muslim rule is very different from that given by historians who have relied primarily on the Muslim chronicles'; in the sequel of this, Richards raises the question of the authenticity of these materials ('The Islamic Frontier in the East: Expansion into South Asia', *South Asia*, 4 (October, 1974), pp. 108–9). The problem at issue is the territorial expansion of a Jat clan in the Doab region just

mean that these Muslim sources would cease to be relevant but that they would have to be reinterpreted, or put in a new perspective which would demonstrate a greater awareness of the resistance of these sources to local formations of power and local expansion, and thereby we should see 'new depths in old evidence' through the eyes of '*fitna mongers*'.

The emphasis may thus shift to new aspects, or newly discovered foundations of the political economy of eighteenth-century India which enable us to observe it without the residue of a teleological perspective which stresses 'lack of effective control', 'poor communications', the absence of 'institutional commitment' on the part of officials, and an array of other 'key weaknesses'.[21] The over-hasty generalizations regarding the deterioration of agriculture and collapse of trade networks which supposedly resulted from over-exploitation by transient *jāgīrdārs* and revenue farmers, pervasive corruption, and corresponding apathy of cultivators, have all become part and parcel of a stereotyped image of 'politically oriented capitalism' set off against the strict autonomy of sovereignty of the colonial state of later times. Here too the Maratha documentation shows that it was not the 'rapacity' of revenue farmers but rather the impact of the colonial government which interfered with the circulation and diffusion of money, credit and resources.

East of Delhi, its 'autonomy and aggressive expansionism', and the degree to which such 'self-sufficient operation of local society' in an area close to Delhi during the heyday of Mughal rule would have been possible or might have been exagggerated in Pradhan's source material or in his own account of this.

21 Cf. M. Adas, 'From Avoidance to Confrontation: Peasant Protest in Precolonial and Colonial Southeast Asia', *CSSH*, 23 (1981), pp. 216–47.

KEY TO SELECTIONS OF PAPERS FROM THE RECORDS AT THE EAST-INDIA HOUSE

vol.3: pp.677–97	Elphinstone's Minute of 6 April 1821
701–6	Minute by Mr. Prendergast, 29 June 1821
814–5	Extract Revenue Letter from Bombay, 27 November 1822
816–8	Extract Revenue Letter to Bombay, 4 May 1825
vol.4: pp.207–17	Report of — (No name, date). Administration of Justice under the Peishwa's Government
217–43	Captain Grant's Replies to Judicial Queries, 30 April 1819; to the Hon. M. Elphinstone, etc.
243–56	Mr. J. Briggs' Replies to Judicial Queries, 13 June 1819; to the Hon. M. Elphinstone, etc.
256–83	Mr. W. Chaplin's Replies to Judicial Queries, 25 June 1819; to the Hon. M. Elphinstone, etc.
283–309	Mr. H. Pottinger's Replies to Judicial Queries, 8 August 1819; to the Hon. M. Elphinstone, etc.
309–451	Report of William Chaplin, Esq., to Chief Secretary to Government, Dated 5 November 1821
340–436	Revenue Enclosures in Mr. Chaplin's Report, 5 November 1821
340–83	J. Briggs, Esq. to W. Chaplin, Esq., Dated 31 October 1821
384–88	H. Pottinger, Esq. to W. Chaplin, Esq., Dated 29 May 1821
388–99	J. Thackeray, Esq. to W. Chaplin, No date
399–436	H. D. Robertson, Esq. to W. Chaplin, 1 May 1820
453–524	Report of William Chaplin, Esq. to the Secretary to Government, 20 August 1822
524–678	Revenue Enclosures in Mr. Chaplin's Report, 20 August 1822
524–600	H. D. Robertson, Esq. to William Chaplin, Esq., Dated 10 October 1821
624–36	Account of the Revenue Management of the Peishwa's Territory during the Administration of Nana Furnaveese

BIBLIOGRAPHY

Archives

Poona Archives (Peshwa Daftar, Alienation Office): a total of 34,972 *rumāls* or 'bundles', each containing 500 to 2,000 loose documents or a number of folded packets, mostly in Marathi (Moḍi script), some in Persian. These archives also contain large amounts of British records, amongst which those of the Inam Commission. For descriptions, see G. S. Sardesai, *Handbook to the Records in the Alienation Office* (Bombay, 1933); V. G. Khobrekar, *Mahārāṣṭrāṇtīl Daftarkhāne* (Bombay, 1968); H. R. Guruji and V. G. Dighe, *Elianeśan Āfis Puṇeṇ yethīl Peśve Daftarācī Mārgadarśikā* (Bombay, 1934); V. D. Divekar, 'Survey of Material in Marathi on the Economic and Social History of India', *IESHR*, 15, 1 (1978), pp. 85–9.

Bombay Archives: Revenue Department. For a description, see P. Desai, *The Handbook of the Bombay Archives* (Bombay, 1978).

India Office Records and Library (London):
MSS, Eur. F.88, Box 14H, 17
Bengal Secret and Political Consultations
Bombay Secret Consultations
Parliamentary Papers

Arabic

Laoust, H., *La Profession de Foi d'Ibn Baṭṭa* (Damas, 1958).
Wafi, A. (ed.), *Muqaddimat Ibn Khaldūn*, 4 vols (Cairo, 1960–2).
Yusuf, Abu, *Kitāb al-Kharāj* (Cairo, 1887).

Persian

Alavi, Azra (ed.), *Ma'āṣir-i-Jahāngirī of Khwaja Kamgar Husaini* (Bombay, 1978).
Shuja ud-Din, M. and Husain, Bashir (eds), *Asrār-i-Ṣamadī* (Lahore, 1965).

Khan, Sayyid Ahmad (ed.), *Tārīkh-i-Fīroz Shāhī of Zia ad-Din Barani* (Calcutta, 1862).
Khare, G. H. (ed.), *Aitihāsik Fārsī Sāhitya*, vol.4 (Poona, 1949).
Pawar, A. (ed.), *Tarabai Papers: A Collection of Persian Letters* (Kolhapur, 1971).
ur-Rahim, Maulawi Abd (ed.), *Akbarnāma of Abul Fazl*, 3 vols (Calcutta, 1878–9).
Shah, In'amullah bin Khurram, *Auṣāf al-Āṣaf* (*ms* 480/1F, Abd us-Salam Collection, Maulana Azad Library, Aligarh).
Verma, D. (ed.), *Newsletters of the Mughal Court* (Reign of Ahmad Shah, 1751–52 AD.) (Bombay, 1949).

Sanskrit

Bendre, V. S. (ed.), *Rājārāmcaritam* (Poona, 1931).
Indian Antiquary (Bombay, 1872–1923).
Kane, P. V. (ed.), *Kātyāyanasmṛtiḥ on Vyavahāra* (Poona, n.d.).
Kangle, R. P. (ed.), *The Kauṭilīya Arthaśāstra*, 3 vols (Bombay, 1965–72).
Nene, G. S. (ed.), *Mānava Dharmaśāstra* (Benares, 1970).
Parvatiya, N. P. (ed.), *Mitākṣara on Yājñavalkya* (Benares, 1914).
Rājyavyavahāra Kośa (Hyderabad, 1956).

Marathi

Apte, D. V. (ed.), *Caṇdracūḍ Daftar* (Poona, 1920).
Apte, D. V. and Kelkar, N. C. (eds), *Śivcaritra Pradīpa* (Poona, 1925).
Avalaskar, S. V. (ed.), *Aitihāsik Sādhaneṇ* (Bombay, 1963).
Banhatti, N. (ed.), *Ājñāpatra* (Poona, 1974).
Bendre, V. S., *Mahārāṣṭre Itihāsācī Sādhaneṇ*, 3 vols (Bombay, 1967).
BISM-Aitihāsik Saṃkīrṇa Sāhitya, vol.1 (Poona, 1931).
BISM-Caturth Sammelan Vṛtt (1910).
BISM-Śivcaritra Sāhitya, 13 vols (Poona, 1926–65).
BISM-Śivkālīn Patrasārsaṃgraha, 3 vols (Poona, 1930–7).
BISM-Vārṣik Itivṛtt (1913–16).
Diskalkar, D. B. (ed.), *Historical Papers of the Sindhias of Gwalior*, 2 vols (Satara, 1934–40).
Gujar, M. V. (ed.), *Pavār Gharāṇyācyā Itihāsācīṇ Sādhaneṇ* (Poona, 1940).
Hervadkar, R. V. (ed.), *Saptaprakaraṇātmak Caritra* (Poona, 1967).
Hervadkar, R. V. (ed.), *Thorle Śāhū Mahārāja yāṇce Caritra* (Poona, 1973).
Historical Selections from Baroda State Records, 5 vols (Baroda, 1934–9).
Joshi, P. M. (ed.), *Selections from the Peshwa Daftar* (New series), 3 vols (Bombay, 1957–62).
Joshi, S. N. (ed.), *Saṃbhājīkālīn Patrasārsaṃgraha* (Poona, 1949).

Khare, G. H. (ed.), *Hiṅgaṇe Daftar*, 2 vols (Poona, 1945–7).
Khare, V. V. (ed.), *Aitihāsik Lekh Saṃgraha* vols 5–13 (Miraj, 1918–26).
Khobrekar, V. G. (ed.), *Records of the Shivaji Period* (Bombay, 1974).
Khobrekar, V. G. and Shinde, S. S. (eds), *Selections from Kolhapur Records: Source Material for the History of Konkan (1692–1828)* (Bombay, 1971).
Lele, K. K. and Oak, S. K. (eds), *Dhār Saṃsthāṇcā Itihās*, 2 vols (Dhar, 1934).
Macdonald, A., *Memoir of the Life of the late Nana Farnavis* (Oxford, 1927).
Mandlik, R. S. V. N., 'Preliminary observations on a Document giving an Account of the Establishment of a New Village named Muruḍa, in Southern Konkaṇa' (with text), *JBBRAS*, 8 (1865).
Nandurbarkar, P. R. and Dandekar, L. K. (eds), *Śivdigvijaya* (Poona, 1895).
Oak, B. P., *Oak Gharāṇyācā Itihās* (Poona, 1973).
Parasnis, D. B. (ed.), *Itihās Saṃgraha* (Poona, 1908–16).
Parasnis, D. B. (ed.), *Dillī yethīl Marāṭhyāṇcīn Rājkāraṇeṇ*, 2 vols (Bombay, 1913–14).
Parasnis, D. B. (ed.), *Brahmendrasvāmī Dhavaḍśīkar* (Bombay, 1945).
Pawar, A. (ed.), *Tārābāīkālīn Kāgadpatre*, 3 vols (Kolhapur, 1969–72).
Phalke, A.B. (ed.), *Śiṇdeśāhīcā Itihāsācīṇ Sādhaneṇ*, vol.1 (Gwalior, 1929).
Poona Akhbars, vol.2 (Hyderabad, 1954).
Purandare, K. V. (ed.), *Purandare Daftar*, vol.1 (Poona, 1929).
Rajvade, V. K. (ed.), *Marāṭhyāṇcyā Itihāsācīṇ Sādhaneṇ*, 22 vols (Poona, Bombay, etc., 1898–1919).
Sabnis, K. G. (ed.), *Paṇt Amātya Bāvḍā Daftar*, vol.1 (Kolhapur, 1937).
Sahāvicār, vol.1, no.4.
Sane, K. N. (ed.), *Aitihāsik Patreṇ Yādī Vagaire* (Poona, 1889).
Sane, K. N. (ed.), *Kāvyetihās Saṃgraha* (n.p., n.d.).
Sardesai Gharāṇyācī Itihās (n.p., n.d.).
Sardesai, G. S. (ed.), *Selections from the Peshwa Daftar*, 45 vols (Bombay, 1930–4).
Sardesai, G. S. (ed.), *Historical Papers relating to Mahadji Sindhia* (Gwalior, 1937).
Sardesai, G. S., Kale, Y. M. and Vakaskar, V. S. (eds), *Kāvyetihās Saṃgraha* (Poona, 1930).
Sardesai, G. S., Kale, Y. M. and Vakaskar, V. S. (eds), *Aitihāsik Patreṇ Yādī Vagaire* (Poona, 1930).
Sardesai, G. S., Kulkarni, K. P. and Kale, Y. M. (eds), *Aitihāsik Patravyavahār* (Poona, 1933).
Shejwalkar, T. S. (ed.), *Nagpur Affairs* (Selection of Marathi letters from the Menavli Daftar), 2 vols (Poona, 1954–9).
Śrī Rāmdās āṇi Rāmdāsī Granthamālā:Śrī Rāmdāsīcīṇ Aitihāsik Kāgadpatreṇ, 1, 'Kārī va Āṃbavaḍe-Jedhe Deśmukh' (Dhulia, 1930).

Śrīsampradāyācīṇ Kāgadpatreṇ (Dhulia, 1915).
Thakur, V. V. (ed.), *Hoḷkarśāhīcā Itihāsācīṇ Sādhaneṇ*, 2 vols (Indore, 1944–5).
Vad, R. B. G. C., Mawji, P. V. and Parasnis, D. B. (eds), *Sanadāpatreṇ* (Bombay, 1913).
Vad, R. B. G. C., Mawji, P. V. and Parasnis, D. B. (eds), *Treaties, Agreements and Sanads* (Bombay, 1924).
Vad, R. B. G. C., Mawji, P. V. and Parasnis, D. B. (eds), *Kaifiyats, Yadis &c.* (Bombay, 1908).
Vad, R. B. G. C., Mawji, P. V. and Parasnis, D. B. (eds), *Decisions from the Shahu and Peshwa Daftars* (Bombay, 1909).
Vad, R. B. G. C., Parasnis, D. B., *et al.* (eds), *Selections from the Satara Rajas' and the Peishwas' Diaries*, 9 vols (Poona and Bombay, 1905–11).
Vaidya Daftarāṇtūn Nivaḍlele Kāgad, 4 vols (Poona, 1944–9).
Vakaskar, V. S. (ed.), *91 Kalamī Bakhar* (Poona, 1962).
Vakaskar, V. S. (ed.), *Sabhāsadācī Bakhar* (Poona, 1973).

Articles and secondary works in Marathi

Bhat, B. V., 'Svarājyāṇtīl Deśādhikārī', *BISM-Tṛtīya Sammelan Vṛtt* (1915).
Bhave, V. K., *Peśvekālīn Mahārāṣtra* (Poona, 1935).
Candarkar, P. M., 'Śahājīrāje va Vataneṇ', *BISMQ*, 2, 1–4 (1922).
Gunjikar, R. B., *Saraswatīmaṇḍaḷa* (Bombay, 1884).
Joshi, P. S., 'Ch.Rājārām mahārāja (1689–1700) hyāṇcā vataneṇ deṇyācā nirṇay', *Bhāratīya Itihās āṇi Saṃskṛti Quarterly*, 7 (1970).
Joshi, S. N., *Arvācīn Mahārāṣṭre-itihāsakāḷāṇtīl Rājyakārbhārācā Abhyās*, vol.1 (Poona, 1959).
Khare, Y. V., 'Lakṣmeśvar Pargaṇyācī Jhaḍatī', *BISMQ*, 18, 2 (1937).
Khobrekar, V. G., 'Marāṭhī Rājyāceṇ Kṣetr va Utpanna', *Bhāratīya Itihās āṇi Saṃskṛti Quarterly*, 4 (1967).
Sardesai, G. S., *Marāṭhī Riyāsat*, Pt.II, vol. 2 (Bombay, 1920).
Sardesai, G. S., *Marāṭhī Riyāsat*, madhya-vibhāg 2 (Bombay, 1921).
Sardesai, G. S., *Marāṭhī Riyāsat*, madhya-vibhāg 1 (Bombay, 1925).
Sardesai, G. S., *Musalmānī Riyāsat*, vol.2 (Poona, 1928).
Sardesai, G. S., *Marāṭhī Riyāsat*, Puṇyaśloka Śahu, 1 Peśvā Bāḷājī Viśvanāth (1707–1720) (Bombay, 1942).
Sharma, G. R., *Sāraswata Bhūṣaṇa* (Bombay, 1950).
Vaidya, C. V., 'Mālojīcī Jahāgīr Puṇeṇ Navhtī', *BISMQ*, 11, 3 (1931).
Vaidya, C. V., 'Cauth āṇi Sardeśmukhī', *BISMQ*, 32, 1 (1953).

Works in European languages

Adas, M., 'From Avoidance to Confrontation: Peasant Protest in Precolonial and Colonial Southeast Asia', *CSSH*, 23 (1981).

Ahmad, Q., 'Mughal–Maratha Relations, 1719–1739', in: Pawar, A. (ed.), *Maratha History Seminar* (Kolhapur, 1971).

Aitchison, C. U., *A Collection of Treaties, Engagements and Sunnuds relating to India and Neighbouring Countries*, 7 vols (Calcutta, 1862–76).

Alam, M., 'The Zamindars and Mughal Power in the Deccan, 1685–1712', *IESHR*, 11, 1 (1974).

Alam, M., 'Mughal Centre and the Subas of Awadh and the Punjab, 1707–1748' (Thesis, Jawaharlal Nehru University, New Delhi, 1976).

Alam, M., 'Sikh uprisings under Band Bahadur, 1708–1715', *Studies in History*, vol.1, no.2 (1979).

Alam, M., 'Aspects of Agrarian Disturbances in North India in the Early Eighteenth Century' (Mimeograph, Jawaharlal Nehru University, 1983).

Anderson, J. N. D., *Islamic Law in the Modern World* (London, 1959).

Anderson, P., *Lineages of the Absolutist State* (London, 1980).

Anquetil Du Perron, A. H., *Législation Orientale* (Amsterdam, 1778).

Anquetil Du Perron, A. H., *L'Inde en Rapport avec l'Europe*, 2 vols (Hamburg and Brunswick, 1798).

Anquetil Du Perron, A. H., 'Observations sur la Propriété Individuelle et Foncière dans l'Inde et en Egypte', in: Paulin de S. Barthélemy, P., *Voyage aux Indes Orientales*, 3 vols (Paris, 1808).

Appadurai, A., and Appadurai Breckenridge, C., 'The South Indian Temple: Authority, Honour and Redistribution', *CIS*, n.s.10, 2 (1976).

Ardant, G., *Histoire de l'Impôt*, 2 vols (Paris, 1971–2).

Ardant, G., 'Financial Policy and Economic Infrastructure of Modern States and Nations', in: Tilly, Ch. (ed.), *The Formation of National States in Western Europe* (Princeton, 1975).

Arkoun, M. and Gardet, L., *L'Islam: Hier-Demain* (Paris, 1978).

Ashton, R., 'Revenue Farming under the Early Stuarts', *Economic History Review*, 2nd ser. VIII (1956).

Athar Ali, M., *The Mughal Nobility under Aurangzeb* (Bombay, etc., 1970).

Athar Ali, M., 'Provincial Governors under Shah Jahan', in: *Medieval India: A Miscellany*, vol. 3 (Bombay, etc., 1975).

Athar Ali, M., 'The Passing of Empire: The Mughal Case', *MAS*, 9, 3 (1975).

Athavale, S., 'Restoration of the Chhatrapati', in: Pawar, A. (ed.), *Maratha History Seminar* (Kolhapur, 1971).

Atmadja, K., *De Mohammedaansche Vrome Stichtingen in Indië* (The Hague, 1922).

Aziz, A., *The Mansabdari System and the Mughal Army* (Delhi, 1972)

Baden-Powell, B. H., *The Land-Systems of British India*, 3 vols (Oxford, 1892).

Baden-Powell, B. H., 'A Study of the Dakhan Villages', *Journal of the Royal Asiatic Society* (April 1897).

Baden-Powell, B. H., *The Origin and Growth of Village Communities in India* (London and New York, 1970).

Baer, G., 'The Evolution of Private Landownership in Egypt and the fertile Crescent', in: Issawi, C. (ed.), *The Economic History of the Middle East, 1800–1914* (Chicago, 1966).

Barbir, K. K., *Ottoman Rule in Damascus, 1708–1758* (Princeton, 1981).

Barnett, R. B., *North India between Empires: Awadh, the Mughals and the British, 1720–1801* (Berkeley, 1980).

Bayly, C. A., *Rulers, Townsmen and Bazaars: North Indian society in the age of British expansion, 1770–1870* (Cambridge, 1983).

Beattie, H. J., *Land and Lineage in China: A Study of T'ung-Ch'eng County, Anhwei, in the Ming and Chi'ing Dynasties* (Cambridge, 1979).

Bechert, H., 'Aśokas "Schismenedikt" und der Begriff Samghabheda', *WZKSOA*, 5 (1960).

Bechert, H., 'Einige Fragen zur Religionssoziologie und Struktur des Südasiatischen Buddhismus', in: *Internationales Jahrbuch für Religionssoziologie*, Bd. IV (Cologne and Opladen, 1968).

Becker, C. H., 'Zur Kulturgeschichte Nord-Syriens im Zeitalter der Mamluken', in: *Islamstudien*, I (Leipzig, 1924).

Becker, C. H., 'Steuerpacht und Lehnswesen', *ibid.*

Bernier, F., *Travels in the Mughal Empire* (London, 1891).

Bhalerao, B. R., 'Exemption from the Jazia Tax secured by Brahmins of Ujjain', *Proceedings of the 15th Session of the Indian History Congress* (Gwalior, 1952).

Bhatt, S. K., 'Holkar–Rajput Relations', in: Pawar, A. (ed.), *Maratha History Seminar* (Kolhapur, 1971).

Biardeau, M. and Malamoud, Cl., *Le Sacrifice dans l'Inde Ancienne* (Paris, 1976).

Binder, L., *Religion and Politics in Pakistan* (Berkeley and Los Angeles, 1961).

Blake, S. P., 'The Patrimonial–Bureaucratic Empire of the Mughals', *JAS*, 39, 1 (1979).

Bloch, M., *Feudal Society*, 2 vols (London and Henley, 1978).

Bonney, R. J., 'The Failure of the French Revenue Farms, 1600–60', *Economic History Review*, 2nd ser. XXXII (1979).

Breloer, B., *Kauṭalīya Studien* (Osnabrück, 1973).

Breman, J., 'The Village on Java and the Early Colonial State', *The Journal of Peasant Studies*, 9, 4 (1982).

Briggs, J. (transl.), *History of the Rise of the Mahomedan Power in India, till the year AD 1612, by Muhammad Kasim Ferishta*, 4 vols (London, 1910).

Broughton, T. D., *Letters from a Mahratta Camp* (Calcutta, 1977).

Brunner, O., 'Das "Ganze Haus" und die alteuropäische Ökonomik', in: *Neue Wege der Sozialgeschichte* (Göttingen, 1956).

Brunner, O., *Land und Herrschaft: Grundfragen der territorialen Verfassungsgeschichte Österreichs im Mittelalter* (Darmstadt, 1973).

Buckler, F. W., 'The Political Theory of the Indian Mutiny', *Transactions of the Royal Historical Society*, 4th series, vol. 5 (London, 1922).

Burghart, R., 'Regional Circles and the Central Overseer of the Vaishnavite Sect in the Kingdom of Nepal' (Mimeograph).

Cahen, C., 'L'Évolution de l'Iqta du IX au XIIIe siècle', *Annales ESC*, 8, 1 (1953).

Calkins, Ph. B., 'The Formation of a Regionally Oriented Ruling Group in Bengal, 1700–1740', *JAS*, 29, 4 (1970).

Candy, E. T., 'Selections, with Notes, from the Records of Government, regarding the Khoti tenure', *BGS*, n.s. no.134 (Bombay, 1873).

Chandra, S., *Parties and Politics at the Mughal Court, 1707–1740* (Aligarh, 1959).

Chandra, S., 'The Deccan Policy of the Mughals – A Reappraisal (1)', *The Indian Historical Review*, 4, 2 (1978).

Chandra, S., *Medieval India: Society, the Jagirdari Crisis and the Village* (Delhi, etc., 1982).

Chaudhuri, P. K., *Political Concepts in Ancient India: A Glossary of Political Terms* (New Delhi, 1977).

Choksey, R. D., *The Aftermath (1818–1826)* (Bombay, n.d.).

Choksey, R. D. (ed.), *The Last Phase* (Bombay, 1948).

Choksey, R. D., *Ratnagiri Collectorate (1821–1829)* (Poona, 1958).

Choksey, R. D. (ed.), *Early British Administration, 1817–1836* (Selections from the Peshwa Daftar, Deccan Commissioner's Files and Pre-Mutiny Records in Gujarat) (Poona, 1964).

Choksey, R. D., *Economic Life in the Bombay Gujarat (1800–1939)* (Bombay, etc., 1968).

Clavel, E., *Du Statut Personnel et des Successions*, 2 vols (Paris, 1895).

Clavel, E., *Le Wakf ou Habous*, 2 vols (Cairo, 1896).

Cohn, B. S., 'Political Systems in Eighteenth Century India: The Banaras Region', *Journal of the American Oriental Society*, 82 (1962).

Cole, J. R. I., 'Imami Shi'ism from Iran to North India, 1722–1856: State, Society and Clerical Ideology in Awadh' (Thesis, University of California, Los Angeles, 1984).

Colebrooke, H. T., *The Law of Inheritance from the Mitacshara* (Calcutta, 1896).

Colebrooke, T. E., *Life of the Honourable Mountstuart Elphinstone*, 2 vols (London, 1884).

Conlon, F. F., *A Caste in a Changing World: The Chitrapur Saraswat Brahmans, 1700–1935* (Berkeley, 1977).

Cooper, J., 'Patterns of inheritance and settlement by great landowners from the fifteenth to the eighteenth centuries', in: Goody, J., Thirsk,

J. and Thompson, E. P. (eds), *Family and Inheritance: Rural Society in Western Europe, 1200–1800* (London, 1976).

Copland, I., *The British Raj and the Indian Princes: Paramountcy in Western India, 1857–1930* (Bombay, 1982).

'Correspondence illustrative of the practice of the Peshwa's government regarding adoptions, and the circumstances under which adopted sons could succeed to property held from the state', *BGS*, n.s. no.28 (Bombay, 1856).

'Correspondence exhibiting the results of the scrutiny by the Inam Commission of the lists of Deccan Surinjams, etc.', *BGS*, n.s. no.31 (Bombay, 1856).

Courtney, W. and Auld, J. W., 'Memoir of the Sawunt Waree State', *BGS*, n.s. no.10 (Bombay, 1855).

Crone, P., *Slaves on Horses: The Evolution of the Islamic Polity* (Cambridge, 1980).

Cruikshank, J., 'Report on the Pitlad Pergunna and the Nepar Tuppa, in the Kaira Collectorate', *BGS*, o.s. no.11 (Bombay, 1853).

Das, V., *Structure and Cognition: Aspects of Hindu Caste and Ritual* (New Delhi, 1977).

Derrett, J. D. M., *The Hoysalas: A Medieval Indian Royal Family* (Madras, 1957).

Derrett, J. D. M., 'The Development of the Concept of Property in India c.AD 800–1800', *Zeitschrift für Vergleichende Rechtswissenschaft*, 64 (1962).

Derret, J. D. M., *The Concept of Property in Ancient Indian Theory and Practice* (Groningen, 1968).

Descriptive List of Mutiny Papers in the National Archives of India, Bhopal, 5 vols (New Delhi, 1960–73).

Dessert, D., *Argent, Pouvoir et Société au Grand Siècle* (Paris, 1985).

Dewar, D. and Garrett, H. L., 'A Reply to Mr. F. W. Buckler's *The Political Theory of the Indian Mutiny*', *Transactions of the Royal Historical Society*, 4th series, vol.7 (London, 1924).

Deyell, J. S., 'Numismatic methodology in the estimation of Mughal currency output', *IESHR*, 13, 3 (1976).

Dharmadhikari, M., 'Gopal Rao Mairal: A Brief Note on Gaekwad Nobility' (Paper submitted to a seminar on the 16th–20th century history of Gujarat and Maharashtra held at the M. S. University of Baroda, 19–21 March 1982).

Dighe, V. G., *Nizam-ul-Mulk Asaf Jah I and the Marathas, 1721–1728* (Paper read at the public meeting of the 14th session of the Indian Historical Records Commission held at Lahore in December 1937) (Simla, 1938).

Dighe, V. G., *Peshwa Baji Rao I and Maratha Expansion* (Bombay, 1944).

Divekar, V. D., 'The Emergence of an Indigenous Business Class in Maharashtra in the Eighteenth Century', *MAS*, 16, 3 (1982).

Dow, A., 'A Dissertation concerning the Customs, Manners, Language, Religion and Philosophy of the Hindoos', in: Marshall, P. J. (ed.), *The British Discovery of Hinduism in the Eighteenth Century* (Cambridge, 1970).

Dumont, L., *Religion, Politics and History in India* (Paris and The Hague, 1970).

Eaton, R. M., 'The Court and the Dargah in the Seventeenth Century Deccan', *IESHR*, 10, 1 (1973).

Eaton, R. M., *Sufis of Bijapur, 1300–1700* (Princeton, 1978).

Elias, N., *Über den Prozess der Zivilisation*, 2 vols (Suhrkamp, 1976).

Elliot, F. A. H., *The Rulers of Baroda* (Bombay, 1934).

Elliot, H. M. and Dowson, J., *The History of India as told by its own Historians*, 8 vols (London, 1867–77).

Elphinstone, M., *Report on the Territories Conquered from the Peshwa* (1809) (Delhi, 1973).

Elphinstone, M., *The History of India* (Hindu and Mohammedan Periods) (London, 1874).

Encyclopaedia of Islam (Leiden and London, 1965–78).

Enthoven, R. E., *The Tribes and Castes of Bombay*, 3 vols (Bombay, 1920–2).

Enzyclopaedia der Islam, Bd. III (Leiden and Leipzig, 1936).

Etheridge, A. T., 'Narrative of the Bombay Inam Commission', *BGS*, n.s. no.132 (Poona, 1873).

'Extract from Manson's Report of 1 May 1853', *BGS*, o.s. no. 12 (Bombay, 1853).

Gagnan, E. (ed. and transl.), *Abou Yousouf Au'Koub: Le Livre de l'Impôt Foncier (Kitāb El-Kharādj)* (Paris, 1921).

Fawcett, E. G., 'Report on the Collectorate of Ahmadabad', *BGS*, n.s. no.5 (Bombay, 1854).

Findley, C. V., *Bureaucratic Reform in the Ottoman Empire: The Sublime Porte, 1789–1922* (Princeton, 1980).

Forrest, G. W., *Selections from the Minutes and other Official Writings of the Honourable Mountstuart Elphinstone* (London, 1884).

Fox, R. G., *Kin, Clan, Raja, and Rule: State–Hinterland Relations in Preindustrial India* (Bombay, 1971).

Fukazawa, H., 'Structure and Change of the "Sharehold Village" (*Bhagdari* or *Narwadari* Village) in the Nineteenth Century British Gujarat' *Hitotsubashi Journal of Economics*, 14, 2 (1974).

Fukazawa, K., 'Some Aspects of Slavery in the Eighteenth Century Maratha Kingdom', *The Journal of Intercultural Studies* (Inaugural number, 1974).

Fussman, G., 'Le Concept d'Empire dans l'Inde Ancienne', in: Duverger, M. (ed.), *Le Concept d'Empire* (Paris, 1981).

Fussman, G., 'Pouvoir central et régions dans l'Inde ancienne', *Annales ESC*, 4, 37 (1982).

Gadgil, D. R., *Origins of the Modern Indian Business Class: An Interim Report* (New York, 1959).

Gazetteer of the Bombay Presidency, vols I-XXIII (Bombay, 1879–96).

Gense, J. H. and Banaji, D. R. (eds), *The Gaikwads of Baroda*, 9 vols (Baroda, n.d.).

Ghauri, J. A., 'Kingship in the Sultanates of Bijapur and Golconda', *Islamic Culture*, 46, 1 (1972).

Ghoshal, U. N., *A History of Indian Political Ideas* (Oxford, 1966).

Gibb, H. A. R. and Kramers, J. H. (eds), *Shorter Encyclopaedia of Islam* (Leiden, 1953).

Cleig, G. R., *The Life of Sir Thomas Munro*, 3 vols (London, 1830).

Gonda, J., *Ancient Indian Kingship from the Religious Point of View* (Leiden, 1966).

Gooddine, R. N., 'Report on the Village Communities of the Deccan', *BGS*, o.s.no.4 (Bombay, 1852).

Goody, J., *Death, Property and the Ancestors* (London, 1962).

Goody, J., 'Inheritance, Property and Women: some Comparative Considerations', in: Goody, J., Thirsk, J. and Thompson, E. P. (eds), *Family and Inheritance: Rural Society in Western Europe, 1200–1800* (London, 1976).

Gopal, S. (ed.), *Selected Works of Jawaharlal Nehru*, 13 vols (New Delhi, 1972–80).

Gordon, S. N., 'Scarf and Sword: Thugs, Marauders, and State-Formation in 18th Century Malwa', *IESHR*, 6, 4 (1969).

Gordon, S. N., 'The Slow Conquest: Administrative Integration of Malwa into the Maratha Empire, 1720–1760', *MAS*, 11, 1 (1977).

Gordon, S. N., 'Legitimacy and Loyalty in some Successor States of the Eighteenth Century', in: Richards, J. F. (ed.), *Kingship and Authority in South Asia* (Madison, Wisc., 1978).

Gordon, S. N., 'Forts and Social Control in the Maratha State', *MAS*, 13, 1 (1979).

Goswamy, B. N. and Grewal, J. S., *The Mughal and Sikh Rulers and the Vaishnavas of Pindori* (Simla, 1969).

Goubert, P., *L'Ancien Régime*, 2 vols (Paris, 1973).

Graham, D. C., 'Statistical Report on the Principality of Kolhapoor', *BGS*, n.s. no.8 (Bombay, 1854).

Grant Duff, J., *History of the Mahrattas*, 2 vols (New Delhi, 1971).

Grover, B. R., 'Nature of Dehat-i-Taaluqa (Zamindari Villages) and the evolution of the Taaluqdari system during the Mughal Age', *IESHR*, 2, 2 (1965) and 2, 3 (1966).

Grover, B. R., 'Nature of Land-Rights in Mughal India', *IESHIR*, 1, 1 (1963).

Gune, V. T., *The Judicial System of the Marathas* (Poona, 1953).

Gupta, B. D., 'Maratha–Bundela Relations', in: Pawar, A. (ed.), *Maratha History Seminar* (Kolhapur, 1971).

Gupta, K. S., *Mewar and the Maratha Relations (1735–1818 AD)* (New Delhi, 1971).

Habib, I., 'Banking in Mughal India', *Contributions to Indian Economic History*, vol. I (Calcutta, 1960).

Habib, I., *The Agrarian System of Mughal India* (Bombay, 1963).

Habib, I., 'The Social Distribution of Landed Property in pre-British India (a Historical Survey)', in: Sharma, R. S. and Jha, V. (eds), *Indian Society: Historical Probings in memory of D. D. Kosambi* (New Delhi, 1964).

Habib, I., 'Usury in Medieval India', *CSSH*, 6 (1964).

Habib, I., 'An Examination of Wittfogel's Theory of "Oriental Despotism"', in: *Studies in Asian History* (Proceedings of the Asian History Congress, 1961) (London, 1969).

Hardy, P., 'Is the *Chachnama* intelligible to the historian as political theory?', in: Khuhro, H. (ed.), *Sind through the Centuries* (Karachi, 1981).

Hardy, P., 'Force and Violence in Indo-Persian Writing on History and Government in Medieval South Asia', in: Israel, M. and Wagle, N. K., (eds), *Islamic Society and Culture: Essays in Honour of Professor Aziz Ahmad* (New Delhi, 1983).

Hasan, A., 'L'Histoire sauf l'Europe, en Inde aux XVIe et XVIIe Siècles: Trésors Américains, Monnaie d'Argent et Prix dans l'Empire Mogol', *Annales ESC*, 24, 4 (1969).

Hasan, I., *The Central Structure of the Mughal Empire* (Lahore, etc., 1967).

Heesterman, J. C., 'Brahmin, Ritual and Renouncer', *WZKSOA*, 8 (1964).

Heesterman, J. C., 'Was there an Indian Reaction? Western expansion in Indian perspective', in: Wesseling, H. (ed.), *Expansion and Reaction: Essays in European Expansion and Reactions in Asia and Africa* (Leiden, 1978).

Heesterman, J. C., 'Power and Authority in Indian Tradition', in: Moore, R. J. (ed.), *Tradition and Politics in South Asia* (Delhi, etc., 1979).

Heesterman, J. C., 'Boer, Bandiet, Bankier en Heilige' (Paper contributed to the KOTA III conference held in Amsterdam, 12–13 May 1982).

Heesterman, J. C., 'Ritual, Revelation and Axial Age', in: *The Inner Conflict of Tradition: Essays in Indian Ritual, Kingship, and Society* (Chicago and London, 1985).

Heesterman, J. C., 'Caste and Karma: Max Weber's analysis of Caste', *ibid*.

An Historical Account of the Settlement and Possession of Bombay by the English East India Company and the Rise and Progress of the War with the Mahratta Nation (London, 1781).

Hobbes, T., *Leviathan* (Oxford, 1946).

Hodgson, M. G. S., *The Venture of Islam*, vol.1 (Chicago and London, 1974).
Hughes, T. P., *Dictionary of Islam* (Lahore, n.d., orig. publ. 1885).
Irvine, W. (ed. and transl.), *Storia Do Mogor by Niccolao Manucci*, 4 vols (Calcutta, 1965–6).
Irvine, W., *Later Mughals* (Delhi, 1971).
Islam, Z., 'Zakāt and its connotation in medieval India', *Islamic Culture* (July 1984).
Islamoğlu, H. and Keyder, Çağlar, 'Agenda for Ottoman History', *Review*, 1, 1 (Summer 1977).
Jain, R. K., 'Kingship, Territory and Property in the Native States of Pre-British Bundelkhand, Northern Madhya Pradesh' (Paper contributed to the Fifth European Conference on Modern South Asian Studies, Leiden, 1976).
Jarrett, H. S. (transl.), *The Ā'īn-i Akbarī of Abul Fazl*, vol.2 (New Delhi, 1978).
Jenkins, T., *Report on the Territories of the Raja of Nagpur* (Nagpur, 1827; reprinted 1923).
Jervis, T. B., *Geographical and Statistical Memoir of the Konkan* (Calcutta, 1840).
Jussawalla, A. (ed.), *New Writing in India* (Penguin Book, 1977).
Kane, P. V., *History of Dharmaśāstra*, 5 vols (Poona, 1968–77).
Karpat, K. H., 'The Stages of Ottoman History', in: *idem* (ed.), *The Ottoman State and its Place in World History* (Leiden, 1974).
Kennedy, H., 'Review of M. G. Morony, *Iraq after the Muslim Conquest*', *The Times Literary Supplement*, September 7, 1984.
Khaur Dhot, J., 'The Pattern of Taxation and Economy of North Gujarat in the Second Half of the 18th and early 19th Century: A Case Study of the Pargana of Nadiad' (Paper submitted to a seminar on the 16th–20th century history of Gujarat and Maharashtra held at the M.S. University of Baroda, 19–21 March 1982).
Khobrekar, V. G. (ed.), *Tarikh-i-Dilkasha of Bhimsen* (English translation by Sarkar, J.) (Bombay, 1972).
Kishore, B., *Tarabai and her Times* (Asia Publishing House, 1963).
Kolff, D. H. A. and Van Santen, H. W. (eds), *De Geschriften van Francisco Pelsaert over Mughal Indië: 1627 Kroniek en Remonstrantie* (The Hague, 1979).
Kolff, D. H. A., 'An Armed Peasantry and its Allies: Rajput Tradition and State Formation in Hindustan, 1450–1850' (PhD thesis, Leiden, 1983).
Kosambi, D. D., *An Introduction to the Study of Indian History* (Bombay, 1975).
Kulkarni, A. R., *Maharashtra in the Age of Shivaji* (Poona, 1967).
Kulkarni, A. R., 'Social Relations in the Maratha Country in the Medieval Period', *Proceedings of the 32nd Session of the Indian History Congress* (Jabalpur, 1970), Presidential Address, Medieval India Section.

Kulkarni, A. R., 'Source Material for the Study of Village Communities in Maharashtra', *IESHR*, 13, 4 (1976).
Kulkarni, G. T., 'Banking in the 18th Century: A Case Study of a Poona Banker', *Arthja Vijñāna*, 15, (1973).
Kulkarni, K. P., *Marathi Etymological Dictionary* (Poona, 1964).
Kumar, R., *Western India in the Nineteenth Century* (London and Toronto, 1968).
Kumar Hans, R., 'The Manotidari System in the Agrarian Economy of Eighteenth Century Gujarat' (Paper read at the 43rd session of the Indian History Congress, Bodh Gaya, 1981).
Lamar, H. and Thompson, L. (eds), *The Frontier in History: North America and Southern Africa Compared* (New Haven and London, 1981).
Lambton, A. K. S., *Landlord and Peasant in Persia* (London, etc., 1953).
Lamotte, E., *Histoire du Bouddhisme Indien* (Leuven, 1958).
Laoust, H., *Essai sur les doctrines sociales et politiques de Taḳī-d-Dīn Aḥmad B. Taimīya* (Cairo, 1939).
Laoust, H., *Les Schismes dans l'Islam* (Paris, 1977).
Leonard, K., 'The "Great Firm" Theory of the Decline of the Mughal Empire', *CSSH*, 21 (1979).
Leonard, K., 'Banking Firms in Nineteenth-Century Hyderabad Politics', *MAS*, 15, 2 (1981).
Leonard, K., 'Indigenous Banking Firms in Mughal India: A Reply', *CSSH*, 23 (1981).
Lewis, B., 'Some Reflections on the Decline of the Ottoman Empire', in: Cipolla, C. M. (ed.), *The Economic Decline of Empires* (London, 1970).
Lewis, B., 'Islamic Concepts of Revolution', in: Vatikiotis, P. J. (ed.), *Revolution in the Middle East* (London, 1972).
Lingat, R., *Les Sources du Droit dans le Système Traditionnel de l'Inde* (Paris and The Hague, 1967).
Løkkegaard, F., *Islamic Taxation in the Classic Period* (Copenhagen, 1950).
Macdonald, A., *Memoir of the Life of the late Nana Farnavis* (Oxford, 1927).
Machiavelli, N., *Il Principe* (Florence, 1857).
Mahalingam, T. V., *South Indian Polity* (Madras, 1967).
Maharashtra State Gazetteer, History, pt.III (Bombay, 1967).
Maine, H. J. S., *Village-Communities in the East and West* (London, 1876).
Maine, H. J. S., *Ancient Law* (London, 1924).
Malcolm, J., *A Memoir of Central India*, 2 vols (New Delhi, 1970).
Malgonkar, M., *Puars of Dewas Senior* (Orient Longmans, 1963).
Malik, M., 'Documents relating to Pargana Administration in the Deccan under Asaf Jah I', in: *Medieval India: A Miscellany*, vol.3 (Asia Publishing House, 1975).
Malik, Z., 'Documents relating to Chauth Collection in the Subah of

Hyderabad, 1726–1748', *Proceedings of the 32nd Session of the Indian History Congress* (Jabalpur, 1970), vol.1.

Markovits, Cl., 'L'Inde Coloniale: Nationalisme et Histoire', *Annales ESC*, 37, 4 (1982).

Marshall, T., *Statistical Reports on the Pergunnahs of Padshapoor, Belgam, Kalaniddee and Chandgarh, Khanapoor, Bagulkot and Badamy, and Hoondgoond, in the Southern Maratha Country, etc.* (Bombay, 1822).

Marshall, T., 'A Statistical Account of the Pergunna of Jumboosur', *Transactions of the Literary Society of Bombay*, vol. 3 (London, 1823).

Massignon, L., 'L'Umma et ses Synonymes: Notion de "Communauté Sociale" en Islam', *Revenue des Études Islamiques* (Cahier unique, 1941–6).

Mauss, M., 'Essai sur le Don', in: *Sociologie et Anthropologie* (Paris, 1973).

Mawji, P. V., 'Shivaji's Swarajya', *JBBRAS*, o.s. 22 (1908).

McGowan, B., *Economic Life in Ottoman Europe* (Cambridge, 1981).

Mernissi, F., *Beyond the Veil* (New York, etc., 1975).

Monier Williams, F., *Memoir of the Zilla of Baroche* (London, 1825).

Monteil, V., *Ibn Khaldūn, Discours sur l'Histoire Universelle*, 3 vols (Beirut, 1968).

Montesquieu, C. L. de Secondat de, *De l'Esprit des Lois* (Paris, 1868).

Moreland, W. H., *India at the Death of Akbar* (London, 1920).

Moreland, W. H., *The Agrarian System of Moslem India* (New Delhi, 1968).

Moreland, W. H., *From Akbar to Aurangzeb* (New Delhi, 1972).

Moreland, W. H. and Geyl, P. (eds and transls), *Jahangir's India: The Remonstrantie of Francisco Pelsaert* (Cambridge, 1925).

Morony, M. G., *Iraq after the Muslim Conquest* (Princeton, 1984).

Mottahedeh, R. P., *Loyalty and Leadership in an Early Islamic Society* (Princeton, 1980).

Mutafcieva, V. P., 'L'Institution de l'Ayanlik pendant les dernières Décennies du XVIIIe Siècle', *Études Balkaniques*, 2–3 (1965).

Nurul Hasan, S., 'Zamindars under the Mughals', in: Frykenberg, R. E. (ed.), *Land Control and Social Structure in Indian History* (Madison, Milwaukee and London, 1969).

Nayeem, M. A., 'Mughal Documents Relating to Land Revenue of the Andhra Districts of Northern Sarkars (1700–1765 AD)', *Itihas-Journal of the Andhra Pradesh State Archives*, VIII, 2 (1980).

O'Hanlon, R., 'Maratha History as Polemic: Low Caste Ideology and Political Debate in Late Nineteenth-century Western India', *MAS*, 17, 1 (1983).

Özkaya, Y., *Osmanli Imparatorluğunda Âyânlik* (Ankara, 1977) (Summary in French).

Pagadi, S. M., *Studies in Maratha History*, vol.2 (Kolhapur, 1971).
Painter, S., *A History of the Middle Ages, 284–1500* (London and Basingstoke, 1979).
'Papers relating to revised rates of assessment for thirteen different Talookas of the Tanna collectorate', *BGS*, n.s. no.96 (Bombay, 1866).
Patterson, M. L.P., 'Chitpavan Brahman Family Histories: Sources for a Study of Social Structure and Social Change in Maharashtra', in: Singer, M. and Cohn, B. S. (eds), *Structure and Change in Indian Society* (Chicago, 1968).
Pawar, A., 'An Episode in the Life of Ramchandra Pant Amatya', *BISMQ*, 28, 1–2 (1947).
Pawar, A., 'Palace Revolution at Kolhapur 1714 AD', in: Mate, M. S. and Kulkarni, G. T. (eds), *Studies in Indology and Medieval History* (Prof. G. H. Khare Felicitation Volume) (Poona, 1974).
Pearson, M. N., 'Shivaji and the Decline of the Mughal Empire', *JAS*, 35, 2 (1976).
Perlin, F., 'Of White Whale and Countrymen in the Eighteenth-century Maratha Deccan. Extended Class Relations, Rights, and the Problem of Rural Autonomy under the Old Regime', *The Journal of Peasant Studies*, 5, 2 (1978).
Perlin, F., 'To Identify Change in an Old Regime Polity: Agrarian Transaction and Institutional Mutation in 17th to early 19th Century Maharashtra', in: Gaborieau, M. and Thorner, A. (eds), *Asie du Sud: Traditions et Changements* (Colloques Internationaux du C.N.R.S.) (Paris, 1979).
Perlin, F., 'Money-Use in Late Pre-Colonial India and the International Trade in Currency Media' (Contribution to the Mughal Monetary Conference at Duke University, June 1981).
Perlin, F., 'The Pre-Colonial Indian State in History and Epistemology. A Reconstruction of Societal Formation in the Western Deccan from the Fifteenth to the Early Nineteenth Century', in: Claessen, H. and Skolnik, P. (eds), *The Study of the State* (The Hague, 1981).
Perlin, F., 'Precolonial South Asia and Western Penetration in the Seventeenth to Nineteenth Centuries: A Problem of Epistemological Status', *Review*, 4, 2 (1980).
Perlin, F., 'Space and Order looked at Critically. Non-Comparability and Procedural Substantivism in History and the Social Sciences' (Revised paper presented to the Colloquium on Bifurcation Theory, Erasmus University Rotterdam, January 1982).
Peterson, E. L., *'Alī and Mu'āwiya in early Arabic Tradition* (Copenhagen, 1964)
Pradhan, M. C., *The Political System of the Jats of Northern India* (Bombay, 1966).
Prakash, S., 'Gujarat in 1857' (Mimeograph, Centre of South Asian Studies, University of Cambridge, 30 January 1985).

Preston, L. W., 'Subregional Religious Centres in the History of Maharashtra: The Sites Sacred to Ganesh', in: Wagle, N. K. (ed.), *Images of Maharashtra: A Regional Profile of India* (London and Dublin, 1980).

Rabi, M. M., *The Political Theory of Ibn Khaldun* (Leiden, 1967).

Rana, R. P., 'Agrarian Revolts in Northern India during the Late 17th and Early 18th century', *IESHR*, 18, 3–4 (1981).

Ranade, M. G., *Rise of the Maratha Power* (Bombay, 1900).

Ranade, M. G., 'Introduction to the Peshwa's Diaries', *JBBRAS*, xx (reprint, 1969).

Rashid, S. K., *Wakf Administration in India* (New Delhi, 1978).

Ray, B. C., 'Maratha Policy in Orissa', in: Pawar, A. (ed.), *Maratha History Seminar* (Kolhapur, 1971).

Raychaudhary, S. C., *Social, Cultural and Economic History of India* (Medieval Age) (Delhi, 1978).

Raychaudhari, T. and Habib, I. (eds), *The Cambridge Economic History of India*, vol. 1 (Cambridge, 1982).

Rayrikar, A., '"Gramanyas" (Caste Disputes) under the Satara State (1825–1838)' (Paper submitted to a seminar on the 16th- to 20th-century history of Gujarat and Maharashtra held at the M.S. University of Baroda, 19–21 March 1982).

Richards, J. F., 'The Islamic Frontier in the East: Expansion into South Asia', *South Asia*, 4 (October 1974).

Richards, J. F., 'The Hyderabad Karnatik, 1687–1707', *MAS*, 9, 2 (1975).

Richards, J. F., *Mughal Administration in Golconda* (Oxford, 1975).

Richards, J. F., 'The Imperial Crisis in the Deccan', *JAS*, 35, 2 (1976).

Richards, J. F., 'Mughal State Finance and the Premodern World Economy', *CSSH*, 23 (1981).

Robinson, R., 'Non-European Foundations of European Imperialism: Sketch for a Theory of Collaboration', in: Owen, R. and Sutcliffe, B. (eds), *Studies in the theory of Imperialism* (London, 1972).

Röhrborn, K., *Untersuchungen zur osmanischen Verwaltungsgeschichte* (Berlin and New York, 1973).

Rousseau, J. J., *Du Contrat Social* (Paris, 1973).

Sadat, D. R., 'Urban Notables in the Ottoman Empire: The Âyân' (PhD thesis, Rutgers University, 1969).

Sadat, D. R., 'Rumeli Ayanlari: The Eighteenth Century', *Journal of Modern History*, 44, 3 (1972).

Sardesai, G. S. (ed.), *Shivaji Souvenir* (Poona, 1927).

Sardesai, G. S., *The Main Currents of Maratha History* (Bombay, 1949).

Sardesai, G. S., *New History of the Marathas*, 3 vols (Bombay, 1971).

Sarkar, J. (ed. and transl.), *Ma'āṣir-i-'Ālamgirī of Saqui Musta'id Khan* (Calcutta, 1947).

Sarkar, J. (ed. and transl.), *Persian Records of Maratha History* (Newsletters from Parasnis' Collection), 2 vols (Bombay, 1953–4).

Sarkar, J., *Fall of the Mughal Empire*, 4 vols (Bombay, Calcutta, etc., 1971).

Sarkar, J., *History of Aurangzib*, 5 vols (Bombay, Calcutta, etc., 1972–4).

Sarkar, J., *The History of Bengal: Muslim Period, 1200–1757* (Patna, 1973).

Sarkar, J., *House of Shivaji* (New Delhi, 1978).

Sarkar, J., Sardesai, G. S. *et al.* (eds), *Poona Residency Correspondence*, 13 vols (Bombay, 1936–58).

Saxena, R. K., *Maratha Relations with the Major States of Rajputana (1761–1818 AD)* (New Delhi, 1973).

Scharfe, H., *Untersuchungen zur Staatsrechtslehre des Kauṭalya* (Wiesbaden, 1968).

Schimmel, A., *Islam in the Indian Subcontinent* (Leiden and Cologne, 1980).

Sen, S. N., *Administrative System of the Marathas* (Calcutta, 1976).

Sen, S. N., *The Military System of the Marathas* (Calcutta, 1979).

Shaban, M. A., *The 'Abbāsid Revolution* (Cambridge, 1970).

Shaw, S. J., *The Financial and Administrative Organization and Development of Ottoman Egypt, 1517–1798* (Princeton, 1962).

Shaw, S. J., *History of the Ottoman Empire and Modern Turkey*, vol. 1 (Cambridge, 1976).

Shulman, D., 'On South Indian Bandits and Kings', *IESHR*, 17, 3 (1980).

Shyam, R., *The Kingdom of Ahmadnagar* (Delhi, 1966).

Siddiqi, N. A., 'The Classification of Villages under the Mughals', *IESHR*, 1, 3 (1964).

Siddiqi, N. A., *Land Revenue Administration under the Mughals (1700–1750)* (Bombay, 1970).

Singh, D., 'Local and Land Revenue Administration of the State of Jaipur (c.1750–1800)' (Thesis, Jawaharlal Nehru University, New Delhi, 1975).

Sinha, R., 'Rajput–Maratha Relations', in: Pawar, A. (ed.), *Maratha History Seminar* (Kolhapur, 1971).

Smith, V. A., *The Oxford History of India* (third ed. by Spear, P., Oxford, 1958).

Sontheimer, G. D., 'Religious Endowments in India: The Juristic Personality of Hindu Deities', *Zeitschrift für vergleichende Rechtswissenschaft*, Bd.67, Heft 1 (1965).

Spencer, G. W., 'Religious Networks and Royal Influence in Eleventh Century South India', *JESHO*, 12 (1969).

Spencer, G. W., 'Royal Initiative under Rajaraja I', *IESHR*, 7, 4 (1970).

Steele, A., *The Law and Custom of Hindoo Castes within the Dekhun Provinces subject to the Presidency of Bombay* (London, 1868).

Stein, B., *Peasant State and Society in Medieval South India* (Delhi, 1980).

Steingass, F., *A Comprehensive Persian–English Dictionary* (London, Henley and Boston, 1977).

Stokes, E., *The Peasant and the Raj* (Cambridge, 1980).
Sućeska, A., 'Bedeutung und Entwicklung des Begriffes A'yān im Osmanischen Reich', *Südostforschungen*, 25 (1966).
Sykes, W. H., 'On the Land Tenures of the Dekkan', *Journal of the Royal Asiatic Society*, 2 (1835).
Temple, R. C. (ed.), *The Travels of Peter Mundy in Europe and Asia, 1608–1667*, 5 vols (London, 1914–24).
Thompson, E., *The Making of the Indian Princes* (London and Dublin, 1978).
Thorner, D., 'The Relevance of Entrepreneurial Economics to Production by Peasant Households', in: *The Shaping of Modern India* (New Delhi, 1980).
Thorner, D., 'Feudalism in India', *ibid.*
Tripathi, R. P., *Some Aspects of Muslim Administration* (Allahabad, 1966).
Twitchett, D., 'The Fan Clan's Charitable Estate, 1050–1760', in: Nivison, D. and Wright, A. F. (eds), *Confucianism in Action* (Stanford, 1959).
Twitchett, D., 'Documents on Clan Administration: I. The Rules of Administration of the Charitable Estate of the Fan Clan', *Asia Major*, 8 (1960–1).
Vaidya, S. G., *Peshwa Bajirao II and the Downfall of the Maratha Power* (Nagpur, 1976).
Van Leur, J. C., *Indonesian Trade and Society* (The Hague and Bandung, 1955).
Van Santen, H. W., *De Verenigde Oost-Indische Compagnie in Gujarat en Hindustan, 1520–1660* (Leiden, 1982).
Vinogradoff, P., *Roman Law in Medieval Europe* (London and New York, 1909).
Wagle, N. K., 'The History and Social Organization of the Gauḍa Sāraswata Brāhmaṇas of the West Coast of India', *Journal of Indian History*, XLVIII, pt. I and II (1970).
Weber, M., *Gesammelte Aufsätze zur Religionssoziologie, II (Hinduismus und Buddhismus)* (Tübingen, 1972).
Weber, M., *Economy and Society*, 2 vols (Berkeley, Los Angeles and London, 1978).
Wellhausen, J., *The Religio-Political Factions in Early Islam* (Amsterdam and Oxford, 1975).
Wensinck, A. J., *The Muslim Creed* (Cambridge, 1932).
Wertheim, W. F., 'Sociological Aspects of Corruption in Southeast Asia', in: Bendix, R. *et al.* (eds), *State and Society* (Berkeley, Los Angeles and London, 1968).
Wilks, M., *Historical Sketches of the South of India*, vol. I (Madras, 1891).
Wilson, H. H., *A Glossary of Judicial and Revenue Terms* (Delhi, 1968).

Wingate, G., 'Reports on the revenue survey settlements of the Hoobullee, Nuwulgoond, Kode, and Dharwar Talookas of the Dharwar collectorate', *BGS*, o.s. no. 12 (Bombay, 1853).

Wink, A., 'The Settlement of the Deccan, c. 1600–1680', *BISMQ*, 60, 1–4 (1981).

Wink, A., 'Maratha Revenue Farming', *MAS*, 17, 4 (1983).

Wink, A., 'Sovereignty and Universal Dominion in South Asia', *IESHR*, 21, 3 (1984).

Wright, W. L. (transl.), *Ottoman Statecraft: The Book of Counsel for Vezirs and Governors (Naṣā'iḥ ül-vüzera ve'l-ümera) of Suri Meḥmed Pasha, the Defterdār* (Princeton, 1935).

Ziegler, N. P., 'Some Notes on Rajput Loyalties during the Mughal Period', in: Richards, J. F. (ed.), *Kingship and Authority in South Asia* (Madison, Wisc., 1978).

INDEX

UNIVERSITY OF CAMBRIDGE
ORIENTAL PUBLICATIONS PUBLISHED FOR THE
FACULTY OF ORIENTAL STUDIES

1 *Averroes' Commentary on Plato's Republic*, edited and translated by E. I. J. Rosenthal
2 *FitzGerald's 'Salámán and Absál'*, edited by A. J. Arberry
3 *Ihara Saikaku: The Japanese Family Storehouse*, translated and edited by G. W. Sargent
4 *The Avestan Hymn to Mithra*, edited and translated by Ilya Gershevitch
5 *The Fuṣūl al-Madani of al-Fārābi*, edited and translated by D. M. Dunlop (out of print)
6 *Dun Karm, Poet of Malta*, texts chosen and translated by A. J. Arberry; introduction, notes and glossary by P. Grech
7 *The Political Writings of Ogyú Sorai*, by J. R. McEwan
8 *Financial Administration under the T'ang Dynasty*, by D. C. Twitchett
9 *Neolithic Cattle-Keepers of South India: A Study of the Deccan Ashmounds*, by F. R. Allchin
10 *The Japanese Enlightenment: A Study of the Writings of Fukuzawa Yukichi*, by Carmen Blacker
11 *Records of Han Administration.* Vol. I *Historical Assessment*, by M. Loewe
12 *Records of Han Administration.* Vol. II *Documents*, by M. Loewe
13 *The Language of Indrafit of Orchā: A Study of Early Braj Bhāṣā Prose*, by R. S. McGregor
14 *Japan's First General Election, 1890*, by R. H. P. Mason
15 *A Collection of Tales from Uji: A Study and Translation of 'Uji Shūi Monogatari'*, by D. E. Mills
16 *Studia Semitica*, Vol. I *Jewish Themes*, by E. I. J. Rosenthal
17 *Studia Semitica*, Vol. II *Islamic Themes*, by E. I. J. Rosenthal
18 *A Nestorian Collection of Christological Texts*, Vol. I *Syriac Text*, by Luise Abramowski and Alan E. Goodman
19 *A Nestorian Collection of Christological Texts*, Vol. II *Introduction, Translation, Indexes*, by Luise Abramowski and Alan E. Goodman
20 *The Syriac Version of the Pseudo-Nonnos Mythological Scholia*, by Sebastian Brock
21 *Water Rights and Irrigation Practices in Lahj*, by A. M. A. Maktari
22 *The Commentary of Rabbi David Kimhi on Psalms cxx-cl*, edited and translated by Joshua Baker and Ernest W. Nicholson
23 *Jalāl al-dīn al-Suyūṭī.* Vol. I *Biography and background*, by E. M. Sartain
24 *Jalāl al-dīn al-Suyūṭī.* Vol. II *"Al-Tahadduth biniŭmat allah"*, Arabic text by E. M. Sartain
25 *Origen and the Jews: Studies in Jewish–Christian Relations in Third Century Palestine*, by N. R. M. de Lange
26 *The 'Visaladevarāsa': A restoration of the text*, by John D. Smith
27 *Shabbetha Sofer and His Prayer-book*, by Stefan C. Reif
28 *Mori Ogai and the Modernization of Japanese Culture*, by Richard John Bowring
29 *The Rebel Lands: An investigation into origins of early Mesopotamian mythology*, by J. V. Kinnier Wilson

30 *Saladin: The politics of the Holy War*, by Malcolm Cameron Lyons and David Jackson
31 *Khotanese Buddhist Texts*, revised edition, edited by H. W. Bailey
32 *Interpreting the Hebrew Bible: Essays in Honour of E. I. J. Rosenthal*, edited by J. A. Emerton and S. C. Reif
33 *The Traditional Interpretation of the Apocalypse of St John in the Ethiopian Orthodox Church*, by Roger W. Cowley
34 *South Asian Archaeology 1981: Proceedings of the Sixth International Conference of South Asian Archaeologists in Western Europe*, edited by Bridget Allchin (with assistance from Raymond Allchin and Miriam Sidell)
35 *God's Conflict with the Dragon and the Sea*, by John Day